Routed West

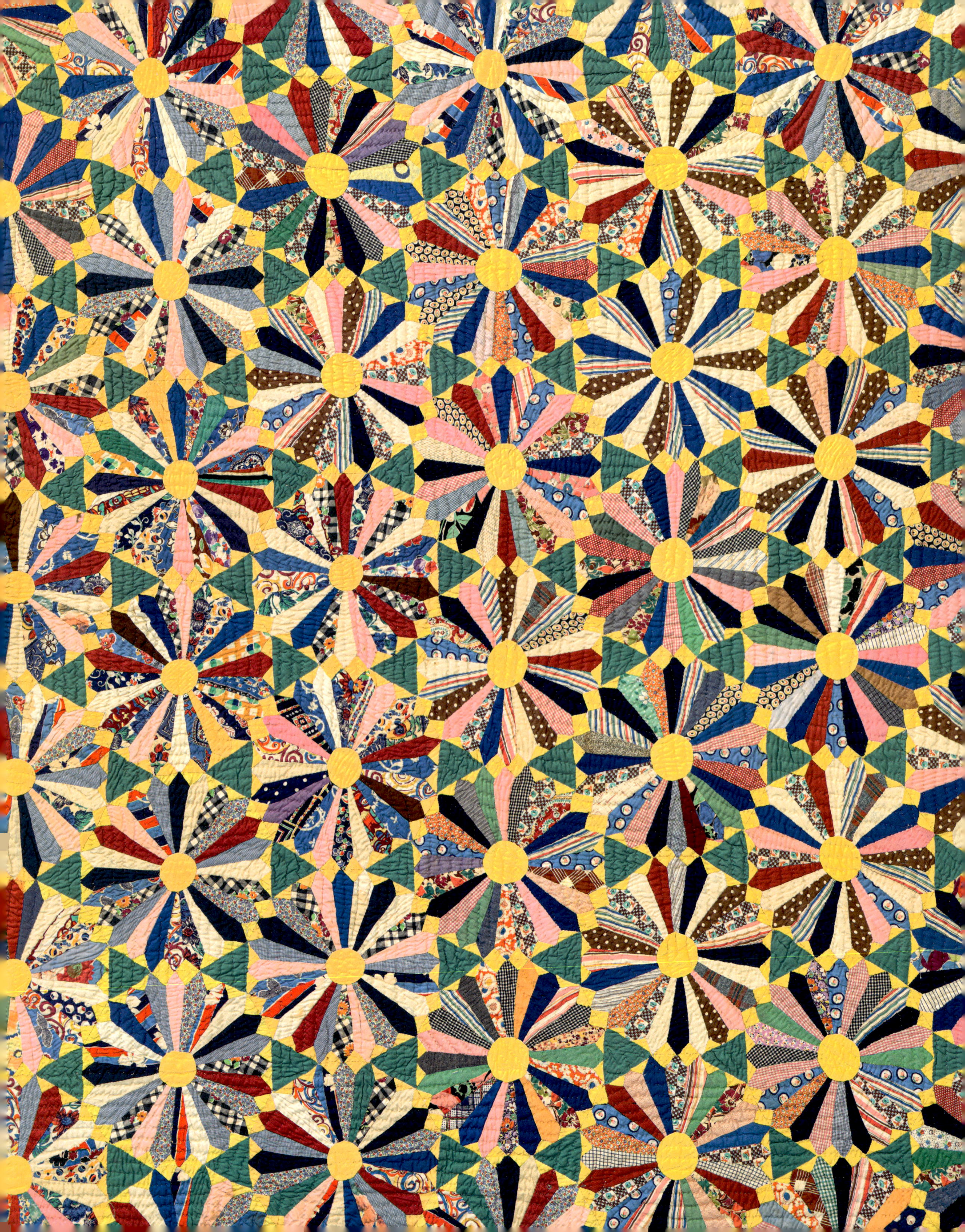

Routed West
Twentieth-Century African American Quilts in California

Edited by Elaine Y. Yau

With contributions by

Daphne A. Brooks
Bridget R. Cooks
Basil Kincaid
Eli Leon
Carolyn Mazloomi
Adia Millett
Matthew Villar Miranda
Sharbreon Plummer
A'donna Richardson
Wendy M. Thompson
Elaine Y. Yau

University of California, Berkeley Art Museum
and Pacific Film Archive

DelMonico Books • D.A.P. New York

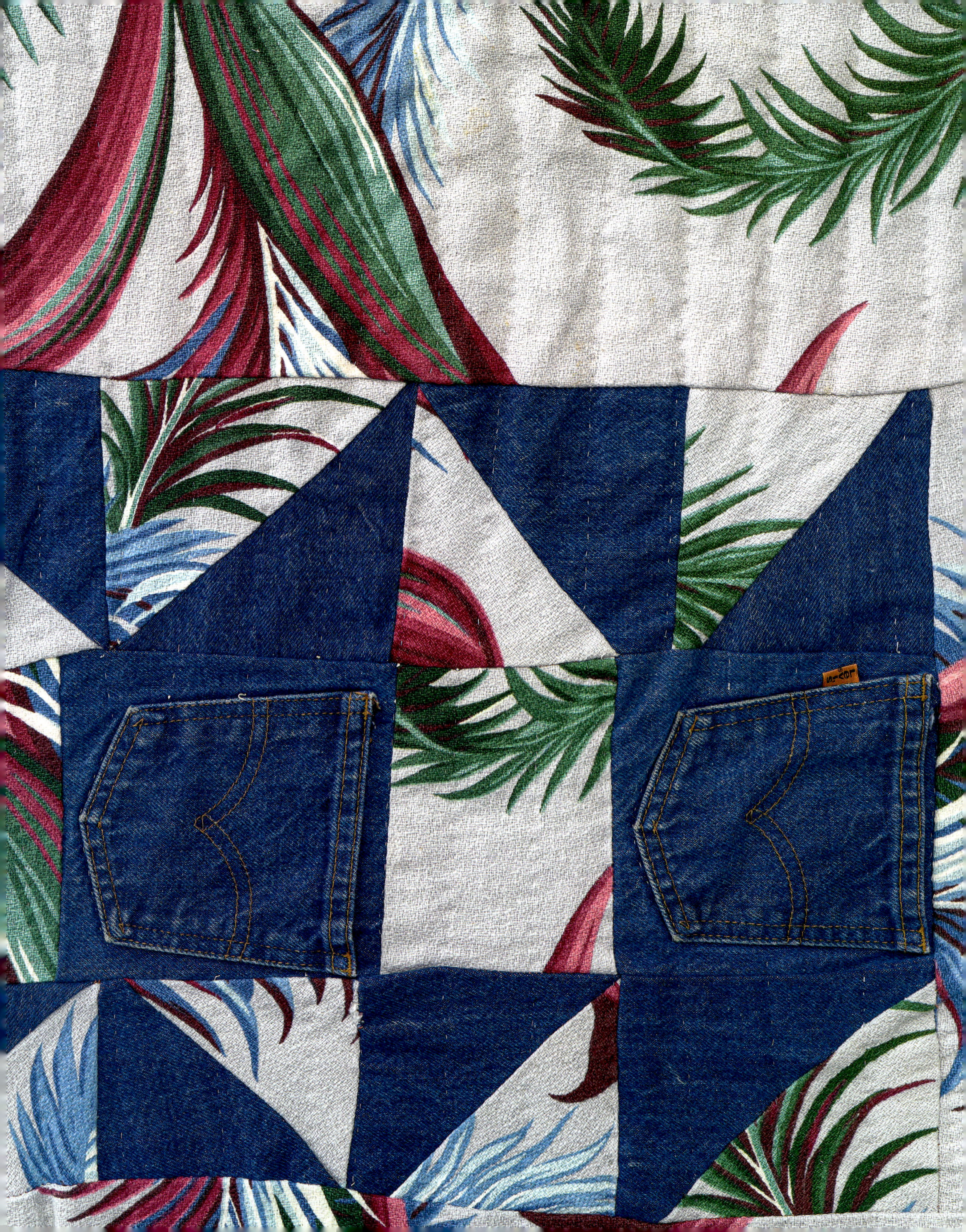

Contents

Director's Foreword

When I joined the University of California, Berkeley Art Museum and Pacific Film Archive, in the summer of 2020, *Rosie Lee Tompkins: A Retrospective* was installed in dark galleries, closed to the public during the COVID-19 lockdown. By the time we were able to reopen more than a year later following unprecedented press coverage and an outpouring of public interest in the exhibition, I understood the immense allure of Tompkins's quilts in particular, and the familiar, if not even familial, resonance of quilts in people's lives in general. Tompkins's quilts were sublime to experience yet humbly crafted from everyday fabrics. Displaying this type of work in an art museum argues for their rightful place in this context, alongside other genres such as photography, craft, video, and installation art that similarly took time to join the more traditional "fine arts" of painting and sculpture in museum collections. In her review, *New York Times* critic Roberta Smith wrote, "The field of improvisational quilting by African-American women is not small, but beyond the great quilters of Gee's Bend, Ala., and a few others, their work is not widely known. Rosie Lee Tompkins's version of what Eli Leon called 'flexible patterning' may have been more extreme than anyone else's. Or perhaps not. It would be gratifying to learn that she did not act alone." And knowing that BAMPFA held more than three thousand artworks by African American quiltmakers that were given as a bequest from the Oakland-based collector Eli Leon in 2019, I felt the responsibility of sharing these stories not only as part of African American material culture and history but also as part of American art history.

A bequest of this size meant that BAMPFA would require many partners to ensure the quilts' physical care for future generations. At the same time, it quickly became apparent that the histories of hundreds of quiltmakers represented by the gift required a different kind of stewardship. The quilts represented the cultural and artistic heritage of generations of African American families even as they physically resided at the University of California, Berkeley. With generous funding from the Terra Foundation of American Art, BAMPFA hosted a series of Quilt Study Days in the fall of 2022 that helped staff and Board members understand more clearly the ethics of care required by these quilts. The Study Days included the first of what will be many cross-disciplinary discussions to map a future for quilts and help us more deeply understand their joyful power in sustaining Black life—as objects of beauty, ingenuity and imagination, collective care, and memory.

We are indebted to the Quilt Study Day participants for their time and candor, giving the museum some guiding principles as we move forward with research and exhibition planning. They encouraged BAMPFA to place historical truth-telling at the forefront of our work, especially around Eli Leon's role as the collection's principal interpreter until now. They also clarified the significance of connecting and building trust with contemporary Black quiltmakers and with the quilts' families of origin. After nearly two and a half years of focused preparation, the result is *Routed West: Twentieth-Century African American Quilts in California*, an exhibition that pays tribute to the quiltmakers and quilt-keepers who were a part of the historic arrival of thousands of African Americans to California—and especially the Bay Area—between 1940 and 1970, following the onset of World War II. As Franklin D. Roosevelt urged the US to become "the arsenal of democracy" abroad, many Black Americans living in the South responded to the president's call to patriotic service by enlisting and entering the workforce to meet the war's demands. At the same time, they forged their own paths toward realizing the nation's promises of equality and the right to a life lived in freedom.

While not specifically about the wartime experience, the quilts in the exhibition speak to larger themes of kinship, survival, and caretaking that underlined the lives that African American migrants during this period were, in effect, defending. Roughly a quarter of the one hundred quilts included in *Routed West* were made in the South before 1950, reflecting the roots of Black quiltmaking and the kinds of objects that migrants kept close during their journeys westward. The remaining quilts were created in California in the postwar period (and mostly after 1970), a time by which many migrants had left the workforce and returned to a craft they were taught as children. Taken together, the quilts in the exhibition exemplify their unique capacity for holding memory and ancestral knowledge and supporting creative expression and spiritual renewal across generations. In many ways it is a local story of national significance told through everyday individuals, who left their creative mark on the history of American art.

I am grateful to Elaine Y. Yau, Associate Curator and Academic Liaison, for recentering our understanding of this medium within the longer history of African American culture and her inclusive vision for this catalogue's group of contributors. They represent fields ranging from academia, contemporary quilt guilds, and individual artistic practices to quilt historians, each offering a fresh perspective on the vitality of African American-made quilts for audiences today and on how BAMPFA can bring others along in the work of stewarding them for the future.

Several partners have been essential supporters from the very beginning. The Henry Luce Foundation was the first to respond to the immense responsibilities facing BAMPFA in caring for the quilt collection. Their generosity allowed the museum to establish a three-year curatorial position dedicated to its physical care and interpretation. They also furnished crucial support in producing the catalog for *Routed West*, providing funds for photography, essayists, and consultants. A major grant from the Bank of America Art Conservation Project underwrote the conservation of more than seven hundred quilts, which allowed the curatorial process for *Routed West* to advance. BAMPFA is able to continue the ongoing work of conservation through a major grant from the Save America's Treasures program of the Institute of Museum and Library Services. The Chancellor's Office of UC Berkeley, led by the now-retired Carol Christ, has also been unflagging in helping the museum conserve the collection. Additional support for the catalog is provided by Brenda and Michael Drake and by a grant from the Black Studies Collaboratory at UC Berkeley, an awardee of the Mellon Foundation's Just Futures Initiative. The Terra Foundation for American Art gave crucial support at the research and implementation stages, the impact of which will continue to reverberate beyond the life of this exhibition. I also extend my deep gratitude to the Shah Garg Women Artists Research Fund for providing additional major support for the exhibition and partnering with BAMPFA to advance conversations around equity and representation.

The care for the quilts and production of the exhibition and this publication have been, and continue to be, twin efforts that BAMPFA's outstanding staff have shouldered for the past five years. I especially wish to thank the following, along with Elaine, for their tireless work in making space, quite literally, for these artworks to enter the museum: John Alexander, Director of Collections and Exhibitions; Laura Graziano, Registrar for Collections and Loans; Laura Hansen, Collections Specialist; and Nada Shalaby, former Senior Grants Officer.

Finally, I wish to extend my profound thanks to the quiltmakers and their descendants with whom we have been able to connect and engage. Being able to present a part of their family stories and celebrate their achievements is one of the great honors in the work museums can do.

Julie Rodrigues Widholm
Executive Director
Berkeley Art Museum and Pacific Film Archive

Acknowledgments

As it often is with quilts, this exhibition and catalog came to fruition through the time, energy, and generosity of many. I would first like to thank Larry Rinder, former director of BAMPFA, for inviting me to work with him on *Rosie Lee Tompkins: A Retrospective* over five years ago. That project marked the beginning of my engagement with quilts, which has enriched my life in ways beyond anything I could have imagined.

Planning for the collection's initial inventory, rehousing, and conservation was a daunting but crucial phase of the project that allowed research for this exhibition to proceed. For their cheerful professionalism that made light work of a long process, I am grateful to Ashley Elieff, Ben Peters, and Atthowe Fine Art Services, especially Malu Beltran, Jenny Galipo, Aaron Gogerty, Taz Johnson, Jordan Konz, and Van McSweeney. The team at Art Conservation de Rigueur led by Elise Rousseau have expertly advised on, undertaken, and continue to implement many rounds of treatment for the quilt collection, and I thank them for their long-term partnership. Amy DiPlacido and Carolina Cuevas provided essential support in cataloging quilts considered for this show, as well as friendship and insights into textiles for which I am deeply appreciative.

I am indebted to the participants of the Terra Foundation-funded Quilt Study Days held in the fall of 2022: Bamidele Agbasegbe-Demerson, Nancy Bavor, Camille Ann Brewer, Ash Brown, Marsha Carter, Ora Clay, Lisa Gail Collins, Bridget R. Cooks, Jenny Hurth, Roderick Kiracofe, Zondra Martin, Adia Millett, Sharbreon Plummer, Amy Reid, Sunny Smith, Patricia A. Turner; and BAMPFA Board and Collections Committee members Brenda Drake, Cathy Koshland, Katrina Traywick, and Cheryl Ward. They formed the first community of advisors for the quilt collection, and their wisdom has been invaluable across the development of this exhibition.

Many individuals lent their gifts to bring this book to print, in particular Kevin Candland for his lush photography and Danica Favorito for her assistance in staging during the photo sessions; Eric Zeidler for his sensitive editing of the entire volume; Jonathan Corum for the lucid maps; and Miko McGinty and Rita Jules for enthusiastically supporting unique aspects of the book and presenting them so elegantly on the page. Julie Silber and A'donna Richardson lent decades of experience to ensure the accuracy of the information included here, while creating new spaces to talk about the future of quilt studies. Nusheen Ghaemi, Guanhong (Andy) Liu, and Abby Simmons were exceptional undergraduates whose research made the maps and visual essay possible. I am profoundly grateful to each of the contributors for saying "yes" to expanding the contexts for African American quilts and elevating them with personal and professional perspectives.

To my BAMPFA colleagues for the support and excellence that made this exhibition and catalog possible, thank you: to Julie Rodrigues Widholm, Executive Director, and Margot Norton, Chief Curator, for their trust and commitment to stewarding the quilt collection with integrity; Anthony Graham, Senior Curator, for his wisdom at various stages of writing and many conversations about the place of quilts in BAMPFA's collection at large; Jess Kreglow, Laura Hansen, Mike Meyers, Scott Orloff, J Pansa, and Laura Graziano on the prep and registration teams, who not only created a new quilt storage space and facilitated their transfers between conservation and the museum, but also beautifully installed the galleries; and Aimée Goggins, Beverly Bradley, AJ Fox, Eva Kalea, and Daria Lugina, who brought many audiences into the world of quilts through their press and marketing work. Justin Glasson, Carrie Kahn, and Nada Shalaby were extraordinary partners in raising funds that impacted every phase of the project; Nada's unparalleled ability to draw out the collection's most compelling narratives, her attention to detail, and her gracious manner in particular deserve a presentation quilt on their own. The programs organized by Sherry Goodman, Karen Bennett, David Wilson, and Sean Carson brought so many aspects of the exhibition to life, and I extend my gratitude to them for their dedication to serving BAMPFA's audiences. I am particularly grateful to John Alexander, Director of Collections and Exhibitions, whose experience steered many complex operations simultaneously and made the everyday realities of conservation, exhibition, and book production run smoothly, and with laughter. My curatorial colleague Matthew Villar Miranda was also an indispensable collaborator in seeing nearly every aspect of the exhibition and catalog through to completion; I am in awe of his organizational wizardry and admire the warmth he imparts to everything he does. I also sincerely thank other current and former BAMPFA staff–Lisa Calden, Stephanie Cannizzo, Alex Confer, Lauren Finch, Claire Frost, Steve Fujimura, Lynne Kimura, Tracy Jones, Albert Liu, Lucia Olubunmi Momoh, Katelyn Nomura-Weingrow, Andrea Rossainz, Orlando Antonio Sanchez, Dave Taylor, Julia M. White, and

Christina Yang–who advanced the project at key points. Like stitches that bind the layers of a quilt together, these individuals perform less visible but essential work that activates BAMPFA's mission. It is an honor to be a part of this team.

Over the course of developing the exhibition's concept, the following individuals offered time and conversation for this project to evolve, and I wish to acknowledge their generosity here: Carin Adams, Barney and Jess Bailey, Laverne Brackens and the entire family in Fairfield, Julia Bryan-Wilson, Sherry Ann and Curtis Byrd, Sonya Clark, Jacqueline Francis and her Visual Critical Studies students at CCA, Sammy Howard, Joyce Hulbert, Lillian LeBlanc, Marsha MacDowell, Danielle Mason, Tracy McCurty, Kathi Neal, Deann Tyler, and Peter Washburn; my cohort at the Townsend Center for the Humanities at UC Berkeley; Barbara Montano, Tianna Paschel, and Leigh Raiford of the Black Studies Collaboratory for including me in their expansive vision for Black Studies; and Berkeley Americanist Group members Susan Eberhard, Elizabeth Fair, Margaretta Lovell, Molly Robinson, and Alberto Sanchez-Sanchez. For their critical insights and encouragement on drafts of the lead essay, I am full of gratitude to Jess Bailey, Nancy Bavor, Lisa Gail Collins, and A'donna Richardson. It has also been a privilege getting to know members of the African American Quilt Guild of Oakland, who taught me so much about quilts and caring for communities in the East Bay. To my husband John, our sons, and our extended families: thank you for making space for this project at home with love and teaching me how to tend generations in a personal way.

Ultimately, this exhibition is dedicated to Black quiltmakers past and present, whose artistry, stewardship, and ethic of care gives more abundantly than any museum show can capture. It is for them and their descendants, foremost and with deep gratitude, that BAMPFA seeks to honor their creative legacy in quilts and in life.

Elaine Y. Yau
Associate Curator and Academic Liaison
Berkeley Art Museum and Pacific Film Archive

NOTE ON TERMINOLOGY

African American and *Black* are related but distinct terms that appear throughout this catalog. The former is used mainly in reference to experiences, practices, communities, and art of people of African descent who are directly connected to the history of enslavement in what is now the United States. The latter term is broader, referring to descendants of Indigenous peoples of Africa and the African Diaspora globally. *Black* is an adjective that is capitalized throughout in recognition of shared senses of identity, community, culture, and history within a widely diverse set of ethnic and racial experiences.

Throughout this catalog, *quiltmaker* appears more frequently as the general term for someone who makes quilts, along with *quiltmaking*, as distinct from *quilter* and *quilting*, terms that emphasize the act of stitching the three layers of a traditional quilt together (that is, the top or more decorative layer, the middle insulating layer or batting, and the back).

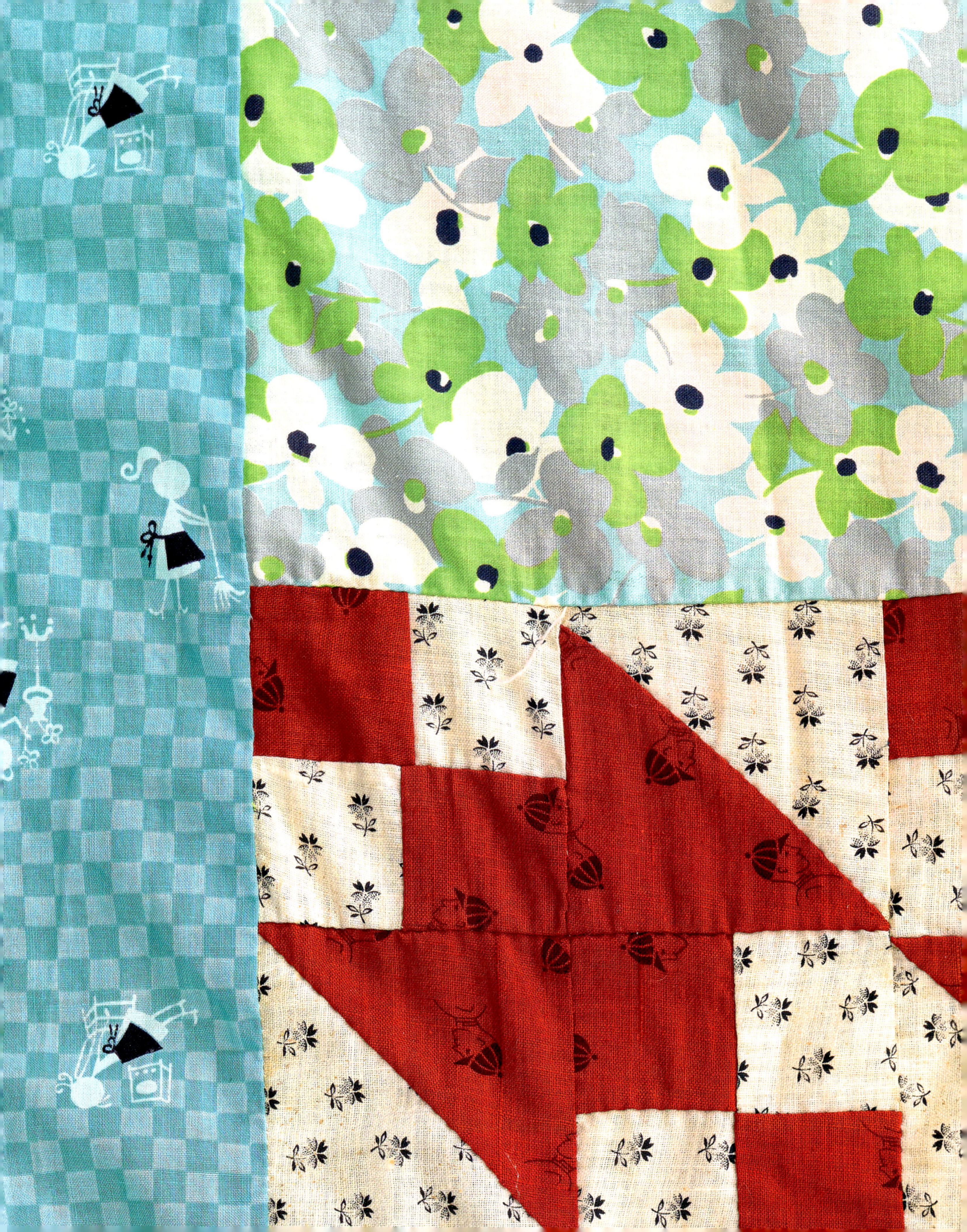

Routed West: Twentieth-Century African American Quilts in California

Elaine Y. Yau

In 1944, well into the United States' involvement in World War II, Selena Foster and her husband, Marvin Foster, left their home in Fort Worth, Texas, to join Selena's brother Floyd Anderson in Richmond, California. Encouraged by Floyd's success in securing higher wages in Richmond's shipyards and by tales of the state's more racially integrated environment, they were determined to make the journey. With a gasoline voucher in hand and family farewells behind them, they began driving west. Four days later, they arrived at Floyd's wartime housing at 52nd Street and Ernest Avenue in Richmond. Marvin began working in the Kaiser shipyards in February, while Selena found work at Leo's Defense Diner (fig. 1). Before long, they purchased their own trailer in El Cerrito and were earning nearly double the amount they had been making back home.[1] They lived the remainder of their lives in northern California's East Bay. For the Fosters, as for the 1.5 million migrants and nearly 340,000 African Americans who came to California between 1940 and 1944 to meet the demands of wartime mobilization, to be "in California" was more than just a geographical location.[2] It was a stake in the dream for a better life.

Along with their 1935 Chevy sedan, suitcases, and hope for the future, Selena carried the roots of her family quiltmaking traditions westward. These roots were first established at the young age of eight, when she would thread her grandmother's needles before leaving for school in rural East Texas, practice piecing with the scraps, and eventually learn to make clothes for her dolls and herself.[3] These talents would flourish more visibly after many years of working, when, in 1966, Selena began quilting more actively as part of her recovery from surgery. She served as chairwoman of the Easter Hill Quilters and sometimes collaborated with her sister Mable Battle, whose family moved from Texas to California shortly after the Fosters (cat. 56).[4] Sewing was a skill she taught to her two grandnieces, whom she was helping to raise when she was interviewed in 1986. As with generations of Black women who hailed from the southern United States, her ability to quilt was more than a functional skill or a hobby rekindled later in life. It embodied an ethic of living inherited from her foremothers—anchored in self-sufficiency, community care, and the creation of beauty—pieced together from thrift and intended to spread love among succeeding generations seeking liberated lives of their own.

A quilt top made by Effie Edwards in the 1960s expresses these themes of Foster's capsule biography in marvelously poetic ways (cat. 37). Although we do not know where

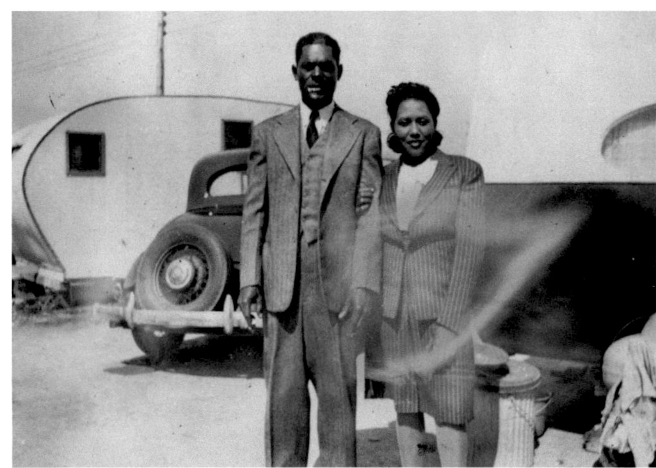

Fig. 1. Marvin and Selena Foster in a trailer court at 1900 Wright Avenue, Richmond, close to the Kaiser Shipyard, September 1944. Photographs of Selena Foster and family, accompanying her oral history interview, BANC PIC 1993.050-PIC, The Bancroft Library, University of California, Berkeley

Opposite: Detail of cat. 37

Edwards pieced this top—it might have been Madera or Fresno, California—we can say that she decided one day to compose a checkerboard pattern from some old blocks that her mother, Sarah Moore, had pieced in the 1890s and 1910s, when they lived in Okfuskee County, Oklahoma. Edwards alternated fifteen Jacob's Ladder blocks with squares of a delicate floral print of lime green, gray, and white. She added another column at the far right, possibly to bring the top up to bed-size. Again, she reached into her fabric stash and incorporated three T blocks that were probably also left over from her mother, using additional strips of fabric to enlarge these smaller blocks and maintain her grid. With precision, Edwards kept the top "beautiful and neat," the way she preferred.[5]

She also crafted a sly statement about her creative lineage through her choice of border fabric (p. 10). In the print she used, small female figures wearing black aprons perform all kinds of household chores against a turquoise and light blue checkerboard: one sweeps, another cooks on a stovetop, while others vacuum, hang laundry, scrub floors, carry dishes, and arrange flowers. In only one instance does she rest, or technically slump, in a chair in front of a radio. Here is menial work that infuses the cliché, "Woman's work is never done," with a cheerful lightness.

While these cartoonish images deflect tedium with humor, in the context of Edwards's top, the idea of women's work takes on a more powerful tone, one where technical skill, know-how, and thrift can reconfigure ordinary scraps of fabric into something exuberantly creative and personal. I want to emphasize *can*, for I do not have Edwards's story about the creation of this pieced top, but like any artwork, it is suggestive. Jacob's Ladder blocks invoke portals to heaven in the space of the quilt top. And of all the blocks Edwards could have placed in the upper right, she chose a pattern called "Farmer's Daughter," possibly as a nod to her relationship with her father, Lee Moore, who worked her family's land in Louisiana and Oklahoma. In distinction from her daytime work as a housekeeper (referenced in the border), we might imagine Edwards with needle and thread or at her sewing machine, "com[ing] back to herself" and reveling in quiltmaking as "a work which renewed the spirit."[6] Kept by Edwards's daughter Zula Mae Johnson (also a quilter), its lessons and memory become enveloped by another layer of intergenerational dialogue.

Read alongside Selena Foster's story, Moore and Edwards's top reminds us that the stuff of westward migration differs from the statistics or lines on a map that record mass movements of people, but all of these need to be kept in view in order to appreciate more fully the aspirations and textures of Black life in California. As cultural geographer Wendy Thompson emphasizes in this volume, such accounts are full of "unmappable things and places, intangible communities and ghost sites, no-longer-existing landmarks and the many public and private objects and practices that can define Black life in the West."[7] In this sense, patchwork quilts by African American makers survive as objects that provide access to dimensions of life that would otherwise remain intangible, like the worlds of individual and collective feeling, creative choices and tastes, or details about a moment in time.[8] In offering an account of the westward flow and flourishing of this artistic medium, *Routed West: Twentieth Century African American Quilts in California* threads the needle of Black people's historical movements in the context of the Second Great Migration with the poetics of their quilts and particulars of their intergenerational stories.

Rather than claiming to offer a comprehensive or authoritative account of quilts in this historical context, *Routed West* explores themes related to a group of over one hundred artworks by ninety individuals. About one-quarter of the quilts included in the exhibition were made in the US South before 1950, representing the cultural roots of African American quiltmaking and its diverse methods and styles. The fact that a substantial number of them were brought to California by succeeding family members and survive today attests to the value that quilts could carry over distance and time. The remaining quilts and patchwork objects were made in the postwar period, and primarily after 1970, when most migrants had left the workforce and taken up quilting traditions that they had known as children. While the sections of this essay unfold across a linear trajectory taking readers from southern states to California, they wend their way around individual stories that demonstrate how quilts can be a nexus for tethering friends and family in these different contexts. They also place special emphasis on quiltkeeping alongside quiltmaking, not only to draw out the memory work involved in both practices, but to illuminate the ethics of care and love underlining quilts' creation and use.

This exhibition is anchored in the history of the Second Great Migration, when nearly five million African Americans left the South between 1940 and 1980 for urban centers throughout the country, including those along the West Coast.[9] As distinct from the earlier arrivals of Southerners that occurred between 1910 and 1940, the Second Great Migration to California was defined by the pull of wartime jobs coupled with migrants' determination to flee the "man-made pestilence" of racist terror that surrounded their lives.[10] The impact of federal spending in drawing workers westward cannot be overstated: California alone received close to 10 percent of all federal spending on war-related

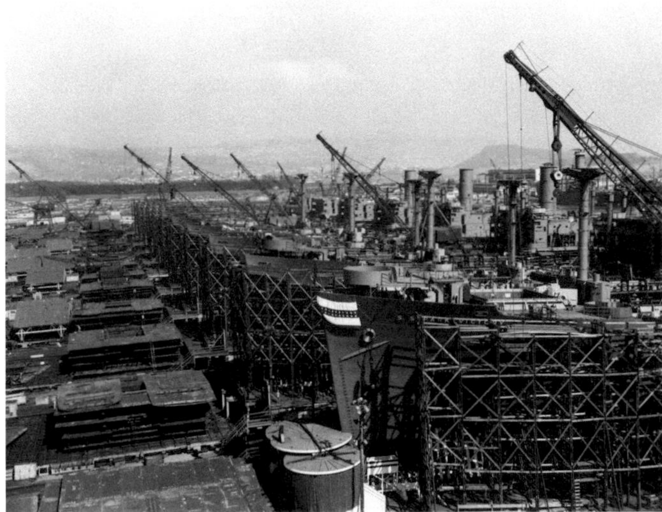

Fig. 2. Richmond Shipyard 2 with the SS *Park Victory* under construction, Richmond, California, 1945. Richmond Museum of History & Culture, Richmond, CA, 3550.37

industries, of which nearly $5 billion accounted for government shipbuilding contracts.[11] The influx of migrants who arrived to fuel this historic growth helped the US reach peak production by 1944, when nearly 40 percent of all war goods produced worldwide were supplied by American workers.[12] The demographic shifts among Black Californians who clustered around the Bay Area and Los Angeles reflect the pull of better jobs and the determination to cut ties with the oppressive environment in the South. By 1950, nearly 80 percent of the African American population of California had been born outside of the state, with the highest number of residents hailing from Texas (22%), followed by Louisiana (18.5%), Arkansas (8.5%), Mississippi (5.4%), and Oklahoma (5.3%).[13] The majority of the quiltmakers in *Routed West* belong to this generation of migrants who arrived during and after World War II (only two, Quinciana Tatmon of Louisiana and Bettie Phillips of Oklahoma, came in the 1930s). As Isabel Wilkerson indelibly writes, Black migrants' resolve initiated "the first mass act of independence by a people who were in bondage in this country for far longer than they had been free."[14]

Population trends in the East Bay, where the majority of the quiltmakers in this exhibition settled, reflect this influx of dream-seekers who transformed small towns into boomtowns. The engines of wartime industry dotted the landscape of the Bay Area (see map, pp. 42-43). Richmond's Kaiser Shipyards, the largest shipbuilding operation in the country (figs. 2-3), were among the first to employ African American workers (along with workers of Chinese, Mexican, and Native American descent), and increased Richmond's Black population from 270 in 1940 to 10,000 in 1945.[15] The Mare Island Naval Shipyard in Vallejo, a town just north of Richmond, and the nearby Port Chicago annex of the Naval Ammunition Depot experienced a tenfold increase in its Black population during the war years, up from 438 people in 1940.[16] Oakland's Black population grew from 8,462 to 21,770 during the war years, absorbing many newcomers who found work in the Moore Dry Dock Company shipyard, the Naval Supply Center and nearby naval installation, and in several

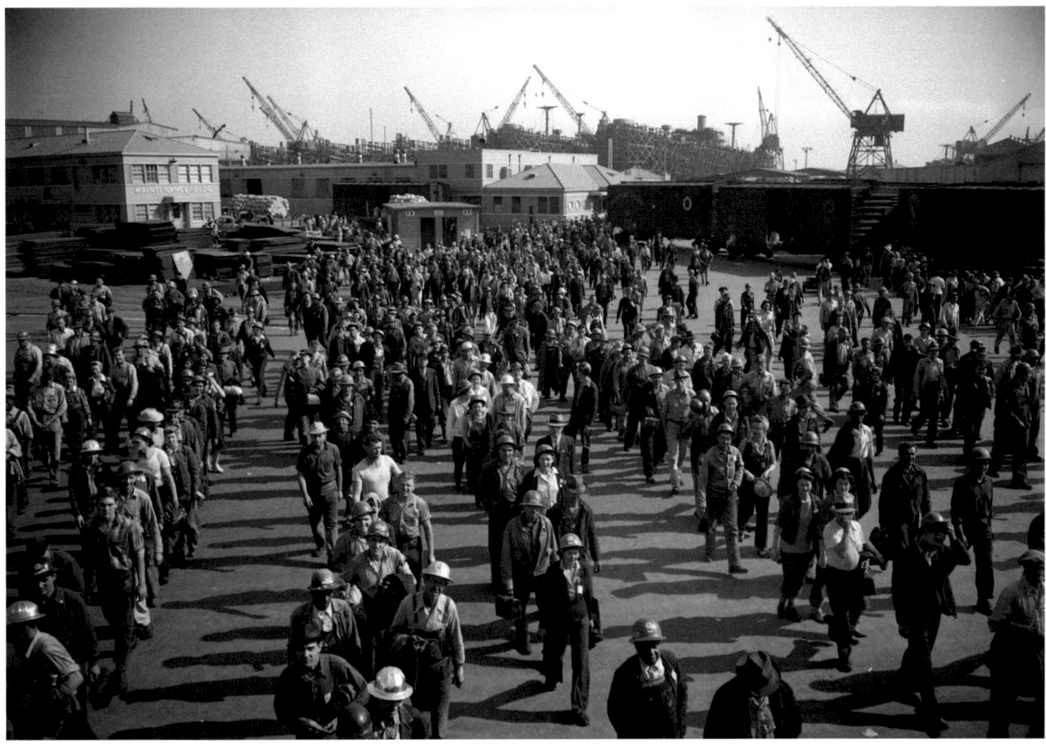

Fig. 3. Dorothea Lange, *Shift Change 3:30 PM, Coming on of Yard 3, Kaiser Shipyards,* 1942. Photonegative. The Oakland Museum of California. Gift of Paul S. Taylor. A67.137.42097.2

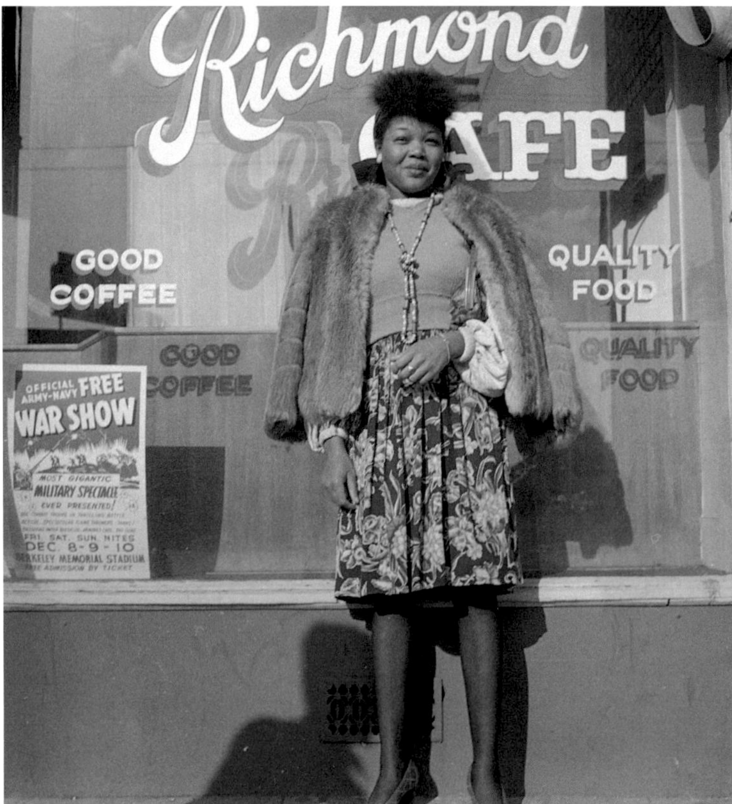

Fig. 4. Dorothea Lange, *Woman Standing in front of Richmond Cafe*, c. 1942. Photonegative. The Oakland Museum of California. Gift of Paul S. Taylor. A67.137.42056.3

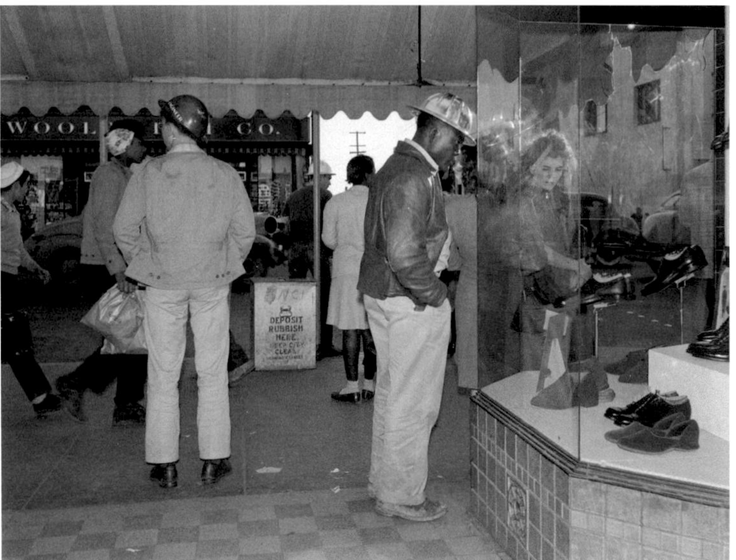

Fig. 5. Dorothea Lange, *Buying Power of Shipyard Workers, MacDonald Ave.*, c. 1943. Photonegative. The Oakland Museum of California. Gift of Paul S. Taylor. A67.137.42059

food processing plants, all of which were crucial in supporting the war effort.[17] Dorothea Lange's iconic photographs capture the scale of this new labor force and accessibility of new wealth that people like the Fosters imagined in "this place that looks like heaven," near the ocean (figs. 3–5).[18] In San Francisco, a Black population of fewer than 5,000 grew nearly sixfold to 32,000.[19] Some, like Isiadore Whitehead, entered the shipyard workforce, while others, like Alice Neal, Arbie Williams, Jimmie Johnson, and Ruth Charlotte Clay, raised families, "kept house," or worked in service sectors while spouses clocked in their shifts. Later migrants followed in the footsteps of family and friends who paved the way.

Against this backdrop of movement and relocation, these individuals infused neighborhoods and cities with Black Southern lifeways—creative acts of living that claimed urban spaces for themselves.[20] They carried and kept quilts from their Southern homes, and with them the memories and roots of an artistic tradition that they would practice well into the twentieth century. Like cooking, planting the kitchen garden, giving newcomers a place to stay, worshiping, singing, gathering, and healing, quilts and quiltmaking were part of a social fabric imbued with the ethic of "love, care, and share" that migrants transplanted to the places where they settled in the West, strengthening communities with things and embodied sensibilities that could be renewed with every visit back home.[21] It is my hope that the quilt stories in this essay, along with the portraits of Black culture evocatively described in the other essays and texts, bring us closer to how quilts and quiltmaking lived with African American families across their migration journeys. These stories not only lend insights into African American women's history, but also help us understand how quilts have the capacity to hold some of life's deeply felt intangibles—memories, presences of loved ones, wishes, prayers, compromises—within their fibers.[22]

The intangibilities of quiltmaking apply also to thinking about a quilt's beginnings and how the medium inhabits worlds of metaphor and matter so seamlessly. In "The Time It Takes," Oakland-based quiltmaker and fiber artist Ora Clay offers this: "For some, the life of a quilt begins with planting cotton seeds like Mother had to do. For me, the clock may start with trying to express my feelings, called to design and create a quilt about important topics in the world."[23] For others, the life of a quilt might germinate with quilt blocks inherited from an aunt, or it could happen when one acts upon the creative urge to piece something new. And for still others, like Alice Walker and poet Marilou Awiakta, whom Walker quotes in her classic anthology *In Search of Our Mothers' Gardens*, a quilt, as an object of creation, has its origins in the "motheroot": that radical channel between generations of women and kin ("two hearts / one to root /

and one to flower") through which creativity flows and blooms, all the while offering a spiritual grounding to those who are suffering ("in time of drouth" and "against winds of pain").[24] These reflections speak to ways that the layers of personal meaning for which quilts are frequently known, especially in ones that do not assume a viewing public, grow out of conditions that are often immediate, ordinary, and profound at the same time. This exhibition lingers on the poetics and cultural roots that course through African American quilts, while recognizing their underexplored journeys to and within California.

In considering the movement of quilts across time and space, *Routed West* also necessarily reckons with their "routings" beyond the networks of quilters and their social circles, namely in connection with the Oakland-based collector Eli Leon (1935–2018; fig. 6) and their current way station, the Berkeley Art Museum and Pacific Film Archive. A white, gay Jewish man from the Bronx, Leon amassed nearly three thousand African American-made quilts and hundreds of unattributed ones by combing flea markets, scavenging dumpsters, purchasing from dealers, trading with other collectors, and eventually buying directly from quiltmakers starting in 1981 and continuing well into the early 2000s. As the three unpublished essays by Leon reproduced in this volume show, he was able to build such a vast collection in large part because of the sheer numbers of African American residents with ties to quilts and quiltmakers who migrated to the Bay Area. Leon's collecting was also directed by his ambition to generate new scholarship about African American quiltmaking and its relationship to African textile production. His ideas reached wide audiences through ten exhibitions he organized during his lifetime, the most influential of which were *Who'd a Thought It: Improvisation in African-American Quiltmaking* (1987) and *Accidentally on Purpose: The Aesthetic Management of Irregularities in African Textiles and African-American Quilts* (2006). Both exhibitions had accompanying publications and toured nationally. Collectively, they advanced a body of research focused on identifying retentions of African aesthetics across the Middle Passage in African American art that included scholarship by Robert Farris Thompson, Maude Southwell Wahlman, and John Michael Vlach.[25] Upon Leon's death, he bequeathed his collection to the University of California, Berkeley—believed to be the largest single gift of African American art and material culture to a museum.

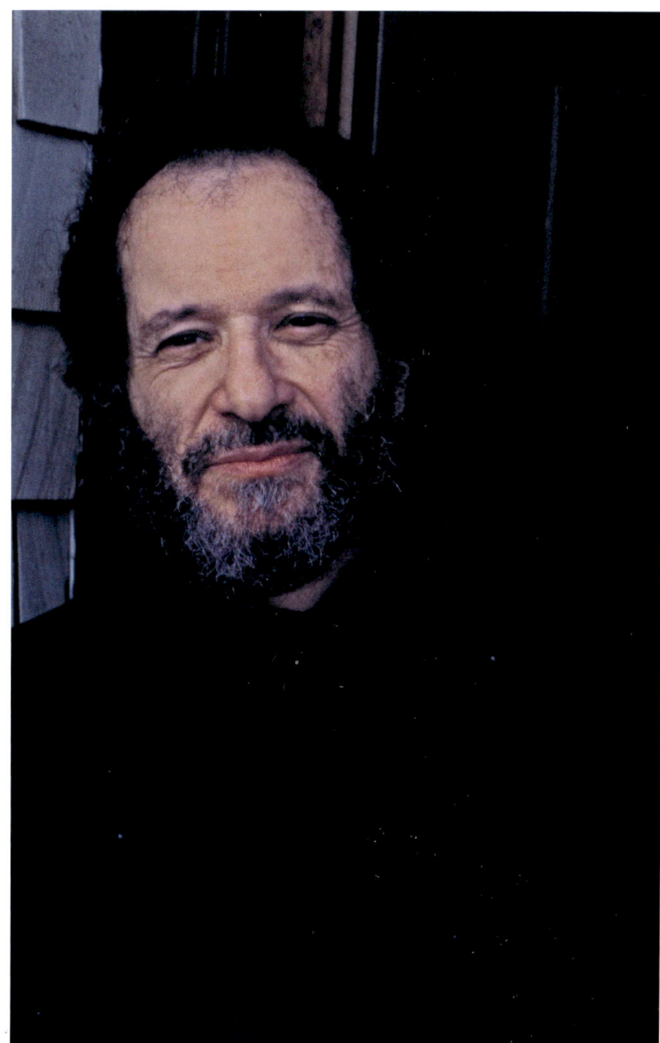

Fig. 6. Eli Leon, 1996

Criticisms of Leon's collecting practices and of his claims regarding African American quilting aesthetics highlight important concerns with his larger project over the past thirty years.[26] Among the most salient are those decrying his reliance on visual qualities over more rigorous historical research. For example, the visual characteristics that Leon and others ascribed to "Afro-traditional" quilts tend to simplify the complexities of quilting as a social practice and ignore the appearance of the same traits in quilts made by white quiltmakers. By attributing qualities like the prevalence of strip piecing, bold contrasting colors, multiple patterns and asymmetrical designs, and symbolic forms to a race-based style, Leon's arguments had the effect of "reduc[ing] African American quiltmaking to a quantifiable, simplistic caricature," in the words of quilt artist Sandra K. German.[27] The problematic aspects of Leon's formalist approach show up in his archive in notes such as the following connected to cat. 21: "From Marie at Alameda Flea. She had a bunch of tops that all looked Black."[28] In effect, African American quiltmakers whose work did not conform to this supposed set of "defining characteristics" often faced dismissal from those in the largely white quilt world, an attitude that also placed them at a disadvantage within the market.

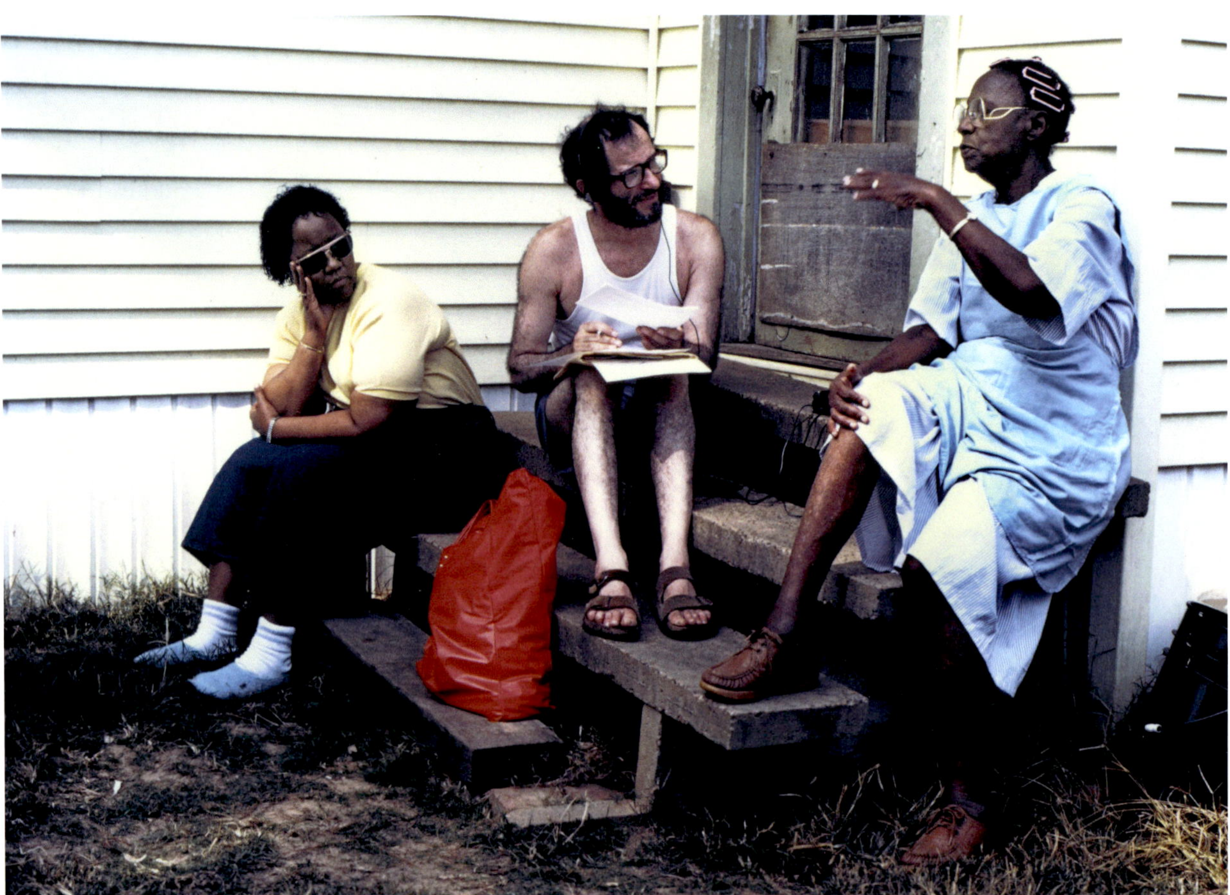

Fig. 7. Eli Leon interviewing Joanna Smiley (right) with her daughter, Sulphur Springs, Texas, 1989

The mixed blessings of Eli Leon's bequest have only become clearer as my colleagues and I have sought to understand its full scope. On the one hand, Leon understood well the precarity of a quilt's survival and sought to document quiltmakers' backgrounds and their methods of construction whenever possible. His written records and interviews with quiltmakers have provided valuable access to the stories assembled here. Because of his advocacy, we know about the extraordinary talents of women like Rosie Lee Tompkins (cat. 110), who expressed her own appreciation for Leon's efforts. On the other hand, his extractive methods of collecting within Black communities have resulted in a legacy fraught with inequities (fig. 7). While Leon recorded interviews and secured consent, he did not prioritize interviewees' interests in their own representation, nor was he interested in centering their lives in the stories of their quilts. The interviews are not, for example, formal conversations but rather touch-and-go phone exchanges, in which the quilters are approached as informants rather than artists or coequals in generating stories about themselves and their quilts. Additionally, Leon's focus on quilts that embodied improvisational abstraction has meant that there are few examples of figurative or story quilts that might offer more legible, first-person accounts of their makers. At the same time, questions about the relationship between his queer identity and advocacy for historically "low" forms of art have not been fully explored,[29] nor have his financial dealings with quiltmakers, which have generated appropriate concerns about his equitable treatment of them.

While these issues remain unresolved for now, they provide important context for the curatorial decisions informing the exhibition. Foremost among them was recognizing the need to consult with those who have been engaged in collecting, making, exhibiting, and researching quilts long before the arrival of Leon's bequest. Indeed, half of the contributors to this book were involved in the Quilt Study Days that BAMPFA hosted in 2022;[30] many others who are named in the acknowledgments are still valued collaborators. Another important decision was recognizing the opportunity for the exhibition to tell a larger (and local) story about artists who made their home in California. In this regard, *Routed West* seeks to uplift Black quilt culture by way of returning to the histories of the quiltmakers whose work Leon championed, allowing their lives and values to take center stage while helping us in the present to best honor their legacies.

SOUTHERN ROOTS

The story of *Routed West* begins in the antebellum South, where the conditions around African American quiltmaking were the most pronounced. Revolving around plantation systems that relied upon the brutal enslavement of Black people to build wealth around the extraction of cotton, tobacco, and other raw materials for white elites, the social relations of the South structure the histories of the quilts made by the two oldest individuals in the exhibition, Monin Brown and Hattie "Strawberry" Mitchell. They were sisters who were born into slavery, lived through the Civil War and Emancipation, and remained linked to white employers until their deaths in 1930 and 1942 respectively. Brown was the live-in caregiver to William M. and Flewellyn Johnston's daughter Viola, and Mitchell was employed as the family's house servant. William Johnston, a banker, was remembered as "one of the leading capitalists" of Macon, Georgia.[31]

What we know of their extant quilts speaks to enduring dynamics of bondage into the early twentieth century, where Black labor was frequently subordinated to white power—and where piecemeal accounts of African American-made quilts came from white storytellers. According to Johnston family oral history, Mitchell's leaf appliqué quilt (cat. 2) was made between 1907 and 1908, following a 1906 trip to France, in which Mitchell accompanied the family and stayed with them at the Hôtel du Jardin. At each of the locations they visited (Champs-Élysées, St. Malo, Jardin du Luxembourg, and Nice, among others), they collected leaves used by Mitchell as patterns for cotton fabric that she then arranged and appliquéd onto undyed natural cloth with decorative stitching. She subsequently embroidered the names of the places, tracing William Johnston's looping cursive and printed handwriting. The final leaf, from the Garden of Gethsemane, was given to Mitchell by Viola in 1914 and is the smallest long green shape in the lower right block embroidered with "PARIS." It was backed and quilted several decades later, around 1930, before it was passed down to Viola's daughter, Valerie Shields, who brought it with her to California. The Johnstons named it "Hattie's Leaf Quilt."

In its harmonious composition of green and red botanical shapes combined into general symmetries, this quilt recalls the visual language of album quilts that were popular among white elites in Maryland as early as the 1840s, and that were known throughout the eastern seaboard (fig. 8). This type of quilt commonly showcased a maker's needlework skills and was presented to notable figures or made to commemorate special occasions. Yet rather than Mitchell's quilt drawing its inspiration from conventional album quilt motifs such as wreaths, stylized flowers, or symbols of friendship and patriotism, the story behind it opens up the possibility that she based it on her own lived experience. She composed an album of her travels abroad with the family, even enlisting her employer to assist her in naming sites they visited. While the quilt documents travels in which Mitchell was the servant—and may have been made at her employer's request—its design could be read as Hattie's in more ways than the family's title lets on: a collection of *her* memories of royal gardens or French coastal towns, voyages across the ocean and back, or her illness that befell her on the trip—which could only be cured once Mr. Johnston "searched the markets and found for her some sweet potatoes and turnip greens."[32] Though we have scant access to her reflections on this trip, her handiwork invites us to think about how they might have emerged during quiet periods of patient, careful stitching.

A patchwork quilt completed in 1932 (cat. 3) differs vastly in look from the leaf appliqué quilt and shows the range of quilting styles that were familiar to Mitchell and her sister. It is constructed of a variety of common patterns ranging from String, Log Cabin, Little Boy's Britches, and Diamond in Square, among others, and utilizes lightweight rayon, cotton, and silk scraps. Mitchell and Brown may have acquired these fabric scraps from the Johnston family or from their own neighbors in Macon's Pleasant Hill neighborhood, where prominent Black residents lived within the segregated city. No larger than the back of a small sofa and quilted without batting, this quilt may have been used as a

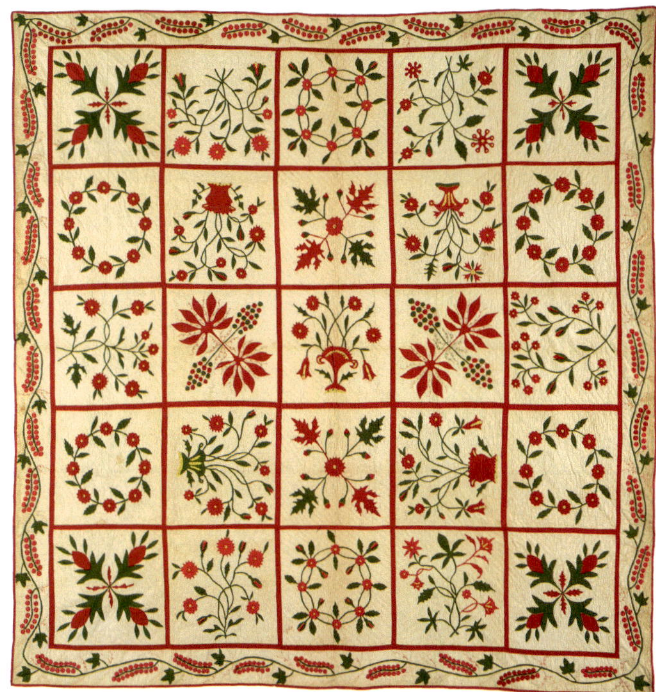

Fig. 8. *Quilt, Appliquéd Maryland Album*, made by Carr and Worthington family members, Anne Arundel County, Maryland, 1840–1855. Plain and printed cottons with wool and silk embroidery threads, 105½ × 103 in. (268 × 261 cm). Museum Purchase, The Friends of Colonial Williamsburg Collections Fund. 2008.609.4

decorative spread in their home at 6 Orchard Avenue that the Johnstons purchased for the sisters.

What, then, did it mean for both of these quilts to end up with the Johnstons' descendants? It is possible that the Johnstons dictated the production of the leaf quilt, giving them full rights to take possession of it. The leaf quilt may have been gifted to the Johnstons in the spirit of an album quilt, or both may have been given as part of Brown's will that included the return of the Orchard Street home to the Johnstons upon her sister's death in 1942.[33] Neither Brown nor Mitchell had living children of their own. Within the mistress-domestic relationship in the years after the Civil War, where "Black women were (in the eyes of whites) servants first and family members only incidentally,"[34] were these quilts left in the spirit of the latter designation as a sign of sincere regard, or as part of a performance of gratitude for those who saw themselves as benefactors? We may never know, but their survival confronts us with these questions from a not-so-distant past.

The other quilts in this section illuminate the range of values, methods, and practices in early twentieth-century African American quiltmaking. By no means exhaustive, they speak to the creative repertoires of many Black women who were born after Emancipation and whose daughters and grandchildren would be the ones to carry them out of the South. Pearlie Rayford's Friendship Dahlia quilt (cat. 12) is a classic example of a popular pattern that appeared in syndicated columns by "Aunt Martha" and "Nancy Cabot" in newspapers like the *Chicago Tribune* from 1932 onward.[35] Whether she saw the pattern in a newspaper or received it from a friend, Rayford's sunny flowers are not only balanced in their array of colors and prints and precisely fanned around the center circle; they also exemplify her careful echo quilting, in which stitches delicately trace each shape and repeat them in the negative spaces. Two flower stems in the upper and lower right corners are the only interruption to this revelry of repetition, and are angled in the opposite direction from the other fifty-four blocks.

Sometimes, fabric given to or inherited from another quilter is a prompt for making, as it may have been for Victoria Ector Cooper of Rusk County, Texas. Cooper had a bag of fabric scraps and pieced blocks from her aunt that may have prompted her to complete the String Hexagon quilt (cat. 19). In the case of Annie Crawford's quilt made of small cotton sacks manufactured to hold tobacco (cat. 13), she gathered her materials over a period of seven years. According to her niece, Estella Brown, Crawford recruited relatives to help her collect the tobacco sacks and bring them to annual family gatherings. Adopting a method similar to that of the velvet and silk Puff or Biscuit quilts that were popular in the 1880s (and again in the 1970s), she washed, dyed, stuffed, and stitched together each group of five hundred and forty "puffs" to construct her singular creation.[36] In her hands, the raw materials central to the trafficking of her ancestors shed their commercial markings as they were crafted into a quilt intended for the enjoyment of her descendants. Crawford's Puff quilt emerges from the South's defining commodities, with Crawford artfully refabricating them as products for her own purposes—a practice of material and symbolic reassemblage that we see unfold across Black quiltmaking in the context of migration.

In Southern rural culture, where sewing was an essential skill for clothing one's family, keeping them warm in wintertime, and mending, it is little surprise that many of the quilters in this exhibition recall first learning to thread needles and piece fabric scraps as early as eight or nine years old (Mattie Lou Henderson, Selena Foster, Arbie Williams, Johnnie Wade, Lee Wanda Jones, Elizabeth Munn, Arbie Major, Georgia Lee Kidd, and Isiadore Whitehead). For others with backgrounds in dressmaking and tailoring (Pearl Nunley, Cora Lee Hall Brown, Chaney Ella Peace, Missie Freeman, and Eula Thomas), their training not only meant that they were highly skilled in handling, measuring, and sewing fabrics and working with patterns; it also meant a ready supply of scraps that they could transform into quilts. One could easily imagine Beatrice Smith, who completed a strawberry appliqué quilt at the age of fourteen over the course of two winters while working outside of the home (figs. 9–10), applying her meticulous needlework to making clothes for herself and her family.

Sewing enabled African American makers to care for kin and community members in the most tangible and personal of ways, and quilts made from work clothes are especially poignant examples. Commonly referred to as "britches quilts" in African American communities, bed coverings made from worn denim and heavier-weight cottons offered materials ready-made for a quilt top in conditions where money was hard-earned and needed for anything that couldn't be made at home. When a yard of material could cost nearly a fifth of a day's wages at ten to fifteen cents, as it did for Roberta Lee Johnson raising a family during the Great Depression, ripping up pocket seams and measuring square blocks from old clothes for a top was the quintessential way for a farmer's daughter to make something out of nothing (cat. 4).[37] Signs of frugality and efficiency characterize Minnie Skinner's tied quilt, in which whole pant legs and swaths of red upholstery or coat fabric provided her with material to assemble her quilt quickly (cat. 25). Joe Washington pieced his backing almost entirely from repurposed cotton sacks, in which the logo for the Double Circle fertilizers and original weight of the product ("100 LBS. NET"), manufactured in Pittsburgh, Texas, remain visible

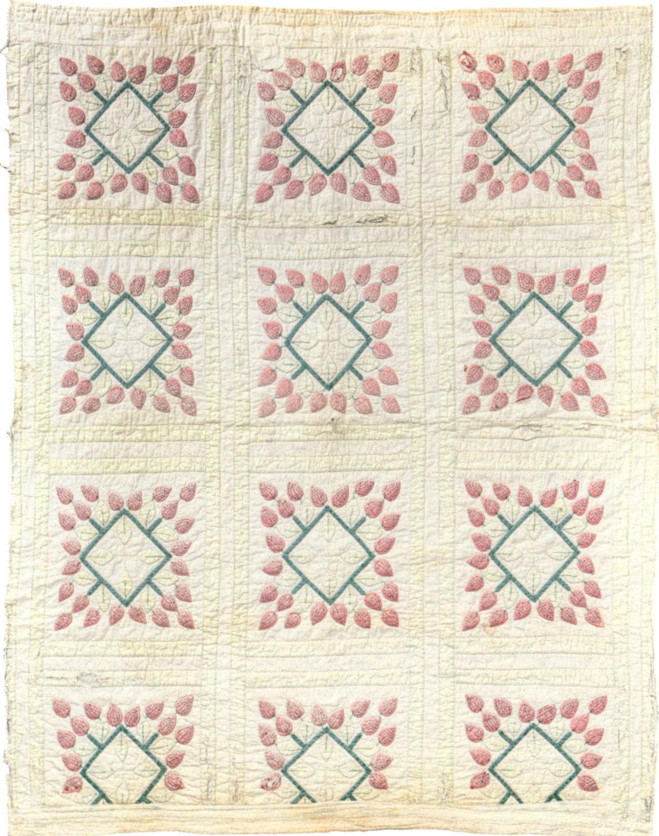

Fig. 9. Beatrice Smith, Untitled (Strawberry Appliqué Quilt), c. 1928–1929, Horatio, Arkansas, BAMPFA

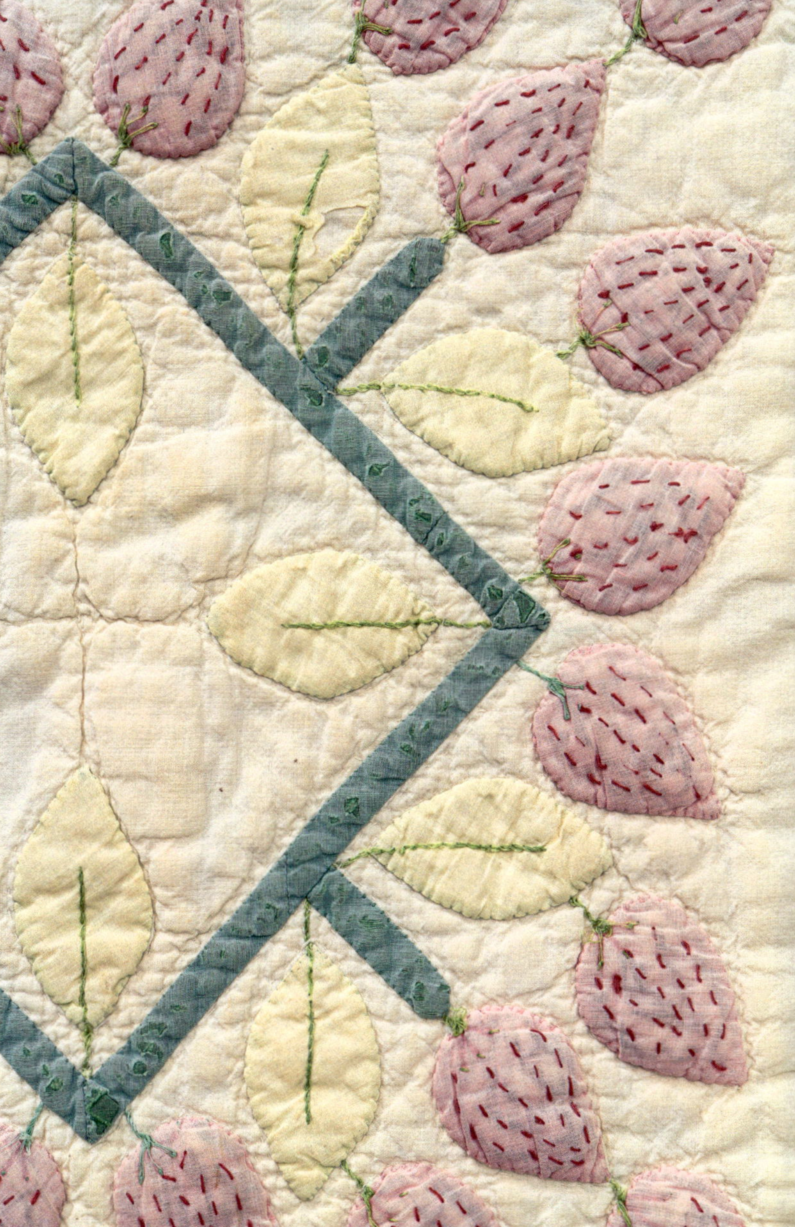

Fig. 10. Detail of figure 9

(cat. 24). In both Skinner's and Washington's quilts, older blankets have been used as batting.

Every softly faded area, tear, stain, lingering commercial stamp, or relief pattern in a quilt is a clue to the social and cultural lives of a quilt and its component parts. The accounts in Lisa Gail Collins's book *Stitching Love and Loss: A Gee's Bend Quilt* enable us to consider the worlds of possibility for Johnson's, Skinner's, and Washington's quilts—the stories of which are not known to us—by illustrating how work clothes are intimately connected to personal memories. For example, Bettie Bendolph Seltzer recalled how her mother made progress on quilts at the end of cotton-picking season, when "she would go to the field and 'scrap' cotton to make bed items . . . [and] Papa would take it to the cotton gin and bring back 'lint' cotton. She would hang those quilting frames from the ceiling and sew quilts throughout the winter months."[38] Quilting could also be tied to the rhythms of daily labor, in the way many women would piece quilts at night after a full day's work. Furthermore, quilts, once made, could be tied to all aspects of life from birth to death, as Collins reminds us: "Babies are conceived under them, mothers labor on top of them, infants are wrapped in them, children eat and sleep on them, and people come of age within them."[39] Quilts also meet individuals in some of the most emotionally intense periods of life. Missouri Pettway created a quilt from her late husband's work clothes with the intention to "remember him, and cover up under it for love," processing her grief through the smell, feel, and warmth of the life she knew with him as it was carried in her quilt. In these brief examples, Collins teaches us that while quilts can be many things, all those things work in supporting human life: as cover, comfort, sometimes currency, a spiritual meeting place, protection or emotional buttress—"like a second skin that holds the body and moves with its breath."[40] No wonder, then, that Venella Tyler, a nurse and midwife, was an avid quilter who was always ready to give away her quilts to those in need (cat. 14; see also p. 251). She was a caregiver by profession who understood how a quilt could offer comfort: for example, when makers give second and third lives to cast-off fabrics (especially from loved ones), they intensify the aura of care imbued in a quilt; or when someone holds or is wrapped under a quilt, its "soft bulk"–its weight and malleable volumes–molds to the body like a customized cure.[41] Understood this way, we might sense how a quilt's preciousness and power grow in proportion to the time invested in its making and number of sentiments imbued in its layers. As Bessie Moore stated, "I just think anybody that receives a quilt as a gift has really received something that they can cherish. Because a quilt is handmade, you know? And it's so much time that has gone into 'em, and love. 'Cause if you sit down and piece a quilt and then quilt it and give it to somebody, it's got to be because you think a lot of them."[42]

TENDING GENERATIONS: QUILTS AND THE SECOND GREAT MIGRATION

In her revelatory study *All That She Carried: The Journey of Ashley's Sack, a Black Family Keepsake*, historian Tiya Miles tells the story of an enslaved woman's gift to her daughter: an ordinary cotton sack filled with physical and spiritual provisions, given to aid her survival when the daughter, Ashley, was sold away from Rose, her mother. The insights that Miles calls forth are too numerous and heartrending to summarize here, but one stands out for its relevance to quiltmaking. In accounting for how enslaved mothers confronted the prospect of separation from their children, she writes, "In the face of devastating mother loss, our ancestors' answer was mother love: a graspingly fierce, imperfect insistence on making and tending generations."[43] She includes Rose in the communion of generations of Black mothers who have activated everyday objects as symbols of their love, strength, and the right to life that they wished to send to their kin in harrowing conditions. To cite just one other example, we might consider the mother of Colonel Allen Allensworth, one of four founders of California's first all-Black town. Faced with the piercing reality that her son was to be sold as a punishment for educating himself, she gave him a silver half-dollar and told him to buy a Bible and a comb. She told him, "Put knowledge from the book into your head, and comb everything else out with the comb."[44]

In these ways, quilts as useful and portable objects could be sent not only to care for bodies escaping the Jim Crow era's cruel forms of anti-Blackness, but as mementos that affirmed and preserved kinship ties as the separation incurred by migration would become increasingly prevalent.[45] To think of quiltmaking as an essential form of "tending generations" and heritage-building, then, is to recognize how functional quilts can serve as a nexus of relationships past, present, and future.[46] They could assist in honoring the passing of one's ancestors, perhaps as J.R. Hall understood when he returned to Merced from Arkansas in 1948, the year his mother, Emma Hall, passed away, with a trunk of her quilts (cat. 16) and a packet of family photographs. Or quilts could convey blessing to future generations. Odessa Doby confirmed that her foremothers put pennies in the corner of quilts "for love and luck," in all quilts that they gave away.[47] In this section, themes of making, carrying, and preserving quilts in the context of migration point to larger storylines about love, collective care, resistance, resourcefulness, and imaginative creativity that Black migrant women practiced while en route to California. Even when we do not have the full story around specific quilts, we can turn to clues in their construction and quilt history to affirm what generations of African American families know about the resilience and humanity of their ancestors.

What is known about Ruth Charlotte Clay and Georgia Lee Kidd's families bears out the story of working-class African Americans continuing to quilt while seeking opportunities in the West. Having grown up in a farming family in Union County in southern Arkansas, Ruth Clay eventually raised her own family with Robert Clay in Oklahoma City, where he worked as a trucker, before they moved to West Oakland. By 1950, their daughter Treva clerked at the Naval Supply Depot while Robert worked as a hauler. Ruth's other daughter, Lavoyce, recalled that her mother had been piecing quilts ever since they were children, and a Dresden Plate quilt top suggests that quilting was a tradition passed from mother to daughter. Two styles of blanket stitches, one longer and the other at a finer scale, and two distinctive stashes of fabric suggest that it was made by two people, possibly Ruth and Treva together (cat. 6). A Roman Stripe quilt also possesses its own distinctive character: flashes of hot orange, pink, red, and black strips jump out from the quilt's muted palette, with a concentration running through the middle column; one square framed with strips stands out from the rest; a single floral print piece in a corner fills in the end of a row (cat. 7). Both the top and the quilt were found in Lavoyce's former home at 3032 Grove Street in Berkeley, right along the redlined boundary that was renamed Martin Luther King Jr. Way.

The fluctuations of the logging industry provide a backdrop for Georgia Lee Kidd and her descendants' migration story. Her father, Edward Neal, is listed as a log cutter in Warren, Bradley County, in the 1920 federal census, a period when businesses like the Arkansas Lumber Company were well-established in Bradley County and voraciously harvested the land's virgin pine trees. Herman Edwards, her husband, was working as a laborer at a lumber mill in 1940, likely supporting the larger timber manufacturing operations that would have expanded by this time. By 1950, however, Georgia, Herman, their four children, and Ed Neal lived in McNary, Arizona, a bustling company town on native Apache lands where roughly half of the population of two thousand were Black. They followed in the footsteps of the initial eight hundred African American laborers brought in by rail in 1924 after two Louisiana businessmen exhausted the resources of their southern operation and sought a new location from which to profit.[48] However, the town's desegregated schools and Black community institutions (a cafe serving Southern food, churches, and a Masonic lodge and nearby theater) were not enough to keep them in this relatively isolated location. The next year, Georgia continued westward to Los Angeles with her daughter Dorothy Edwards. In 1980 she moved back to Camden, Arkansas, before returning to California in 1984.

In a tied quilt from 1983 that Kidd and Edwards created together, pieced blocks with necktie-like patterns and sashing epitomize the neat work that Kidd learned from her mother (cat. 64). At the same time, the pieces of irregular length and pattern forming the top and bottom borders speak to the practical resourcefulness that was common among their generation of quiltmakers who came of age in the Great Depression. This combination of technical know-how and improvisational problem-solving was an essential skill for Black rural women of Kidd's generation, which they relied on to care for their families when opportunities for education and building economic independence were limited. Georgia recalled her mother telling her, "I'm glad you learning [quilting]. When you get grown you won't have to ask no one to do it for you; you do it for yourself, 'cause I won't be with you always."[49] The family's quiltmaking traditions passed on to Angelia Tobias, who made quilts for family and for sale—adapting this family tradition for her own livelihood, as her grandmother Georgia had two generations before her (cats. 68, 72, and 95). She also made Black dolls, participating in the powerful tradition of creating positive images of the self when white ideals of beauty dominated the commercial market (cats. 96–103).

Migration and quiltmaking take a different trajectory for Sherry Ann Byrd, a native Texan whose time in California was the context for reconnecting to the long tradition of quiltmaking in her family. She first came to Richmond, California, with her two young children in 1977 with the help of a relative who was already living there. Her husband, Curtis, joined them a few months later, finding work as a truck driver for the Alameda Naval Base. Drawn to the Bay Area's social diversity and liveliness, they made a life in North Richmond in the Easter Hill Projects. Weathering a postwar climate characterized by divestment from Richmond's once-bustling downtown, dramatic population decline, and the shift from manufacturing to service-sector jobs in the 1960s and 1970s, they stayed twenty years before returning to Fairfield, Texas, in 1997.

Observing her maternal grandmother, Gladys Henry (affectionately known as "Big Mama"), making quilts and helping her tie some as a young girl planted a love for quiltmaking that Byrd did not have opportunities to nurture while she completed college, married, and started a family. As she recalls, "I didn't get started until the stillborn death of my son Micah in 1984. For years I had saved pieces of cloth that excited me . . . saving them for the quilts. . . . When I finally got started, I drew from my memories of how Big Mama did it." Intuitively reaching for quiltmaking in this period of intense grief, Byrd continues, saying, "I wrote home to her and asked if she would send me some of her already pieced blocks to learn from, [be]cause I was now trying to create my own quilts. She responded with quite a few."[50] These blocks are now a part of a series of story quilts entitled *Jazz With a Needle and Thread*, and they show "the offbeat, asymmetrical uniqueness" towards piecing that Byrd calls "m-provisational": a word with a sense of swagger and playfulness used to describe the quilt created in a "relaxed but fast-paced manner, without a lot of fuss or precision" and made mostly for family use.[51]

In her Double Medallion quilt of 1984, Byrd's "m-provisational" flair achieves maximal effect in the most efficient of ways (cat. 67). Between stacking squares in the central feature (the medallion) and using fabric patterns somewhat systematically—that is, reserving smaller-scale dot patterns for the medallion and matching them with paler colors, while pairing darker solids with stripes and other distinctive prints in the series of frames around the medallion—her quilt radiates restless energy and generates a sense of grandness that is casual but not imposing. A later quilt made of salvaged Marimekko fabrics carries a similar sense of visual dynamism with a more limited palette of colors and the playful curves of the original print (cat. 87). She passed these lessons on to her daughter Bara, who completed her first quilt tops at the age of twelve and became the seventh-generation quilter in her family (cat. 82).

African American migration to California, as with its pathways to northern and midwestern cities, was frequently made within familial contexts. Many couples moved together, but also common was a two-stage movement with husbands, uncles, and fathers going first and women and children arriving after jobs and housing were secured.[52] Older relatives who followed their migrant children were conduits for Black Southern cultural practices like quiltmaking, as well. Anna Nicholson, who migrated from Vicksburg, Mississippi, lived with both her son and husband in Pittsburgh, California, by 1947. While they worked at the Port Chicago Naval Magazine—it is not known if they were direct survivors of the tragic explosion in 1944—Nicholson's daughter Rosalie and her husband, Thaddeus Brown, also from Vicksburg and who served as a Tuskegee Airman, were residents of San Francisco. Perhaps utilizing surplus twill from these military contexts, she made a heavy Log Cabin quilt (cat. 20), constructed in a "quilt-as-you-go" method where pieces are sewn directly onto a backing fabric. While there is scant information about Gracie Pigrum, who was born and died in Mississippi, she had a daughter who moved to San Francisco. Perhaps on one of her visits, Pigrum passed the time by repurposing a rice bag, packed by a South San Francisco merchant, as the base for precisely folded and stitched pieces of polyester and athletic wear in an innovative floor mat (cat. 57). Sarah Turnage brought her quiltmaking practice to California when she settled there with her son Lonnie; her quilts demonstrate a fluency in both improvisational and pattern piecing styles that were common among Southern Black women (cat. 59 and figs. 11–12).

CARRIED AND KEPT

Roland L. Freeman's book *A Communion of the Spirits: African-American Quilters, Preservers, and Their Stories* was and continues to be a pathbreaking project, not least for its scope as the first national survey of African American quilting conducted from 1974 to 1996. Freeman recognized quiltkeepers as essential figures in maintaining a quilt's ties to the past. For as his title suggests, preservers—whether they are physical keepers of quilts, storytellers, family historians, teachers of the craft, or many times all of the above—constitute a core part of the community in which quilts are the most alive: alive to the cultural contexts that inform their creation, alive to the creative minds of makers, and alive to affirmations and meanings that permeate their fibers. The quilt Lily Chiles created with her grandchildren (cat. 92) exemplifies these cultural connections in practice and theme: as the elder quilter, she guided Tina and Clarence Jackson in piecing and embroidering names of African countries on this quilt. In its final form, the quilt presents and celebrates a vision of pan-African identity, past and future. Freeman understood this social and spiritual communion fostered by quilts as "the continuity of black expressive culture" that "gives common meaning to the world of quilting by African Americans."[53] He proceeded to document Black quiltmaking with this holistic view, recording a multitude of stories and encounters that quilts opened up over the course of his fieldwork. Following in Freeman's footsteps, this section acknowledges quiltkeepers for their role as the preeminent stewards of these quilts and their

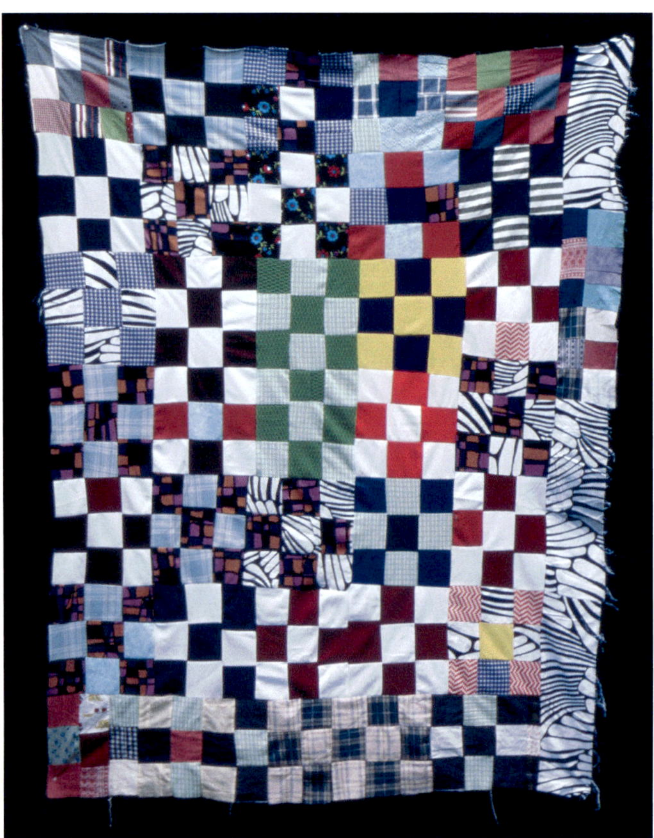

Fig. 11. Sarah Turnage, Untitled top (Nine Patch), before 1980, San Francisco, California, BAMPFA

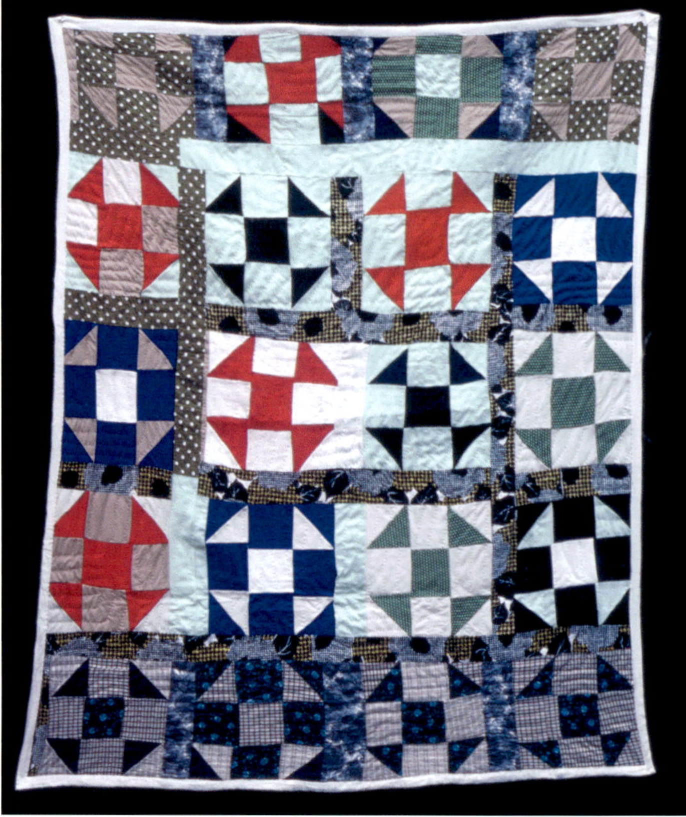

Fig. 12. Sarah Turnage, Untitled (Shoo-Fly), before 1980, San Francisco, California; quilted by Mary Thompson, 1992, San Francisco, California, BAMPFA

stories (curators in the truest sense of the Latin verb *curare,* "to take care of"), and honors accounts of Black life they have made available to us today.

In many cases, quiltkeepers are those who have left their family's Southern homegrounds but remain connected to their elders through the quilts they have inherited from them. For Carlena White of Oakland, California, her family's quilts represented her parents' differing approaches to quiltmaking that made for a spiritually rich home life in Wesson, Mississippi, with her three brothers and two sisters. Her mother, Laura Covington, "always wanted them to be pretty" with some kind of specific pattern, and set out to make a quilt for each of her children that incorporated a special piece of their clothing. She also went out of her way to give quilts to those who did not have any. By contrast, her father tended to use assorted squares and long and short strips of fabric (cat. 41 and fig. 13). White remembers that her father preferred piecing experimentally over the repetition of patterns, an approach that could yield unexpected results, remarking, "We liked his. We always thought that his were funny, [laughs] but he didn't care how we felt about it. He was just doing something because he liked to do it . . . some pieces were straight, some were not. He always enjoyed doing that."[54] For this son of enslaved parents, who eventually owned his farm, piecing quilts was simply one of many skills–from building homes, fixing rooftops, shoeing horses, breaking in wild horses, to growing all of the family's food–that he wielded to realize freedom for himself and his family.[55] Covington's quilt visually conveys his sense of artistic abandon within a white masculine world referenced in the coats of arms, equestrian imagery, pheasants, chinoiserie, and European landmarks that appear on the fabrics he uses. Not only does he create his own shapes with strips of novelty prints and plain cotton, but their gentle arcs and jagged, strippy triangles interrupt the rigid orthogonals that typically structure a quilt's grid. What remains is an image of daring improvisation that is uniquely Covington's and is resonant with modes of Black being characterized by invention, individuality, and challenges to fixed social relationships.[56]

The family quilts kept by Laura Johnson Battise attest to the ways quilts and quiltmaking practices could tether family members together across time and space. For example, the Shadow Star quilt she owned (cat. 5) was made in Bastrop, Louisiana, around 1930, when Battise was living in a multigenerational household that included Betty Chafford, who raised her, and a younger sister, Inez. Rebecca Smith, Chafford's mother, lived in the same parish at this time, affording both women ample opportunities to share patterns, pull from larger sources of fabric, and sew together the one hundred and twenty-one pieces required for each block.

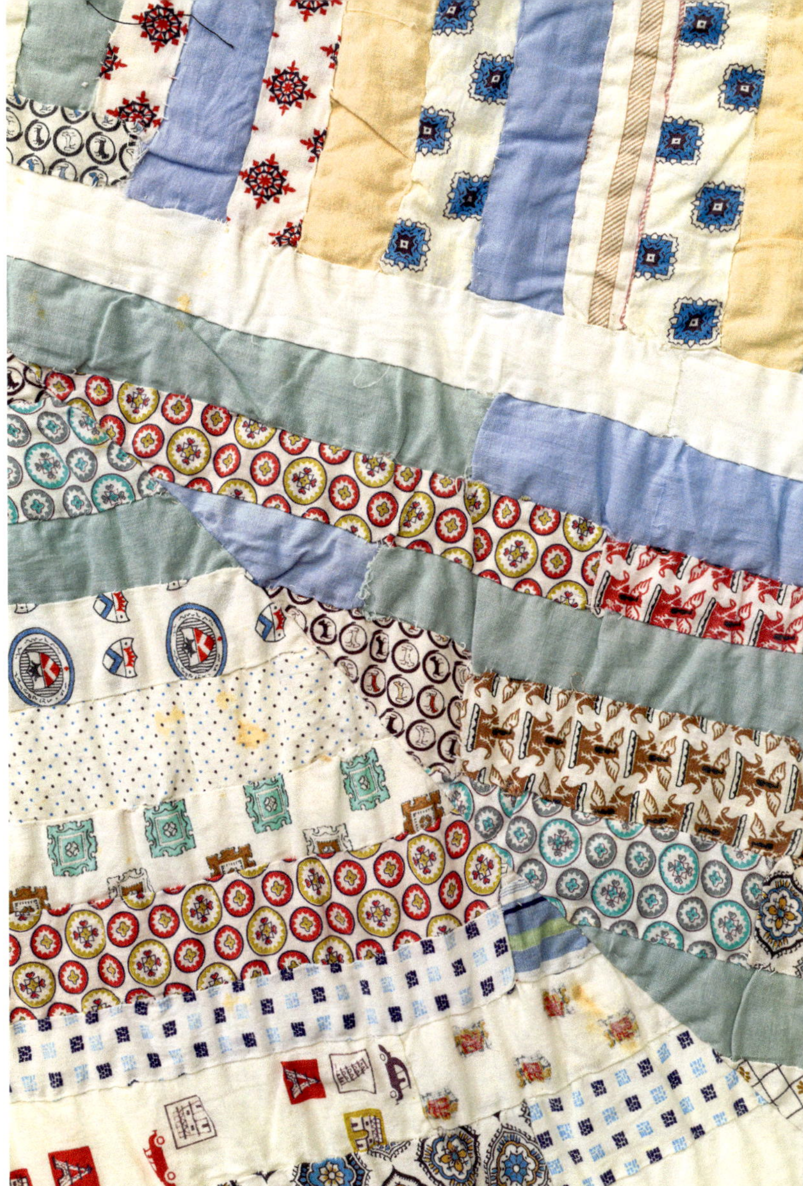

Fig. 13. Detail of cat. 41

We can see some of their exacting work in a quilt that Battise pieced with her sister-in-law Jimmie Johnson (cat. 27). Its central pattern, Fifty-Four Forty or Fight, takes its name after the popular political slogan from 1846 in support of annexing the Oregon Territory. Perhaps not coincidentally, Battise reported helping Johnson piece its central blocks in the early 1940s after Jimmie arrived in Oakland. By 1950, federal census records show that Chafford and other relatives migrated as well: Chafford, then fifty-eight years old, lived with her son Robert (a machine operator at the Dry Docks) and his wife Lula, while Johnson, her husband, Elmore (listed as a scrap metal worker), Battise (an upholstery machine operator), and Inez (a practical nurse) shared a home just a few blocks away.

For others, memories of family and Southern homes are directly preserved in quilts. To make her nearly ten-foot-long quilt titled *Post Oak Grapevine*, Mable Battle proceeded with an organic yet intentional process of alternating bright solid fabrics with florals in each of the blocks (many of which contain a small piece interrupting a border) and fitting them together to form the top (cat. 105). Her design pulses with the unbridled energy and willful disregard for perfect geometries that she connected to the landscape of East Texas. Of this quilt she remarked, "My daddy told me when I didn't know the name of anything we had on the farm [in Cherokee County, Texas]–especially something wild–say 'Post Oak.' The grapes grew wild on the farm."[57] The salvaged Nine Patch block made by her great nieces and included in the quilt's upper left corner activates yet another memory. Commenting on her artistic process as a whole, she emphatically stated, "I do not do anything without giving it a thought."[58]

For Rosie Lee Tompkins, denim was especially evocative of her rural upbringing and farming family. She frequently used it whenever she was thinking of herself in Arkansas and memorializing her ancestors (cat. 77). While Tompkins tended to source secondhand fashion jeans rather than denim from work clothes, the fabric's distinctive blue color, weight, and weave easily elicit such personal associations. In this quilt and its related pillows, she pairs denim with commercial barkcloth containing characteristic tropical prints of lush botanicals (cats. 78–80). Although she was famously reticent about her art, we might speculate on what meanings she desired to activate with this combination. Was it her way of celebrating her aesthetic of luxury and abundance with a nod to the past? Do the patches of animal fur bring these things closer in their appeal to the tactile?

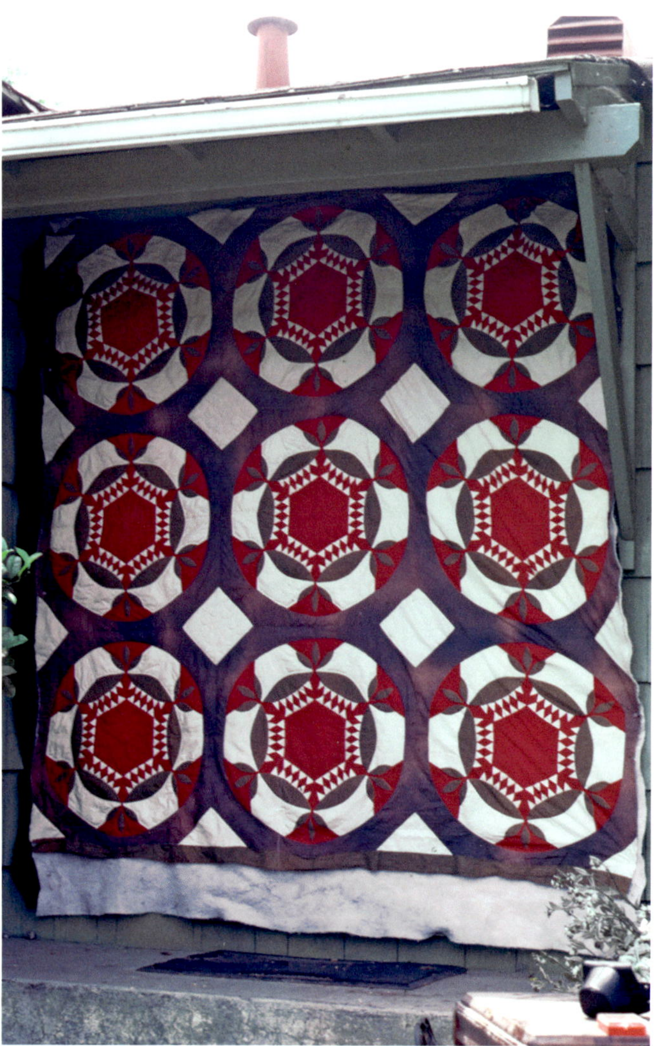

Fig. 14. Jane Traylor, Untitled (Lotus Blossom variation or Whig's Defeat), c. 1918, Litroe, Louisiana; shown here with quilting in progress by Alice Neal, 1980s, Oakland, California, BAMPFA

Handmade objects are natural containers for memories of their makers, offering a tangible connection to distant and deceased relatives. Rose R. McDowell expresses the role of quilts in mediating loss and longing: "I don't remember my mother but my grandmother had quilts that she made. My cousin's wife wanted this quilt, but my grandmother wouldn't give it to her. She said my mother made it, she wanted to keep it–that particular one–for me. When you can't remember your mother, it seem like you could just get something she made, you feel more close. That was something my mother done and I wanted to keep it."[59] Quiltkeeping is not just tending to the life of the object, but to the life of the woman who created it.

Growing up in Marion, Louisiana, Alice Neal recalled that, especially among poor families, quilts were ways of recording and safeguarding family genealogies in a culture where family bibles were scarce. Two quilts that she worked on extend this commemorative tradition. The first involves an unfinished top made by Neal's grandmother Jane Traylor (fig. 14). According to family history, Traylor believed that it would have been bad luck to complete it, since eight or nine of her eleven children died in the 1918 influenza epidemic while she was working on it. It survived a fire (Neal's brother J.D. rescued it). But its story might have ended there had not Orene, Neal's sister, claimed it. Upon Orene's death, Neal stepped forward when no other family members wanted it. As the only one among her siblings who learned and continued to quilt, she added her own meticulous skills to those of her grandmother in working on the family's Lotus Blossom variation top. Her stitches complement her grandmother's neat piecework, adding a floral design in the red hexagons and undyed corner pieces before backing it. Although it is unclear whether Neal never completed the quilting process by happenstance or by choice (perhaps in order to avoid bad luck, just as Traylor had done before her), this quilt richly captures a family story across three generations. Its survival and final form demonstrate how certain quilts "[call] for a conversation between the dead and the living."[60]

After her mother, Mary Bright, died in December 1954, Neal began work on her exquisite portrait quilt, imbuing

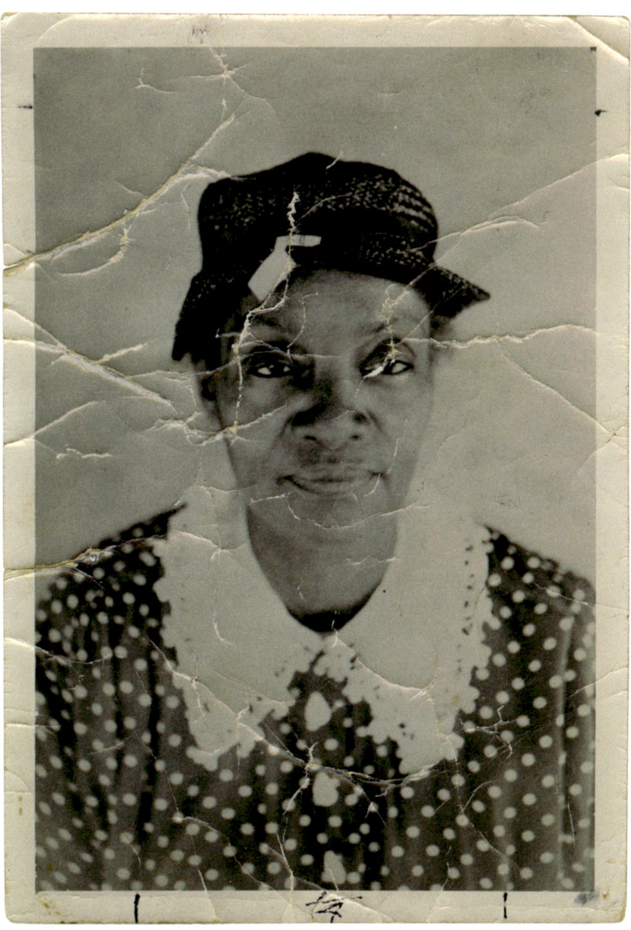

Fig. 15. Photograph of Mary Bright, Alice Neal's mother, used as inspiration for cat. 33

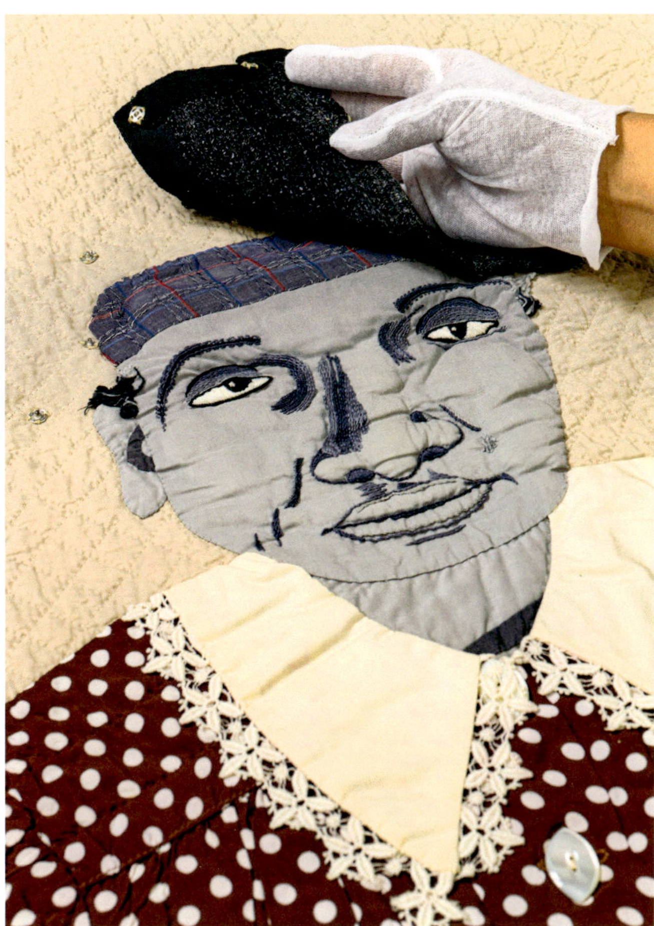

Fig. 16. Detail of cat. 33 showing the hat unbuttoned and revealing the sitter's silk cap

nearly all aspects of its design and execution with the memory of her mother (cat. 33). At its center is a figurative portrait of Bright that Neal reproduced from a photograph (fig. 15), using leftover material from a dress Bright had sewn for herself, a lace collar, buttons, and embroidery. She also crafted a replica of one of Bright's hats, which snaps off to reveal a silk cap that she sometimes wore (fig. 16). The other patterned blocks that appear throughout carry personal meaning as well. Four Nine Patch blocks anchoring the portrait's frame symbolize the first pattern that Neal learned from her mother; Stars of Lemoyne blocks appearing just outside the frame are a nod to her lifetime spent in Louisiana. Her portrait is also flanked on both sides by a cascade of blocks—Fan, Wild Goose Chase, Basket of Flowers, Monkey Wrench, and Dresden Plate—that reproduce patterns that her mother had once made. Above Bright's likeness are two Churn Dash blocks representing the rural labor that provided her family with milk and butter, and below are two stars to invoke one of her favorite hymns, "Will There Be Any Stars in My Crown?" Over nine types of intricate quilt stitching designs and embroidery embellish the top, like line drawings accentuating the plain areas with another display of Neal's fine handwork. Taken as a whole, Neal's quilt offers its familial tribute in the language of her artistic inheritance. How fitting, then, that the embroidered life dates of her mother echo the start and finishing dates for the quilt, which Neal has also stitched onto the top layer. The life of the object nestles within the memory of its source.

There is one more layer to this quilt's story. Neal wished for it to be displayed in a museum that her family was planning to establish and dedicate to Bright near Monroe, Louisiana, on ten acres of family land that was originally homesteaded and bequeathed by her aunt. Neal wanted Bright's picture to be seen "so that people would know who gave the property [to the museum]."[61] These plans never materialized, due to a local television station purchasing the land from the family. As a concession, Neal sold her quilt to Eli Leon, believing him to be the best person to take care of the quilt and its story.[62] Holding onto this lost context for the quilt's display emphasizes the larger significance that Bright's family wished to publicly commemorate: the legacy of Black land ownership and pride in tending to generations

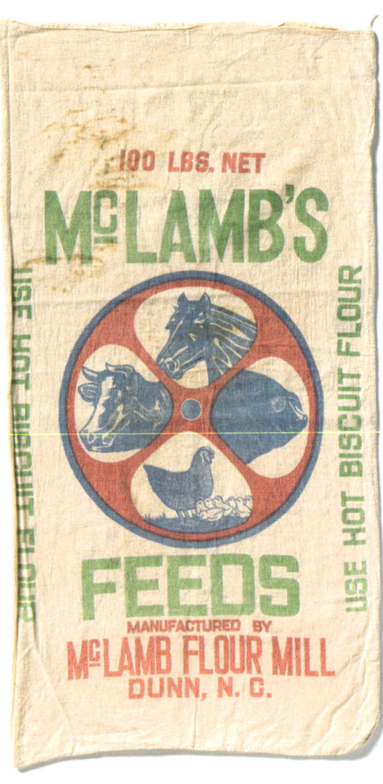

Fig. 17. Flour sack, c. 1930, Dunn, North Carolina. Cotton. BAMPFA. In this example the manufacturer's logo and text have not been washed or bleached out.

through these hard-won possessions. Neal's quilt was meant to be a visible tribute to the wealth that her mother—the first generation born into freedom—had acquired and exercised the power to give.

Willia Ette Graham was a prolific and skilled quiltmaker who was also a keeper of two family quilts, one made by her grandmother, Lucinda Ballenger (cat. 1), and another by her mother, Louise Hicks (cat. 15). As Graham recalled, Ballenger was born in Tennessee under enslavement and sold from her mother. Her sewing skills were likely learned from other enslaved women prior to emancipation or possibly other family members upon forging a new life under freedom in Rusk County, Texas. All that considered, her Six Point Star variation from c. 1900 was made when she was an older woman. We might imagine how, in its freshest condition before light, time, and handling aged the yellow and blue prints, it offered her family a starry design that was by turns cheerful and calming. A young Willia Ette would sometimes assist her in making quilts, picking up a love for sewing. Graham's mother, Louise Hicks, was a schoolteacher (imparting to her pupils the literacy that Ballenger had passed on to her), leaving her less time to quilt. This might partially explain the efficiency of her plain quilt from around 1939. It consists of seven rectangular pieces of undyed cotton, whose sizes and ripped seams suggest that Hicks repurposed flour sacks (fig. 17), which she bound together with broad quilt stitches (cat. 15). Compared with her mother's quilt, which requires sixteen pieces per Six Point Star block alone, Hicks's quilt would have required far less labor to create than the typical patterned quilt top. It also accords with the spirit of Depression-era campaigns that encouraged women to reuse cotton sacks, thereby supporting struggling US cotton farmers who were competing with jute exports from India, while also bringing down the national surplus of commodity cotton during the 1930s.[63]

Graham was not only a keeper of family quilts; she was also a bearer of quiltmaking traditions. Two of her quilts in the exhibition demonstrate the fluency and freedom she possessed as a third-generation quilter and carried with her to California. The String blocks in her Medallion quilt (so-called for the long "strings" of material left over from trimming) exemplify the thrifty use of scraps that she made in 1944, prior to leaving the area around Henderson, Texas, for Oakland (cat. 26). Once in California, she eventually bordered them using the Courthouse Steps variation of a Log Cabin design, epitomizing how improvisational approaches can interact with conventional patterns (see cat. 44 for an example of a Courthouse Steps variation quilt). Graham's inventive process in creating her 1981 quilt began with constructing a right triangle of orange square pieces that is typical for Basket patterns (cat. 63 and fig. 18). But instead of smoothing out its sawtooth edges with half-square triangles, she continued piecing with more squares of other colors and patterns, resulting in the woven look of the final quilt. Clearly steeped in knowledge of traditional patterns, Graham

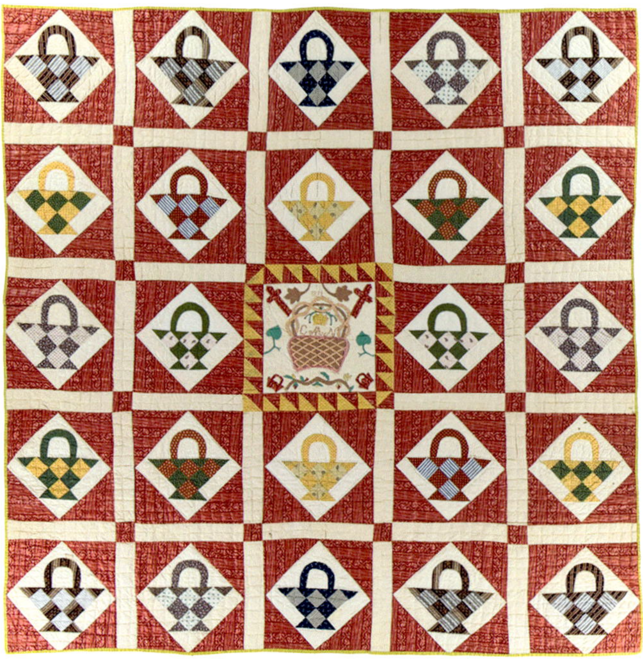

Fig. 18. Maker Once Known/Unidentified Artist, Untitled (Basket), 1877–1900, Canada. Cotton; hand and machine appliquéd, embroidered, 83 x 83 in. (211 x 211 cm). Ardis and Robert James Collection, International Quilt Museum, University of Nebraska-Lincoln, 2006.043.0082

nonetheless was never beholden to them, motivated to keep experimenting and seeking the surprise and discovery as part of the process—for herself and the beholder. As she shared with Eli Leon during an interview, "That's the way I go with most of my quilts, trying to match the pieces where it don't just keep your sight beared down on one thing. It keeps the flow of your sight going on instead of stopping. You move on to see the next step. You [are] searching for something else to see."[64]

QUILTMAKING IN POSTWAR CALIFORNIA

In "Meeting Mrs. Murphy" (p. 188), Eli Leon describes the flurry of activity that ensued when he instigated a trip with Bettie Phillips, Missie Freeman, Arbie Williams, and Graham to visit another Black quiltmaker, Mable Murphy, in 1986. Having registered many "lamentations on the scarcity of quiltmakers in the California cities [his interviewees] found themselves in after their westward migrations" over the course of his research, Leon grew elated when these feelings were dispelled for one afternoon as bags of quilts were unpacked, handwork admired, and patterns exchanged.[65] It took a nearly one-hundred-thirty-mile drive from Oakland, but this gathering of older quiltmakers over quilts, chicken, and cake brought about not only a communion of quilters, but a space full of Southern aromas, things, and stories.

Leon, frustratingly, does not include any reflections from his traveling companions about this visit with Mrs. Murphy, but he suggests that this get-together "provided a direct line to their roots."[66] Many migrants tread this line across physical space by making regular trips back to their Southern homes to reconnect with loved ones, get caught up on the latest news, attend to family business, celebrate a wedding or mourn at a funeral, and bring back tastes from home in the process. As Gretchen Lemke-Santangelo writes in her study of African American migrants in the East Bay, "By returning regularly to their birthplaces, migrant women brought the West to the South and the South to the West. Thus, Southernness was not a finite essence trapped in memory but a fluid, renewable resource."[67] These visits were opportunities for spiritual renewal that contributed to the cohesiveness of migrant communities in California and especially in the East Bay.

Rather than the more downward growth of tree roots, however, the cultural roots that quiltmakers from the South carried with them to California are more akin to rhizomes that move outward and send up shoots from nodes without a central locus; the direction of their growth depended on external environmental factors.[68] For the generation of quiltmakers considered in *Routed West*, many women were taught quilting as young girls by their mothers or grandmothers, who were intent on passing down the useful skills of sewing and quiltmaking, and they recalled seasonal gatherings when extended family and neighbors would finish quilts for the upcoming winters. However, they did not always continue quilting as young adults navigating relationships, jobs, or young families during the 1940s to the 1970s, when store-bought blankets were an affordable, time-saving alternative to handmaking quilts. As their children grew up and left the house, or they faced the prospect of retirement, quiltmaking was something they returned to as older adults.

For Lily Chiles, Laverne Brackens, and Selena Foster, quilting offered a way to fill their time and aid in recovery following debilitating accidents later in life. In many cases, memories about quiltmaking—observing the magic of creating something out of nothing (Selena Foster), sensing a mother's patient love as she taught them how to piece (Lee Wanda Jones), fondly recalling how her mother would have the children thread a bunch of needles to stay out of trouble (Ruby Richard)—were roots of creativity and community that they carried their whole lives until they had more time to take up the craft. Once they entered that season of retirement (forced or otherwise), when they could cease attending to the immediate needs of their children or demands of employers, quilting could usher in a period where one could seek rest for her mind and body, and, in bell hooks's poetic phrasing, "come back to herself."[69] Even if the latter half of their lives were still busy with family responsibilities and other activities, some women regarded their quilts as inheritances to pass down to their grandchildren and into the larger community.[70]

As older individuals living in postwar geographies, the quiltmakers in the exhibition adapted traditional values learned from their foremothers to new social and cultural realities. Many thrifty and resourceful women turned to secondhand stores, flea markets, or the remnant bin at fabric shops as sources for affordable material. Other times, remnants could be sourced from people in their network. For example, Irene Bankhead's sister used to work at a dress factory; Laverne Brackens had a friend who worked at a factory that manufactured medical staff uniforms; and Gerstine Scott was known to send her aunt Cora Lee Hall Brown fabric from a factory in Emeryville (cat. 62). Neighbors aware of a quilter's practice were also natural sources of donated fabric. Scott's remarkable necktie quilt was made from ties given to her by a neighbor; Isiadore Whitehead commemorated friends who donated fabrics to her by embroidering their names on one of her Double Wedding Ring drapes (cats. 49 and 50).

Perhaps the most dramatic difference for older Southern migrants who were now living in an urban context was quilting in solitude and frequently without a frame. Quiltmaking during their youth was typically a seasonal and communal affair. For Annie Crawford's niece, Estella Brown, their family

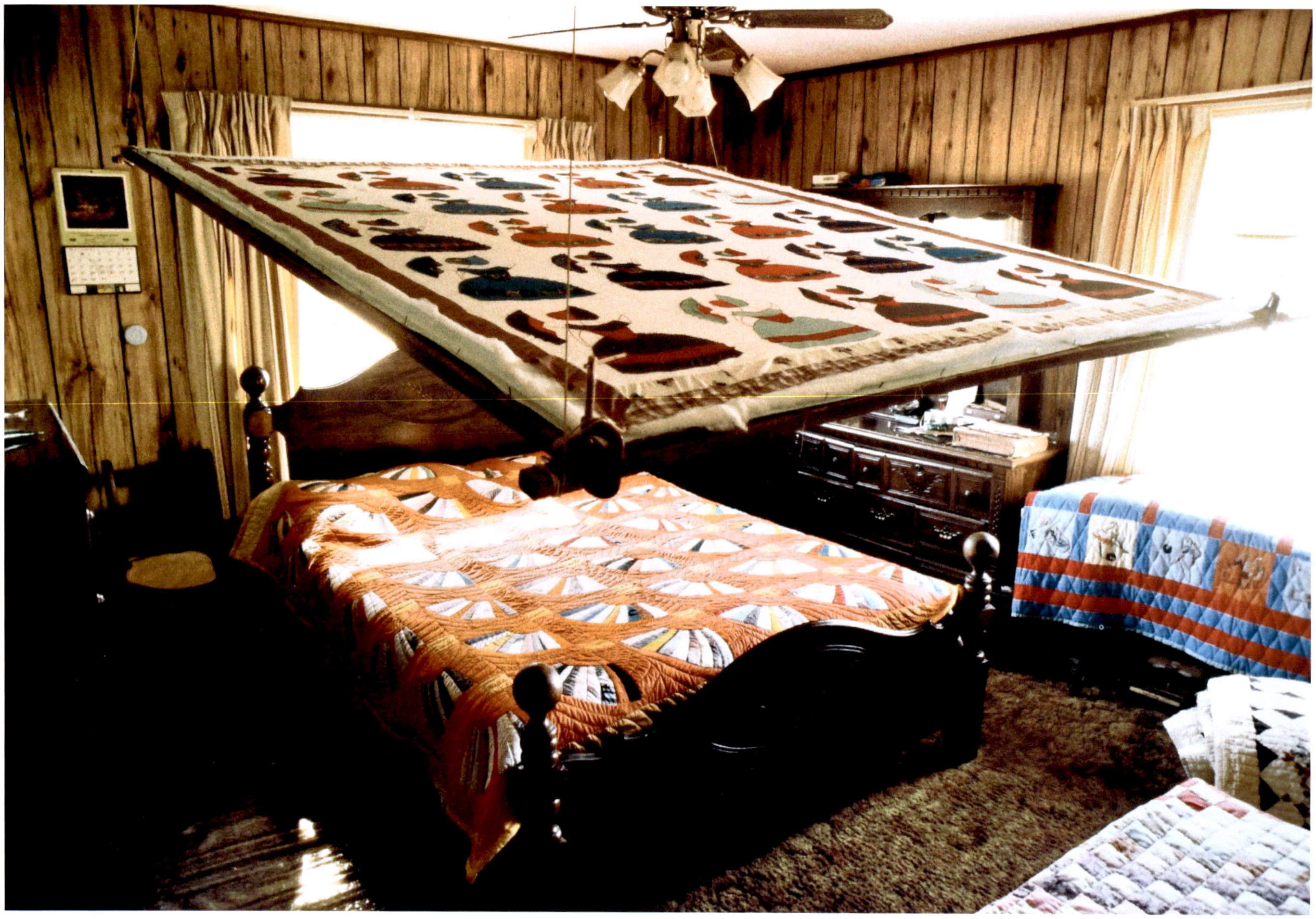

Fig. 19. Example of a quilting frame suspended from the ceiling in Myrtis W. Lord's bedroom, Bienville Parish, Louisiana, 1990, Roland L. Freeman Photographic Collection (70147), Southern Folklife Collection at Wilson Special Collections Library, University of North Carolina–Chapel Hill

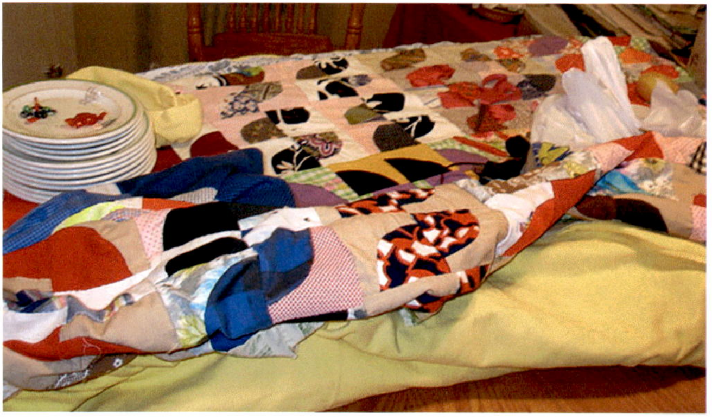

Fig. 20. Quilt in progress on Irene Bankhead's kitchen table, c. 2002. Note the stack of plates used as a weight to create tension.

couldn't afford new materials, and so the summers were spent collecting old clothes, cutting out sections of the strongest fabrics, and working with her extended family to complete quilting for one cover in a day.[71] Graham remembered her grandmother's quilting frame that could seat up to eight quilters at a time swung from the ceiling in her bedroom, and could be drawn up when it was time to sleep, similar to the ones Thomas Covington's and Susan Pless's descendants remembered having in the home while growing up (fig. 19). In her recorded conversations with Eli Leon from 1984, Whitehead shared about her family and neighbors in Arkansas gathering for large dinners and quilting sessions to help finish one another's quilts; by contrast, she commented, "Now I just quilt mine on my bed by myself."[72] Irene Bankhead, who quilted alongside her mother and other women at quilting bees, was known later in life to quilt on her bed and at her kitchen table (fig. 20), ingeniously using stacks of dinner plates as a weight to create tension for the quilt in progress.

The individuals featured in *Routed West* were making quilts before the founding of the region's first formal organization of Black quilters, the African American Quilt Guild of Oakland, in 2000, and for the most part never quite re-created the scale of community gatherings that many had known back in the rural South of their youth. Instead, some forged new friendships and smaller communities in the Bay Area through quiltmaking. Lily Chiles's senior citizen club at New Hope Baptist Church in West Oakland quilted some of her tops, and she actively enlisted family and neighbors in creating quilts that she could sell at the Berkeley Flea market (fig. 21).[73] Charles Cater and his wife integrated their quiltmaking into their business at Cater's Nook, a notions shop on Grove Street that they operated from roughly 1980 to 1987 before it was destroyed in a fire (fig. 22). In a pattern similar to that of many women quilters, Cater pieced his first quilt around the age of eight, but didn't make them more regularly until the early 1980s. By his own count, he created roughly fifty to seventy-five quilts per year, a quantity that speaks to a local demand for handmade quilts over commercially produced covers.

An ethic of care derived from Black Southern traditions of hospitality and religious belief and especially directed toward the less fortunate was an integral part of many quilt-making practices of African American migrants. Gussie Wells donated quilts regularly to her church for mission work. Sherry Ann Byrd recalls specific instances of giving her quilts to families with newborns and to neighbors in a pinch that reinforced her belief that quiltmaking was a powerful way to respond to the immediate needs of others. Isiadore Whitehead's immense achievement of creating one hundred quilts for humanitarian need in Ethiopia is another manifestation of the close relationship between quiltmaking and a culture of care. For others like Rosie Lee Tompkins, quilting was a process of spiritual meditation, in which she could offer up prayers for family members near and far.[74]

Intimate friendships founded on a shared love of quilting were also common. For example, Mattie Lou Henderson and her friend Tennie Edwards regularly traded quilt patterns and borrowed ideas from each other for their own quilts. While caring for Gussie Wells's mother in the mid-1980s, Arbie Williams suggested that the two begin piecing and quilting together to pass the time. Before long, they began collaborating and discovered a shared aesthetic sensibility around bright colors, vivid contrasts, and novel materials (cat. 86). Johnnie Wade first approached Willia Ette Graham as a teacher and mentor before the two became friends. While Wade knew how to piece quilts, she was eager to learn how to quilt by hand, preferring the look to those quilted by machine. A neighbor in Wade's building connected her to the elder quilter, and, starting in 1988, she was regularly assisting Graham on quilting commissions from Eli Leon and carrying forward the pleasure in completing quilts in community as generations of women before them had done (cats. 83 and 90). Through their friendship, too, Wade could realize her own creations, such as her Texas Star accented with String-pieced sections, which she quilted with playful verve (cat. 108). For these two Texas women only five years apart in age, the roots of their love for quiltmaking both crossed and emerged together in Oakland. The results are a set of contemporary quilts they created together, far from their Southern homes of origin but inextricably tied to the Southern traditions of those homes, neither blindly copying nor diluting them. Quite the opposite: they, like the plurality of quilts appearing throughout *Routed West*, spring forth from and channel the same ethic of Black collective care and community knowledge-sharing Wade and Graham knew as young women.

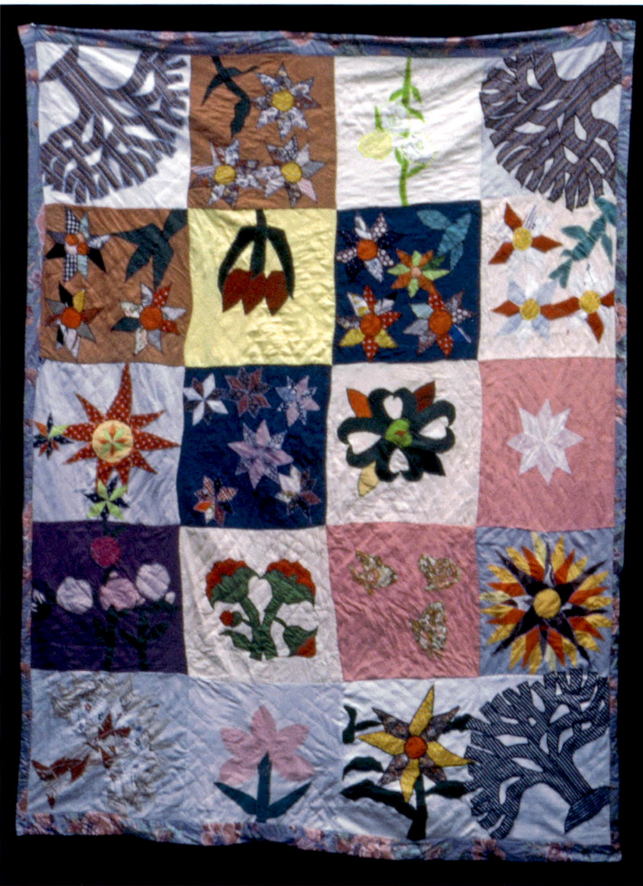

Fig. 21. Lily Chiles, with relatives and neighbors, Untitled (Oakland Tree Sampler), 1989, Oakland, California, BAMPFA

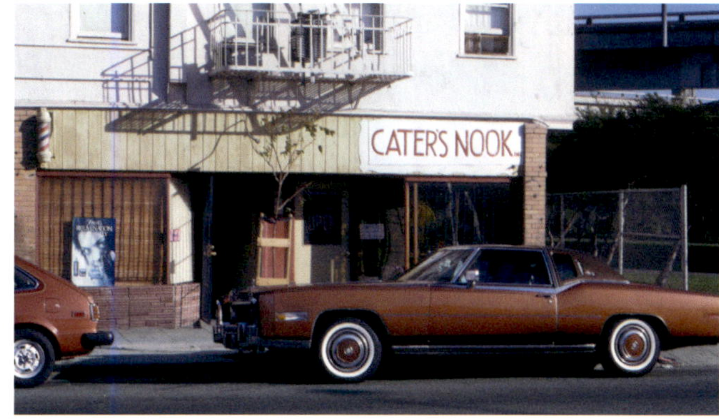

Fig. 22. Cater's Nook, Oakland, California, 1985

THE BEAUTY THEY HOLD

Quiltmaking is a practice that opens oneself to the heavens. Louisa Fite may have considered something to this effect when she placed pieces of light blue flannel at the center of her Log Cabin blocks (cat. 34). Replacing the traditional red square that typically signifies the hearth of the home with blue fabric printed with white feathers, she deftly invites us to consider her quilt as an aperture to the sky, a space where vision and spirits may be directed upward. bell hooks wrote about this process, noting how art in general allows "the creator to move beyond the self into a place of transcendent possibility . . . where all is possible."[75] But hooks also knew how this dynamic served Black women in particular, for whom quiltmaking was a survival strategy and daring choice in circumstances riddled with poverty and physical and psychic violence. Writing about the wisdom she derived from watching her grandmother Sarah Oldham (Baba) sew, hooks recalls observing Baba patiently attuned to "the divine voice speaking" and "the life-sustaining energy of the imagination" that flowed through her. hooks, citing curator Alvia Wardlaw on quiltmakers of Gee's Bend, helps us understand how the process of making bold and uniquely beautiful objects like quilts affirms a self outside of subjugation.[76] That is, in the zone of creative exploration, the quiltmaker occupies a space of aliveness apart from assaults on her personhood, away from the needs of others, free to return to herself more centered and self-aware. Laverne Brackens, who was guided to the power of quiltmaking by her quiltmaker-mother Gladys Henry (another wisdom-keeper), deeply understood this interplay between creativity and survival when she called the quiltmaker a "warrioress." As an outlet for peace and meditation, her turn to quiltmaking offered her an immediate tool for maintaining her sanity, peace, and serenity amid all that life had dealt her.[77]

In fact and in practice, the dignifying powers of quilting tend to accrue in spaces like the porch, kitchen table, bedroom, living room, or even the school bus (in Isiadore Whitehead's case), where tops get pieced and quilts are finished. While Leon did not invite all of the quilters he interviewed to talk explicitly in these terms, their quilts offer a bounty of ways for us to glean how their minds and hands moved in boundlessly creative and decisive ways. Dorothy Perkins punches up the simplicity of a crossword puzzle with polka dotted, striped, and plaid squares and enhances the asymmetrical patterns with contrasting hits of bright and pastel solids with gray throughout (cat. 55). Although the two never met, Perkins would have understood Graham's aesthetic dictum of giving the eye "something else to see" by breaking up areas of color and shapes that she realized in her more improvisational compositions. "It won't make your sight just sit," Graham would express in another context, "It keep[s] the eyes up lifted, you know, flowing over the quilt kind of like water moving in a pond or in the ocean. That's the beauty of the water, that changing of scenes."[78] Even for quilts that consist of patterns like Louella Harris's Wheel of Fortune (cat. 61) and Mattie Lou Henderson's Sailboats (cat. 69), the subtle irregularities of their piecing complement the poetics of motion, travel, and journeying in their names. This impulse to keep the eye moving, to acknowledge that what you see is not the final state of things, feels akin to keeping one's vision on vastness that one can step into.

The pursuit of constant visual movement that Graham describes encourages experimentation and openness to all kinds of formal results. Some quiltmakers may start with a single parameter, as Irene Bankhead often did. In Bars (cat. 111), the mode of construction invites the quiltmaker to seek variations in the length of pieces and color. In the Half-Square Triangle quilt, her decision to make this basic quilt block out of a striped fabric opens the door to a kaleidoscopic effect when the pieces are recombined (cat. 66). In a departure from her signature use of velvet, a creation by Rosie Lee Tompkins (cat. 76) offers the eye and hand a glossy topography of satin and embroidered silks that might, as it did for Alice Walker when she owned this quilt for a time, make someone "feel real snazzy" and transport them into a soiree of their own imagining.[79] In her sensitive handling of plaid flannel and wide-wale corduroy, Maple Jean Swift's Medallion plays with soft and hard variations of grids and its orthogonal lines to the point where gradients of color seem to glow within nets of gray threads (cat. 39).

For Venella Tyler, the lessons learned from her mother inform her unfinished Pinwheel top (cat. 14 and figs. 23-24). Her use of a red-dotted navy cotton to surround pastel-colored wedges typifies the method of "showing up," which entails placing light and dark colors near one another to make the blocks stand out better.[80] Two of her blocks, one in the upper left and another just right of center, in which four of the wedges match the navy "ground" and create a dark pinwheel shape, demonstrate Tyler's clever application of this principle. While beholders might initially see the overall pattern as circles with multicolored segments, Tyler's strategic placements of dark wedges contribute to a wholly new pattern that activates the larger curved cross shapes making up the center piece of the block (while Tyler has sensibly reused blue wedges created by cutting out quarter sections from each square's corner). Angelia Tobias similarly could be strategic in designing her quilts with existing materials. When working on a patchwork top (cat. 72), she was initially dissatisfied with the overall composition (fig. 25) and eventually opted to slice an entire swath of fabric off and move it entirely to the other side. By effectively creating two borders

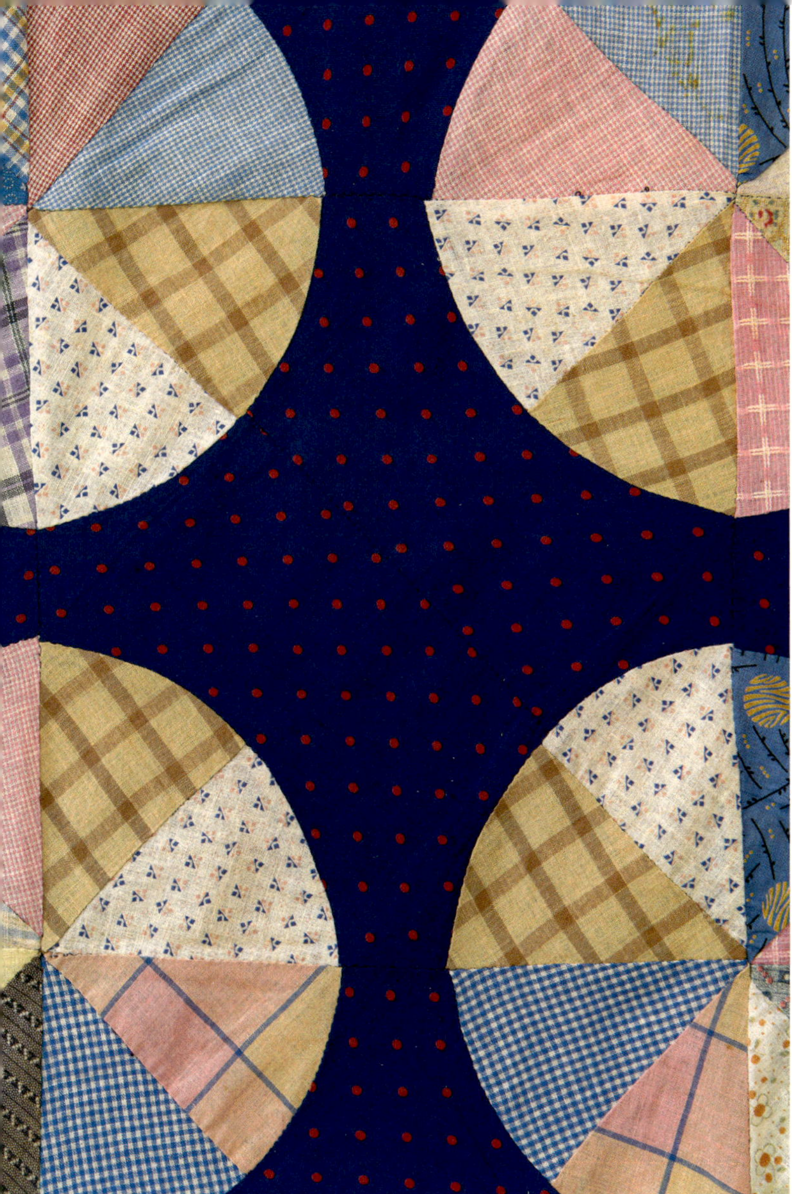

Fig. 23. Detail of cat. 14

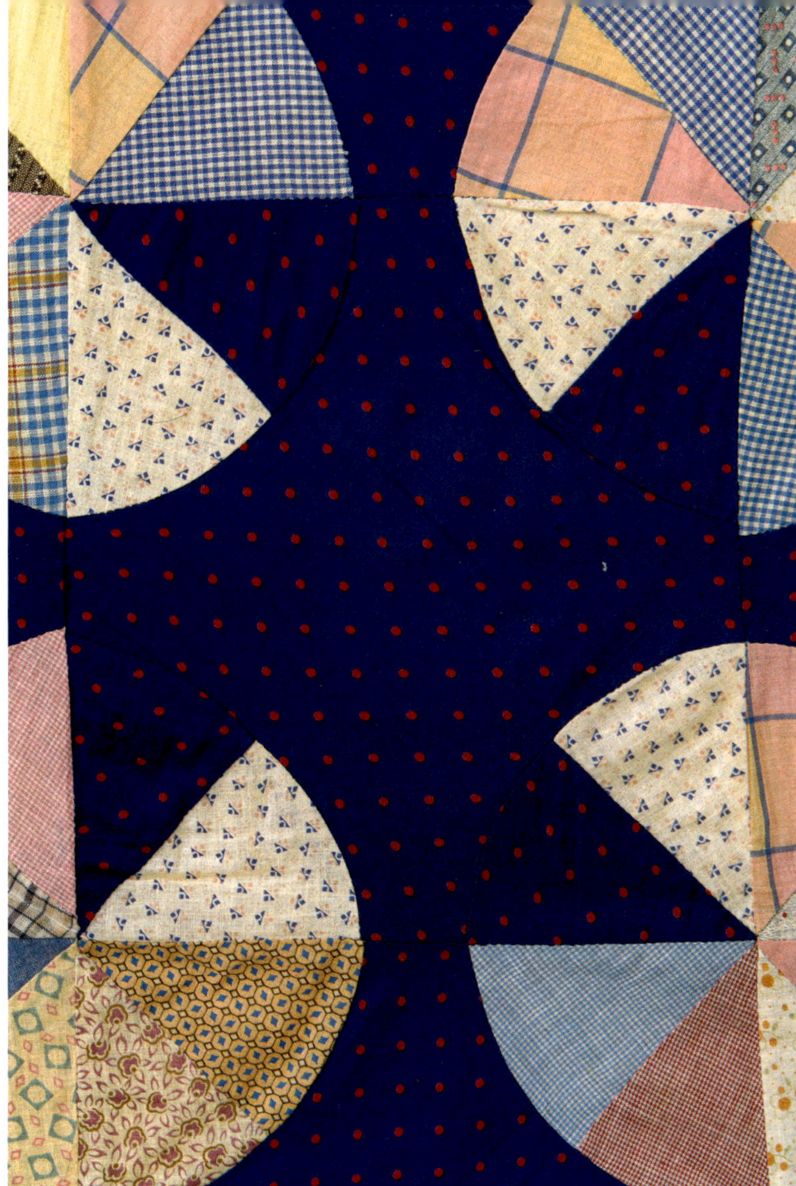

Fig. 24. Alternate detail of cat. 14

for her top, she generated a composition that is balanced in its irregularity.

Beauty Vaughns and Arbie Major, sisters who acquired their technically accomplished piecing skills from their seamstress mother, Pearl Nunley, created two quilts that demonstrate their aptitude for organizing otherwise unruly scrap bags into visually engrossing compositions. Vaughns's Ocean Wave (cat. 38) is not consistently made with the same dark red or teal fabric throughout, nor does Major's Snowball (cat. 30) have equal-sized borders. But these quilts are evidence of the meticulous process of measuring, cutting, arranging, piecing, composing, cutting again, joining, stitching, pausing to look, stitching, and stitching some more until one's vision for a quilt's design is fully realized. The entire process is repetitive, but not necessarily tedious; repetition can release one into mindfulness, in the same way as walking or breathing, and can bring one in closer touch to the present. Their quilts, along with Nunley's Sunflower Garden (cat. 17), invite us to consider all of the intangible dimensions of Black women's quilting and especially bring to mind the radiant image of Black women artists that Alice Walker calls forth at the end of her essay, "In Search of Our Mothers' Gardens." In describing her own mother, who cultivated brilliant and ambitious gardens, Walker recognized the spark of the creator and artist: "hand and eye . . . involved in the work her soul must have. Ordering the universe in the image of her personal conception of Beauty." More than the fact of the garden itself, her mother's artistry is "a legacy of respect she leaves to me . . . for all that illuminates and cherishes life" and is proof of her intent to grasp it in the midst of an anti-Black world that would oppose it.[81] In reclaiming this lineage of African American women's creativity, Walker honors, as she extends, the artistic spirit of her foremothers.

Gerstine Scott's necktie quilt (cat. 85), as with the skills manifest in Vaughns's and Major's quilts, has its roots in the work of her elders. It was modeled after a quilt made by her

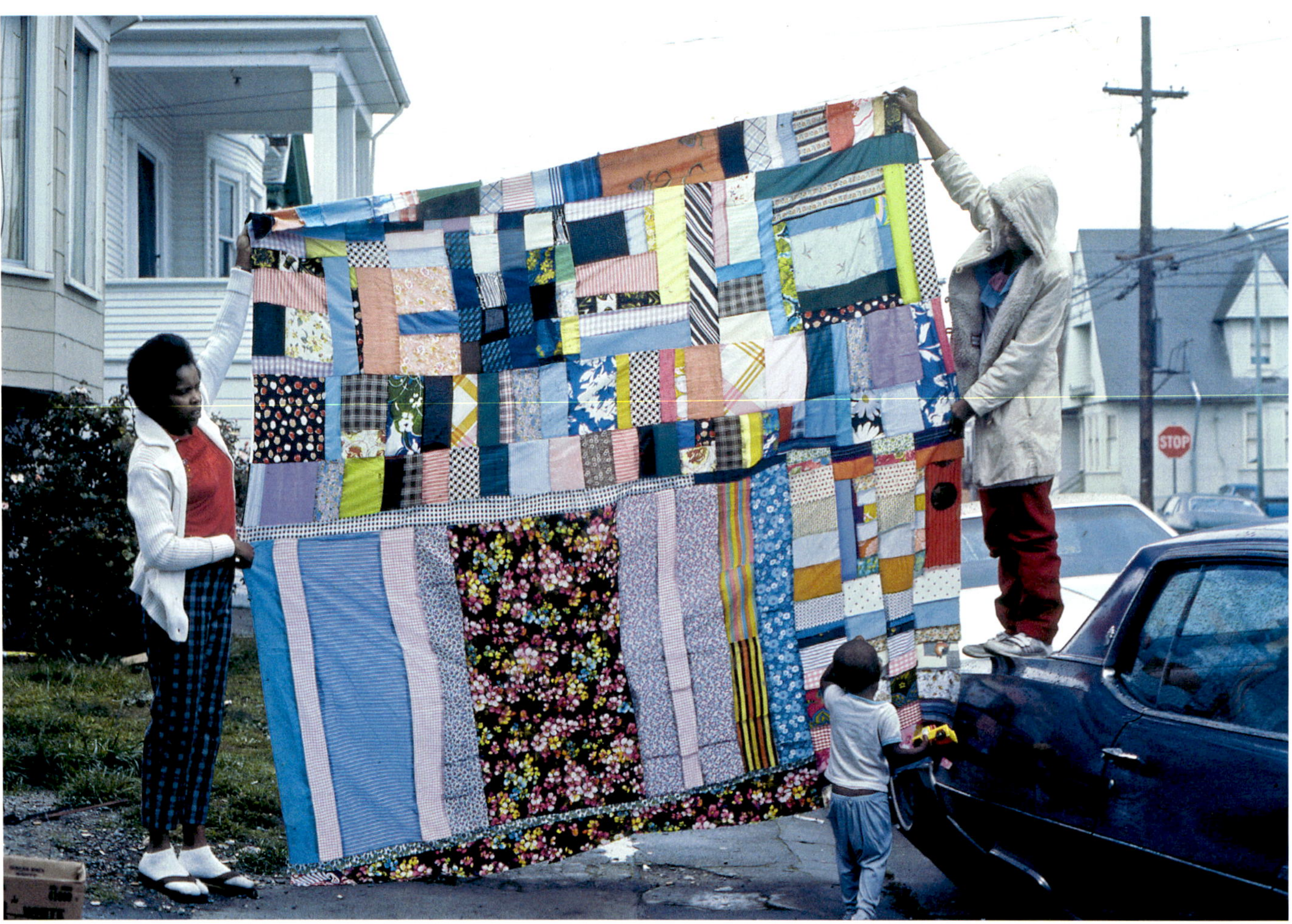

Fig. 25. Angelia Tobias and friend holding a quilt top in progress (see cat. 72), c. 1985

grandmother Laura Hall that her aunt Othella Moss kept at her home in Texas. Preferring that the quilt stay with her rather than make the move to California, Moss let her niece copy it on paper. The drawing is no longer extant, but we might regard this quilt's primary forms as the signature aesthetic of Hall's quilt, which is seen in the rivulets of silk fabrics that narrow and flare along one another's edges. As we see in many of the improvisational and pattern-based quilts exhibited in *Routed West*, Black women have long understood the value of everyday materials in making objects of functional beauty, a kind of ingenuity channeled in Gladys Henry's woven mat made of cotton T-shirts (cat. 89) or registered in the newspapers that Cora Lee Hall Brown used as interfacing (yet to be removed) for her String Medallion top (cat. 45). Selena Foster succinctly articulated the power of this alchemy, saying, "I take your nothing and make something out of it."[82] Willie Mae Chatman underscores the responsibility she accords to the creative ability involved in quilting, believing that if a talent is not used, then it can be taken from you.[83]

Anchored in an artistic tradition of creating objects meant to care for people—those in need of warmth or protection from drafty and dusty floorboards, those in need of comfort or reminders of where they came from—the quiltmakers in *Routed West*, like many quiltmakers, were familiar with the humble, liberating power that quiltmaking lent them. The gift of such creativity blooms into a full environment in the hands of Isiadore Whitehead, who adorned her home's guest room with Double Wedding Ring quilts, drapes, floor mats, and a chair seat (cats. 46–53 and fig. 26). In many ways, it is reminiscent of the 1970s, when the "pattern-on-pattern" trend entered popular interior design vocabularies; Gloria Vanderbilt's "patchwork bedroom" exemplifies this revelry in all-over decoration (fig. 27).[84] Yet in contrast to Vanderbilt's cosmopolitan eclecticism, Whitehead's Double Wedding Ring Room is self-made, anchored in the artist's personal vision and community. She began piecing the quilts, drapes, and floor mats during quiet moments on the job as a bus driver waiting for school to let out, and before long, teachers and parents began donating fabric to her. Akin

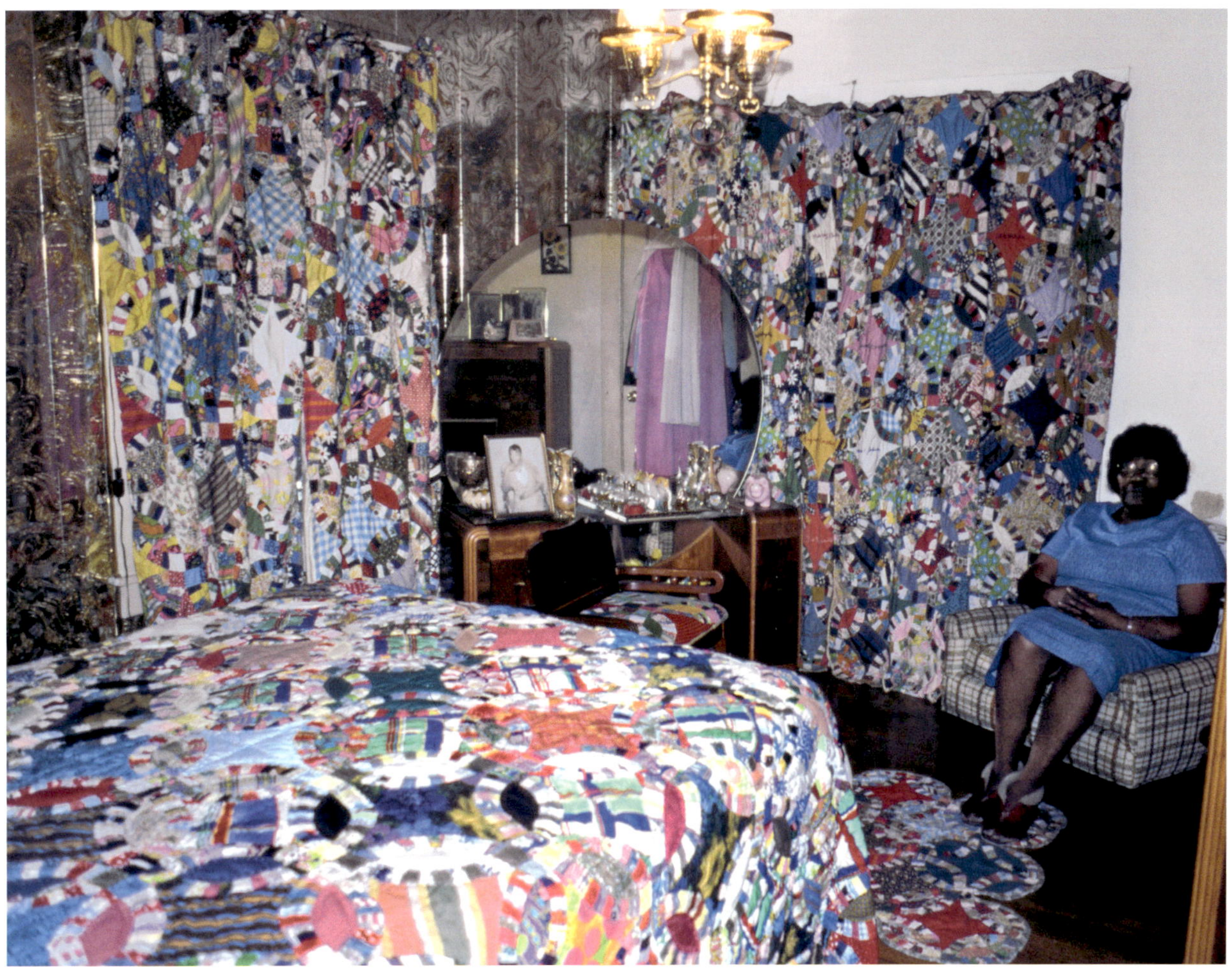

Fig. 26. Isiadore Whitehead in her guest bedroom decorated with Double Wedding Ring quilt, drapes, mats, and chair (cats. 46–53), Oakland, California, 1984

to the manner of friendship quilts, she embroidered their names on the drapes in appreciation. To recite their names today is like performing a roll call of Whitehead's multicultural network: Kazue Granich, Mary Burkes, Robert King, Edith Eddington, Velma Miles, Virginia Hernandez, among many others. Installed with a chandelier, gold-veined mirrors, and full vanity displaying perfume bottles, her Double Wedding Ring Room is a dazzling testament to her "will to adorn"–the outpouring of her inner vision, crafted by hand.[85] This might be the highest (and humblest) lesson that the quiltmakers in the exhibition leave for audiences today: to recognize through their quilts the spirit of interconnectedness, pleasure in beauty, resilience, and love released towards self and others across generations.

COLLECTIVE CAREGIVING FOR THE FUTURE

At present, the quilts in this exhibition are housed at the Berkeley Art Museum and Pacific Film Archive as part of the bequest of Eli Leon, which the museum received in 2019 upon his death. Numbering nearly three thousand patchwork

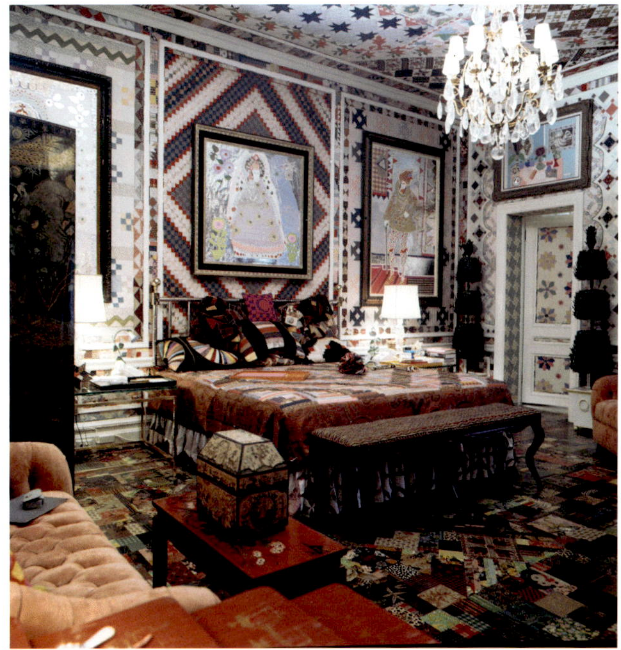

Fig. 27. Gloria Vanderbilt's Patchwork Bedroom, published in *Vogue*, February 1, 1970

quilts attributed to Black makers (the bequest also includes hundreds of unattributed quilts), the African American quilt collection gathers objects that have traced diverse routes before their arrival at this institution. Even a museum flush with resources would be hard-pressed to meet the demands of its physical care, but as I hope to have shown, the quilts and their stories make a compelling case for their preservation as artworks and objects of cultural heritage. Along with the important insights presented by the other contributors to this catalog, I wish to lay out a few considerations in this final section regarding what stewardship for the African American quilt collection might look like. What is the museum's role in conveying the ethic of love that is imbued in these quilts?

Once again, Alice Walker brilliantly provides essential insights about quilts and their relationship to the past in ways that can inform museum practice today. In her well-known short story of 1973, "Everyday Use," the central plot revolves around the narrator's revelation about her two daughters: Maggie, a thin, homely young girl with scarred arms and legs who lives with her mother in rural Georgia, and Dee, her lighter-skinned, stylish sister who has left home, scorning her family's poverty and what she views as their cultural backwardness. When Dee makes her appearance in the story, she has returned home with a Black revolutionary mindset, and a new name, "Wangero," along with revived interest in her Black roots that she expresses toward objects like the butter churn she wishes to display as home décor and quilts made by her namesake, her grandma Dee. The story's tension rises to a pitch when Wangero learns that their grandmother's hand-pieced quilts are already destined for Maggie by their mother. Enraged, Wangero argues that her unsophisticated sister would put the quilts to "everyday use" rather than hang them on a wall like a treasured object. The narrator of the story, the sisters' mother, ultimately gives the quilts to Maggie in a flash of recognition about her "backward" daughter when she says, "Maggie knows how to quilt." That is, she has embraced the spiritual inheritances of her Black Southern family and has the ability, through quiltmaking, to craft her own cultural survival by remembering, practicing, and passing on the values of her foremothers. Maggie, Walker's story seems to say, exemplifies the most honest and sustained engagement with one's heritage; she remains closest to the idea of the "motheroot" discussed at the outset of this essay.

By contrast, Wangero's ambivalence toward her Black past and susceptibility to popular fashions position her as a latecomer to what was always already there. That said, like folklorist Patricia A. Turner, I am struck by the cultural moment that Wangero/Dee symbolizes at large. Turner writes, "Using quilts as an example, Walker captures the realization that occurred in the 1960s and 1970s, when many formally educated blacks shared a genealogical epiphany. In spite of the economic deprivation endured by African Americans, the cultural legacy was a rich one, worthy of celebration and reverence. . . . After family quilts were retrieved from trunks, attics, and basements, they remained as particularly revered commodities."[86] In other words, even if Walker portrays Wangero's interest in her family's quilts as superficial and belated, it is nevertheless a legitimate one, representative of unprecedented levels of popular interest in and desire to reclaim one's Black past—not unlike the impact that Alex Haley's *Roots* had on generations of African American viewers when it premiered on television in 1977. Through Wangero's character, we can appreciate that, for many, the physical survival of quilts symbolizes broader truths about ancestral resilience and artistry that directly fed into Black radical imaginaries struggling against postwar economic decline and a growing carceral state. There is no one authentic way to enter the worlds of African American-made quilts, for they generate meaning across a complex terrain of Black identity, where personal histories, political identification, craft knowledge and traditions, aesthetic experience, and physical preservation all play a vital part in quilts' multiple valences as cultural heritage, material culture, and art.

With these strands of culture in mind, the collective labor of various entities seems best equipped to document, preserve, and interpret the significance of African American quilt stories for public audiences. Quilt documentation projects, in the mold of state initiatives from the 1980s, are foundational in this sense; they are designed to record stories about quilts and their quiltmakers. The California Heritage Quilt Project, founded in 1984 as a nonprofit organization, was one of the thirty-six such state documentation projects that were organized during the wave of popular interest in quilts that gained momentum throughout the 1970s. Over the course of thirty-two days, residents of California brought in 3,300 quilts for documentation and entry into the historical archive. Among them was Dorinda Green Mansfield's Nine Patch Variation dating from 1920–1940 (fig. 28), the only documented quilt made by a Black woman that would appear in the publication emerging from the CHQP, *Ho for California! Pioneer Women and Their Quilts* (1990).[87] Had the project moved its documentation cut-off date beyond 1945 and conducted more extensive outreach, Mansfield's story might have been affirmed by the thousands of cultural kin who moved westward just decades later, energized by the same "snap and ambition" that W.E.B. Du Bois noted in 1913 among Black Californians seeking to better their lives.[88]
In this vein, historical research of the kind grounding this exhibition is one way of reconnecting the quilts that Leon collected to their histories, geographical places, lineages, and

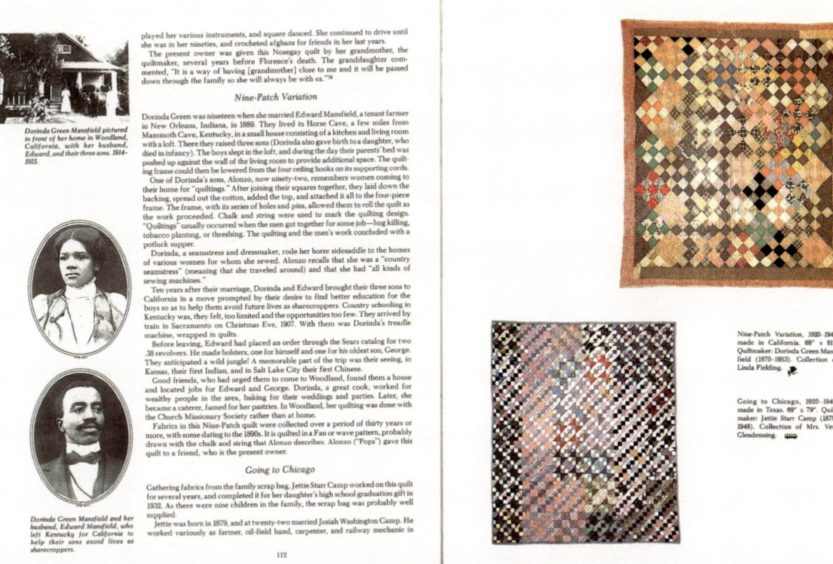

played her various instruments, and square danced. She continued to drive until she was in her nineties, and crocheted afghans for friends in her last years.

The present owner was given this Nosegay quilt by her grandmother, the quiltmaker, several years before Florence's death. The granddaughter commented, "It is a way of having [grandmother] close to me and it will be passed down through the family so she will always be with us."[78]

Nine-Patch Variation

Dorinda Green was nineteen when she married Edward Mansfield, a tenant farmer in New Orleans, Indiana, in 1889. They lived in Horse Cave, a few miles from Mammoth Cave, Kentucky, in a small house consisting of a kitchen and living room with a loft. There they raised three sons (Dorinda also gave birth to a daughter, who died in infancy). The boys slept in the loft, and during the day their parents' bed was pushed up against the wall of the living room to provide additional space. The quilting frame could then be lowered from the four ceiling hooks on its supporting cords.

One of Dorinda's sons, Alonzo, now ninety-two, remembers women coming to their home for "quiltings." After joining their squares together, they laid down the backing, spread out the cotton, added the top, and attached it all to the four-piece frame. The frame, with its series of holes and pins, allowed them to roll the quilt as the work proceeded. Chalk and string were used to mark the quilting design. "Quiltings" usually occurred when the men got together for some job—hog killing, tobacco planting, or threshing. The quilting and the men's work concluded with a potluck supper.

Dorinda, a seamstress and dressmaker, rode her horse sidesaddle to the homes of various women for whom she sewed. Alonzo recalls that she was a "country seamstress" (meaning that she traveled around) and that she had "all kinds of sewing machines."

Ten years after their marriage, Dorinda and Edward brought their three sons to California in a move prompted by their desire to find better education for the boys so as to help them avoid future lives as sharecroppers. Country schooling in Kentucky was, they felt, too limited and the opportunities too few. They arrived by train in Sacramento on Christmas Eve, 1907. With them was Dorinda's treadle machine, wrapped in quilts.

Before leaving, Edward had placed an order through the Sears catalog for two .38 revolvers. He made holsters, one for himself and one for his oldest son, George. They anticipated a wild jungle! A memorable part of the trip was their seeing, in Kansas, their first Indian, and in Salt Lake City their first Chinese.

Good friends, who had urged them to come to Woodland, found them a house and located jobs for Edward and George. Dorinda, a great cook, worked for wealthy people in the area, baking for their weddings and parties. Later, she became a caterer, famed for her pastries. In Woodland, her quilting was done with the Church Missionary Society rather than at home.

Fabrics in this Nine-Patch quilt were collected over a period of thirty years or more, with some dating to the 1890s. It is quilted in a Fan or wave pattern, probably drawn with the chalk and string that Alonzo describes. Alonzo ("Pops") gave this quilt to a friend, who is the present owner.

Going to Chicago

Gathering fabrics from the family scrap bag, Jettie Starr Camp worked on this quilt for several years, and completed it for her daughter's high school graduation gift in 1932. As there were nine children in the family, the scrap bag was probably well supplied.

Jettie was born in 1879, and at twenty-two married Josiah Washington Camp. He worked variously as farmer, oil-field hand, carpenter, and railway mechanic in

112

Dorinda Green Mansfield pictured in front of her home in Woodland, California, with her husband, Edward, and their three sons. 1914–1915.

Dorinda Green Mansfield and her husband, Edward Mansfield, who left Kentucky for California to help their sons avoid lives as sharecroppers.

Nine-Patch Variation, 1920–1940, made in California. 68" x 81". Quiltmaker: Dorinda Green Mansfield (1870–1953). Collection of Linda Fielding.

Going to Chicago, 1920–1940, made in Texas. 69" x 79". Quiltmaker: Jettie Starr Camp (1879–1948). Collection of Mrs. Vera Glendenning.

Fig. 28. Dorinda Green Mansfield's quilt (top) as featured in *Ho for California! Pioneer Women and Their Quilts*, 1990

traditions so that more quiltkeepers might recognize the stories held by family heirlooms, or begin a quiltmaking tradition for themselves.

Taking a clear-eyed view of Eli Leon's collecting practices is also critical to understanding the intentions behind the cultural work around the collection at BAMPFA and to charting future paths. Leon launched his personal quest for African American quilts around 1981 with the purchase of Emma Hall's Double Wedding Ring (cat. 16), pursuing his own interest in improvisational quilt practices around the same time that the CHQP was organizing its efforts. Whereas the CHQP compiled its documentation from self-selected volunteers who brought in their family quilts for recording, Leon's work was indebted to the African American individuals whom he pursued and from whom he ultimately acquired quilts. The essays "Trips South" and "Meeting Mrs. Murphy" make clear the extent to which he relied upon the familial networks of Black women quilters in the Bay Area for an entrée into their communities to conduct his research and collecting. His African American informants entertained Leon's countless questions, impromptu phone calls, and regular home visits as he built his collection. His research was, for the most part, disengaged from questions about quiltmakers' active participation in the market for their works, whether belonging to well-established cooperatives like the Tutwiler Quilters (cat. 88), founded in 1988 to help its members living in the Mississippi Delta region earn money from selling their quilts, or based on his and others' patronage of artists like Rosie Lee Tompkins, Arbie Williams, and Laverne Brackens. Indeed, Leon's singular focus on improvisational quiltmaking and the outsized impact of his exhibitions have overshadowed other vital histories of African American quilts. In addition to quilting cooperatives, of which the Freedom Quilting Bee is the best known, these other histories include—among many others not mentioned—the story quilt tradition that traces back to the nineteenth-century work of Harriet Powers, the ways that the interracial Negro History Quilt Club of Marin City and Sausalito or Jessie Telfair mobilized quilts as a form of political consciousness-raising during the Civil Rights movement, and how Marion Coleman as a quilt artist, teacher, and president of the African American Quilt Guild of Oakland used quilts as a vehicle for community art education to advance social justice and community change throughout the 1990s and early 2000s.[89] This is to say that understanding what Leon *did not* collect alongside what he did acquire, and how, is crucial for historically situating quilts in BAMPFA's collection within the myriad of ways that African American makers have engaged the medium throughout history.

Essays in this volume make strides in this direction. In "A Table of Our Own: A Conversation on Repair, Reclamation, and Rootedness," Sharbreon Plummer, Carolyn Mazloomi, and A'donna Richardson offer a firsthand account of Leon's research and the ways it reactivated harmful stereotypes about Black women's quilts within a majority-white quilt world. The resulting lack of trust is still being addressed today. In her essay "Collecting and Exhibiting Quilts," Bridget R. Cooks incisively locates Leon's enterprise within a longer history of "white preoccupation with Black possession" and, through her critical reading of his essays, highlights how culturally extractive his collecting practices were, and for the benefit (in the main) of himself. Both contributions affirm the ways museums more broadly (including BAMPFA), can respond reparatively to these histories, most importantly by providing a platform for living Black quiltmakers to speak, teach, and share about their art directly with audiences. The Women of Color Quilter's Network has been doing this work—along with educating its members about the market, documenting African American-made quilts, and providing practical tools for sustaining its members' practices—for nearly four decades, since it was founded by Dr. Mazloomi in 1985. Its model of inclusivity and artistic empowerment has led the way in bringing visibility to Black quilt artists across the country and in safeguarding their legacies.[90] African American guilds throughout the country continue to teach and foster quilting practices among their members.

The formation of quilt guilds and other quilt organizations, especially from the 1970s onward, points to the inescapable truth that quilts and the practices around their making have thrived apart from art museums for at least two centuries by virtue of their historical exclusion from these very spaces. Fine arts and modern art museums have, by definition, been founded on aesthetic hierarchies in which quilts, "women's work," craft, and folk art were marginalized and held the least value in comparison with the "fine arts" of painting and sculpture. This marginalization was compounded when African American women artists were the ones struggling for recognition. As Cooks has shown, art museums have historically been exclusionary places for Black art and artists, even when they exhibit their work. As a key example, when the quilts made by the African American women of Gee's Bend were shown across the country in places like the Whitney and the Museum of Fine Arts, Houston, the terms of their reception still privileged the values and forms of fine art, rather than those belonging to the quiltmakers.[91] Along similar lines, Eli Leon's investments in quilts confirmed their value even if, in practice, his collecting enterprise did not always place community care over his own interests. We could say that museums at large have been outsiders to the world of quiltmaking. And because many still rest upon colonialist foundations that prize objects over people, structural transformation remains necessary if museums wish to respect and include a medium that has thrived without them *and* meaningfully support the grassroots nature of quilt production. Reflecting on this past has informed several aspects of this exhibition's preparations, from seeking to reconnect quilts with descendant families, to securing permissions for using images of quilts in this book and the exhibition's programs and marketing, to inviting family participation in the presentation of their ancestors' quilts. As the museum continues a multiyear initiative to preserve the quilts' physical condition, this work of preserving quilt-centered stories about family and Black culture is also an integral part of the museum's stewardship responsibilities.

Plummer, Mazloomi, Richardson, and Cooks offer recommendations that further reorient museum conversations around the future of African American quilts. They emphasize the critical importance of documentation efforts, whether at BAMPFA and other museums or in private family collections, to raise awareness about and preserve the history of African American quilts, a movement that Richardson's African American Quilt Documentation Study Group is leading.[92] They also encourage museums through their programs, exhibitions, or collecting initiatives to reflect a range of artistic backgrounds, aesthetic values, and cultural histories. The final two essays of this volume, by contemporary artists Adia Millett and Basil Kincaid, bring readers back to the space of kinship—the grounds where so many quilts originate—and reflect on the impact of their family's quiltmaking traditions on their contemporary artistic practices. Their personal essays illustrate how quilts have much to teach us through the ancestral wisdom they carry, encouraging us to converse honestly about the history from which they come and to seek new ways of channeling their lessons in art and life.

At its foundation, *Routed West* is about an ethic of care that underlines the flow and flourishing of quilts within African American communities. It is an ethic that guides how fabrics are salvaged and chosen, puts hands to work to fill physical or emotional needs, tends to past memory as much as it does to present and future kin, and calls forth the quiltmaker's own image of beauty from the sovereign space of the imagination. That the stories gathered here include California as part of their journey is specific to these quilts, but they are not exclusive to the Golden State; in terms of their other destinations and travels, one need only look at a map of other African American migration routes for a view of where quilts, made and kept for sustaining Black life, can likely be found.

Edith Gross's *Generational March* is one such map, whose rust-dyed fabric eloquently registers the "permanent stain of slavery" within the history of the United States (fig. 29).[93] Her quilt is a powerful reminder that this history, along with that of Black resistance to these inequities, informs the lives of African American quiltmakers and migrants, as well as the abstract, improvisational, and patterned splendor of their quilts. The "motheroot" of African American quiltmaking carries these complex realities in its fibers. When we are able to hold and understand these connections, then we may be that much closer to honoring, in our practice of them, the lessons of care and repair that the quilts carry forward.

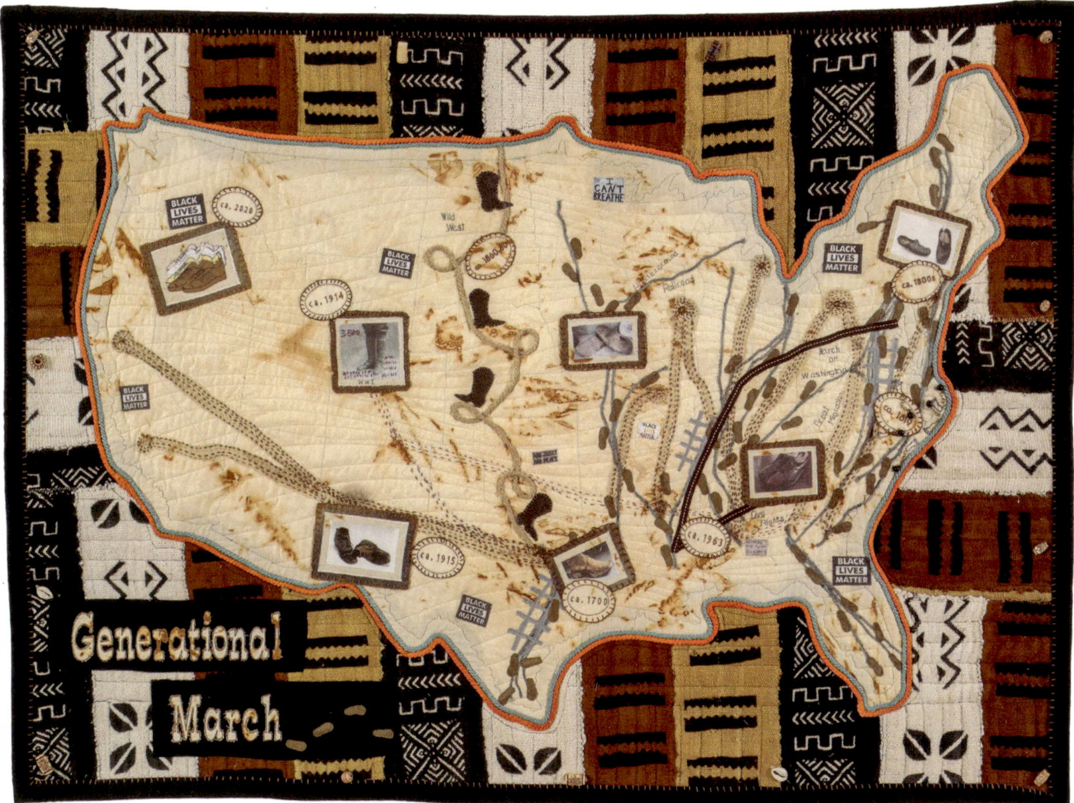

Fig. 29. Edith Gross, *Generational March*, 2020. Rusted-dyed fabric, printed pictures, mud cloth; pieced, hand-stitched, 37 x 51 in. (94 x 129.5 cm)

Notes

1. Selena Foster, "Selena Foster: A Longtime Richmond Resident from Cherokee County, Texas," interview by Judith K. Dunning in 1986, *On the Waterfront: An Oral History of Richmond, California*, Oral History Center, The Bancroft Library, University of California, Berkeley, 1992, 64-69, 118.

2. "Historic Overview," chap. 2 in *Rosie The Riveter/World War II Home Front National Historical Park: General Management Plan/Environmental Assessment* (Richmond, CA: National Park Service, U.S. Department of the Interior, 2008), 24 and 26. Accessed April 17, 2024, http://npshistory.com/publications/rori/gmp-ea-2008.pdf. See also Isabel Wilkerson, *The Warmth of Other Suns: The Epic Story of America's Great Migration* (New York: Random House, 2010), 187.

3. Foster, "Selena Foster," 61.

4. Foster, "Selena Foster," 219.

5. Zula Johnson, interview by Eli Leon, 1987, African-American Quilt Maker Interviews, BAMPFA, CD065, 8/87, side B, track 6.

6. bell hooks, "Aesthetic Inheritances: History Worked by Hand," in *yearning: race, gender, and cultural politics* (Boston: South End Press, 1990); reprinted in *Belonging: A Culture of Place* (New York: Routledge, 2008), 155.

7. Wendy Thompson, this volume, 45.

8. "[Quilts] were history as life lived." hooks, "Aesthetic Inheritances," 160.

9. James N. Gregory, "The Second Great Migration: A Historical Overview," in *African American Urban History: The Dynamics of Race, Class and Gender since World War II*, ed. Joe W. Trotter Jr. and Kenneth L. Kusmer (Chicago: University of Chicago Press, 2009), 19-38.

10. "Historic Overview," 179.

11. "Historic Overview," 24. See also Gretchen Lemke-Santangelo, *Abiding Courage: African American Migrant Women and the East Bay Community* (Chapel Hill, NC: University of North Carolina Press, 2000), 50.

12. "Historic Overview," 23.

13. James N. Gregory, "Black Migration History for Individual States, 1850-2017," in *America's Great Migrations Project* (accessed April 22, 2024), https://depts.washington.edu/moving1/black_migration_states.shtml. In 1950, the Black population in California numbered 469,439 people, compared to 128,337 in 1940. Population increases among African Americans in California, broken down by state of birth, are as follows: from Texas, 21,545 Black migrants in 1940 increased to 103,745 in 1950 (382% increase); from Louisiana, 16,061 to 86,953 (441%); from Arkansas, 4,287 to 39,718 (825%); from Mississippi, 5,264 to 25,292 (380%); and from Oklahoma, 8,946 to 24,669 migrants (176%).

14. Wilkerson, *The Warmth of Other Suns*, 10.

15. "Historic Overview," 35. See also Lemke-Santangelo, *Abiding Courage*, 50-51, and "Richmond Took a Beating: From Civic Chaos Came Ships for War and Some Hope for the Future," *Fortune* 31 no. 2 (February 1945): 264.

16. Lemke-Santangelo, *Abiding Courage*, 51.

17. Lemke-Santangelo, *Abiding Courage*, 51. In Los Angeles, the Black population grew from 63,700 in 1940 to 763,000 in 1970. See also Kelly Simpson, "The Great Migration: Creating a New Black Identity in Los Angeles," *PBSSoCal* (February 15, 2012), https://www.pbssocal.org/history-society/the-great-migration-creating-a-new-black-identity-in-los-angeles.

18. Foster, "Selena Foster," 68.

19. Gary Kamiya, "When WWII brought blacks to the East Bay, whites fought for segregation," *San Francisco Chronicle*, Nov 23, 2018, https://www.sfchronicle.com/chronicle_vault/article/When-WWII-brought-blacks-to-the-East-Bay-whites-13417228.php.

20. The phrase "acts of living" is drawn from a quotation by artist Noah Purifoy memorialized at the Watts Towers Art Center: "One does not have to be a visual artist to utilize creative potential. Creativity can be an act of living, a way of life, and a formula for doing the right thing." It has been creatively expanded by the sixth iteration of the Hammer Museum's *Made in L.A.* biennial of contemporary art in Los Angeles, which opened in 2023.

21. Onnie Lee Logan, quoted in Lemke-Santangelo, *Abiding Courage*, 140 and 147-150.

22. Feminists of the 1970s have long championed quilts as a rich source of insight into women's history. For addressing quilts and Black women's history in particular, see, for example, Darlene Clark Hine, "Quilts and African-American Women's Cultural History," in Marsha L. MacDowell, ed., *African American Quiltmaking in Michigan* (East Lansing, MI: Michigan State University Press, 1997), 13-17, and Sharbreon Plummer, *Diasporic Threads: Black Women, Fibre & Textiles* (Norwich, Norfolk, UK: Common Threads Press, 2022).

23. Ora Clay, "The Time It Takes," *Quiltfolk* 16 (Special theme issue, "Family"), 51.

24. Alice Walker, "In Search of Our Mothers' Gardens," in *In Search of Our Mothers' Gardens, Womanist Prose* (New York: Harcourt Brace Jovanovich, 1983), 230.

25. Robert Farris Thompson, *Flash of the Spirit: African and Afro-American Art and Philosophy* (New York: Vintage, 1984); John Michael Vlach, *The Afro-American Tradition in Decorative Arts* (Cleveland: Cleveland Museum of Art, 1978); and Maude Southwell Wahlman, *Signs and Symbols: African Images in African-American Quilts* (New York: The Museum of American Folk Art, 1993).

26. My summary of the critical responses to Eli Leon's work and the discourse on African retentions in quiltmaking are drawn from Cuesta Benberry, "African American Quilts: Paradigms of Black Diversity," *The International Review of African American Art* 12, no. 3 (January 1995): 30-37; Stacy Hollander, "African-American Quilts: Two Perspectives," *Folk Art* (Spring 1993): 44-51; Teri Klassen, "Representations of African American Quiltmaking: From Omission to High Art," *Journal of American Folklore* 122, no. 485 (Summer 2009): 297-334; Carolyn Mazloomi, *Spirits of the Cloth: Contemporary African American Quilts* (New York: Clarkson Potter, 1998), including Benberry's foreword; and Patricia A. Turner, *Crafted Lives: Stories and Studies of African American Quilters* (Jackson, MS: University Press of Mississippi, 2009).

27. Sandra K. German, "Surfacing: The Inevitable Rise of the Women of Color Quilters' Network," *Uncoverings* 14 (1993): 142.

28. Collecting Ledger 2, Eli Leon Archives, BAMPFA, 79.

29. For additional readings on the intersection of queerness and craft, see, for example, Julia Bryan-Wilson, *Fray: Art + Textile Politics* (Chicago: University of Chicago Press, 2017); John Chaich and Todd Oldham, *Queer Threads: Crafting Identity and Community* (Los Angeles: Ammo, 2017), based on an exhibition held in 2014 at the Leslie-Lohman Museum of Art in New York; Michael Moon, "Quilts as Koans," in *Boundary Trouble in American Vanguard Art, 1920-2020*, Lynne Cooke, ed., Studies in the History of Art Series 84 (Washington, DC: National Gallery of Art; New Haven, CT: Distributed by Yale University Press, 2022), 37-58; and the work of Zak Foster, Grace Rother, and Sunny Smith.

30. For more information, see the Director's Foreword, this volume, 6.

31. Find a Grave, database and images (https://www.findagrave.com/memorial/56200047/william_mcewen-johnston: accessed December 8, 2023), memorial page for William McEwen Johnston (20 Jul 1850-16 Dec 1913), Find a Grave Memorial ID 56200047, citing Riverside Cemetery, Macon, Bibb County, Georgia, USA; Maintained by steve s (contributor 47126287).

32. Copy of pages from the diary of Fllewellyn Johnston, Eli Leon Archives, BAMPFA.

33. Brown's Probate Inventory, if available, has not been located.

34. Jacqueline Jones, *Labor of Love, Labor of Sorrow: Black Women, Work, and the Family from Slavery to the Present*, 2nd ed. (New York: Basic Books, 2009 [1985]), 110.

35. "Friendship Dahlia," *90 Years Ago: 1934 Patchwork and Stories*, last modified December 19, 2021, https://chestercriswellquilt.blogspot.com/2021/12/friendship-dahlia.html;. For background on Loretta Leitner, the author behind Nancy Cabot, see Barbara Brackman, "Nancy Cabot/Loretta Leitner: A Short History," last modified October 4, 2022, https://barbarabrackman.blogspot.com/2022/10/nancy-cabotloretta-leitner-short-history.html

36. A similar quilt made by Effie Roe in 1935 is in the Kathleen McCrady Quilt History Collection at the Briscoe Center for American History, University of Texas, Austin. See "Historical Quilts," accessed March 15, 2024, https://briscoecenter.org/collections/historical-quilts/. Some historians question the practicality of using these quilts as coverings, noting their weight and lumpiness. For additional background on Puff quilts, see Judy Anne Breneman, "Those Peculiar Biscuit and Puff Quilts," 2006, https://quiltindex.org//view/?type=publications&kid=51-149-53.

37. Roberta Lee Johnson, interview by Eli Leon, 1989, African-American Quilt Maker Interviews, BAMPFA, CD112, 10/89, side B, track 9.

38. Lisa Gail Collins, *Stitching Love and Loss: A Gee's Bend Quilt* (Seattle, WA: Washington University Press, 2023), 62.

39. Lisa Gail Collins, *Stitching Love and Loss*, 88.

40. Lisa Gail Collins, *Stitching Love and Loss*, 84, 111.

41. Zak Foster, *Soft Bulk* video series, https://www.zakfoster.com/softbulkhome.

42. Bessie Moore, interview by Eli Leon, 1987-1988, African-American Quilt Maker Interviews, BAMPFA, CD082, 12/87 to 2/88, side A, track 10.

43. Tiya Miles, *All That She Carried: The Journey of Ashley's Sack, a Black Family Keepsake* (New York: Random House, 2021), 125-126.

44. Alice C. Royal, *Allensworth, The Freedom Colony: A California African American Township* (Berkeley, CA: Heyday Books, 2008), 1.

45. The Equal Justice Initiative's "Lynching in America" interactive map graphically displays the frequency with which racist lynchings occurred in the same states and counties in which the quiltmakers in the exhibition were born and from which they migrated. Accessed April 11, 2024, https://lynchinginamerica.eji.org/explore.

46. "Black women's notions of relationality move in circular/overlapping time." LaKisha Michelle Simmons, "Black Feminist Theories of Motherhood and Generation: Histories of Black Infant and Child Loss in the United States," *Signs: Journal of Women in Culture and Society* 46, no. 2 (2021): 330, cited in Miles, *All That She Carried*, 125-126.

47. Eli Leon, "But Now I See: African-American Quilt Revelations" (unpublished essay, January 5, 2006), Bequest of the Eli Leon Living Trust, BAMPFA.

48. Curtis W. Wienker, "McNary: A Predominantly Black Company Town in Arizona," *Negro History Bulletin* 37, no. 5 (August-September 1974): 282-285.

49. Georgia Lee Kidd, interview by Eli Leon, 1992, African-American Quilt Maker Interviews, BAMPFA, CD167, 5/92 to 10/92 and 7/97, side A, track 10.

50. Sherry Ann Byrd, email correspondence with author, June 13, 2021.

51. Roderick Kiracofe, *Unconventional & Unexpected: American Quilts Below the Radar 1950-2000*, 2nd ed. (Atglen, Oregon: Schiffer Publishing and Quiltfolk, 2021), 69.

52. Lemke-Santangelo, *Abiding Courage*, 57-62.

53. Roland L. Freeman, *A Communion of the Spirits: African-American Quilters, Preservers, and Their Stories* (Nashville, TN: Rutledge Hill Press, 1996), 376-377.

54. Carlena White, interview by Eli Leon, 1997-98, African-American Quilt Maker Interviews, BAMPFA, CD176, 7/97 to 2/98, side A, track 2.

55. Carlena White, interview by Eli Leon, 1992, African-American Quilt Maker Interviews, BAMPFA, CD168, 5/92 to 10/92, side B, track 7, and 1997–98 interview, tracks 2–3.
56. Kevin Gaines, "Artistic Othering in Black Diaspora Musics: Preliminary Thoughts on Time, Culture, and Politics," *Uptown Conversation: The New Jazz Studies* (New York: Columbia University Press, 2004), 205, 208–209. I am grateful to Professor Daphne A. Brooks for the prompt to connect improvisational quiltmaking to this body of scholarship in Black music history.
57. Collecting Ledger 4a, Eli Leon Archives, BAMPFA, 234.
58. Mable Battle, interview by Eli Leon, 1995, African-American Quilt Maker Interviews, BAMPFA, CD175, 10/94 to 10/95, side A, track 5.
59. Quoted in Eli Leon, *Models in the Mind: African Prototypes in American Patchwork*, exh. cat. (Winston-Salem, NC: Diggs Gallery, Winston-Salem State University, 1992), 37.
60. bell hooks, "Piecing It All Together," in *Belonging: A Culture of Place*, 166.
61. Alice Neal, interview by Eli Leon, 1984, African-American Quilt Maker Interviews, BAMPFA, CD001, Interview 4-84a, track 1.
62. Neal, interview by Eli Leon, 1984, track 1.
63. Janneken Smucker, *A New Deal for Quilts* (Lincoln, NB: International Quilt Museum, 2023), 104–6.
64. Quoted in Eli Leon, *Something Else to See: Improvisational Bordering Styles in African-American Quilts*, exh. cat. (Amherst, MA: University Gallery, University of Massachusetts, Amherst, 1997), 17.
65. Eli Leon, "Meeting Mrs. Murphy," this volume, 189.
66. Leon, "Meeting Mrs. Murphy," 191.
67. Lemke-Santangelo, *Abiding Courage*, 147–48.
68. I wish to thank Sharbreon Plummer for her presentation at BAMPFA's Quilt Study Days, October 2022, and for enriching this idea of the rhizomatic. See also her essay "Of Salt and Spirit: A Love Letter to Black Southern Women," in *Of Salt and Spirit: Black Quilters in the American South*, ed. Sharbreon Plummer (Jackson, MS: University Press of Mississippi; in association with the Mississippi Museum of Art, 2024).
69. hooks, "Aesthetic Inheritances," 155.
70. As women over the age of forty and steeped in a Southern ethic of care, some Black women quilters might be considered "othermothers," those who assist blood mothers in the responsibilities of childcare and community care in situations where resources were scarce and persistent racial discrimination necessitated the wisdom of an older individual who knew how to survive and resist such assaults. See Stanlie M. James, "Mothering: A Possible Black Feminist Link to Social Transformation?" in *Theorizing Black Feminisms: The Visionary Pragmatism of Black Women*, ed. Stanlie M. James and Abena P.A. Busia (London and New York: Routledge, 1993), 44–54.
71. Estella Brown, interview by Eli Leon, 1987–1988, African-American Quilt Maker Interviews, BAMPFA, CD078, 12/87 to 1/88, side A, track 2.
72. Isiadore Whitehead, interview by Eli Leon, 1984, African-American Quilt Maker Interviews, BAMPFA, CD007, 5/84(2), side A, track 5.
73. From research conducted to date, only a few quiltmakers represented in BAMPFA's collection belonged to quilting groups, and only one object (cat. 88) is from a quilting cooperative, an organization that helps its members earn wages from selling their quilts.
74. For deeper explorations of spirituality in Tompkins's quilts, see *Rosie Lee Tompkins: A Retrospective*, exh. cat., (Berkeley, CA: University of California, Berkeley Art Museum and Pacific Film Archive), 2020.
75. hooks, "Piecing It All Together," 163.
76. hooks, "Piecing It All Together," 162, 163.
77. Sherry Ann Byrd, email correspondence with the author, Feb 5, 2024. See also Adia Millett, "Conversations," this volume, 210.
78. Willia Ette Graham, interview by Eli Leon, 1990, African-American Quilt Maker Interviews, BAMPFA, CD138, 10/90 to 11/90, side B, track 3.
79. Quoted in Freeman, *A Communion of the Spirits*, 152.
80. Eli Leon, *Accidentally on Purpose: The Aesthetic Management of Irregularities in African Textiles and African-American Quilts*, exh. cat. (Davenport, IA: Figge Art Museum, 2006), 85.
81. Walker, "In Search of Our Mothers' Gardens," 241–42.
82. Nanci Valcke, "Remember When I Saw Richmond for the First Time," *West County Times*, July 22, 1990, reprinted in Foster, "Selena Foster," 225.
83. Willie Mae Chatman, interview by Eli Leon, 1987, African-American Quilt Maker Interviews, BAMPFA, CD080, 12/87(1), side A, track 2.
84. Kayleigh Perkov, "Pattern Consciousness: Counterculture-Influenced Interior Design," in *With Pleasure: Pattern and Decoration in American Art 1972–1985*, Anna Katz, ed. (Los Angeles: Los Angeles Museum of Contemporary Art, 2020), 215–23.
85. As Zora Neale Hurston elaborates, "The feeling back of such an act is that there can never be enough of beauty, let alone too much." Zora Neale Hurston, "Characteristics of Negro Expression," in *The Negro: An Anthology*, Nancy Cunard, ed. (London: Published by Nancy Cunard at Wishart, 1934), 25.
86. Turner, *Crafted Lives*, 133–34.
87. Jean Ray Laury and the California Heritage Quilt Project, *Ho for California! Pioneer Women and Their Quilts* (New York: E.P. Dutton), 1990.
88. W.E.B. Du Bois, "Colored California," *The Crisis* 6, no. 4 (August 1913): 192 and 194.
89. This list could also include ways that contemporary quiltmakers categorize genres for themselves, as exemplified in "Modern Quilt," "Art Quilt," "African American Heritage Quilt," and "Traditional Quilt" categories used to jury quilt competitions that are held nationwide today.
90. The generational movement of the Black Diaspora in the 1980s was also the condition for its founding, which incidentally occurred in California. As Dr. Mazloomi recalled, "I enjoy quilting and had a small group of quilters in Los Angeles. Maybe four—four of us that met at a museum in Los Angeles and started to quilt, but I wondered where were the others. Where were the other African-American quilt-makers, and [I] consequently placed an ad in the *Quilter's Newsletter* magazine asking any African-American quilters out there reading the magazine to get in touch with me. And as a result, nine people wrote. . . . And the one commonality that we had together was the fact that we all thought we were the last of the African-American quilters in the country quilting." Oral history interview with Carolyn Mazloomi, September 17–30, 2002, Archives of American Art, Smithsonian Institution, https://www.aaa.si.edu/collections/interviews/oral-history-interview-carolyn-mazloomi-11504.
91. See Bridget R. Cooks, "Collecting and Exhibiting Quilts," in this volume and her book *Exhibiting Blackness: African Americans and the American Art Museum* (Amherst, MA: University of Massachusetts Press), 2011.
92. The array of recent initiatives between the Souls Grown Deep Foundation and the quiltmakers of Gee's Bend (described at www.geesbend.org) are innovative examples of cultural partnerships that honor local histories and support the agency of quiltmakers.
93. Edith Gross, artist statement, in Carolyn Mazloomi, *We Are the Story: A Visual Response to Racism*, in collaboration with the Textile Center, Minneapolis, MN, and Women of Color Quilters Network (West Chester, OH: Paper Moon Publishing, 2021), 52.

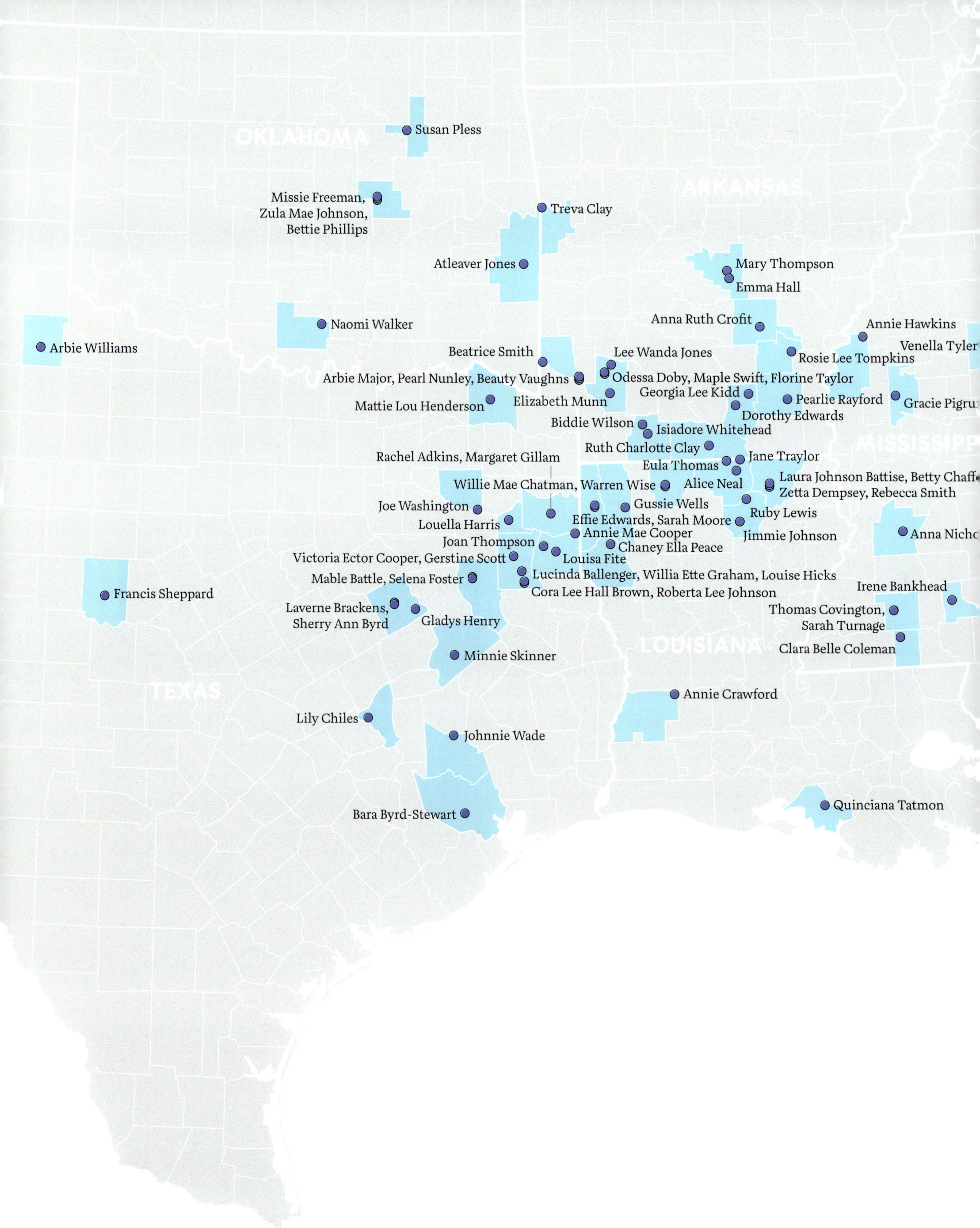

OKLAHOMA

Susan Pless

ARKANSAS

Missie Freeman,
Zula Mae Johnson,
Bettie Phillips

Treva Clay

Atleaver Jones

Mary Thompson

Emma Hall

Naomi Walker

Anna Ruth Crofit

Annie Hawkins

Arbie Williams

Venella Tyler

Beatrice Smith

Lee Wanda Jones

Rosie Lee Tompkins

Arbie Major, Pearl Nunley, Beauty Vaughns

Odessa Doby, Maple Swift, Florine Taylor

Georgia Lee Kidd

Pearlie Rayford

Gracie Pigru

Elizabeth Munn

Mattie Lou Henderson

Dorothy Edwards

Biddie Wilson

Isiadore Whitehead

MISSISSIPP

Ruth Charlotte Clay

Rachel Adkins, Margaret Gillam

Jane Traylor

Eula Thomas

Laura Johnson Battise, Betty Chaff

Willie Mae Chatman, Warren Wise

Alice Neal

Zetta Dempsey, Rebecca Smith

Joe Washington

Gussie Wells

Ruby Lewis

Louella Harris

Effie Edwards, Sarah Moore

Annie Mae Cooper

Jimmie Johnson

Anna Nicho

Joan Thompson

Chaney Ella Peace

Victoria Ector Cooper, Gerstine Scott

Louisa Fite

Lucinda Ballenger, Willia Ette Graham, Louise Hicks

Mable Battle, Selena Foster

Francis Sheppard

Cora Lee Hall Brown, Roberta Lee Johnson

Irene Bankhead

Laverne Brackens,
Sherry Ann Byrd

Gladys Henry

Thomas Covington,
Sarah Turnage

LOUISIANA

Clara Belle Coleman

Minnie Skinner

TEXAS

Annie Crawford

Lily Chiles

Johnnie Wade

Quinciana Tatmon

Bara Byrd-Stewart

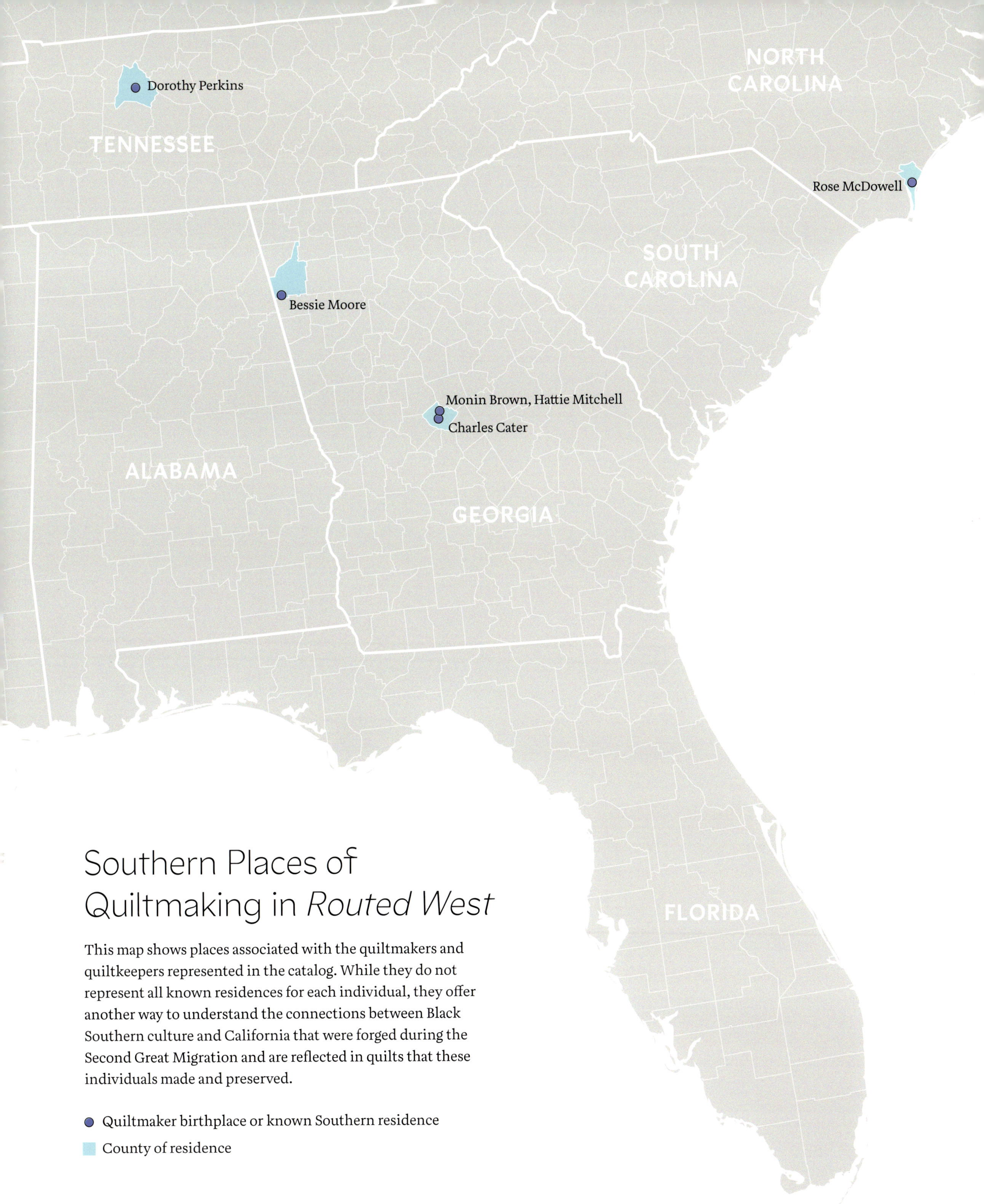

NORTH CAROLINA
Dorothy Perkins
TENNESSEE
Rose McDowell
SOUTH CAROLINA
Bessie Moore
Monin Brown, Hattie Mitchell
Charles Cater
ALABAMA
GEORGIA
FLORIDA

Southern Places of Quiltmaking in *Routed West*

This map shows places associated with the quiltmakers and quiltkeepers represented in the catalog. While they do not represent all known residences for each individual, they offer another way to understand the connections between Black Southern culture and California that were forged during the Second Great Migration and are reflected in quilts that these individuals made and preserved.

- Quiltmaker birthplace or known Southern residence
- County of residence

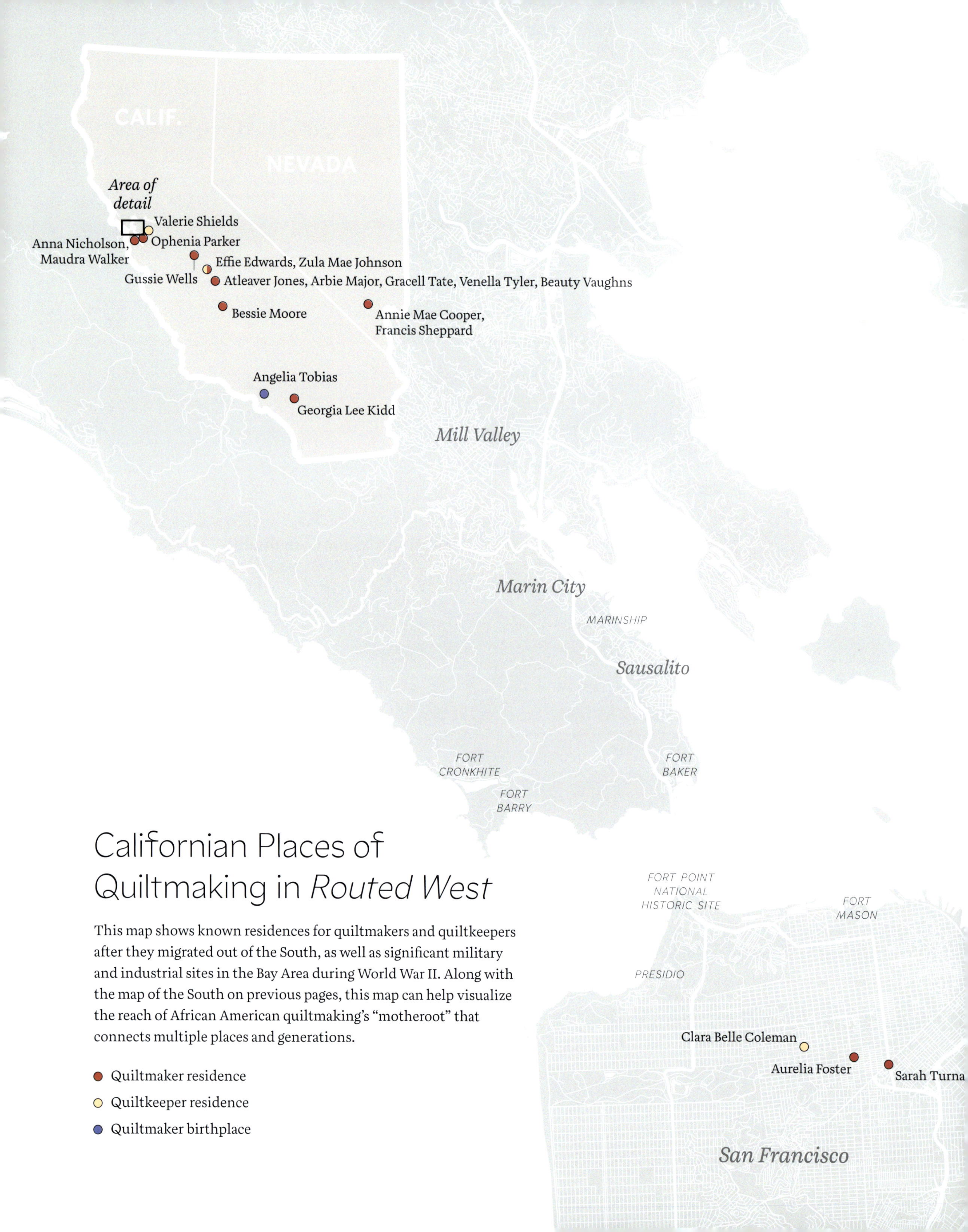

CALIF.

NEVADA

Area of detail

Valerie Shields

Ophenia Parker

Anna Nicholson, Maudra Walker

Effie Edwards, Zula Mae Johnson

Gussie Wells

Atleaver Jones, Arbie Major, Gracell Tate, Venella Tyler, Beauty Vaughns

Bessie Moore

Annie Mae Cooper, Francis Sheppard

Angelia Tobias

Georgia Lee Kidd

Mill Valley

Marin City

MARINSHIP

Sausalito

FORT CRONKHITE

FORT BAKER

FORT BARRY

FORT POINT NATIONAL HISTORIC SITE

FORT MASON

Californian Places of Quiltmaking in *Routed West*

This map shows known residences for quiltmakers and quiltkeepers after they migrated out of the South, as well as significant military and industrial sites in the Bay Area during World War II. Along with the map of the South on previous pages, this map can help visualize the reach of African American quiltmaking's "motheroot" that connects multiple places and generations.

- Quiltmaker residence
- Quiltkeeper residence
- Quiltmaker birthplace

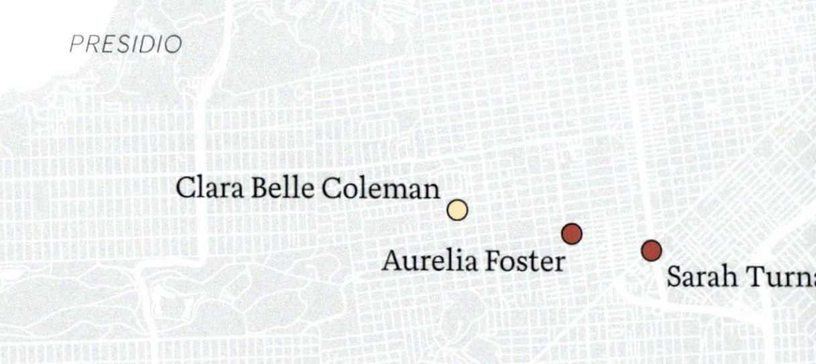

San Francisco

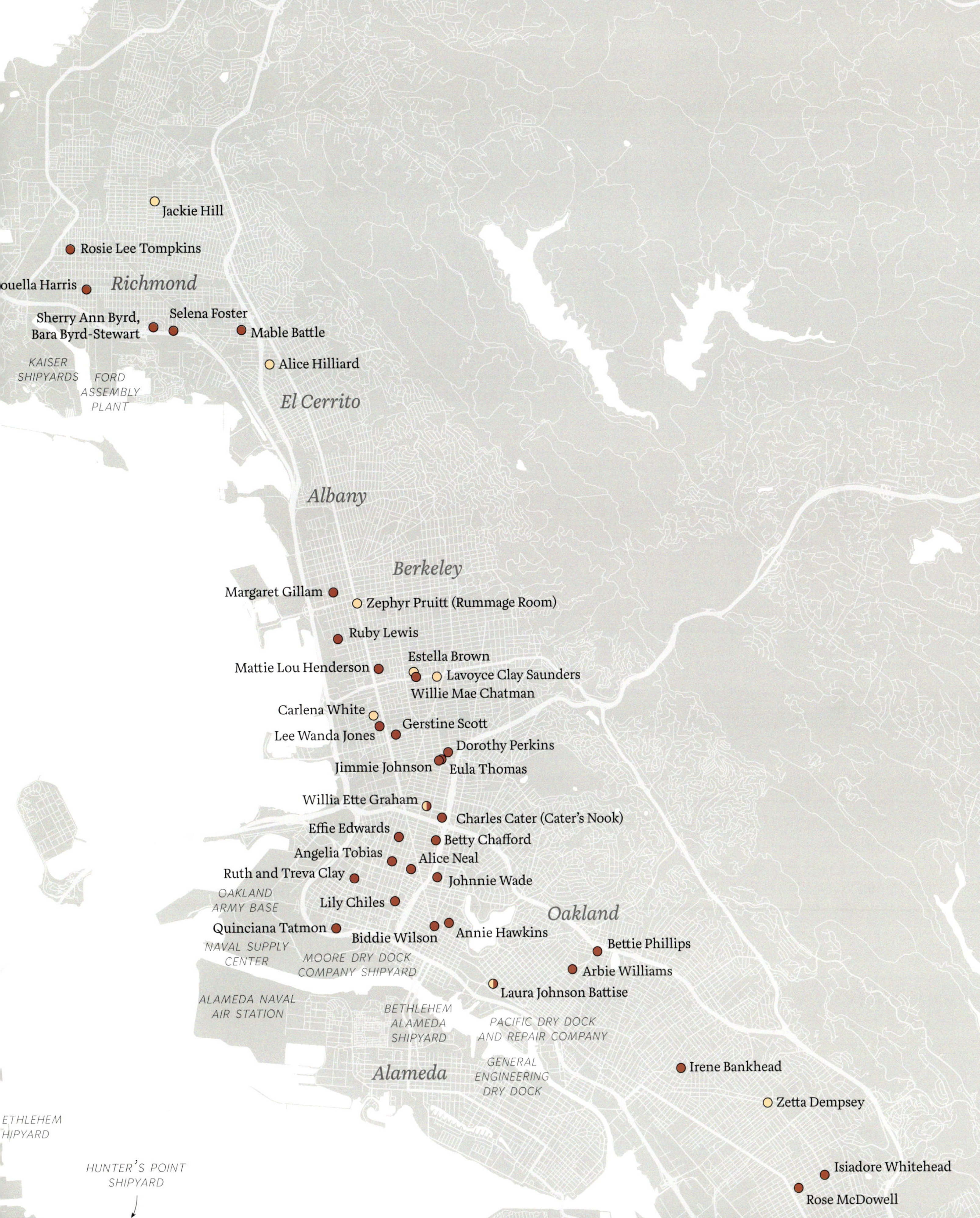
Jackie Hill
Rosie Lee Tompkins
ouella Harris
Richmond
Sherry Ann Byrd,
Bara Byrd-Stewart
Selena Foster
Mable Battle
Alice Hilliard
KAISER SHIPYARDS
FORD ASSEMBLY PLANT
El Cerrito
Albany
Berkeley
Margaret Gillam
Zephyr Pruitt (Rummage Room)
Ruby Lewis
Estella Brown
Mattie Lou Henderson
Lavoyce Clay Saunders
Willie Mae Chatman
Carlena White
Gerstine Scott
Lee Wanda Jones
Dorothy Perkins
Jimmie Johnson
Eula Thomas
Willia Ette Graham
Charles Cater (Cater's Nook)
Effie Edwards
Betty Chafford
Angelia Tobias
Alice Neal
Ruth and Treva Clay
Johnnie Wade
OAKLAND ARMY BASE
Lily Chiles
Oakland
Quinciana Tatmon
Biddie Wilson
Annie Hawkins
NAVAL SUPPLY CENTER
MOORE DRY DOCK COMPANY SHIPYARD
Bettie Phillips
Arbie Williams
Laura Johnson Battise
ALAMEDA NAVAL AIR STATION
BETHLEHEM ALAMEDA SHIPYARD
PACIFIC DRY DOCK AND REPAIR COMPANY
Alameda
GENERAL ENGINEERING DRY DOCK
Irene Bankhead
Zetta Dempsey
ETHLEHEM HIPYARD
HUNTER'S POINT SHIPYARD
Isiadore Whitehead
Rose McDowell

Rooted to the Ground, Stitched Together Like Patchwork: Southern Migrant Landscapes in the Black Bay Area

Wendy M. Thompson

THE SUN WAS NOT THE ONLY THING THAT (WAS) SET IN THE WEST

It began with an idea, a desire to chase the promise of a sun-soaked edge of a delicious life in the Golden State. Stacked high on a shelf, it was a tangible future that simple and extraordinary Black folks saw as promising the possibility of abundance outside of a world tied to backbreaking labor or domestic service, punctuated by the physical repression and threat of lynching presented by Jim Crow. It was a door to a new world with fruitful job opportunities and integrated public services. A country paved with miles of freeway interchanges and kissed by a mild climate—all sunny skies and light breezes. The belief went that once they got here, they would blend into the larger social and cultural milieu as uniquely Californian, reinventing themselves as they went: a proud, sophisticated, cultured, urban people, poised to take on anything.

They saw their newly expanded freedom as possible in a region mythologized as a multicultural, racially progressive, exceptional promised land (fig. 30).

All they had to do was reach it.

And for many Black Southerners who arrived during the period of the Second Great Migration, this future seemed within reach: a state whose reputation was defined by sudden prosperity, good luck, and easy-won progress.

Because who could turn away from that romantic vision—the California dream—that was sold to them on the pretense of economic advancement, social mobility, and a broader sense of freedom than one could ever fully attain back home? This was what drove Black Southerners west.

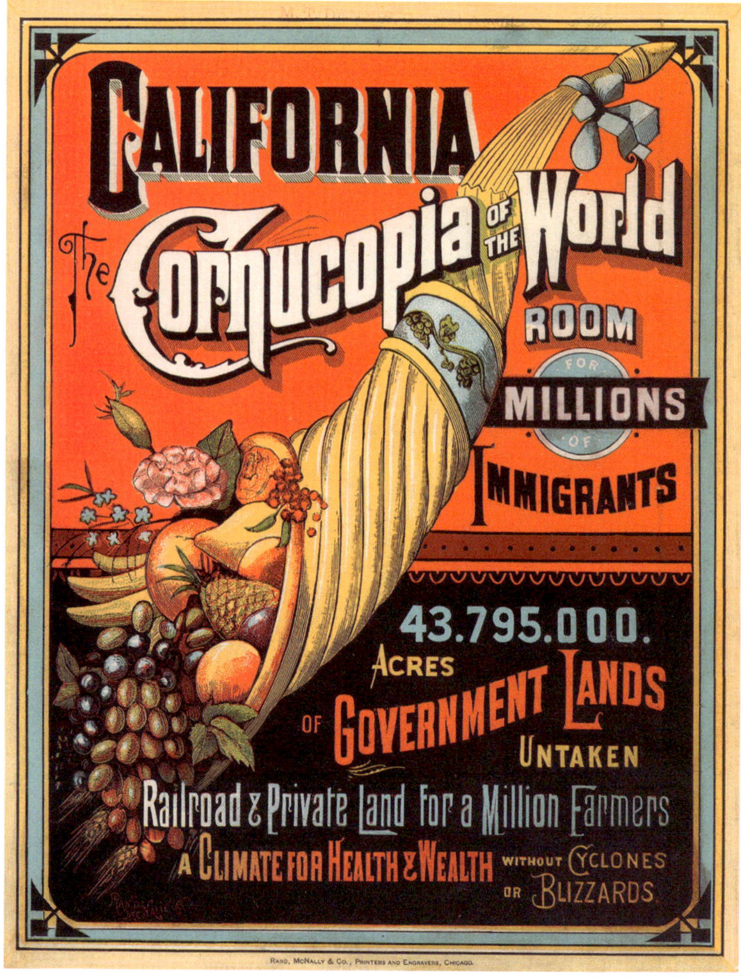

Fig. 30. *California: The Cornucopia of the World*, advertisement created by the California Immigration Commission, 1885. BANC; Box 928:4, The Bancroft Library, University of California, Berkeley

WHAT THEY BROUGHT WITH THEM

Tracing the geography of the Black Bay Area, it is important to note the significance of unmappable things and places: intangible communities and ghost sites, no-longer-existing landmarks, and the many public and private objects and practices that have come to define Black life in the West. Black migrants brought with them a toolkit of survival techniques, mechanisms, and intuitive capacities to navigate a region known for its idyllic landscapes and beautiful sunsets, making a home in their new surroundings. For example, among those who hailed from New Orleans were individuals who carried with them an infrastructure of business interests, churches, and fraternal organizations. Others brought folk healing practices, political organizing experience, blues and gospel music, inventive foodways that turned a handful of yesterday's kitchen scraps into today's hearty, mouthwatering meal, and the art of quilting.

This has become part of the cultural and social fabric that sustained migrants and their descendants during periods of precarity and gave Black Bay Area communities strength. Grounded in a Black Southern ethos of collectivity, spontaneous action, and individual expression, this fabric would be passed down generationally through memory work–from grandparents to grandchildren, mothers to daughters, elders to descendants–to form a Black, deeply rooted, West. The many traditions and cultural expressions that Black Southerners carried with them would also undergo reinvention as ties to the South were stretched. New identities and experiences, along with new sounds, textures, and paces of life, meant changes in outlook, taste, and values. And in a familiar pattern of mobility, the back-and-forth movements of migrants like Gussie Wells (p. 252), who relocated to San Francisco in 1945 but traveled back and forth between the city and the country, would further keep this fabric alive.

WAR AND HOUSING IN THIS DECADENT AMERICAN SOCIETY

The Second World War and a series of push-pull factors[1] led to a massive shift of Black people out of the South and into urban "Norths" across the country. This single largest Black population shift in American history would send migrants west to fill jobs in federal defense industries and shipyards, including the Kaiser shipyards in Richmond, the Moore Dry Dock, and a new army base, all just east of the Bay Bridge in Oakland. The majority of Black Southerners came from Louisiana, Texas, and Oklahoma, followed by smaller streams from Mississippi and Arkansas. They left behind plantation economies where acres of crops were left to bend and die without the vigilant care of their exploited labor, and joined friends and kin to chase after the sun.

Of all the Southern states, Louisiana, which had one of the highest rates of occupational mobility, watched as its cotton-growing parishes became the epicenter of a population exodus that ranged from 4 to 31 percent in the 1940s.[2] In total, more women than men would pack and leave the South, with those between the ages of nineteen and twenty-four outnumbering their male counterparts two to one.[3]

The war effort generated a direct link between the corridor of defense industries and shipyards that lined the West Coast and local Bay Area economies. Given the lucrative jobs, mild climate, and newfound freedoms, California saw the largest influx of migrants to urban centers from Marin City to San Diego during the Second Great Migration. As a prime destination, the Bay Area experienced massive changes, with new settlements blooming around the circumference of defense installations and shipyards leading to "a new migration geography" that connected Louisiana, Texas, Arkansas, and Oklahoma to the region.[4] These changes would unsettle older Black communities, where residents had brokered a system of delicately and unequally balanced race relations with local whites.

The arrival of newcomers, who differed, sometimes greatly, from established, longtime Black Bay Area residents, would test the waters of social change, forcing city leaders to grapple with insufficient infrastructure, provoking proponents of West Coast racism, and accelerating political, social, and demographic change in Black communities. In Richmond, where the war boom launched the small bayside town into full-on defense production mode, city leaders and planners, hoping to control demographic growth and retain prewar boundaries, did little to develop municipal infrastructure or provide adequate additional housing. They reasoned that after the war, only one of the four shipyards, which included the one where Isiadore Whitehead (p. 252) worked as a welder, would still be in production, and that the housing authority would raze any temporary war workers' housing to the ground.

But with thousands of migrants flooding the city, civic leaders found themselves overwhelmed and faced with the depletion of city resources and the breakdown of existing infrastructure. This led the Richmond Housing Authority to contract private developers to build around 2,400 structures for defense workers and their families in 1941, applying racial preferences and exclusions to specific buildings, blocks, and divisions–practices that continued well into the 1950s.[5] As a result of the decisions made by the Richmond Housing Authority, Black families tended to be assigned units in the housing projects south of Cutting Boulevard (fig. 31), a major east-west artery that led to the shipyards.

Outside of the projects, the search for housing would force Black homeseekers to confront racially restrictive covenants, predatory landlords, and real estate agents who were bound to uphold white racial exclusivity. All of this led to Black residents being redlined in North Richmond, an area that extended into an unincorporated part of a nearby county and was located next to a garbage dump, replete with inadequate utilities, poor sanitation, no waste disposal, sewage backups, and a lack of local medical facilities.

In West Oakland, where migrants settled at the edge of Grove Street (since renamed Martin Luther King Jr. Way) and San Pablo Avenue, the Black business and entertainment district that ran along Seventh Street would quickly become a cultural magnet. Lauded by the San Francisco Chamber of Commerce as the "the largest shipbuilding center in the world" in 1943, the region would see exponential growth, with Oakland's Black population jumping from 3 percent in 1940 to 12 percent ten years later.[6] To serve this growing population, new restaurants, cafes, cleaners, markets, barbers, hotels, and nightclubs would emerge along Seventh Street, making it the center of Black public life in the East Bay well into the sixties (fig. 32). Eula Thomas (p. 248), for example, who migrated to Oakland from Louisiana in the early 1940s, ran a cleaning and pressing business in the area with her husband.[7] In this way, West Oakland would come to represent one of the cultural gateways to Black California, just as Louisiana, Texas, Arkansas, and Mississippi served as Southern homelands of a significant number of East Bay migrants.

Unlike their counterparts in Richmond, Oakland civic leaders sought to prepare for the influx of newcomers, with the Oakland Housing Authority building a series of low-income housing projects in West Oakland. In 1941 and 1942, the brand-new Campbell Village and Peralta Village would open their doors to new tenants,[8] adhering to an integrated policy that stood in contrast to those of the majority of other public housing developments. With racial segregation exacerbating an already tight private housing market and Black residents confined to historically redlined West Oakland neighborhoods, the Maritime Commission and Moore Dry Dock Company would construct alternate housing such as Chestnut Court for war workers.

It wasn't until the efforts of Black realtors like Edith Hill, who was central to opening up neighborhoods in North and East Oakland for Black homeseekers in the 1950s,[9] that the boundaries of settlement began to expand, sending Black people into other parts of Oakland and the East Bay, sowing their seeds through each mortgage and deed they acquired.

Across the bay in San Francisco, the city's Black population ballooned by more than 600 percent between 1940 and 1945.[10] Prior to the war, this population remained small in number and scattered across the city, but following the forced evacuation and incarceration of persons of Japanese ancestry in 1942, homes and property ownership would open up to

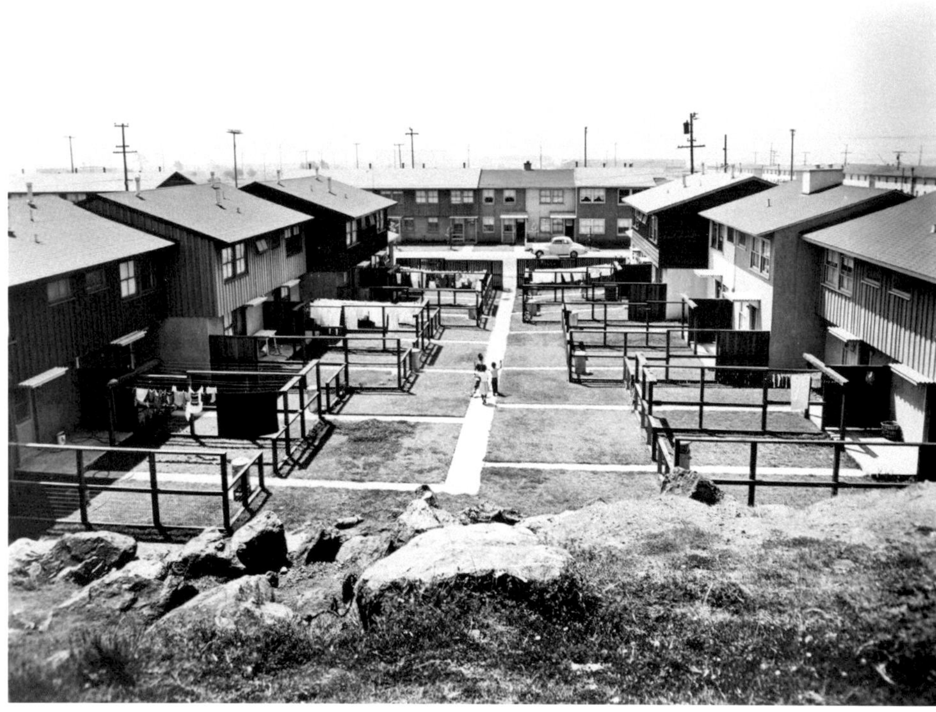

Fig. 31. Easter Hill Village, Richmond, California, 1950. Vernon DeMars and Donald L. Hardison Collections, College of Environmental Design Archives, University of California, Berkeley

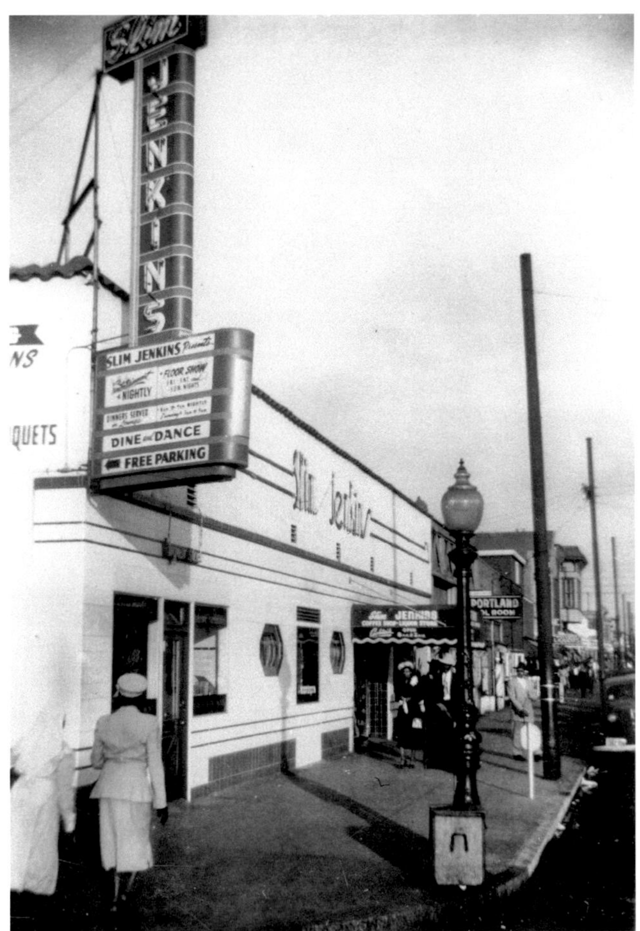

Fig. 32. Pedestrians walking on sidewalk in front of the Slim Jenkins Bar and Restaurant, Oakland, California, c. 1940s. Jenkins (Harold) Photograph Collection, Box MS11_B1_F3_076, African American Museum & Library at Oakland (Oakland, Calif.)

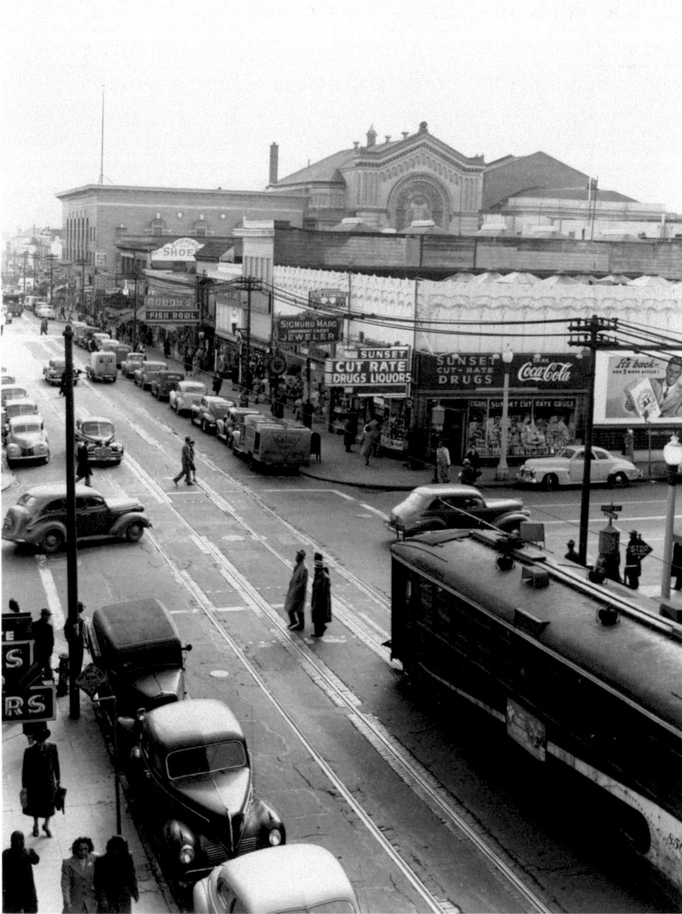

Fig. 33. David Johnson, *Looking South on Fillmore Street*, n.d. David Johnson Photograph Archive, BANC PIC 2017.001, PIC_box 1, The Bancroft Library, University of California, Berkeley

Black tenants and buyers, as it did in other cities along the West Coast. As they confronted western iterations of Jim Crow in their war-industry jobs by brokering alliances with established Black leaders and white progressives, a number of migrants would move beyond defense-installation prejudice and shipyard politics to take on racial barriers and anti-Black discrimination in employment, education, and housing. They would face a long road in a city where Black residents made up a disproportionate number of those housed in the Western Addition, an area located about one mile west of downtown, annexed to the city's westernmost boundary in 1858.[11]

But it was in a neighborhood that residents referred to as the Fillmore, so named for its major thoroughfare, that the highest concentration of Black migrants would build a life (fig. 33). Confined to an older grade of housing and plagued by overcrowding, dilapidated units, broken fixtures and appliances, rat and roach infestations, and overall unsanitary living conditions, Black migrants endured these daily indignities that would further weigh on already heavy lives. At the same time, such conditions informed the actions of civic leaders and planners who, in reenvisioning the future of the city, would gut large swaths of neighborhoods like the Fillmore District. At a public hearing in 1948, State Senator Gerald J. O'Gara identified the Fillmore as San Francisco's most blighted area, offering it as a prime candidate for renewal.[12]

Connecting substandard living conditions and declining property values with the presumed criminality, poor health, and overall deprivation of its residents, a series of systemic decisions affected the Fillmore and other areas of the city following the passage of the 1949 Housing Act, a landmark expansion of the federal legislation that laid the groundwork for slum clearance and urban renewal.[13] The legislation stipulated that property and land would be seized, buildings would be demolished, and public housing would be constructed, with the result that Black residents, in the midst of it all, would become further marginalized in this model of a new international city.

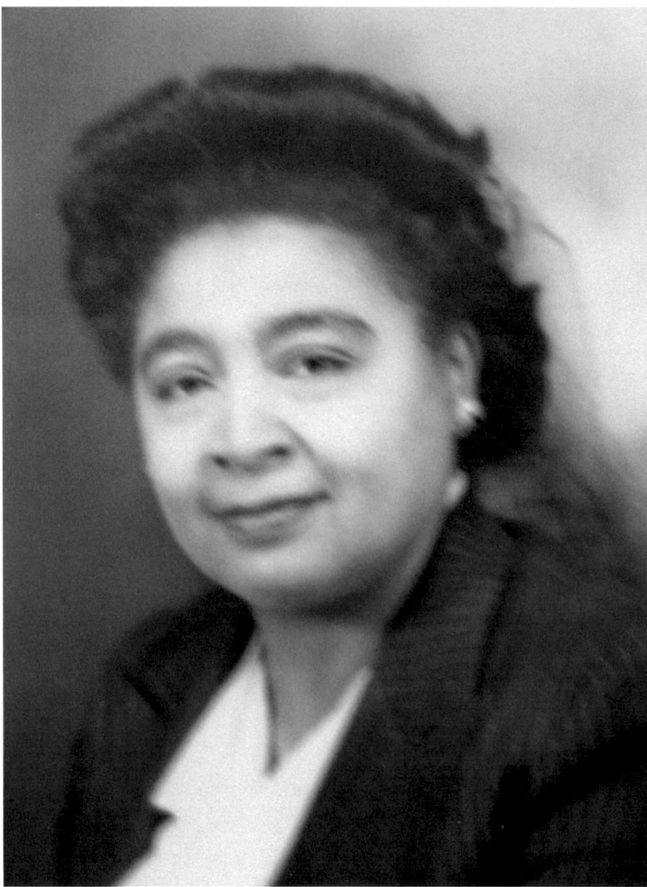

Fig. 34. Willia Ette Graham, 1946, two years after her arrival in California from Texas

Despite the uneven gains experienced by Black migrants in Bay Area cities, most chose to stay. A northern California industry survey conducted in 1944 revealed that only 15 percent of Black defense workers planned to return home.[14] Continuing to arrive in the postwar era, Black Southerners catalyzed a demographic shift on a scale not seen since the Gold Rush in 1849. As they settled around the Bay Area, a lucky few would find a comfortable quality of life, having quietly purchased homes during the war years in white neighborhoods like those "above the numbered streets to Ashby Avenue in Berkeley" by way of white proxies.[15] For these affluent Black homebuyers, Berkeley was seen as the most desirable step up in a succession of moves that went from West Oakland to North Oakland and, if one was particularly successful and landed a coveted civil service job, South Berkeley.[16]

This trajectory pushed Black middle-class professionals further into all-white neighborhoods in Oakland, San Francisco, and Berkeley, each family seeking upward mobility and security for their children in the middle class. As each family became part of a new area code, they would shift the map of the Black Bay Area, little by little.

A STITCH THAT MEANS MANY THINGS

In the midst of the war boom, migrants worked to set up homes and adapt to their new surroundings: spending good money, making ends meet, caring for children, perfecting a new recipe, finding a man, falling out of love, tending a garden, going out with friends, learning to sew patchwork. All of these small chores and pleasures required balancing one's time between business and personal affairs. As wartime shipyards and defense installations tended to run around the clock with production spilling into evening "swing shifts," migrants found themselves sometimes working long, irregular hours that kept them from enjoying the very homes and lifestyles they worked so hard to maintain. As the primary wage earners during the war, some Black single mothers were forced to rely on the labor of other women or older children to care for their young ones, leading to profound changes in family life.

Many would watch the disintegration of parental authority and control and the surge in juvenile delinquency and crime rates firsthand in their own families and communities. Stuart Cosgrove notes that by the summer of 1943, it was common for young adults to be left unsupervised while their parents were on active duty or working in the defense industry.[17] In the face of this, any time set aside for personal hobbies, creative expression, or crafting was precious. Not exclusive to Black women, quilting became a way for migrants to indulge in private pleasures as well as a means to supplement their incomes. This was true for such individuals as Charles Cater and Lily Chiles (both p. 227), who quilted while spending time with spouses, children, and grandchildren.

For some, the making and gifting of quilts served as an extension of migrants' friendship and kinship networks, stretched far across state lines and regions. They would provide a source of connection and comfort, as in one home where Mary Lue Brown created a quilt, *Hit and Miss* (see fig. 36, p. 187), for her lifelong friend, Helen. This quilt, which was likely sent from Mary Lue in Dallas to Helen in San Francisco in the 1940s, was referred to as "the loud quilt" and was a regular fixture on the family couch, where members would drape themselves in it while watching TV.[18]

THE POSTWAR YEARS AND QUILTING AS BLACK FUTURITY

In the postwar years, the presence of the Southern diaspora bled into every aspect of urban Bay Area life. Migrants' desires, dreams, frustrations, and disappointments shaped the contours of industry, education, housing, politics, and cultural institutions. The shaky race relations that prewar Black communities brokered with whites would be transformed by migrants and their descendants, who sought to cash out what they had invested during the war years: political access, financial stability, and a higher quality of life denied to them in the South. When they found these promises empty and whites reluctant to budge, they engaged in both organized conflict and spontaneous acts of resistance.

In the face of ongoing anti-Black racism, urban renewal schemes, aggressive displacement, and white flight, the next generation, the "soul babies"[19] born in the 1960s and 1970s, would come into a sense of home that rested on decommissioned shipyards, industrial decline, and structural unemployment despite a thriving Cold War economy. The tools their parents and grandparents brought with them and used to navigate the world would have less resonance in 1964 when the federal government officially declared Oakland a "depressed area" replete with rising unemployment, unmaintained public housing, inadequate schools, and rampant police brutality. Here, like elsewhere in the Bay Area, the Black revolutionary practices that emerged from the political unrest of the late 1960s–organized armed patrols, community survival programs, socially conscious music and art, and a vibrant car and motorcycle culture–became some of the chosen tools of resistance. Inevitably, those tools and the communities they were designed to empower would be met by conservative backlash, deindustrialization, the crack epidemic, the appearance of so-called "murder capitals," and the rise of the carceral state.

By the 1980s, the decade that I was born in Oakland, the daughter of a San Francisco-born father and Louisiana-descended grandparents, our mantel places, grandparents' stories, and local connections to home would proclaim just how far we'd come and the miles we'd have yet to travel. Many quilters of the migrant generation would find themselves aging, their hands and eyes becoming all the more unsteady and strained, their time and energy being consumed with raising grandchildren and sheltering adult children from life's storms. Nevertheless, the quilts they continued to produce would offer comfort, a space for beauty, and friendship in the age of displacement.

In so many ways, the quilt itself becomes a metaphor for the Black Bay Area, each piece of fabric representing the unique vision of the hands that contributed to its making; the batting, the migrant generation and their descendants, providing insulation and warmth to families over the course of multiple generations and through multiple storms; the backing, the most intimate part of the textile, providing comfort to the body on the coldest nights; and the stitching, lessons learned and taken to heart, holding all the layers together: first and last loves, saving for another rainy day, finding out about the outside children, struggling to keep the family home, making peace with the truth and regrets, insisting on the retention of traditions, giving them up, trying to make gumbo for the first time following the handwritten recipe of a great-grandmother on your father's side, the stories, the stories, the stories, and the friendships spanning over forty-plus years.

The freedom in this West. We wrap ourselves in it.

Notes

1. The main push-pull factors were oppressive Jim Crow laws and widespread disenfranchisement, cycles of debt that kept Black people tied to sharecropping and the cotton economy, environmental disasters like boll weevil infestations, floods, and storms that wreaked havoc on the land, and brutal racial hostility in the forms of nightriding, lynchings, and vigilante violence.
2. Donna Jean Murch, *Living for the City: Migration, Education, and the Rise of the Black Panther Party in Oakland, California* (Chapel Hill, NC: University of North Carolina Press, 2010), 19.
3. Murch, *Living for the City*, 19.
4. Murch, *Living for the City*, 16-17.
5. Shirley Ann Wilson Moore, *To Place Our Deeds: The African American Community in Richmond, California, 1910-1963* (Berkeley, CA: University of California Press, 2000), 84.
6. Murch, *Living for the City*, 16.
7. Eli Leon, *Accidentally on Purpose: The Aesthetic Management of Irregularities in African Textiles and African-American Quilts* (Davenport, IA: Figge Art Museum, 2006), 114.
8. Murch, *Living for the City*, 25.
9. Murch, *Living for the City*, 25.
10. Albert S. Broussard, *Black San Francisco: The Struggle for Racial Equality in the West, 1900-1954* (Lawrence, KS: University Press of Kansas, 1993), 133.
11. Clement Lai, "The Racial Triangulation of Space: The Case of Urban Renewal in San Francisco's Fillmore District," *Annals of the Association of American Geographers,* 102, no. 1 (January 2012): 155.
12. Lai, "The Racial Triangulation of Space," 157.
13. Arnold R. Hirsch, "Searching for a 'Sound Negro Policy': A Racial Agenda for the Housing Act of 1949 and 1954," *Housing Policy Debate* 11, no. 2 (2000): 393.
14. Broussard, *Black San Francisco*, 206.
15. Murch, *Living for the City*, 24.
16. Murch, *Living for the City*, 24.
17. Stuart Cosgrove, "The Zoot-Suit and Style Warfare," *History Workshop*, no. 18 (Autumn 1984): 79.
18. Leon, *Accidentally on Purpose*, 76.
19. See Mark Anthony Neal's *Soul Babies: Black Popular Culture and the Post-Soul Aesthetic* (New York: Routledge, 2001).

Staggering Quilt Works of Sonic Genius

Daphne A. Brooks

In memory of Juanita Kathryn Brooks and Nathaniel Hawthorne Brooks, Sr. and Lodell Matthews and Ernie Matthews

> Now that's a real heartbreaker there.
> Where's she from? Texas?
>
> –Arbie Williams, 1993[1]

You can hear it around the edges of these striking and varied patterns, swirling across these "galaxies of spidery constructions,"[2] pulsating at the center of squares and circles and all sorts of geometric shapes attesting to the intricacy, precision, and purpose of these wildly innovative makers who set their hands to creating glorious things of beauty. Embedded in the designs of the exquisite quilts that constitute *Routed West: Twentieth-Century African American Quilts in California* are legacies of sound that reflect and convey the magnitude of Black women's artistic genius: pivoting and arcing and turning like the sharp and spirited choices made by an ensemble of brilliant Black women musicians stretching across the modern era–from polymath ethnographer Zora Neale Hurston to Queen of Soul Aretha Franklin.

Just as the philosopher Fred Moten famously suggests that "photographs in general bear a phonic substance . . .," an auditory thickness, a "phonographic content" that both captures and yet forcefully exceeds the very image in the frame, overflows with the history and material circumstances informing the very image before our eyes, we might think too about the sonic language of these quilts made by an indomitable generation of women who stitched parables and prophecies, heirlooms and keepsakes, quotidian cultural memory and fragments of family history into humbly majestic tapestries of aesthetic wonder and grace.[3] Most were made in the wake of enormous upheaval, by women riding a mid-century, second stream, Great Migration westward wave that carried them to a California coast that was worlds away from hometowns like Summit and Prentiss, Mississippi; Le Flore County and Castle, Oklahoma; Magnolia, Gould, Ozan, and Paraloma, Arkansas; and Fairfield and Henderson, Texas. Like the classic Black music of this era willed into being by pathbreaking women artists with Southern roots in places like Hurston's Eatonville, Florida; like Billie Holiday's Baltimore; like Ella Fitzgerald's Newport News, Virginia; like Nina Simone's Tryon, North Carolina; like Odetta's Birmingham, Alabama; like Mahalia's New Orleans and Aretha's Memphis, Tennessee, these *Routed West* quilters tapped into the infinite potential of their own aesthetic talents as a means to repeatedly reinventing themselves through material expression. They turned to cultural work as a strategy to contest and explode the Jim Crow tyranny which sought to shrink, corner, and imprison their personhood on the regular. Along with their northern peers (with the Supremes coming of age in Detroit, Michigan, and Sarah Vaughan in Newark, New Jersey), these musicians and their sister quilters played with colors and moods, with textures and dimensions, to instead tell big stories of their limitless personhood and the precious fullness of their humanity, like the kinds of stories one finds in an Alice Neal quilt (cat. 33; see also p. 250). The creative parallels between their work and that of the musicians who would have inevitably contributed to the soundscapes of their lives invite profoundly poignant contemplation.

The quilts are, themselves, testimonies of enormous skill and staggering imagination shaped by intergenerational

Opposite: Detail of cat. 104

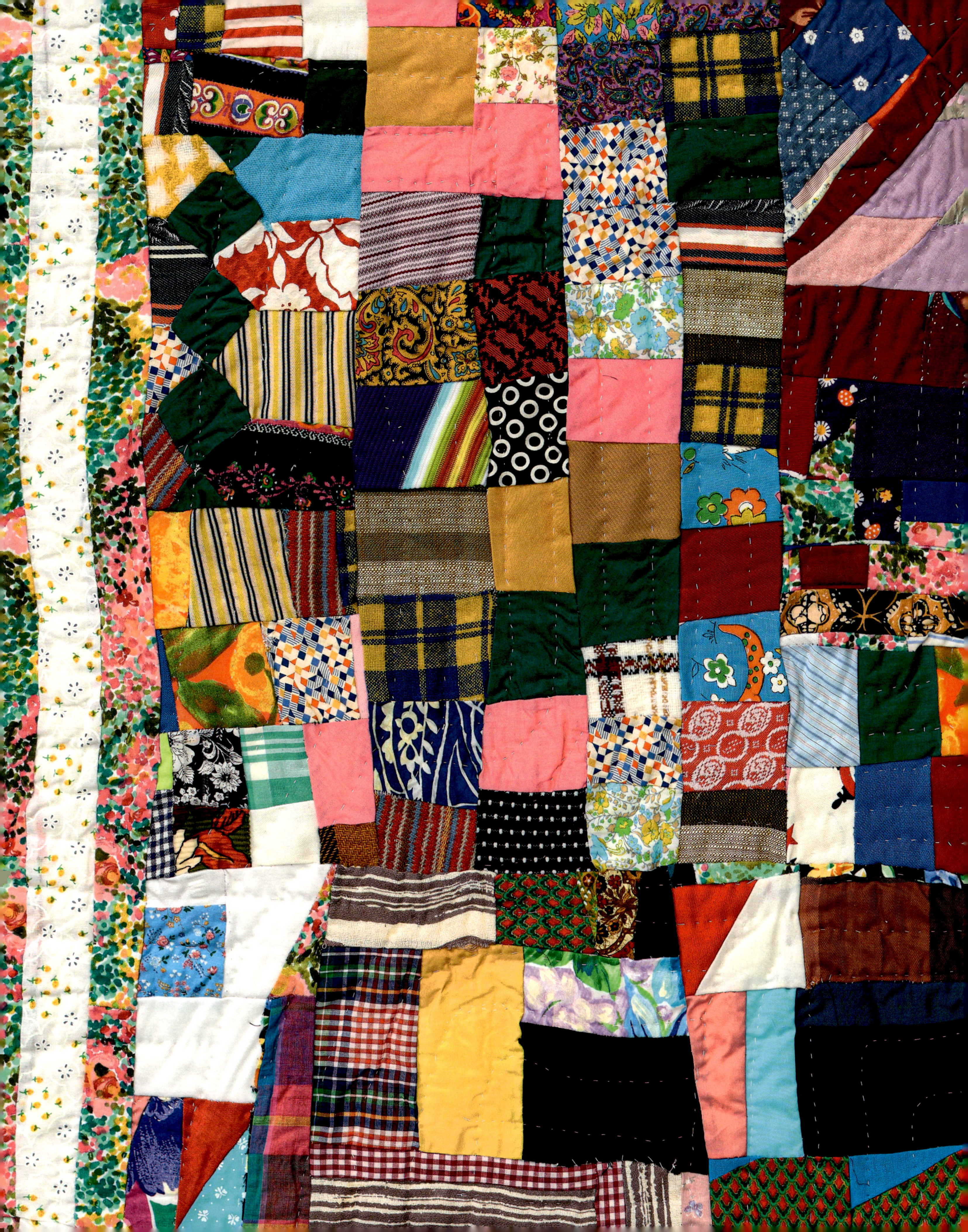

wisdom, communal love, and care. And they are, just as much, works whose aesthetics and forms of style and craft resonate oh so deeply with a formidable archive of Black women's landmark musicianship. This sensorial women's work is the kind of which Alice Walker would speak in her classic short story, "Everyday Use,"[4] which fused Black Power movement ideas about art's worth (as being "collective, functional and committing")[5] with burgeoning modern Black feminisms that center the value of everyday Black women's creations and care (in the form of quilting, gardening, and storytelling) as radical and necessary forms of communal survival. It is the kind of work made by women who led lives as farmers and seamstresses; as housekeepers and nurses; as welders, bus drivers, and shipyard workers; laundresses, cooks, factory workers, and truck drivers–while also loving partners, raising children, and giving of themselves selflessly to their communities. They would gather up and reclaim fragments of their days by turning to a craft they'd learned from their ancestors–mothers, aunts, and grandmothers. And one imagines the music that likely constituted the sonic fabric of these women's lives–that which perhaps provided them with the inspiration to pursue their own striking works of self-expression. One thinks of the legendary Rosie Lee Tompkins (p. 249) turning up her beloved opera and disco as she went to work on her sprawling array of masterpieces, or any of these women setting themselves for hours at a time to their tasks with the radio on in the living room, or Isiadore Whitehead (p. 252), Lily Chiles (p. 227), and Arbie Williams (p. 245) each carrying home the sacred sounds of the choir from their weekly services, holding on to that righteous tune in her head and letting the music guide her fingers (cats. 46–53, 76–80, 86, 92, and 94).

Each quilt of theirs stands as its own gorgeously original, boldly ambitious statement that–at least to these listening eyes and seeing ears–complements and reflects the conceptual and interpretative approach of some of our greatest performers. Think of the way that Roberta Smith so aptly describes the dazzling Tompkins's astonishing and daring ability to create quilts that could be "deliriously akimbo, imbued with a mesmerizing pull of differences and inconsistencies that communicates impassioned attention and care . . . "[6] and then consider Hurston's groundbreaking theories of Black performance in the years leading up to her Depression-era field recordings. It was Hurston the anthropologist who insisted that we take seriously Black vernacular culture's "will to adorn"; its fascination with "angularity" in art; its interest in the "beauty" of "asymmetry."[7] Her own amateur recordings in the late 1930s as an ethnographer of Black folk culture ring with the kind of vocal twists and narrative turns that rhyme with dimensions of Tompkins's and her fellow quilters' vast and prodigious quilting repertoire.

So often likened to "free jazz," these quilters' practices hold as well the kinds of experimentations that ripple through the sounds of the iconic sisters. The riddles of Holiday's trademark timing, her pauses, her interrogative delivery, for instance, saturate some of Laverne Brackens's singular work (cats. 91 and 104; see also p. 232), and the abstractions of the First Lady of Song Ella Fitzgerald's bottomless scat lexicon dance across the arrangements made by Sherry Ann Byrd (cats. 67 and 87; see also p. 233). The density of the dark blue corduroy panels in work by Elizabeth Munn (cat. 32; see also p. 242) or the indigo depth in the work of Rachel Adkins (cat. 44; see also p. 223) and Bettie Phillips (cat. 70; see also p. 236), among many others, conjures the oceanic dimensions of Simone's contralto or a Jackson spiritual, a Franklin solo, or the cosmic expansiveness of Vaughan's swooping range. And the two-tone color blocks of some of Atleaver Jones's work (cat. 43; see also p. 238) seem ready-made for a glamorous Motown trio's precision pop. The sheer resourcefulness and focused labor of any one of these quilters calls to mind the ethos of folk legend Odetta's excavation of music made by the enslaved, her intent to repurpose it as history and armor during the long Civil Rights era like the fertilizer sacks that Joe Washington salvaged and transformed into what we might think of as a kind of living memorial material (cat. 24; see also p. 252). Refulgent with the spirit of what Hurston once described as Black folks' pleasure and ability to revel in artistic excess, detail, and lavishness, these sisters made quilts with affectionate monikers like "Damn It to Hell" that summed up the showstopping nature of the artistry stored up in the object. They made quilts that sang ballads so beautiful and sorrowful and full of history and specificity that expert makers like Arbie Williams would dub one with a star "surrounded by improvisational piecing" as nothing short of "a heartbreaker" (cat. 104).[8]

Leon himself, an ardent champion and steward of the improvisational fearlessness of these West Coast and westward-leaning quilting artisans, would bear witness to the distinctiveness of their quilts' styles, how "alive with the moment" they are; how these quilts "invited audience participation. Rather than the consummate expression of an archetype ideal," he argues of the legendary Double Wedding Ring quilt, "it was something new and something different. Its vital force elicited a whole-body response."[9] In this way, these quilts are instructive, offering especially to the "one who is black" and "in the totality of a black world," as Black feminist scholar Kevin Quashie might put it, a means of "conceptualiz[ing] 'how to be' as a reckoning of human capacity, as the right and burden of being."[10]

The quilts, like the music, were road maps for a people on the move, the people of Toni Morrison's epic novel *Jazz* who uprooted themselves in order to make themselves new, in order to "hear themselves in an audience, feel themselves moving down the street among hundreds of others who moved the way they did and who, when they spoke, regardless of the accent, treated language like the same intricate, malleable toy designed for their play."[11] Quilts, like music, constituted forms of place-making and served as sources of archival memory, as ways of determining who they were in a new world, the directions in which they were headed as well as the people, places, and keepsakes infusing their past, like the kinds of materials carried by Zetta Dempsey (cats. 10 and 11; see also p. 229). People like my Aunt Lodie and my Uncle Ernie and my mother, Juanita, and my father, Nathaniel, who, by train and car, packed up their belongings, said goodbye to their birthplace and extended family, and planted a flag in the East Bay in the late 1940s and early '50s. They discovered the score to their foreign surroundings in the repertoires of these women musicians who built the culture of the twentieth century, and they drew on these sounds to curate a new world. And though neither my mother nor my Aunt Lodie nor perhaps most of their immediate fellow Cal-Berkeley friends and neighbors were quilters, I like to think about their Bay Area proximity to the sister artists who, like them, were "busy being original, complicated, changeable," as Morrison would say of her striving, risk-taking migrants.[12] Tompkins and her brethren made a place for them all in their fabric monuments, in their denim, satin, cotton, polyester, and wool meditations as magically opaque and multifaceted as a Nina Simone early '60s Town Hall concert set, as kaleidoscopic and sublime as the miracle of Black life itself.

Notes

1. Eli Leon, "Trips South," this volume, 192.
2. Eli Leon, "But Now I See: African-American Quilt Revelations" (unpublished essay, January 5, 2006), Bequest of The Eli Leon Living Trust, BAMPFA, 3.
3. Fred Moten, *In the Break: The Aesthetics of the Black Radical Tradition* (Minneapolis, MN: University of Minnesota Press, 2003), 236, 242.
4. Alice Walker, *Everyday Use*, ed. Barbara T. Christian (New Brunswick, NJ: Rutgers University Press, 1994).
5. Looking back on the Black Arts Movement in the 1980s, Amiri Baraka would remind us that "[b]y revolutionary art, we meant, as Ron Karenga said, that it had to be collective, functional and committing." Amiri Baraka, "Black Culture in the Second Renaissance–1954-1970," *The Black Scholar* 18, no. 1 (January/February 1987): 24.
6. Roberta Smith, "The Radical Quilting of Rosie Lee Tompkins," *New York Times*, June 26, 2020, https://www.nytimes.com/interactive/2020/06/26/arts/design/rosie-lee-tompkins-quilts.html.
7. Zora Neale Hurston, "Characteristics of Negro Expression," in *The Jazz Cadence of American Culture*, ed. Robert O. Meally (New York: Columbia University Press, 1998), 298-310.
8. Leon, "Trips South," 192.
9. Eli Leon, *Accidentally on Purpose: The Aesthetic Management of Irregularities in African Textiles and African-American Quilts* (Davenport, IA: Figge Art Museum, 2006), 93.
10. Kevin Quashie, *Black Aliveness, or A Poetics of Being* (Durham, NC: Duke University Press, 2021), 12.
11. Toni Morrison, *Jazz* (New York: Vintage Reprint, 2007), 31.
12. Morrison, *Jazz*, 218.

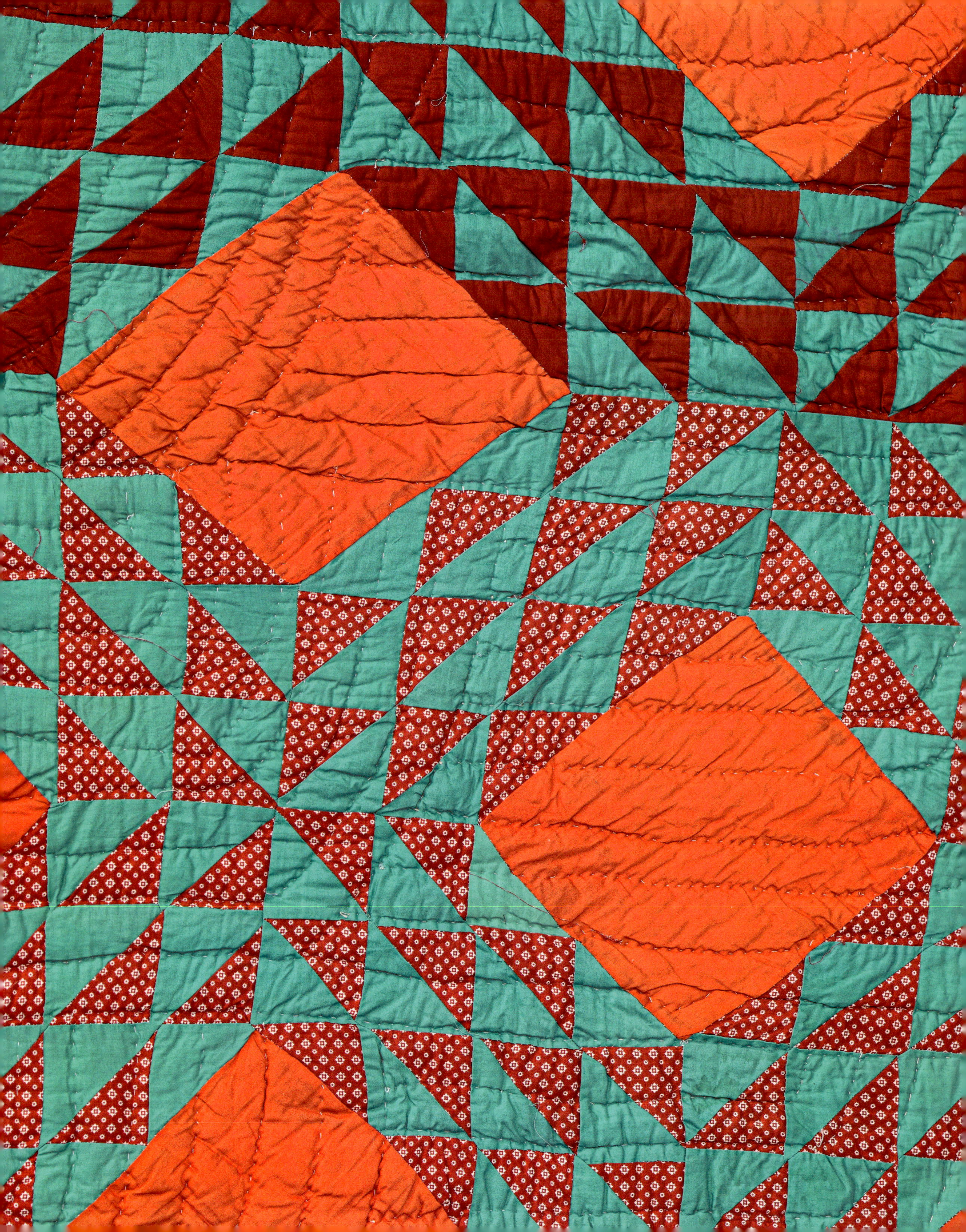

Plates

The following plates appear in rough chronological order. Circa ("c.") is used when a probable date of construction is known; date ranges by decade are given as estimates based on a combination of fabric dating and available information about the quiltmaker(s).

All artworks are from the bequest of the Eli Leon Living Trust, University of California, Berkeley Art Museum and Pacific Film Archive, unless otherwise noted. When applicable, plate captions identify the family keepers of individual quilts prior to their acquisition by Eli Leon. The terms "keeper" and "kept" recognize the person's role in preserving family histories that are intertwined with the physical care of a given quilt.

Opposite: Detail of cat. 38

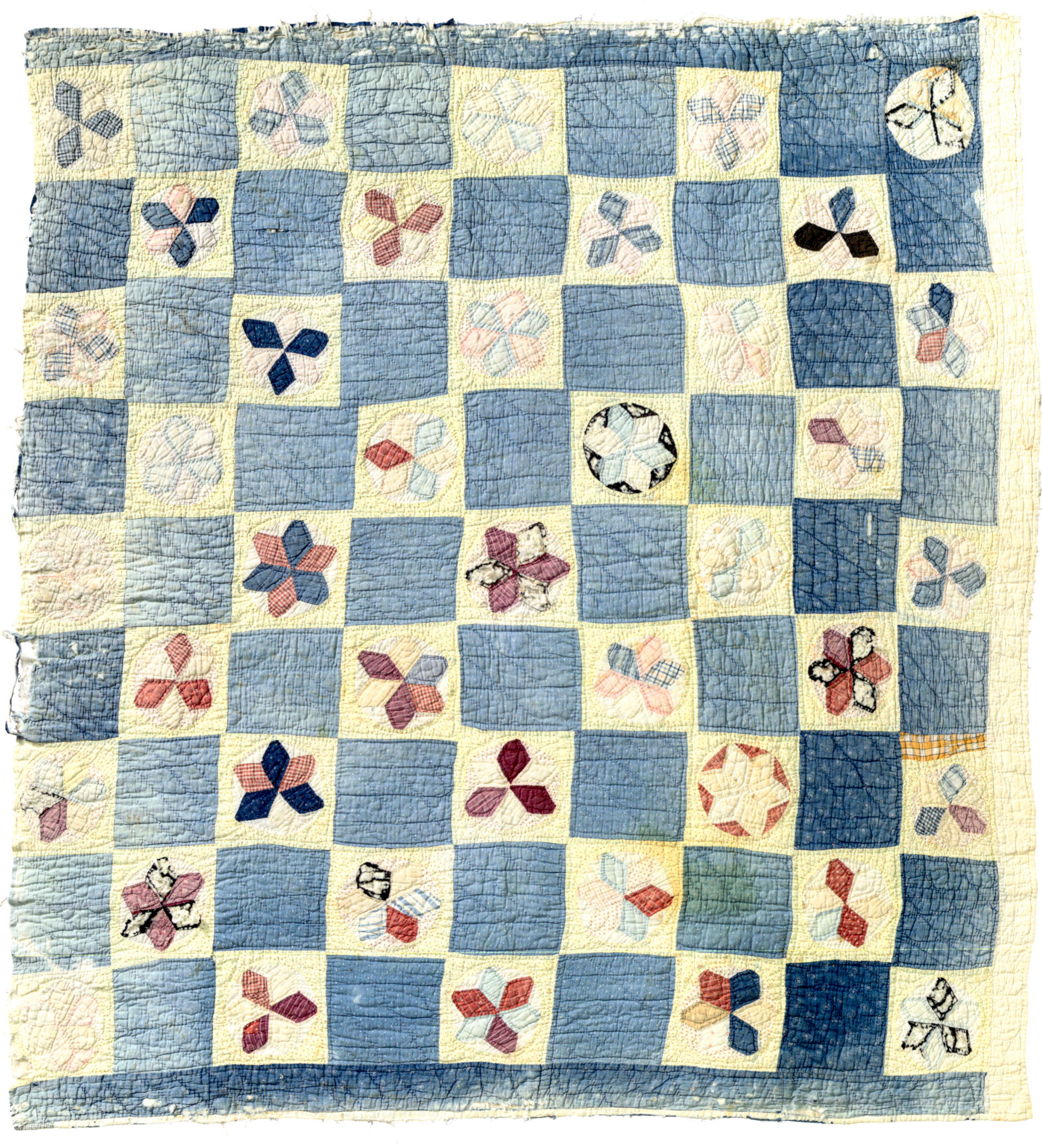

1. Untitled (Six Point Star variation)
Lucinda Ballenger, c. 1900; Henderson, Texas
Willia Ette Graham, Ballenger's granddaughter, was the keeper of this quilt until 1985.

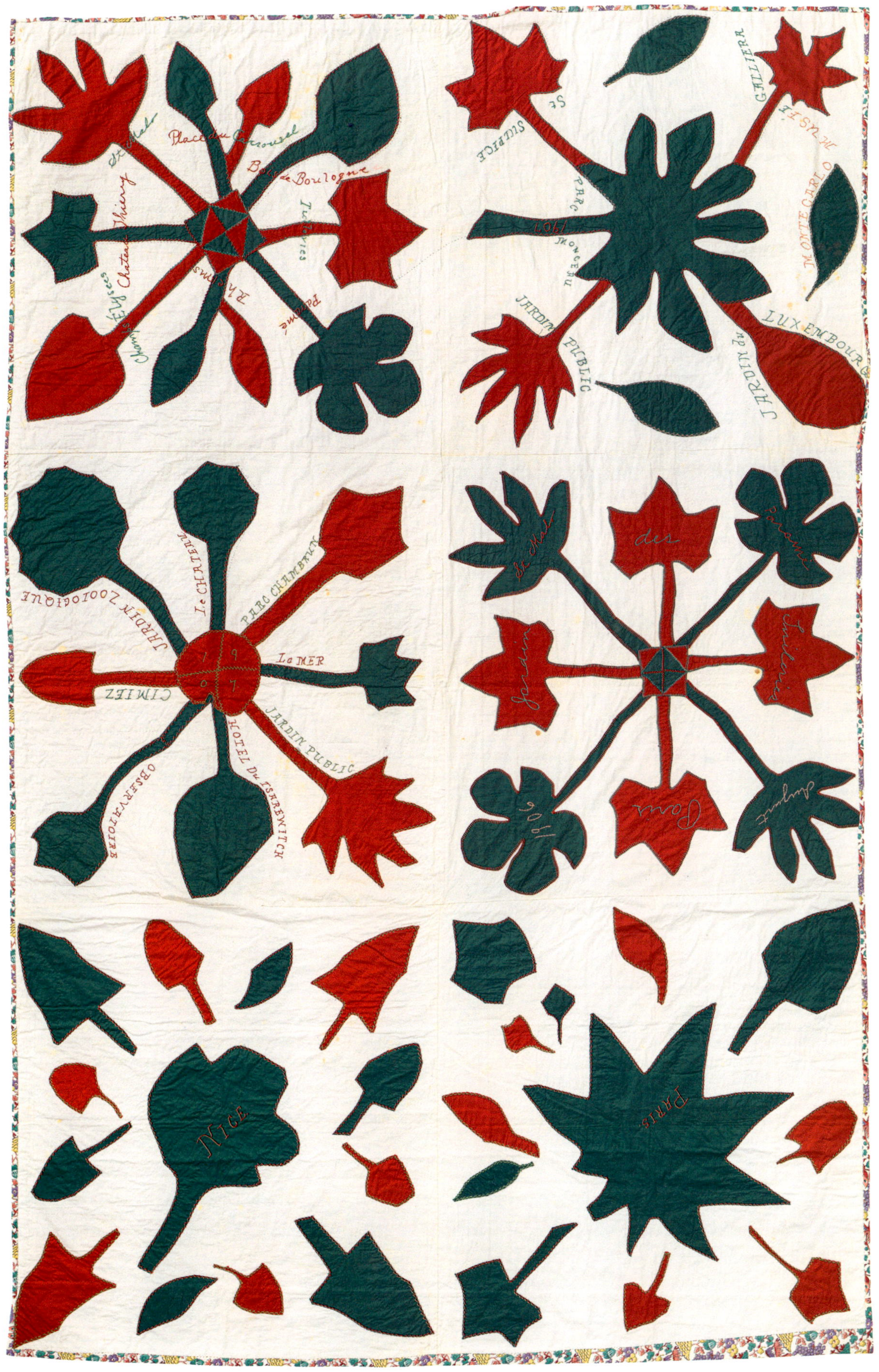

Front

2. Untitled (appliqué with embroidery)
Appliquéd and embroidered by Hattie Mitchell, 1906–08, 1914; Macon, Georgia
Quilted and finished by Hattie Mitchell, c. 1930; Macon, Georgia

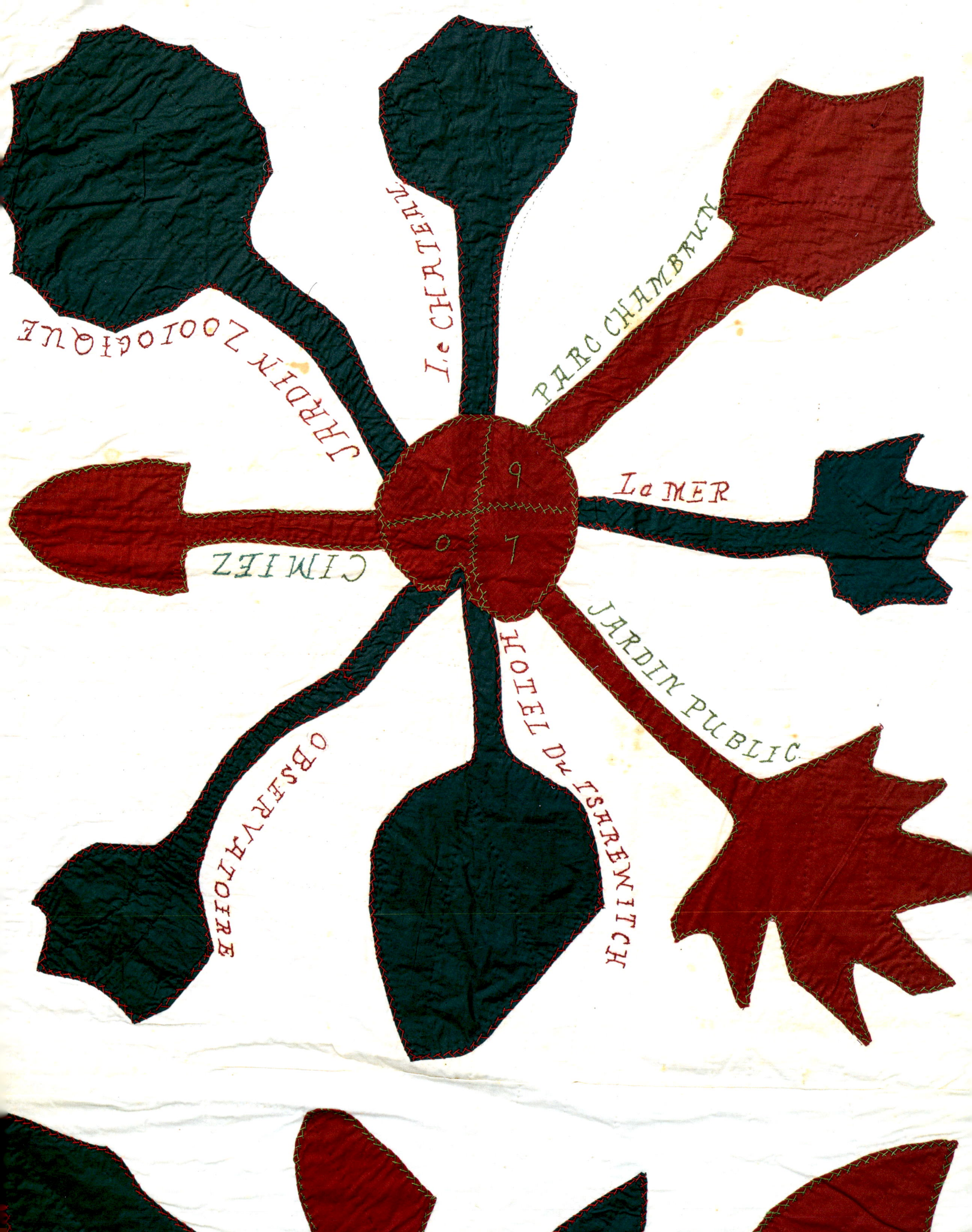
JARDIN ZOOLOGIQUE
Le CHATEAU
PARC CHAMBRUN
La MER
1907
CIMIEZ
JARDIN PUBLIC
HOTEL Du TSAREWITCH
OBSERVATOIRE

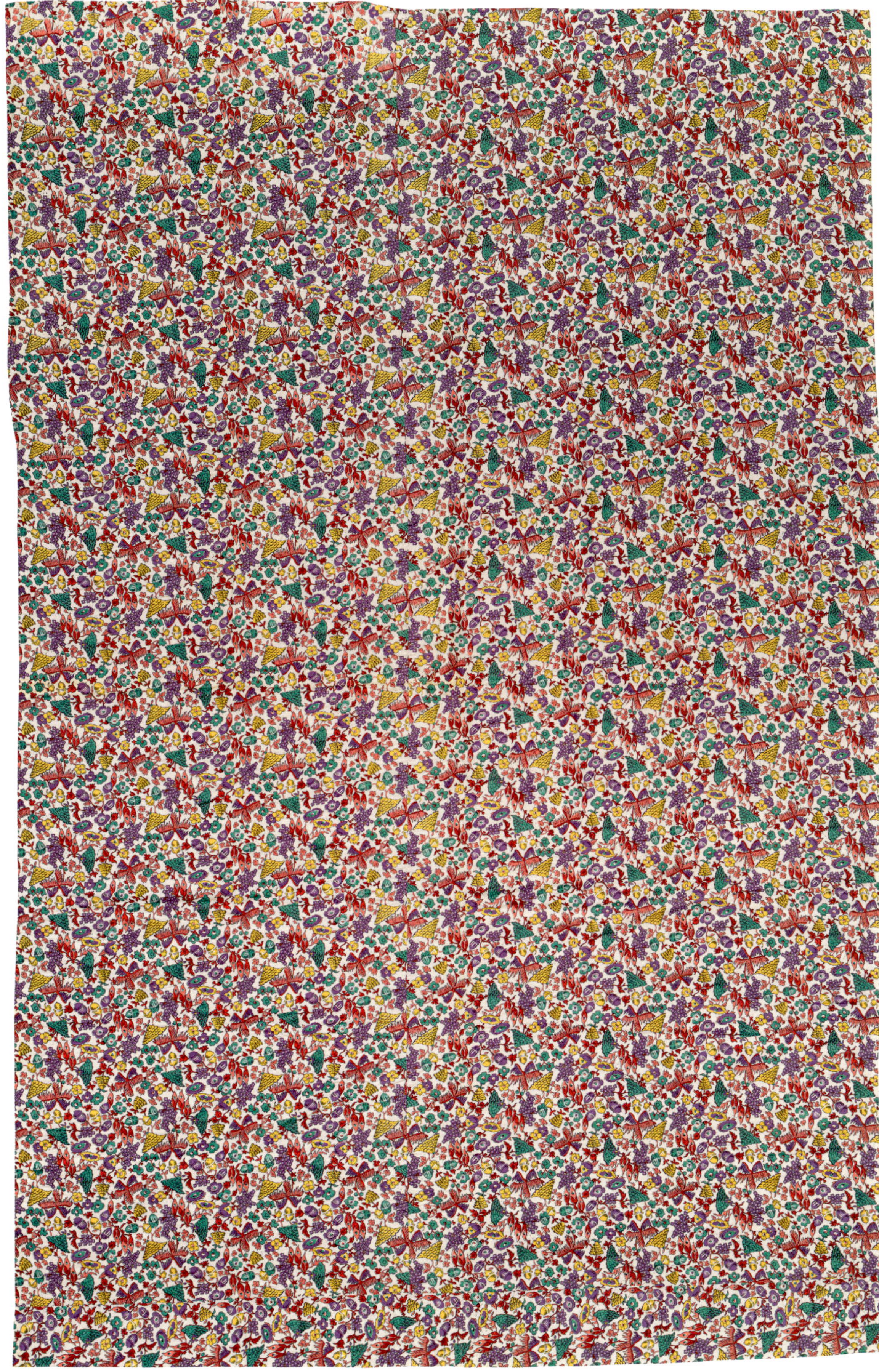

Back of cat. 2

Opposite: Detail from front of cat. 2

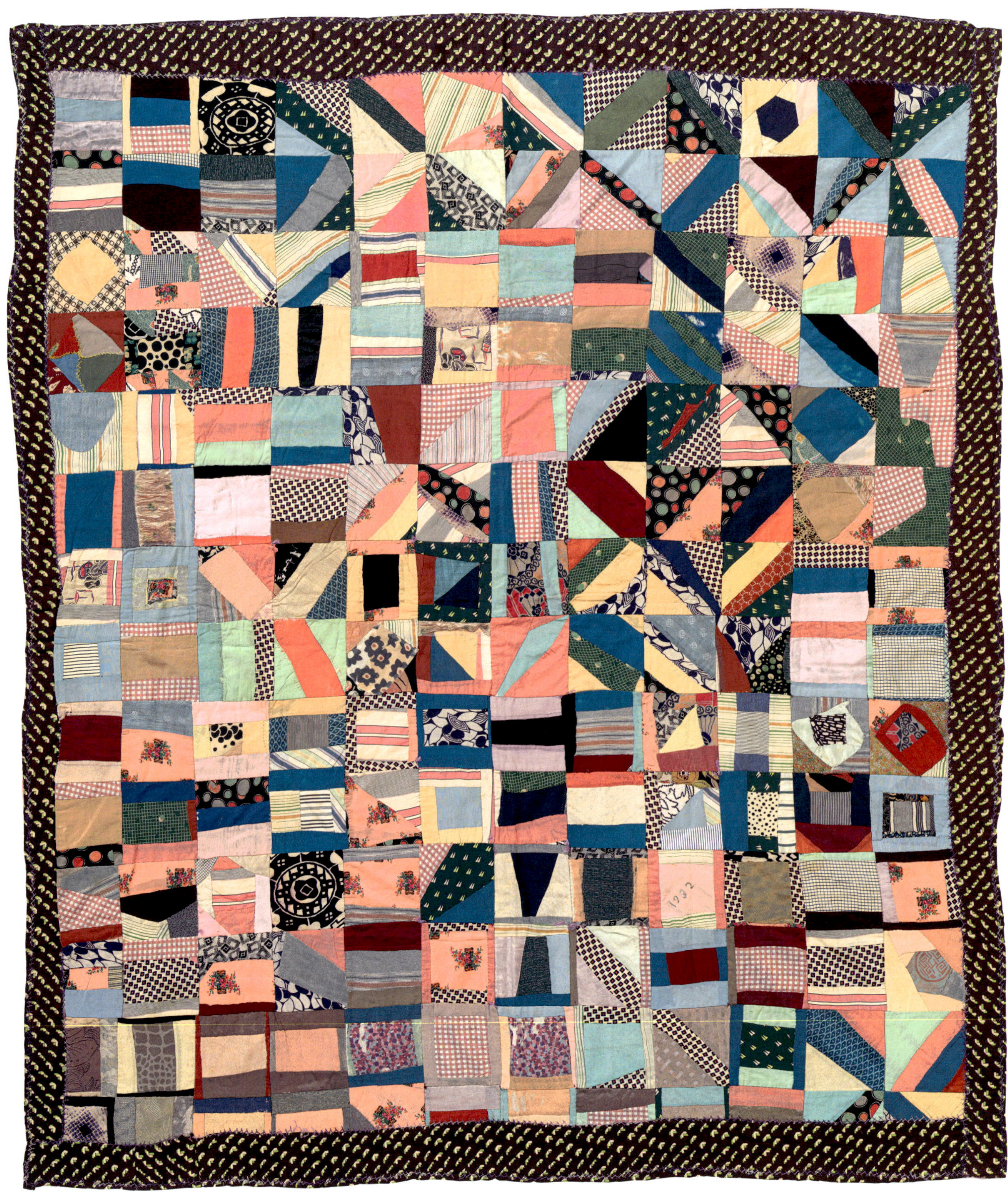

3. Untitled (Patchwork)
Pieced by Monin Brown and/or Hattie Mitchell, possibly before 1930; Macon, Georgia
Bordered and finished by Hattie Mitchell, 1932; Macon, Georgia

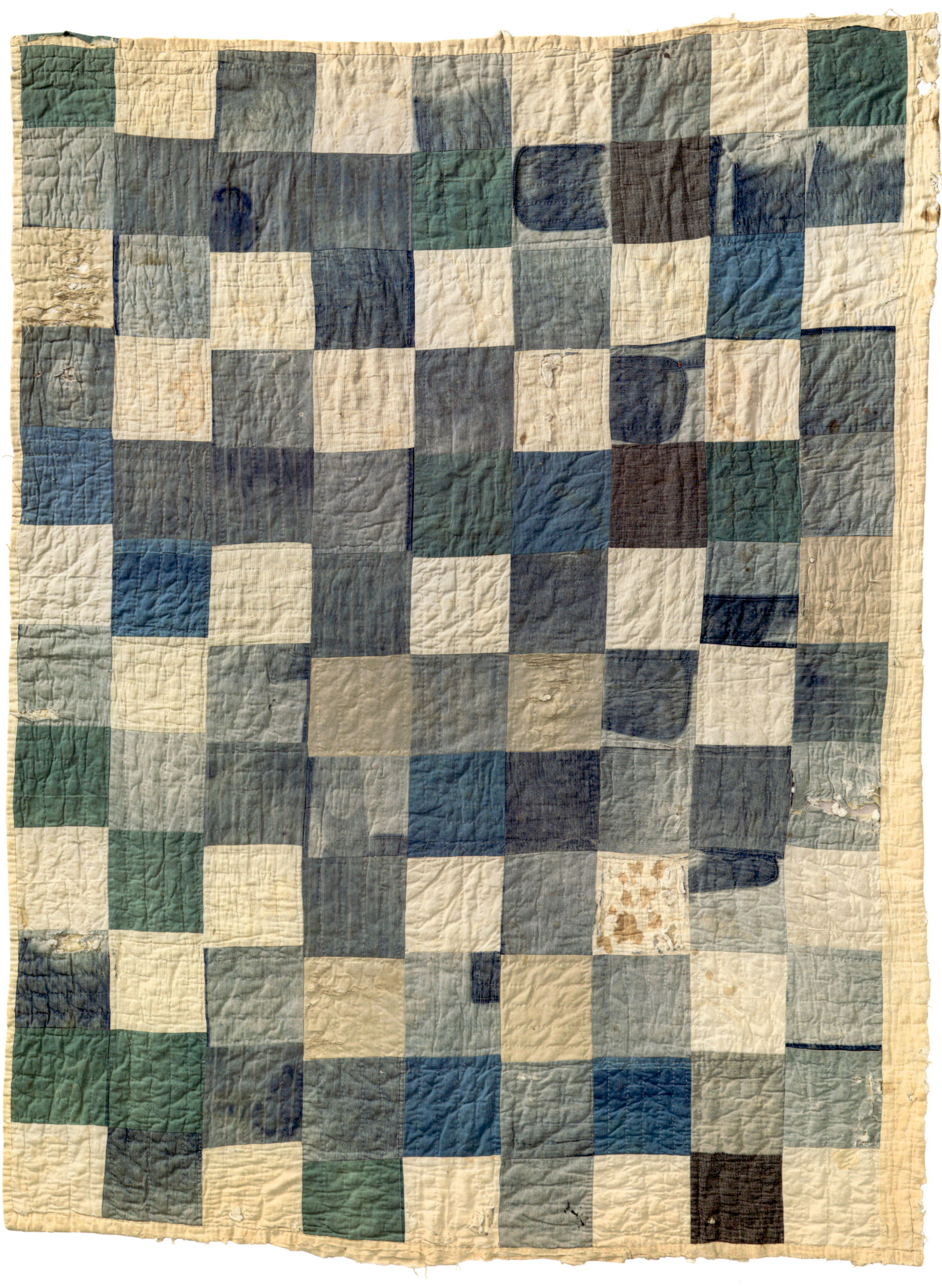

4. Untitled (One Patch, Strip)
Roberta Lee Johnson, c. 1928; Cushing, Texas

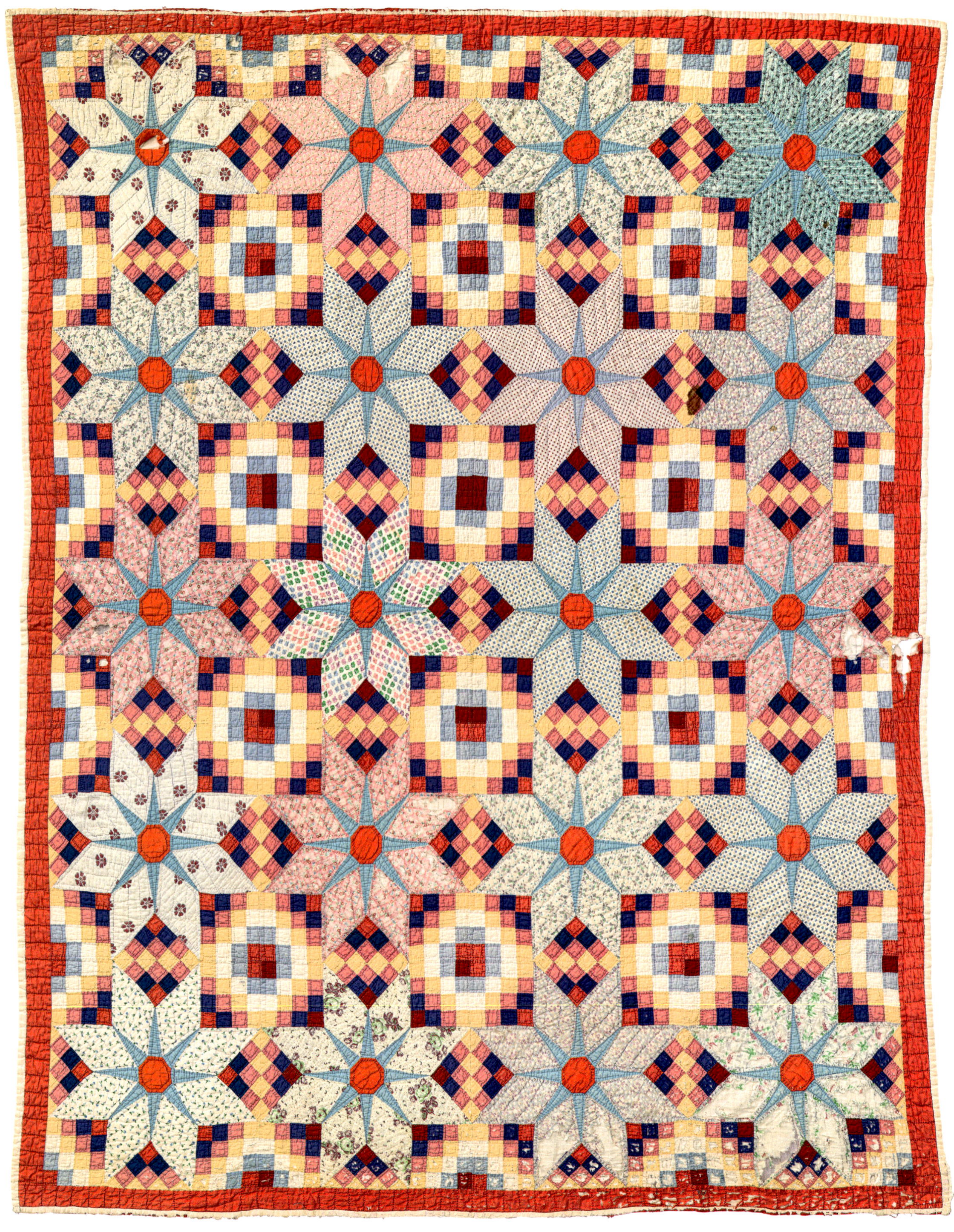

5. Untitled (Shadow Star)
Betty Chafford and Rebecca Smith, 1920s–1930s; Bastrop, Louisiana
Laura Johnson Battise, Chafford's granddaughter and Smith's daughter, was the keeper of this quilt until 1984.

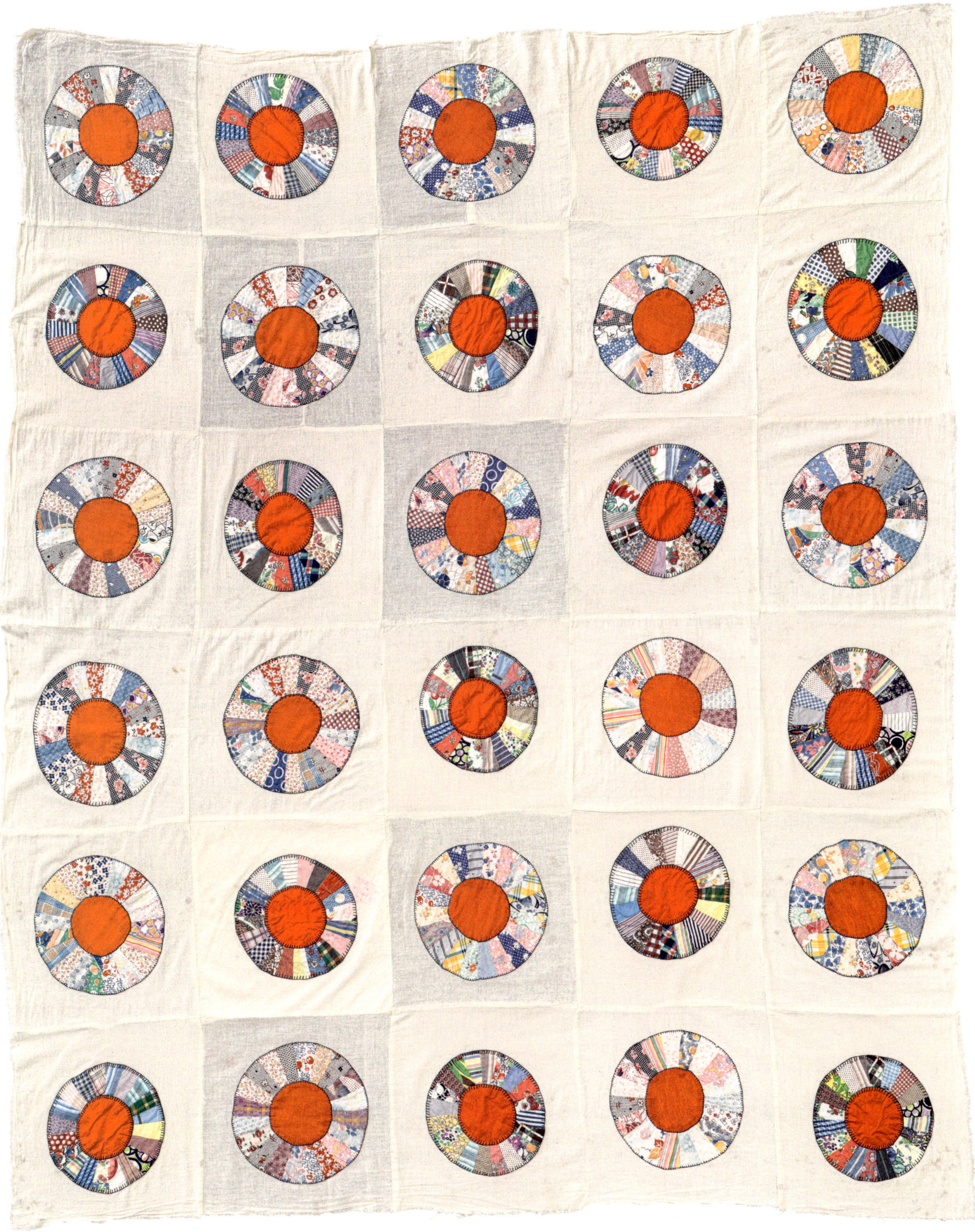

6. Untitled top (Dresden Plate)
Ruth Charlotte Clay and possibly Treva Clay, 1930s–1940s; location unknown

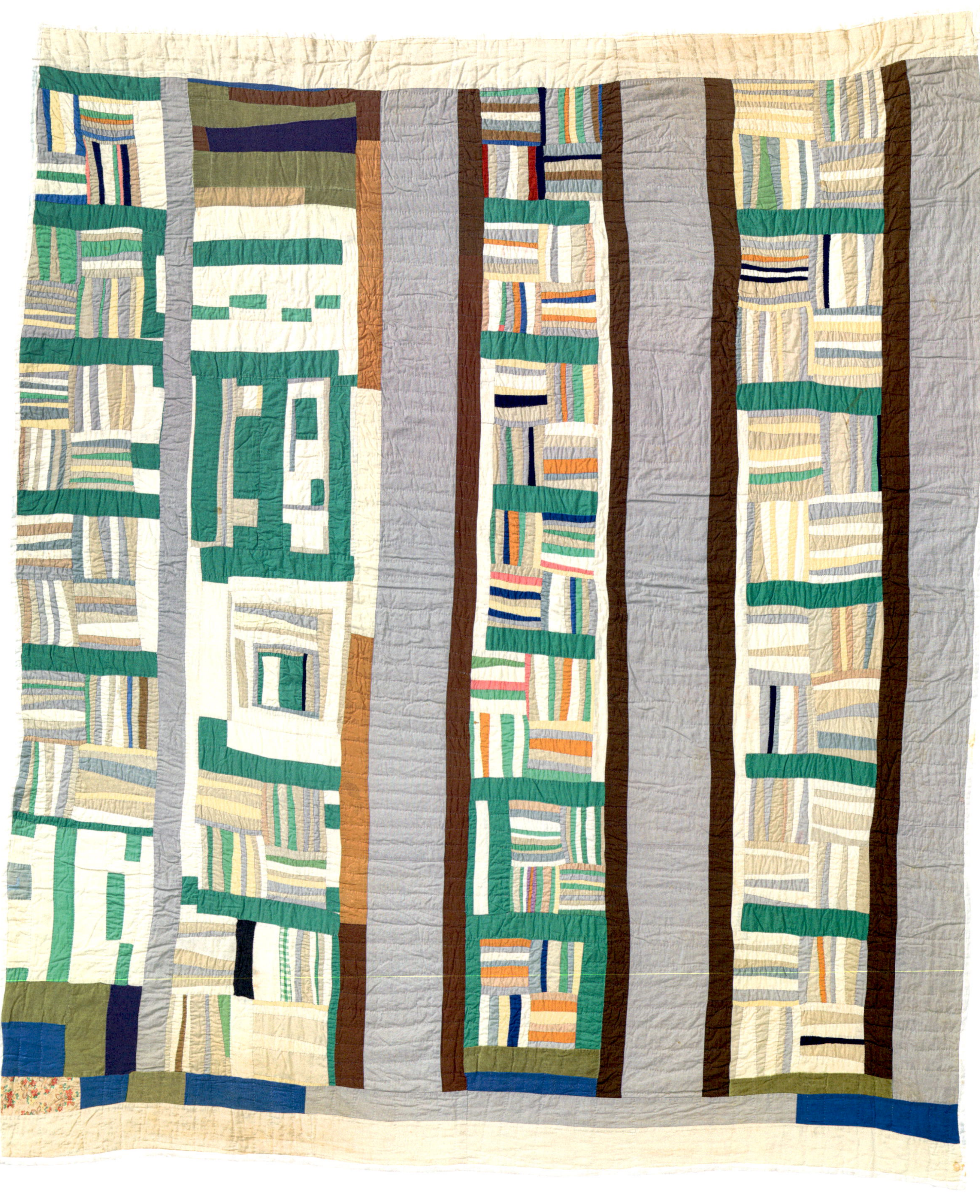

7. Untitled (Roman Stripe)
Pieced by Ruth Charlotte Clay and possibly Treva Clay, 1930s–1940s; location unknown
Quilted by Irene Bankhead, 1998; Oakland, California

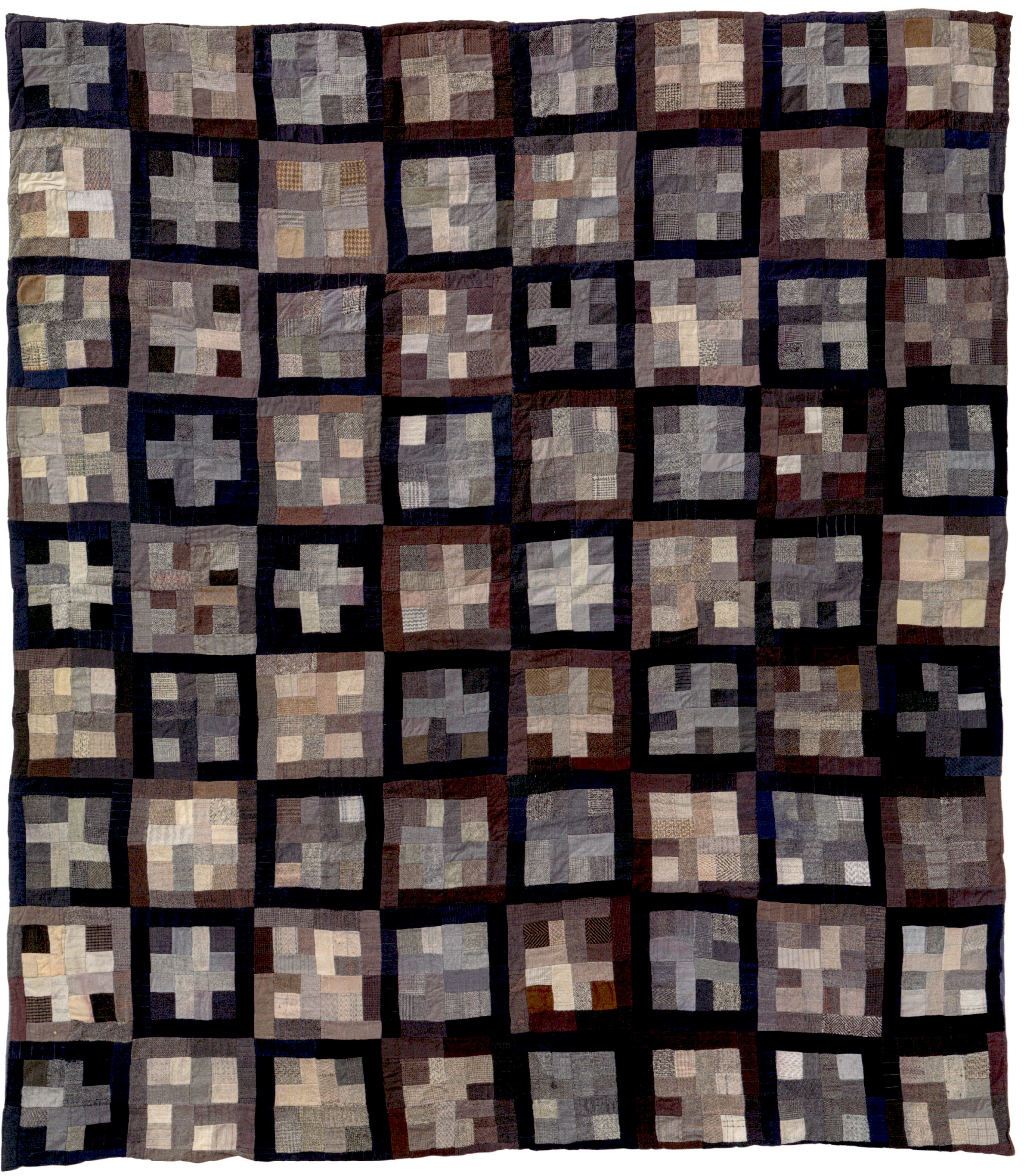

8. Untitled (Four Patch Log Cabin variation)
Maker Once Known/Unidentified Artist
1930s; location unknown

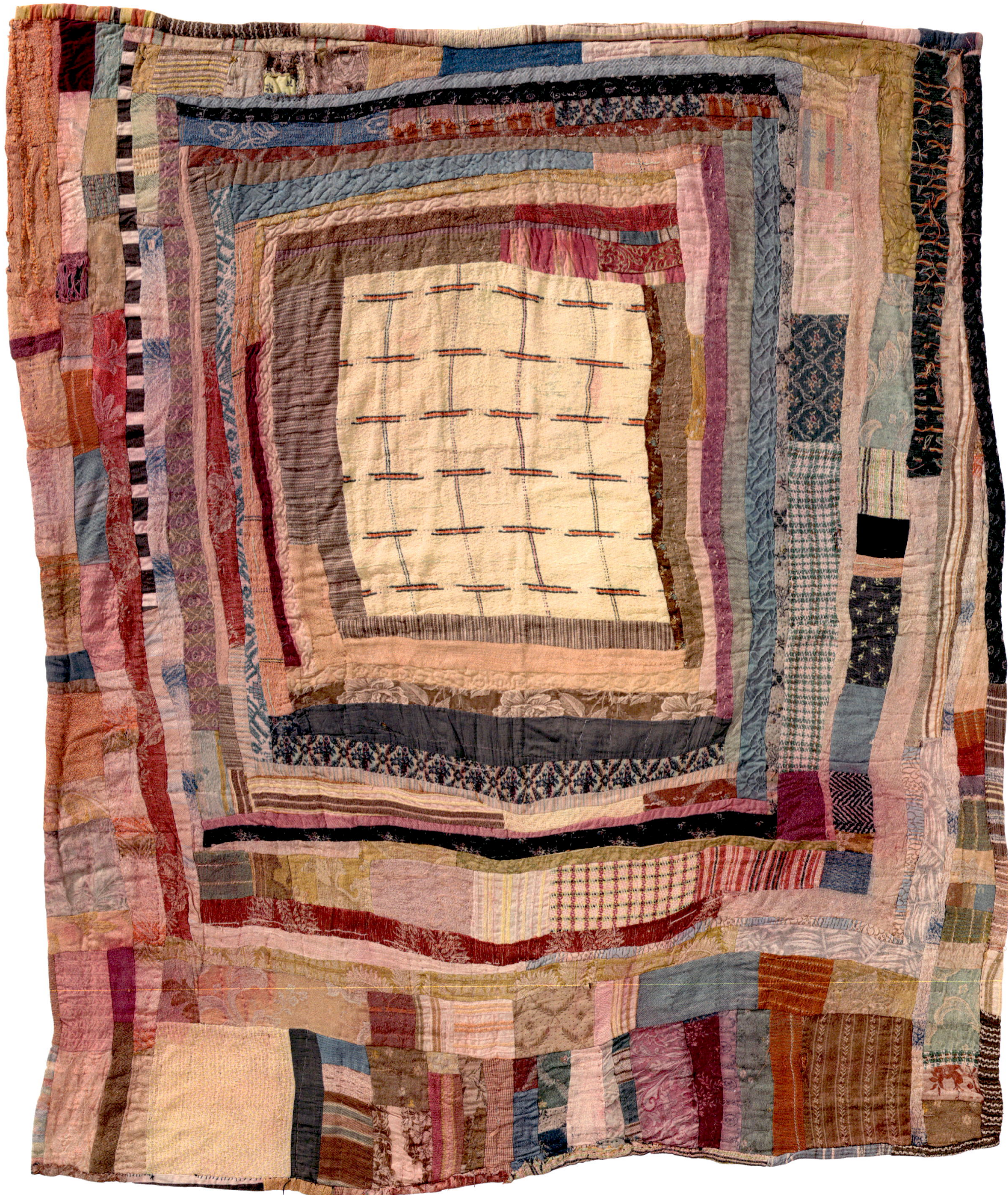

Front

9. Untitled (Medallion)
Maker Once Known/Unidentified Artist
Probably 1930s; near McComb, Mississippi, or San Francisco, California
Clara Belle Coleman and her descendants were the keepers of this quilt until 1987.

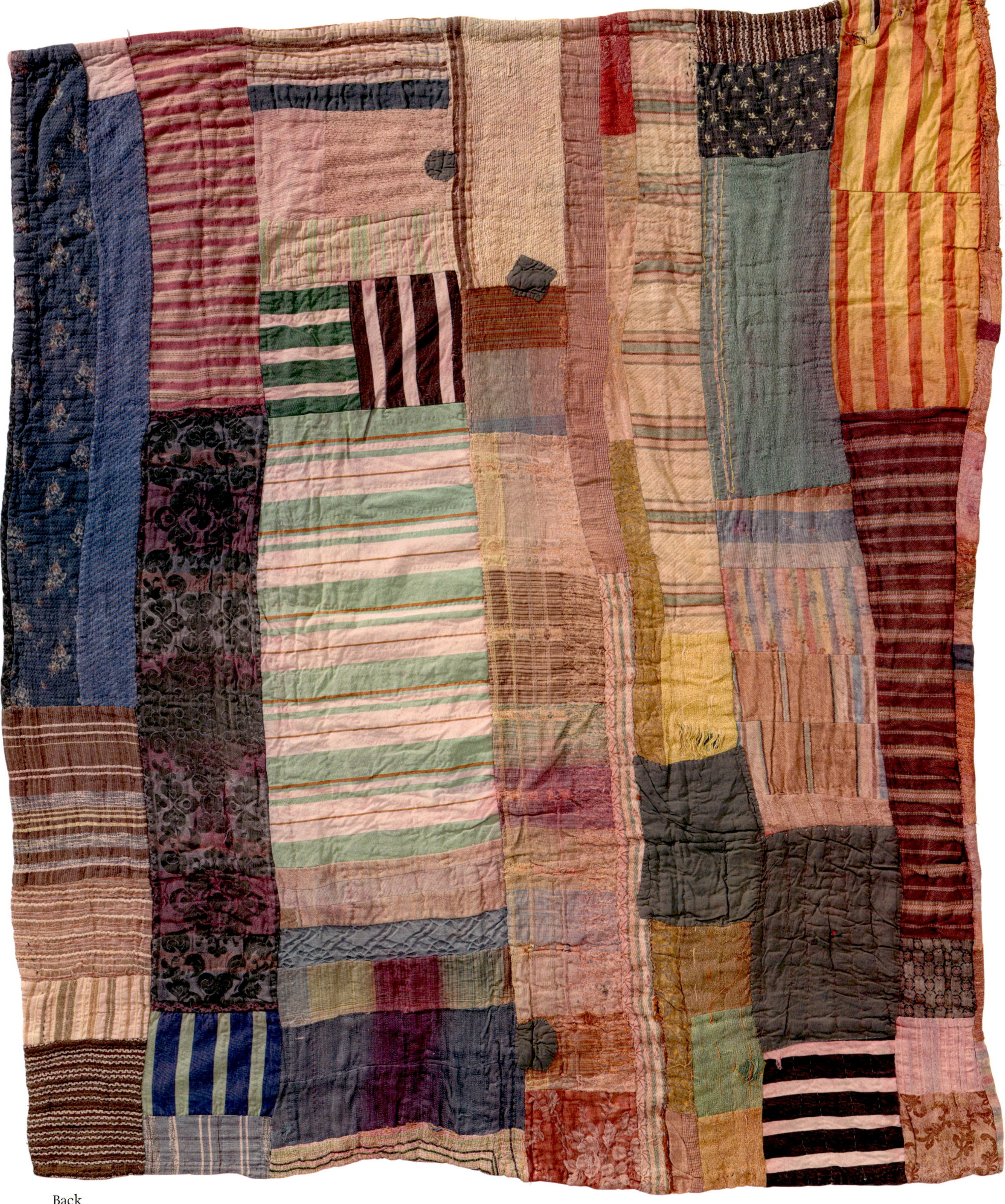

Back

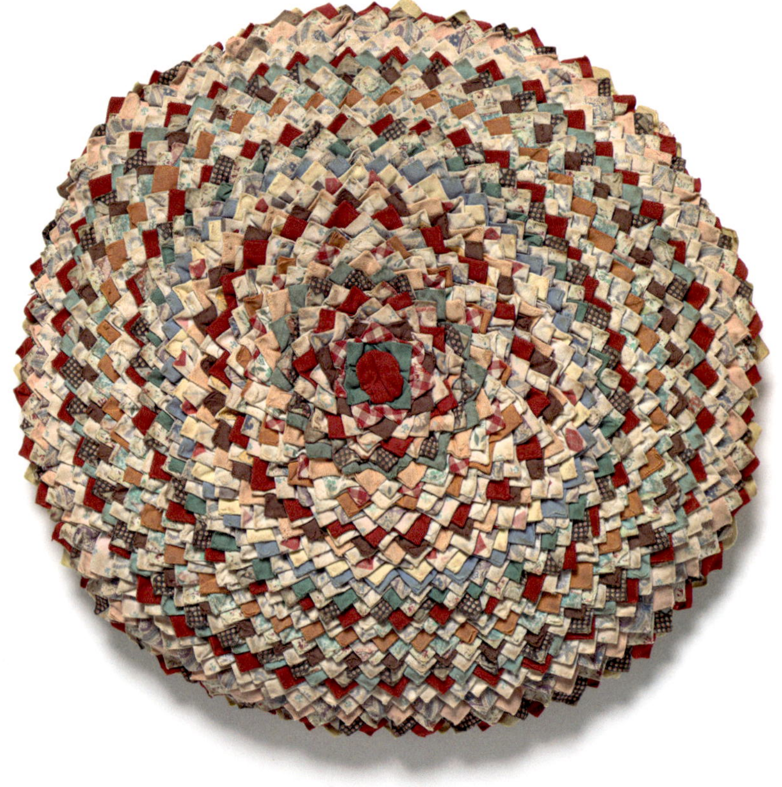

Front

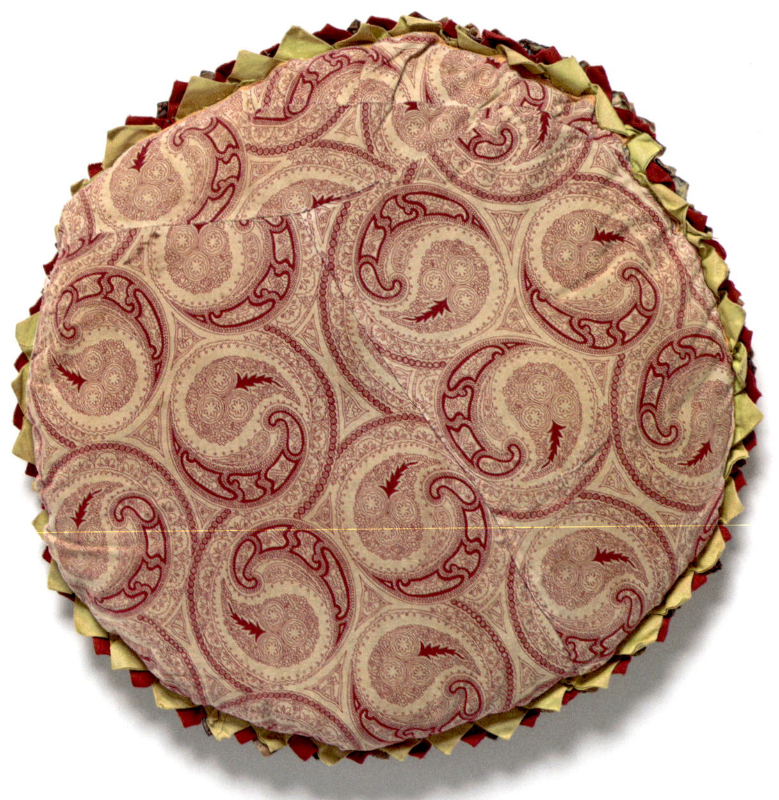

Back

10. Pillow (Pine Burr)
Maker Once Known/Unidentified artist, 1930s–1940s; location unknown
Zetta Dempsey was the keeper of this pillow until sometime in the mid-1980s.

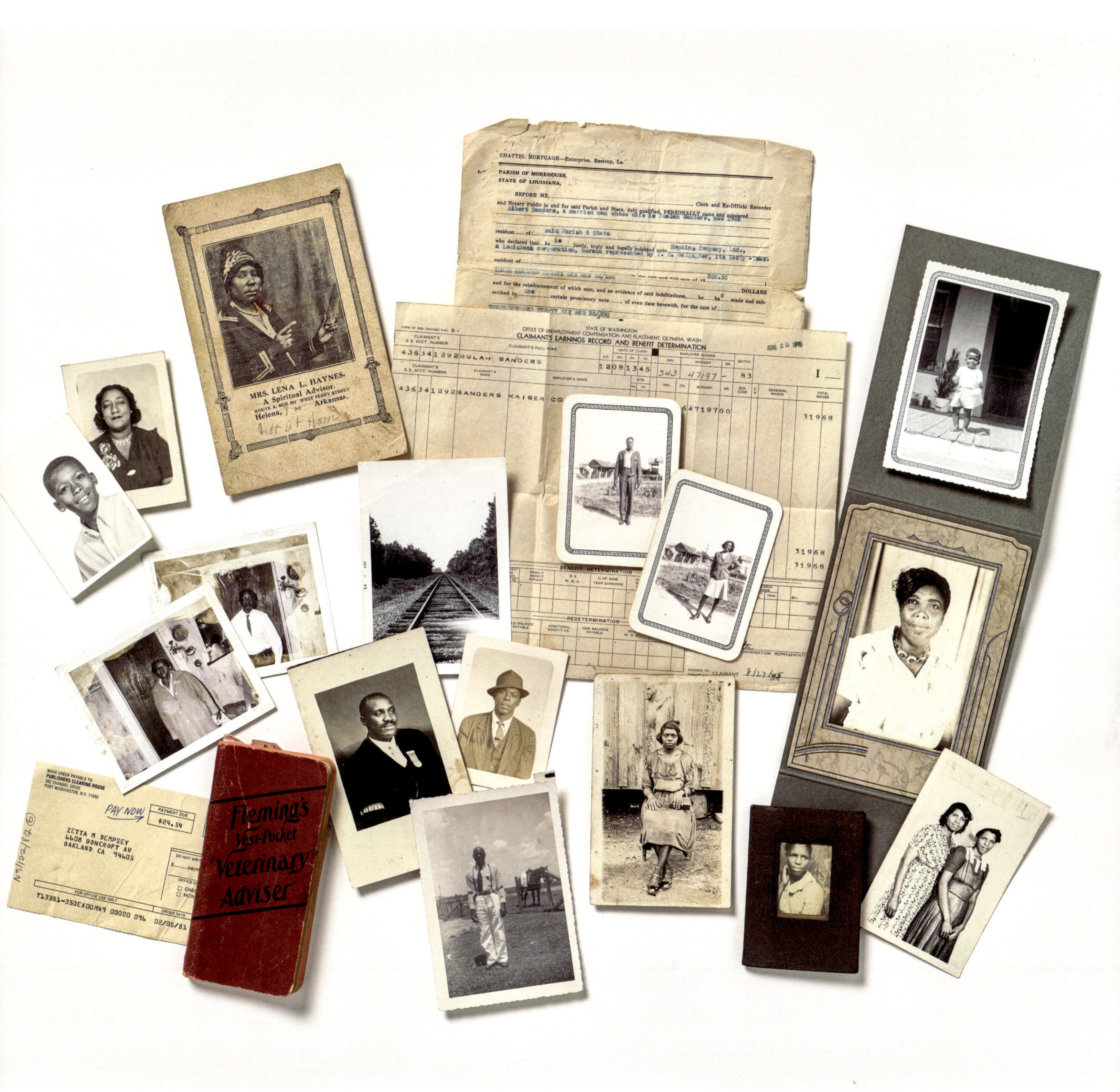

11. Assorted ephemera and photographs
1920s–1980s; location unknown
Zetta Dempsey was the keeper of these materials until sometime in the mid-1980s.

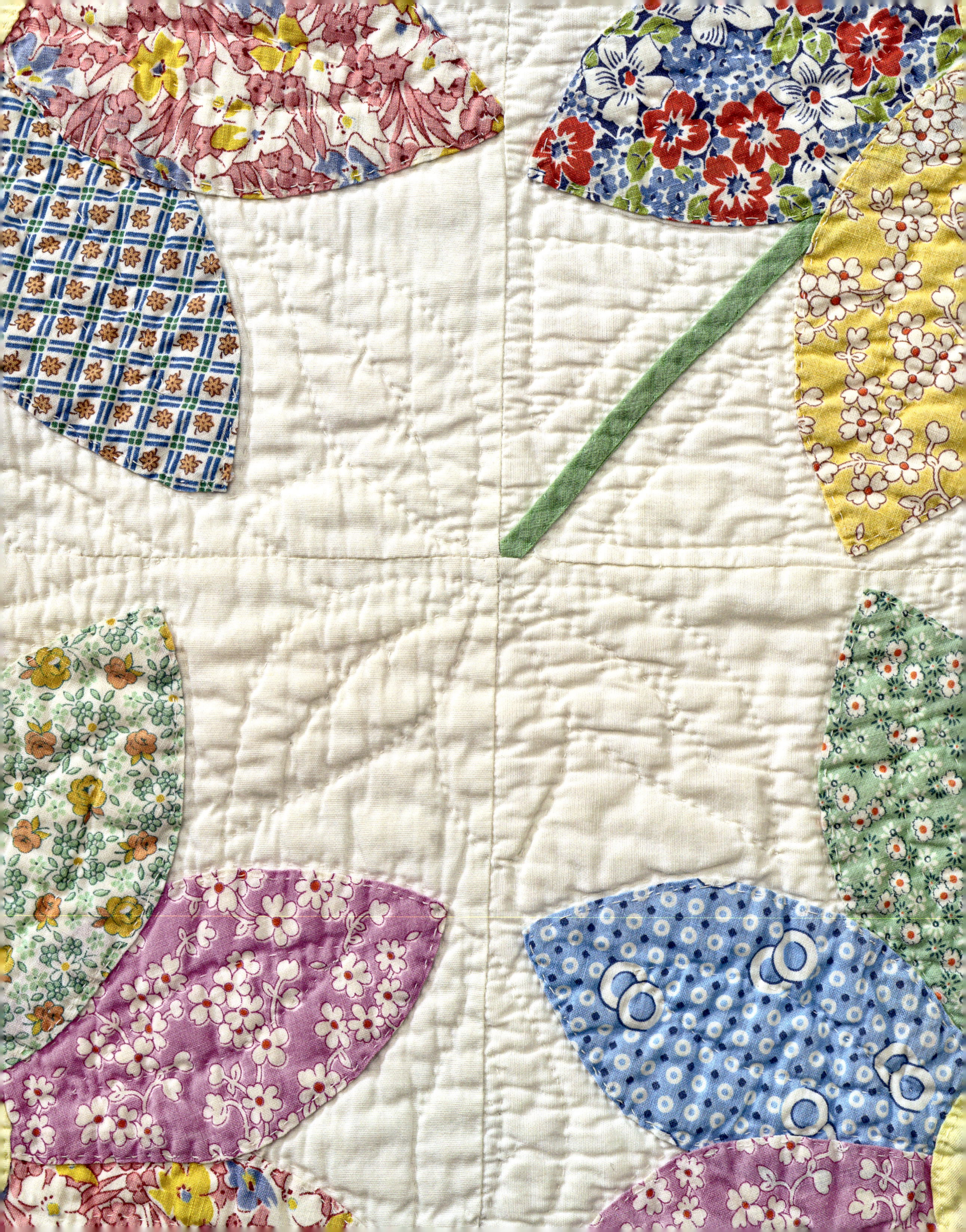

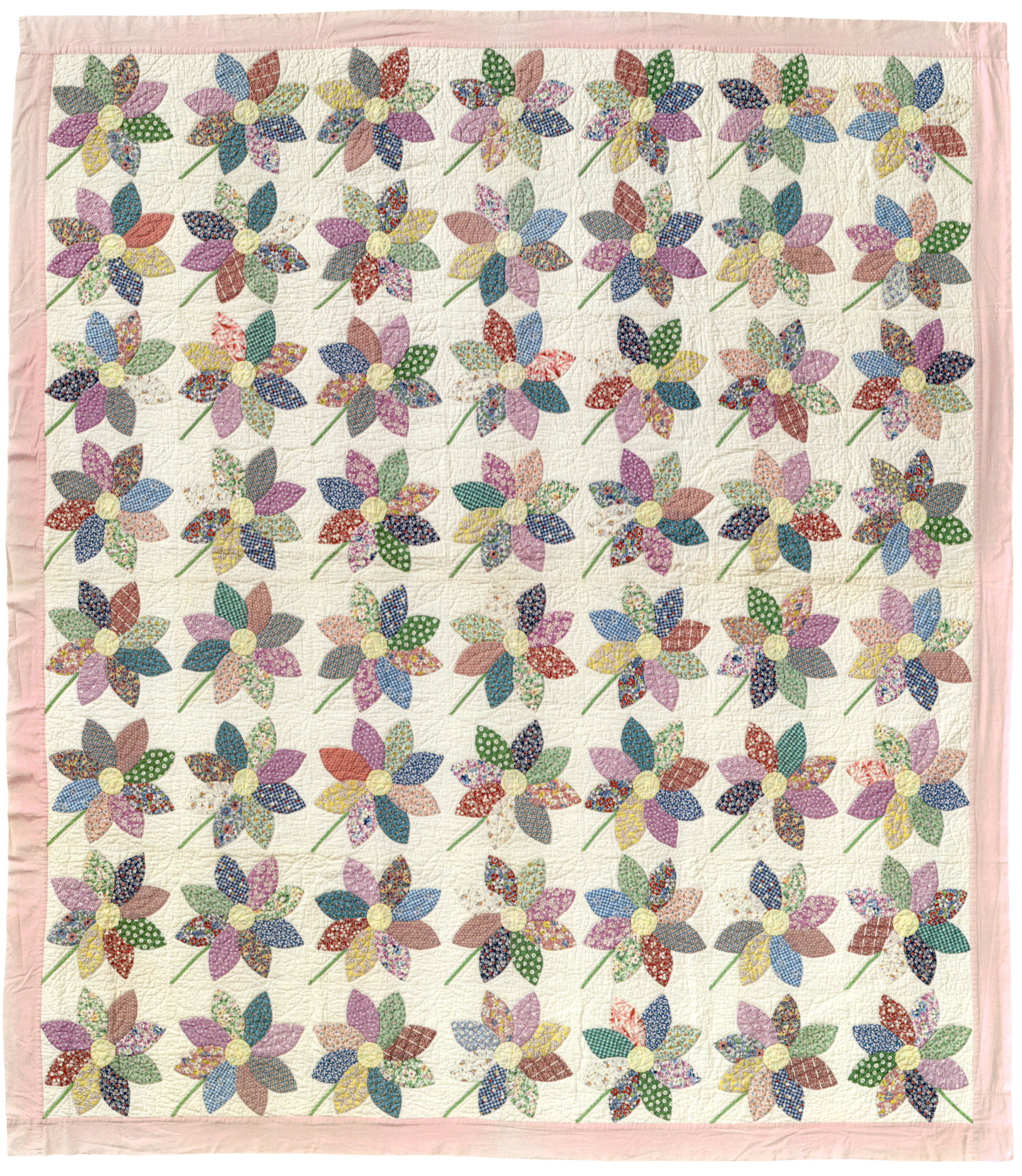

Detail

12. Untitled (Friendship Dahlia)
Pearlie Rayford, 1930s–1940s; Little Rock, Arkansas

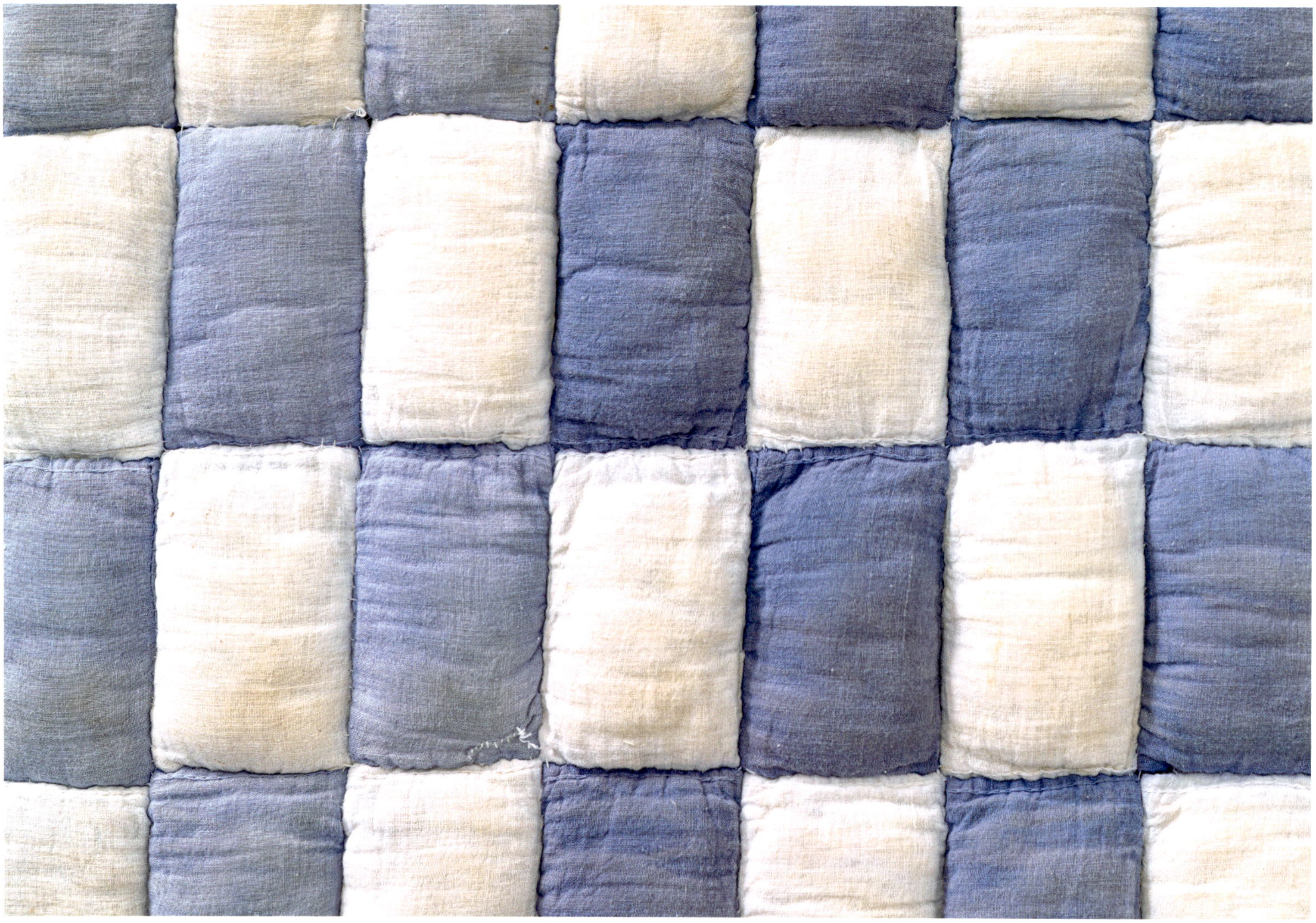

Detail of cat. 13

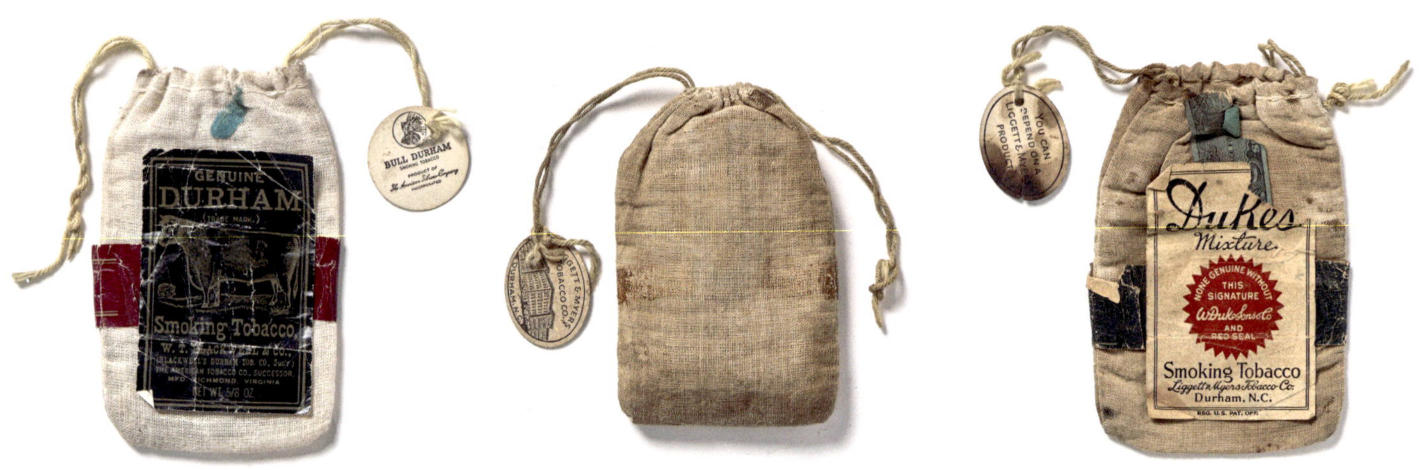

Fig. 35. Tobacco sacks, 1910s–1940s

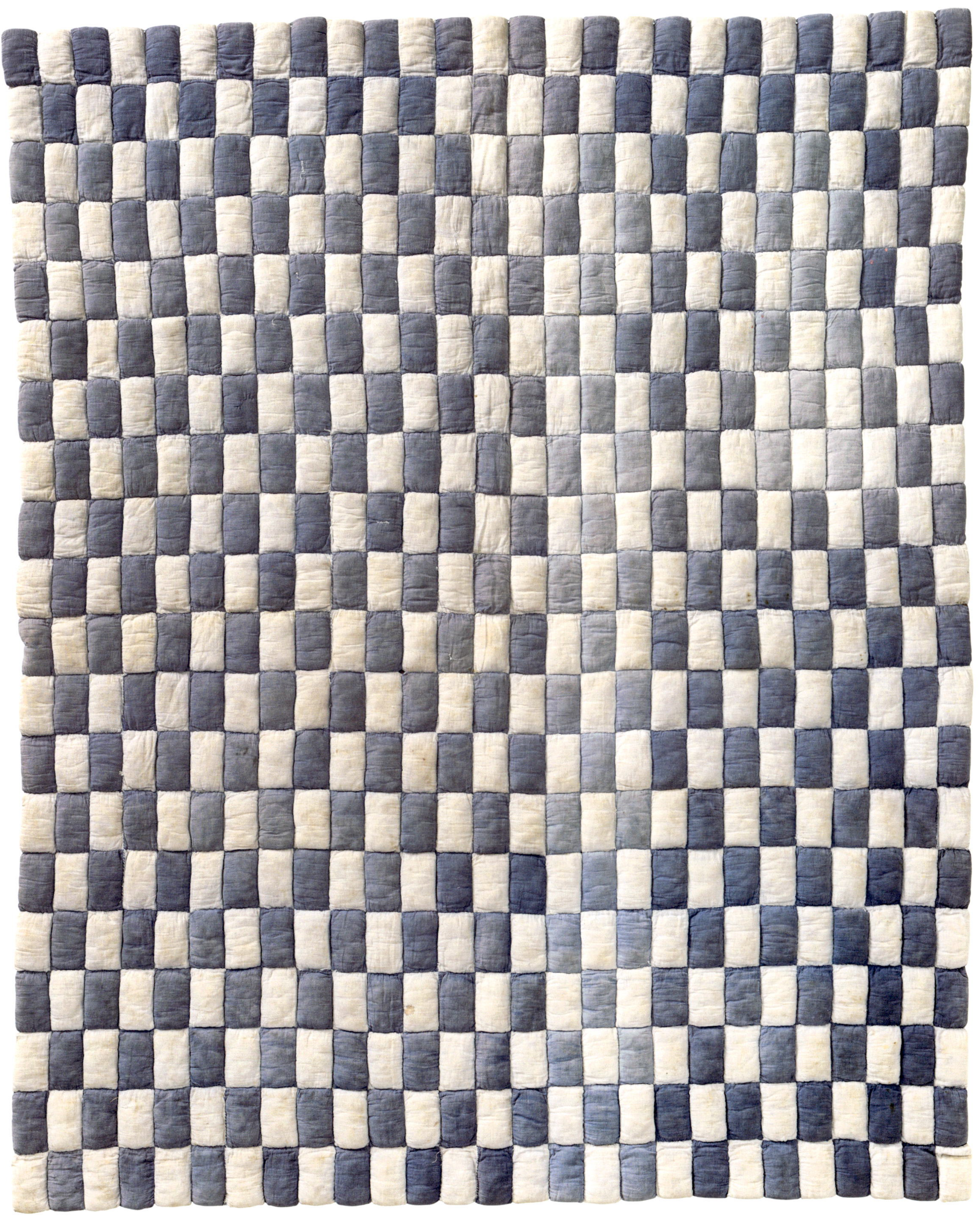

13. Untitled (Puff quilt with tobacco sacks)
Annie Crawford, 1933–1940; Call, Texas
Estella Brown, Crawford's niece, and her relatives were keepers of this quilt in Berkeley, California, until 1980.

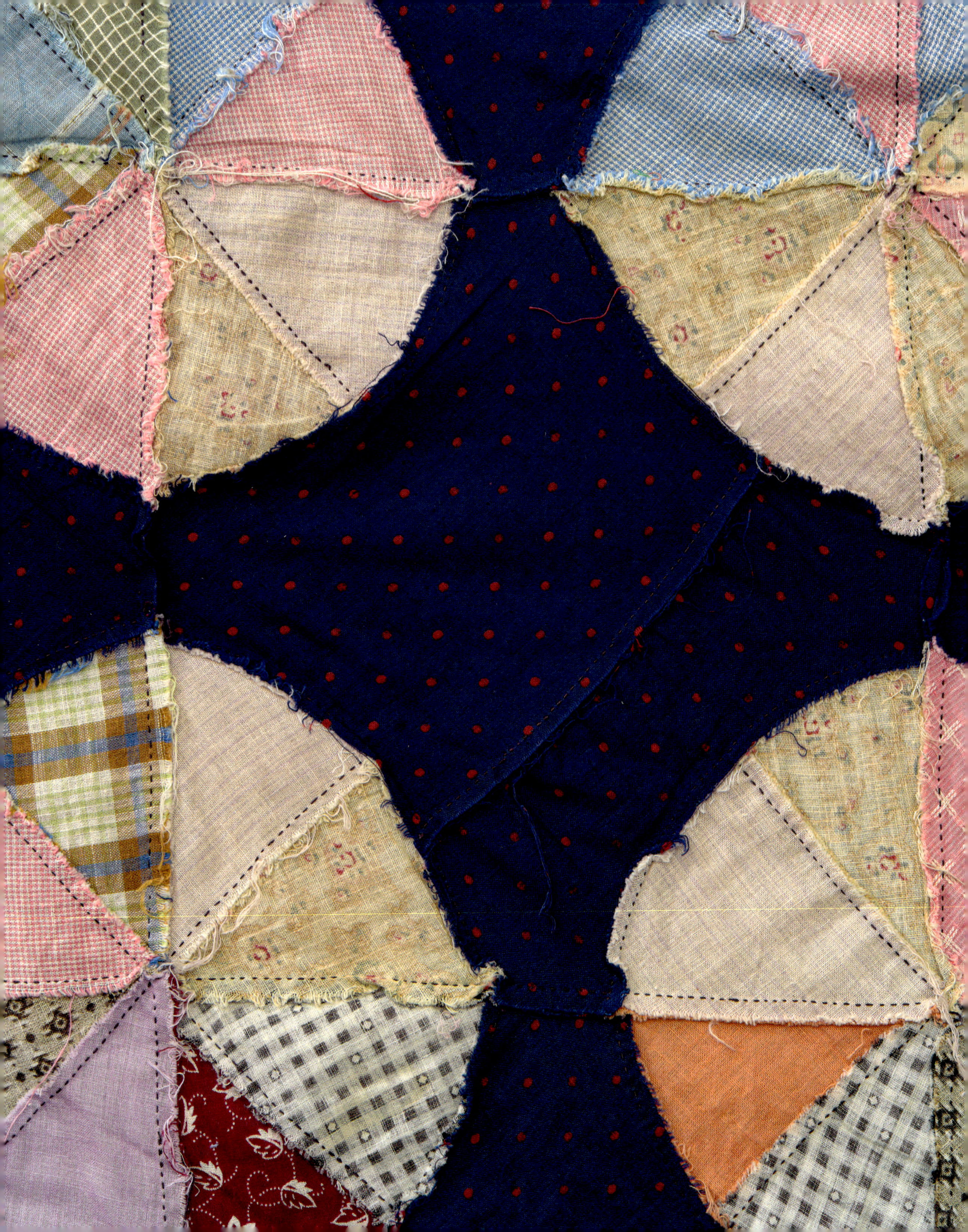

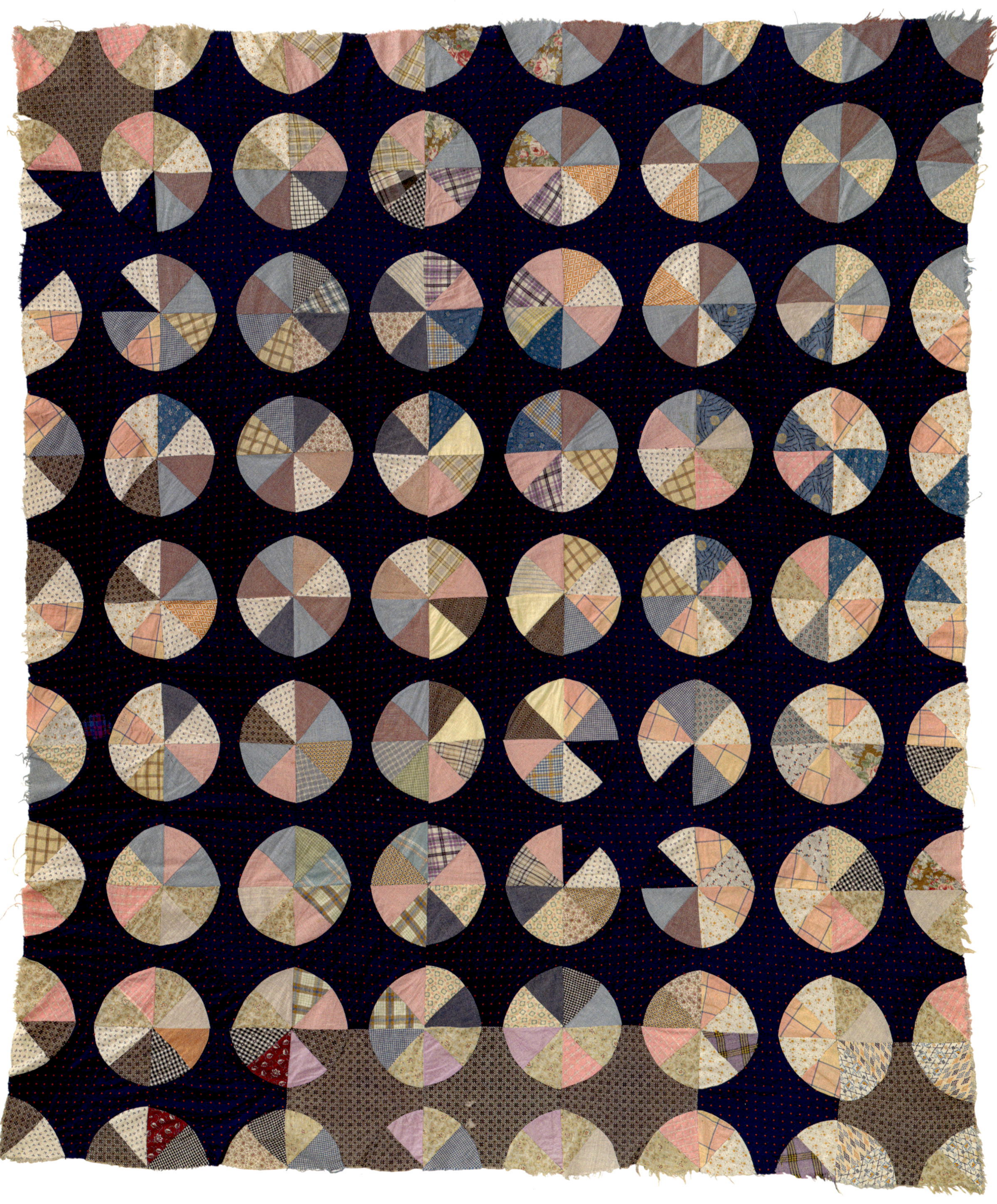

14. Untitled top (Pinwheel variation)
Venella Tyler, c. 1936; Greenwood, Mississippi

Detail of back

15. Untitled (Plain quilt)
Louise Hicks, c. 1939; Henderson, Texas
Willia Ette Graham, Hicks's daughter, was the keeper of this quilt until 1985.

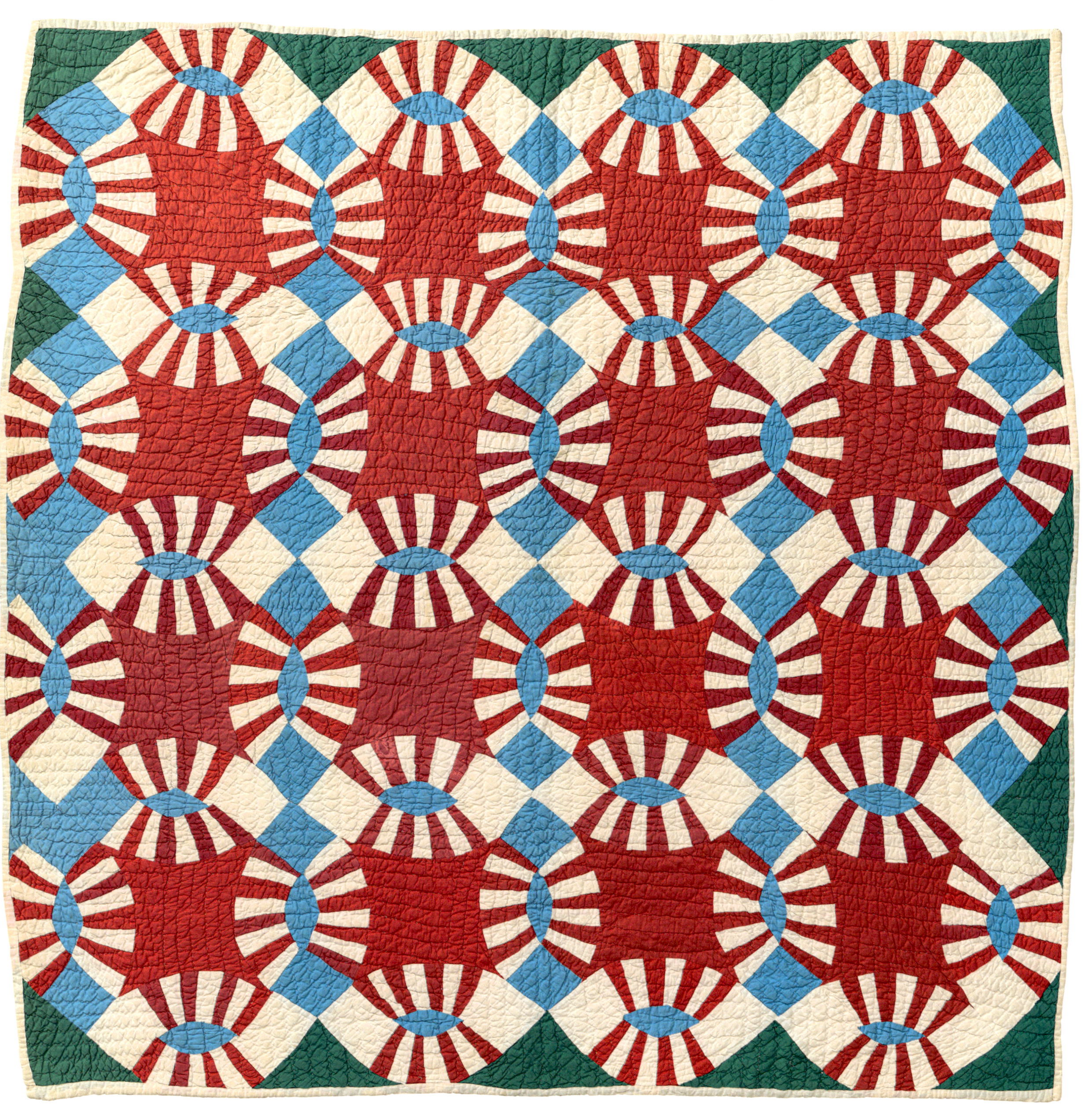

16. Untitled (Double Wedding Ring)
Emma Hall, c. 1940; Sweet Home, Arkansas
James R. Hall, the quiltmaker's son, and Gussie Wells were keepers of this quilt until 1981.

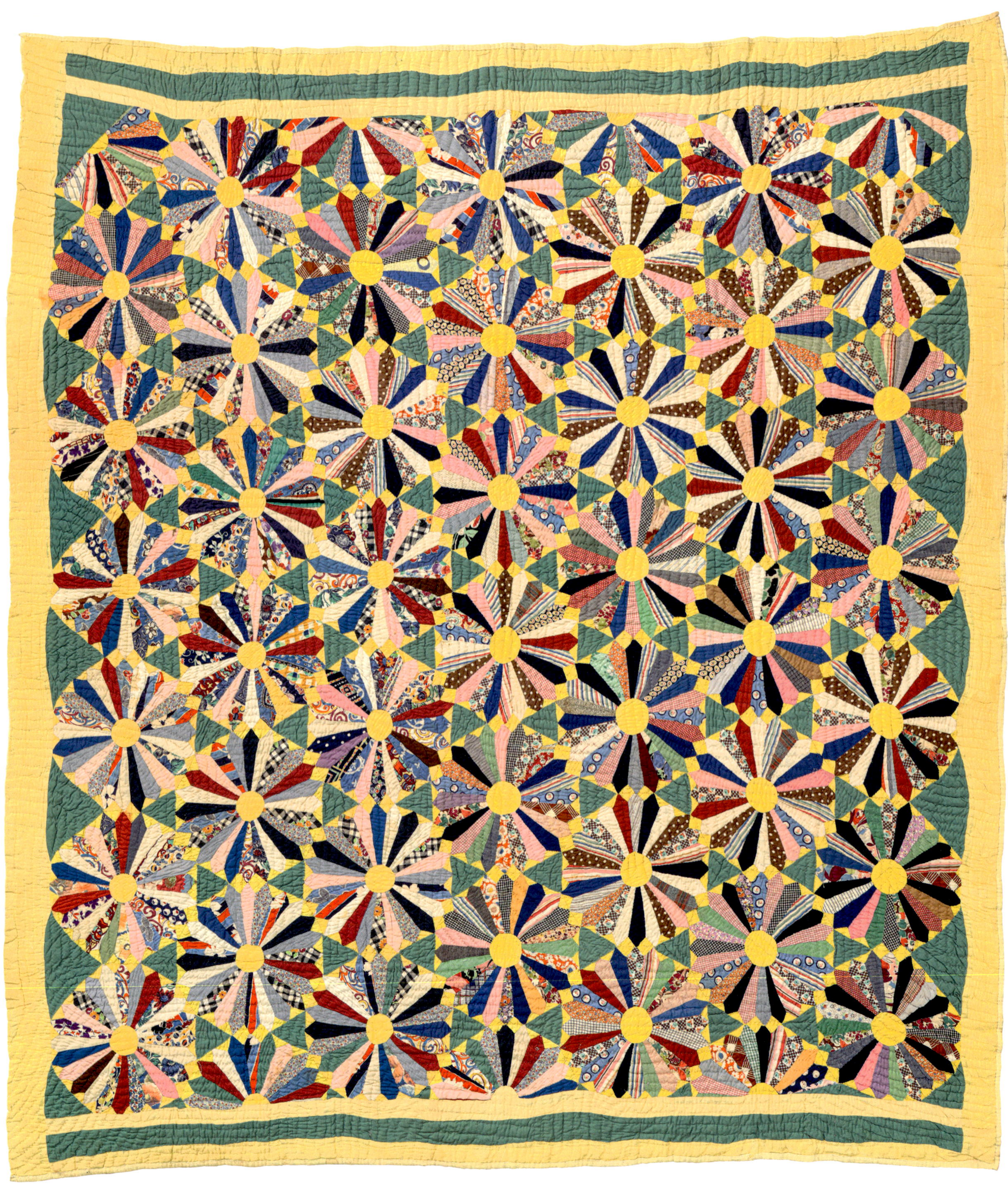

17. *Flower Garden* (Sunflower variation)
Pearl Nunley and Beauty Vaughns, 1940; Paraloma, Arkansas
Vaughns was the keeper of this quilt until 1984.

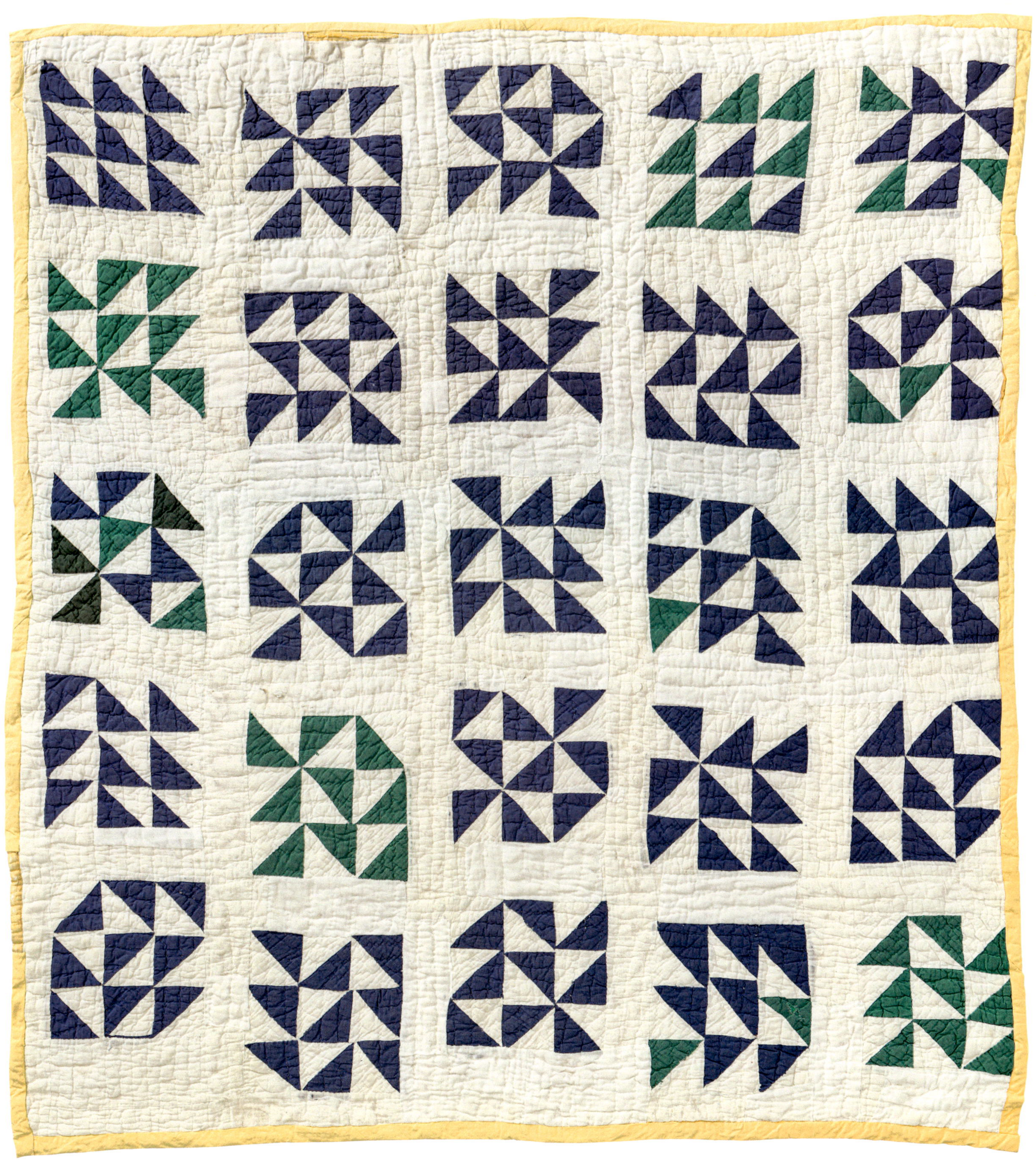

18. Untitled (Broken Dishes)
Odessa Doby, 1940s; Ozan, Arkansas
Restored by Willia Ette Graham, 1987; Oakland, California

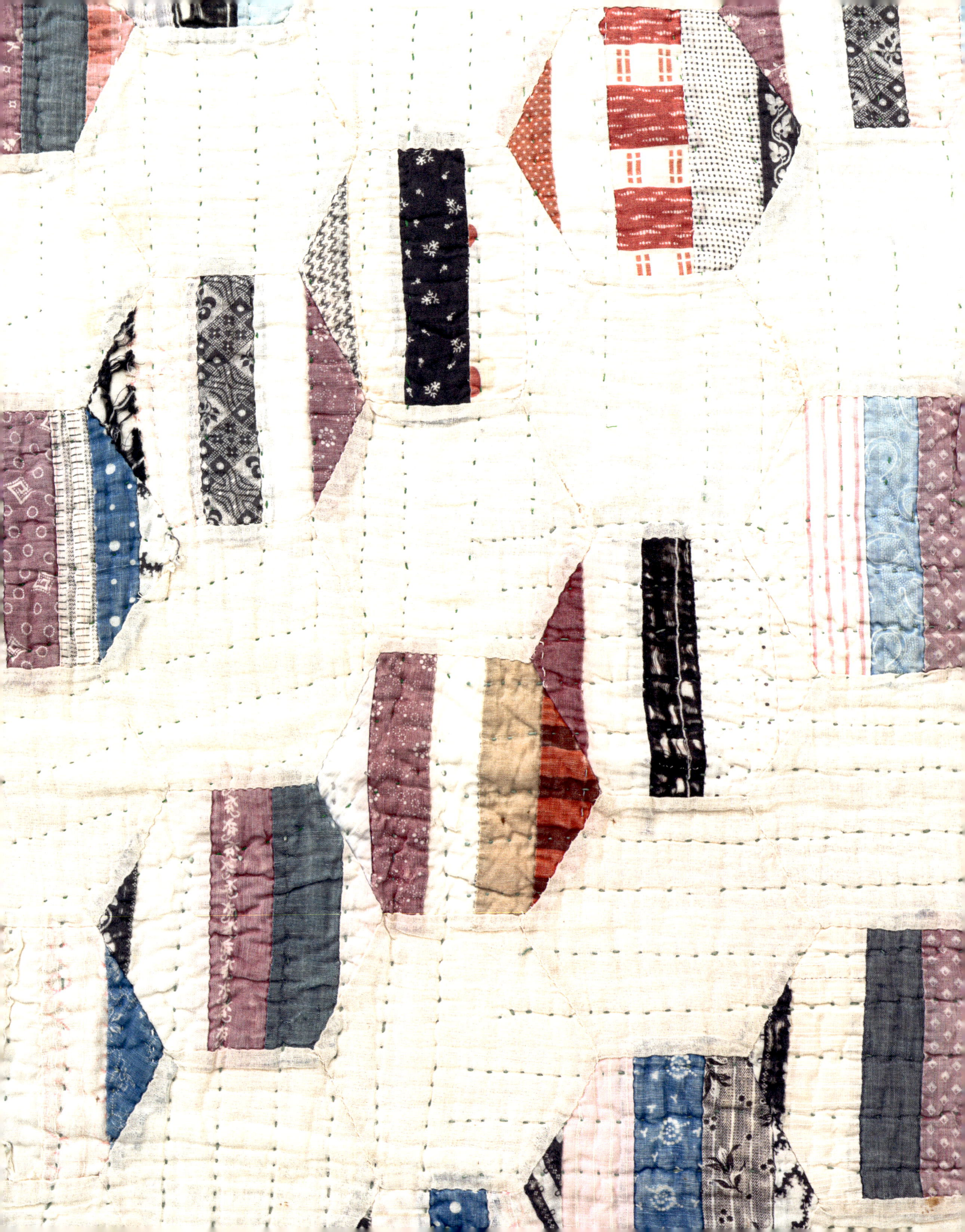

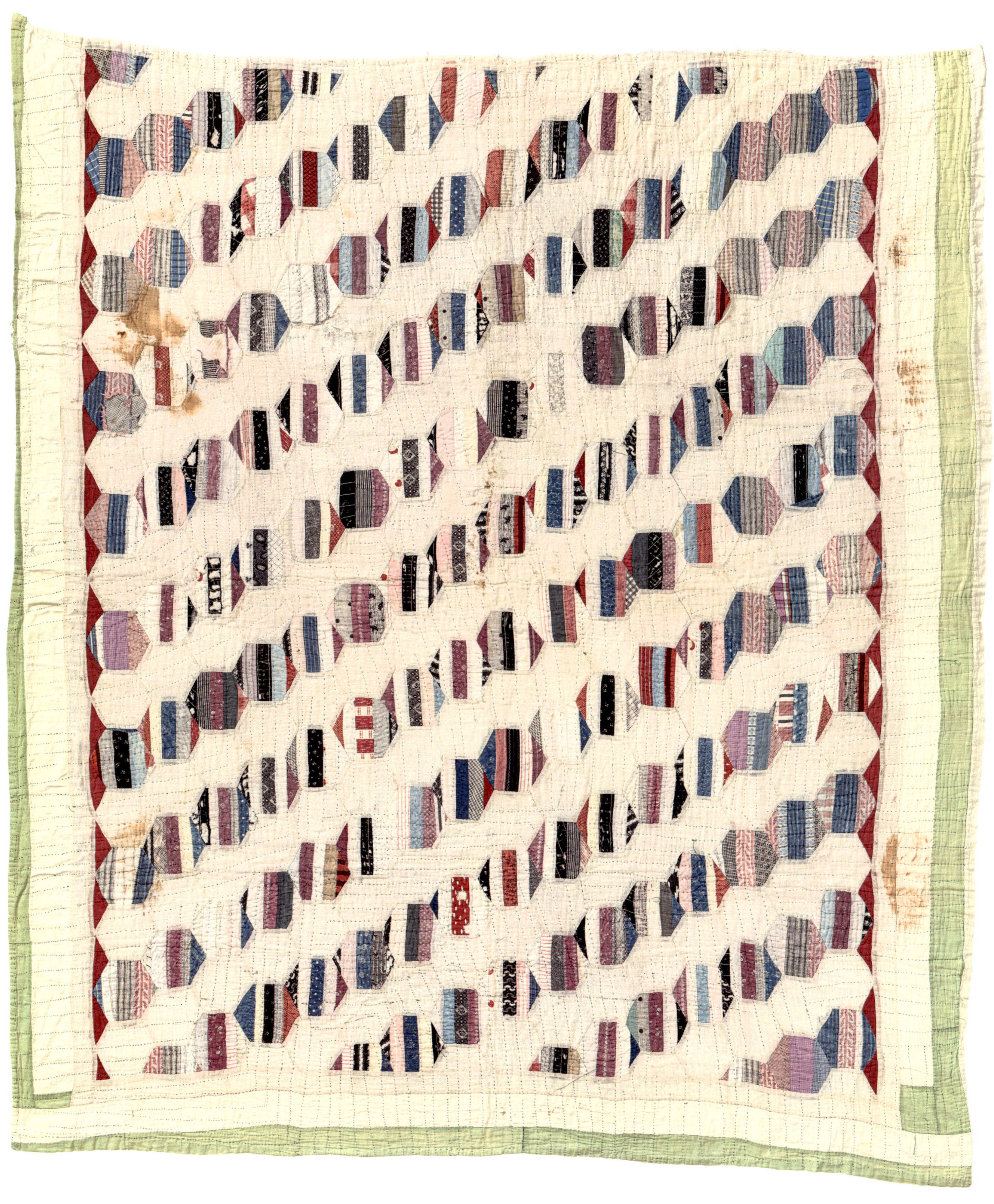

19. Untitled (String Hexagons)
Victoria Ector Cooper, 1940s; Rusk County, Texas

Detail

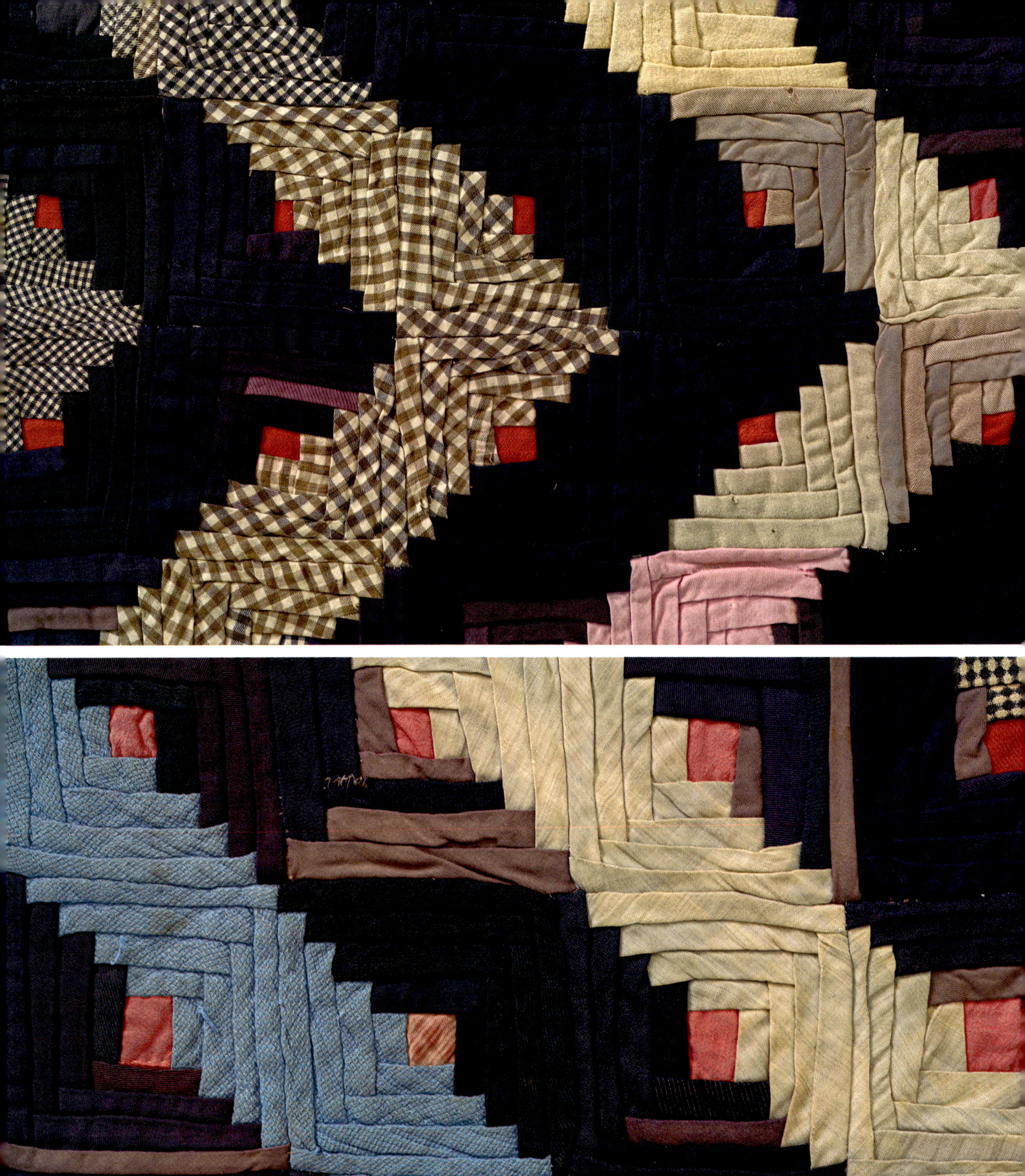

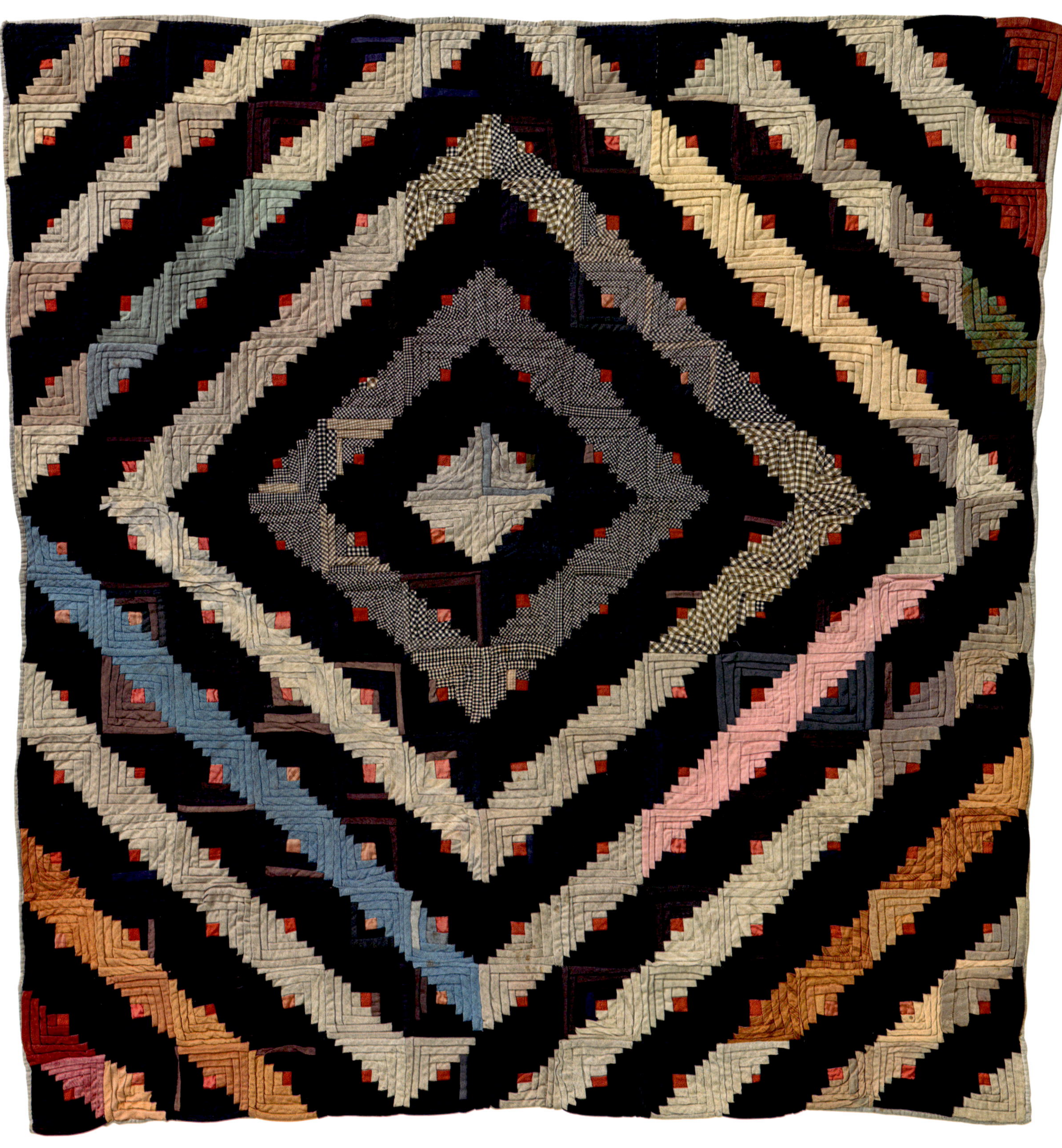

20. Untitled (Log Cabin, Barn Raising variation)
Anna Nicholson, 1940s; Vicksburg, Mississippi, or California Bay Area

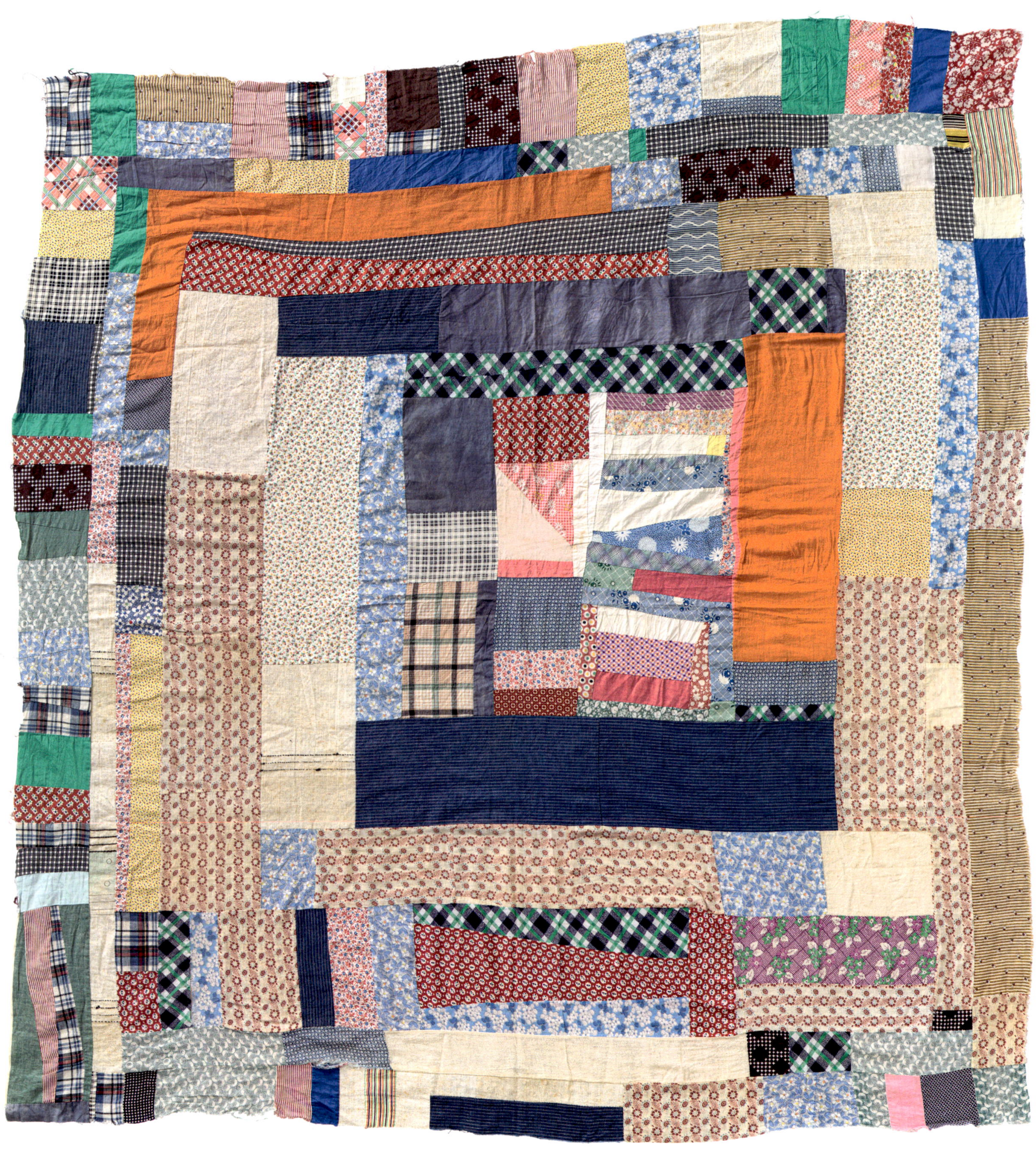

21. Untitled top (Medallion)
Maker Once Known/Unidentified Artist
1940s; location unknown

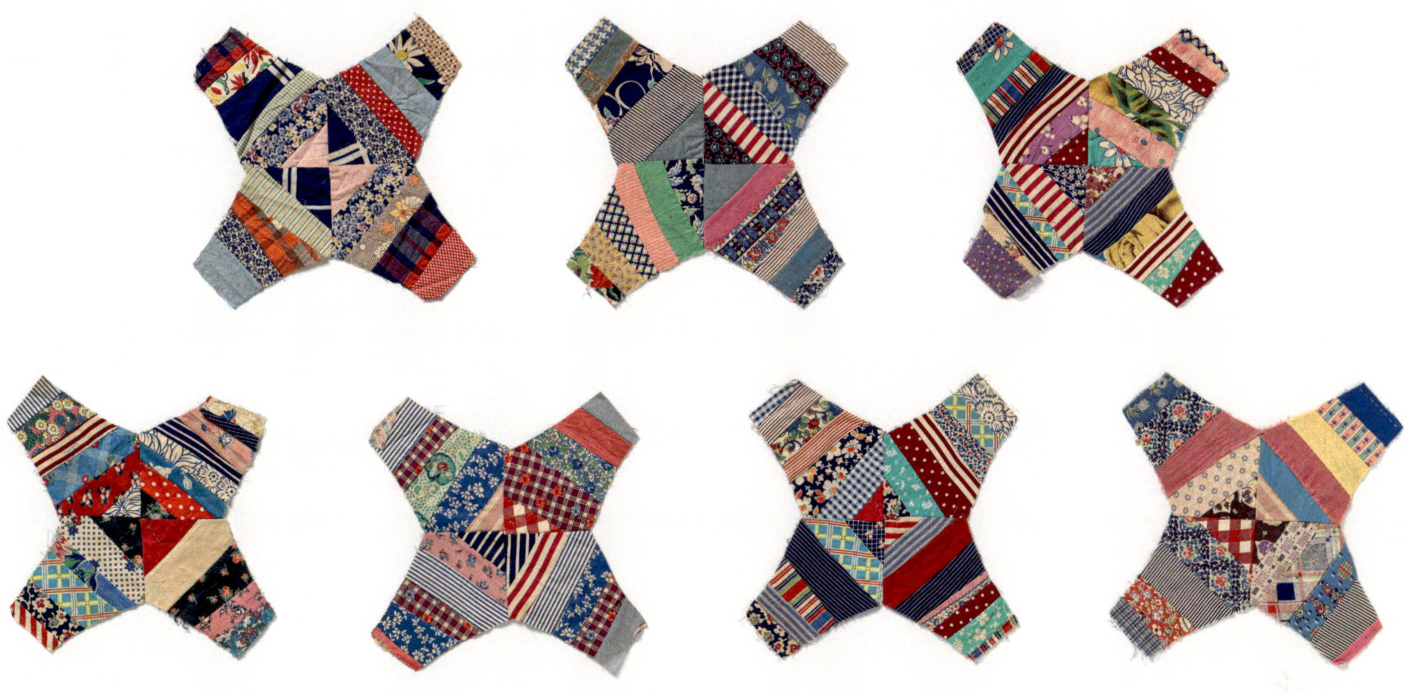

Front

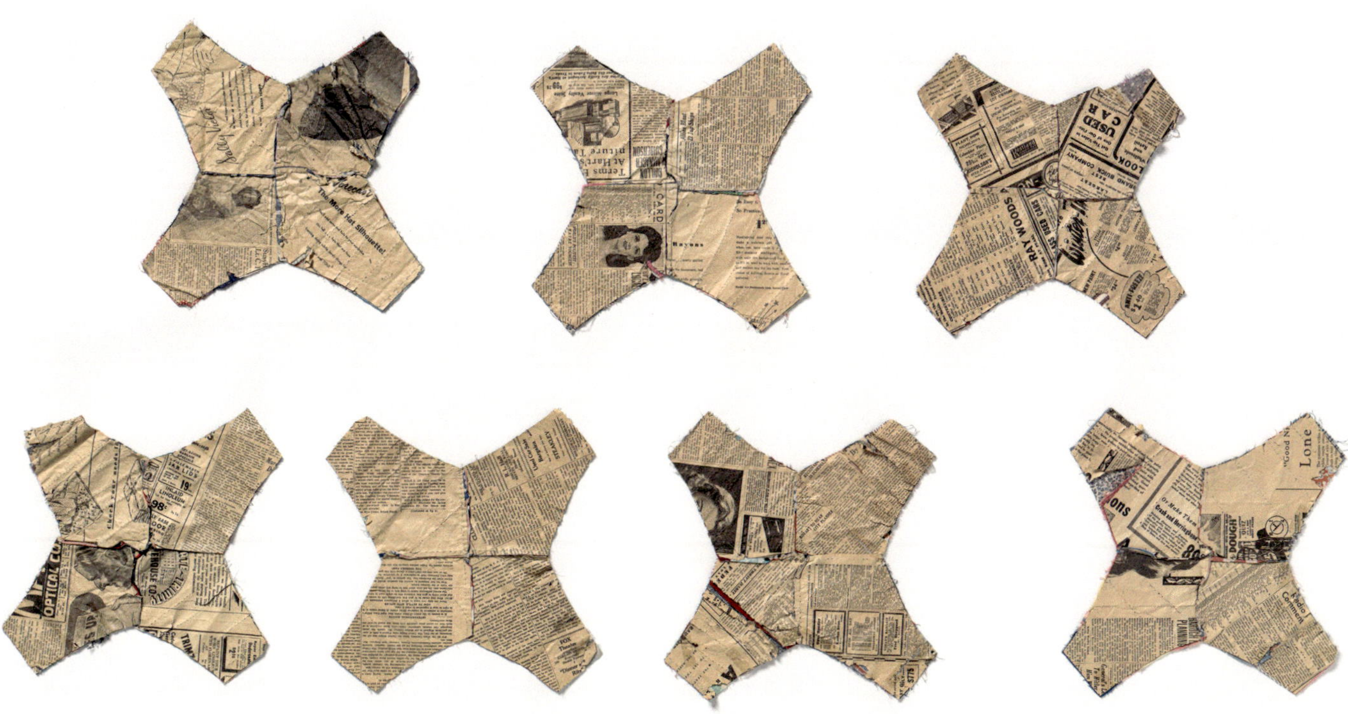

Back

22. Untitled (String crosses with newspaper backing)
Naomi Walker, after 1943; near Gene Autry, Oklahoma

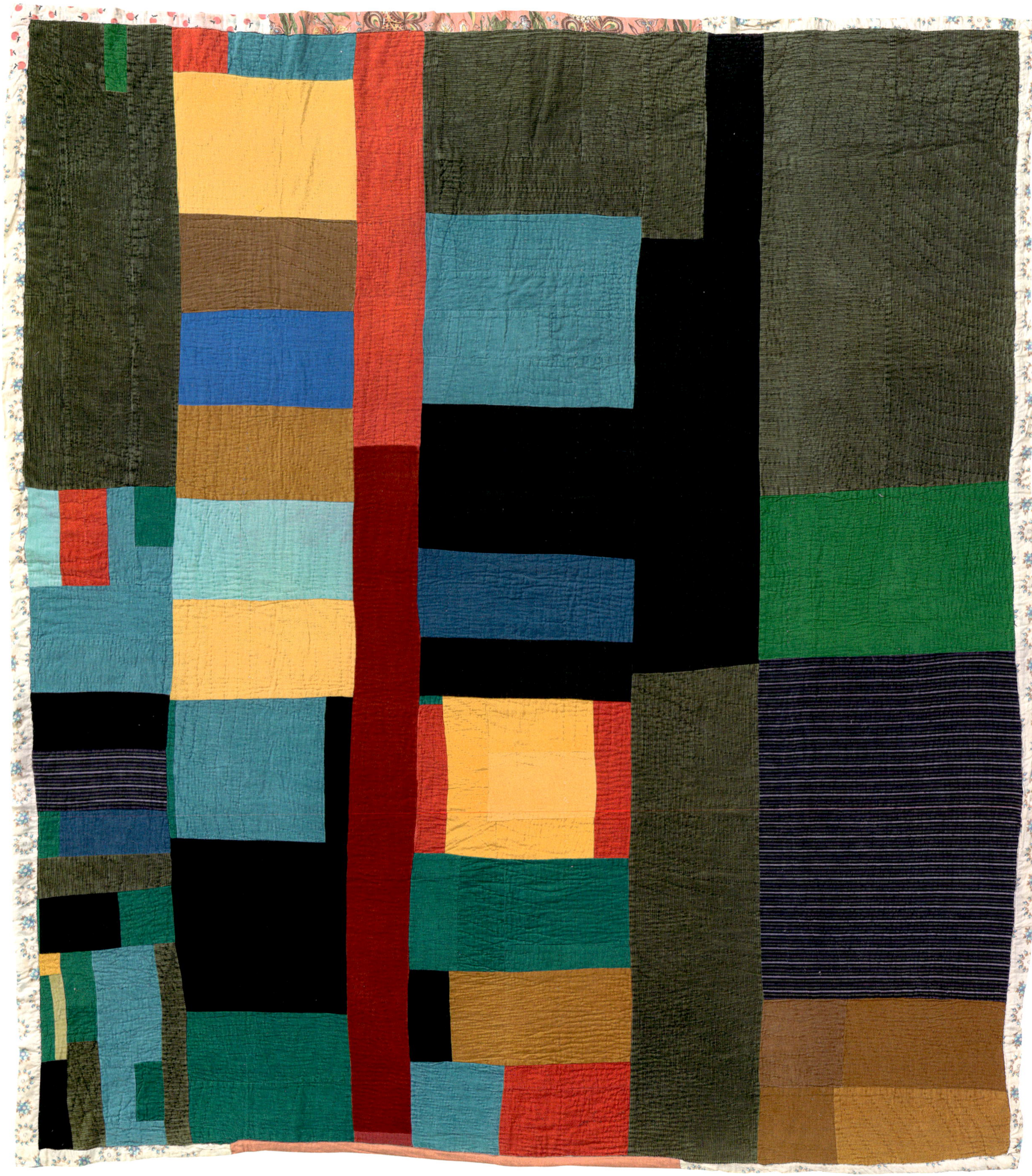

Front

23. Untitled (Strip)
Susan Pless, before 1944; Okfuskee County, Oklahoma
Gracell Tate, Pless's granddaughter, was the keeper of this quilt in Fresno, California, until 1993.

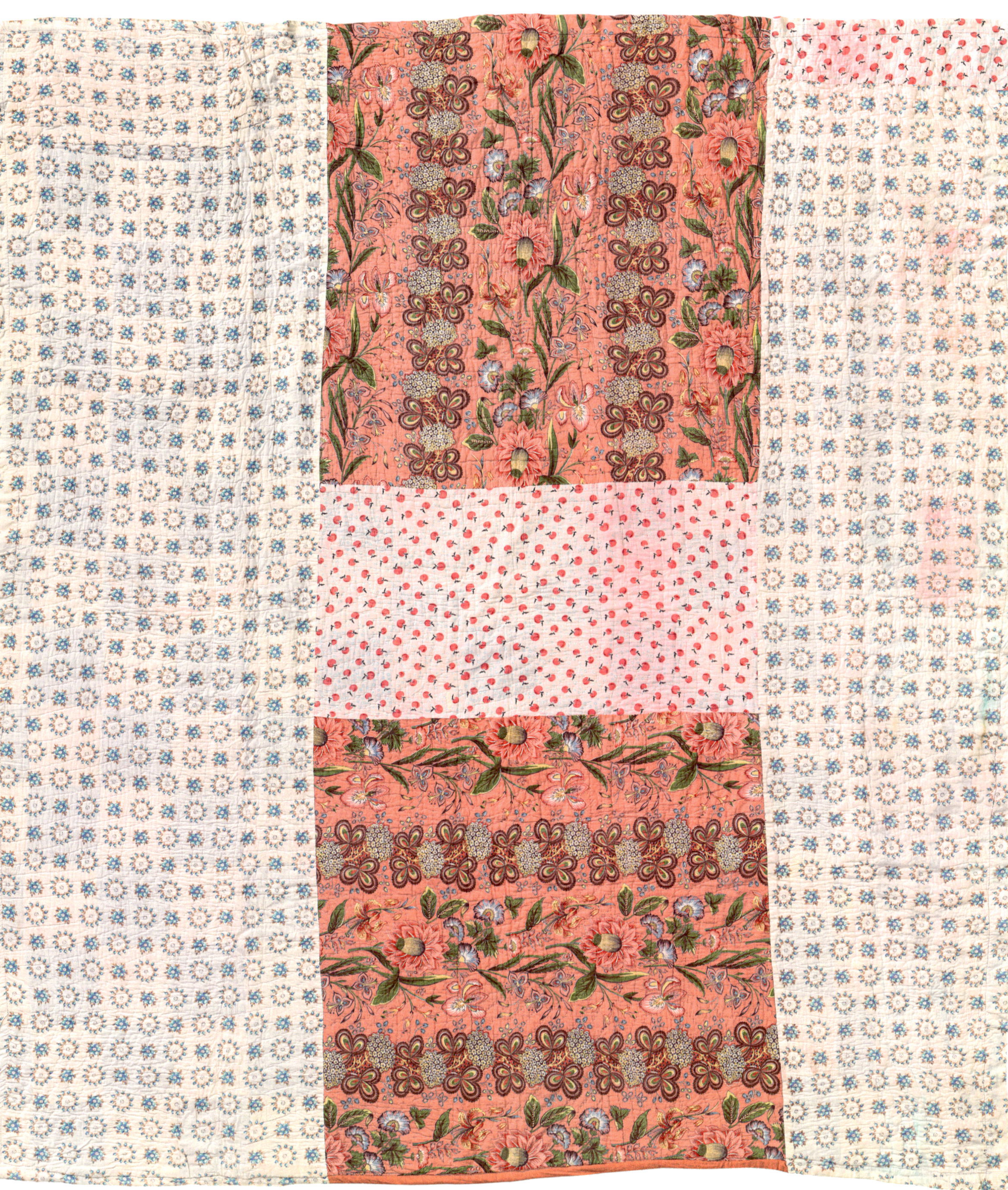

Back

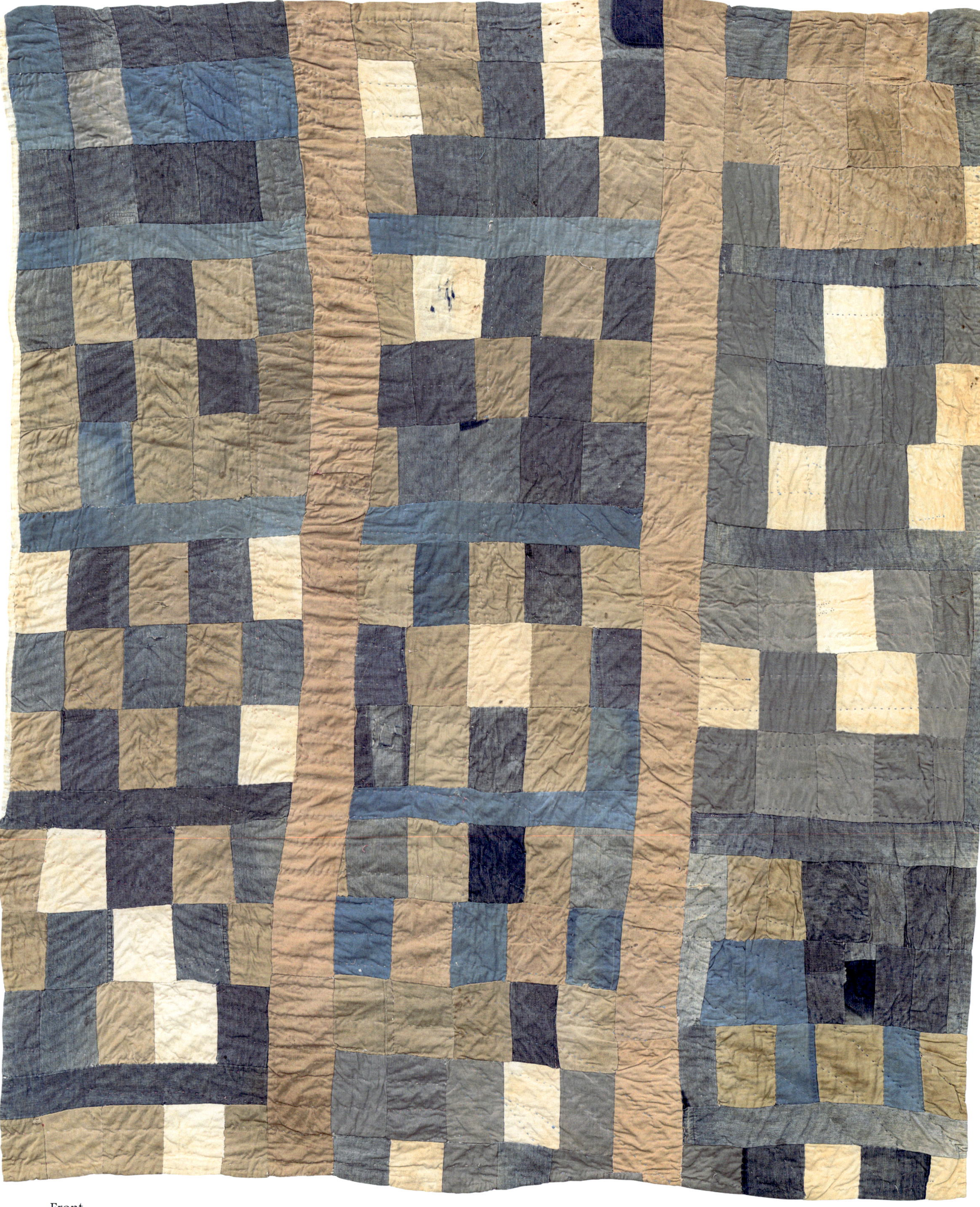

Front

24. Untitled (Fifteen Patch variation)
Joe Washington, 1940s–1950s; near Hawkins, Texas
Ruby Richard, Washington's daughter-in-law, was the keeper of this quilt until 1990.

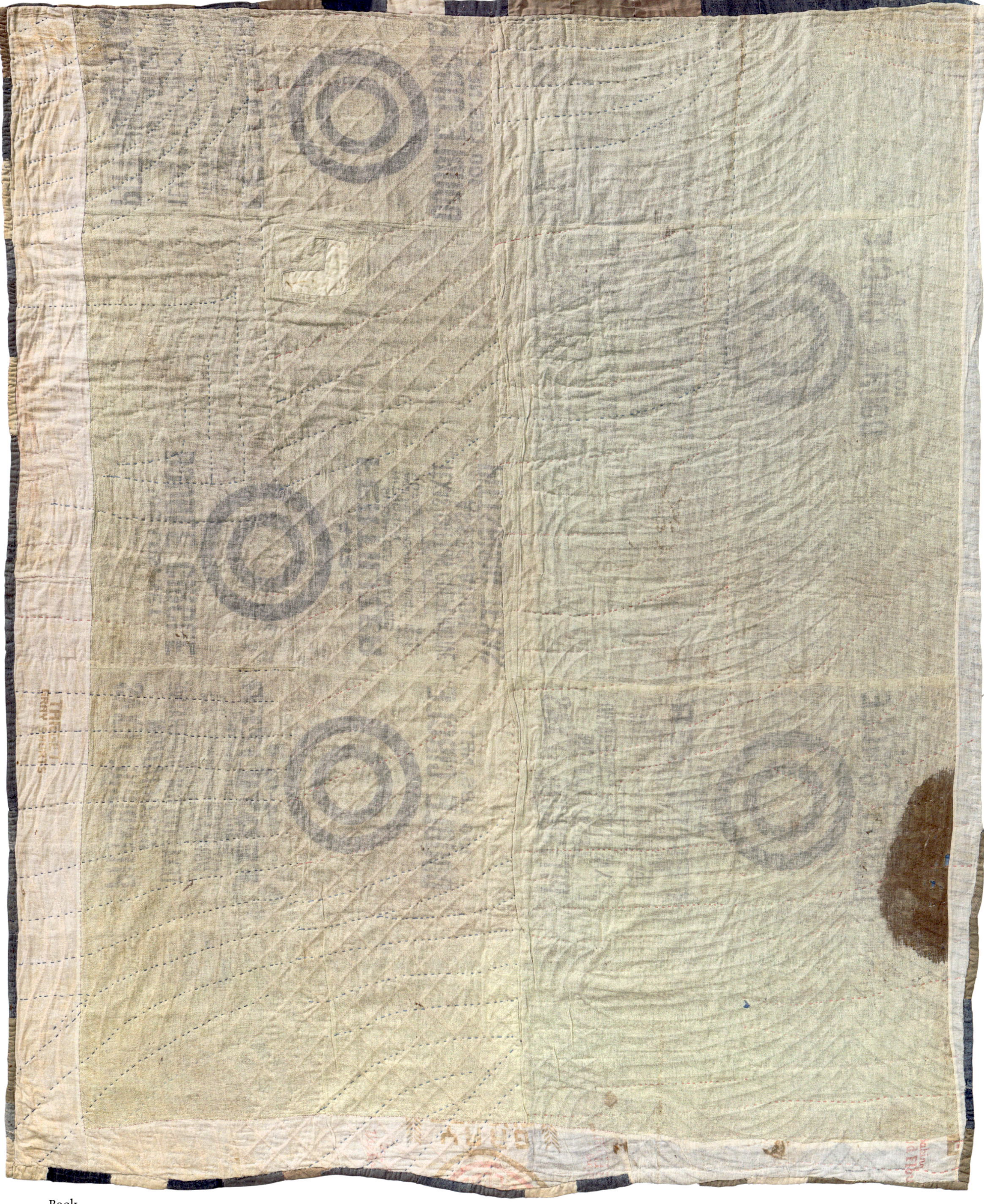

Back

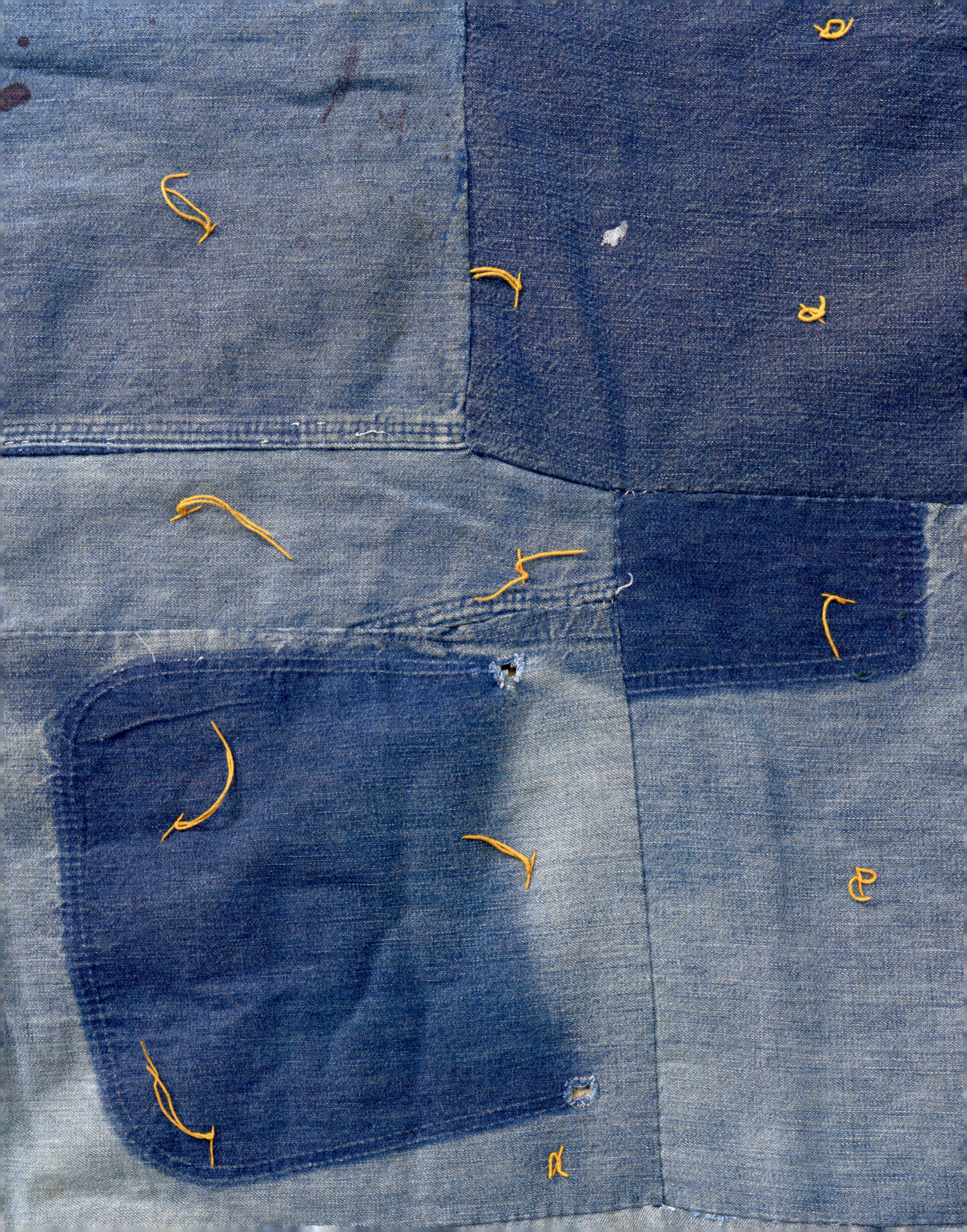

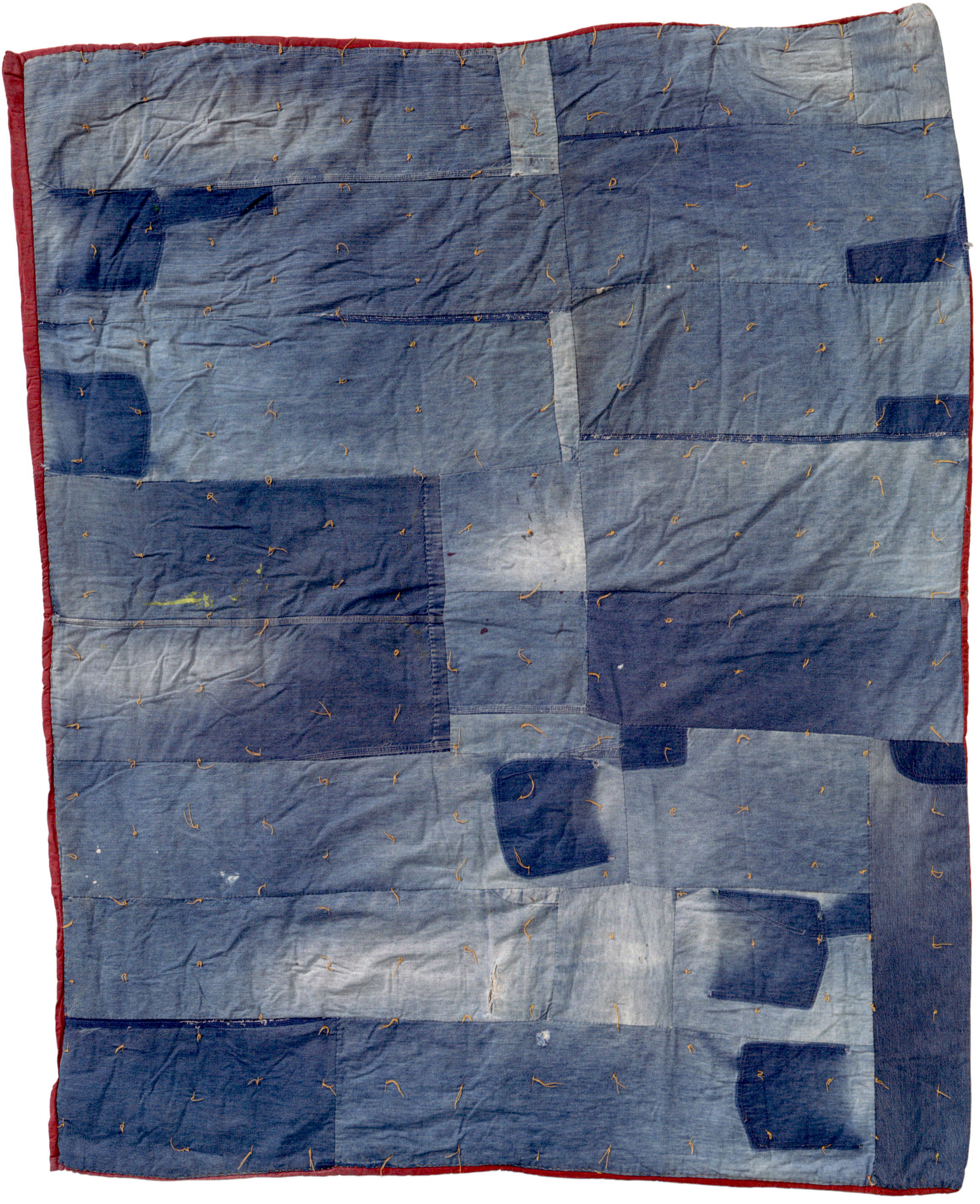

25. Untitled (Patchwork with work clothes)
Minnie Skinner, late 1940s; Alto, Texas

Detail

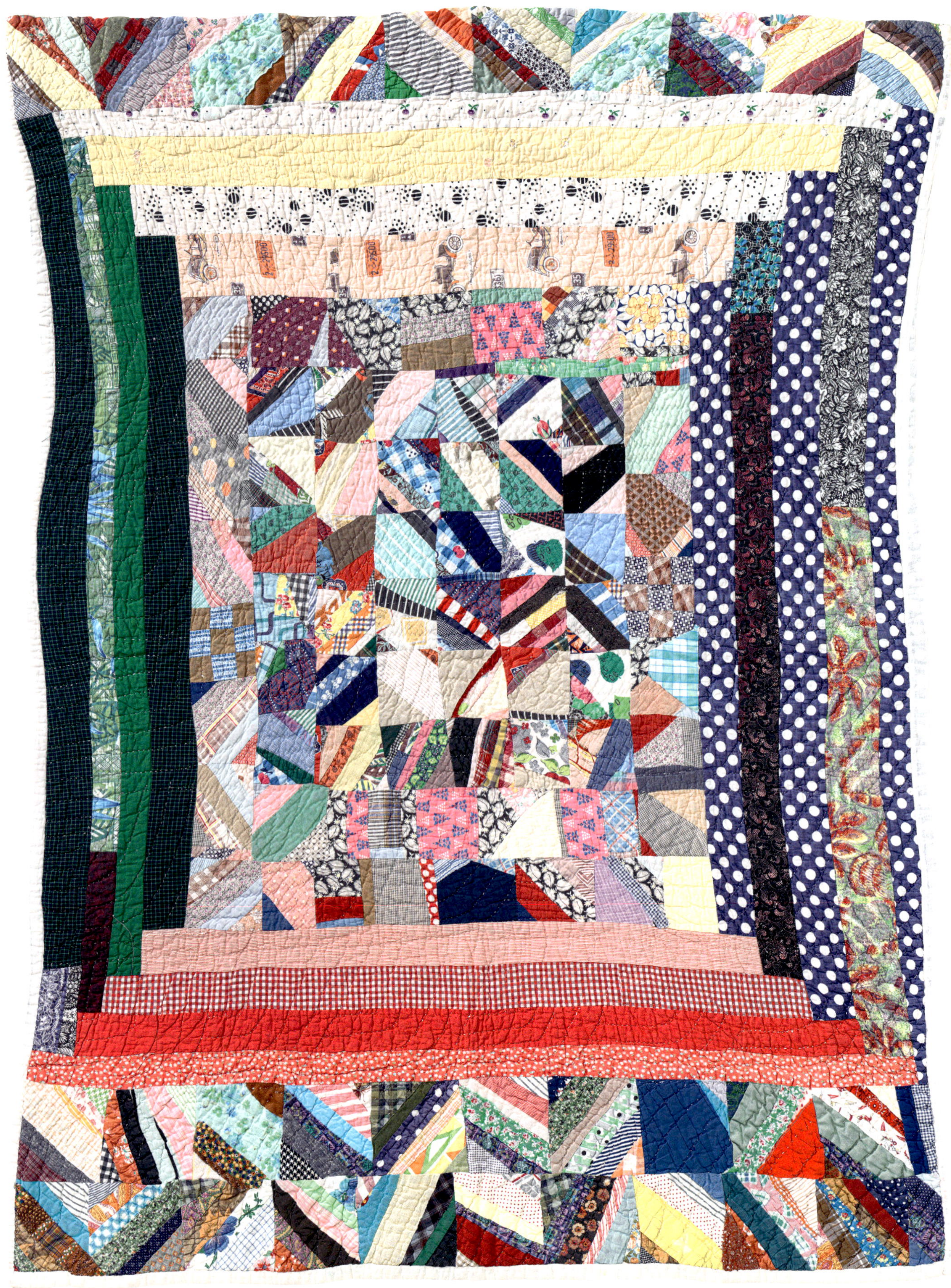

26. Untitled (String Medallion)
Some blocks pieced by Willia Ette Graham, before 1944; Texas
Completed by Willia Ette Graham, 1950s; Oakland, California
Repaired by Willia Ette Graham, 1985; Oakland, California

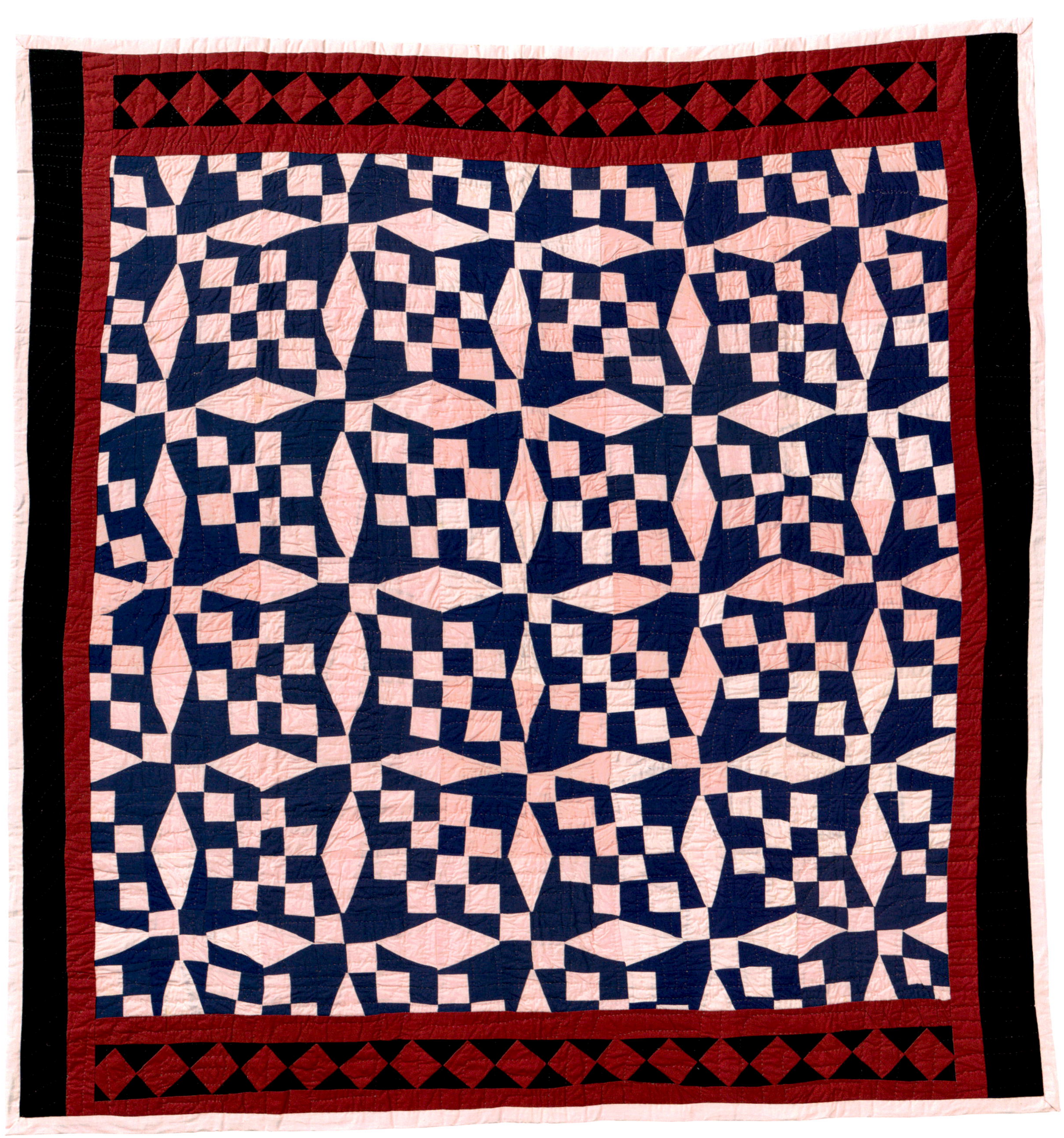

27. Untitled (Fifty-Four Forty or Fight)
Pieced by Jimmie Johnson and Laura Johnson Battise, 1940–1978; Oakland, California
Bordered by Arbie Williams, 1988; Oakland, California
Quilted by Willia Ette Graham, 1988; Oakland, California

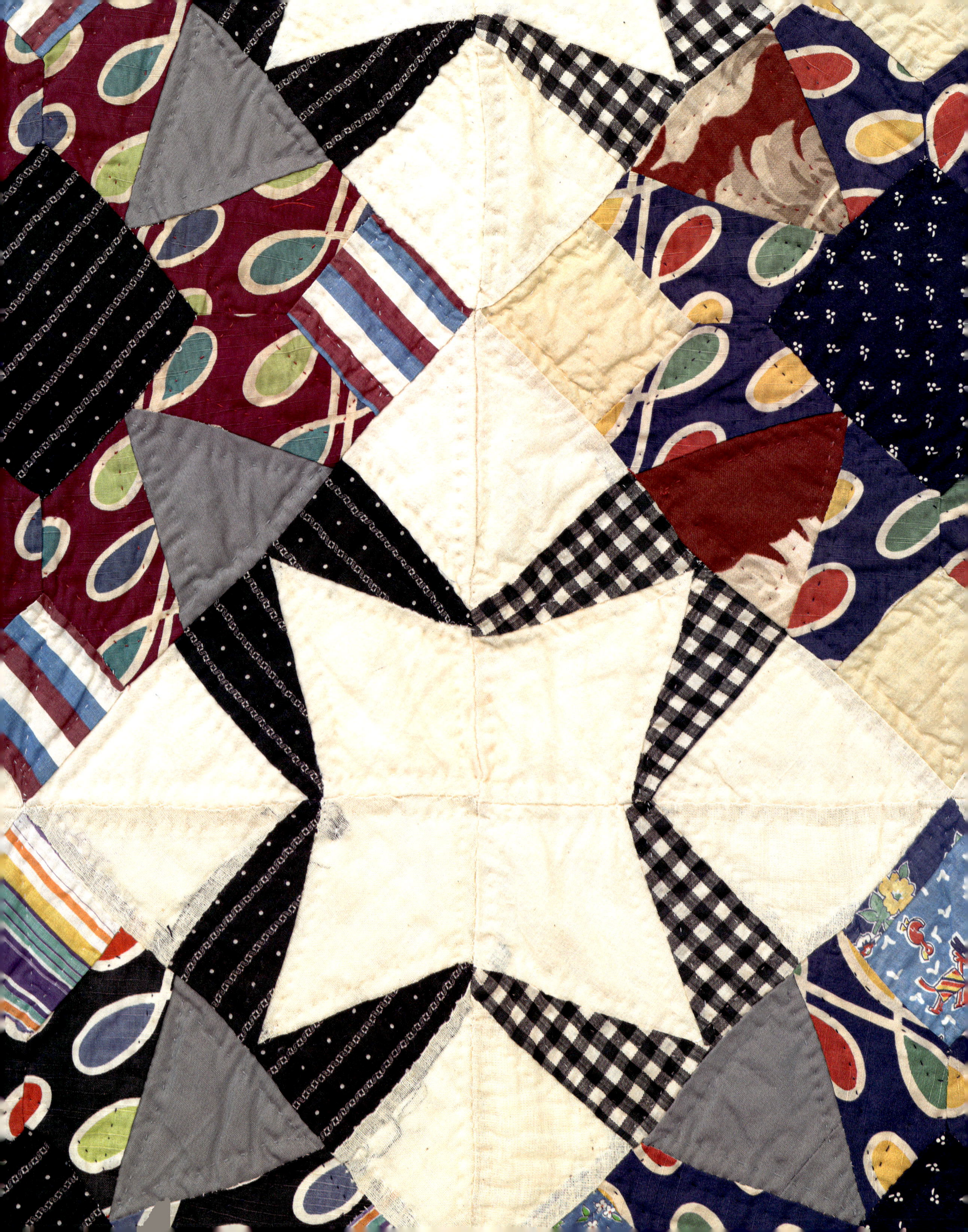

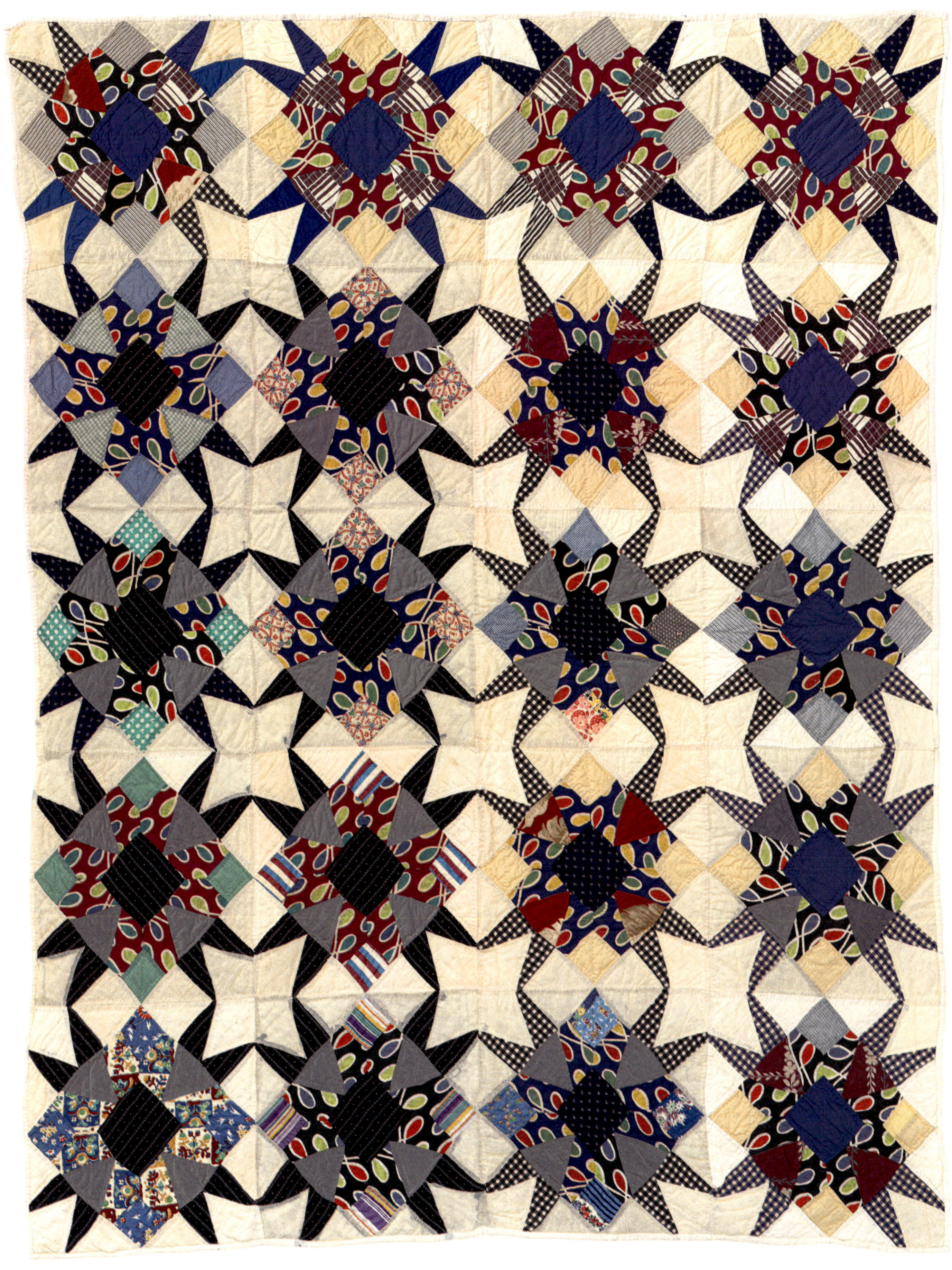

28. Untitled (Royal Star, Dog Tooth Violet, and Britches variations)
Pieced by Chaney Ella Peace, c. 1950; Shreveport, Louisiana
Quilted by Bessie Moore, c. 1989; Oakland, California
Lula Belle Zanders, Peace's niece, was the keeper of this quilt as a top until 1981.

Detail

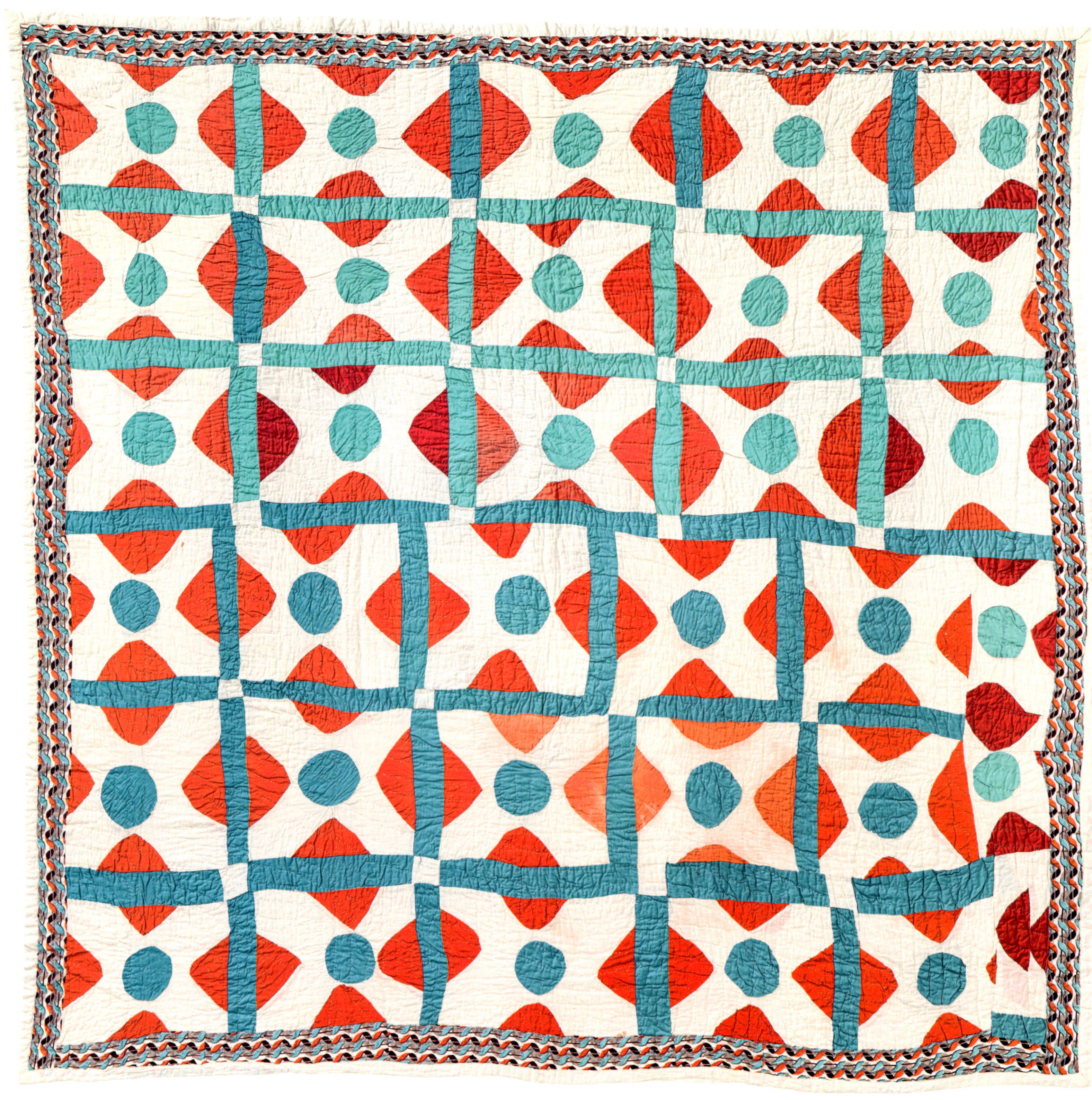

29. Untitled (Cross and Circles)
Pieced by Warren Wise, c. 1950; Prescott, Arkansas
Quilted by Willia Ette Graham, 1985; Oakland, California

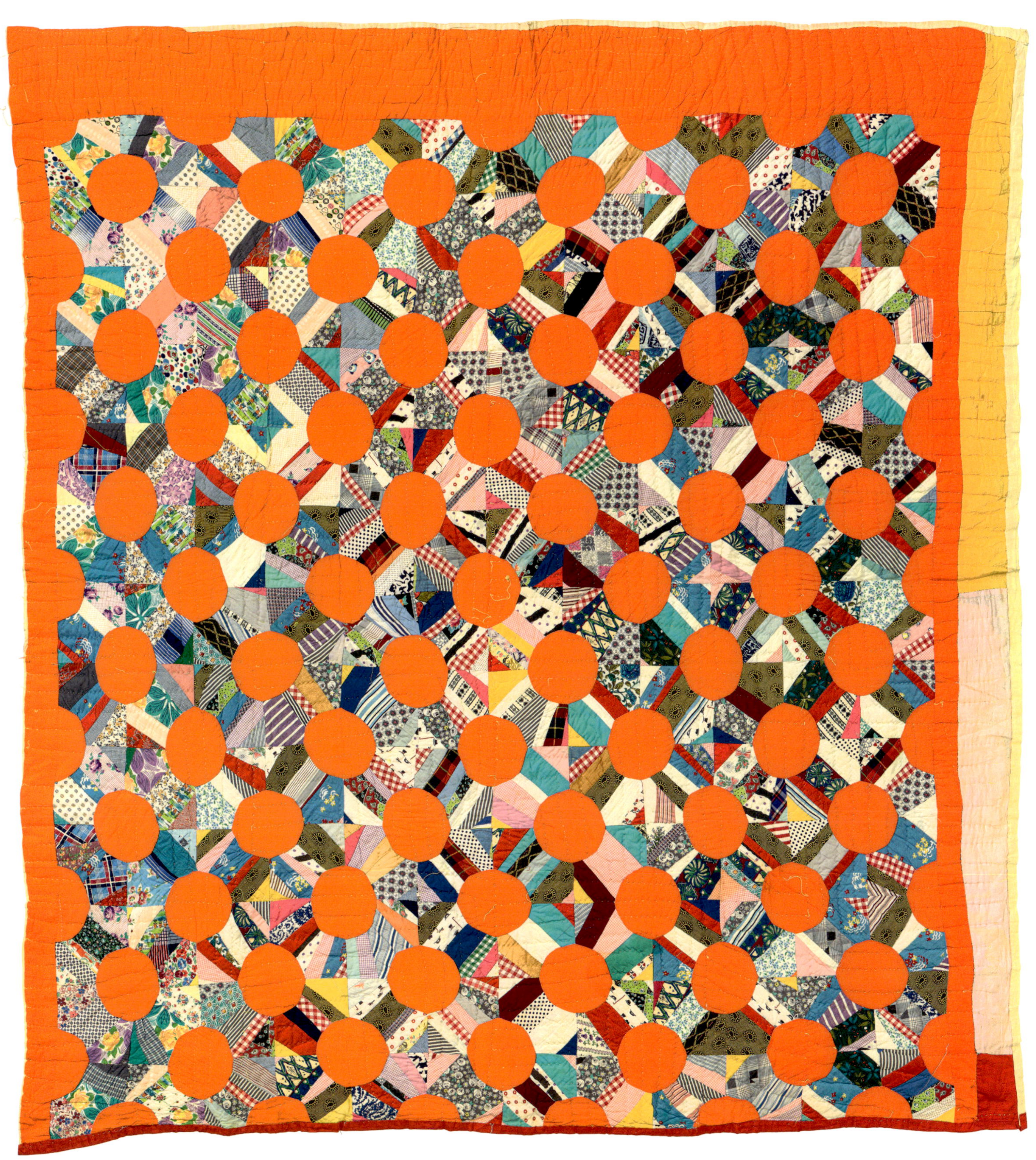

30. Untitled (Snowball String)
Arbie Major, c. 1950–1952; Paraloma, Arkansas

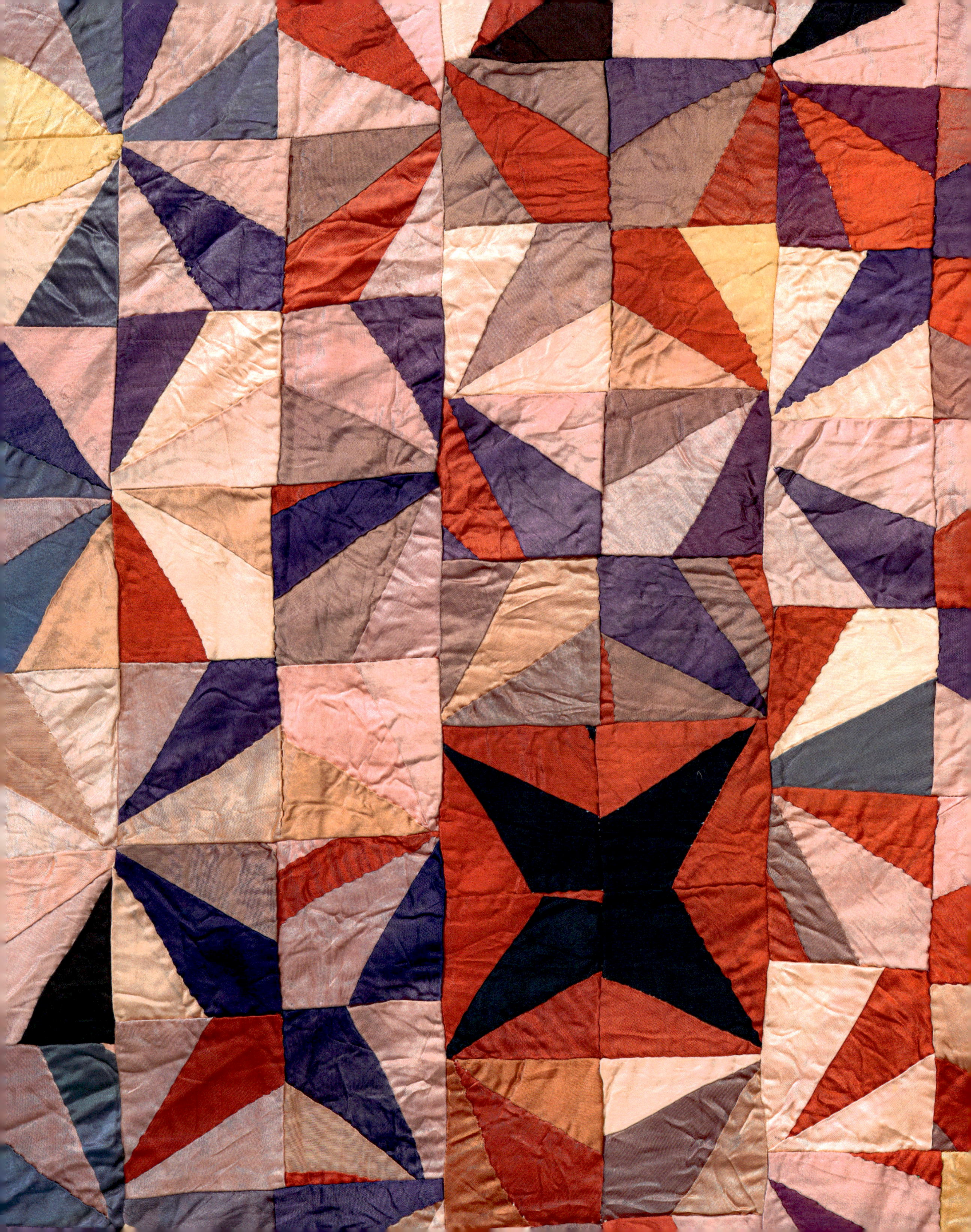

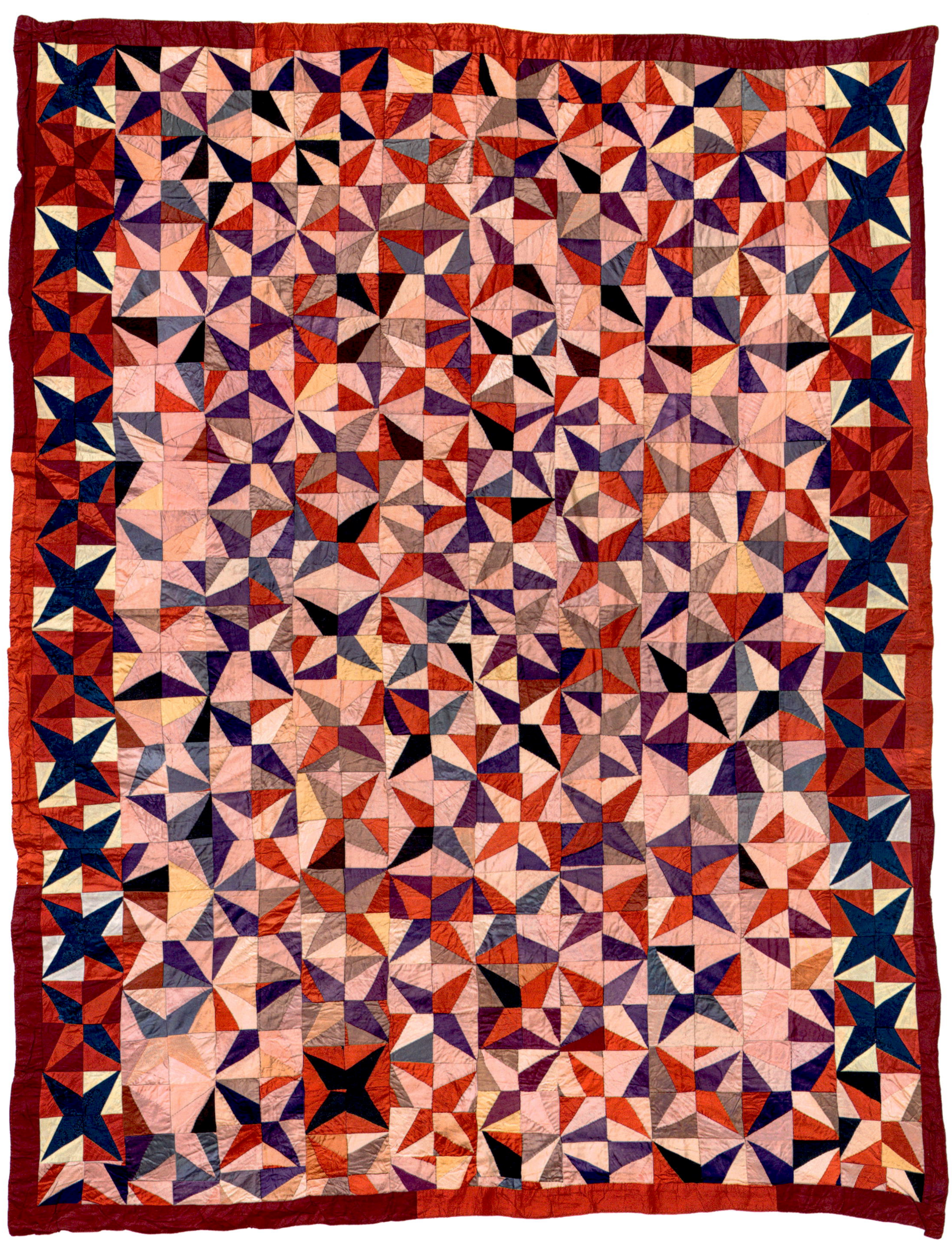

31. Untitled (Crossed Canoes variation)
Zula Mae Johnson, 1951; Oakland, California

Detail

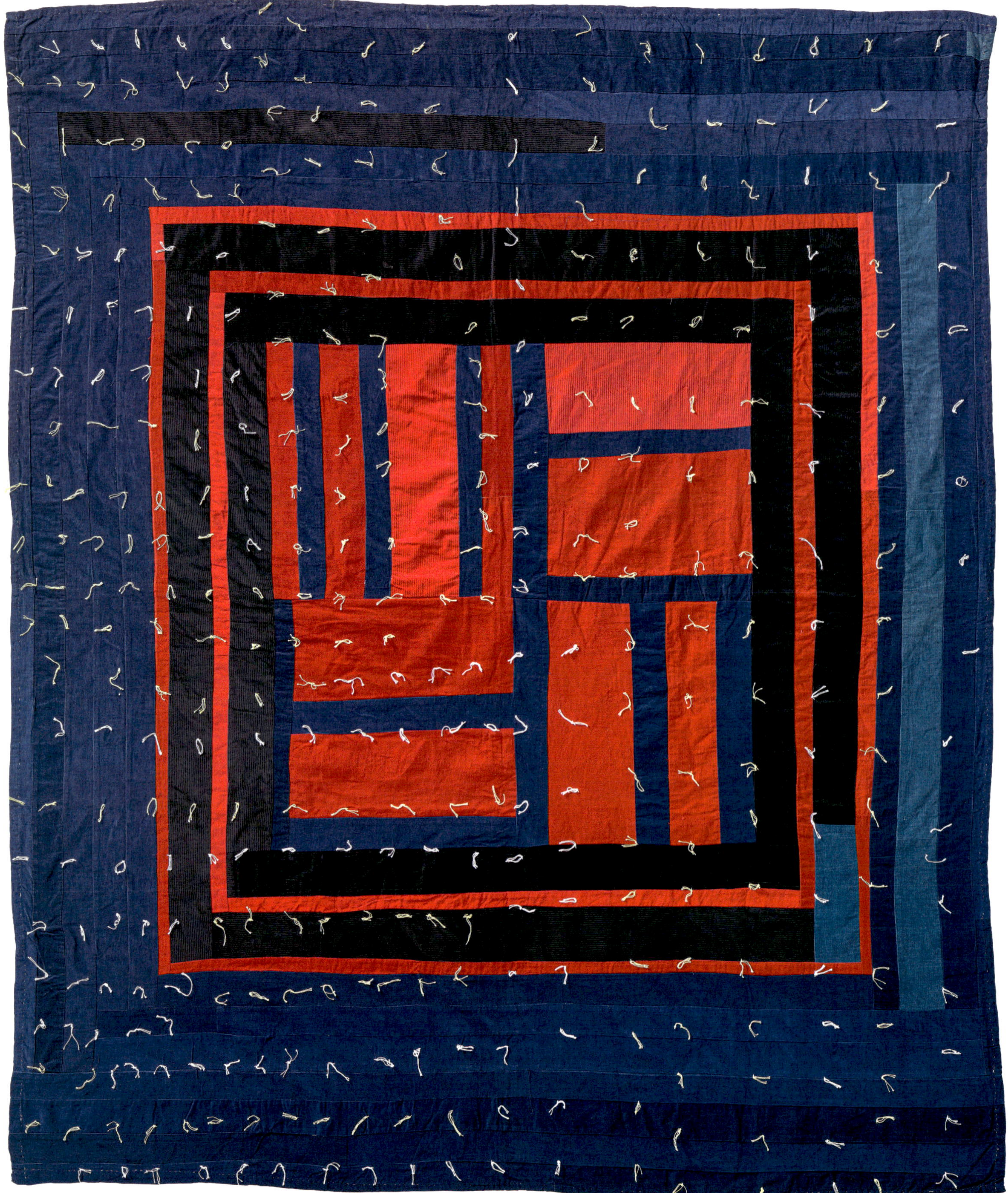

Front

32. Untitled (Roman Stripe Medallion)
Elizabeth Munn, c. 1951–52; Ozan, Arkansas

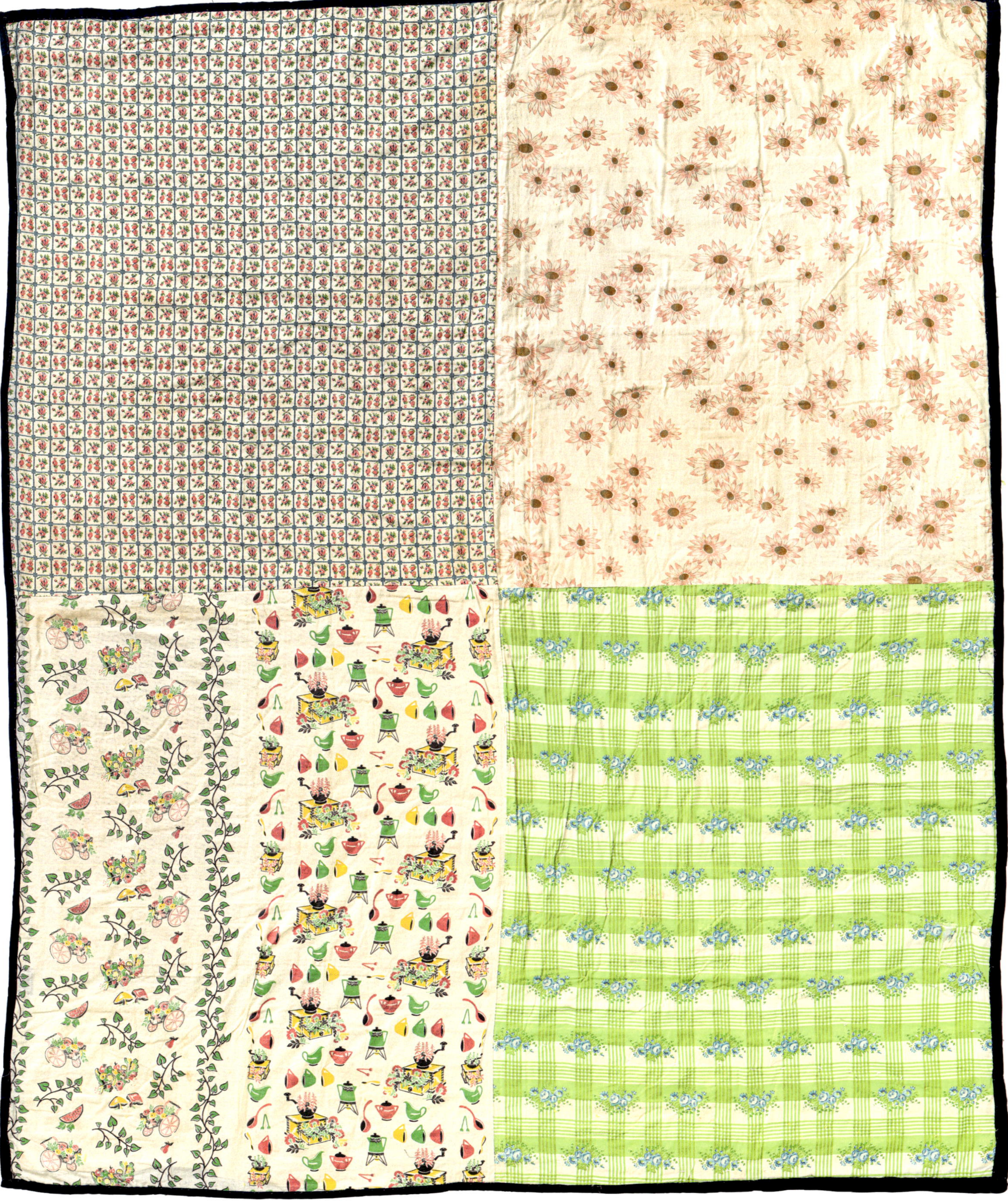

Back

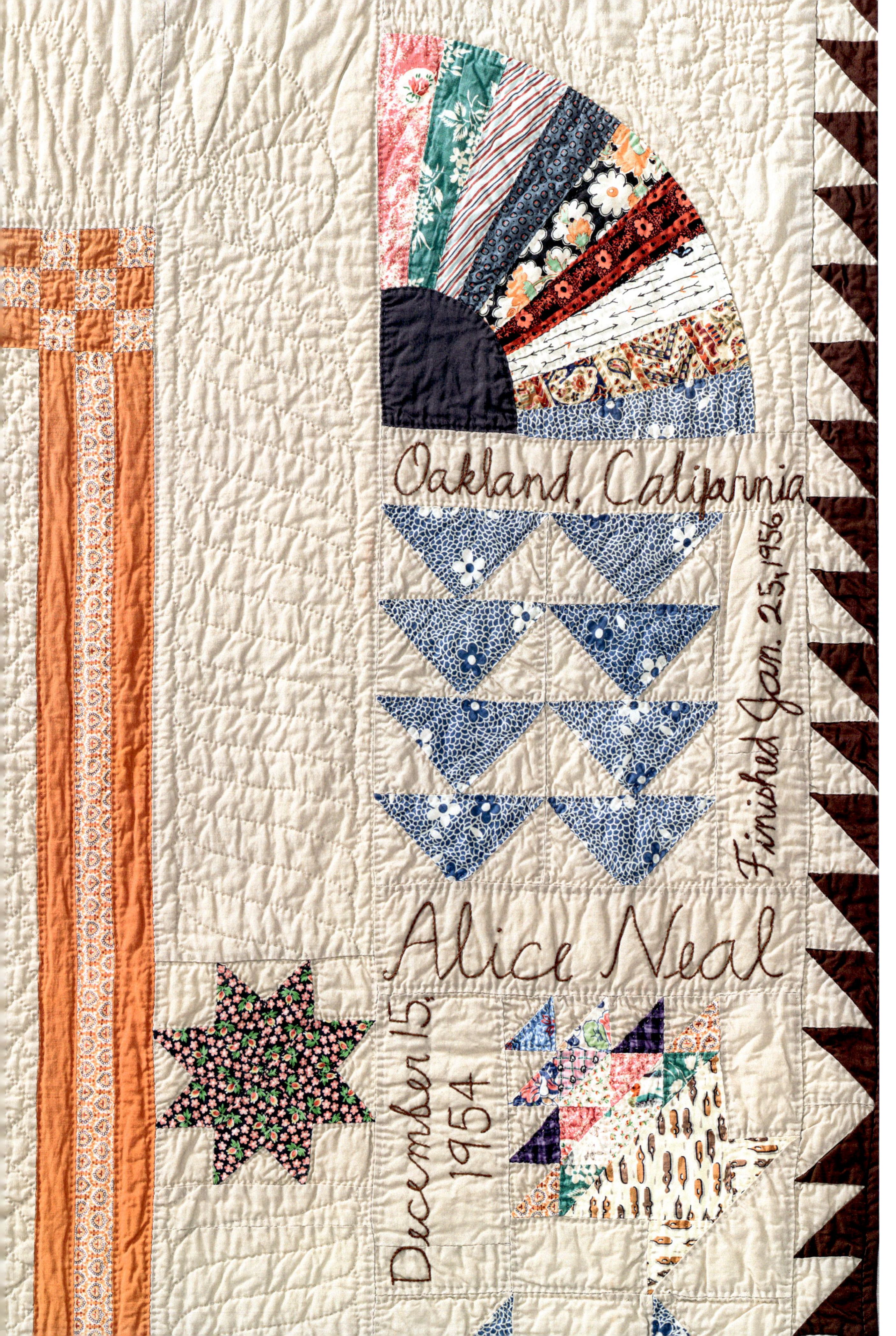

Detail of embroidered text

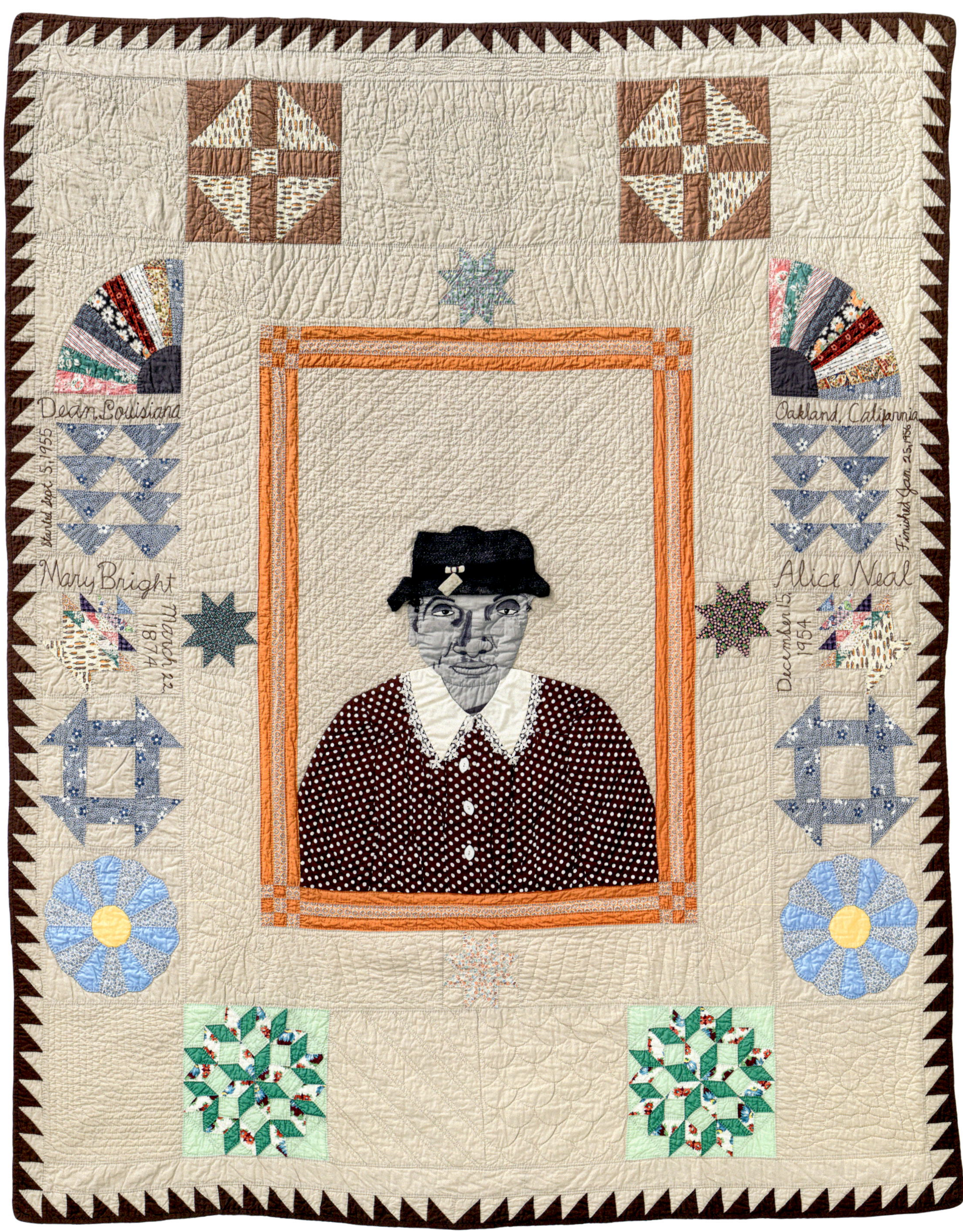

33. Mary Bright Commemorative Quilt (with Dresden Plate, Monkey Wrench, Wild Goose Chase, Fan, Basket of Flowers, Star of Lemoyne, Nine Patch blocks)
Alice Neal, 1955-1956; Oakland, California

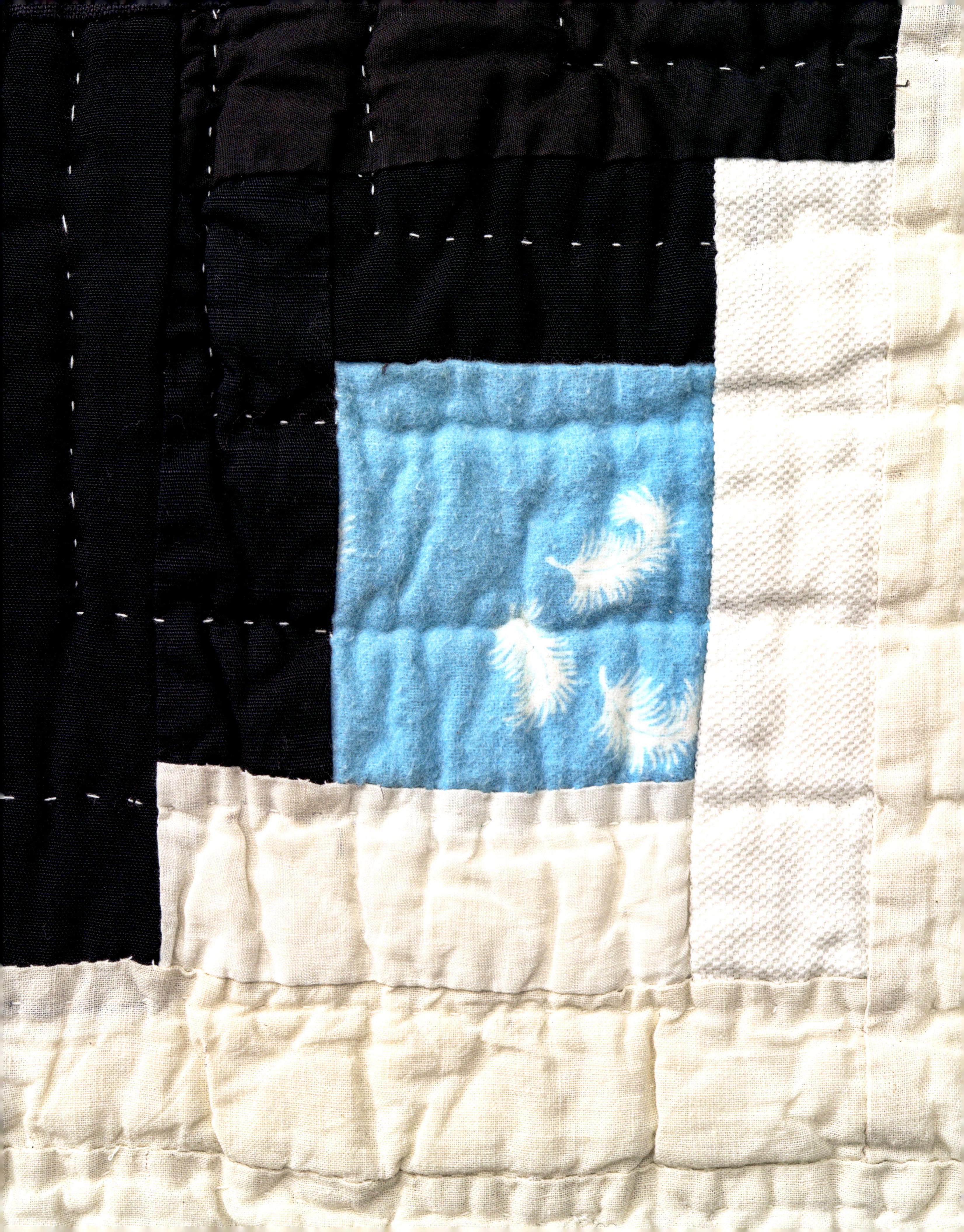

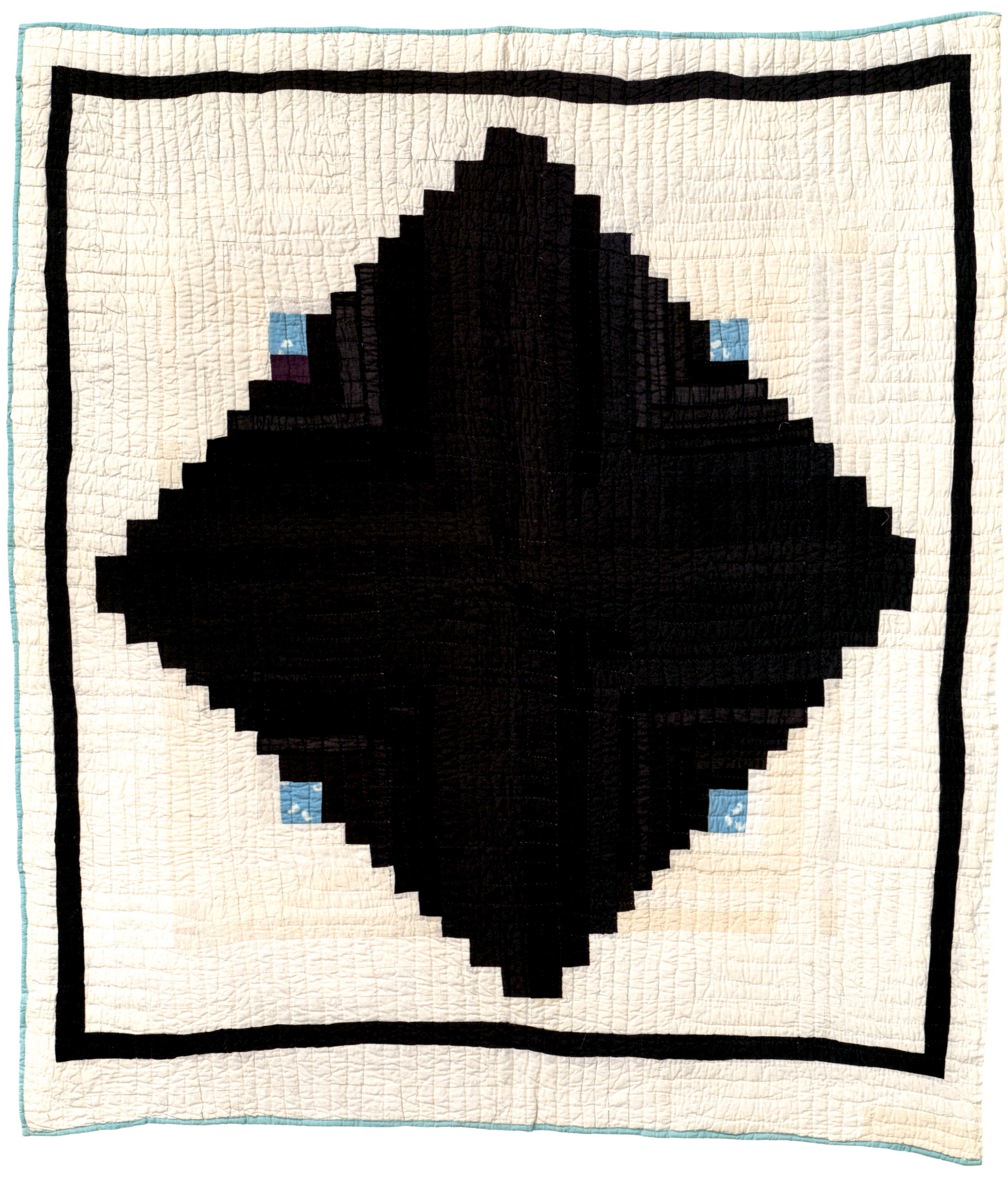

34. Untitled (Log Cabin)
Pieced by Louisa Fite, 1950s–1960s; Beckville, Texas
Quilted by Joan Thompson, c. 1970; Holland Quarters community (Carthage), Texas

Detail

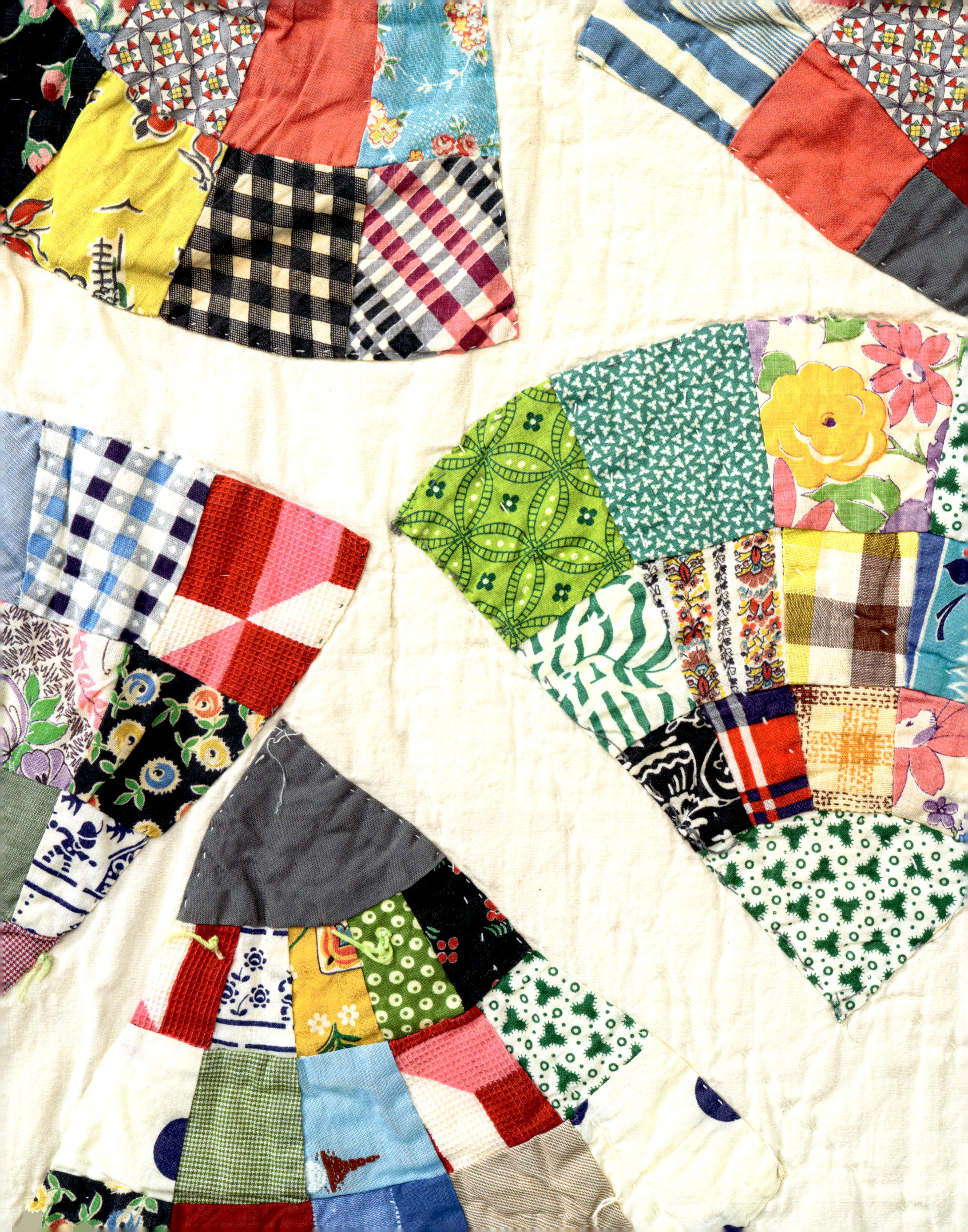

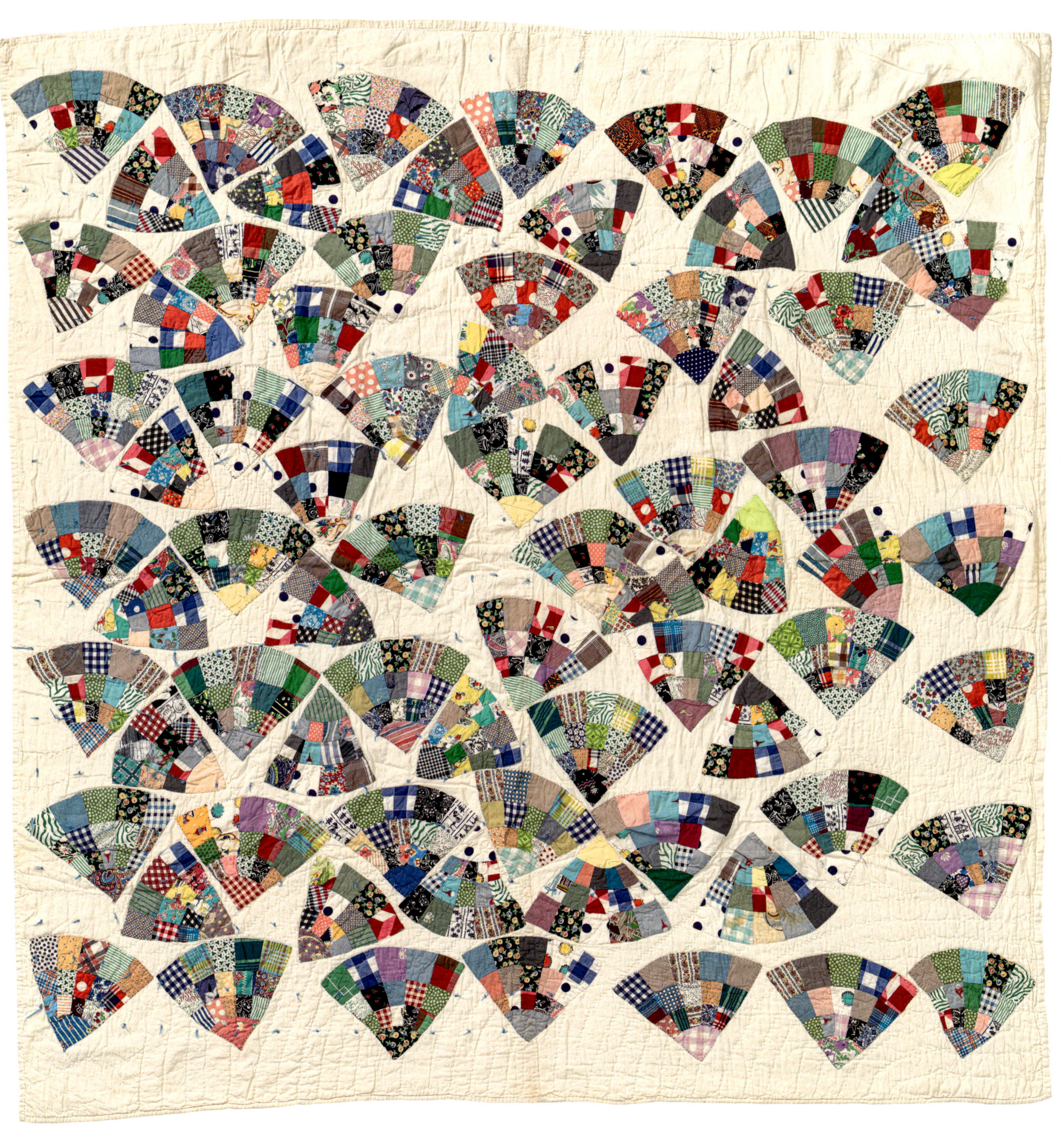

35. Untitled (Fans)
Quinciana Tatmon, 1950s–1960s; Oakland, California
Annabelle Pace, Tatmon's daughter, was the keeper of this quilt until 1992.

Detail

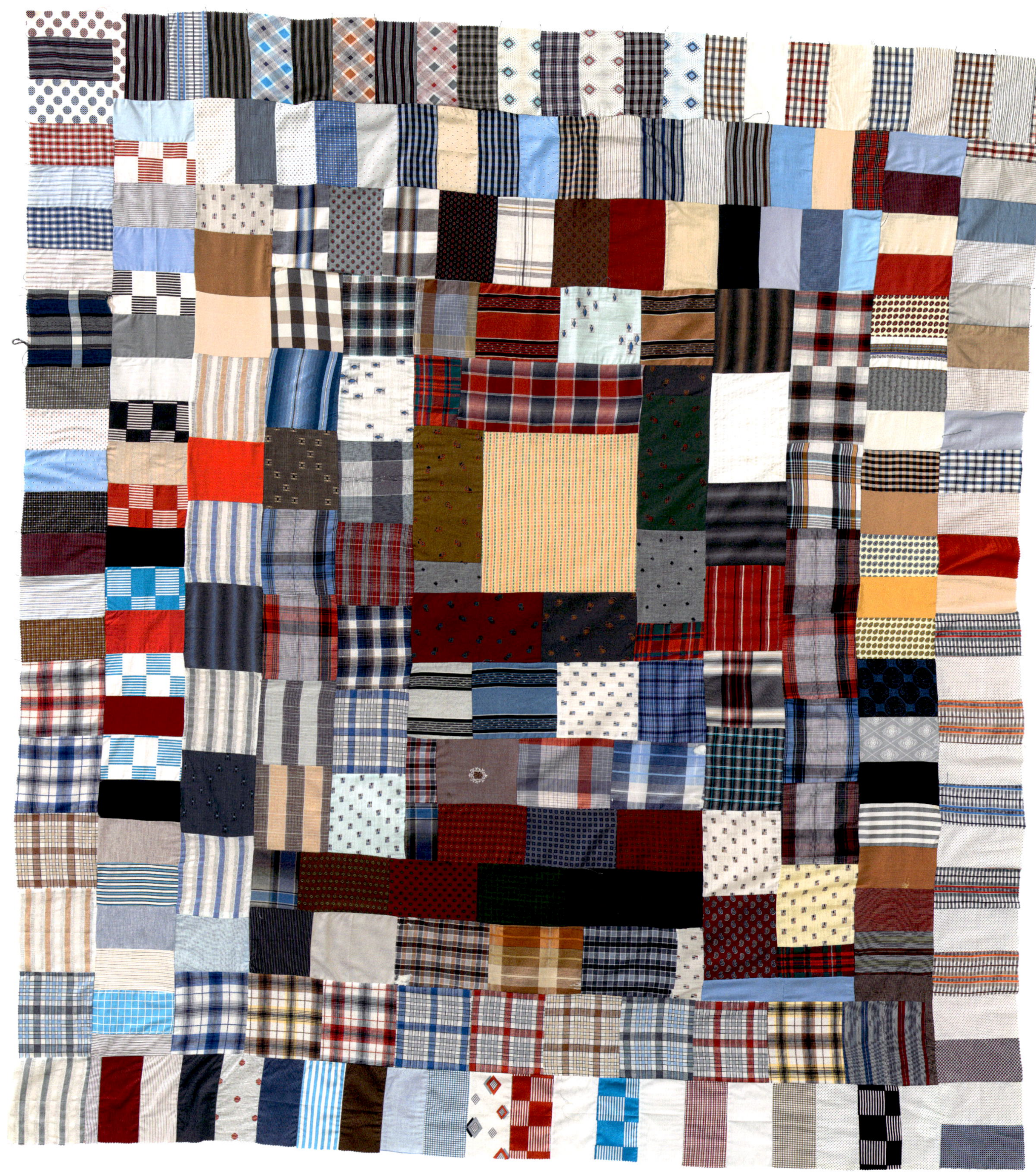

36. Untitled top (Medallion)
Attributed to Emma Smith, possibly 1950s–1970s; Monroe, Louisiana, or San Francisco, California

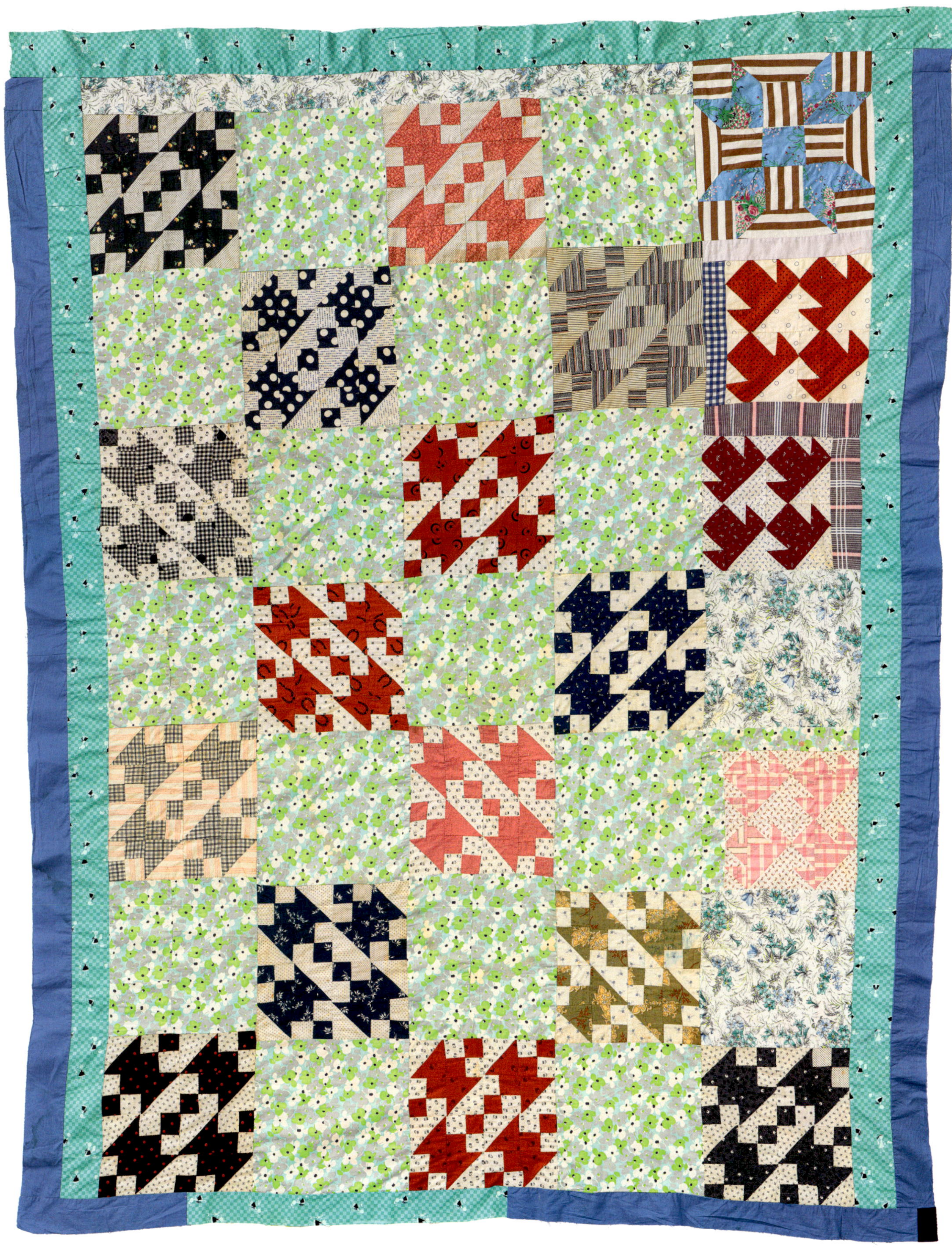

37. Untitled top (Jacob's Ladder, T, Farmer's Daughter)
Some blocks pieced by Sarah Moore, 1890s–1910s; Ruston, Louisiana, and/or Oklahoma
Pieced by Effie Edwards, 1960s; California
Zula Mae Johnson, Moore's granddaughter and Edwards's daughter, was the keeper of this quilt until 1982.

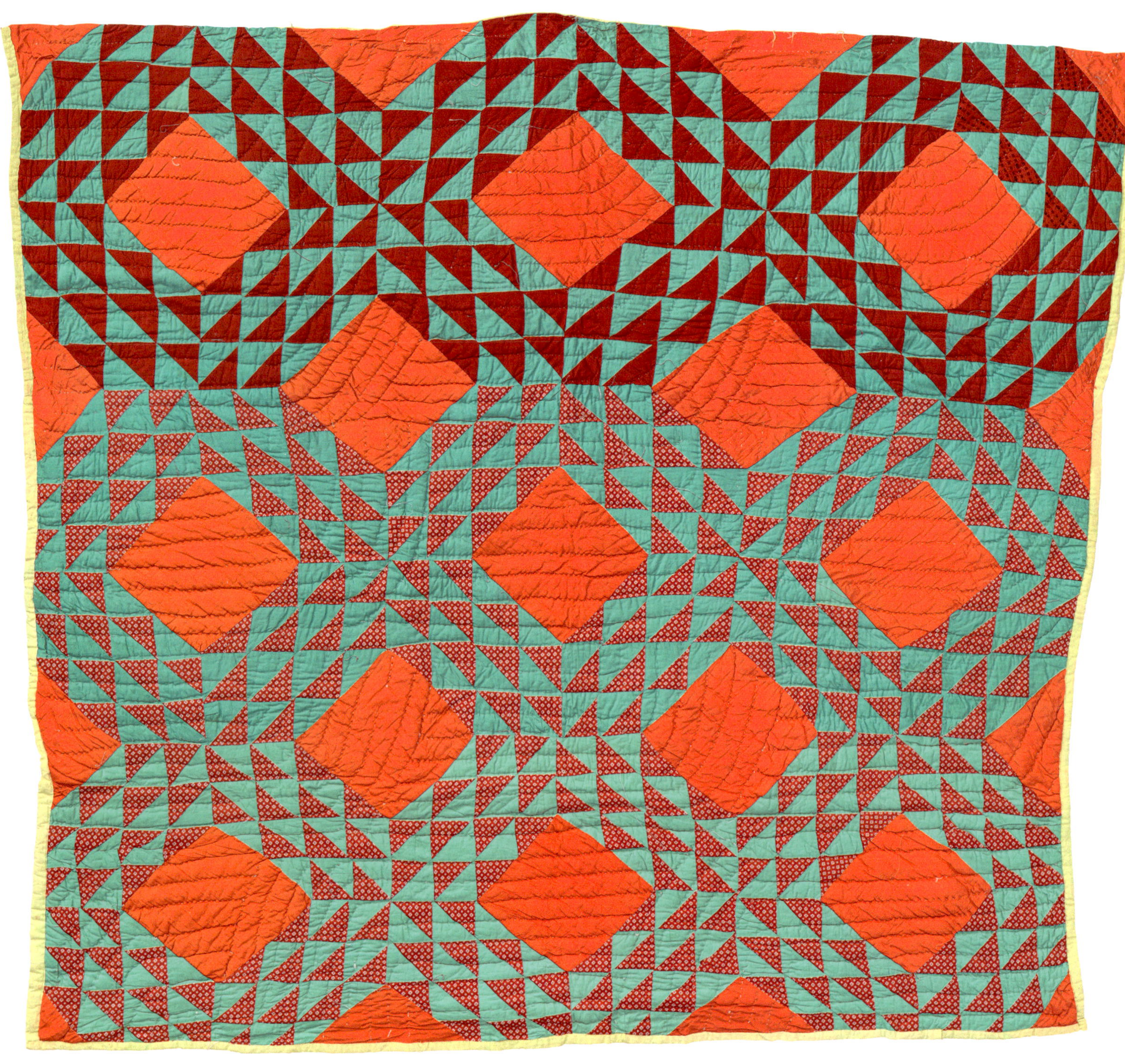

38. Untitled (Ocean Wave)
Beauty Vaughns, 1963; Fresno, California

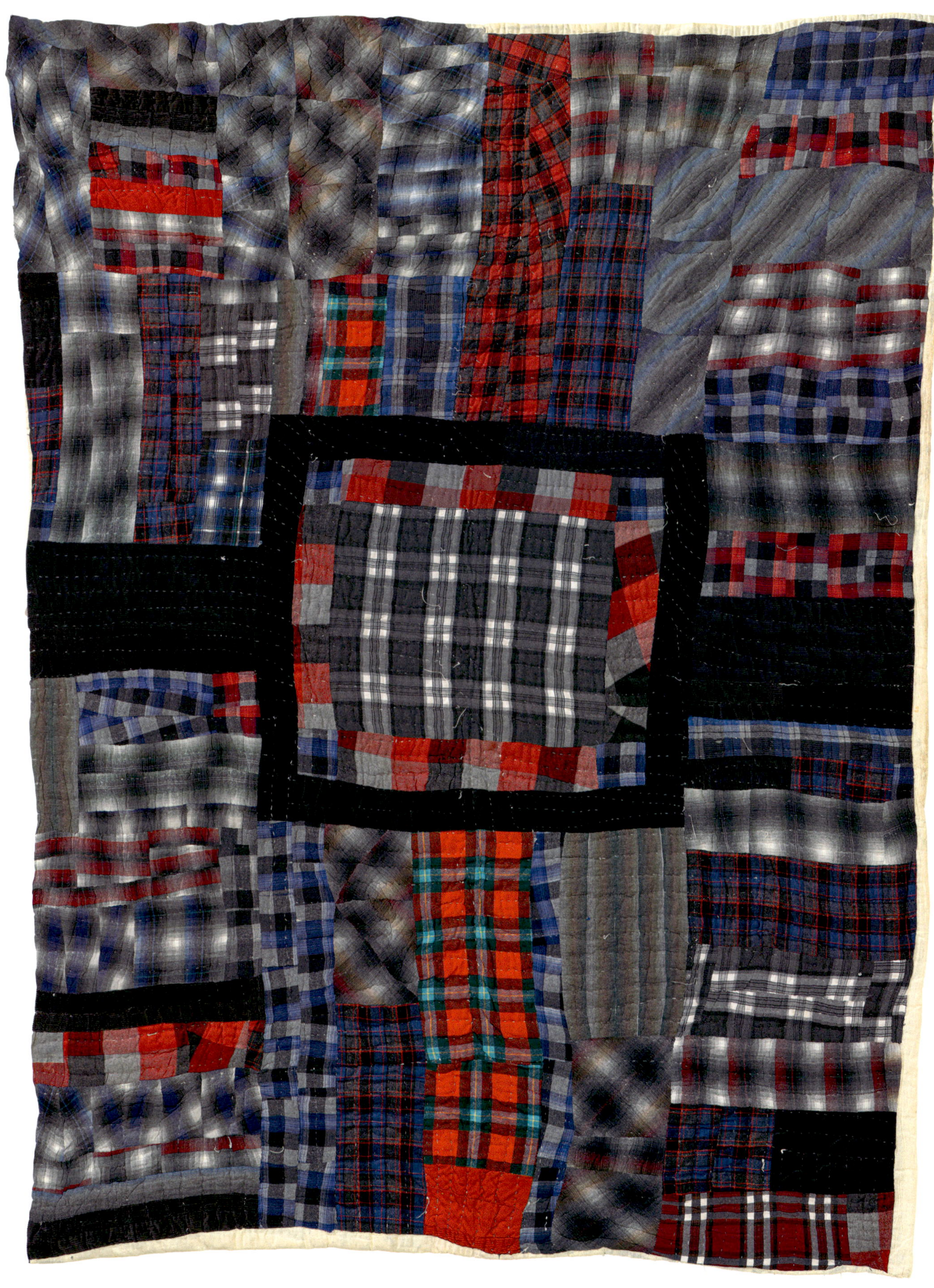

39. Untitled (Medallion)
Pieced by Maple Jean Swift, 1960s; St. Luke's community, Ozan, Arkansas
Quilted by Florine Taylor, 1960s; Ozan, Arkansas

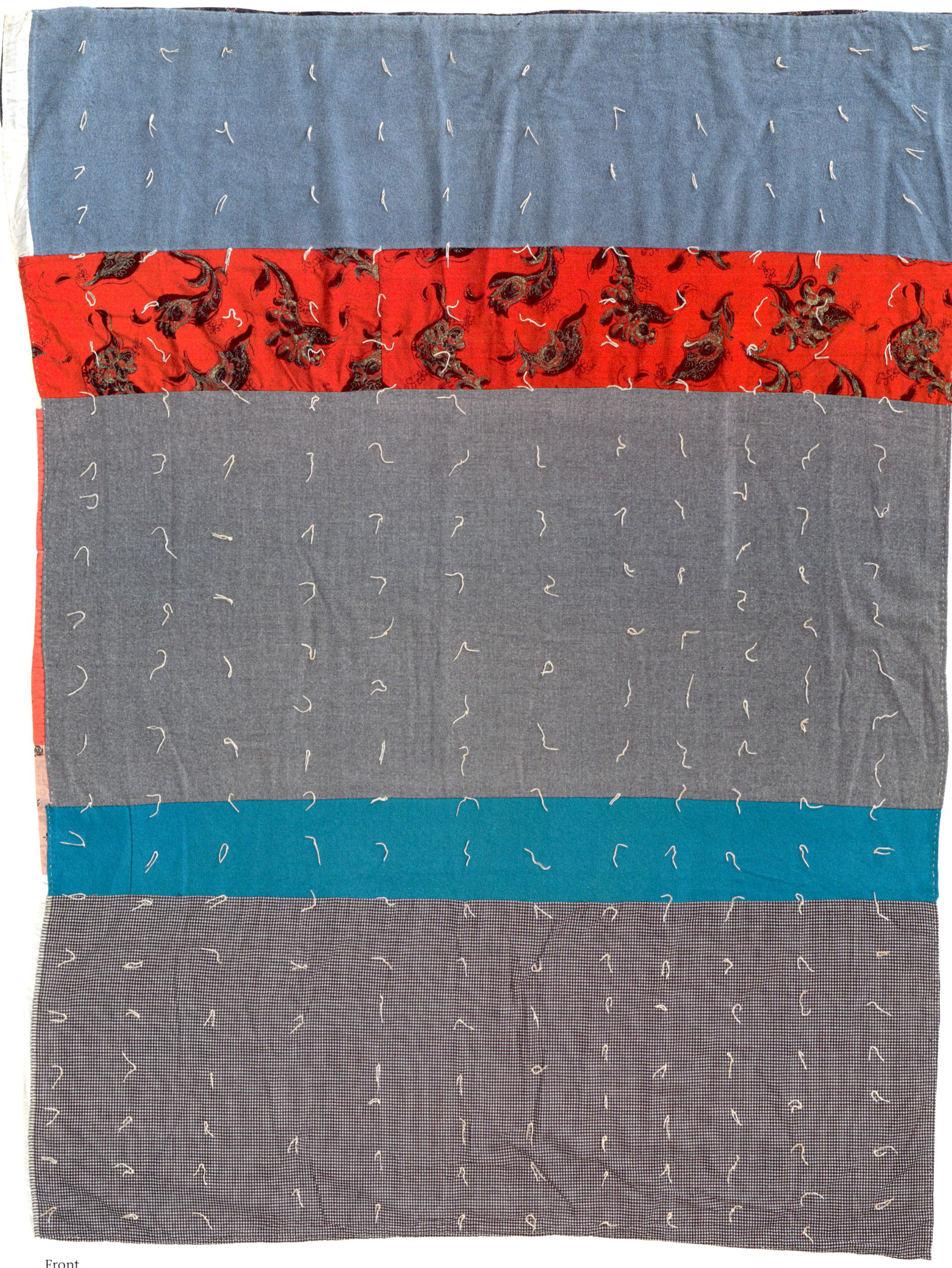

Front

40. Untitled (Strip)
Maudra Walker, 1960s–1970s; Oklahoma or San Mateo, California

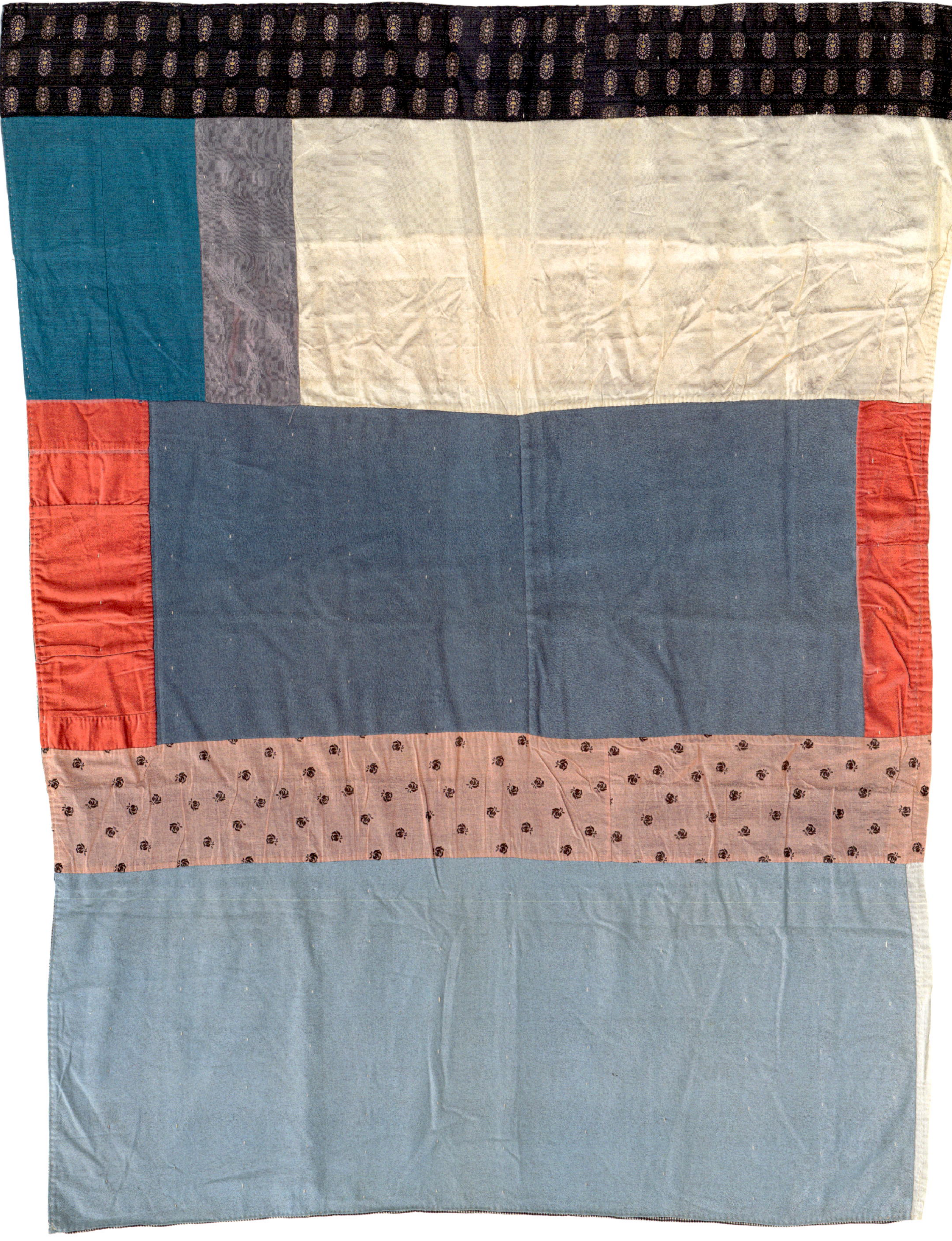

Back

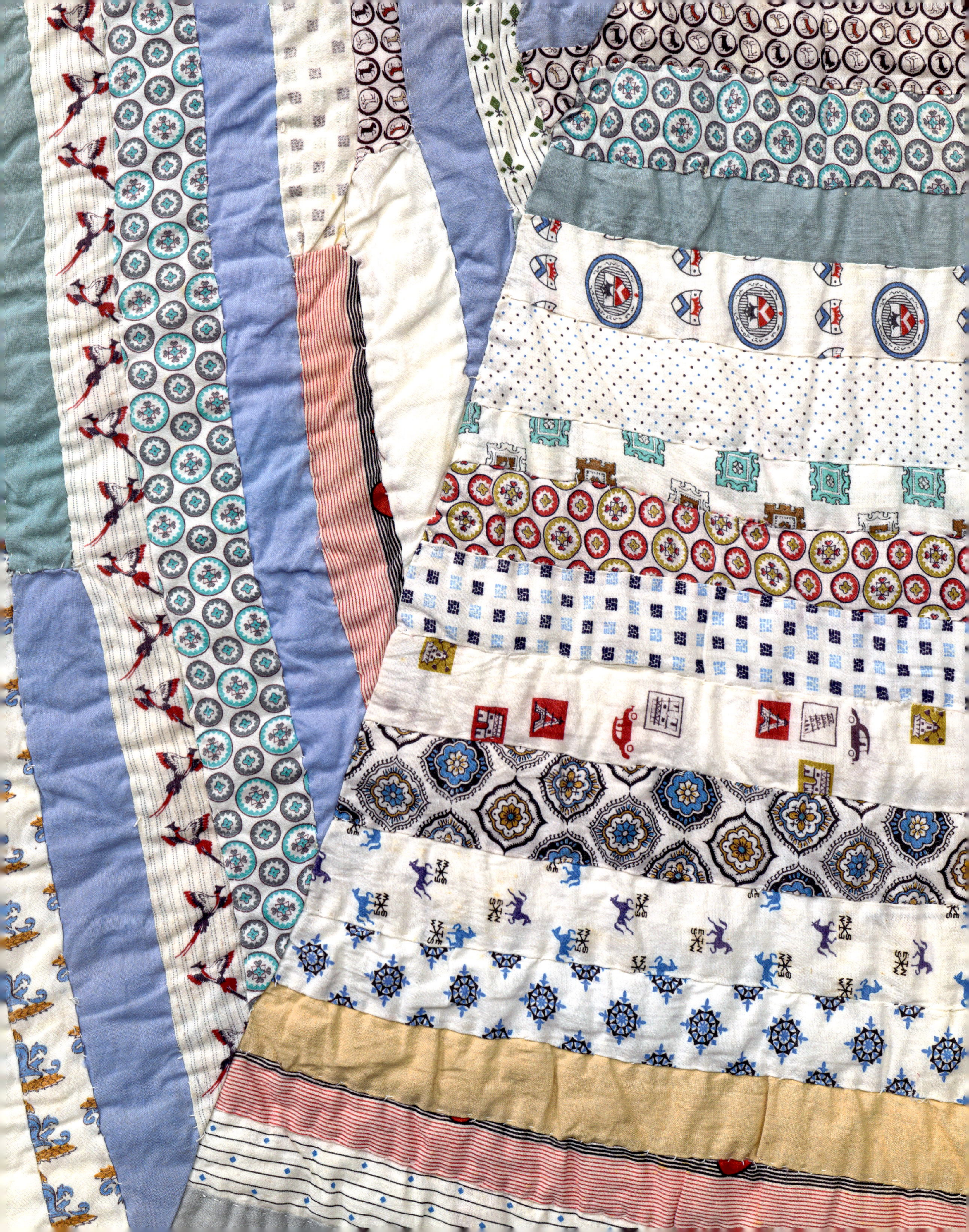

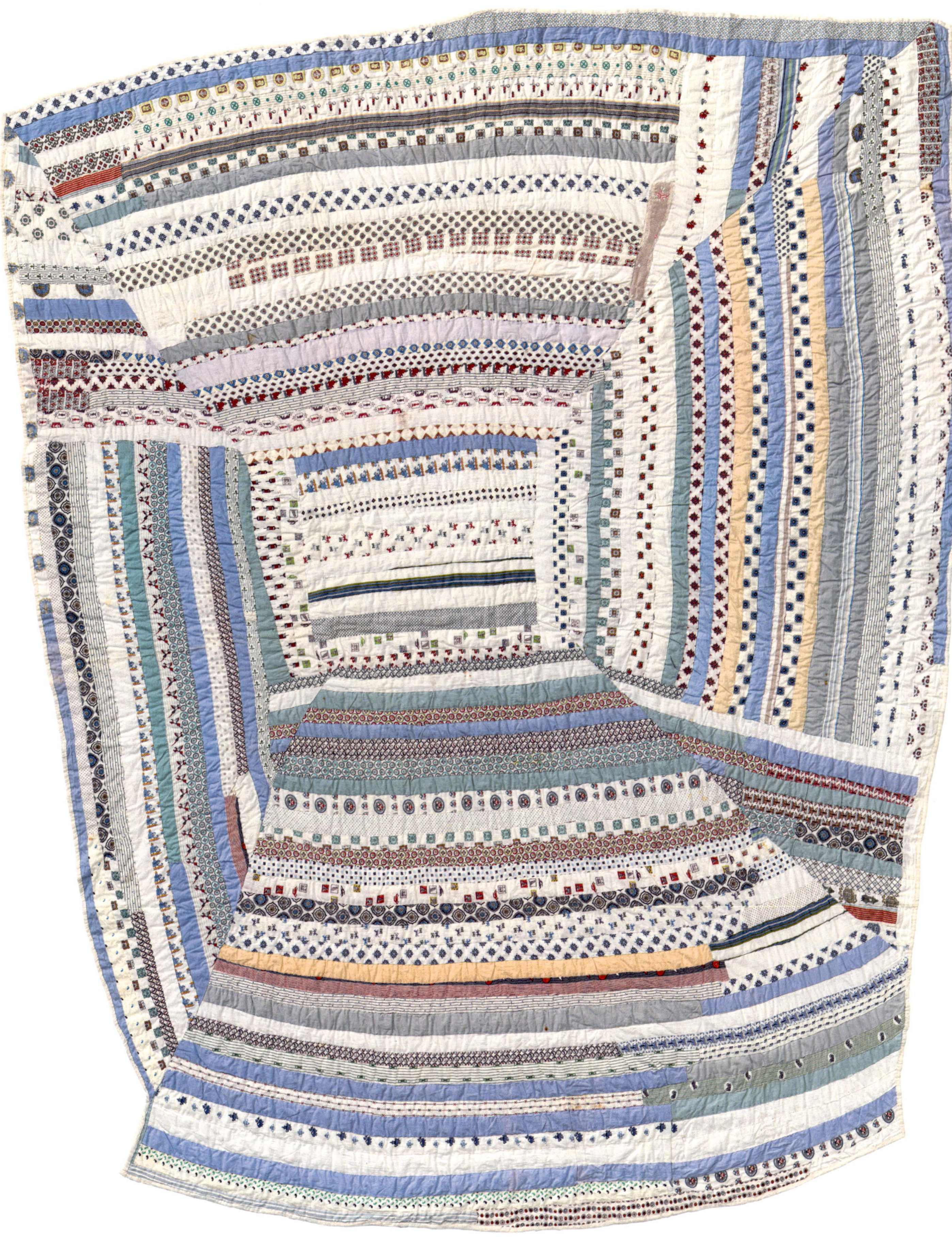

41. Untitled (Medallion)
Pieced by Thomas Covington, c. 1965; Grand Bay, Alabama
Quilted by Irene Bankhead, 1997; Oakland, California
Carlena White, Covington's daughter, was the keeper of this quilt in Oakland until 1997.

Detail

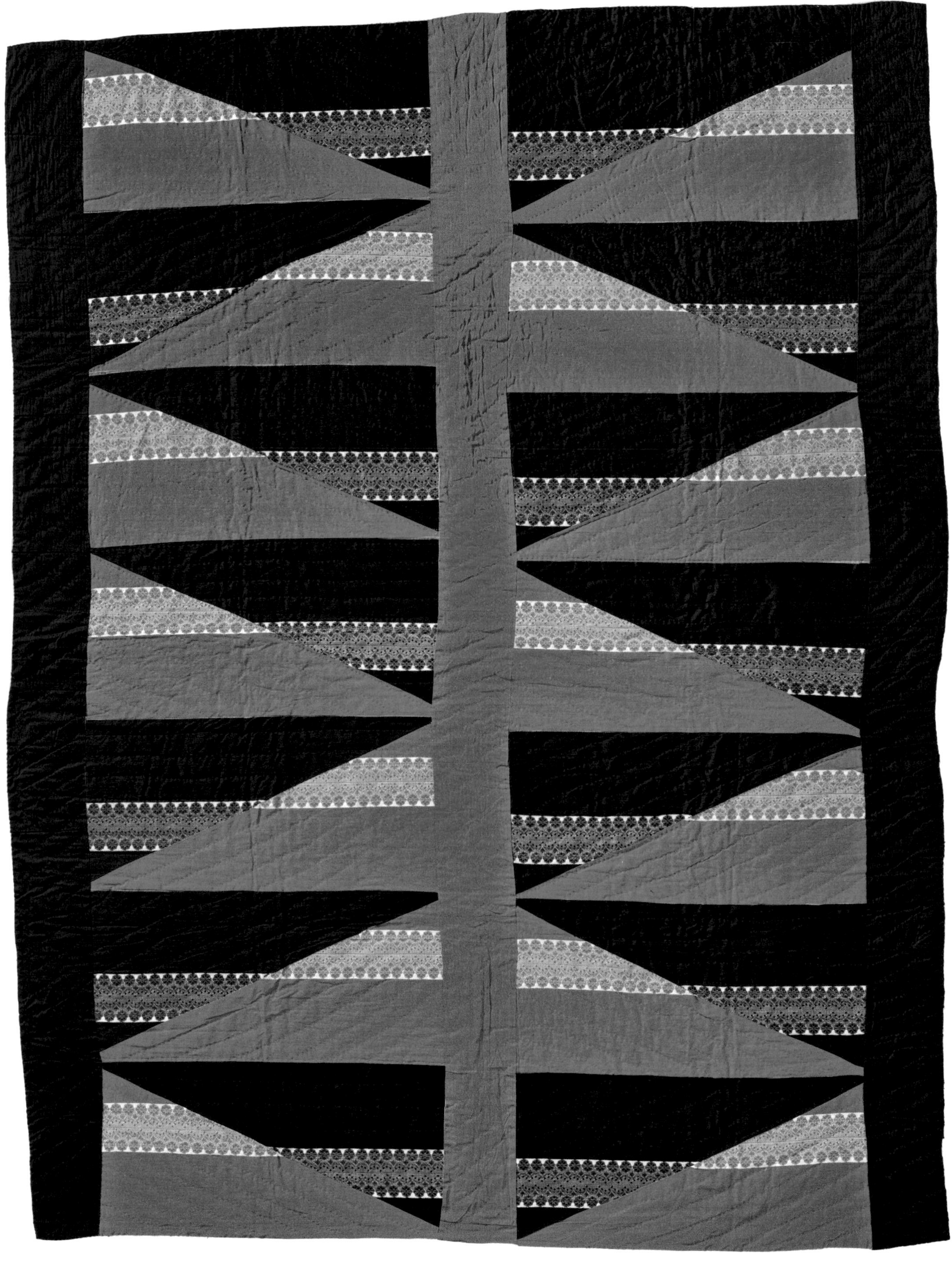

42. Untitled (original design)
Pieced by Annie Hawkins, c. 1969; Oakland, California
Quilted by Willia Ette Graham, 1984; Oakland, California

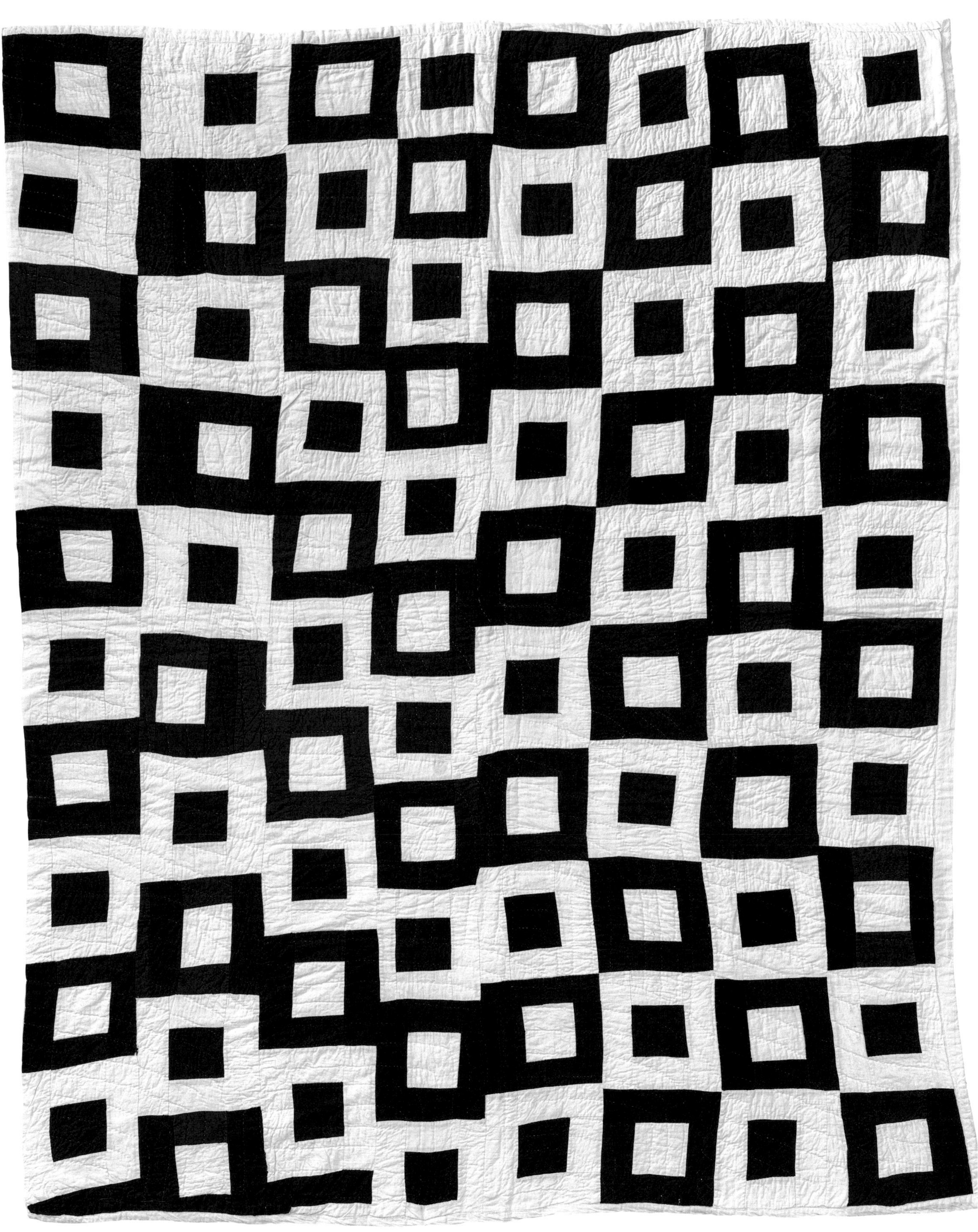

43. Untitled (Square in a Square)
Pieced by Kitty Gladys Jones, before 1970; Forest, Mississippi
Quilted by Atleaver Jones, c. 1978; Fresno, California

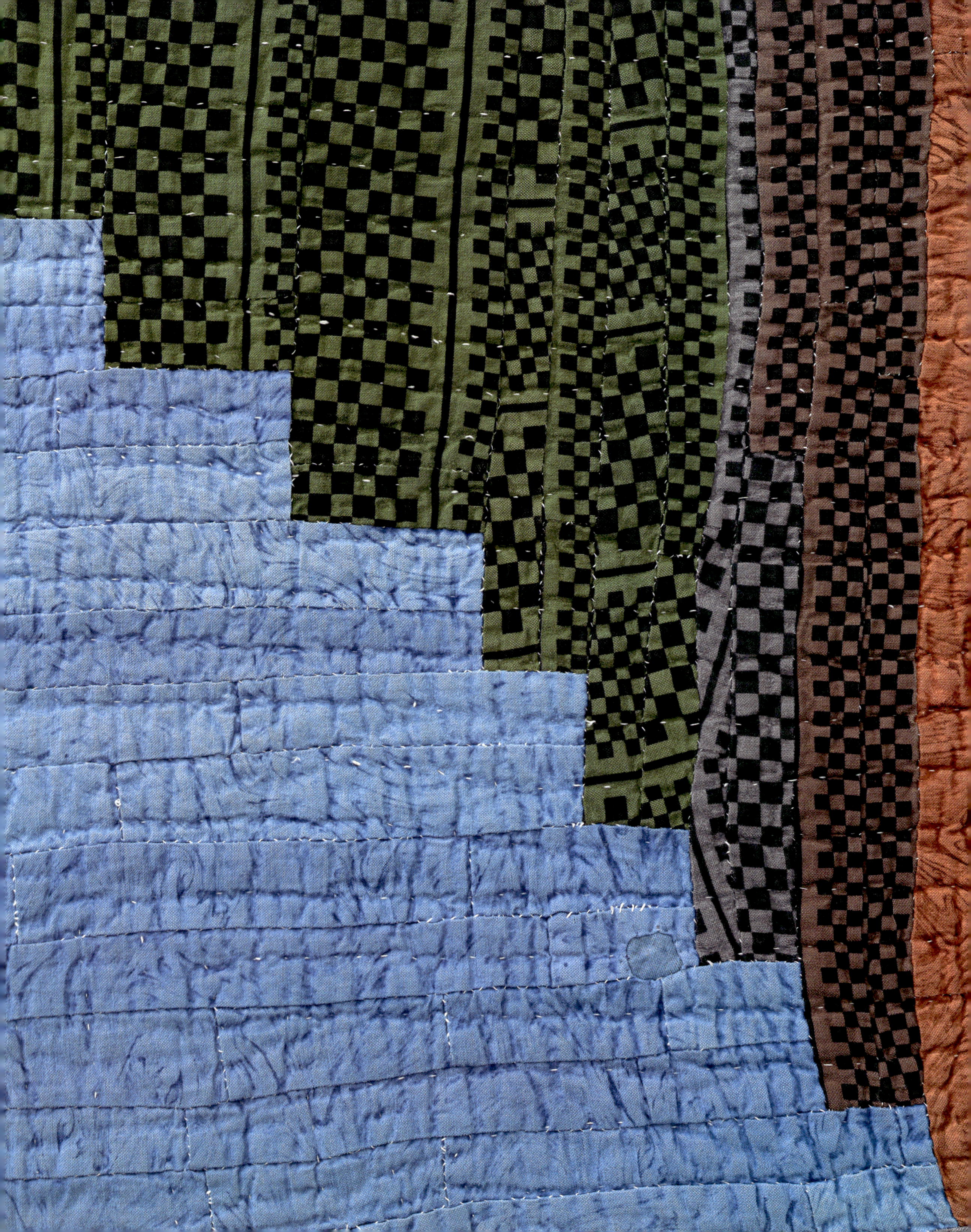

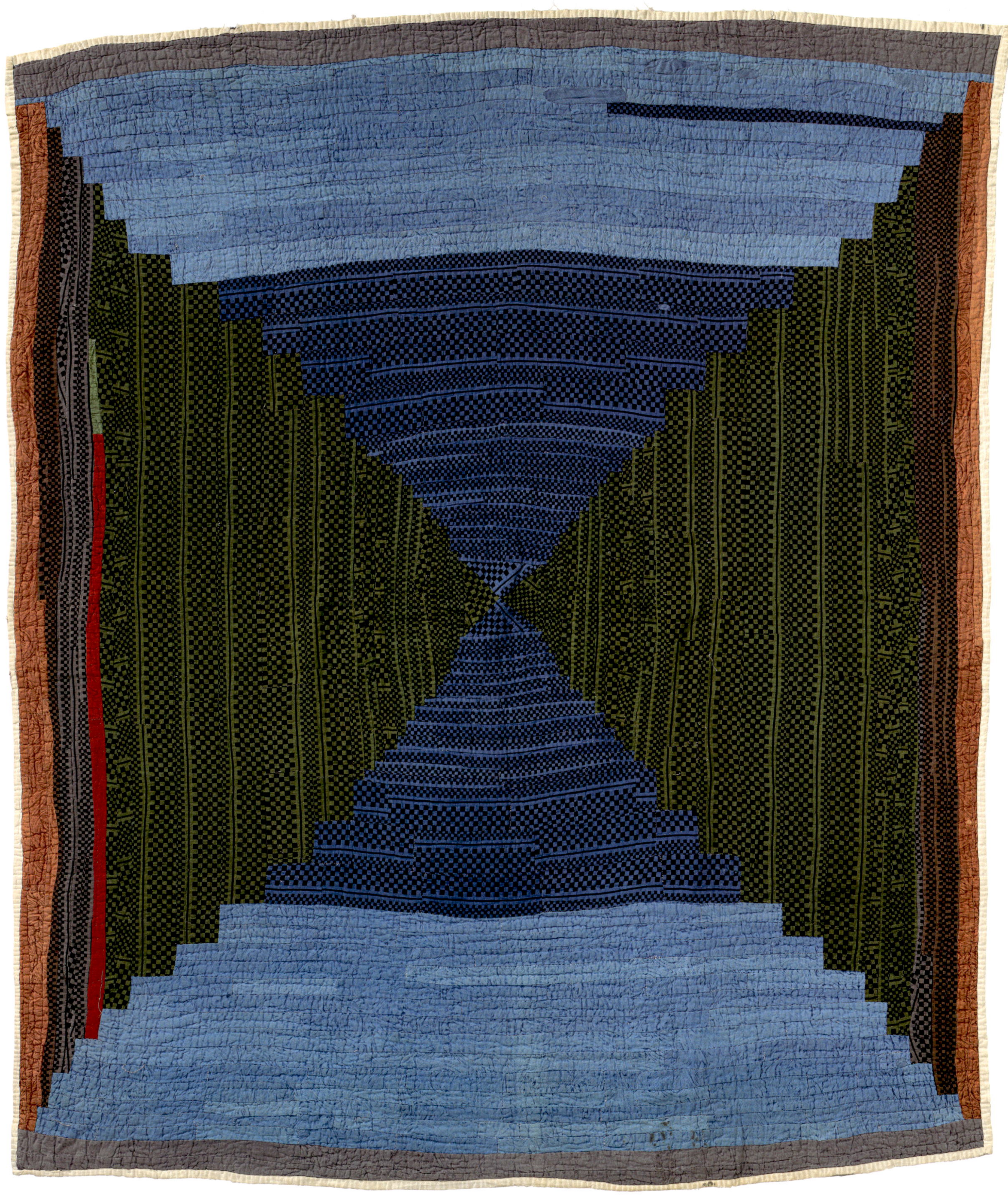

44. Untitled (Log Cabin, Courthouse Steps variation)
Pieced by Rachel Adkins, c. 1970; Houston, Texas
Quilted by Margaret Gillam, c. 1970; Berkeley, California
Zephyr Pruitt was the keeper of this quilt in Berkeley until 1987.

Detail

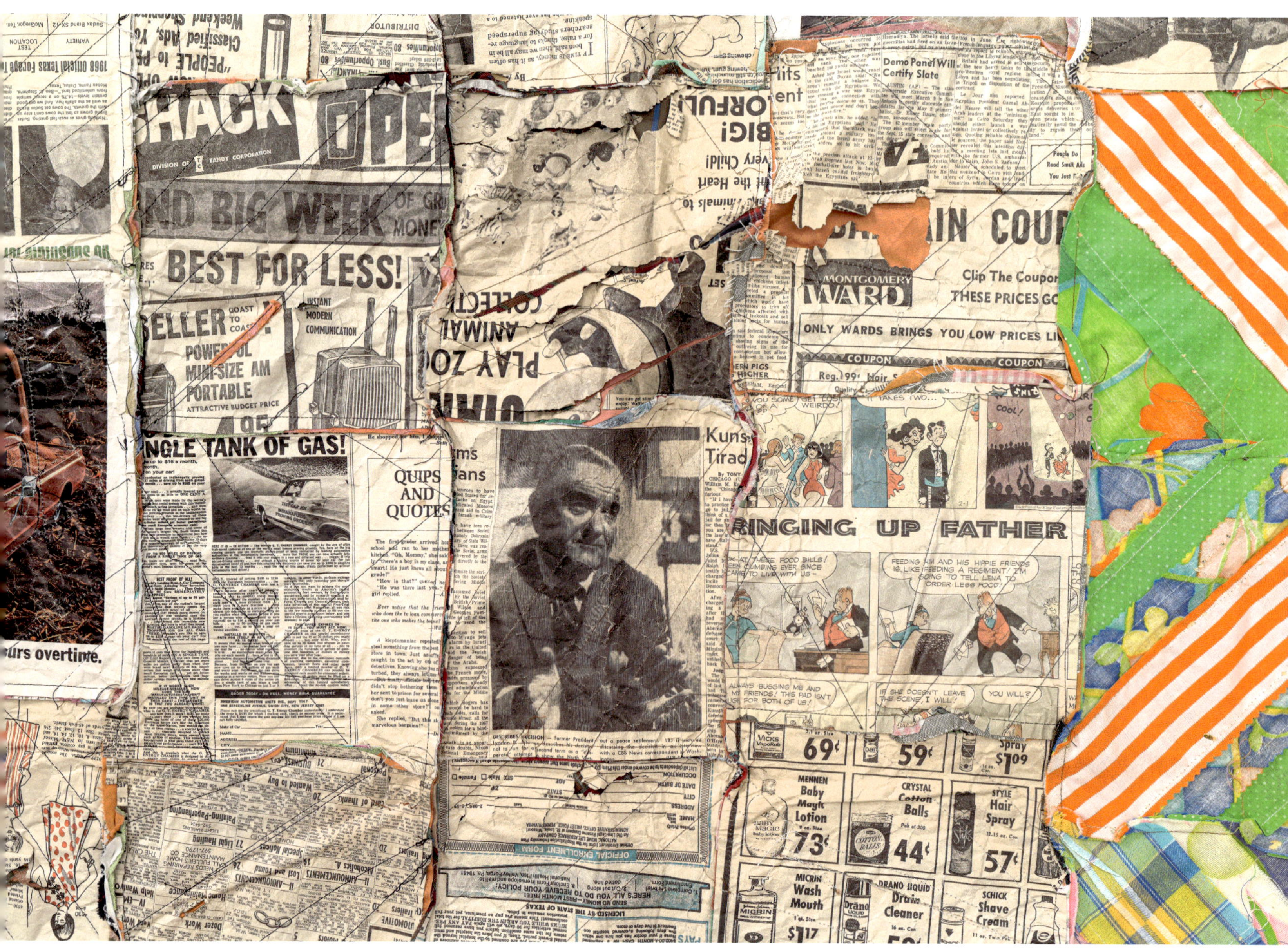

Detail, back of cat. 45

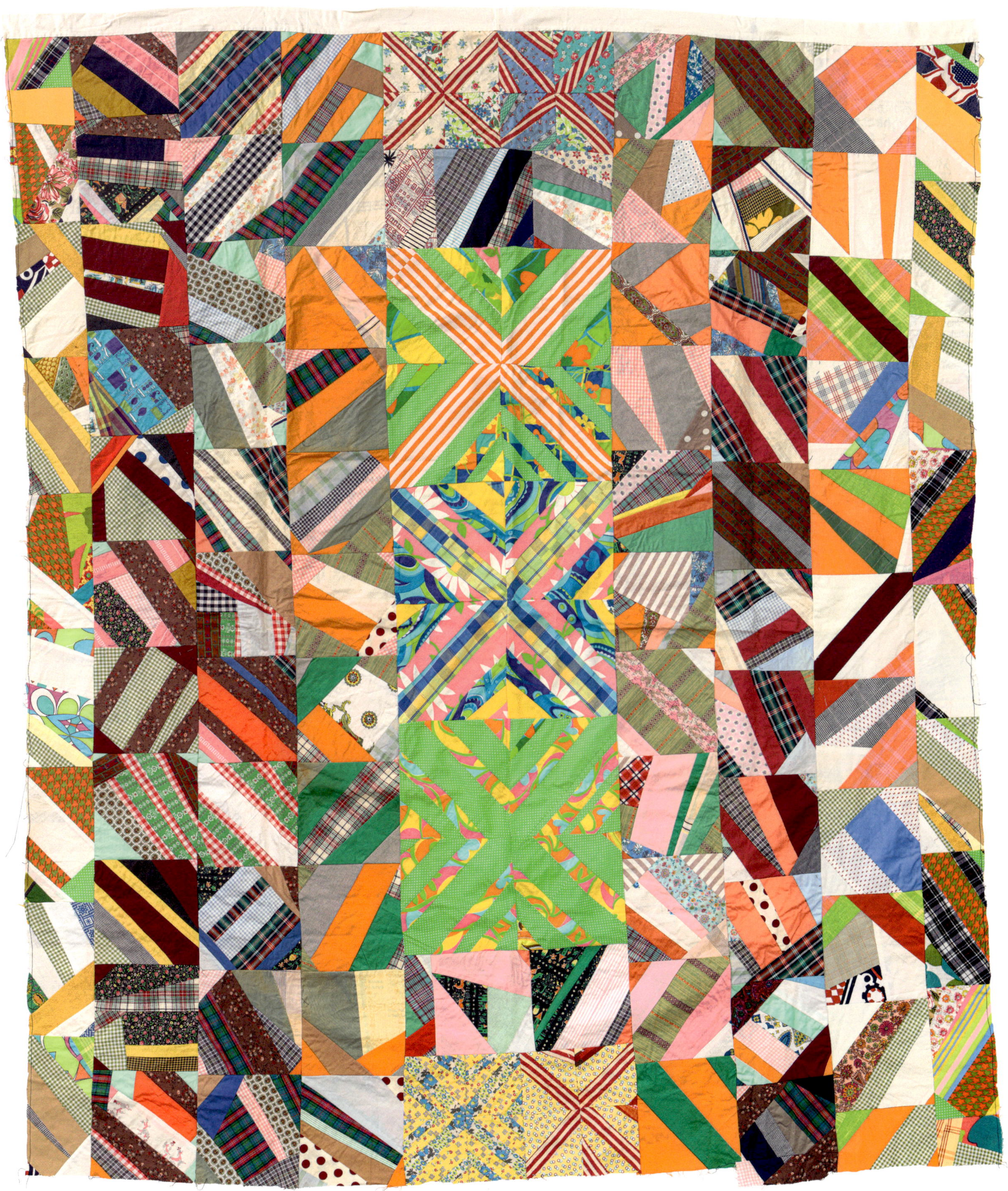

45. Untitled top (String Medallion with newspaper backing)
Cora Lee Hall Brown, c. 1970; Mount Enterprise, Texas

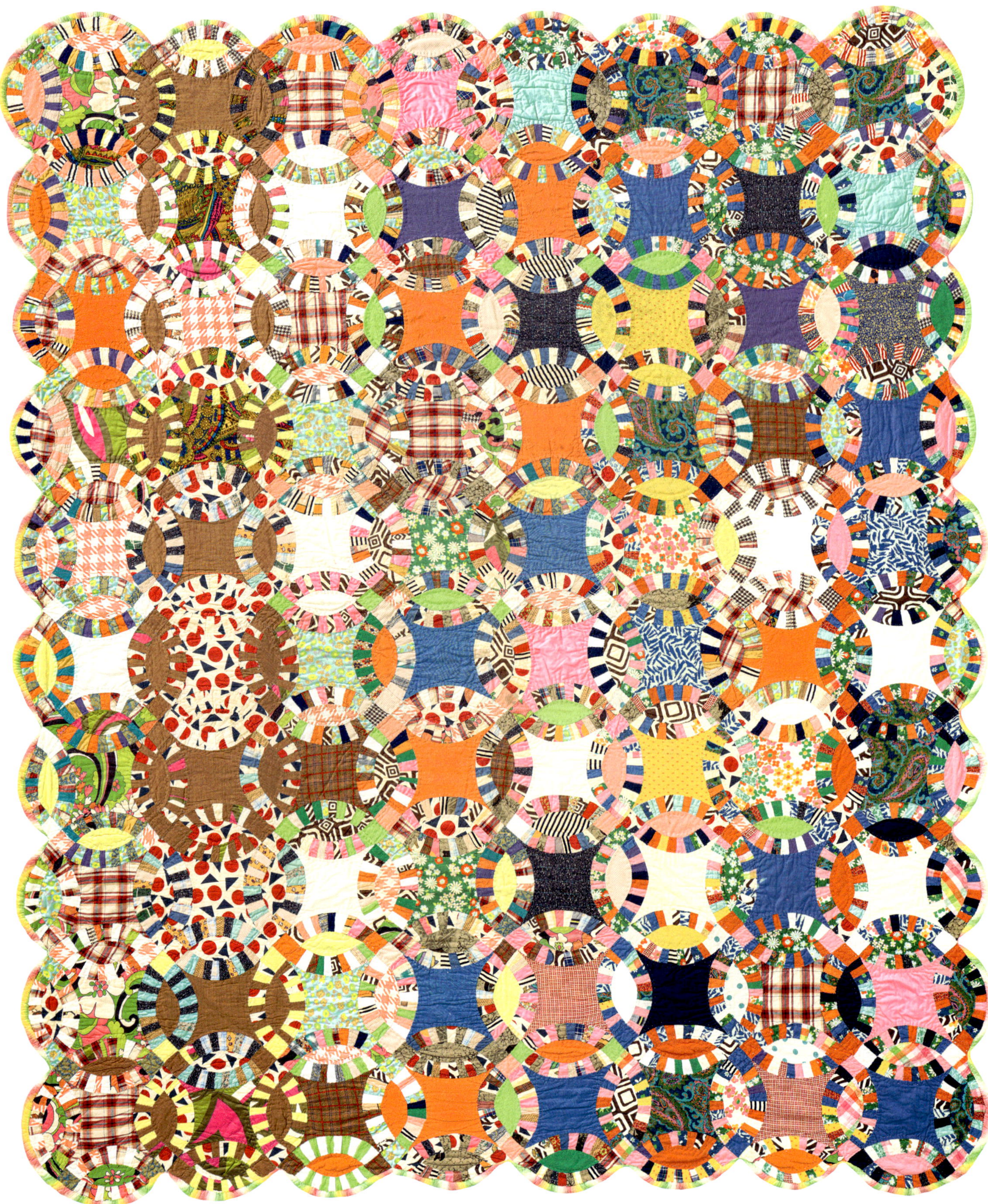

Front

Above and following pages:
ISIADORE WHITEHEAD DOUBLE WEDDING RING ROOM

46. Untitled (Double Wedding Ring)
Isiadore Whitehead, c. 1970; Oakland, California

Back

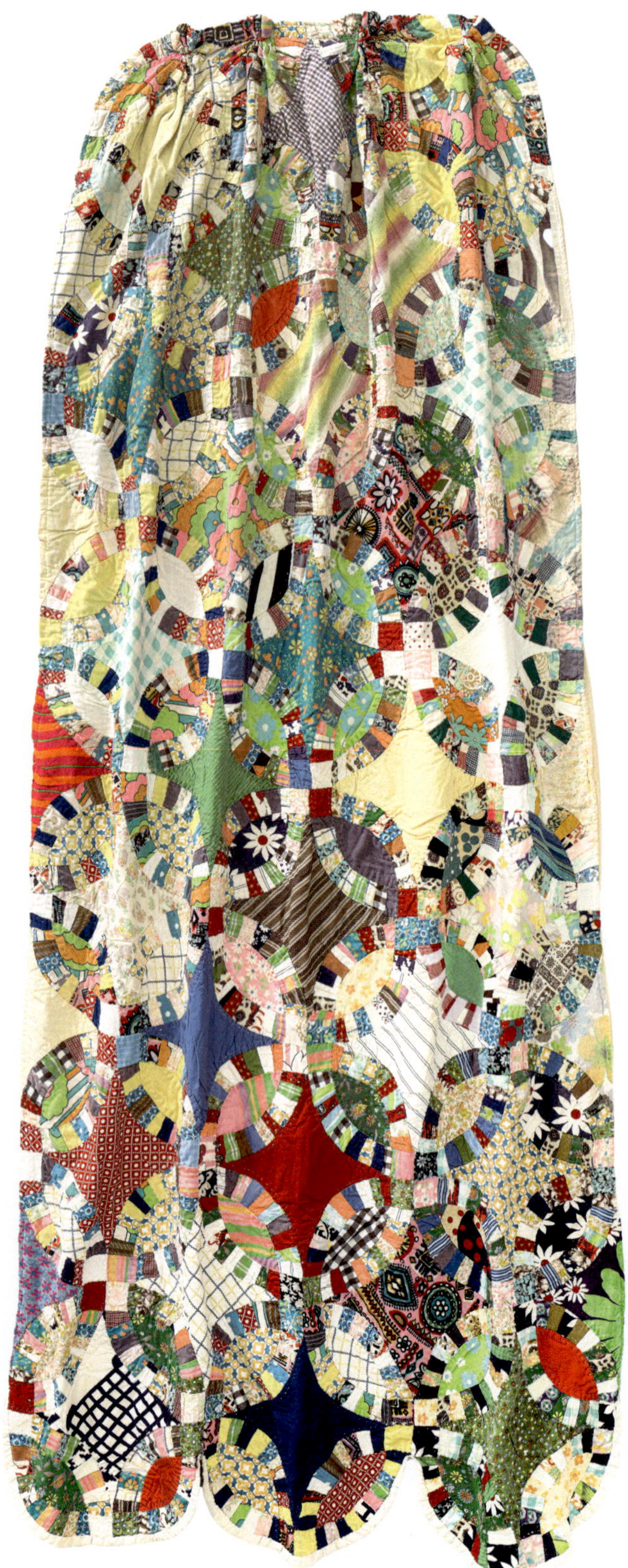

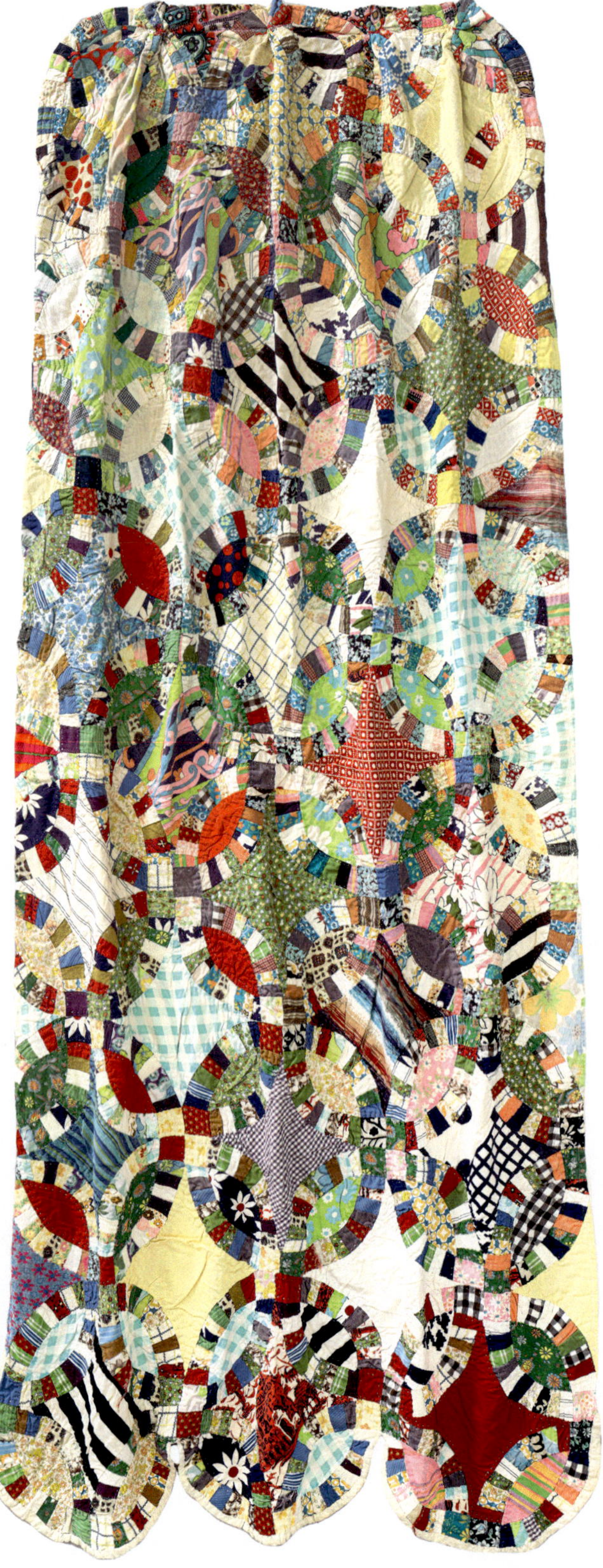

47. Drape (Double Wedding Ring)
Isiadore Whitehead, c. 1970; Oakland, California

48. Drape (Double Wedding Ring)
Isiadore Whitehead, c. 1970; Oakland, California

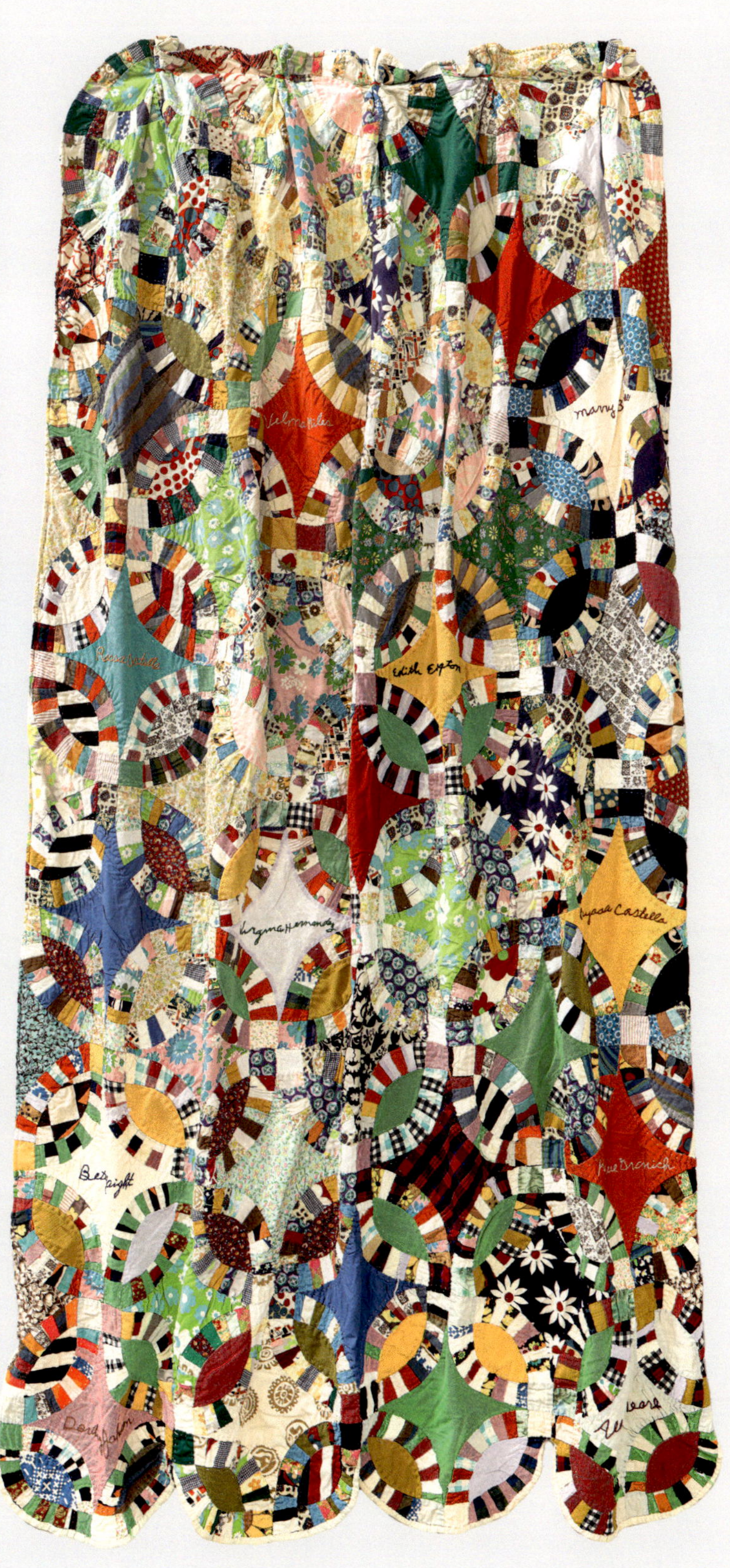

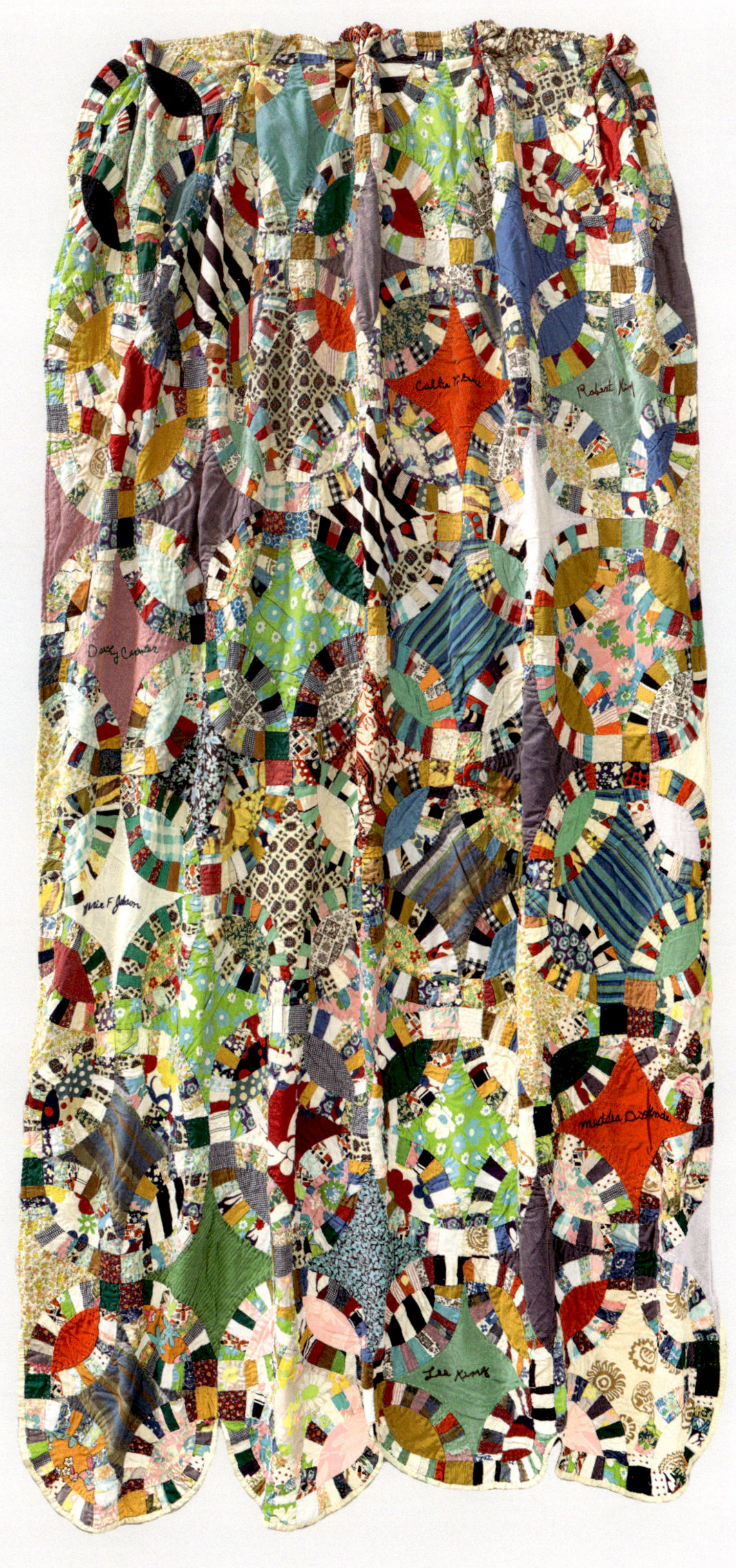

49. Drape with embroidered names (Double Wedding Ring)
Isiadore Whitehead, c. 1970; Oakland, California

50. Drape with embroidered names (Double Wedding Ring)
Isiadore Whitehead, c. 1970; Oakland, California

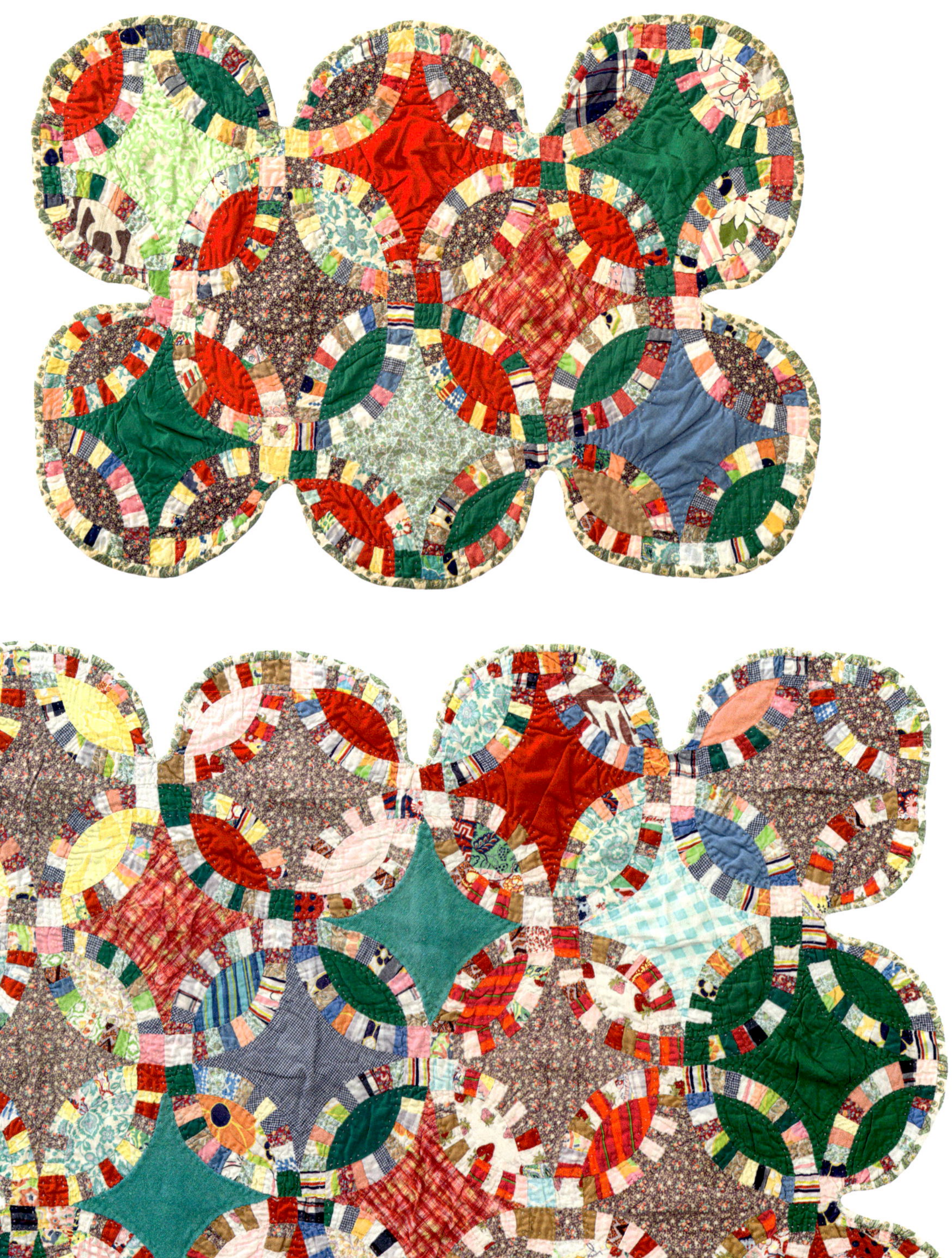

51. Floor mat (Double Wedding Ring)
Isiadore Whitehead, c. 1970; Oakland, California

52. Floor mat (Double Wedding Ring)
Isiadore Whitehead, c. 1970; Oakland, California

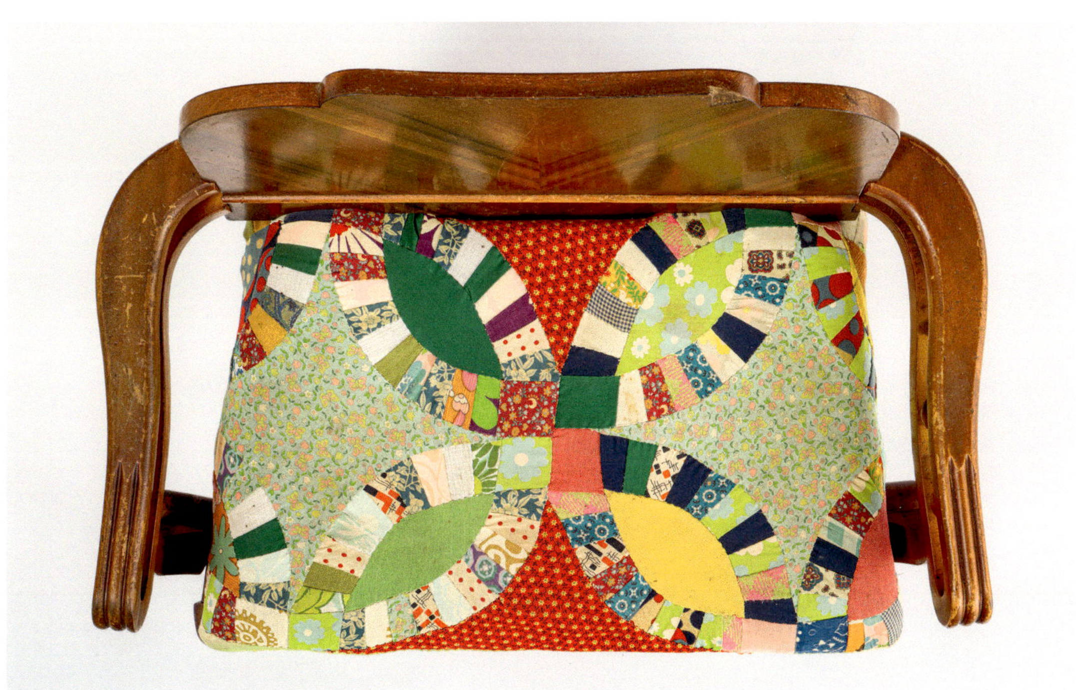

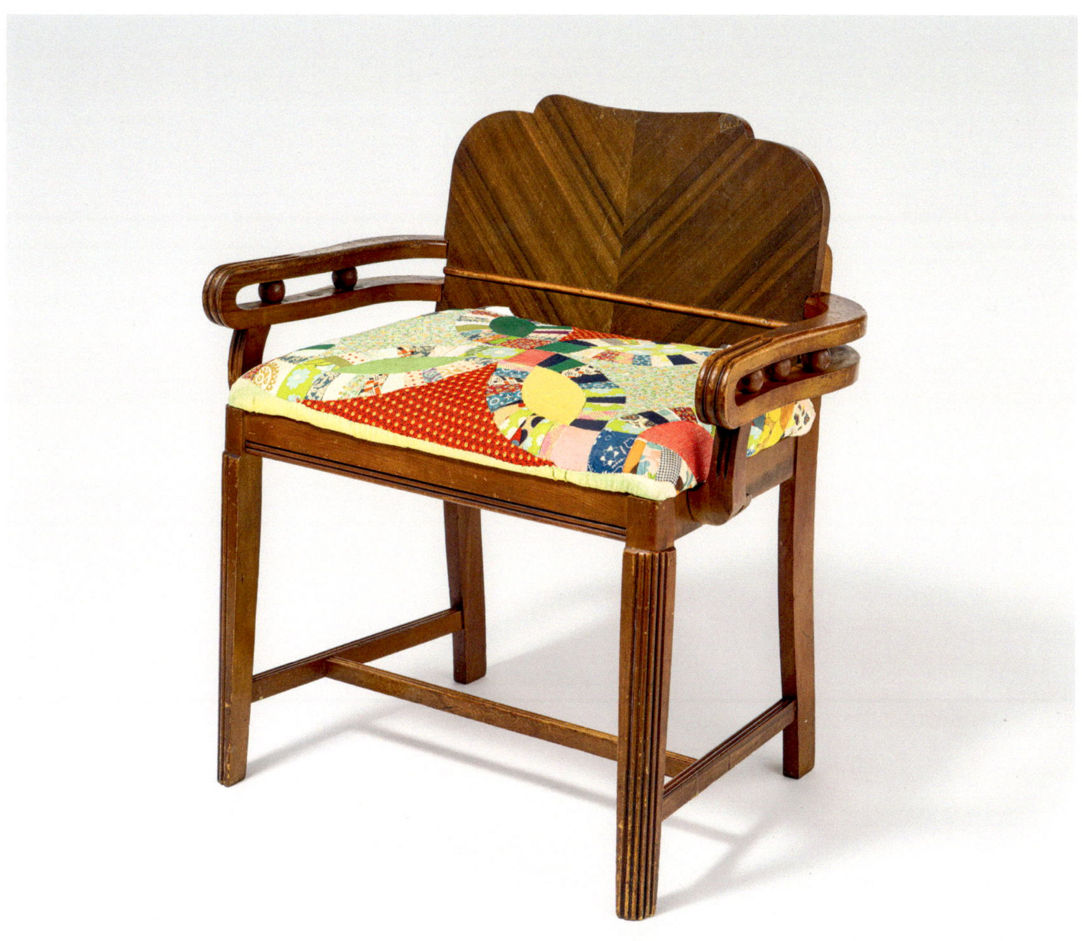

53. Chair with Double Wedding Ring seat cushion
Isiadore Whitehead, c. 1970; Oakland, California

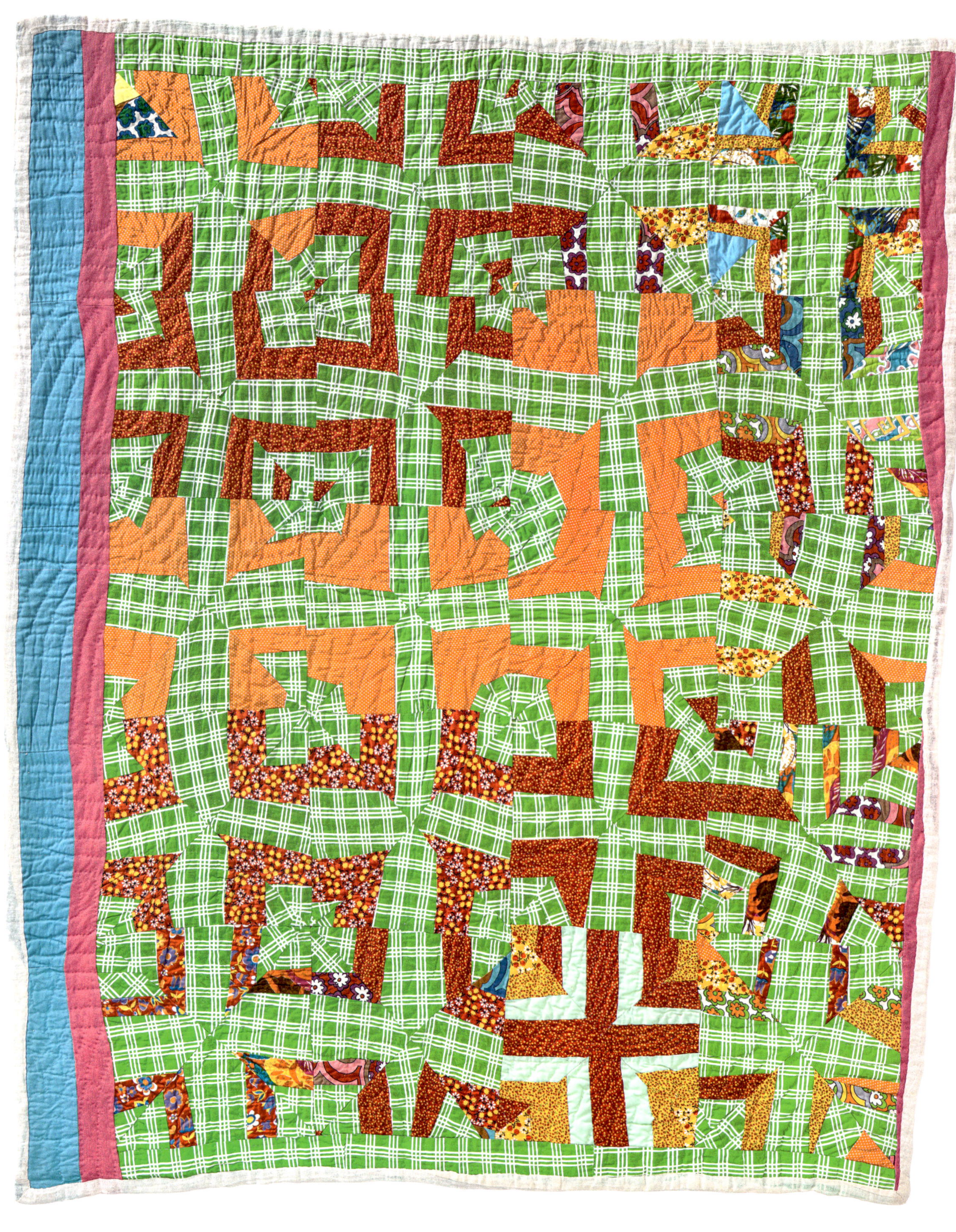

54. Untitled (String)
Pieced by Eula Thomas, 1971; Oakland, California
Quilted by Willia Ette Graham, 1984; Oakland, California

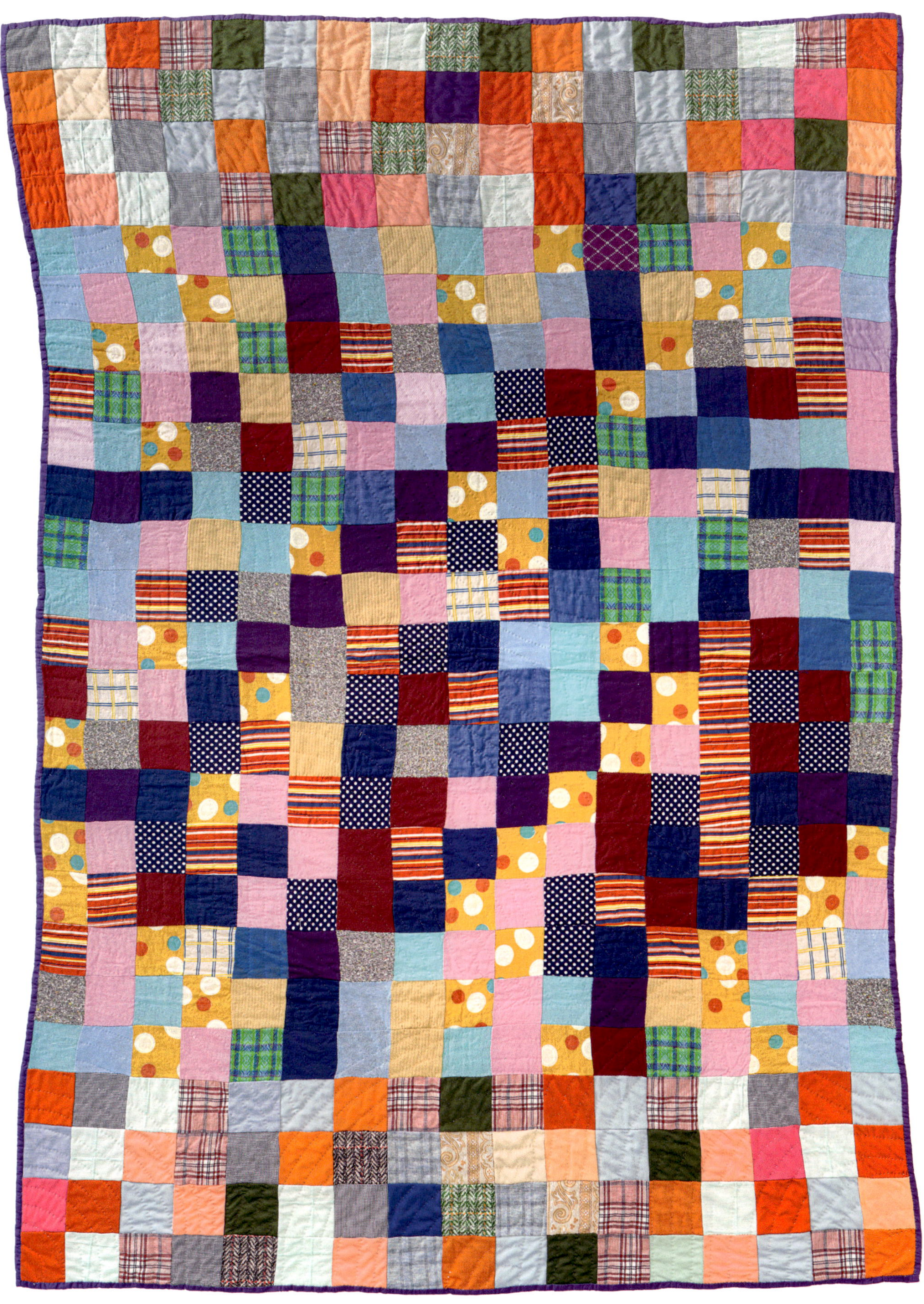

55. Untitled (Crossword Puzzle)
Pieced by Dorothy Perkins, c. 1974; Oakland, California
Quilted by Irene Bankhead, 1987; Oakland, California

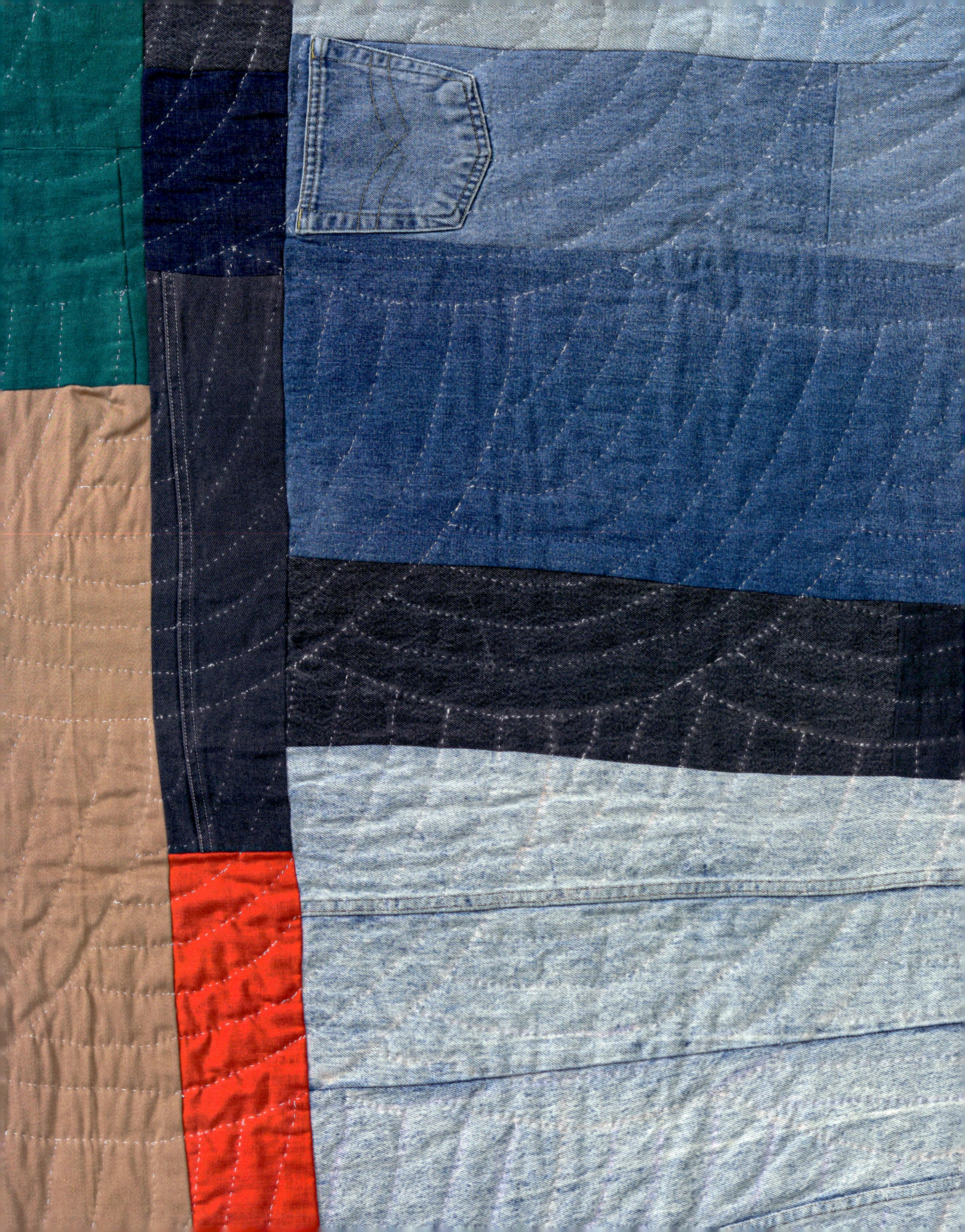

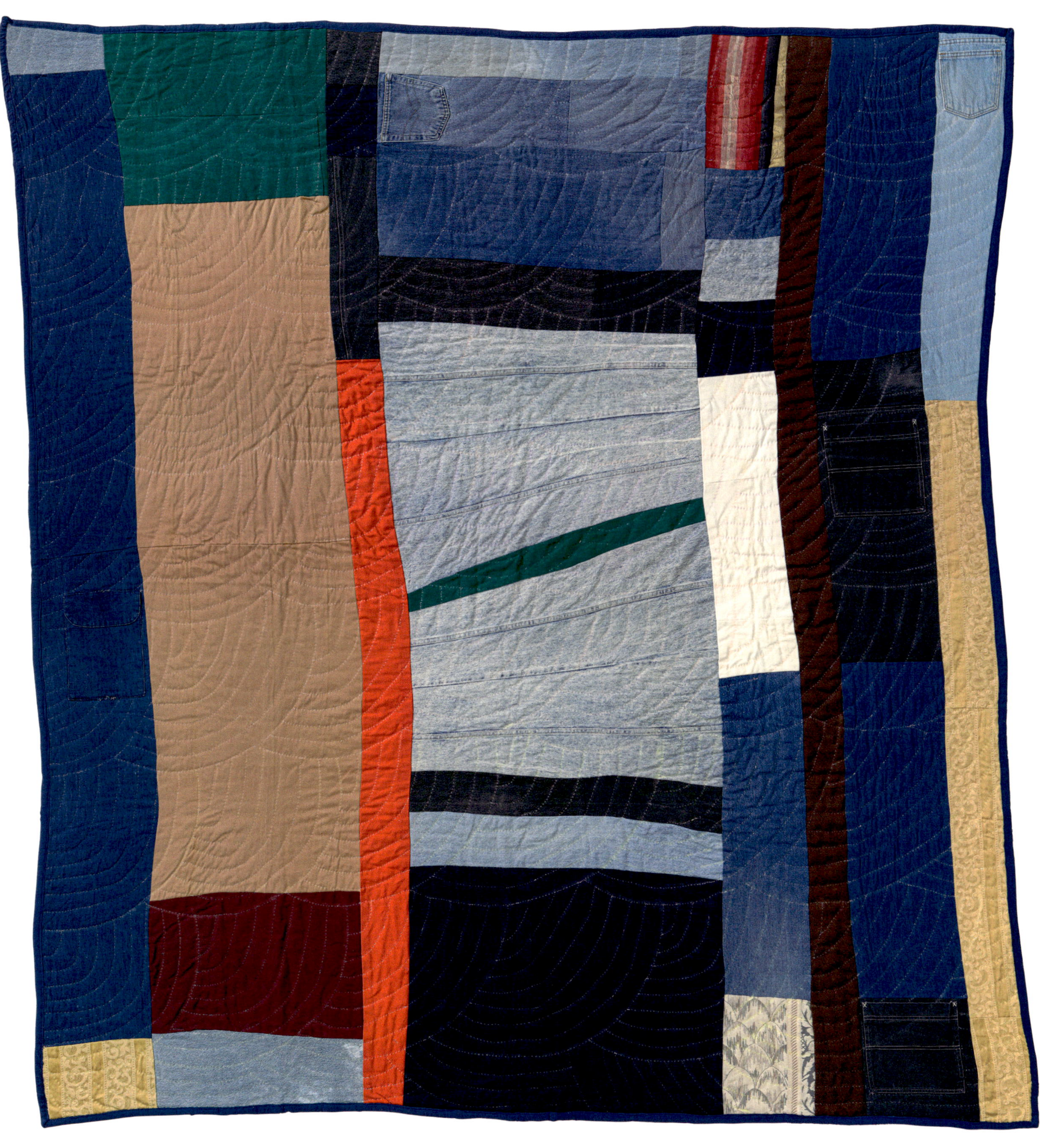

56. Untitled (Medallion)
Pieced by Mable Battle, 1978–1979; Richmond, California
Quilted by Selena Foster, 2004; Richmond, California
Lena Fay Forte, Battle's daughter and Foster's niece,
was the keeper of this quilt as a top in Richmond until 2003.

Detail

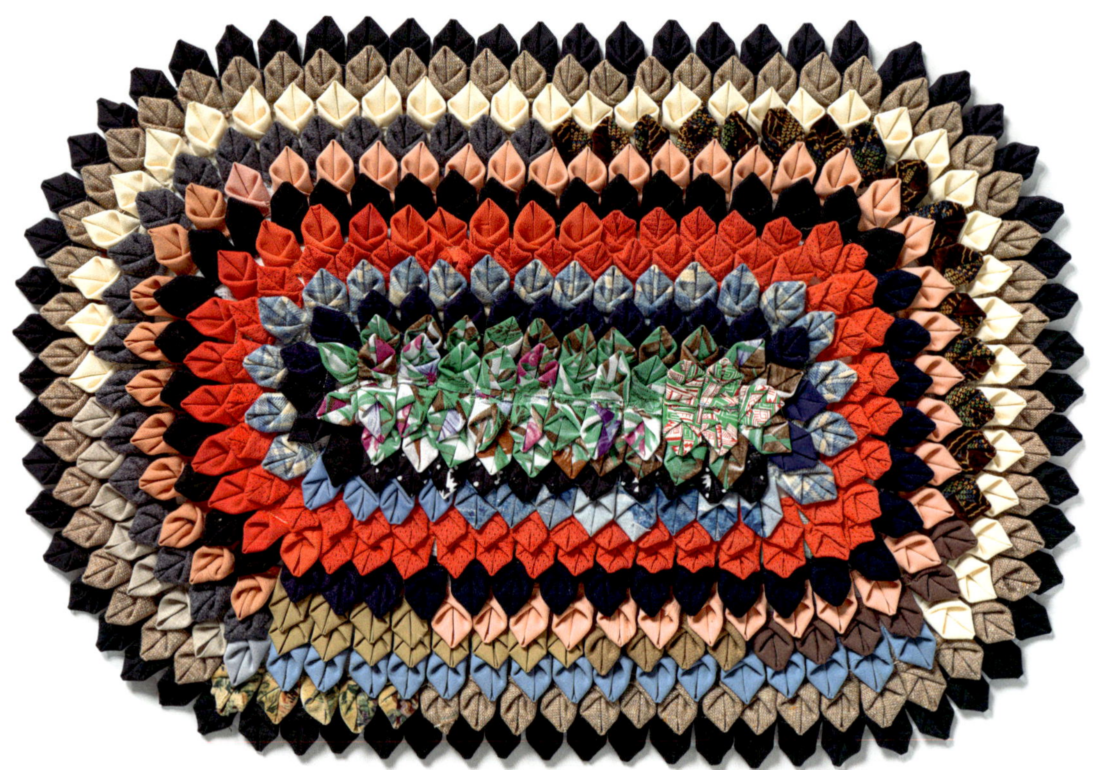

Front

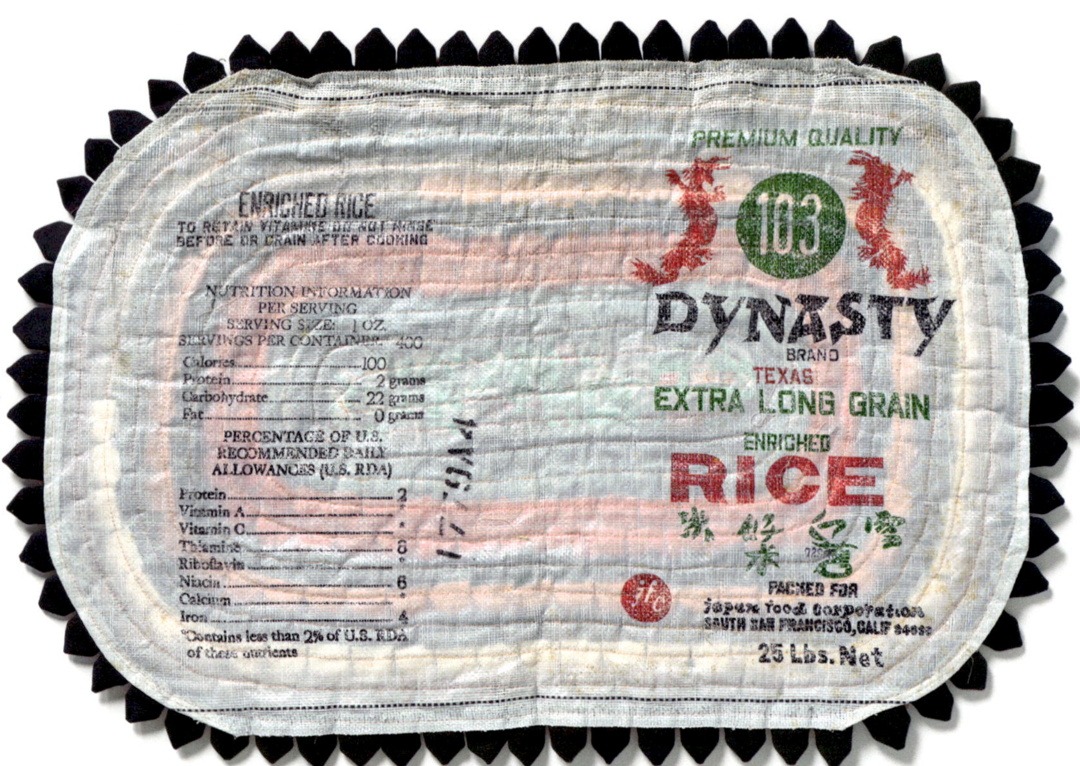

Back

57. Floor mat (Pine Burr variation?)
Gracie Pigrum, 1970s or early 1980s; San Francisco, California

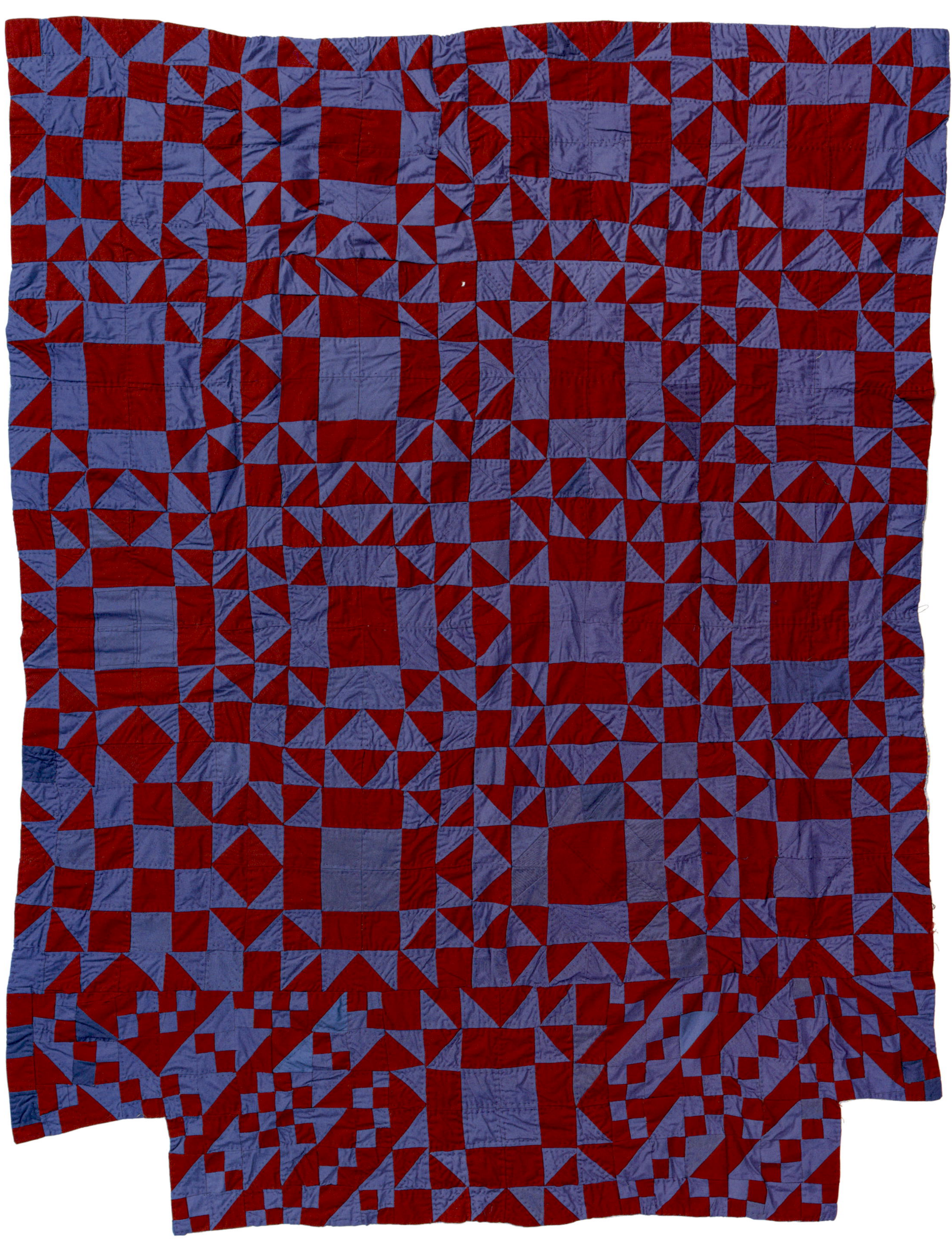

58. Untitled (Robbing Peter to Pay Paul, Jacob's Ladder)
Biddie Wilson, 1970s–1990s; likely Oakland, California
Lily Chiles, Wilson's friend in Oakland, kept this quilt until 2000.

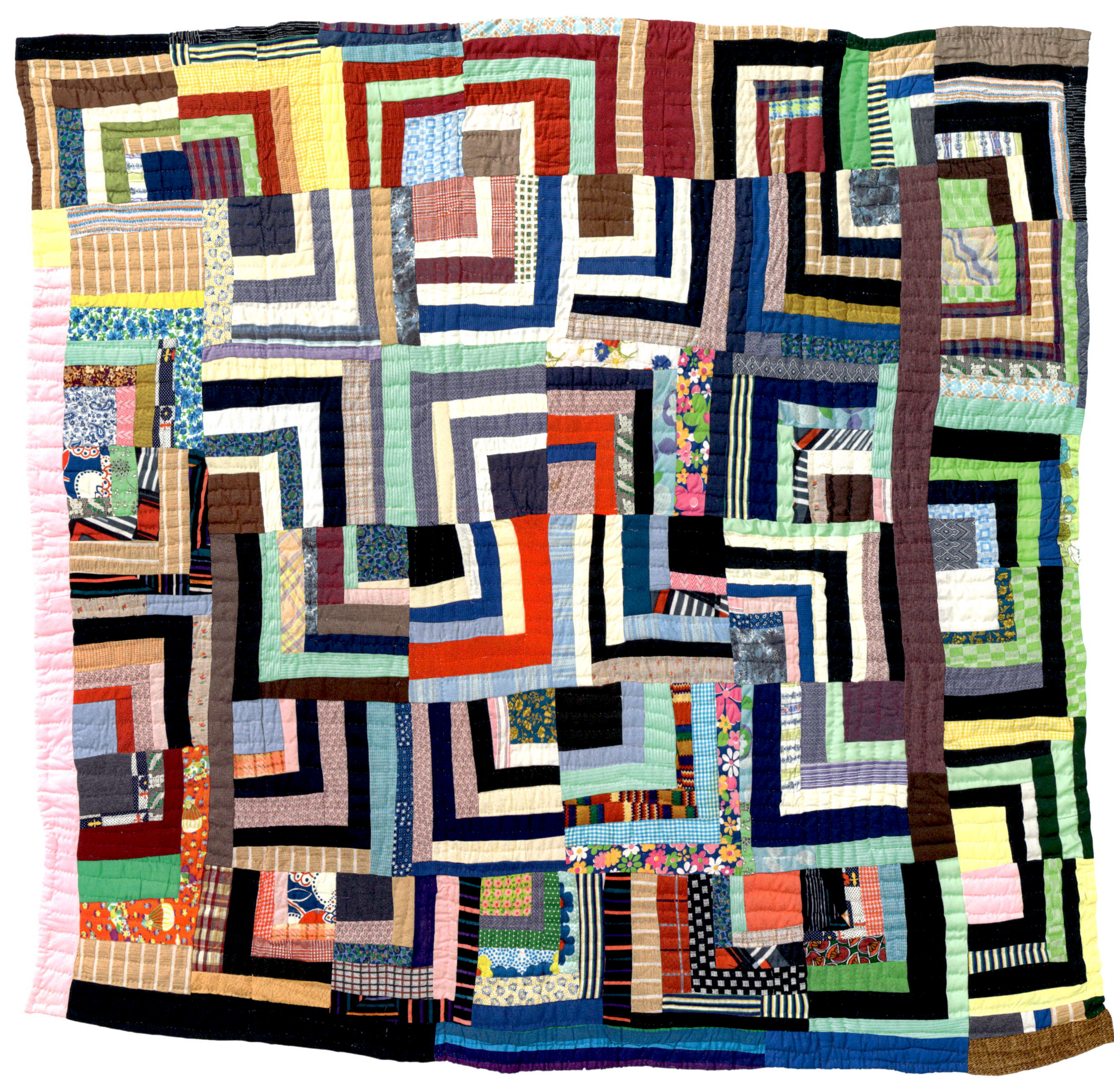

59. Untitled (Fractured Log Cabin)
Pieced by Sarah Turnage, 1970s; San Francisco, California
Quilted by Mary Thompson, 1990; San Francisco, California
Quilted by Aurelia Foster, 1990; San Francisco, California

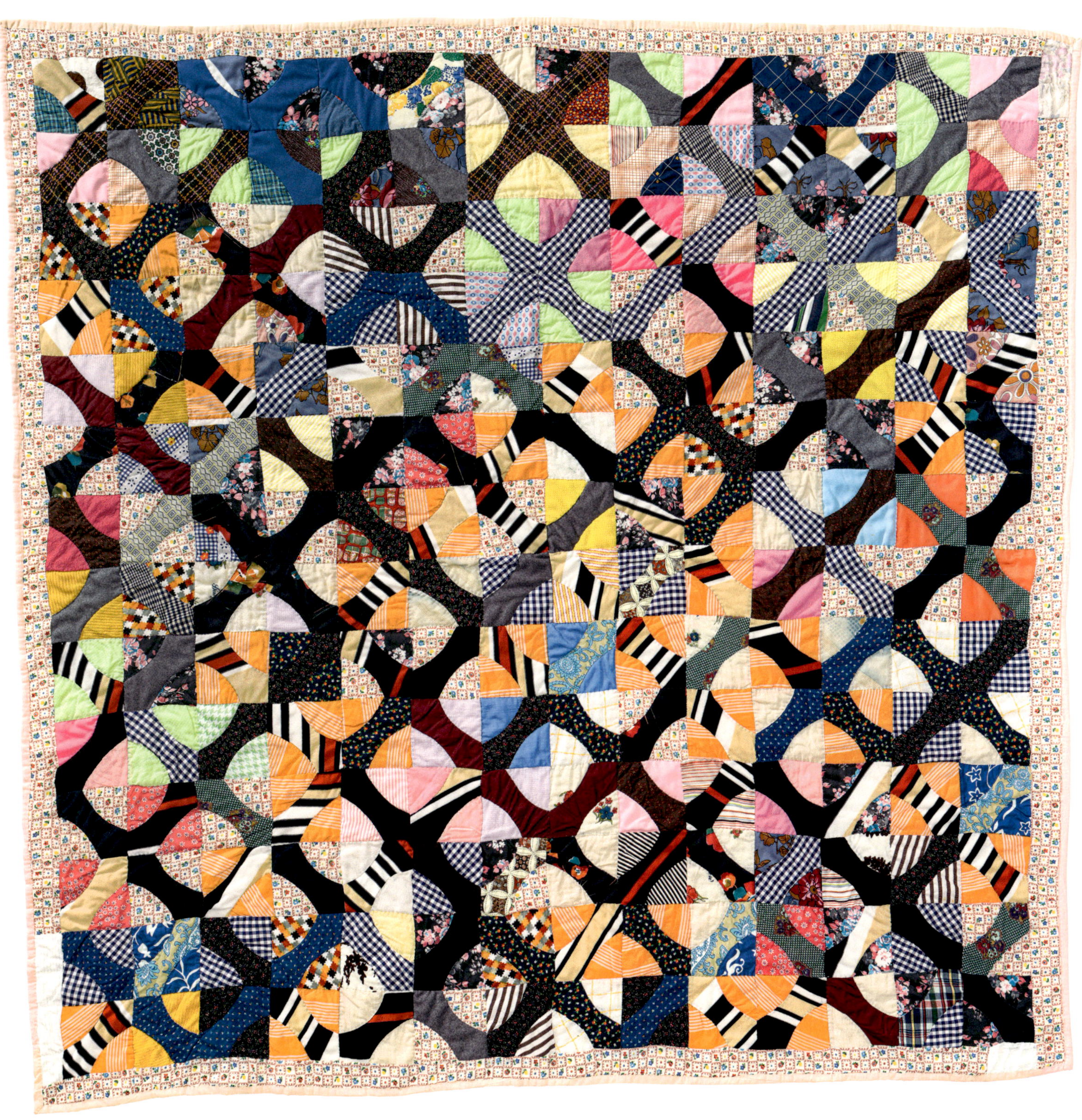

60. Untitled (Boston Puzzle or Marble)
Pieced by Francis Sheppard, 1980–1985; Las Vegas, Nevada
Quilted by Irene Bankhead, 1991; Oakland, California
Arbie Williams, Sheppard's daughter, was the keeper of this quilt as a top until 1985.

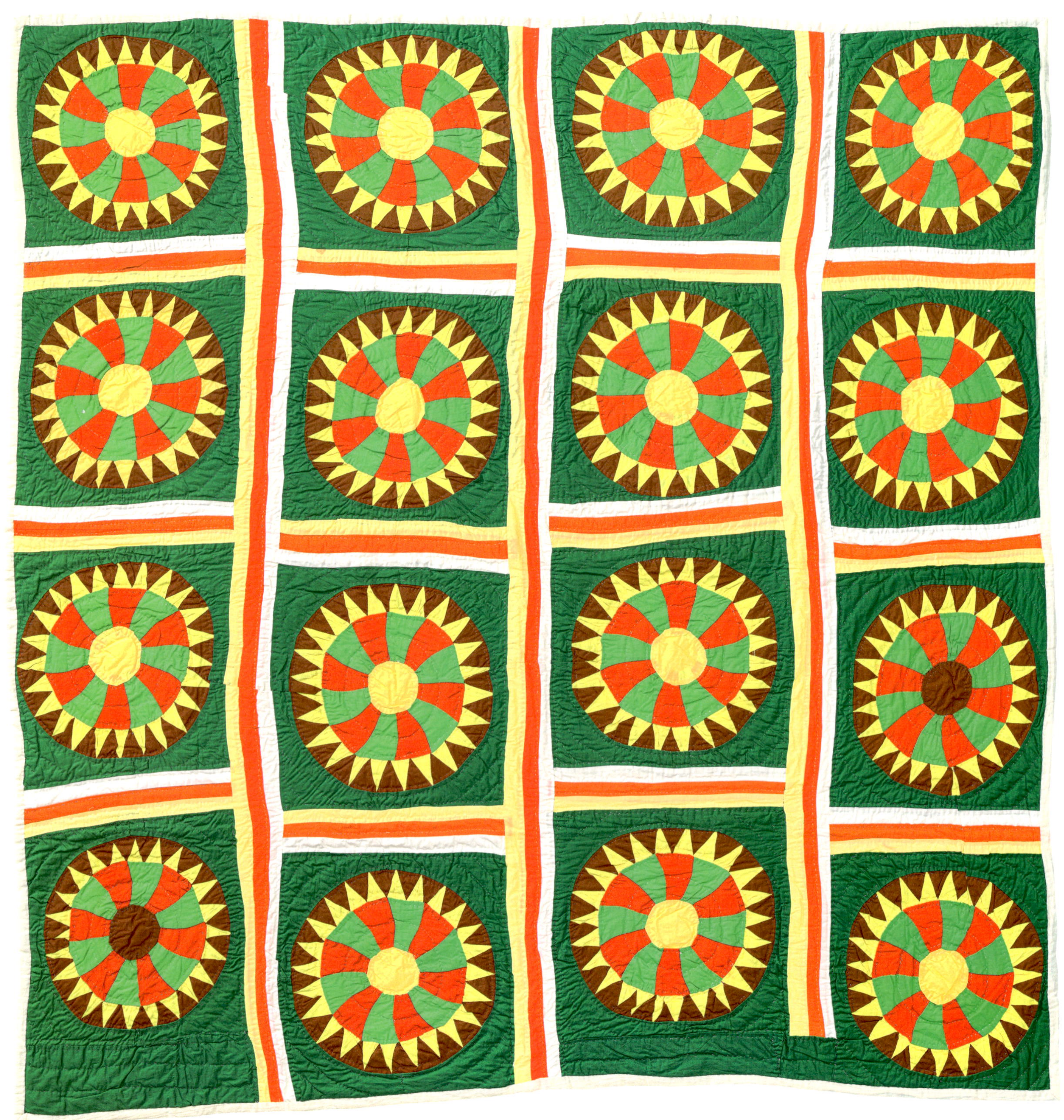

61. Untitled (Wheel of Fortune)
Pieced by Louella Harris, 1980s; Richmond, California
Quilted by Willia Ette Graham and Johnnie Alberta Wade, 1994; Oakland, California
Alice Hilliard, Harris's daughter-in-law, was the keeper of this quilt until 1994.

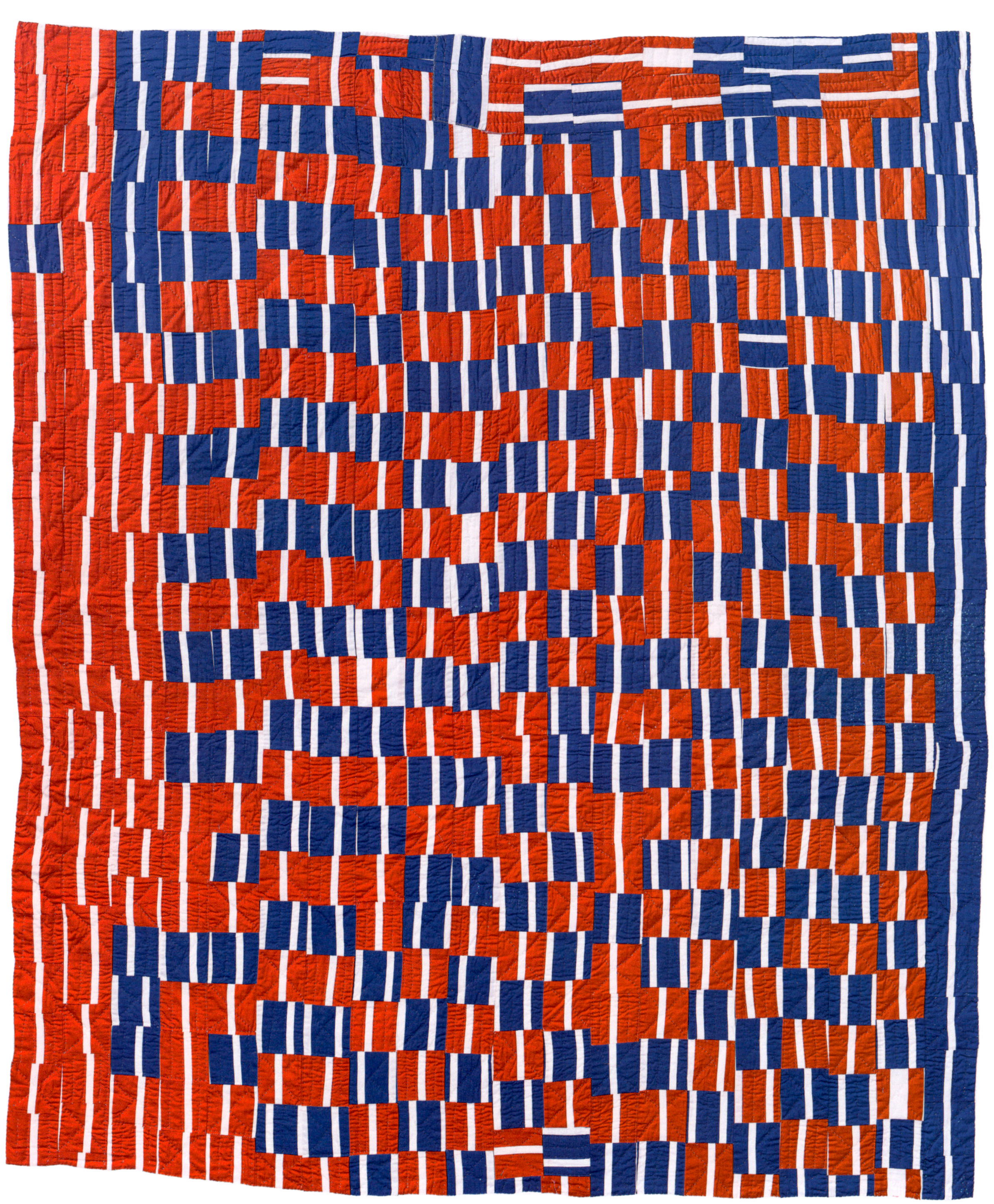

62. Untitled (One Patch)
Pieced by Cora Lee Hall Brown, 1981; Mount Enterprise, Texas
Quilted by Willia Ette Graham, 1985; Oakland, California

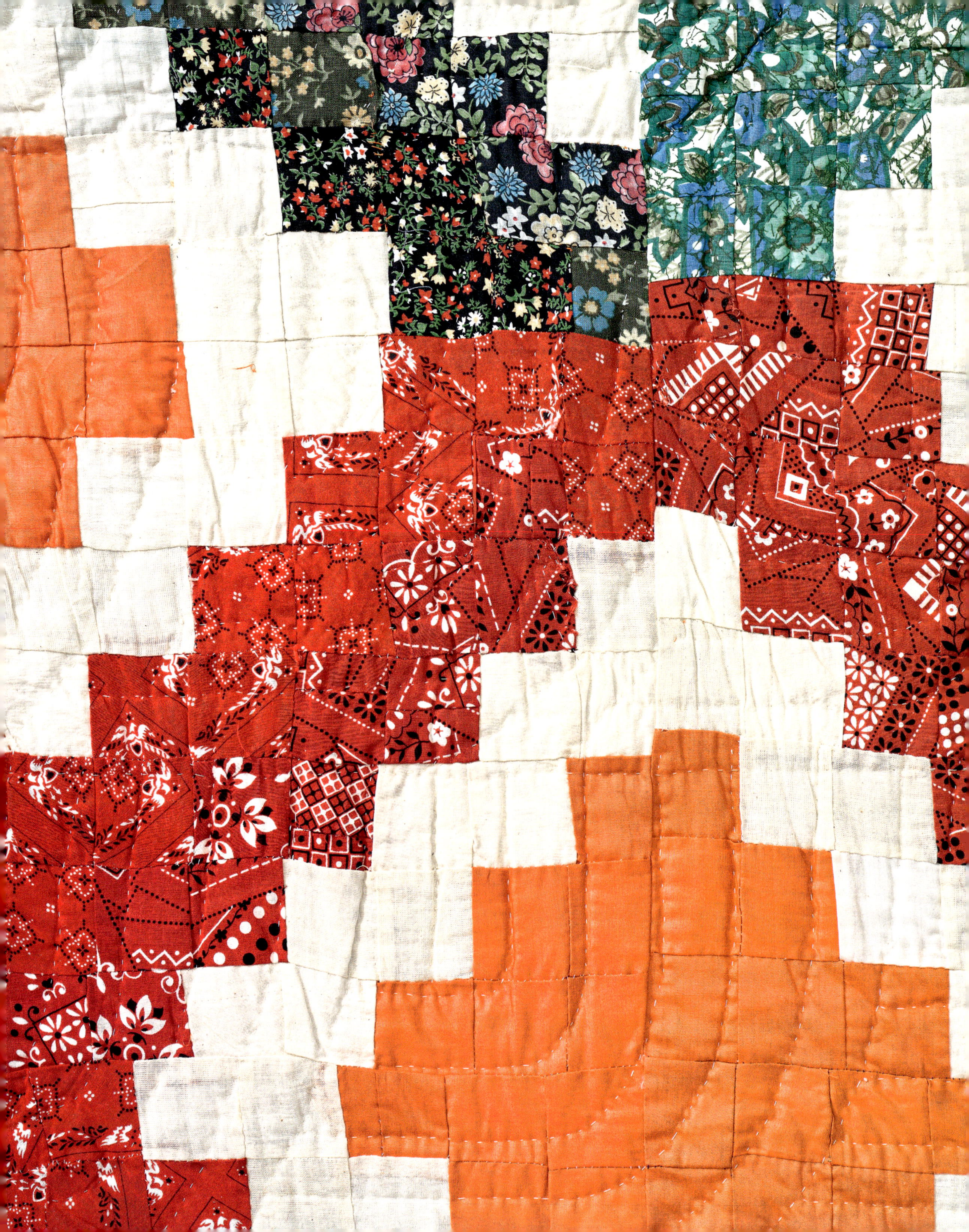

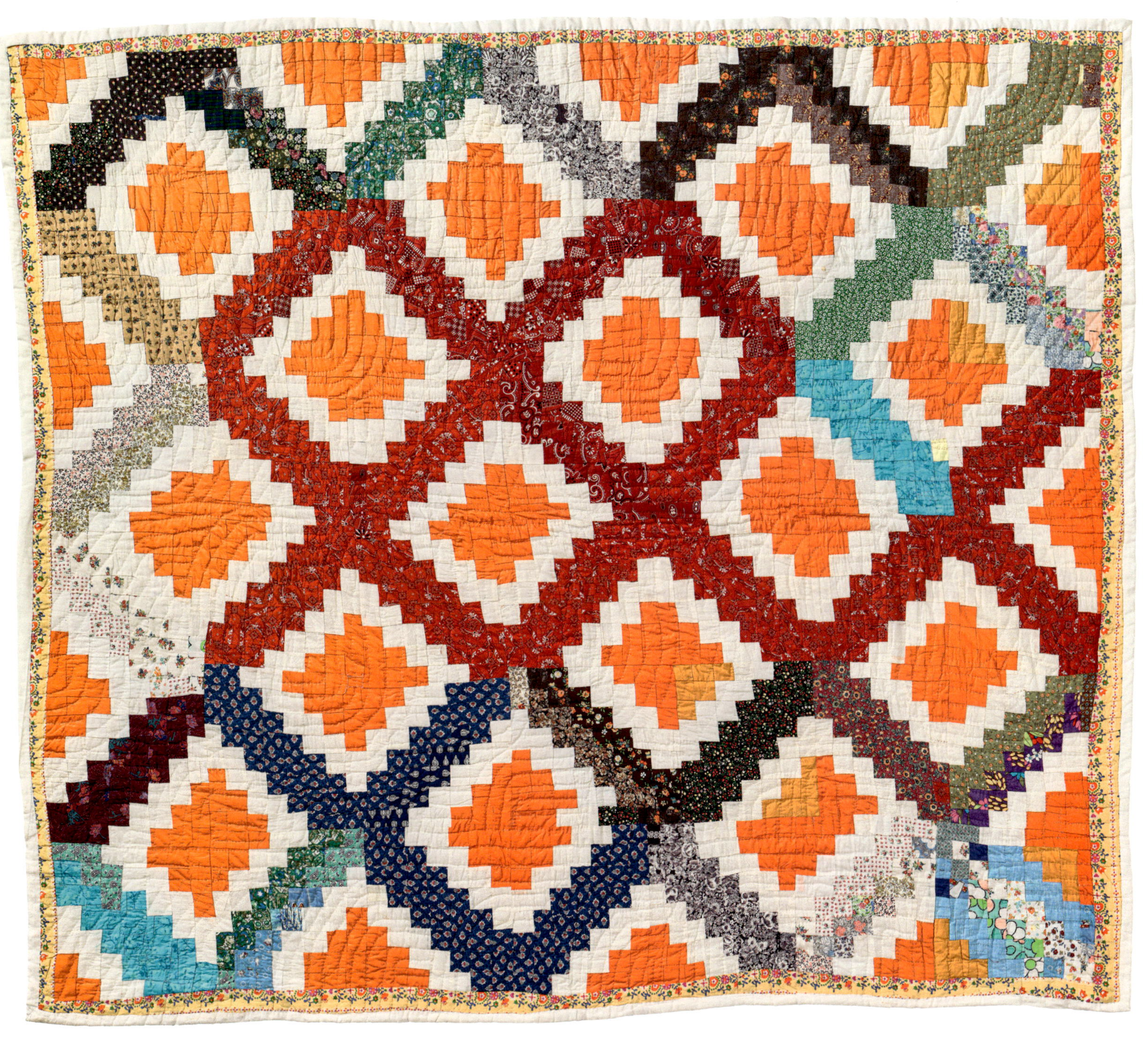

63. Untitled (original design)
Willia Ette Graham, 1981; Oakland, California

Detail

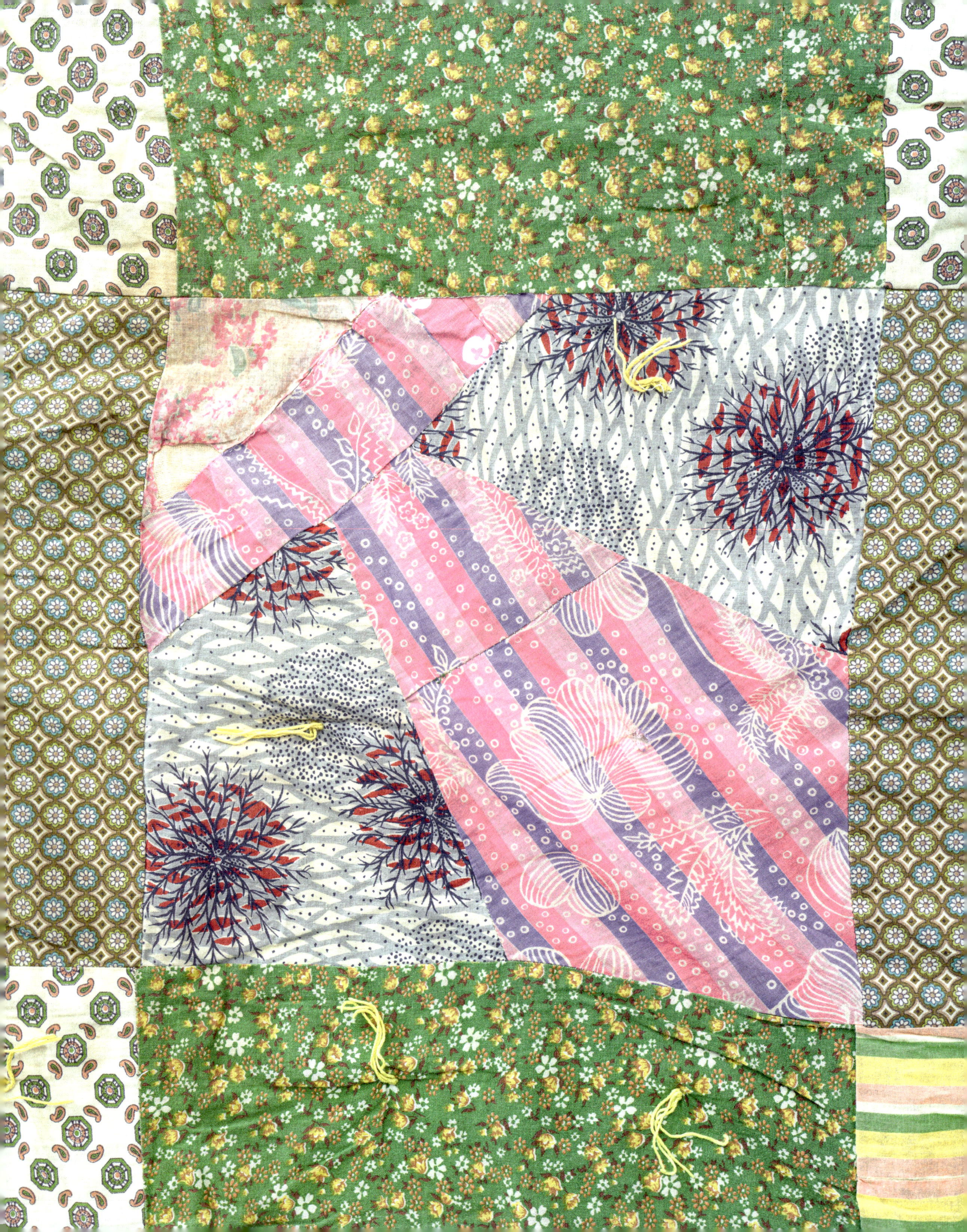

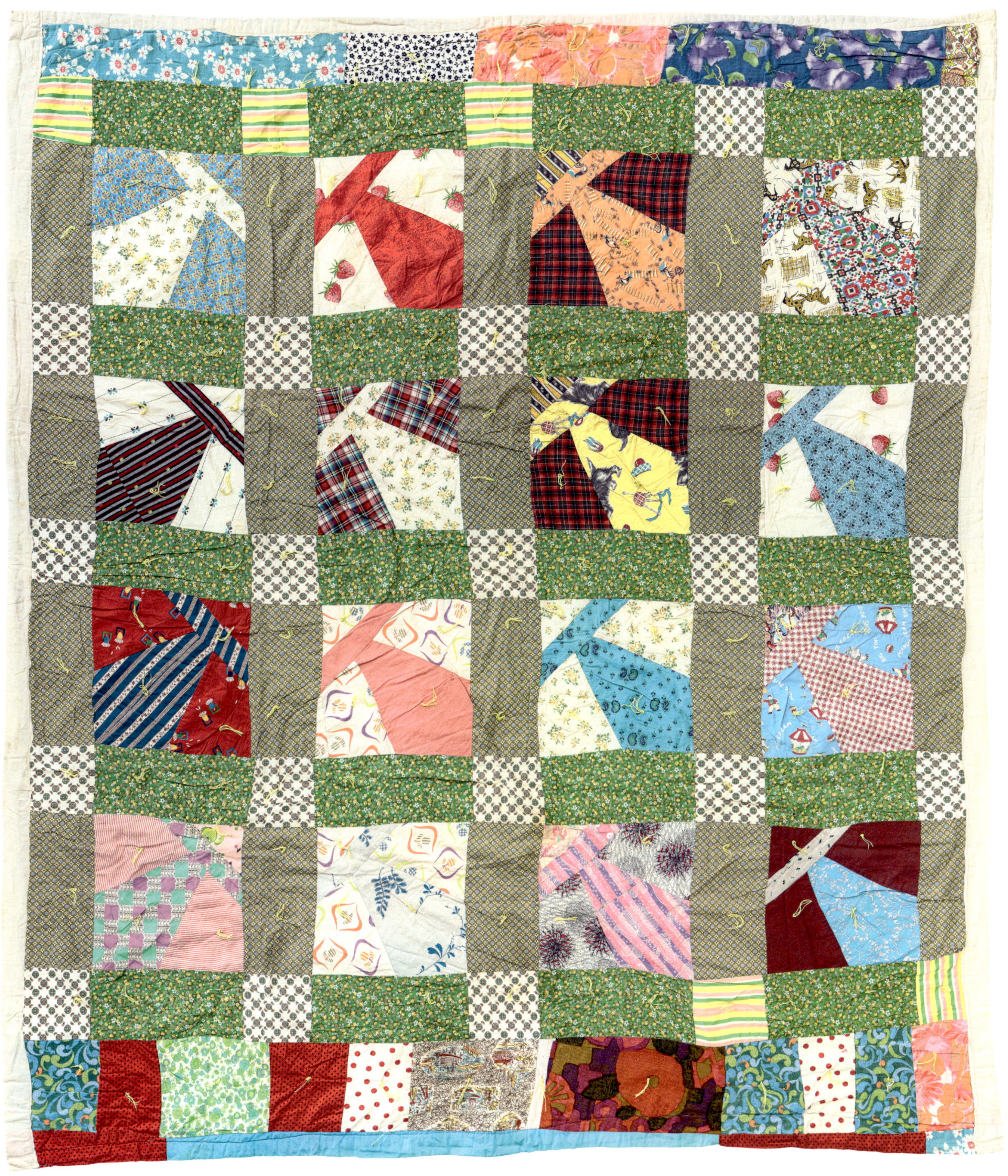

64. Untitled (unidentified pattern)
Dorothy Edwards and Georgia Lee Edwards, 1983; Fordyce, Arkansas
Angelia Tobias, Dorothy's daughter and Georgia's granddaughter, was the keeper of this quilt in Oakland, California, until 1991.

Detail

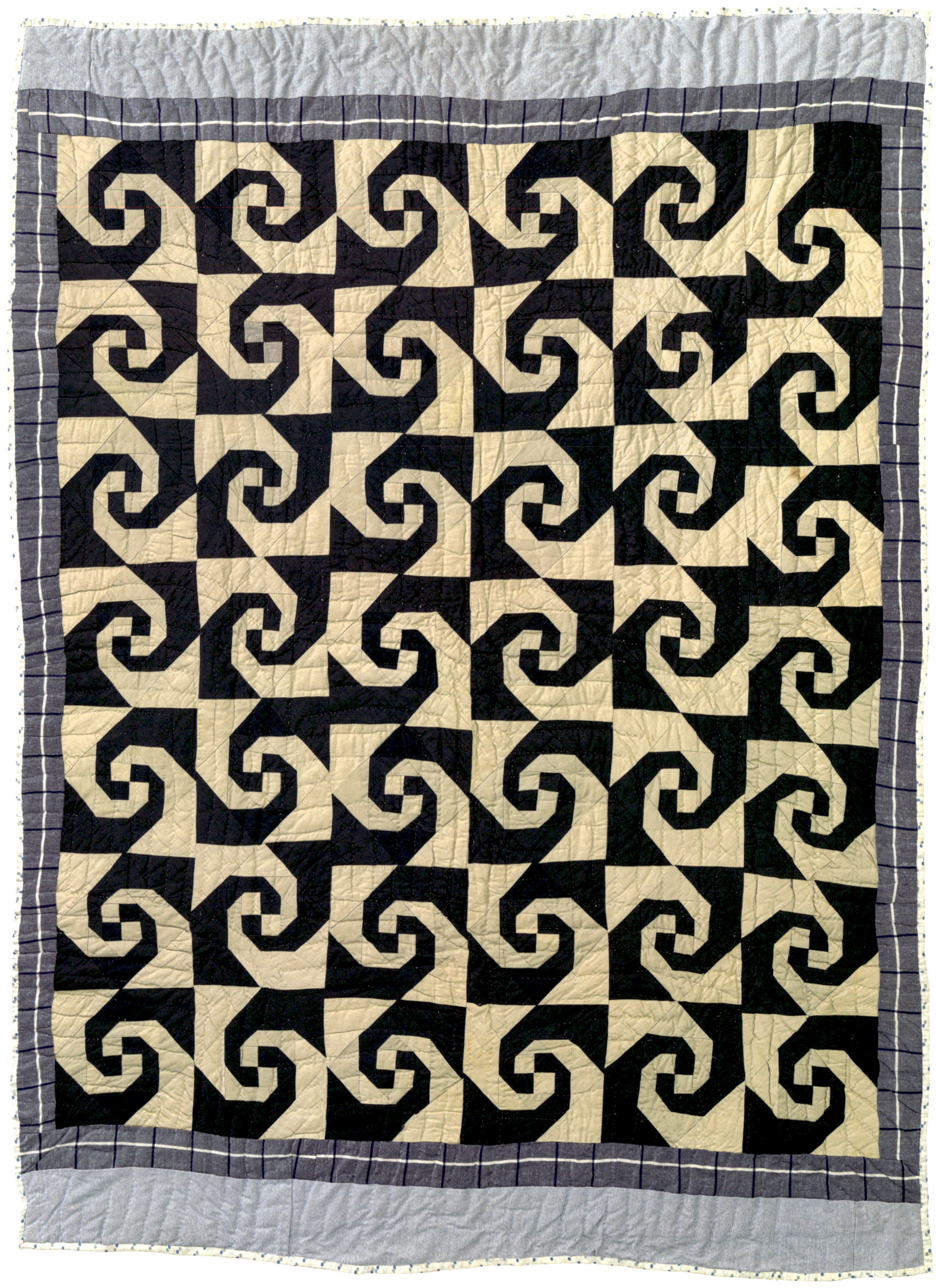

65. Untitled (Snail's Trail or Indiana Puzzle)
Anna Ruth Crofit, before 1983; Pine Bluff, Arkansas

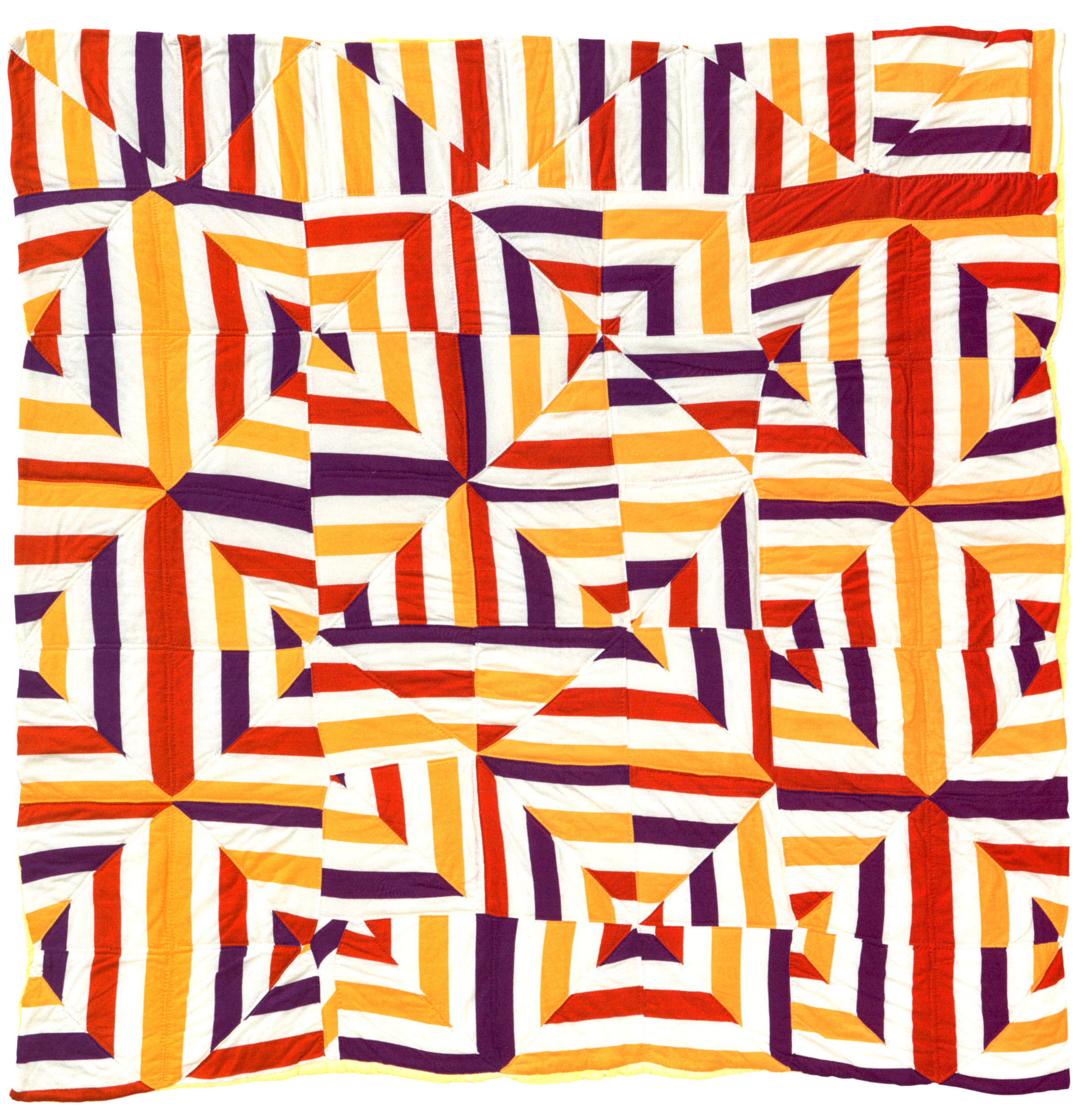

66. Untitled (Half-Square Triangles)
Irene Bankhead, 1984; Oakland, California

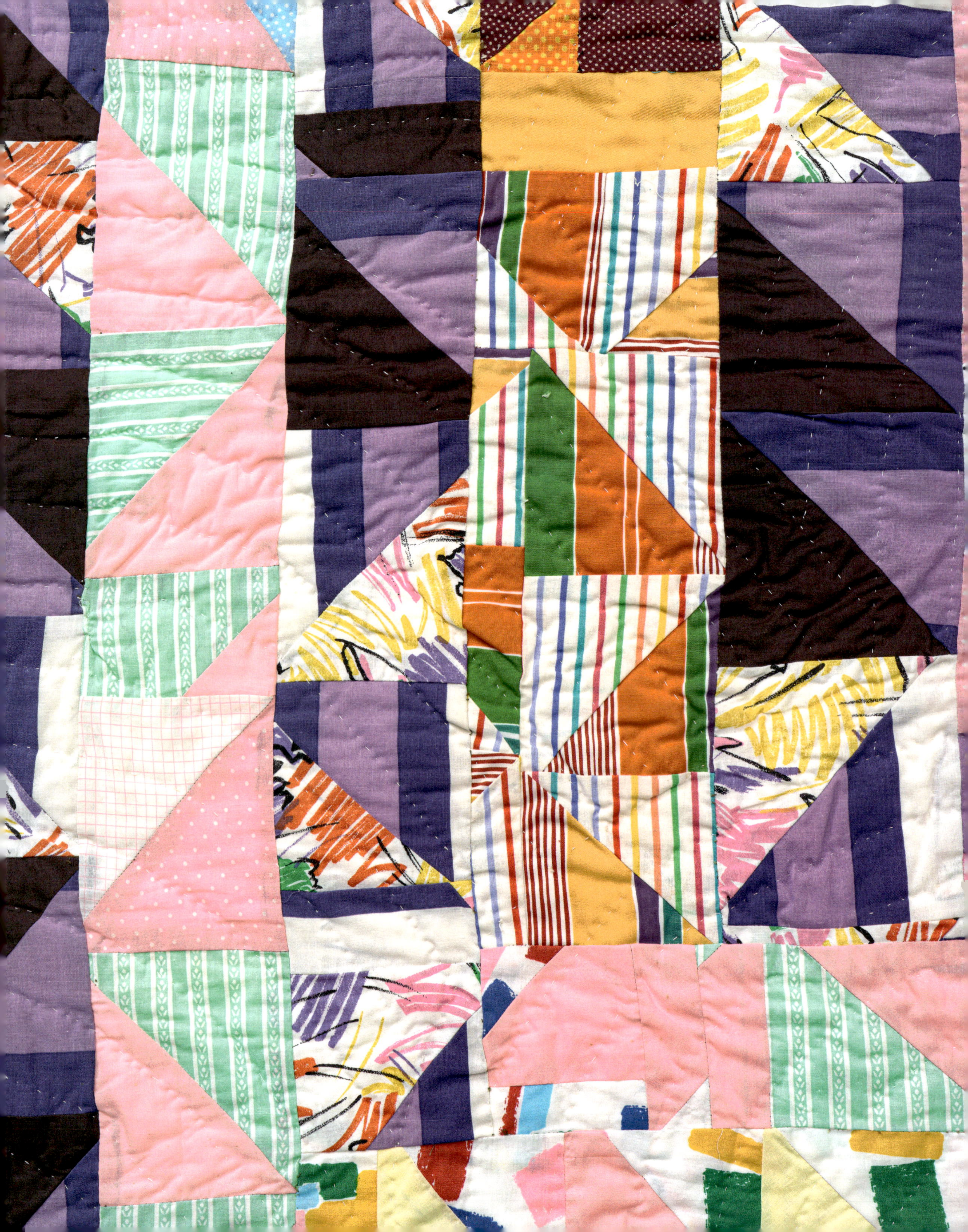

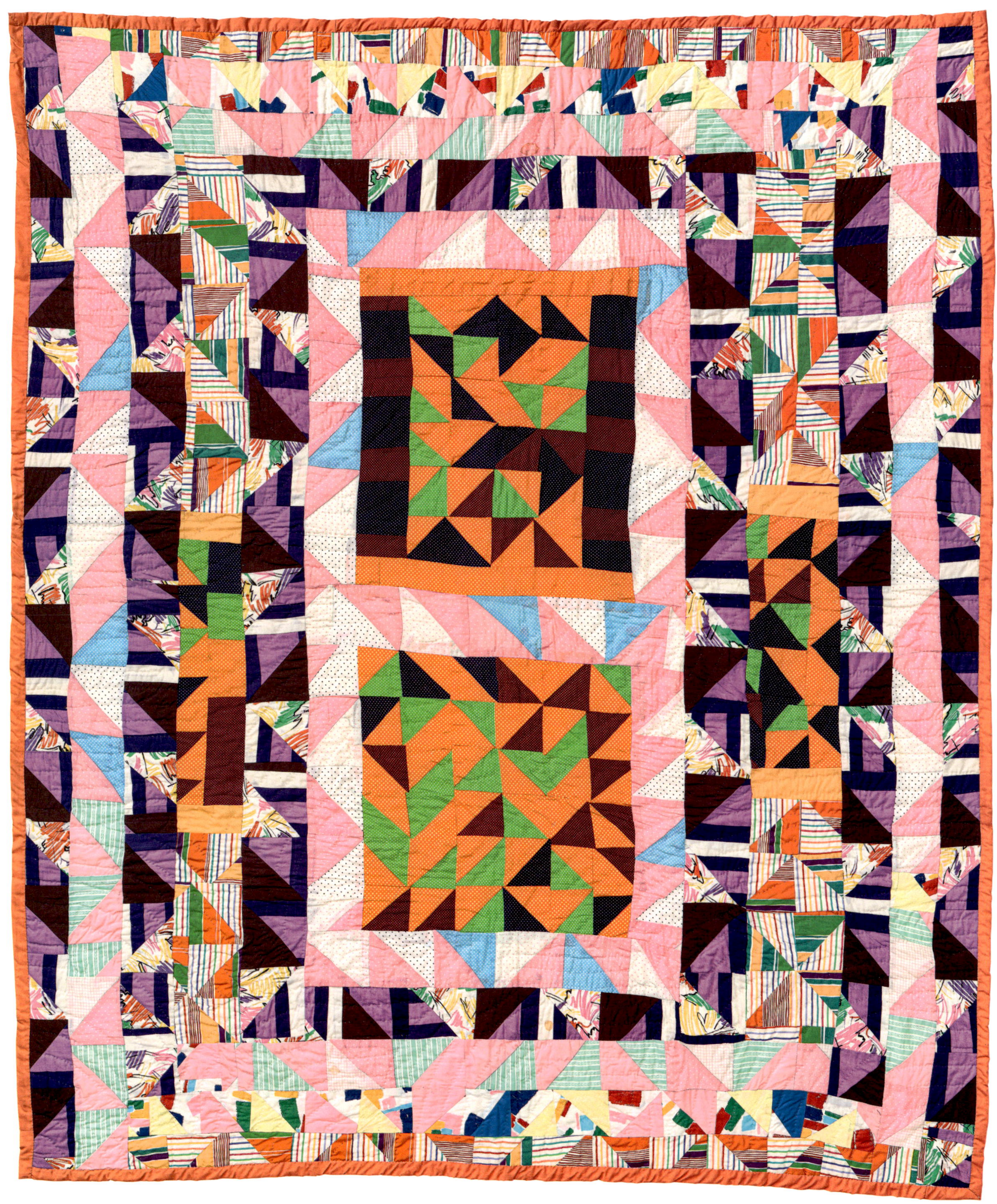

67. Untitled (Double Medallion, Half-Square Triangles)
Pieced by Sherry Ann Byrd, 1984, finished 1987; Richmond, California
Quilted by Irene Bankhead, 1987; Oakland, California

Detail

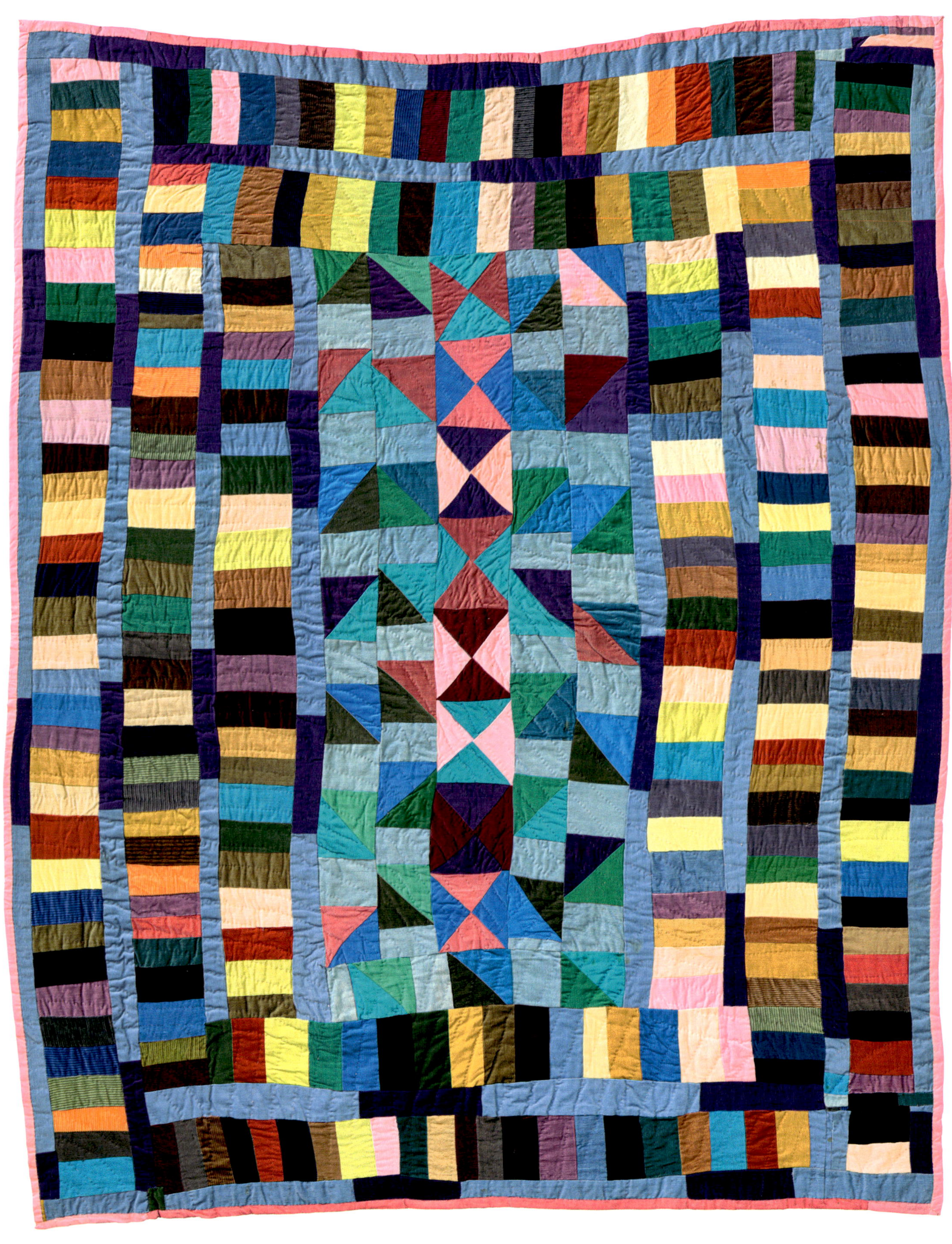

68. Untitled (Medallion)
Pieced by Angelia Tobias, 1984; Oakland, California
Quilted by Irene Bankhead, 1987; Oakland, California

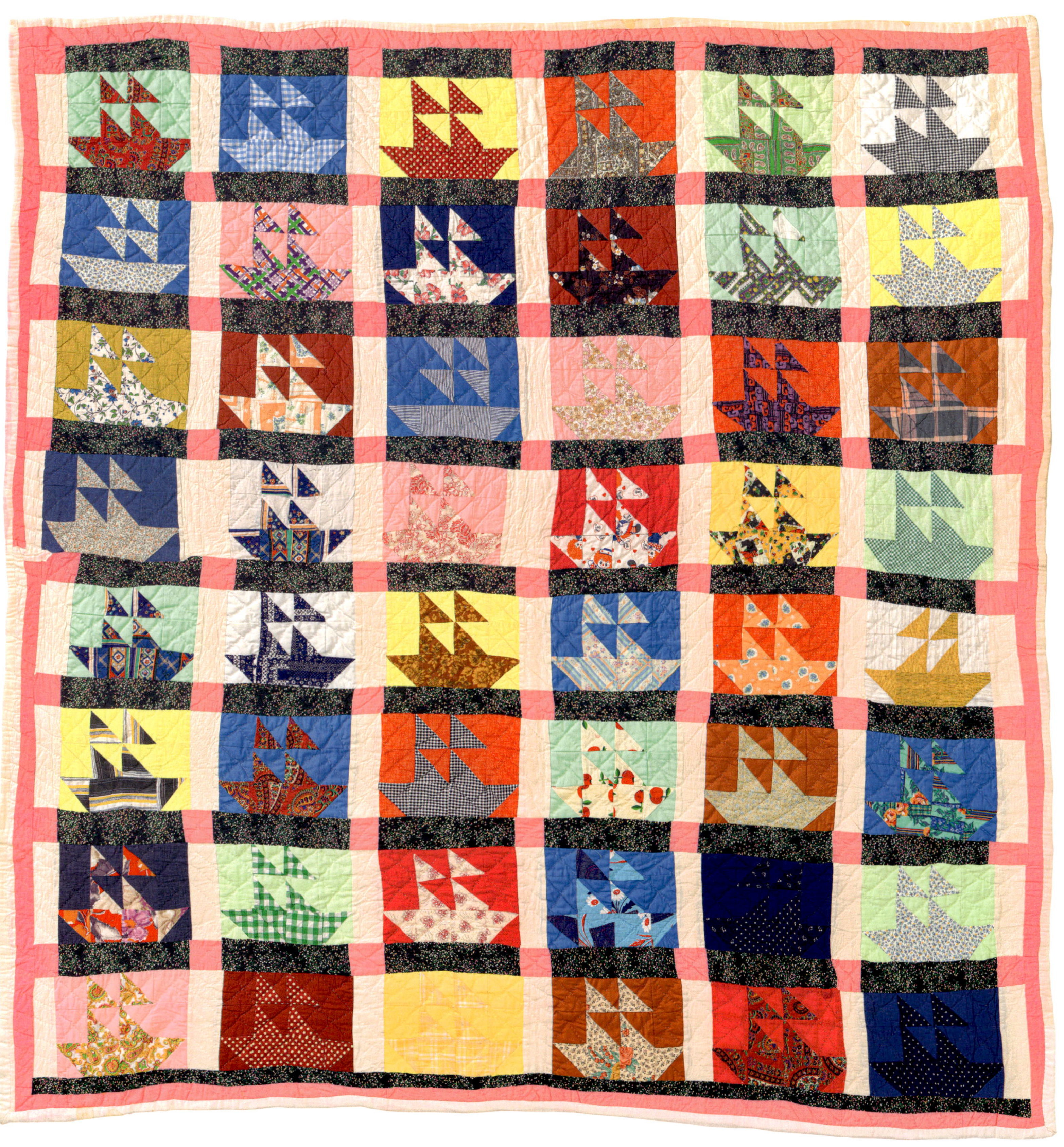

69. Untitled (Sailboats)
Mattie Lou Henderson, c. 1984; Berkeley, California

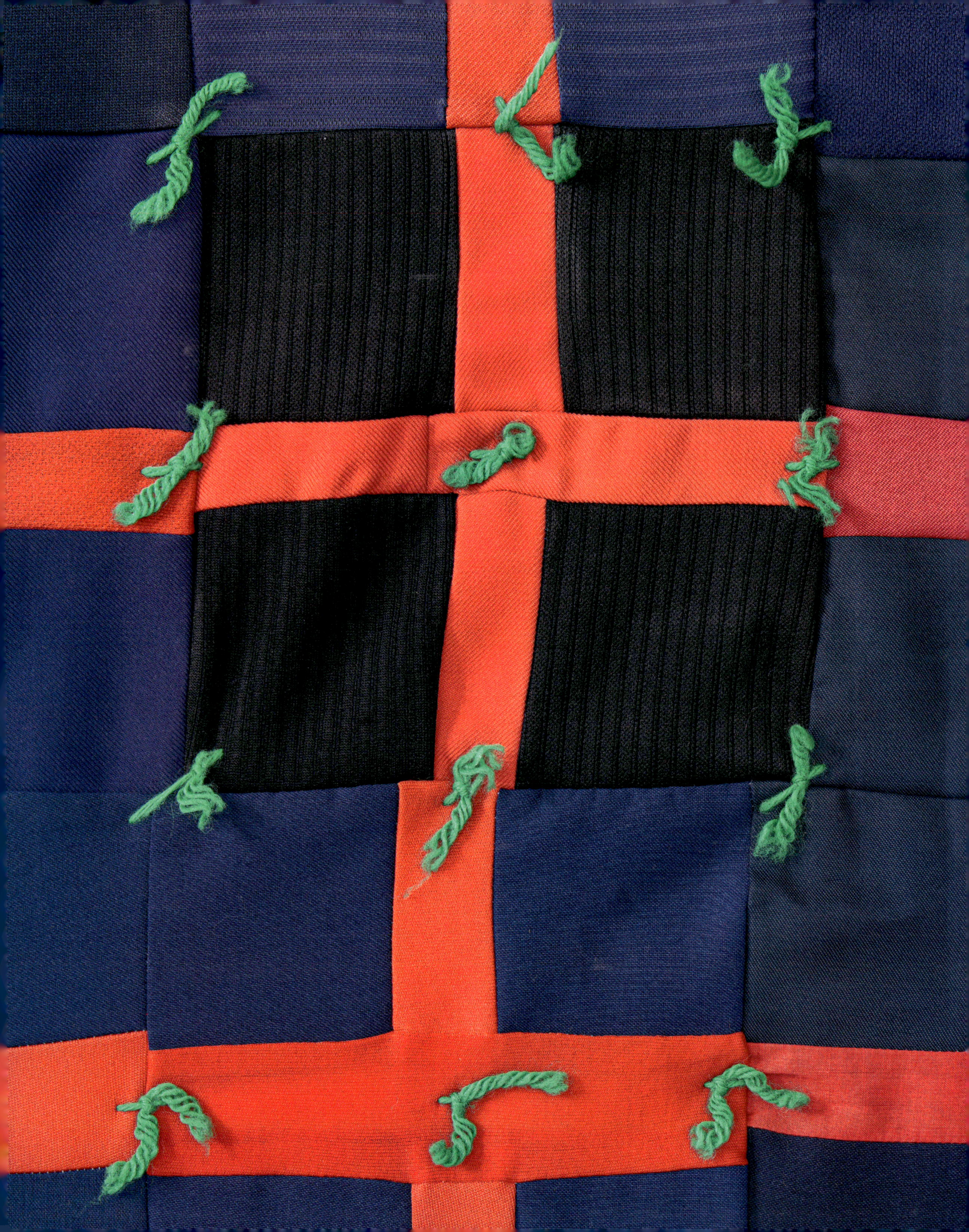

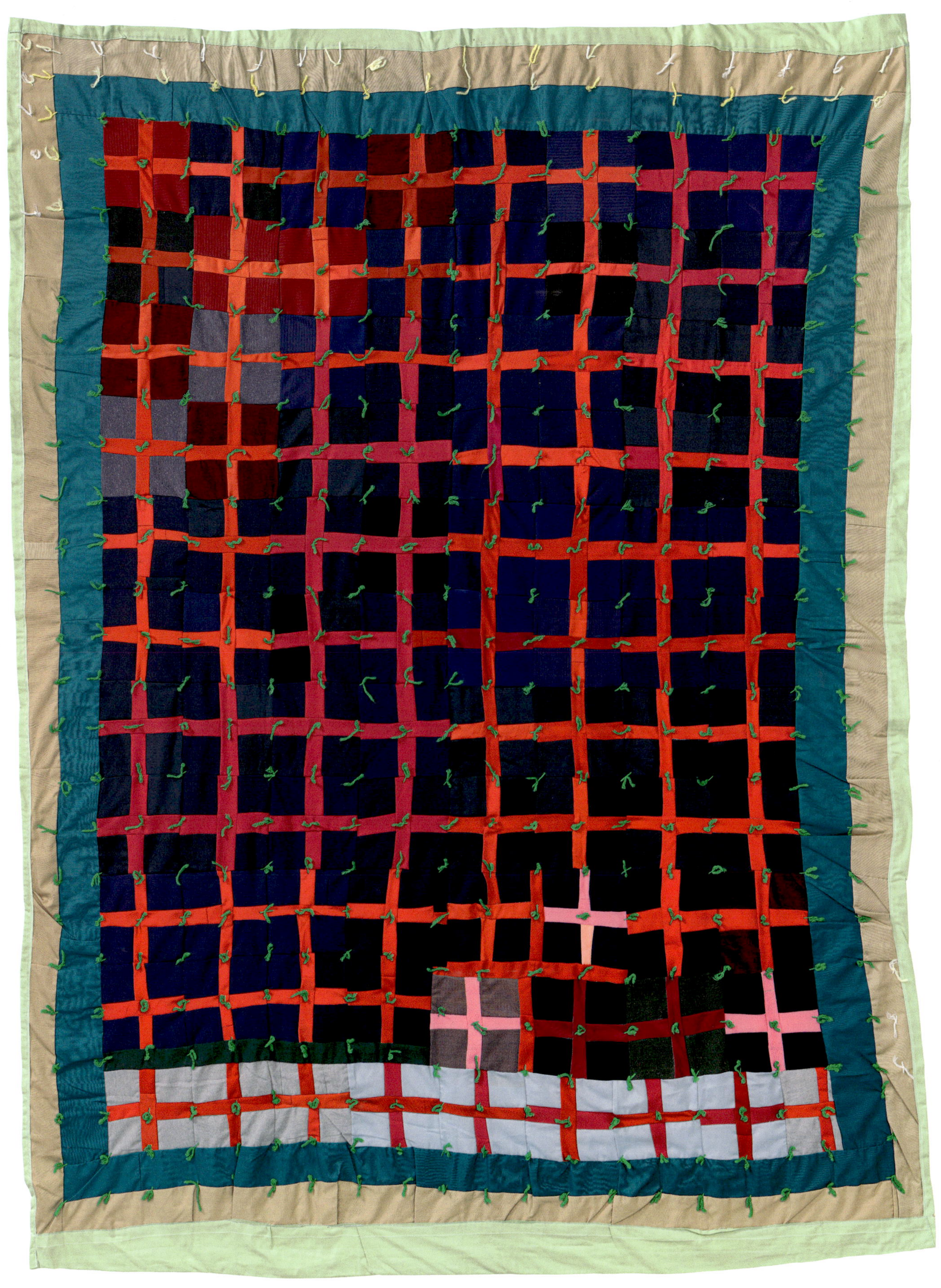

70. *The Fence*
Bettie Phillips, 1985; Oakland, California

Detail

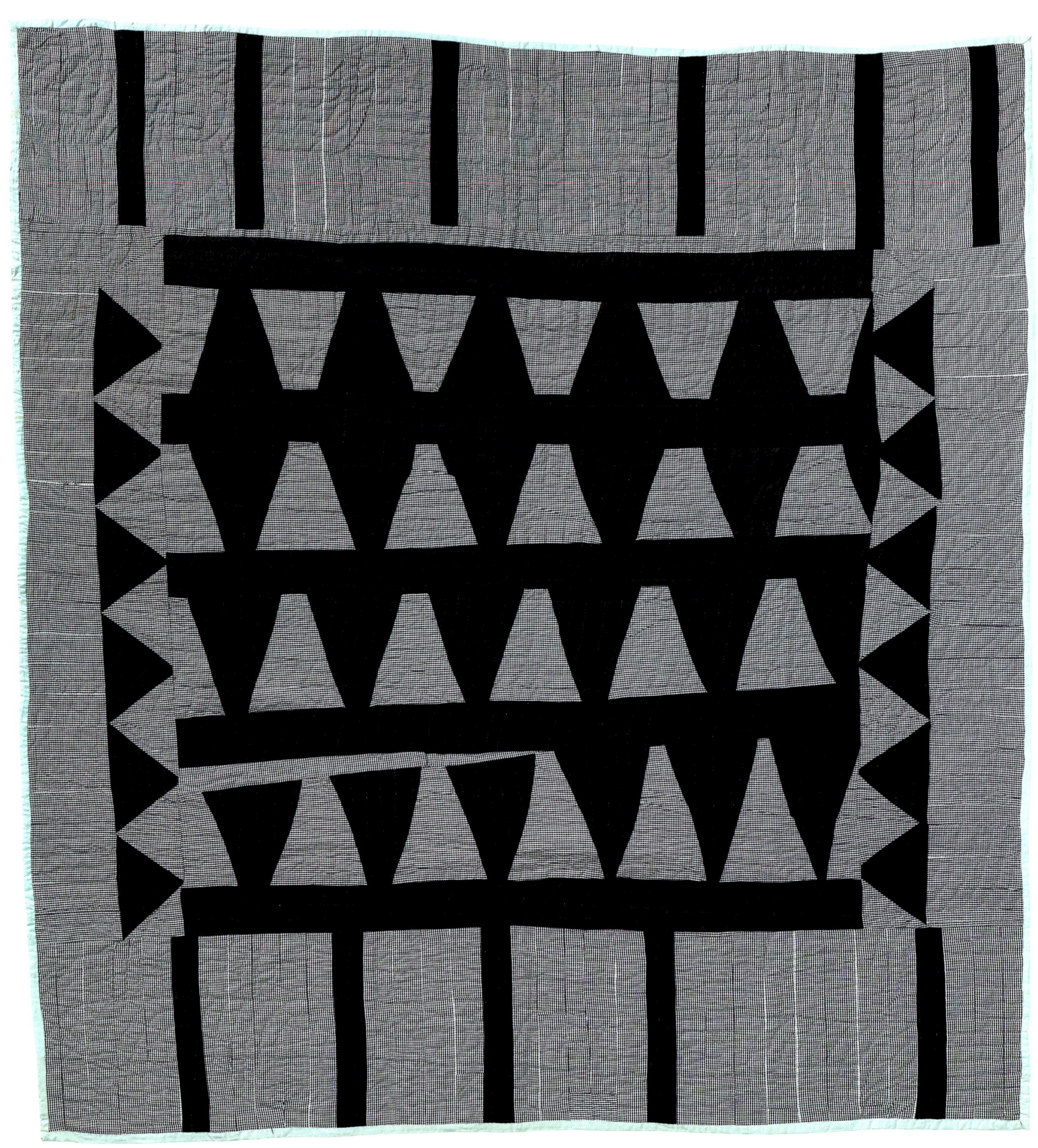

71. Untitled (Medallion)
Pieced by Charles Cater, 1985; Oakland, California
Quilted by Willia Ette Graham, 1986; Oakland, California

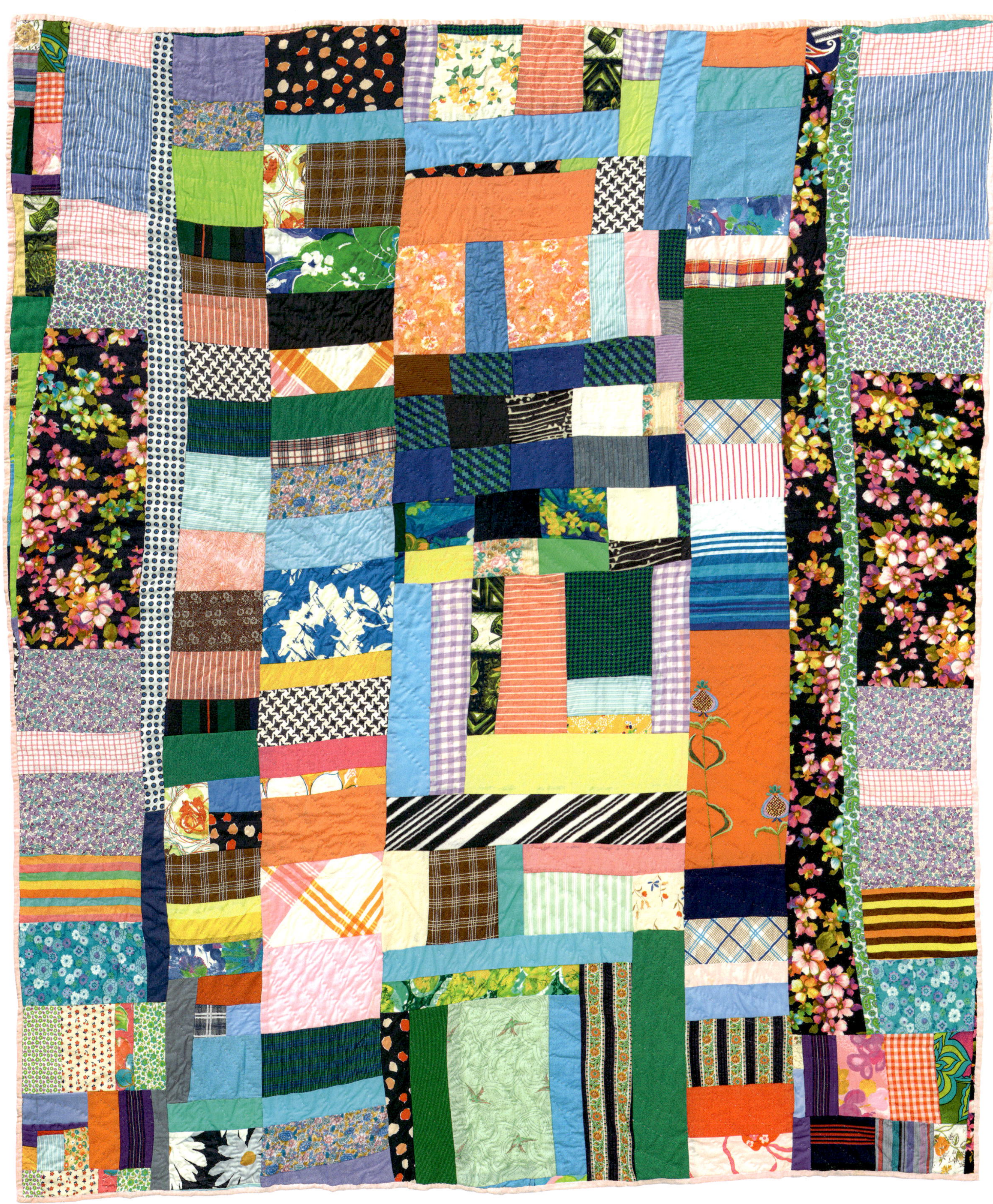

72. Untitled (Patchwork)
Angelia Tobias, 1985; Oakland, California
Quilted by Irene Bankhead, 1986; Oakland, California

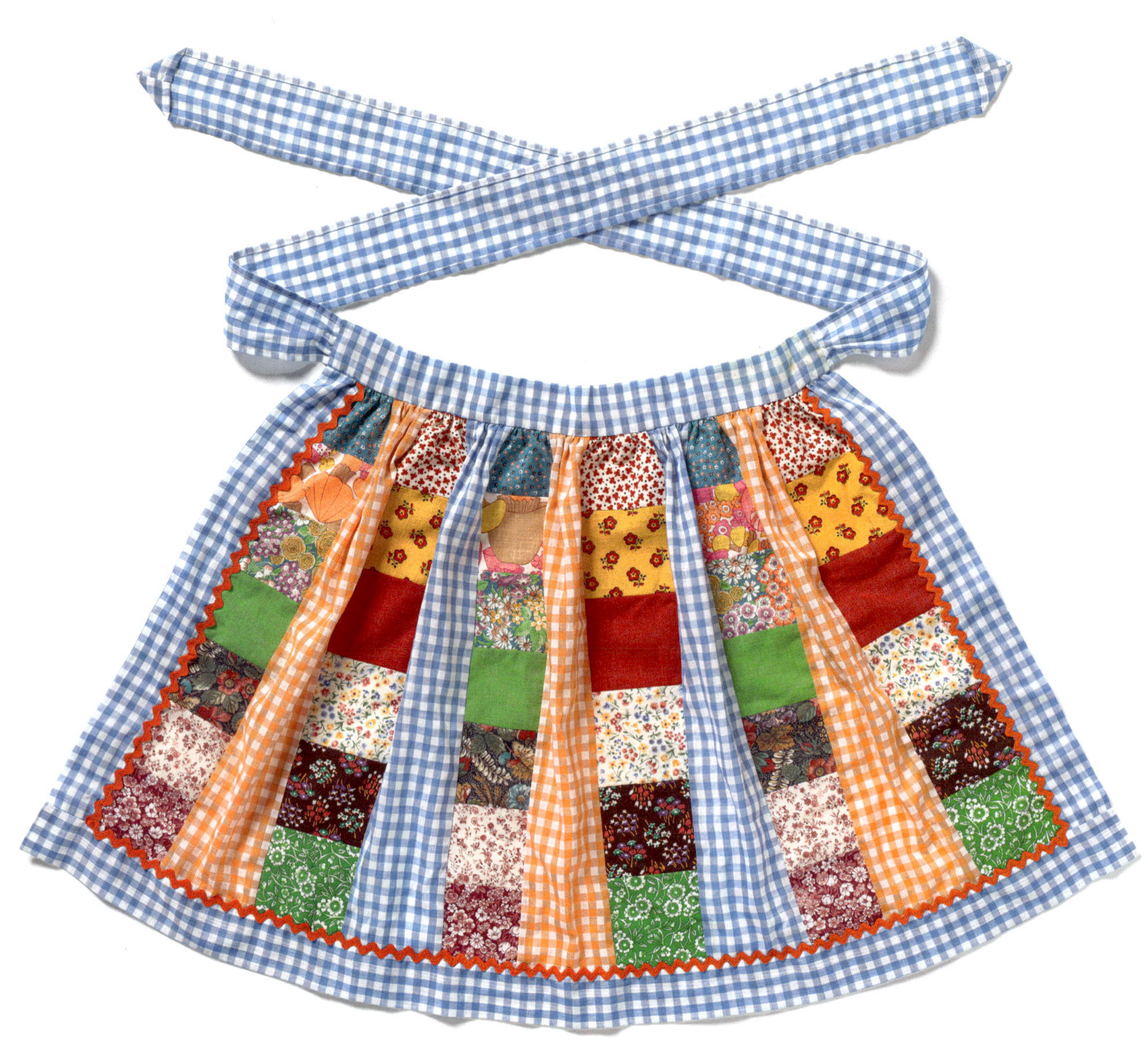

73. Half apron (One Patch)
Lee Wanda Jones, c. 1985; Berkeley, California

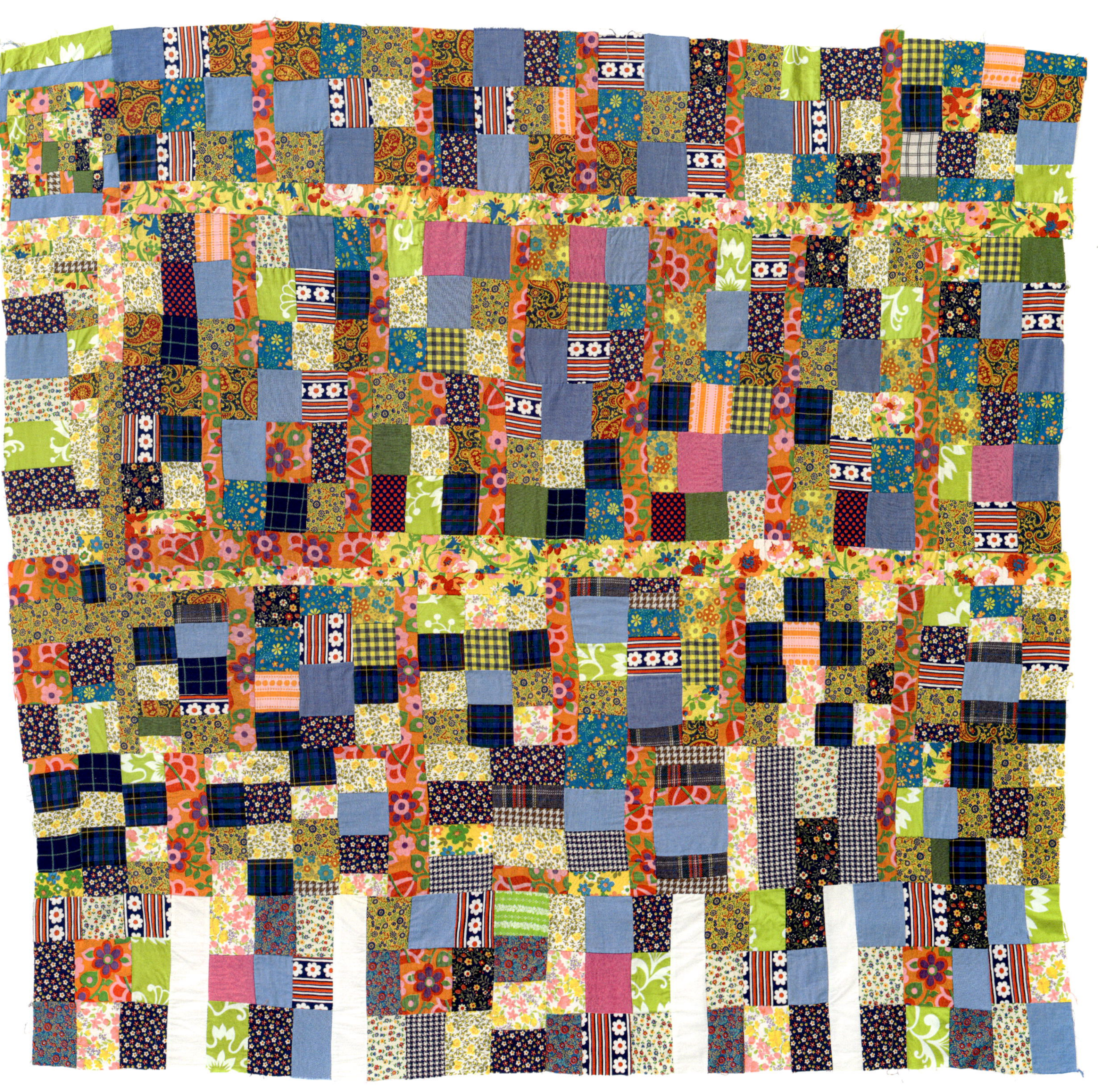

74. Untitled top (One Patch)
Ruby Lewis, c. 1985; Berkeley, California

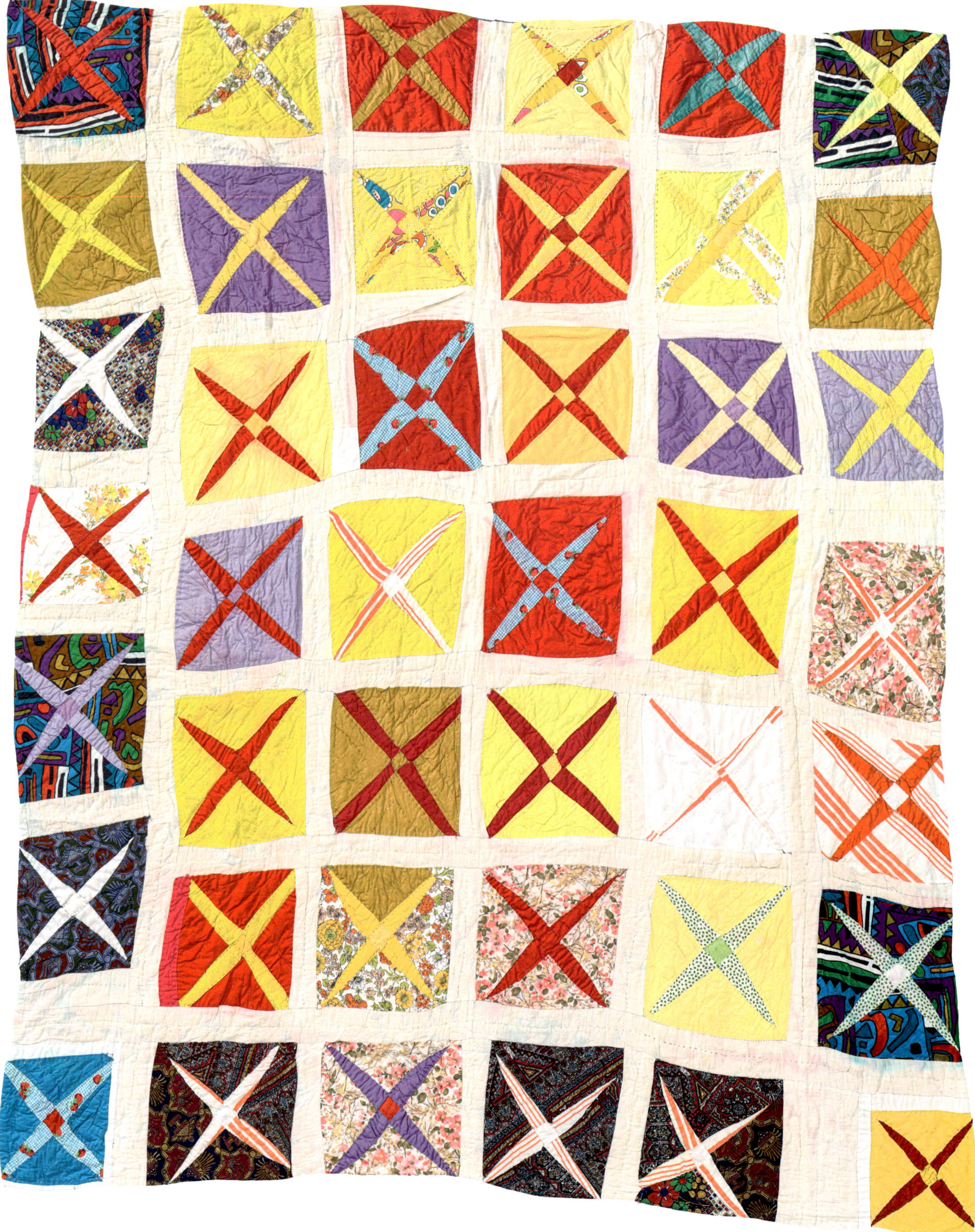

Front

75. Untitled (Crossed Canoes or Evening Star)
Willie Mae Chatman, 1986; Berkeley, California

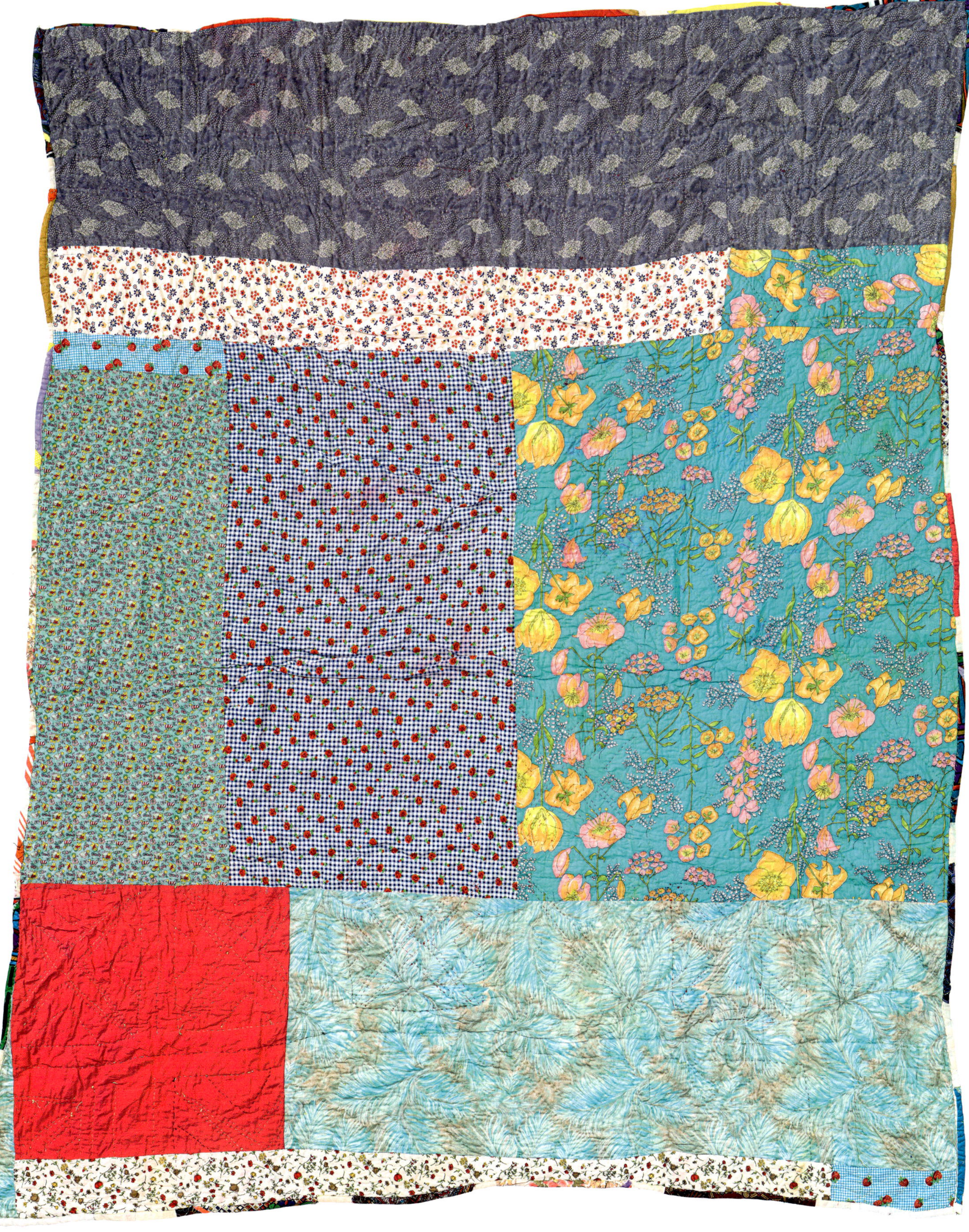
Back

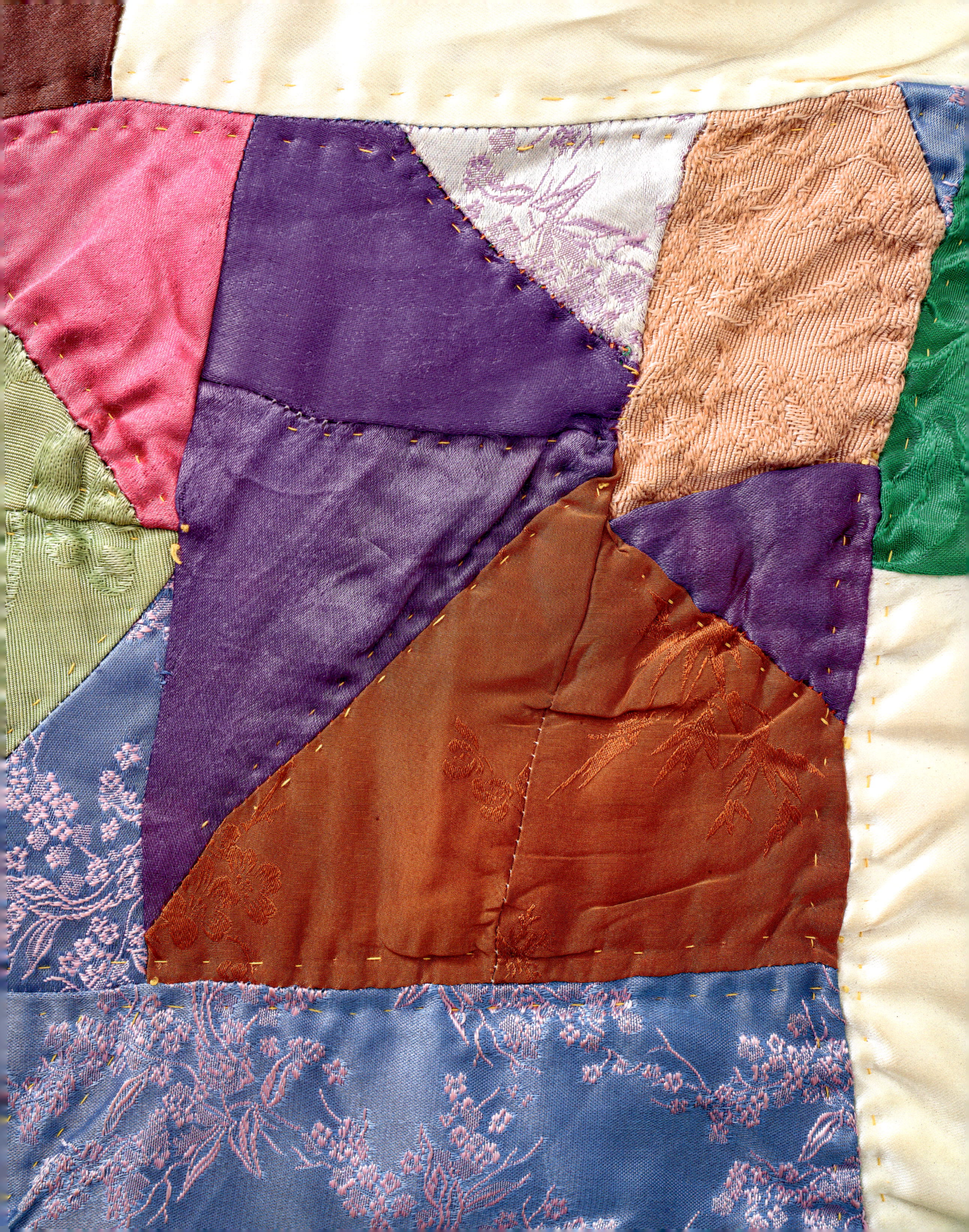

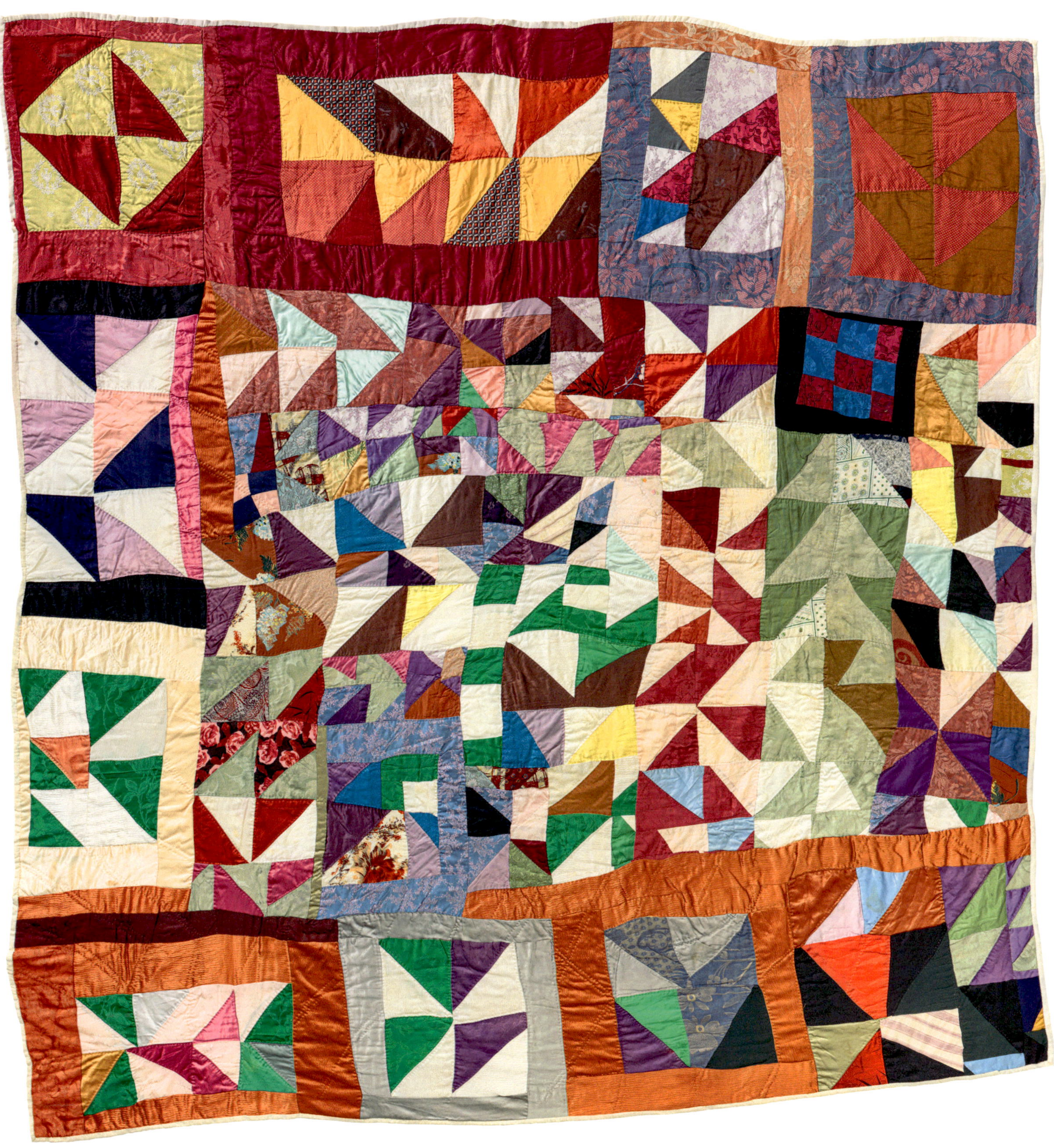

76. Untitled (Half-Square Triangles, Nine Patch)
Pieced by Rosie Lee Tompkins, 1986; Richmond, California
Quilted by Irene Bankhead, 1987; Oakland, California

Detail

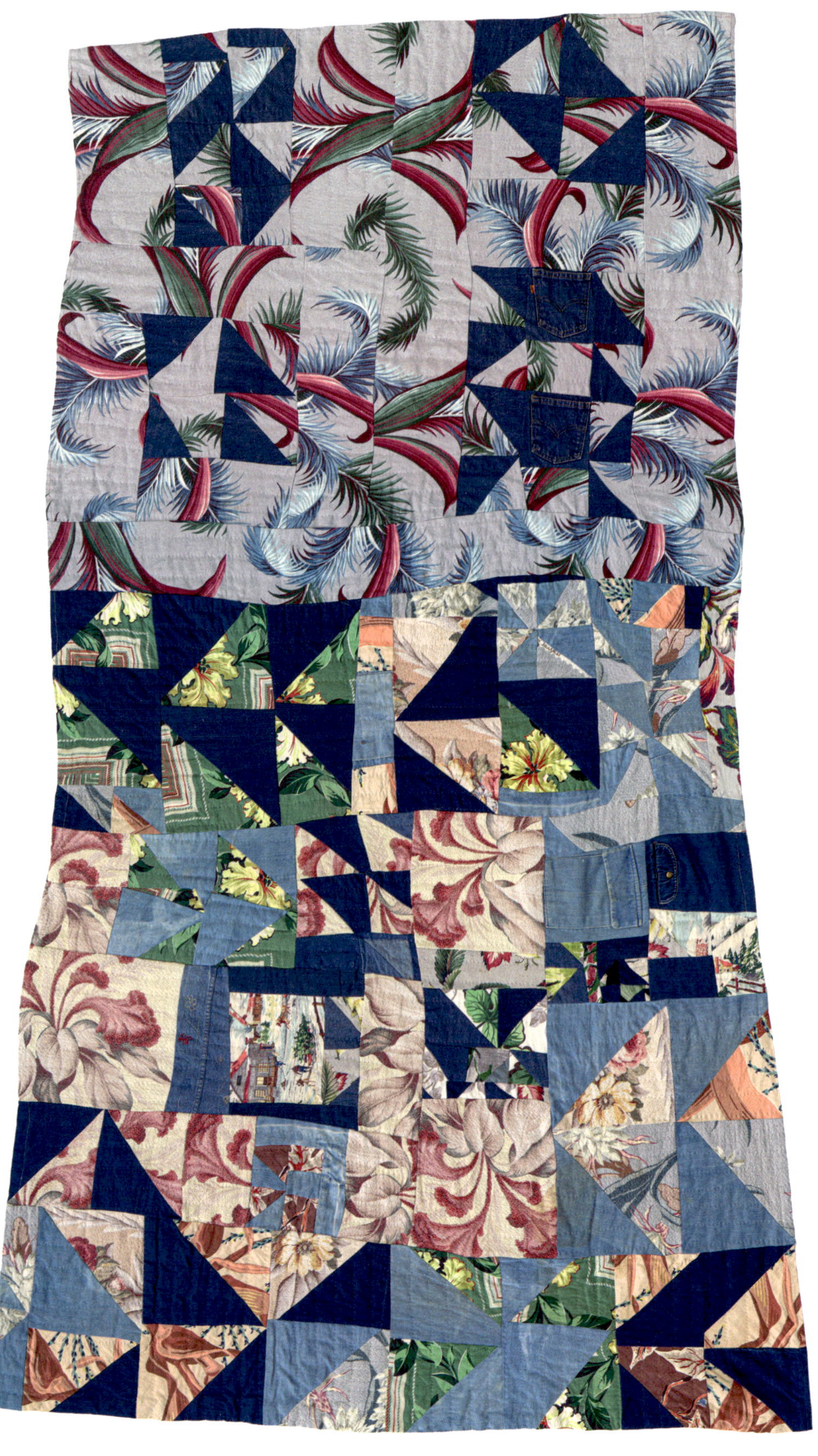

77. Untitled (Half-Square Triangles)
Pieced by Rosie Lee Tompkins, 1986; Richmond, California
Quilted by Irene Bankhead, 1996; Oakland, California

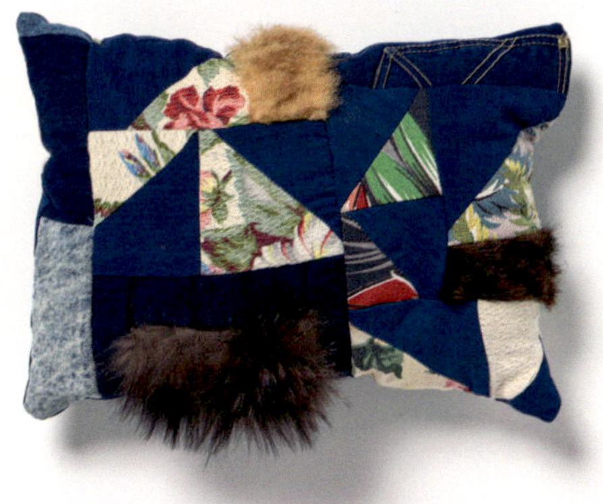
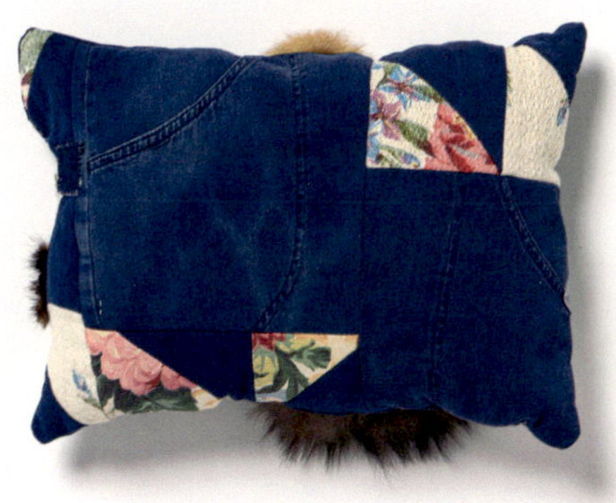
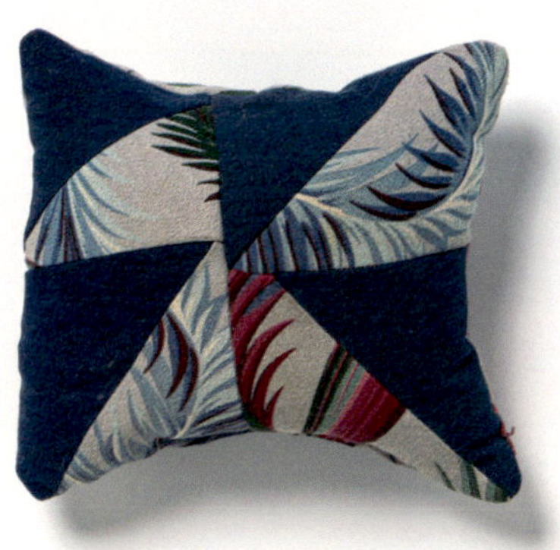
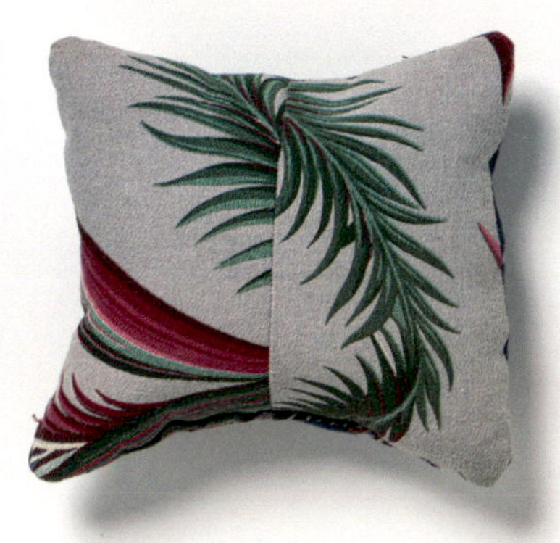
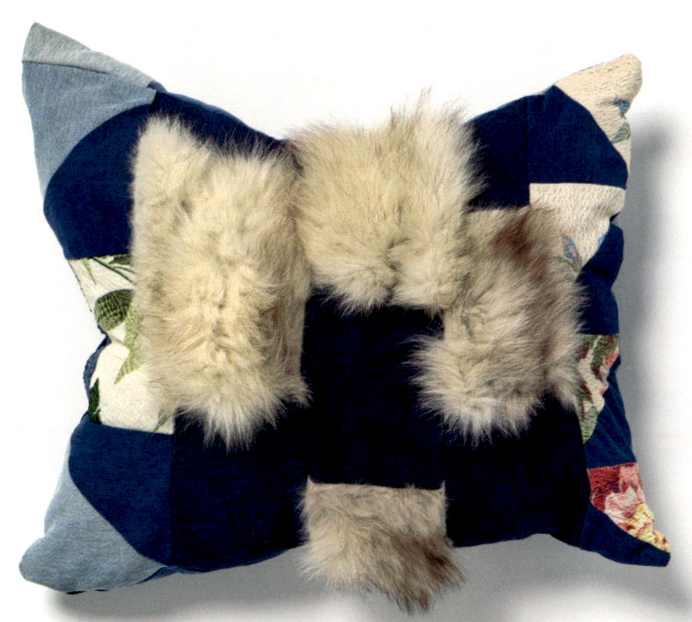
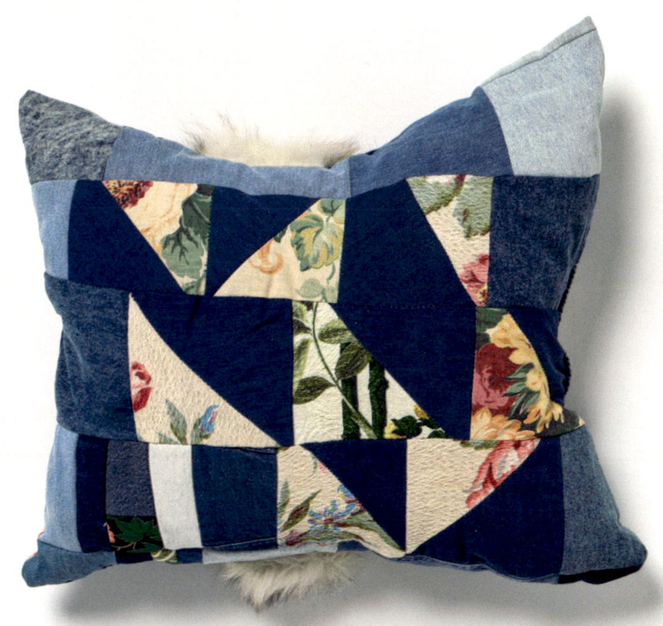

Front

Back

78. Pillow (Half-Square Triangles)
Rosie Lee Tompkins, 1997; Richmond, California

79. Pillow (Half-Square Triangles)
Rosie Lee Tompkins, 1988; Richmond, California

80. Pillow (Half-Square Triangles)
Rosie Lee Tompkins, 1997; Richmond, California

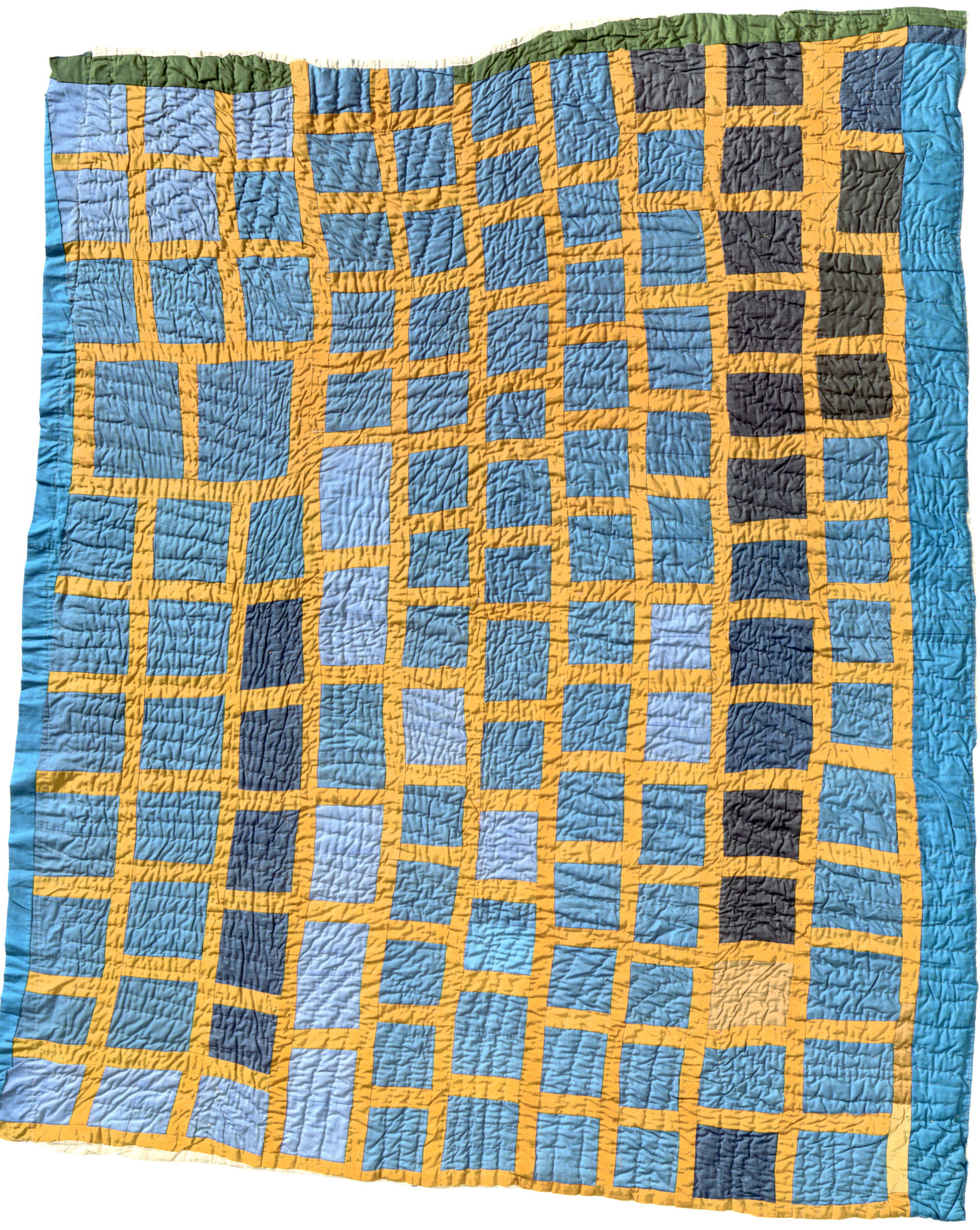

81. Untitled (One Patch with borders)
Florine Taylor, 1987; Ozan, Arkansas

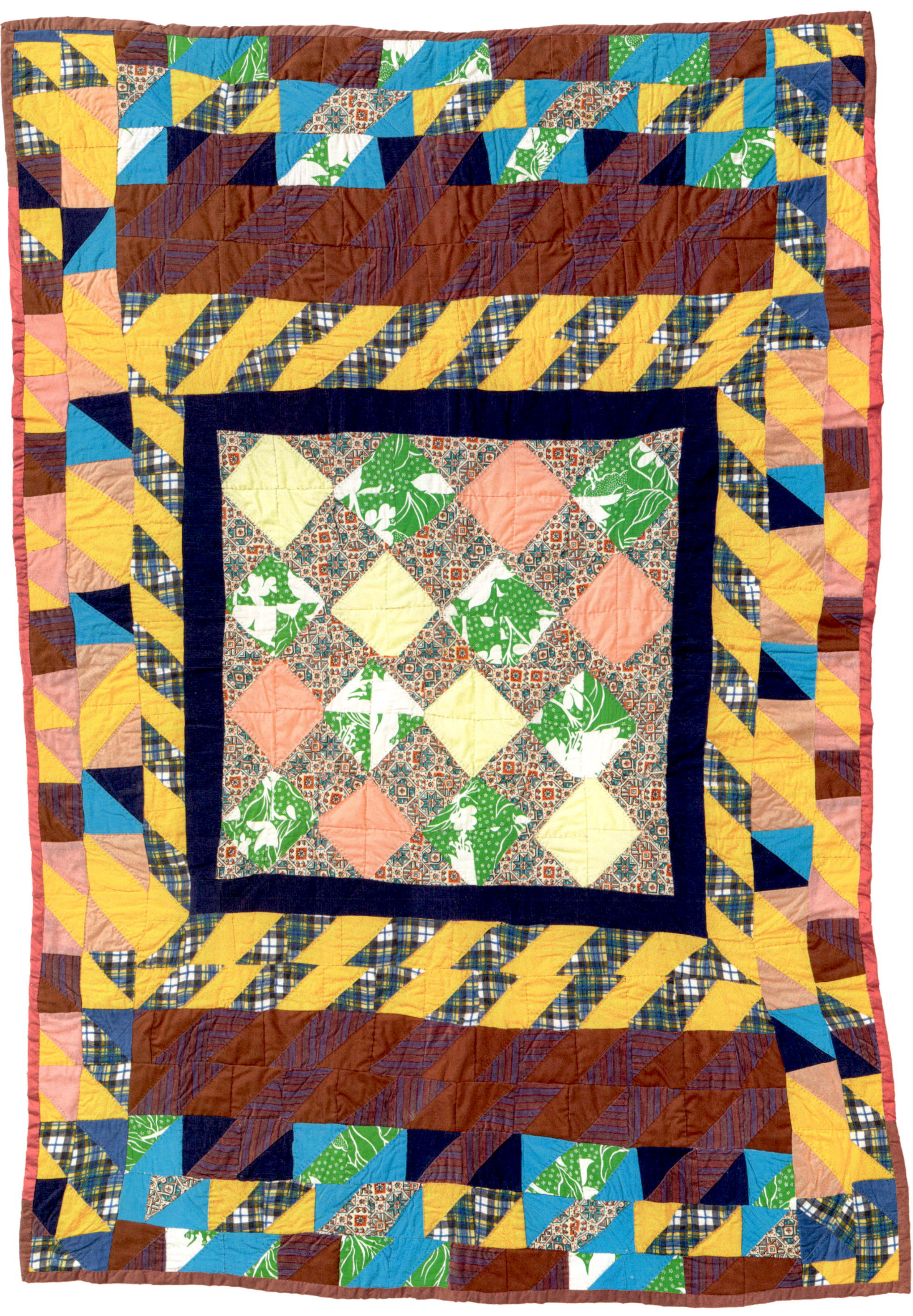

82. Untitled (Medallion, Broken Dishes Variation, Half-Square Triangles)
Pieced by Bara Byrd-Stewart, 1988; Richmond, California
Quilted by Irene Bankhead, 1989; Oakland, California

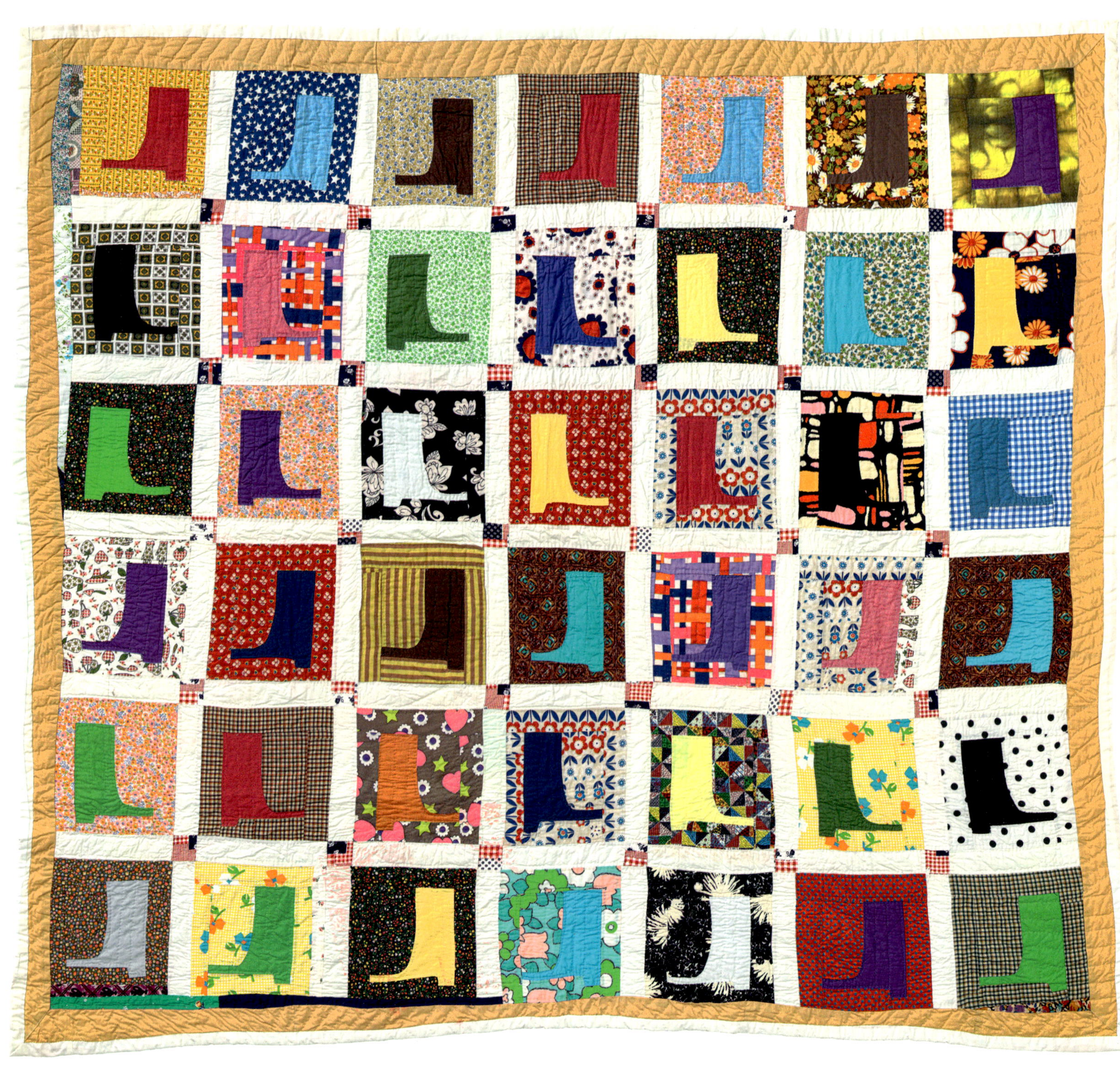

83. Untitled (Boots)
Pieced and quilted by Willia Ette Graham, 1988; Oakland, California
Quilted by Johnnie Wade, 1988; San Francisco, California

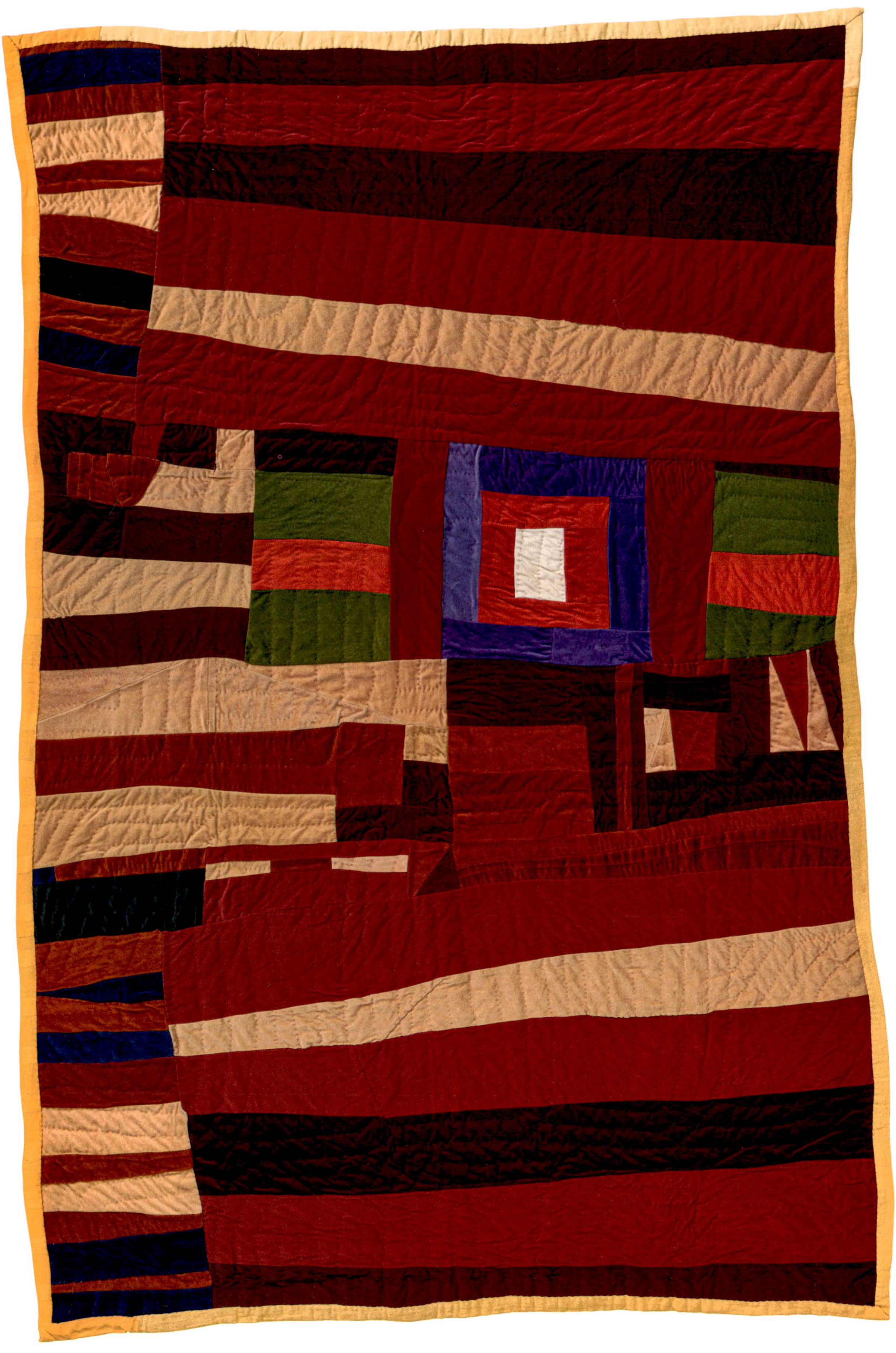

84. *Road to Nowhere*
Pieced by Lee Wanda Jones, 1988; Oakland, California
Quilted by Willia Ette Graham and Johnnie Wade, 1988; Oakland, California

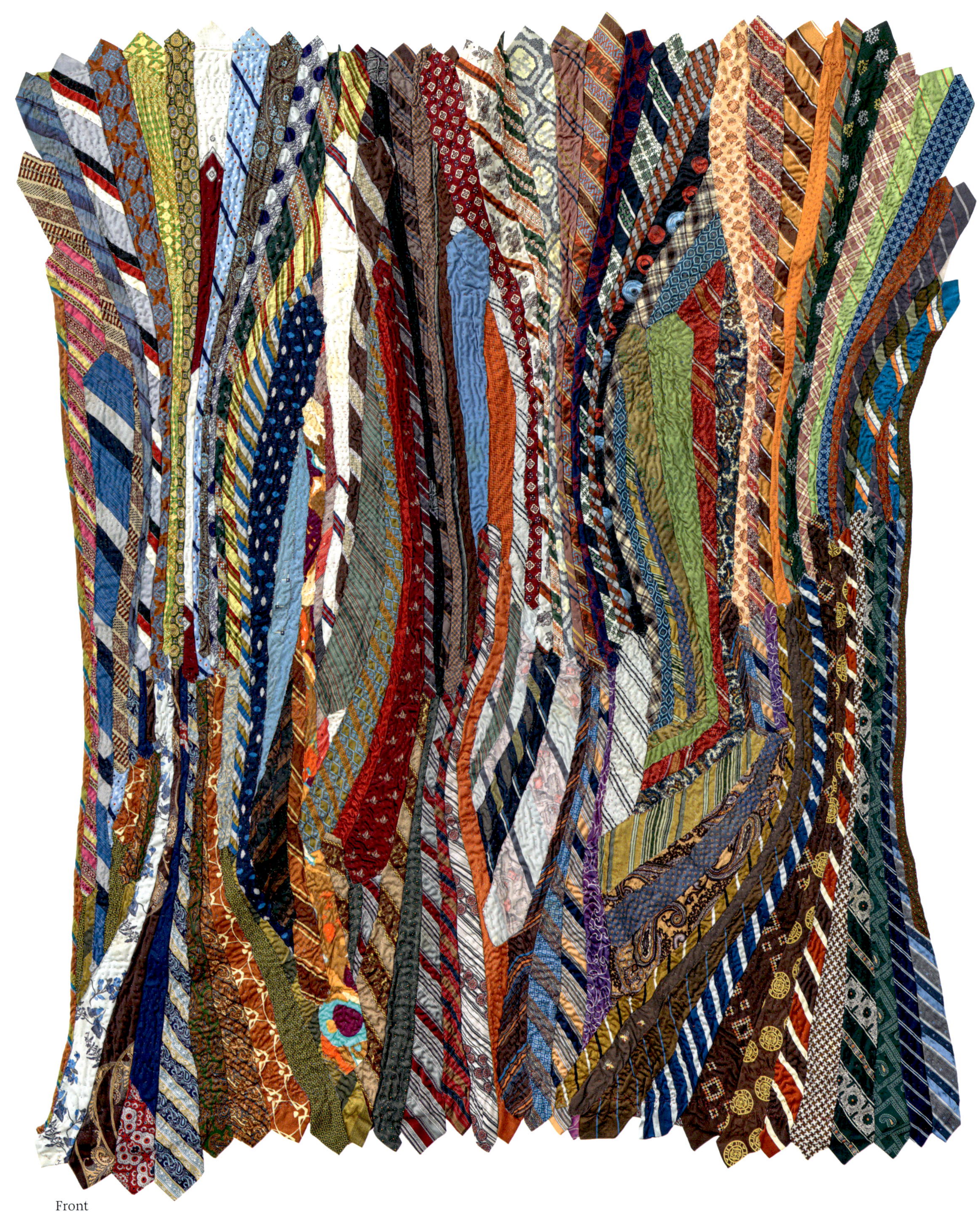

Front

85. Untitled (Necktie quilt)
Gerstine Scott, 1989; Oakland, California

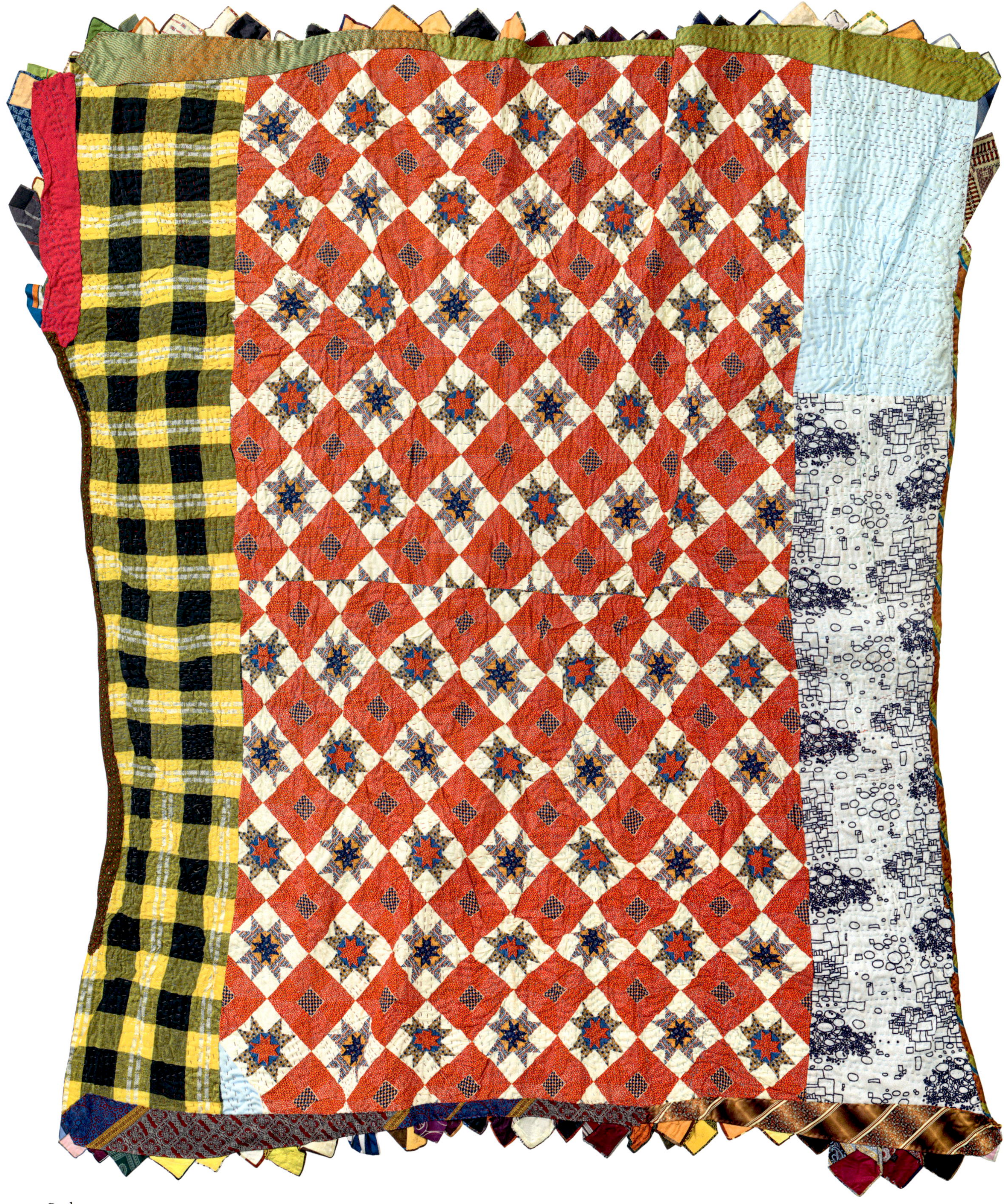

Back

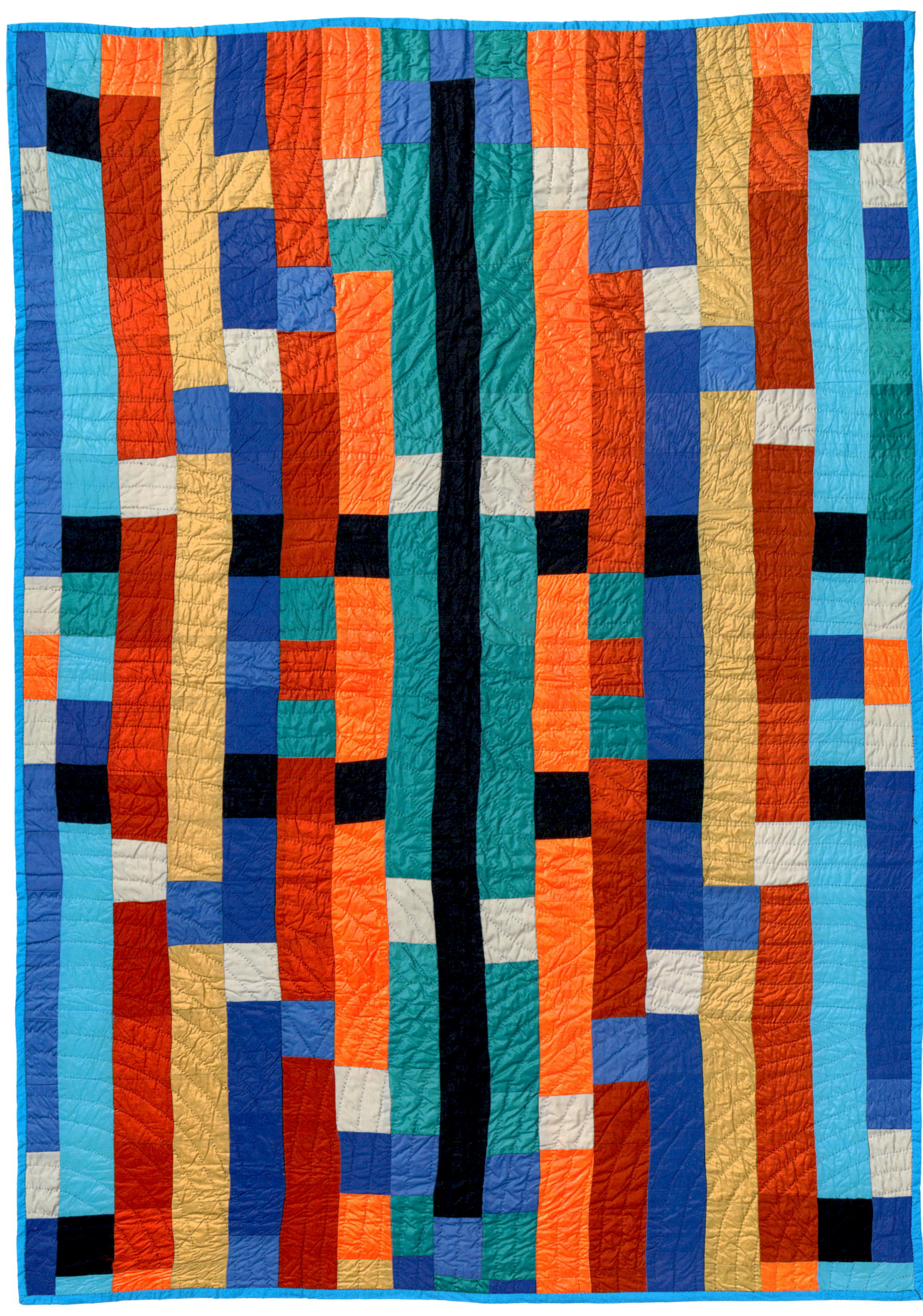

86. Untitled (Strip)
Pieced by Gussie Wells and Arbie Williams, 1989; Oakland, California
Quilted by Irene Bankhead, 1989; Oakland, California

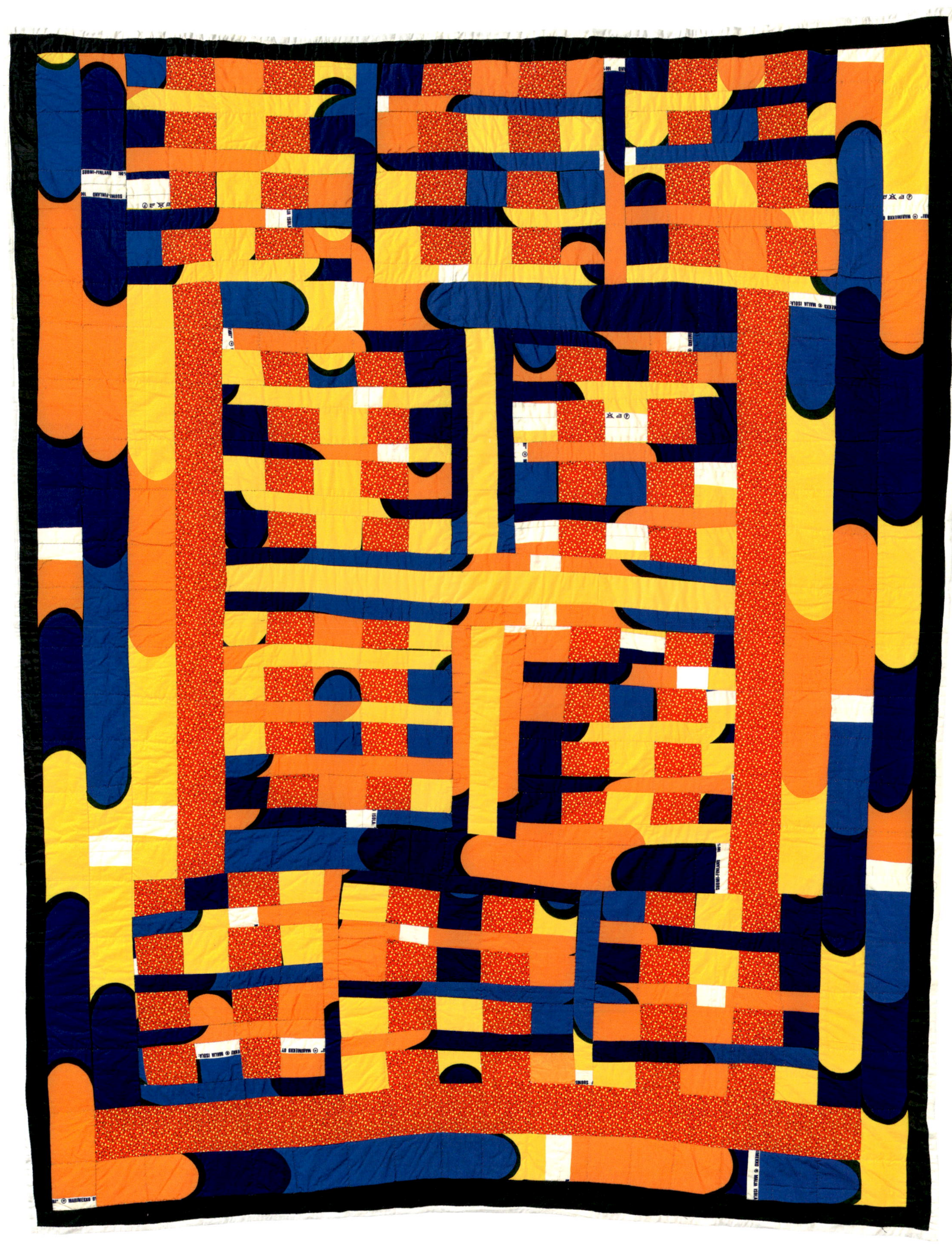

87. Untitled (Medallion)
Pieced by Sherry Ann Byrd, 1990; Richmond, California
Quilted by Irene Bankhead, 1990; Oakland, California

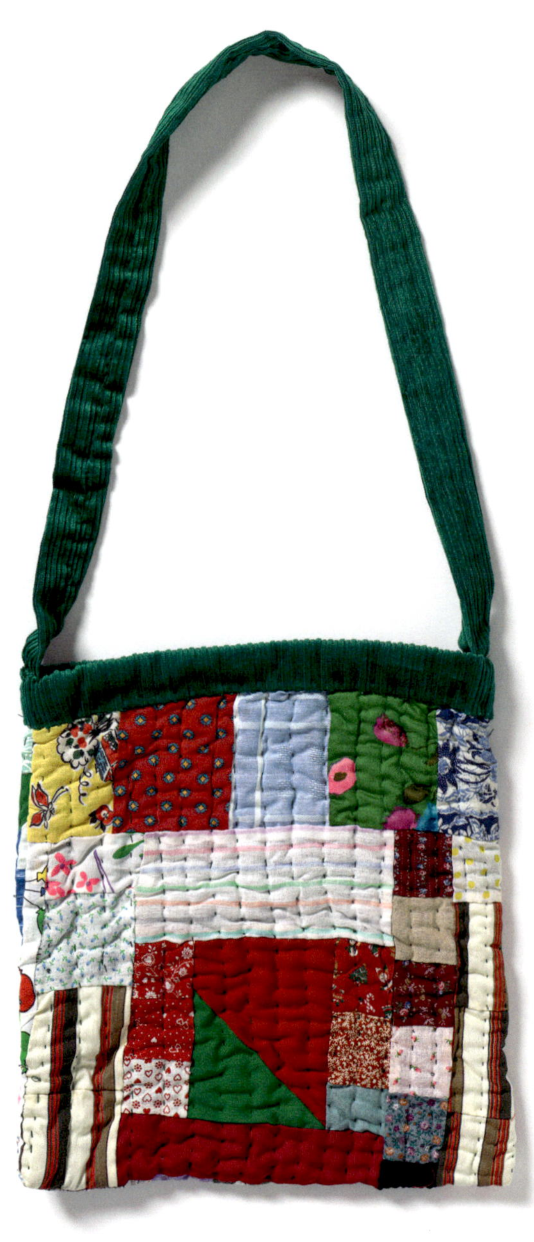

88. Handbag (Patchwork)
Maker Once Known/Unidentified Artist, c. 1990; Tutwiler, Mississippi

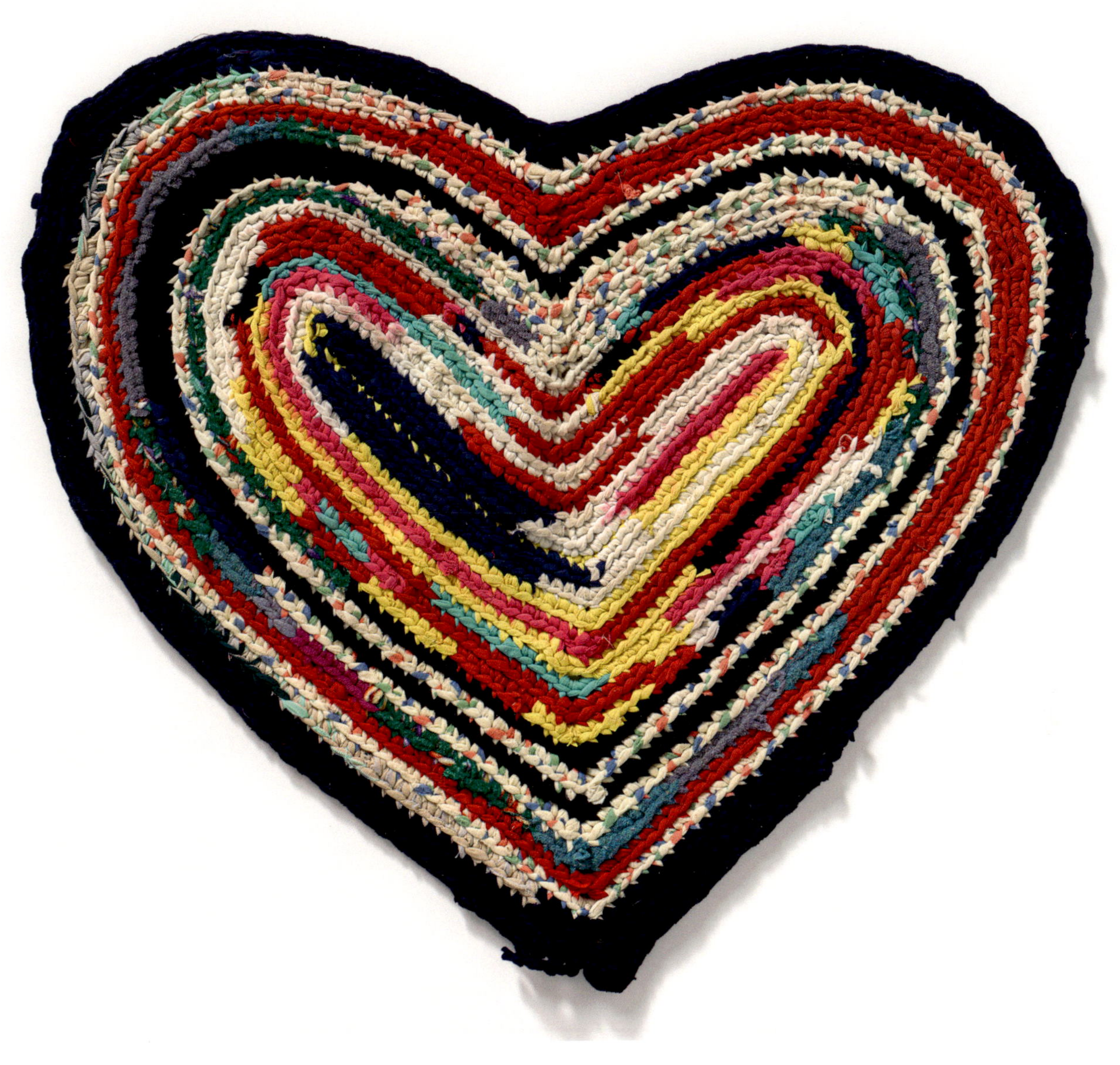

89. Crocheted rug
Gladys Henry, c. 1990; Butler, Texas

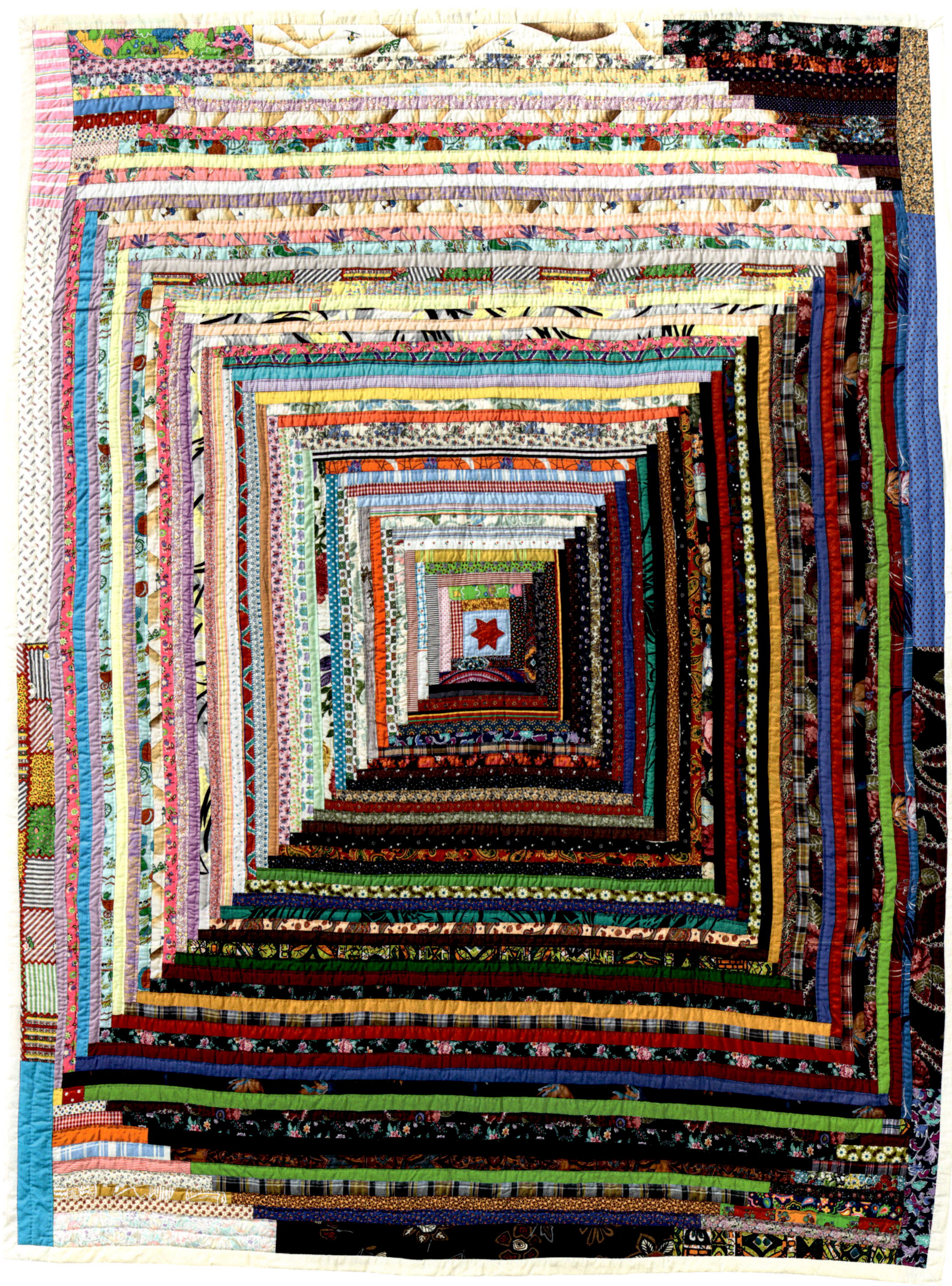

90. Untitled (Log Cabin)
Pieced and quilted by Johnnie Wade, 1990; Oakland, California
Quilted by Willia Ette Graham, 1990; Oakland, California

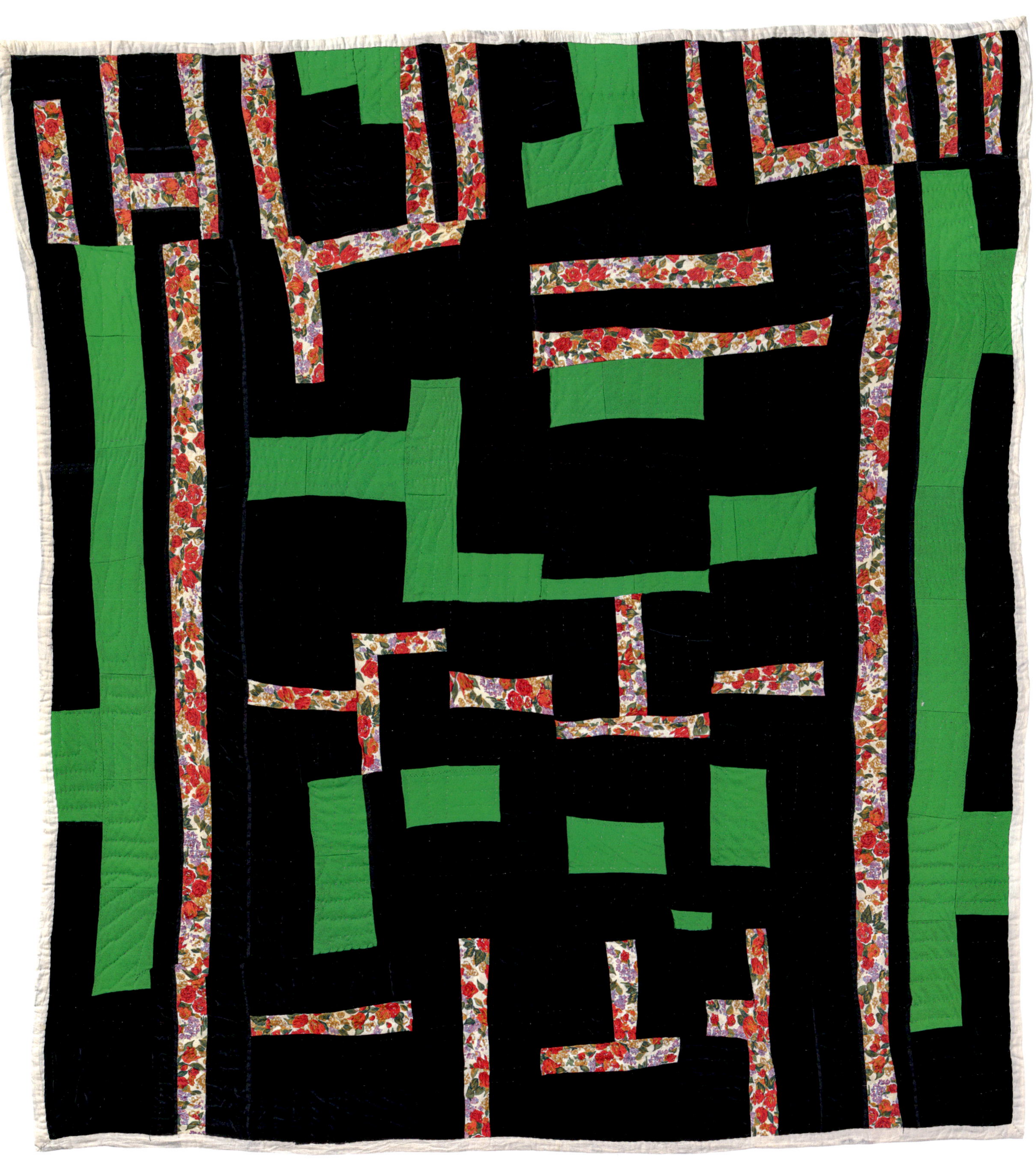

91. Untitled (Bars)
Pieced by Laverne Brackens, 1990–1991; Fairfield, Texas
Quilted by Willia Ette Graham and Johnnie Wade, 1992; Oakland, California

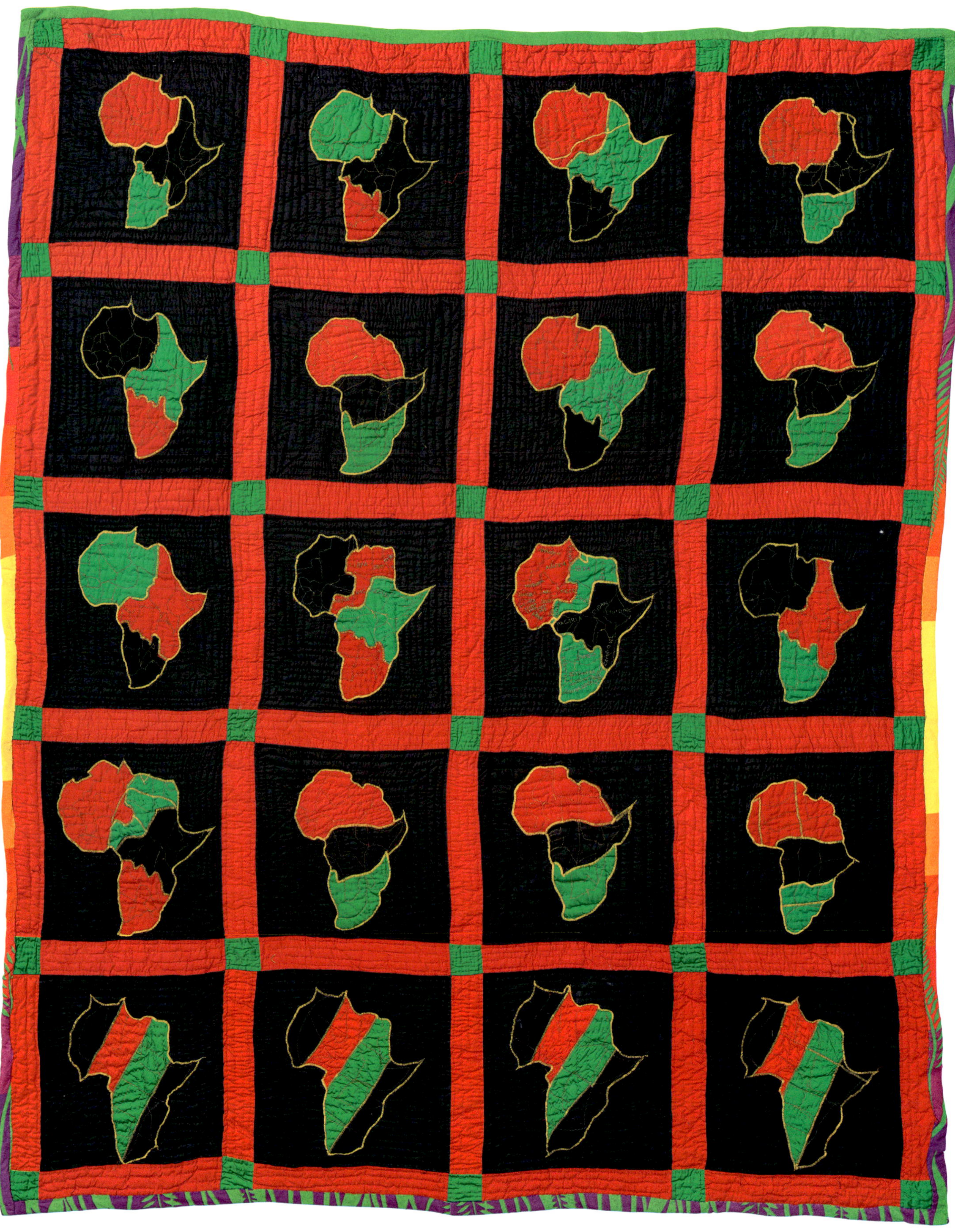

Front

92. Untitled (Africa blocks)
1991; Oakland, California
Pieced and quilted by Lily Chiles
Embroidered by Clarence Jackson and Tina Jackson
Quilted by Tina Jackson and Ruthie Love

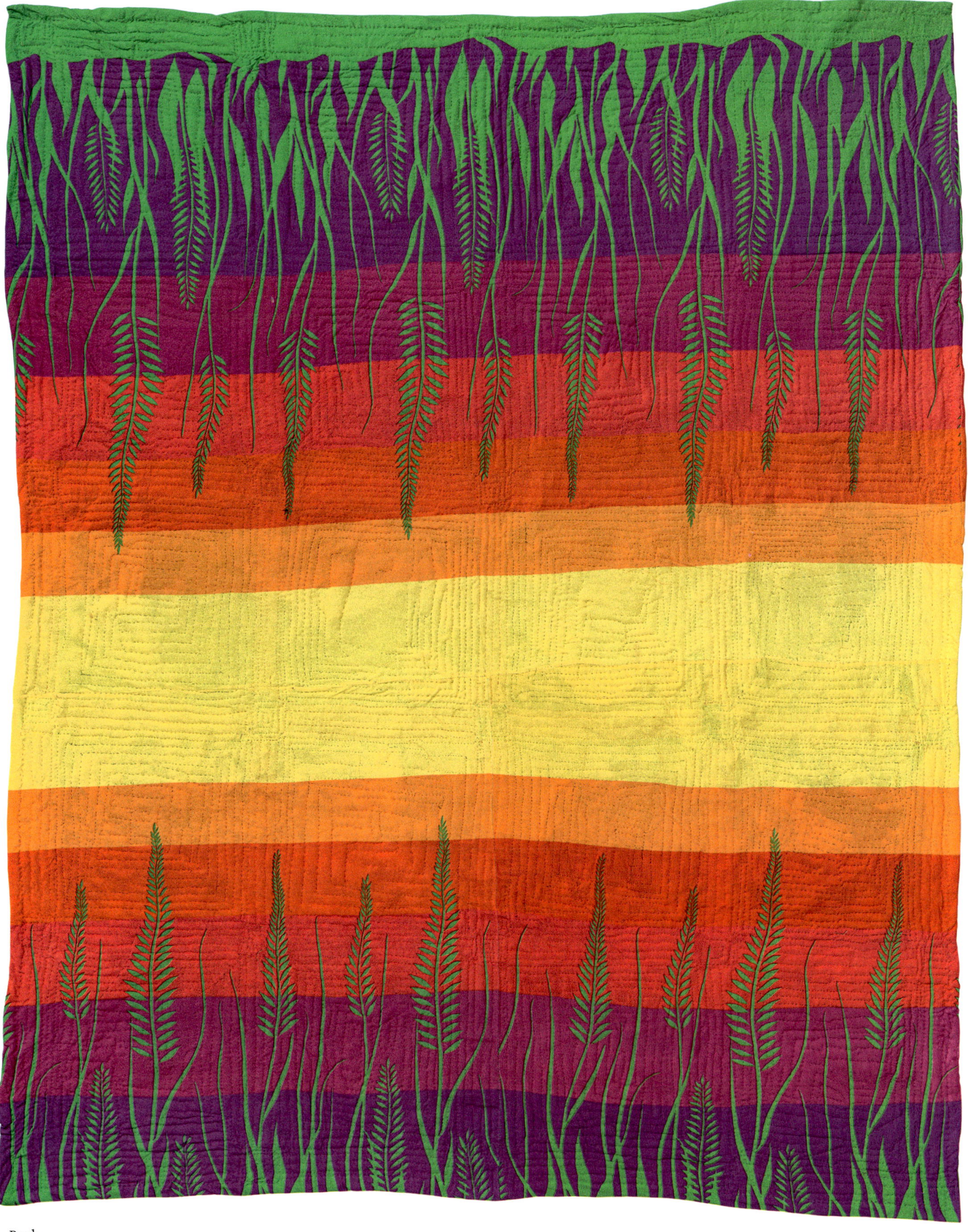

Back

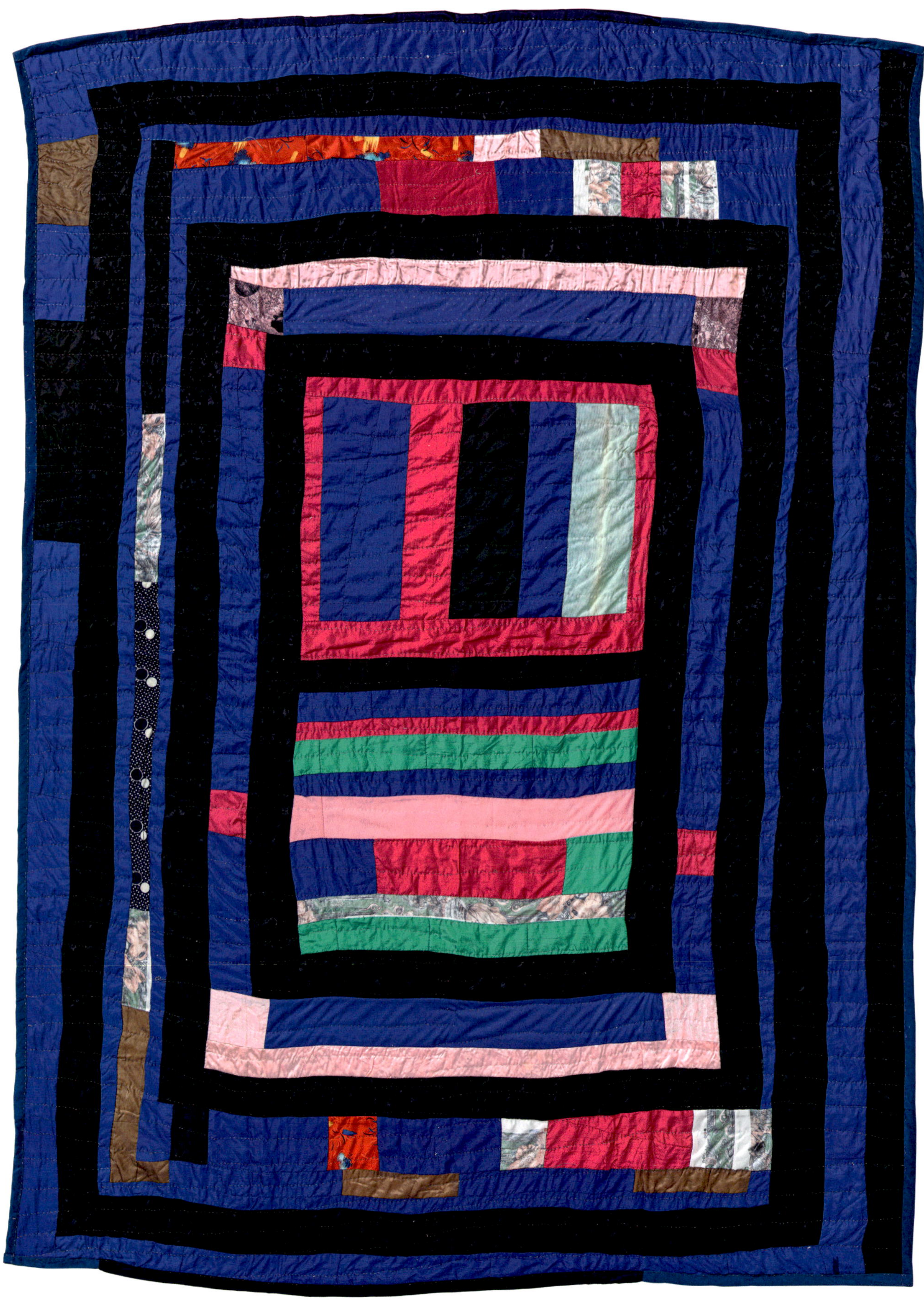

93. Untitled (Double Medallion)
Pieced by Gladys Henry, 1993; Butler, Texas
Quilted by Rose McDowell, 1993; Oakland, California

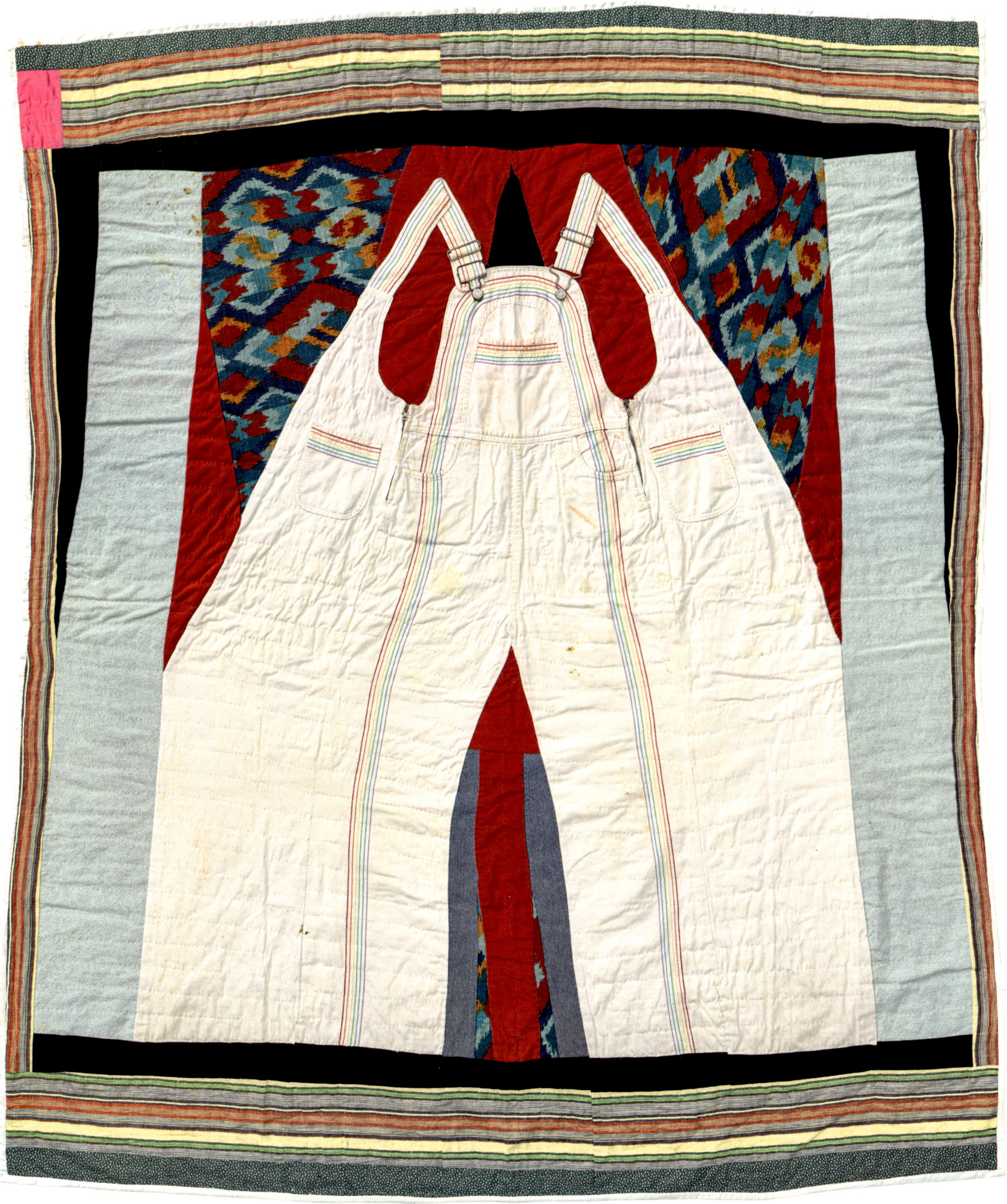

94. Untitled (Overalls quilt)
Pieced by Arbie Williams, 1993; Oakland, California
Quilted by Irene Bankhead, 1993; Oakland, California

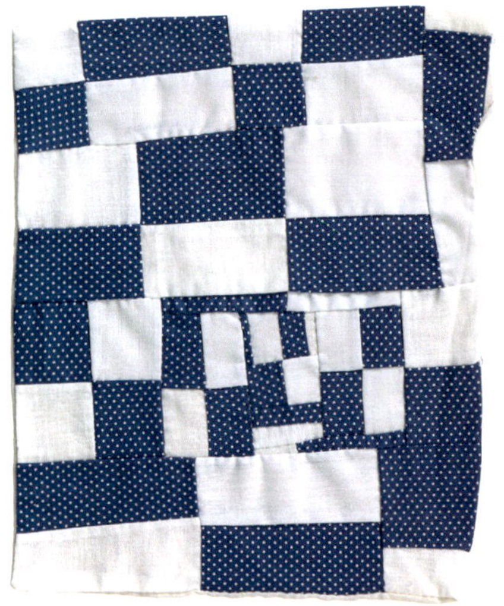

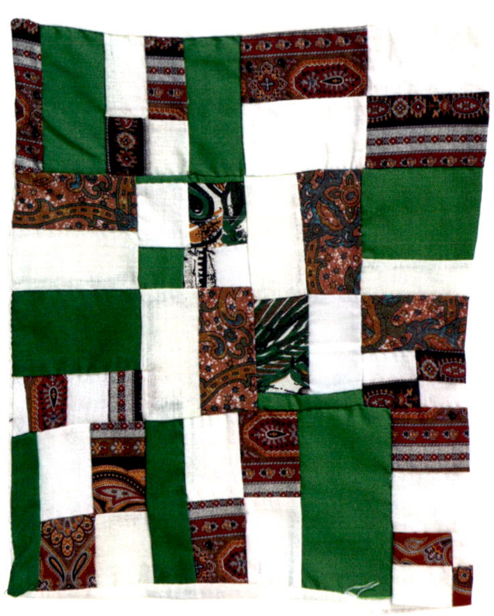

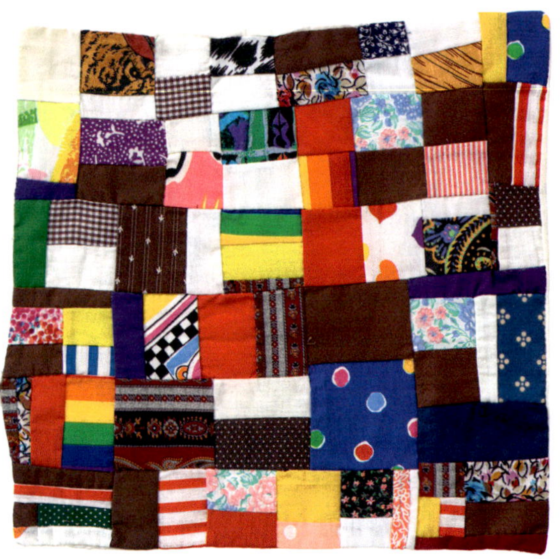

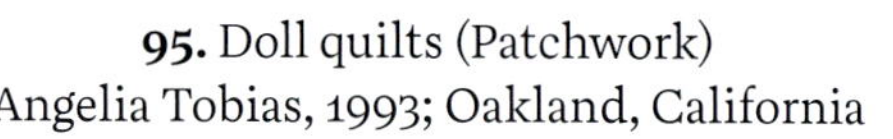

95. Doll quilts (Patchwork)
Angelia Tobias, 1993; Oakland, California

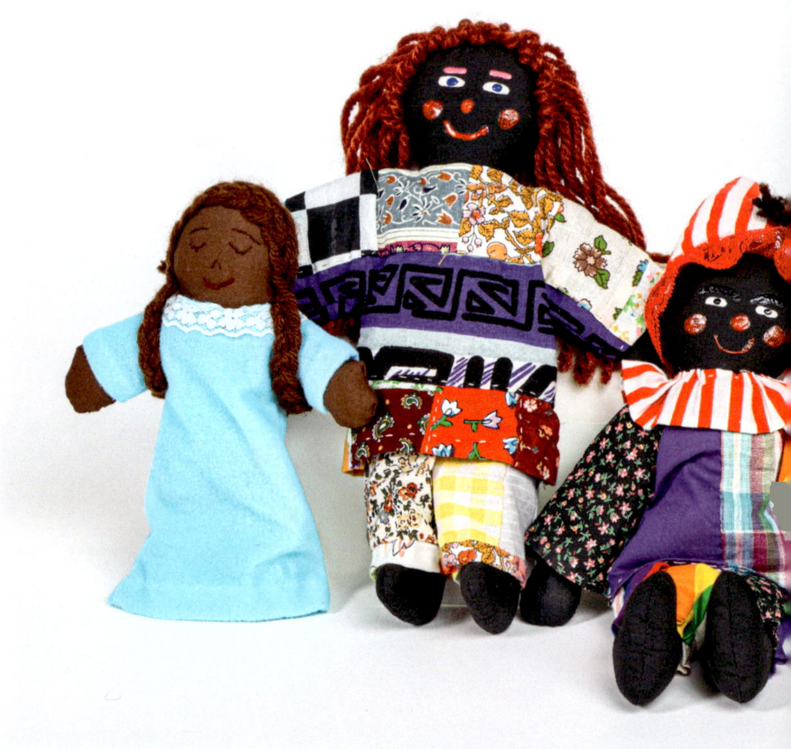

Left to right, all by Angelia Tobias:

96. Sleeping doll with braids
1996; Merced, California

97. Double-sided doll with patchwork clothes
1992; Oakland, California

98. Doll with patchwork clothes and striped hat
1992; Oakland, California

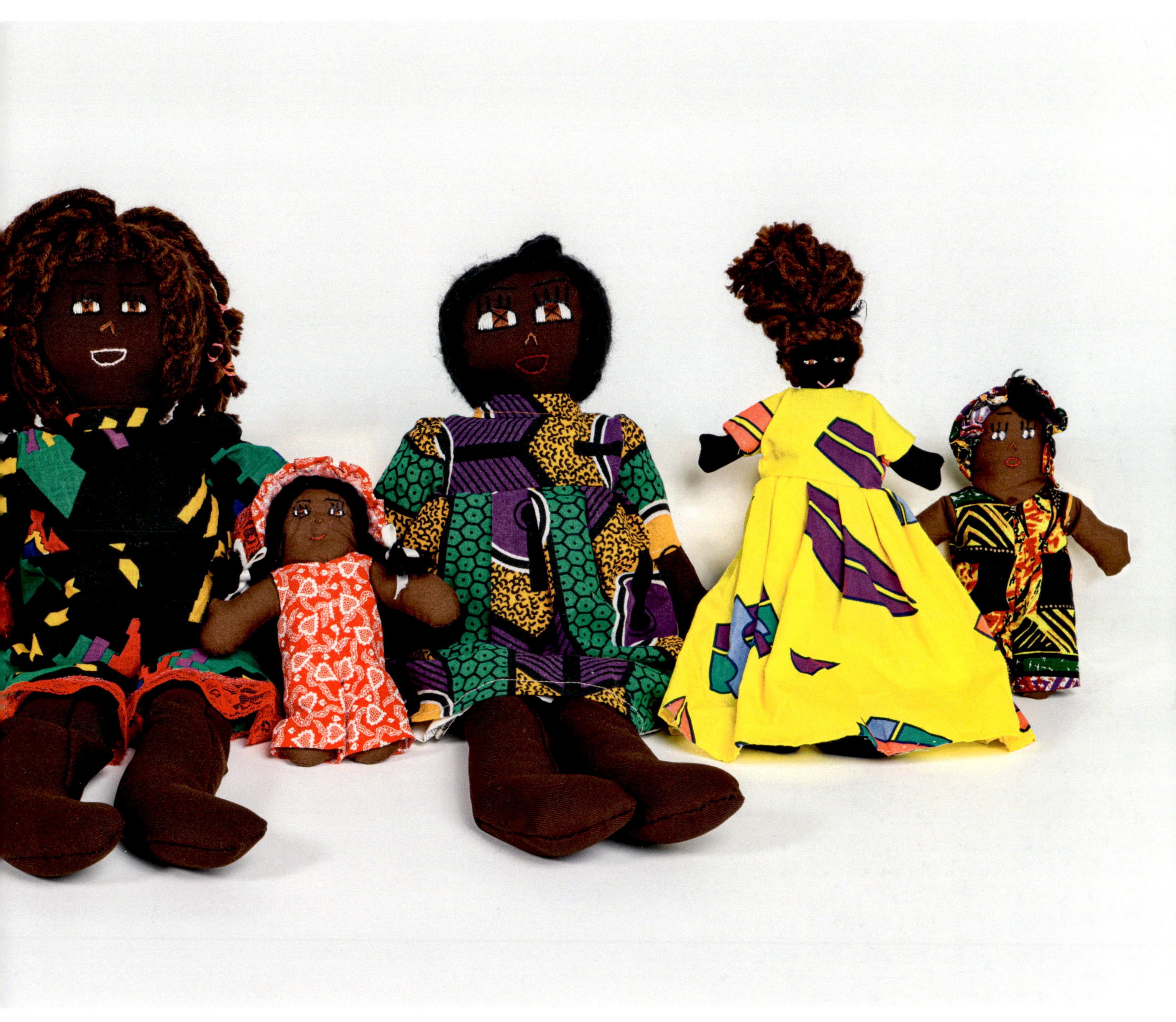

99. Doll with romper and lace trim
1996; Merced, California

100. Doll with braided pigtails, cap, and red dress
1996; Merced, California

101. Doll with braided hair and dress
1996; Merced, California

102. Doll with yellow dress
1993; Merced, California

103. Doll with jumpsuit and cap
1996; Merced, California

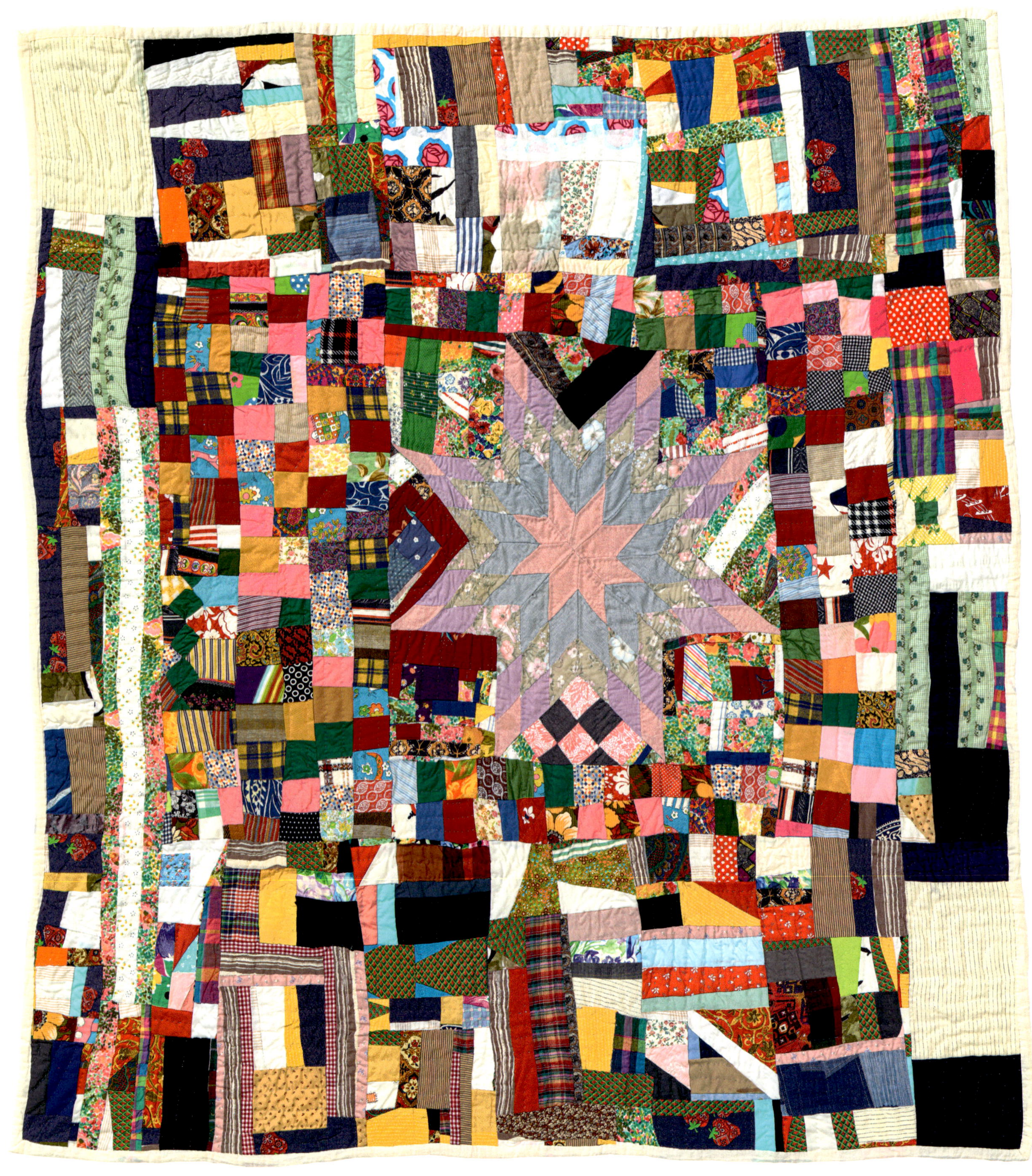

104. Untitled (Star put-together)
Pieced by Laverne Brackens, 1994; Fairfield, Texas
Quilted by Willia Ette Graham and Johnnie Wade, 1994; Oakland, California

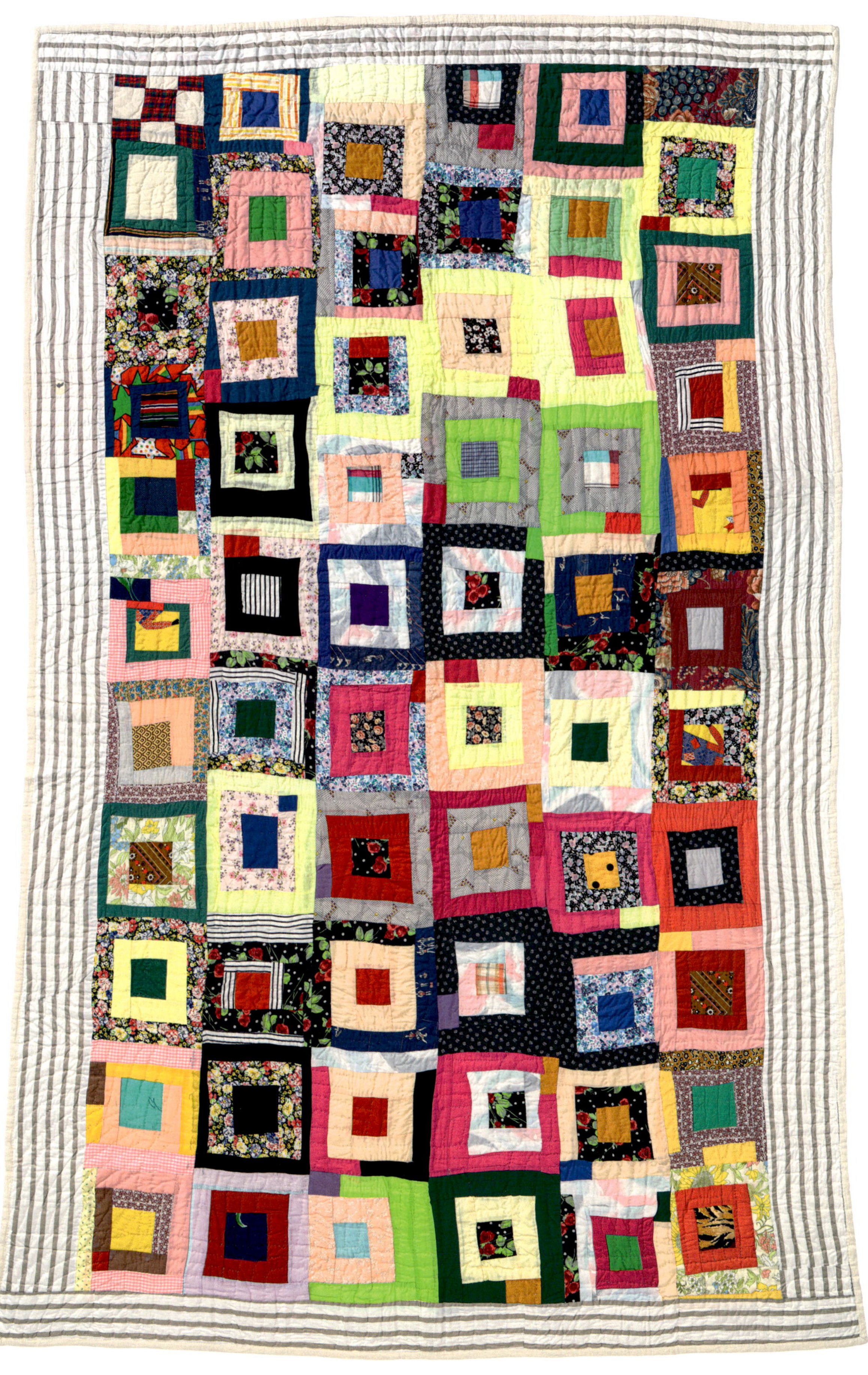

105. *Post Oak Grapevine* (Square in a Square, Nine Patch)
Pieced by Mable Battle, 1995; Richmond, California
Quilted by Willia Ette Graham and Johnnie Wade, 1995; Oakland, California

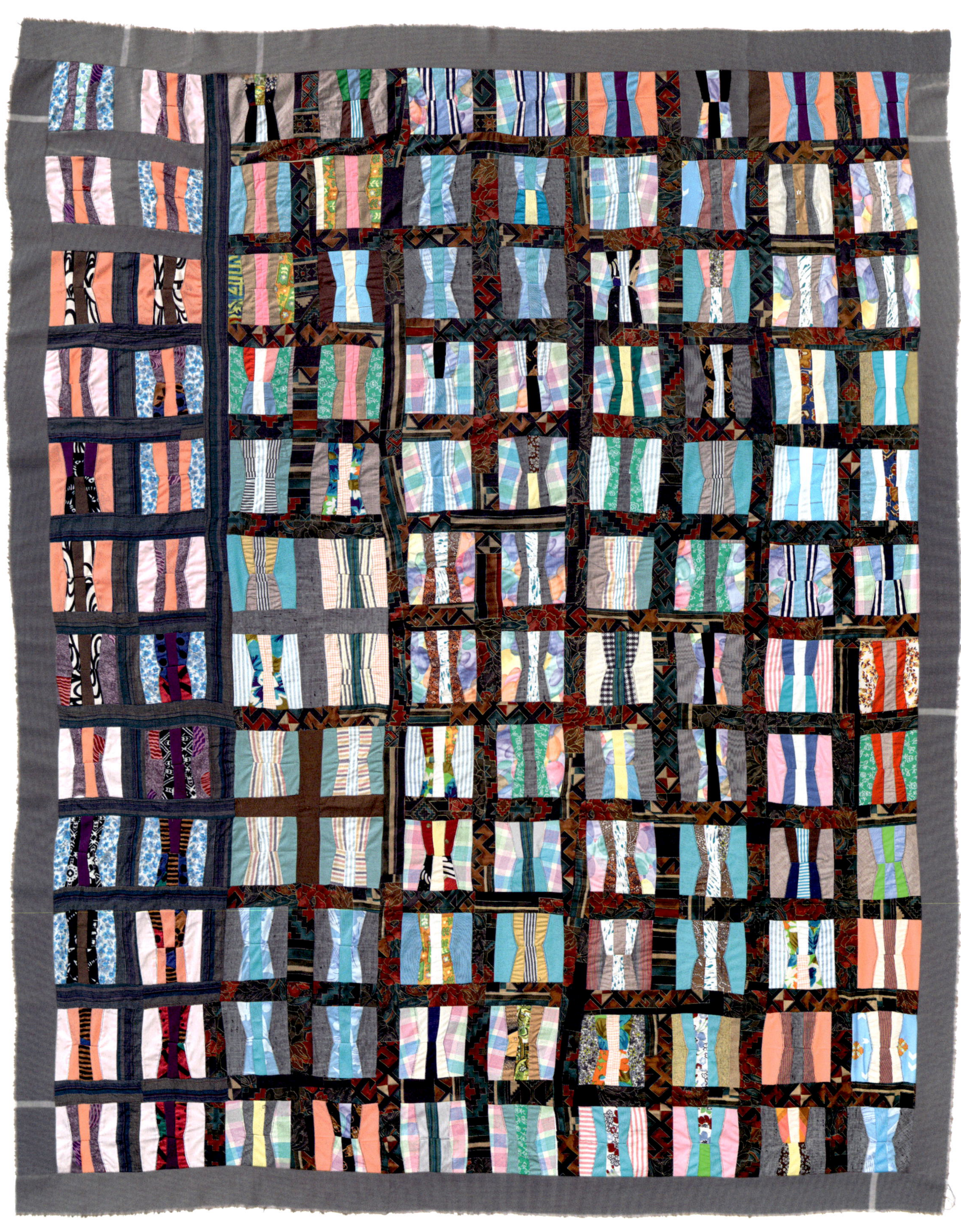

106. Untitled top (Little Boy's Britches)
Missie Freeman, 1995; Oakland, California

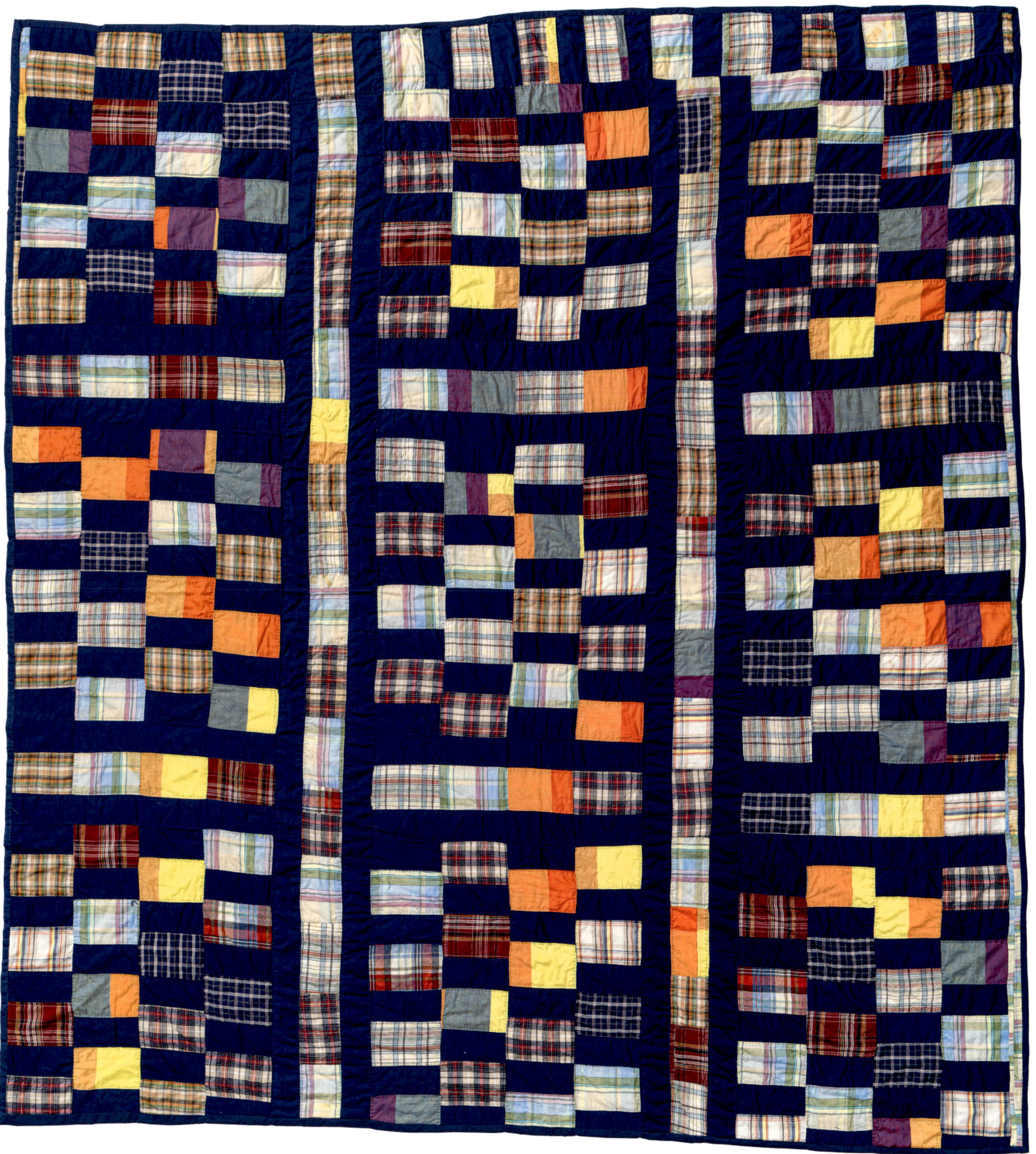

107. Untitled (One Patch)
Irene Bankhead, 1996; Oakland, California

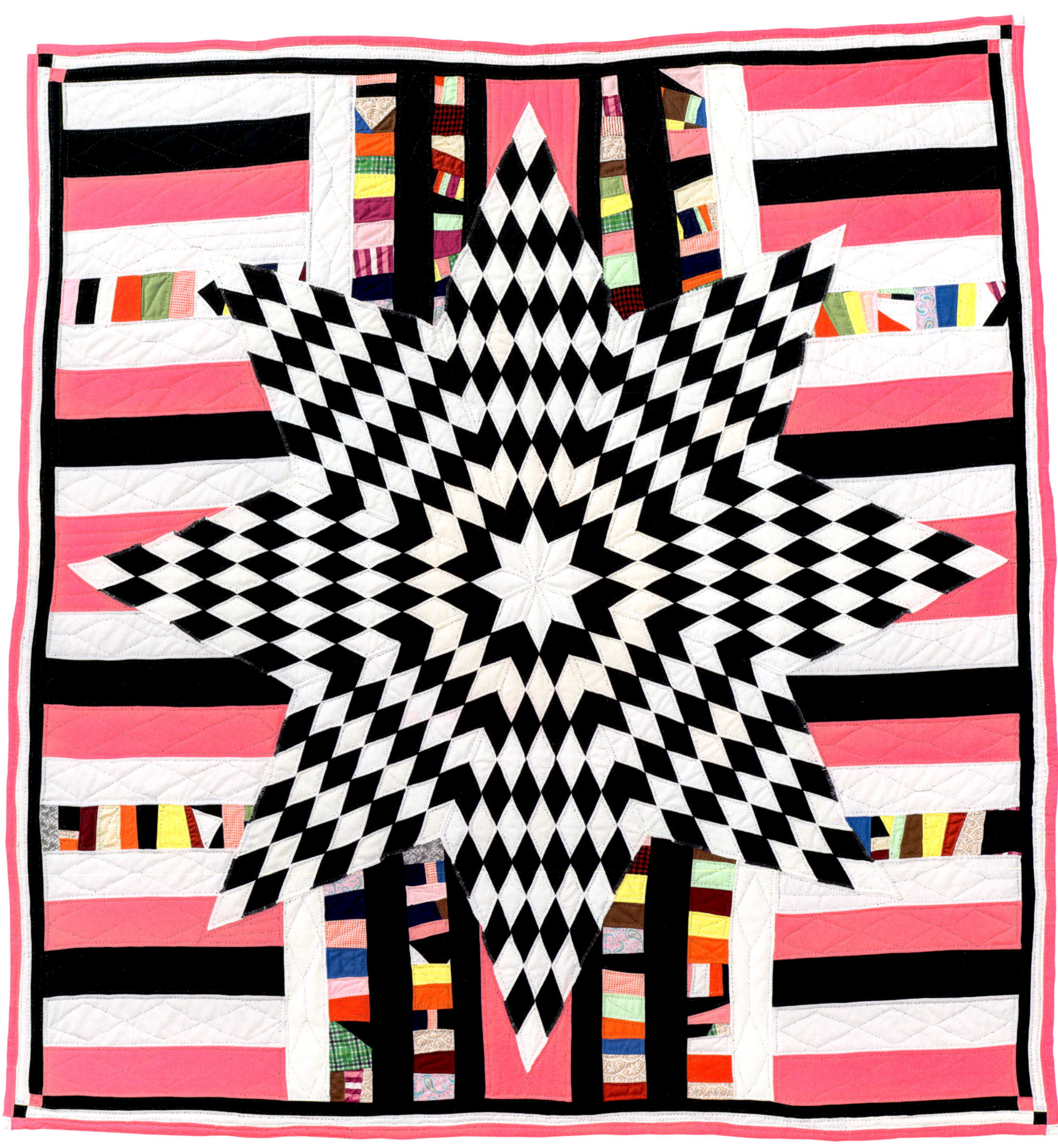

108. Untitled (Texas Star)
Johnnie Wade, 1996; Oakland, California

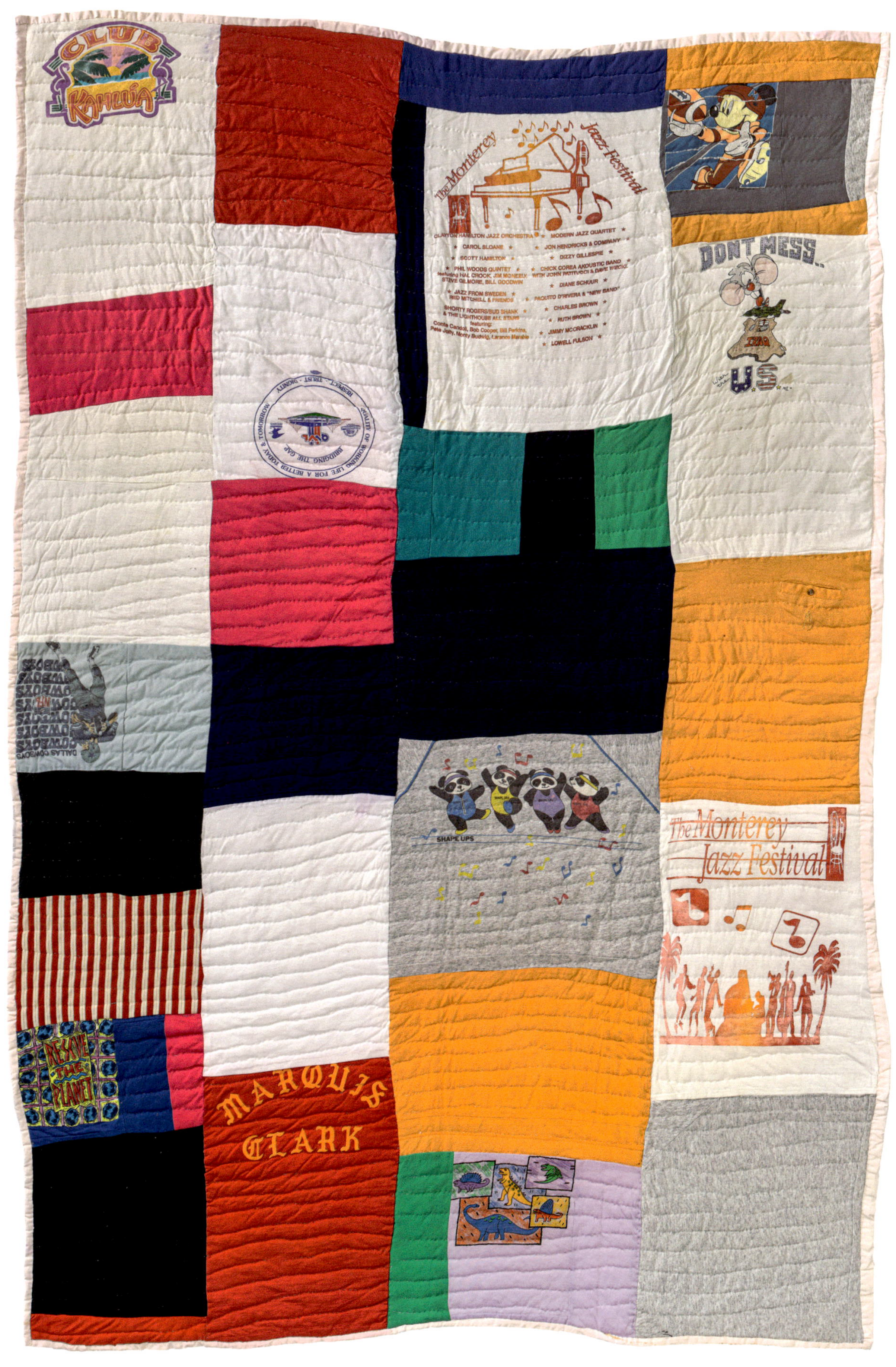

109. Untitled (T-shirt quilt)
Mable Battle, 1997; Richmond, California

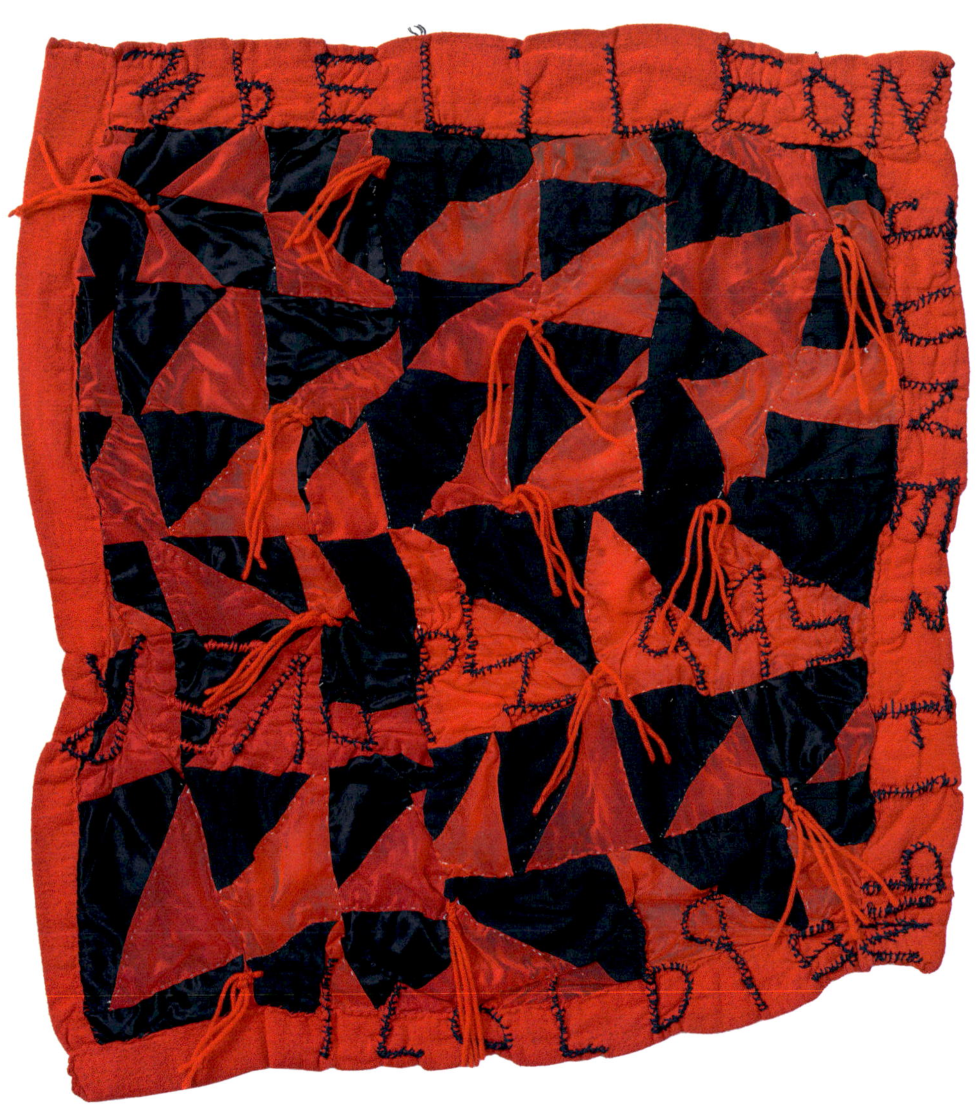

110. Untitled (Half-Square Triangles)
Rosie Lee Tompkins, c. 2000; Richmond, California

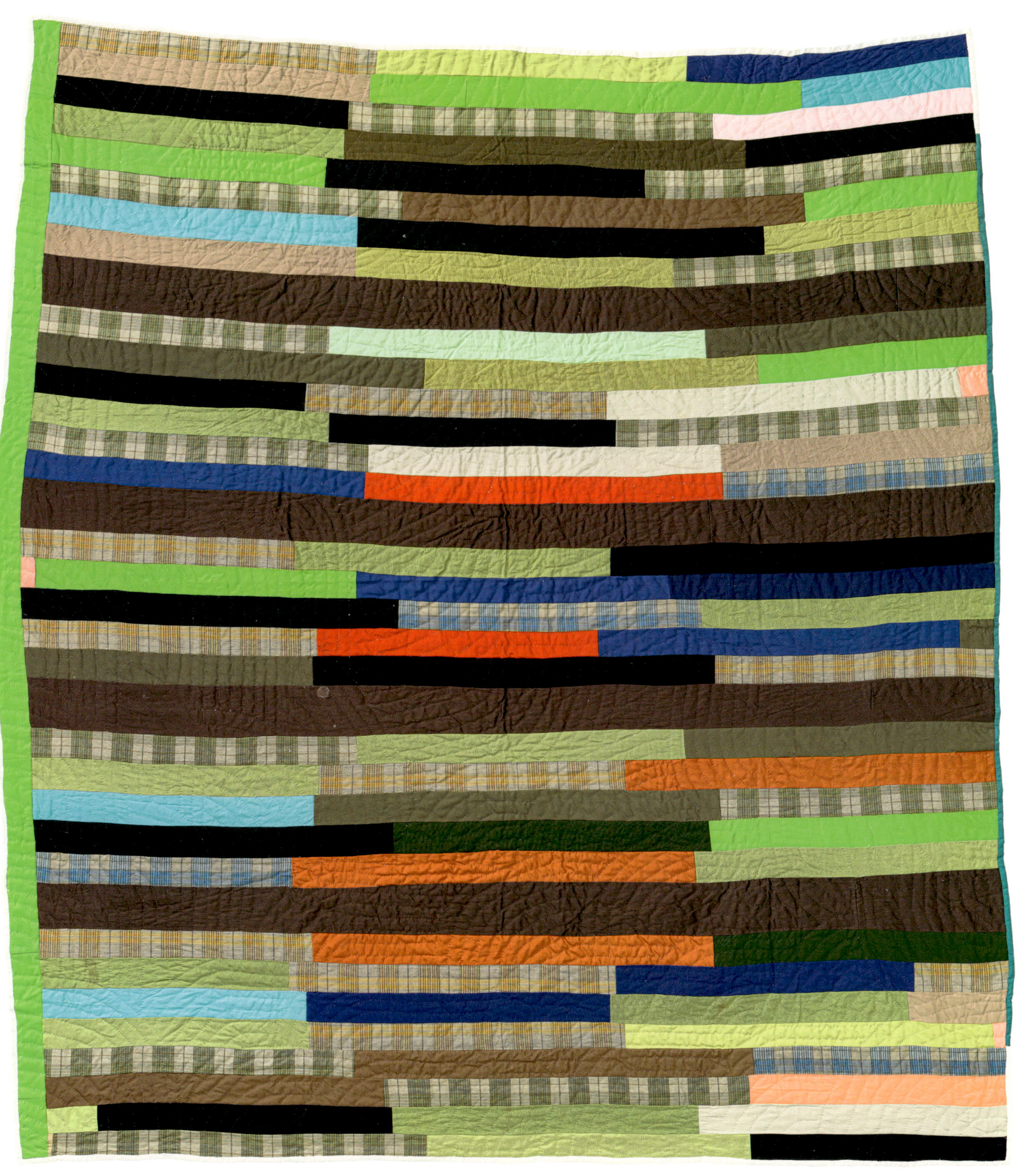

111. Untitled (Bars)
Irene Bankhead, 2001; Oakland, California

Quilt Collecting Stories

Eli Leon

From 1999 to around 2011, Eli Leon participated in a writing group that met in Oakland, focused on gay and lesbian autobiography. In addition to circulating excerpts of his memoir, Leon wrote nearly two dozen short essays about his various experiences collecting and researching African American quilts. Often lively and engaging as stories, they also offer valuable insights into Leon's acquisition process, interactions with quiltmakers and their families, and his personal motivations. The following essays were written in the spring and summer of 2005 and have been transcribed from Leon's original typed manuscripts that came to the University of California, Berkeley Art Museum and Pacific Film Archive, as part of his bequest. They incorporate Leon's handwritten line edits and have been lightly edited for clarity.

I. RECLAIMING A MISSING LINK

I first saw Mother Brown's [1891–1979] missing-link strip quilt [fig. 36] one drizzly Saturday morning at a great distance across the enormous Oakland, California, Alameda flea market. It was the early 1980s. The quilt was wrapped around an African American quilt enthusiast and occasional dealer of my acquaintance named Alberta. As a new scholar of improvisational African American patchwork and a proponent of the theory of African influence on African American quiltmaking, I was very much on the lookout for survivals of African aesthetic values in the American work. Spotting Mother Brown's quilt, even from afar, I was pretty sure I'd hit pay dirt.

I zipped across the flea market, my extra-large shopping cart bouncing behind me, and bought the quilt out from around Alberta. I'd arrived in the nick of time. Alberta and her friend Bettie, who turned out to be the quilt's owner, were about to get rained out. Thrilled to find what I considered to be a repository of Africanisms so close to what I assumed was the quilt's community of origin, I readied pencil and paper to take notes and started firing questions. Needless to say, I was crestfallen to discover that Alberta and Bettie had no information to give me, or so they believed. Bettie had bought the quilt at auction and knew nothing whatever about its origins. Short of a miracle, its maker would forever remain anonymous.

Within the decade, this quilt would dazzle the American museum-going public in *Who'd a Thought It: Improvisation in African-American Quiltmaking*—my first cataloged exhibition of African American quilts,[1] whose twenty-some-odd venues would include the Renwick Gallery at the Smithsonian Institution, Chicago's Field Museum, and the American Craft Museum in New York City. Later, paired with a stripwoven Hausa cloth from West Africa that makes use of a similar randomized checkerboard pattern, it would grace the cover of my second catalog, *Models in the Mind: African Prototypes in American Patchwork*.[2] And although I would make repeated research/collecting trips to East Texas, Northern Louisiana, and Southern Arkansas (the region from which most of my California quiltmaking contacts had migrated) and see hundreds of improvisational African American quilts, Mother Brown's would remain my best example of a "two-pair" bordering arrangement, thereby providing critical support for one of my strongest arguments for African antecedents. In short, if its origins could be established, this quilt was destined to be of particular importance to my work; I couldn't have been more disheartened by the news that Alberta and Bettie had no clue as to who made it.

When told of my belief that the quilt was African American, Alberta assured me that it was. I asked how she knew. She made gestures in its direction ("*Look* at it!") and explained that you could just tell. Bettie could not have agreed more. Well, *I* was pretty sure it was African American, and *they* were pretty sure it was African American, but mere opinions were of limited use for my scholarly purposes.

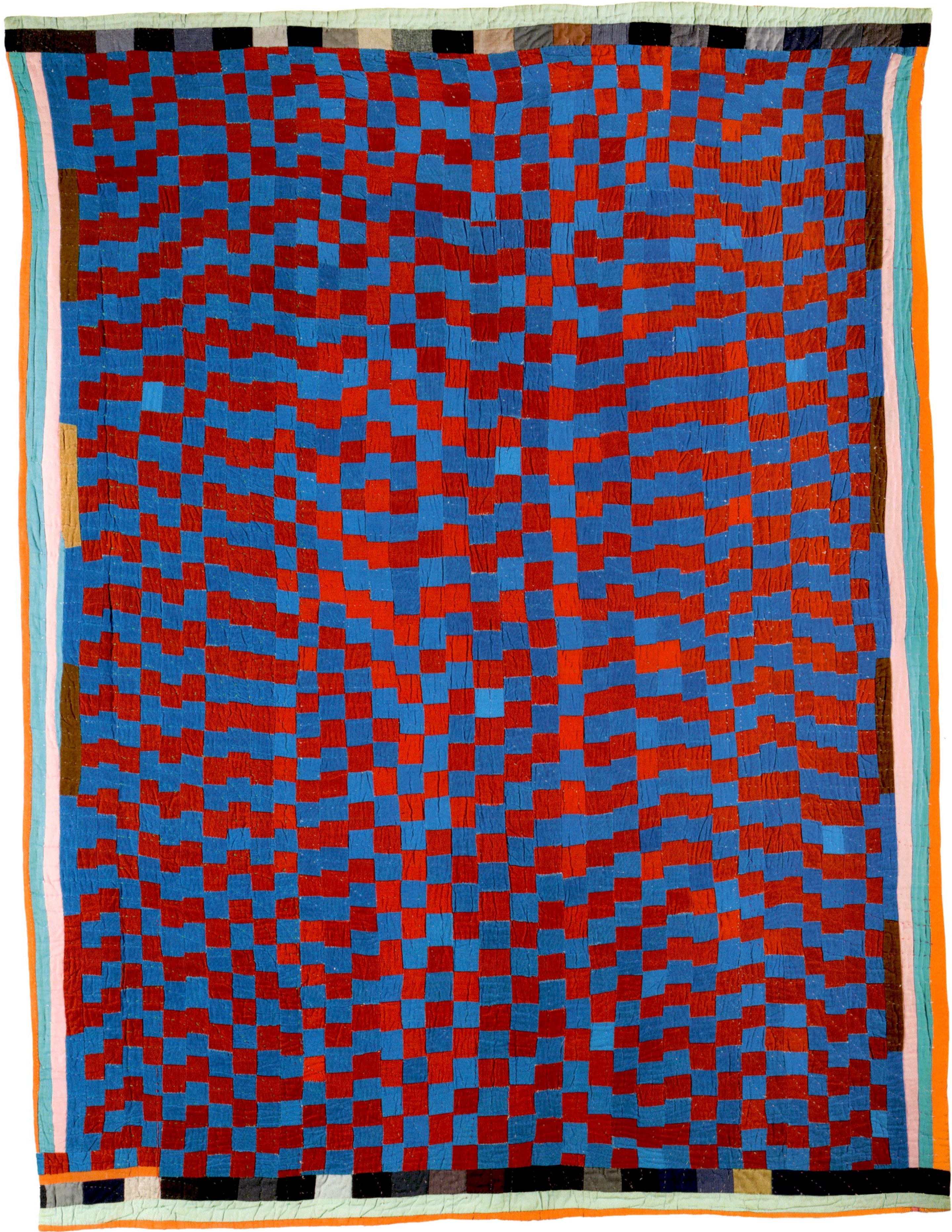

Fig. 36. Mary Lue Brown, *Hit and Miss*, c. 1945. Cotton corduroy, wool twill, wool plain weave, acrylic plain weave, rayon damask, cotton/polyester twill, cotton plain weave with warp patterning, and rayon plain weave (crepe); pieced and quilted, 98⅜ × 78½ in. (249.9 × 199.4 cm). Gift of the 2019 Collectors Committee, Los Angeles County Museum of Art, Los Angeles, California, M.2019.219.1

Although the rain got steadily worse, I was unable to tear myself from the spot. I hung around, sinking onto a folding chair and asking pesky questions while Alberta and Bettie packed. Did they get anything else with this quilt? Had it by any chance been in a carton with some kind of label or other stuff written on it? How long ago had this auction taken place? Which one was it, anyway? Finally, Bettie perked up. "Hey," she said, poking around in her glove compartment for a Butterfields catalog, "wait a minute." She still had it, a thirteen-page list of several thousand items. She'd circled the items she'd bid on, and there it was: #640; PATCH QUILT. She'd got it for ten bucks, sold it to me for thirty.

Bettie turned the catalog over to me. Contacting Butterfields, I was soon informed that I was wasting both my time and theirs. The last thing I might expect, I was roundly assured, was that an auction house would be giving out the names of its sellers. I insisted on speaking to someone in authority and, eventually, was put in touch with a woman who gave me the time to explain that I was writing a book about African survivals in African American quilts and that this particular quilt evidenced several such survivals, but that it would be of little use to me without its history. Sympathetic to my mission, the woman agreed to look the sale up. (A year or two later, in my attempt to reclaim the heritage of another stray quilt, I tried this again, found that my helper at Butterfields had moved on, butted against a wall of impatience and sarcasm, and had no choice but to give up the quest.)

The San Francisco estate that this quilt had been part of, it turned out, had been under a conservatorship. My informant was not allowed, by law, to tell me the company name, but was willing to contact them herself and seek permission for me to talk to the party that had handled the transaction. Again, I was lucky. Apprised of the nature of my research, the conservator was so intrigued that she agreed to talk to me personally. Black conservatorships were extremely uncommon in her experience, but, as she couldn't help blurting out, the man to whom this quilt had belonged was indeed Black. How, she wondered aloud, could I know? This was a peak moment for me. My audience couldn't have been readier for the theory of African influence. Quite aside from which, I was in ecstasy. Even if I were to get no further, I now had some measure of authentication.

But I was on a roll. My latest helper called the daughter-in-law of the old man who had once owned the quilt and got permission for me to talk to her myself. Lodesta, as it turned out, was delighted to hear from me. She'd worried about the family's quilts and was relieved to learn that this one had found a good home. We arranged for me to bring it across the Bay that next day for a hands-on identification. She was amused when she saw it. Turned out, it was the quilt they used the most. Kept it on the sofa to wrap up in while watching TV. Called it "the loud quilt."

There had been several other, "better," quilts that had been sold as higher-class merchandise in another section of the auction. I tried to track them down, but in each case the buyer refused to talk to me. Mine, according to Lodesta, was made by Mother (Mary Lue) Brown, a woman who'd died in 1979. Mother Brown had a special relationship with Helen, the deceased wife of the man whose possessions had been auctioned. In the 1930s, Helen had gone to college with Mother Brown's daughter. When Helen, an orphan, had had her first child, she'd had no one to help her. Mother Brown had stayed with her until she'd been able to handle the situation herself. The two formed an attachment that was to last a lifetime.

Lodesta put me in touch with Mother Brown's now elderly daughter, Elfreda, in Southern California, who speculated that the quilt (of whose existence she'd until then been unaware) had been made in Dallas in the 1940s and given to Helen as a present. Her telephone hearing was spotty, so we corresponded. Elfreda agreed to send me a photo of her mother from the forties but didn't get around to it. Eventually, on the occasion of my (and Mother Brown's) first museum show, I had the sponsoring institution (the then San Francisco Craft and Folk Art Museum) ask her again, with better results. The photo has since accompanied the quilt in my exhibitions and catalogs.

Many "anonymous" quilts would be reclaimable as the products of Black craftspeople if I were able to engage all of the gatekeepers encountered along the way (in this case I was dependent on the goodwill and cooperation of five separate informants, six if I count Alberta and Bettie as two, plus one museum), but most of my collecting stories don't turn out this well. The search ends when I can't overcome suspicion or indifference at one or another critical point. The times that—as in this case—it all works out, however, go a long way toward compensating for the disappointments.

II. MEETING MRS. MURPHY

Early in 1986, quiltmaker Bettie Phillips [p. 236] told me about a ninety-two-year-old friend of hers, a Mrs. Mable Murphy (1894–1996), who lived in the little town of Dos Palos, California, and had a house full of quilts, many of which were for sale. Bettie estimated there to be at least fifty, and raved about their great beauty. I wanted to meet Mrs. Murphy (as she preferred to be called) right away of course, but there turned out to be obstacles. Mrs. Murphy was hard of hearing, for one. Unable to understand me when I telephoned, she had her son, a smoker, handle the call. When I mentioned that I had a cigarette-smoke allergy, he got enraged and hung up. On top of that, my car became mysteriously unreliable. The meeting with Mrs. Murphy, it seemed, would have to wait for more favorable conditions.

Then Bettie informed me that Mrs. Murphy was giving up her house for smaller quarters. In all probability, some of her quilts would be inaccessible after the move. For them, it was now or never. I had, meanwhile, learned that Mrs. Murphy's son didn't actually live with her, although he was often around. I'd also changed cars. So I tried to get Bettie to make the trip with me, imagining that having her along would smooth the way, but she showed no interest in the project. Resolving to take my chances and go didn't work either; it just led to my feeling guilty whenever Mrs. Murphy came to mind, which was often, since my strategically placed to-do list was headlined, "INTERVIEW MRS MURPHY."

When I asked quiltmaker Willia Ette Graham [p. 224], however, if she'd like to visit an elderly quilter in the San Joaquin valley, she jumped at the chance. Suddenly everything was looking up. Graham was warm, friendly, and generally relaxed. The thought of her supportive presence was all I needed to lend courage to my convictions. I called Bettie to tell her that Willia Ette and I were hoping to give it a go that Monday, which happened to be a holiday, and Bettie did an abrupt turnabout; she would accompany me after all. Springing into action, she straightaway called Mrs. Murphy, ascertained that the son wouldn't be around that day, and made all the arrangements–even deciding to fix a bring-along lunch featuring fried chicken and homemade cake.

Why the sudden change? It baffled me for a moment; then I got it. Bettie was as eager to meet Willia Ette as Willia Ette was to meet Mrs. Murphy! This expedition was taking on a new character. For some years I'd been listening to my informants' lamentations of the scarcity of quiltmakers in the Califiornia cities they'd found themselves in after their westward migrations; they were longing to meet one another. And witnessing these meetings might very well be as informative for me as interviewing Mrs. Murphy.

I now wanted to include Gussie Wells [p. 252] and Arbie Williams [p. 245], two of my closest quiltmaker contacts, in what was promising to be a memorable get-together, but there wasn't room for five in my car. When I floated the idea past Bettie, though, she immediately latched on to it. Again, I was taken by surprise. Why all the fuss? But we needed a few more participants, I finally realized, for a critical mass. Wells and Williams were best buddies, however; we couldn't invite one without the other. After mulling the thing over, Bettie and I decided to go ahead with the invitations. If both of them accepted, we'd devise a new plan.

Bettie volunteered to drive, but her car was no bigger than mine. The obvious solution would be to go in two cars, but not wanting to miss any of the fireworks I was anticipating, I was intent on all of us riding together. As it turned out, Gussie couldn't make it. Arbie, however, was raring to go. Right off the bat, moreover, she notified me that she would be wearing pants. I dutifully passed this information on to Bettie and Willia Ette.

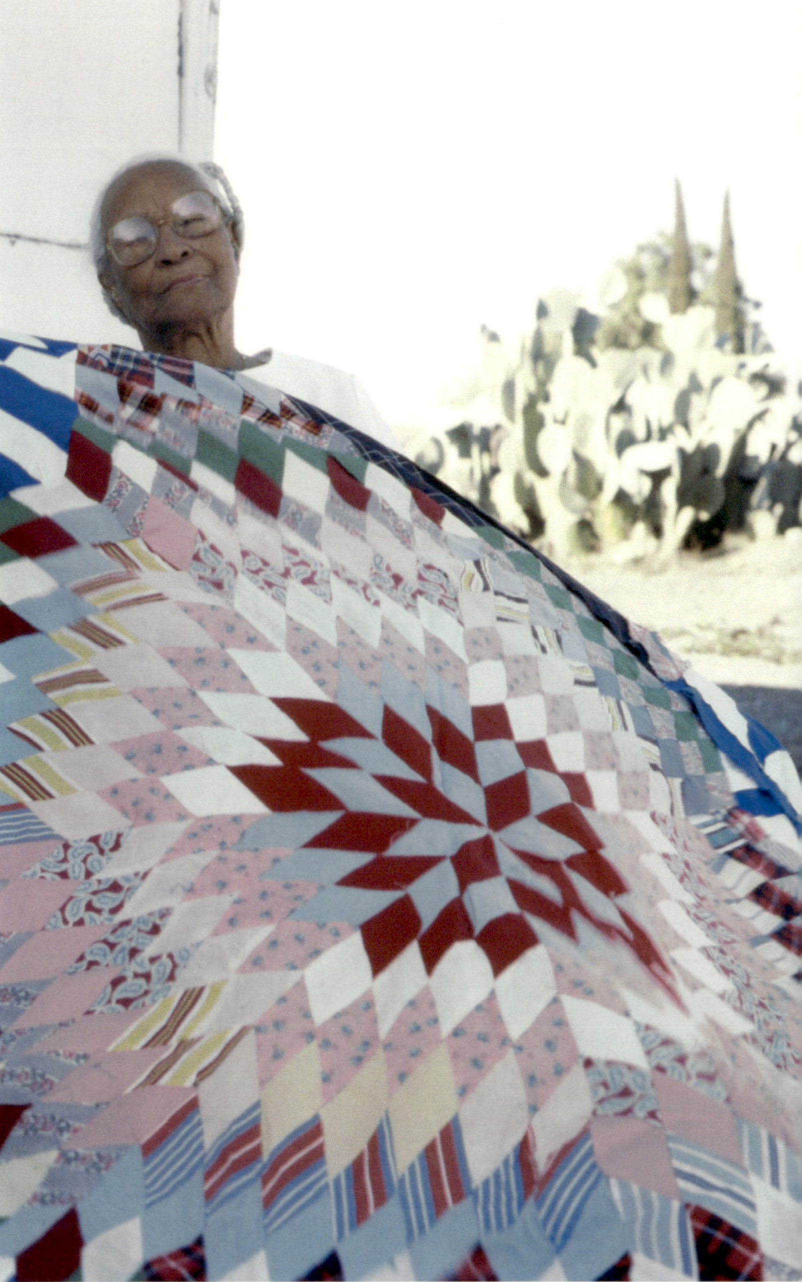

Fig. 37. Mable Murphy holding one of her quilts, Dos Palos, California, 1987

So, on January 19, 1987, Martin Luther King Jr.'s fifty-eighth birthday, the bunch of us assembled on the sidewalk in front of the Phillipses' house. At the last minute, Bettie announced that she was taking her car after all. She never went anywhere, she informed us, without her deaf-mute sister, quiltmaker Missie Freeman (b. 1914 [p. 235]). I had no choice but to take the two-car solution in stride. Getting

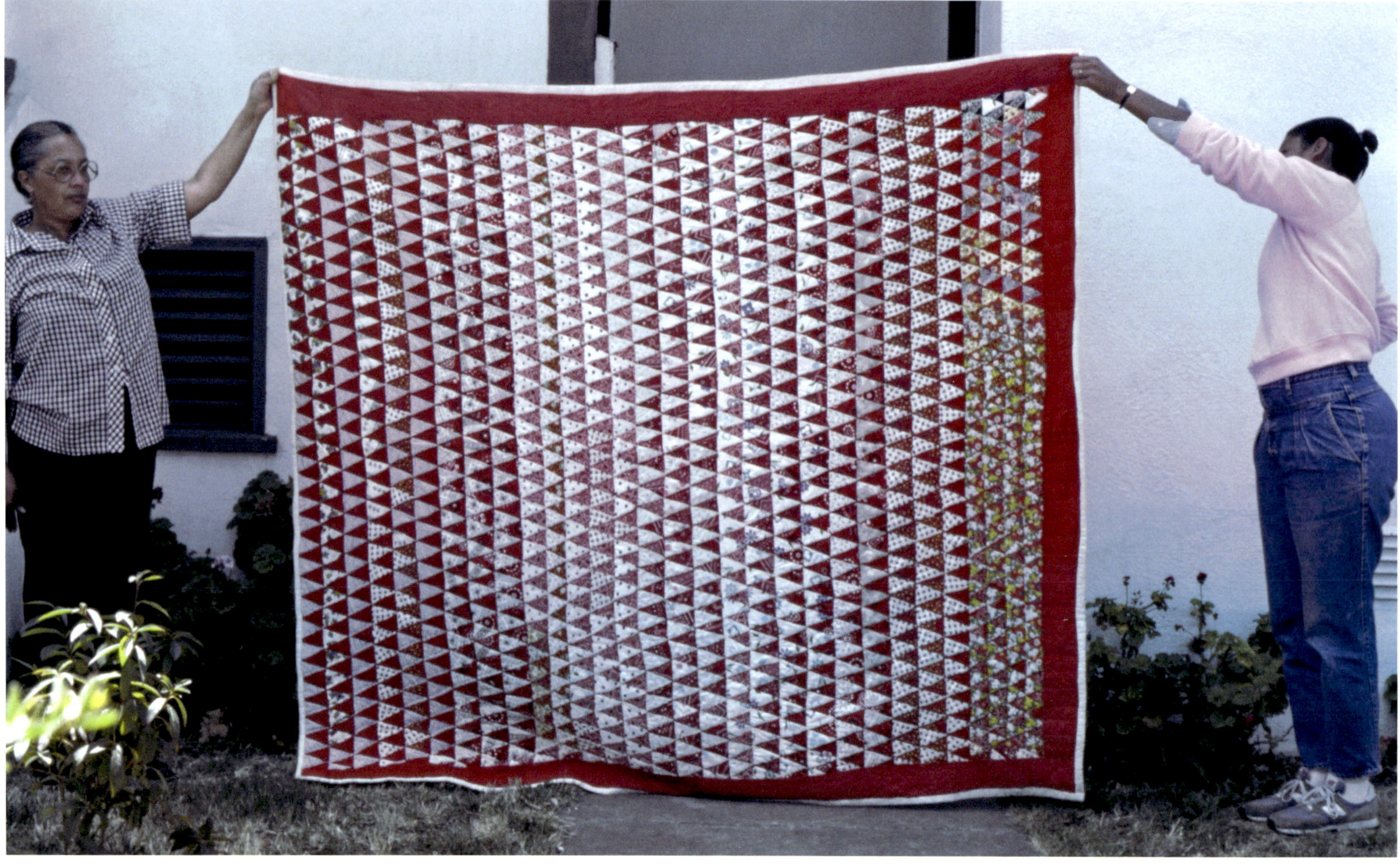

Fig. 38. Mable Murphy's daughter and granddaughter holding her "Teepee quilt" made in 1963–64, Dos Palos, California, 1987

acquainted before leaving, meanwhile, the women were bustling with excitement. An aroma of fried chicken filled the air. Everyone but Missie was wearing pants.

With wistful goodbyes and much slamming of car doors, we finally set off. Arbie, Willia Ette, and I followed Bettie and Missie in the slow lane of the freeway at such a crawl that I (then a mere fifty-one years old and feeling like a teenager keen on getting on with it) expected any minute to be pulled over by the highway patrol. The time, however, passed quickly. Williams was a scintillating talker, Graham was an enthusiastic listener, and I got to be a fly on the wall. I was not surprised to discover an aspect of Williams's quiltmaking history that I hadn't accessed in our prior conversations. Turned out Arbie, as a young woman living in a railroad workers' community in Beckville, Texas, in 1943, had organized a quilting group:

> Well our idea was, we [pieced] all the quilts we could in the winter and wouldn't let either one know what we were buildin' on. If one come to the house and you was piecin' quilts, you'd roll it up and put it in a bag and shove it up under the bed right quick 'for you let 'em come in. They didn't get to see what you were piecin.'[3]

In the spring and summer, the eight women would assemble at one of their houses and quilt all day, easily completing two quilts a session. By 1945, when Arbie and her husband moved west to take advantage of the high-paying war-industry jobs that were springing up in California, Williams had amassed seventeen quilt tops and can't remember how many quilts. She left them behind, though, never to be seen by her again. Nor would she again achieve the level of quiltmaking camaraderie that she'd almost effortlessly brought about in Beckville. In Oakland, as we all knew, the quilters were few and far between.

When we arrived at Mrs. Murphy's, we found a spry, high-spirited lady who seemed much younger than her ninety-three years, waiting to greet us at the front door. She steered a little clear of me at first, but, taking her cues from the other women, soon accepted me as part of the crowd. I wondered how long she'd been standing watch. She must have been as deprived of quiltmaker companionship as the rest of the company. Plus, this was to be her red-letter day. This bevy of quilt aficionados were keyed to sustain an undue interest in her handwork as we emptied closets, drawers, and trunks, bringing out dolls, beadwork, endless crochet (my favorite was a miniature soup bowl and spoon in red thread), and quilts, quilts, quilts.

All of these women were so passionate about their craft that it had taken over the better part of their living quarters; they must have felt right at home. No matter how often I encountered a house full of quilts, however, this guided tour of an artist's lifework would remain a special treat. And this time it would be in the most distinguished of companies.

As for my nostalgic companions, this get-together was providing a direct line to their roots. In their formative years in rural Missouri (Murphy, Freeman, and Phillips), Texas (Williams and Graham), and Oklahoma (again, Murphy, Freeman, and Phillips), quiltmaking had largely been a communal activity; six participants would comprise only a modest bee. Now, light-years from the rural 1940s South, where virtually all of the neighboring women could be expected to quilt, these women were compelled to work singly or, at best, in pairs.

So they lived it up as I, with Willia Ette's unstinting help, and frequent visits from the rest of the company, went to town. We were extremely thorough, emptying each storage space entirely before refilling it with carefully examined goods. In a few hours we'd, in all probability, seen everything. Mrs. Murphy's recent works were splendid examples of highly complex, published patterns expertly repeated over king-sized surfaces in consistent color schemes requiring great quantities of store-bought fabric. She sold these professional-level wares through a connection in Los Angeles. I regretfully refrained, however, from collecting any of them. Precisely executed quilts from printed patterns are not what my research is about, and my resources were limited.

A red-and-white Teepee quilt (as she called it) that Mrs. Murphy had made in the early 1960s and which won the Dos Palos Ladies Sewing Group's top prize of $25 in 1981 or thereabouts took my breath away [fig. 38]. I was not, at the time, familiar with similarly patterned Central African bark-cloth ceremonial skirts like the one later pictured near the end of my *Something Else to See* catalog,[4] [and] I'd never seen this pattern before. It wasn't for sale, but Mrs. Murphy agreed to let me photograph it at a future date, when her daughter and granddaughter could hold it up for me in the shade.

Willia Ette was the only one who was as intent as I on not missing a trick. Or maybe it was the shyness that had come over her today, which I'd never seen when the two of us were alone. She painstakingly undid the ties of a mountain of plastic bags of cloth scraps and went through each one to find an occasional pieced section of quilt top. I found a completed older top that very much interested me, and which was for sale among the unfinished pieces, a Lone Star with Maple Leaf Corners, later quilted by Irene Bankhead.

Afterwards we ate our chicken and cake and took pictures of each other with Mrs. Murphy's polaroid camera. Mrs. Murphy gave each of us a photo as a souvenir [fig. 39]. In response to my questions, she got to talking about her parents, who had been born in slavery. I was impressed by the extent of her knowledge of those times; her descriptions of the whippings, forced matings, and so on were consistent with hundreds of accounts by former slaves that I'd read in WPA narratives of the 1930s. None of which seemed to be news to my companions.

Mrs. Murphy's grandmother lived to be emancipated but was not able to find a single one of the thirteen children (from a total of sixteen) who'd been sold away from her; their names changed as they passed from owner to owner. It is this background of dehumanization, I imagine, that makes a respectful form of address so essential to her granddaughter.

After lunch, we moved on to other things. Arbie copied one of Mrs. Murphy's crochet patterns under Missie's vigilant supervision. Missie, who had been profoundly deaf since birth and communicated with nods, gestures, and grunts, would issue a volley of wordless admonitions each time Arbie slipped up, then smile when she finally got it right. Willia Ette wanted to buy a pair of Mrs. Murphy's crocheted shoes, but Mrs. Murphy didn't have them in her size. Bettie

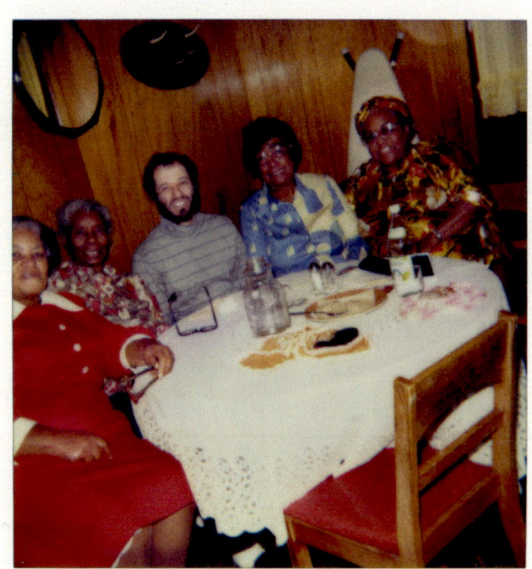

Fig. 39. Polaroid taken by Mable Murphy picturing (left to right) Missie Freeman, Arbie Williams, Eli Leon, Willia Ette Graham, and Bettie Phillips; Dos Palos, California, 1987

borrowed a Maple Leaf from Mrs. Murphy's collection of sample blocks; I noted that it was pieced of fabric that was at least seventy years old. At all times there was too much going on for one person to keep track of, but it was an ongoing joy to watch these elderly, uprooted women connect through their shared interests and an affinity for an art form that I suspected had origins in their ancestral homelands.

Eventually it was time to go. Bettie and Missie went on to see other friends in Dos Palos, and Arbie, Willia Ette, and I scooted off and into the fast lane of the freeway with Mrs. Murphy's invitations to return ringing in our ears. For most of the trip home, we were silent. We had finally run down.

Then too, we had a lot to think about. I don't know about Arbie and Willia Ette, but I couldn't get the thirteen missing children out of my mind.

III. TRIPS SOUTH

I used my Guggenheim money to extend my quilt research to the South. By 1989, when I got the fellowship, I'd connected with scores of Bay Area quiltmakers who were well positioned to direct me to friends and relatives still living in the places from which they had migrated. Most of my informants were extremely helpful. Inadvertently, I would be investigating their roots.

I bought a used RV, compiled hundreds of names, addresses, and phone numbers, mostly in east Texas, southern Arkansas, and northern Louisiana, recruited photographer Helen Wallis as traveling companion for my first trip, and was on my way. I also had people to look up in the California valley, Southern California, Nevada, New Mexico and Oklahoma, some of which are places I could arrange to pass through.

Arbie [Williams, p. 245] was delighted that I was going south to look for quilts. "Some of those sisters down there," she told me, "make some quilts that'll make your *eyes* swim."[5] She sent me to Aunt Jewell Harts [1907-2003], a legendary quiltmaker in Beckville, Texas, who lived next door to Arbie's brother. Aunt Jewell, in fact, was the only quiltmaker to whom more than one informant directed me. "Never make all your quilt blocks alike," her grandmother and grandmother's friends used to tell her, "make 'em different."[6] I bought just about everything this woman had for sale, including the Marsalis Avenue Missionary Baptist Church Quilt (fig. 40). When the church that her minister son-in-law presided over burned down, Aunt Jewell rescued its tattered flag from the ashes, salvaging enough fabric to make the cross at the quilt's center. Then, when the new church held its first service, she embroidered everything [printed] on the program's cover, along with a stick figure of her son-in-law, onto the quilt.

Willia Ette [p. 224] sent me to the Big Springs community out from the little town of Henderson, Texas—the first of many all-Black rural settlements way out of town with which I was to become familiar—where I met her cousins Dymon Moreland [1910-1998], Minnie Nobles [1901-2004], and Bettie Mae Hart [1902-1991], all of whose quilts would appear in my subsequent cataloged exhibitions. These women had once made up a quilting group, but age and infirmity had taken their toll, and the group no longer met.

Lee Wanda Jones [p. 230] sent me to her cousin, Maple Jean Swift [p. 231], in Ozan, Arkansas, who, in turn, introduced me to just about every member of her extended family. Maple and her mother and quilting partner, Florine Taylor [p. 230], lived next door, both houses full of quilts, ten or fifteen under each mattress. When I got through looking at these, Maple personally escorted me far and wide to view quilts made by or given to her friends and family members, some of whom likewise had them stored under their mattresses.

Angelia Tobias [p. 239] put me in touch with her grandmother and quilt teacher, Georgia Lee Kidd [p. 238]. Kidd didn't have a phone. I had to leave messages with relatives across town and ended up arriving at Kidd's place when she was off fishing. I was especially interested in seeing the quilts of relatives of the quiltmakers whose work I admired, particularly when the relative was their teacher, so I hung around for hours waiting for Kidd to come home. I was well rewarded for my efforts.

Sherry Ann Byrd [p. 233] sent me to her mother, Laverne Brackens [p. 232], and grandmother, Gladys Henry [p. 231], two of the most exciting quiltmakers I was to meet. Years later, working on their nomination for National Heritage Fellowships (which, well-deserved as they would have been, they didn't get), I showed Arbie Williams (herself a National Heritage fellow) slides of this family's work, recorded her reactions, and included her assessment in the nomination application. "That's a 'Damn It to Hell' quilt," Williams said of one of Henry's. "See, you can't get a pattern like that. She workin' with what she had, so she didn't have enough to fix it exactly—and, too, when you're an artist, you really don't want to fix it exactly like it's supposed to do."[7]

Holding a slide of one of Brackens's quilts [cat. 104] to the light, Williams commented: "Oh, bless her heart—what you doing, gal? She want it different from what she's seen it, so that's the reason you see so much of them flashing with different corners one way—now that's a real *heartbreaker there*. Where's she from? Texas? Oh God, I sure want to go see her when I go there."[8]

About one of Byrd's, she said: "Oh, mercy. I didn't know nobody went through with all that stuff but me—oooh my! *Well glad I went to Washington first, girls*. Where she stay?"[9]

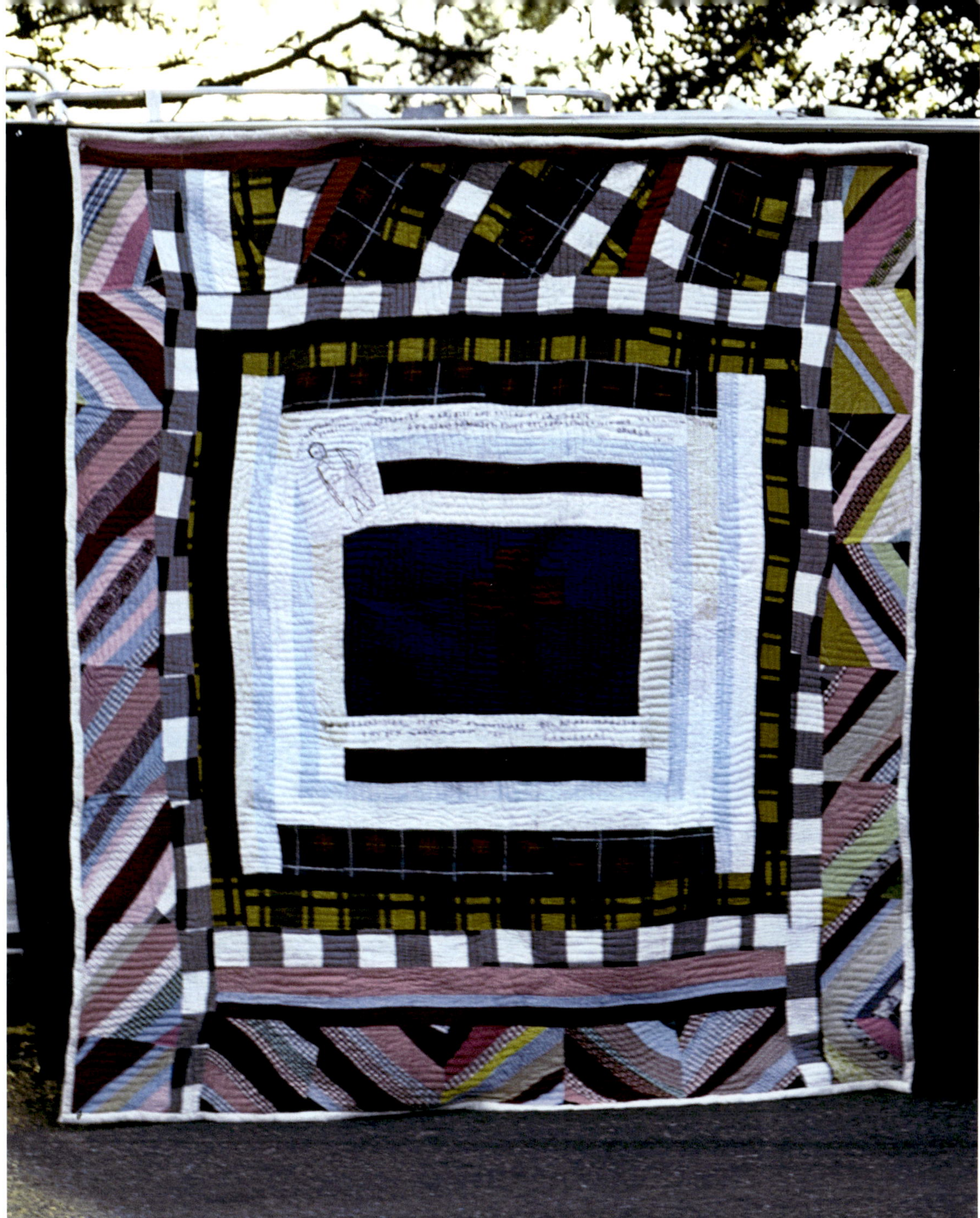

Fig. 40. Jewell Harts, Marsalis Avenue Missionary Baptist Church quilt, 1985, Beckville, Texas

Once in the field, of course, quilters would introduce me to each other. Which is how I met Roberta Lee Johnson [p. 237], who turned out to be one of my regulars. I not only checked in with her on every trip; I was encouraged to park my RV in her yard, use her phone for local calls, and generally visit with her and her friends [figs. 41–42]. She was a larger-than-life figure with a radiant personality, evident in her photos. She also furnished one of the most important pieces of evidence for African survivals I have ever come upon.

Johnson had been a schoolteacher in her younger days—until integration came to Texas, and all Black teachers were fired. She knew how to follow the rules. Indeed, she had a closet full of precisely measured standard-traditional quilts that she was planning to pass on to her children. She also had the two ragged, late 1920s britches quilts that, for sentimental reasons, she was loath to discard, but was doubtful that any of her children would want. One of these is the treasure to which I allude.

Making do with worn-out work clothes, Roberta Lee and her mother-in-law Georgia Ann Johnson [1884–1965] mindfully ordered dark and light squares in their lengthwise strips to alternate paired checkerboard "cross-strip bands"

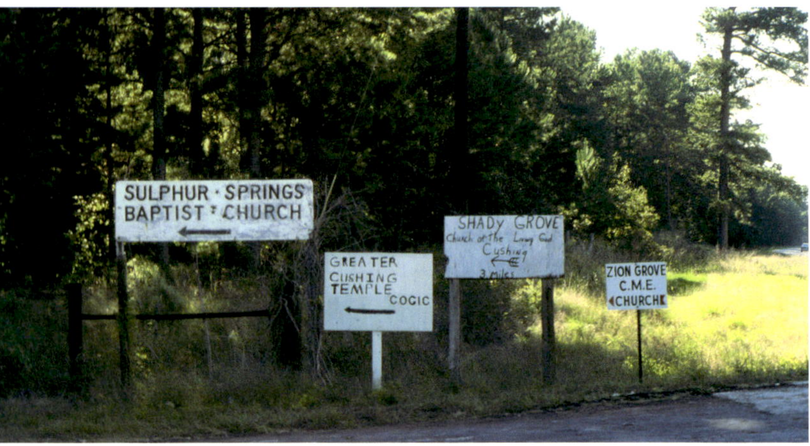

Fig. 41. Turn-off to Roberta Lee Johnson's home in the Sulphur Springs community near Cushing, Texas, 1990

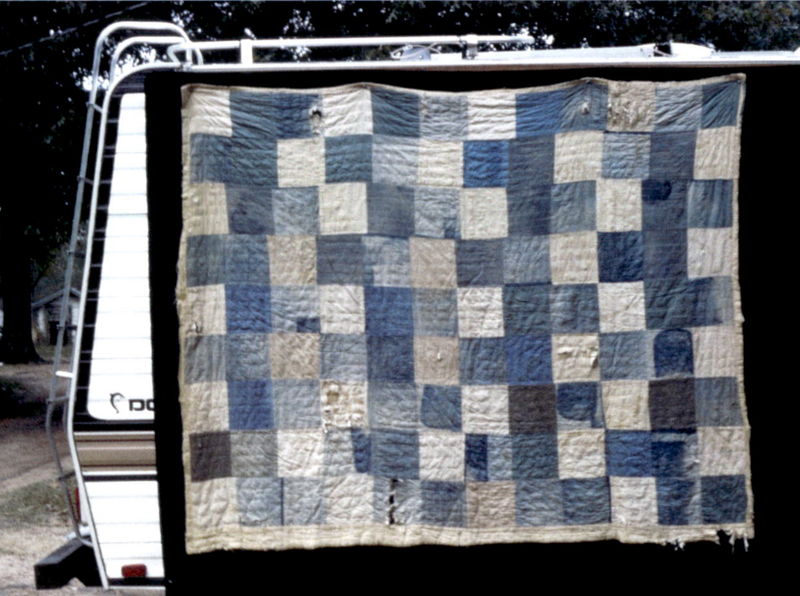

Fig. 42. Roberta Lee Johnson's quilt (cat. 4) hanging from Eli Leon's RV, Sulphur Springs community near Cushing, Texas, 1989

(widthwise stripes traversing the lengthwise strips[10]) with single solid bands, bordered top and bottom with single checkerboard bands. "We didn't have no design or pattern," Roberta Lee, who learned to quilt from Georgia Ann, told me, "We just blend them together to please our sight."[11]

This practice of alternating cross-stripped bands of contrasting colors, values, or patterns, however, is common to the strip-woven cloths of a wide variety of African peoples.[12] The similarity of the Johnson quilt to a Mandingo men's weave, exclusive of the central medallion, is uncanny [fig. 43]. (In the African example, pinstriped instead of solid bands alternate with wider checkerboard bands.) The Johnsons may not have had a printed pattern, but they conceived a systematic assembly embodying a prototypical design that, among many African peoples, would be carried as a model in the mind.[13]

Needless to say, I was thrilled to find such a treasure in the hands of its actual maker. Johnson was similarly thrilled to have found such a good home for her quilt.

In Shreveport, I visited Susan Roach, a quilt scholar who'd written a doctoral thesis on the quilting practices of northern Louisiana women, Black and white. Roach had concluded that, although improvisation was somewhat more prevalent among her Black constituents, there was not that much difference between the two populations. I wanted to see for myself but was only able to reach one of Roach's informants who still had quilts on hand–Jossie Shelton [1917-2009]. Her quilts were pretty much standard-traditional–at least the ones she was ready to show me. Again, however, sticking around paid off. After many repetitions on my part of my interest in "put-togethers" and my lack of concern with the quilt's condition, Jossie pulled out her oldest quilt–one she'd made when first married–which turned out to be a masterpiece of improvisation.

Poking around a little crafts store that Roach had helped start, I also found a quilt top by Essie H. Intoe [1909-2005] that was pieced of diamond-shaped patches like a Lone Star but–due to an innovational use of color–read as a Cross. Again, a striking improvisation. The quilt had not been photographed or recognized as an improvisation on the Lone Star pattern. Had it left the shop before my arrival, its value as an example of African American improvisation would have been lost.

And then there was Rosie Lee [Rosie Lee Tompkins, see p. 249], who told me that the last time she'd been home, her mother (I'll call her "Lucy") had a closet full of quilts. Prior to my second major trip, Rosie Lee gave me her mother's number in eastern Arkansas and prepped her for my visit. Nevertheless, when I called from a phone booth in Pine Bluff, Lucy was reluctant to let me come by. I called Rosie Lee and asked for more help. She called her mother. I called back. "You better get over there," Rosie Lee told me. "Did she agree to see me?" I asked. "No," Rosie Lee said, "but she sure won't let you in after it gets dark."

So I scooted off to eastern Arkansas, only to find a huge padlock on the outside of Lucy's front door. I asked the neighbor across the street if she had any idea of Lucy's whereabouts. "She's not home," she told me, squinting at the oversized lock, "that's for sure."

Luckily, I'd gotten the names of a few of Lucy's quilting friends in town. I spent the day interviewing them, asked them to call Lucy when she returned to assure her that I was okay, got permission to park my RV overnight in a church parking lot, and was knocking on Lucy's door bright and early the next morning. She opened it a crack. There was Rosie Lee's double, peering at me through the slit. I held up a copy of *Who'd a Thought It* with her daughter's quilt on the cover.

We talked for a while through the crack. "Can I come in?" I finally ventured to ask. "Okay," she said. "You can come *in*." By which emphasis I understood her to mean that she wasn't planning on showing me anything. But she and I sat down in her front room and started getting acquainted. [. . .][14]

Rosie Lee had always insisted that she didn't know the first thing about quilting. She was God's instrument; he showed her what to do. One thing I hoped to find out by looking at Lucy's quilts was how much they were like Rosie Lee's. I'd already established that one neighbor's quilts showed the hit-and-miss piecing so typical of Rosie Lee's work and been informed by this neighbor that Rosie Lee had watched her work as a girl, but I still hoped to see Lucy's.

At one point, after I'd learned that Lucy had a raggedy old quilt stuffed in her sofa as protection from a broken spring, but before she agreed to tear the setup apart for my benefit, I went out [to the RV parked outside]. As luck would have it, [I was] sitting up front in the RV with a copy of *Who'd a Thought It* in my lap, when one of Rosie Lee's brothers stopped by to say hello. He saw the book with Rosie Lee's quilt on the cover and blurted out, "That's one of my mother's, isn't it?" He hadn't known that Rosie Lee quilted and said his mother made quilts just like that.

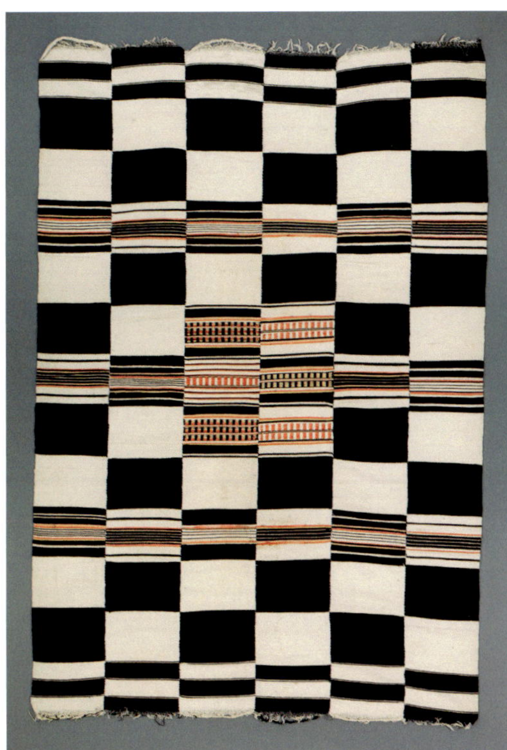

Fig. 43. Illustration of strip-woven cloth from Guinea, reproduced in Leon's book, *Accidentally on Purpose*, The Division of Anthropology, American Museum of Natural History, New York, Catalog # 90.2/1934

Eventually, Lucy undid the sofa. She was amazed when I offered to buy the excavated quilt and only too happy to sell it to me. As for me, my mission was accomplished. Both Rosie Lee's hit-and-miss piecing and the large medallion format she sometimes uses were represented in her mother's work. Not that this explains Rosie Lee's genius–just that her work has some connection to that of prior generations.

So my collecting trips were a great success. I had, however, bitten off more than I could chew. I soon filled up the two-story storeroom addition I'd built onto my house. I'd also spent a good deal of the money I'd earmarked for my retirement. And my short-term memory was going; it was increasingly difficult to keep the masses of objects and information I was accumulating in usable order.

I'd envisioned training a fleet of grad students to carry on my work, perhaps for the Smithsonian. I'd even been nominated for a MacArthur [fellowship], which would have facilitated getting such a project going. But my critics had prevailed. I didn't get the award, and the Smithsonian wasn't beating a path to my door. Something would have to give.

Notes

1. Eli Leon, *Who'd a Thought It: Improvisation in African-American Quiltmaking* (San Francisco: San Francisco Craft and Folk Art Museum, 1987). – Ed.
2. Eli Leon, *Models in the Mind: African Prototypes in American Patchwork* (Winston-Salem, NC: Diggs Gallery, Winston-Salem State University, 1992). – Ed.
3. Arbie Williams, interview by Eli Leon, date unknown, African-American Quilt Maker Interviews, BAMPFA.
4. Eli Leon, *Something Else to See: Improvisational Bordering Styles in African-American Quilts* (Amherst, MA: University of Massachusetts, 1997). – Ed.
5. Arbie Williams, interview by Eli Leon, June 1989, African-American Quilt Maker Interviews, BAMPFA.
6. Jewell Harts, interview by Eli Leon, November 1989, African-American Quilt Maker Interviews, BAMPFA.
7. Arbie Williams, interview by Eli Leon, December 18, 1993, African-American Quilt Maker Interviews, BAMPFA.
8. Williams, interview, December 18, 1993.
9. Williams, interview, December 18, 1993.
10. *Strips* designates units of construction, which may or may not also be units of design. *Stripes* are units of design only.
11. Roberta Lee Johnson, interview by Eli Leon, October 1989 , African-American Quilt Maker Interviews, BAMPFA.
12. Roy Sieber, *African Textiles and Decorative Arts* (New York: The Museum of Modern Art, 1972), 184, 186-89, 191 (top). See also Peggy Stolz Gilfoy, *Patterns of Life: West African Strip-Weaving Traditions* (Washington, DC: National Museum of African Art 1987), figs. 1-5.
13. For a more extensive discourse on cross-strip patterning, see Eli Leon, "Cross-strip Patterning in African Textiles and African-American quilts," *Surface Design Journal* 15, no. 1 (Fall 1990): 6-8, 38.
14. To maintain the focus on Leon's interactions with quilters, the editor has decided not to include a handwritten addition to this essay that narrates an incident with Leon's traveling companion. – Ed.

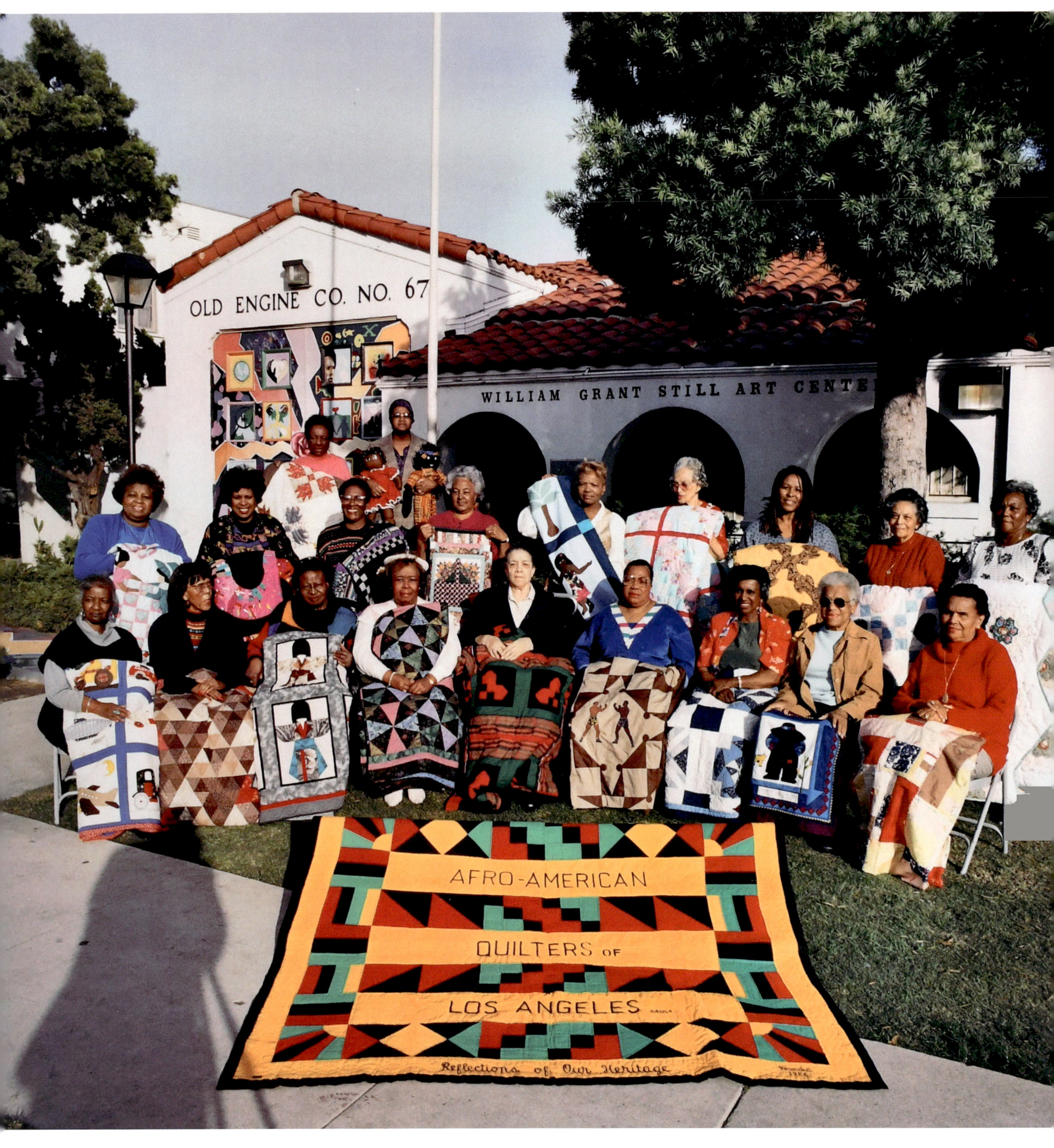
OLD ENGINE CO. NO. 67
WILLIAM GRANT STILL ART CENTE
AFRO-AMERICAN
QUILTERS OF
LOS ANGELES
Reflections of Our Heritage

A Table of Our Own: A Conversation on Repair, Reclamation, and Rootedness

Sharbreon Plummer with Carolyn Mazloomi and A'donna Richardson

Quilting within Black quilt communities remains a deeply relational practice—shaped by rich social and cultural contexts. Quilters' connections to geography, lived experiences, and one another are integral to how quilts are made and how quilters come to know themselves. Historically, quilt scholarship has attempted to capture the meaning of quilts produced by Black women through a lens that is both shortsighted and removed from its makers. This removal led to the imposition of artistic frameworks that did not consider the diverse sources of inspiration shaping the makers' work. Most non-Black scholars did not take into account how their biases and their commitment to proving their own assertions diminished the fullness of Black quilters' humanity and creative expression. The scholars' efforts, especially when circulating in mainstream art museums, placed so much emphasis on "improvisation" and "African retentions" as themes that they came to define African American quiltmaking. For decades, the surprise and awe at the ability of poor and working-class Black women to be stewards of beauty went without question or critique. Meanwhile, quilting grew and evolved as a tool for storytelling, veneration, and memory, with Black women sitting at the helm as griots who continued to take risks visually and conceptually.

There remains a need for repair in how the work of Black women, specifically Black quilters, is discussed and theorized. This conversation is an attempt at repair and reclamation. We, as a collective, have each been touched and molded by the act of quilting. We view it as an extension of love and care that our foremothers seeded within us. Thus, we feel particularly protective of how their stories are preserved and disseminated. Just as our elders surrounded their quilt frames to conspire and commune, we find it necessary to convene around our roles in protecting the practice that sustains us. As we enter into another quilt revival, we hope this intergenerational dialogue illuminates the role that each of us has in ensuring that legacies of Black quiltmaking don't succumb to the distortions and diminishments of the past.

Sharbreon Plummer: Let's begin with each of us introducing ourselves and describing our relationship to quilts or quiltmaking. My name is Sharbreon Plummer, and I am a scholar and artist who focuses on Black quilt practices.

Carolyn Mazloomi: I'm Carolyn Mazloomi, and I am an artist, quilter, collector, and writer.

A'donna Richardson: I'm A'donna Richardson, and I'm also a quilter—primarily art quilting. I consider myself an aspiring historian and an advocate for African American quilts that are still out there, left to be uncovered.

SP: I'd love to hear a little bit about both of your personal experiences with migration and how that may have shaped your practice or perspective on quilts.

CM: I was born and raised in the South and always say I'm a product of the Jim Crow segregated South. As an adult, I moved to California. Initially, my childhood introduction to quilts included the very traditional patchwork quilts and improvisational quilts—not unlike the ones you see from Gee's Bend. Those were the quilts that my aunts and my grandmothers made, and the ones I was familiar with. When I started quilting, I started out making traditional quilts. Once I moved to California, my work morphed into something

Opposite: Fig. 44. Members of the African-American Quilters of Los Angeles, 1992. University of North Carolina Libraries, Digital Collections Repository—Part of Roland L. Freeman Photograph Collection (70147), Southern Folklife Collection at Wilson Special Collections Library, University of North Carolina-Chapel Hill

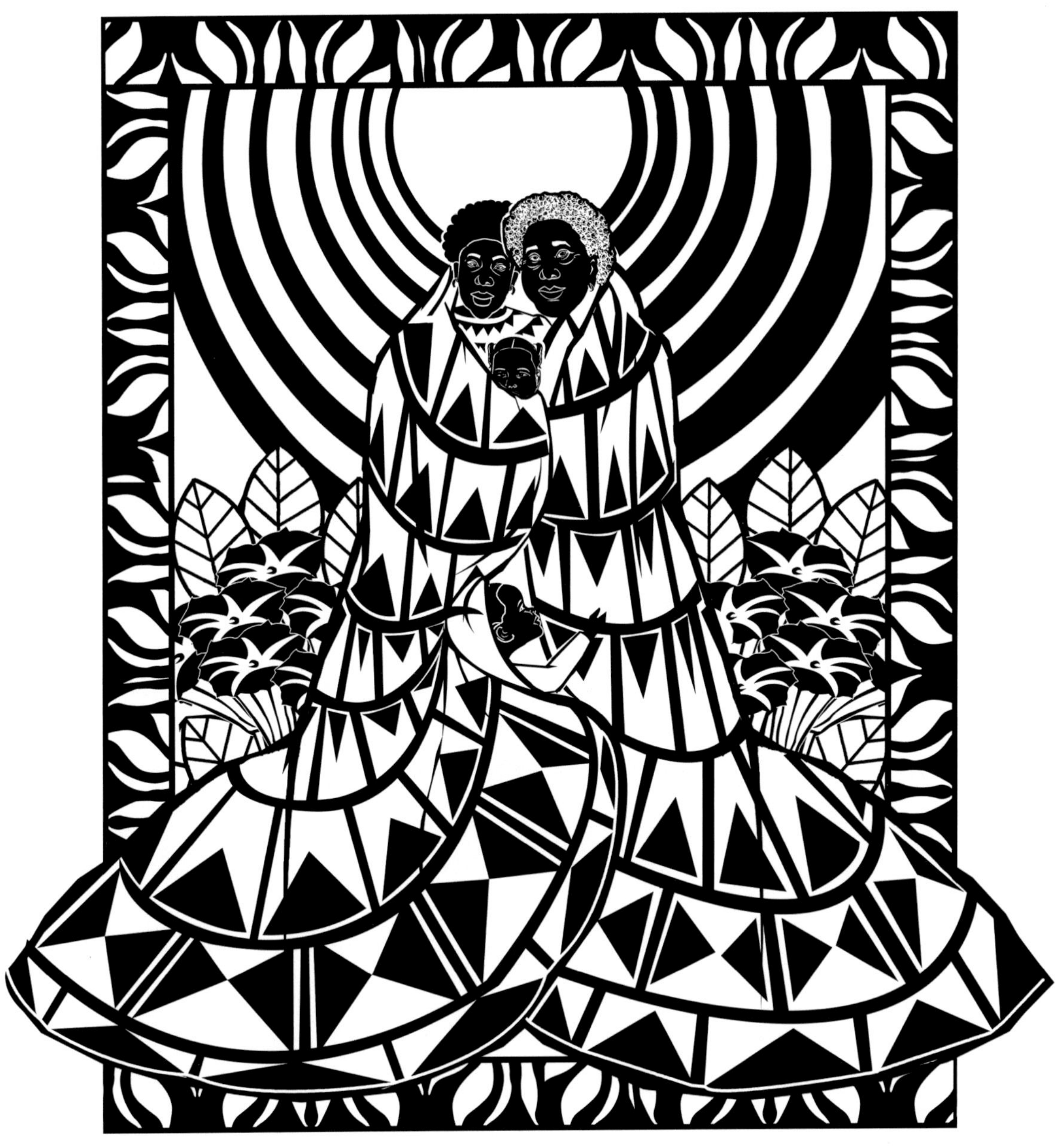

Fig. 45. Carolyn Mazloomi, *Wrapped in Love*, 2016. Cotton, India ink, textile paint, cotton thread, and cotton batt. Claire Oliver Gallery, Harlem

else. I switched to making narrative quilts (fig. 45). I was also introduced to the art quilt during my time in LA. The art quilt movement had a big impact on quilting as well. Moving just opened up a whole new arena to a different type of quilt. It also introduced me to all the hoopla about improvisational quilts, which I really didn't take very well to. As we all know, those were not the definitive quilts.

I also became familiar with the collection of Eli [Leon] at the African American Museum of Los Angeles. To this day, I get frustrated that people see Eli Leon—who in turn saw Bill Arnett—as a pioneer and a true advocate for Black quilts. To me, it was just the opposite. He collected quilts, and we know he didn't pay much for those quilts. His scholarship was fraught with controversy, and I don't want people to walk away thinking that he was an angelic figure in African American quilt history. He had a hand in shaping the whole conversation around what did or did not make an African American quilt, but I'll save that for later.

AR: With regard to migration in a broader sense, people brought their unique styles and techniques with them as they left the South during the Great Migration. Long before that, forced migration and displacement from the transatlantic crossing, enslavement, and segregation created legal and societal barriers that separated us from the rest of the population. These oppressive systems created distinctive experiences and histories for African Americans in the different regions of the country.

As people moved around, they carried their quilts and their quilting knowledge and techniques with them. This migration enabled the cultural exchange of quilting practices between different regions. With most changes affecting African Americans, quilters adapted their techniques and designs based on the materials and patterns available to them in their new environments. Customs, techniques, and patterns continued to be shared and swapped, leading to the evolution of new and different quilting styles. This blended traditional African American quilting methods (customs) with influences from other regions.

My personal story isn't as colorful as Carolyn's! [*Laughter*] I was getting ready to retire from my second career. We were visiting my husband's parents in Texas, like we do every year. It just so happened this one year that I was getting ready to retire, I realized that every bed in the home we visited had these beautiful handmade quilts on them. I thought to myself, "My family in Washington [State], nor my grandkids, have nothing made with such love and care to pass on from generation to generation." So I turned to my husband and I said, "I want a sewing machine. I'm going to quilt" (figs. 46 and 47). Once I got into quilting, I became aware of, and was very much influenced by, Carolyn Mazloomi, Gee's Bend, and Roland Freeman's *A Communion of the Spirits*.[1]

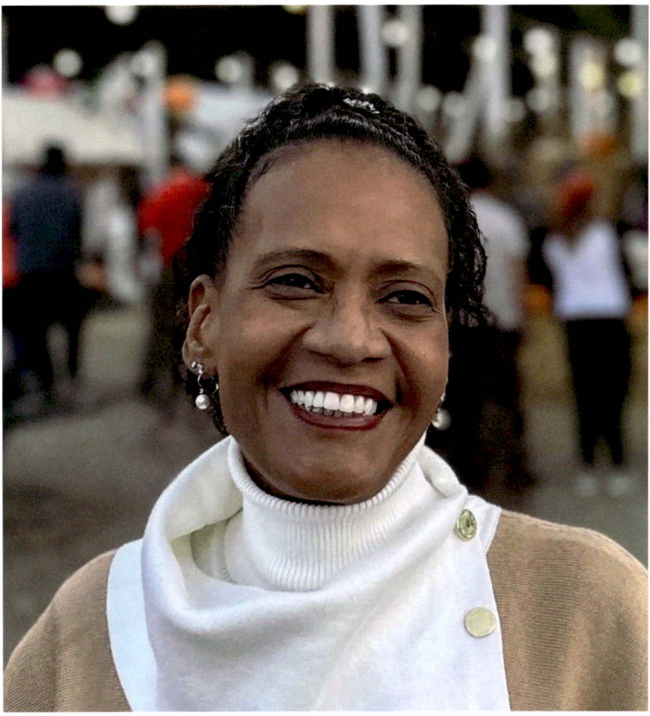

Fig. 46. A'donna Richardson, founder of the African American Quilt Documentation Study Group

SP: Thank you for mentioning scholarship. That actually brings me to my next question, if we think back to the particular time in which the majority of this exhibition's quilts were made (1940s–80s) and subsequent scholarship. Dr. Mazloomi, you in particular have a very beautiful and specific relationship to quilt scholarship. You were a part of the voices, along with Roland Freeman and Cuesta Benberry,[2] that later pushed against white scholars of that time. What did those scholars' work do to/for Black quilters and what tensions arose from that critique?

CM: Those early books about Black quiltmaking did nothing but harm to the Black quilt community, because they pigeonholed the work. The early scholars came up with a set of criteria to define the "African American quilt." It should be stated that it's one of the reasons why there were hardly any Black quilts in the state quilt research projects.[3] I heard often, during the era of the state quilt research projects, that Black quilters would bring in quilts to be documented on documentation days, and if they didn't look "improvisational," they weren't archived. I also observed this myself.

They were looking for asymmetry, the large stitching, and the bold, bright colors. They wanted to see these so-called subconscious African signs and symbols that related to our heritage. Much of that was untrue and based on opinion. If we have quilts that are made with African signs and symbols, it's because we made a concerted effort to study that and put them in our quilts. It didn't come by osmosis! It doesn't work that way. Overall, the scholarship was very limiting, and that was proven by the state research projects. That's why I feel nobody can define us but us.

SP: Absolutely. By not having those voices present to provide context, it strips away the agency and ability to clarify.

AR: They were underrepresented and ignored, and almost stripped from the mainstream of what was happening at the time. When I say underrepresented, I mean both the quilts and Black women. It's not that they weren't active. Quilts were absolutely being made at that time, but these women were also, sometimes, dealing with uninviting environments. They had to melt into the fabric of white guilds, which wasn't always the best experience. Eventually several

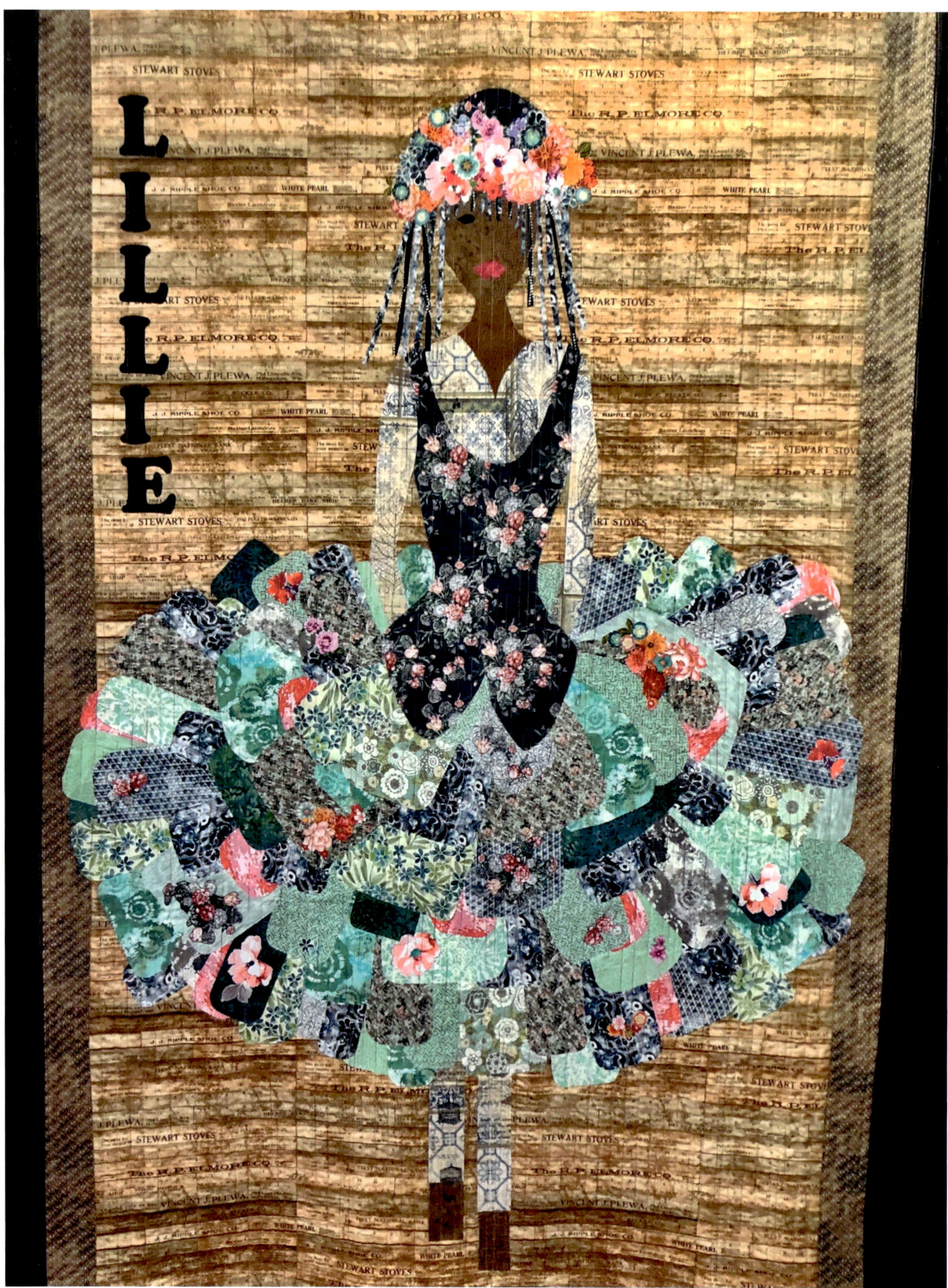

Fig. 47. A'donna Richardson, *Lillie*, 2018. Courtesy of the artist

African American quilt guilds started (fig. 44), but before they were formalized, people were working at home or in community spaces. Back in the 80s, Black women always did things together, like sisters, but not attached to an organization, so to speak. The people in charge of state quilting projects would not have invited or interacted with us, because they weren't interested.

CM: Well, that was the idea. I feel that's why so many people from outside of the culture take the worst of what we have, or what they think nobody cares about, and position it as the best we can do. It makes them look better. I recall when I was in Indianapolis with Cuesta Benberry for a lecture series. We were waiting outside of the auditorium for me to be called in for my lecture. I overheard this man speak about a quilt made by an African American with all these wonderful signs. He talked about the symbols, what they meant and how they were used on this quilt. I thought, "Damn! I have to see this." It was intriguing to hear about all the symbolism that this quilter used in their quilt. I opened the door to look at the piece that he was talking about on the projector screen, and it was one of my pieces! Here I was, listening to this man, and would never have known that it was my work. This was because nothing he said was the actual intention when I created the quilt.

This is the importance of voice. This is the importance of artists speaking for themselves. This is the importance of documentation that includes statements from the artist(s). This is what earlier scholars like Wahlman,[4] Vlach,[5] Thompson[6] did not do. Wahlman ultimately came back and released a second edition of a book where she *did* ask some of the original quilters who were living about the meaning of their quilts. I can remember [discussing this with] Gwen McGee, who was a founding member of the Women of Color Quilters Network and lived in Jackson, Mississippi. Gwen was friends with a lot of the Mississippi artists that were documented in Maude Wahlman's book, and she spoke on how they would talk about the interpretation of their quilts. Primarily because that was *her* (Wahlman's) interpretation and not *theirs*. So it became a big thing [internally].

It was always important for me, with every book I write and every show I curate, to have a statement from the quilter. I want people to know what the artist intended, how they interpret their work, and what it means to them (fig. 48). It's the same thing for myself with my own work. I want to document it. I've documented every show I've ever curated. It's important to have that, so nobody can come back and interpret—or in our case, misinterpret—what the artist is trying to say.

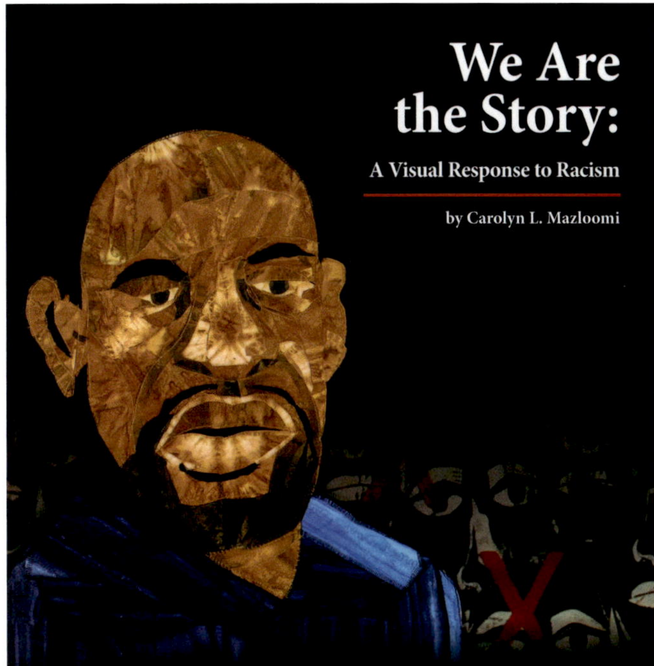

Fig. 48. Cover of *We Are the Story: A Visual Response to Racism*, catalog accompanying the exhibition curated by Carolyn L. Mazloomi and co-presented by the Textile Center, Minneapolis, Minnesota, and the Women of Color Quilters Network, 2021

SP: I appreciate you saying that, because it brings up something I believe in naming explicitly. Part of why the harm and misinterpretation was able to happen is because of how, societally, people treat and view us as Black women. There's almost this unspoken feeling of, "Oh. They don't care. It's fine. They're just glad to be represented." Because who, especially at that time—who truly was going to advocate for us and counter that? I think your legacy is an example of us doing the work for ourselves, because if not us, then who?

CM: It's true, and you know what's disheartening? We had those early scholars who told their viewpoint. Then you had Gladys Fry,[7] Roland Freeman and Cuesta Benberry, and myself. I'm producing catalogs and they're discussing the diversity of quiltmaking within the national African American quilt community. All of us talked about that. So it disputed what was written earlier by white writers.

AR: You know, mainstream white scholars and other enthusiasts don't put that out there . . . the disputed part.

CM: Right! So there was a period, for nearly twenty years, where quilt appreciators and historians outside of the culture saw what we put out about narrative quilts. They've seen numerous art quilts. They've seen these masterful traditional quilts made by African Americans. So, we were sailing along smoothly. Then along comes Gee's Bend. For me, it's wonderful that the women of Gee's Bend got notoriety for their quilts, and they're known for their quilt work. However, Bill Arnett saw those quilts in Roland Freeman's book *Communion of the Spirits*. He even called Roland to ask Roland about the women in Mississippi and Alabama who made those quilts.

I believe putting those quilts into the public made it so easy for people to revert back to the beginning, when we had early white quilt scholars talking about improvisational quilts. Because they don't believe in there being room for all of us, Gee's Bend became the be-all end-all of quilt discussion for African American quilts. Again, people were looking at that kind of improvisational quilt as being definitive, and all the research we put out didn't mean anything.

SP: I think it's important for people to interrogate why they feel so drawn to improvisational quilts. They are beautiful.

That's not up for debate. However, there's also been the continuation of an implied narrative that we should almost be shocked that women of humble means would happen to put something so lovely together. Even improvisation requires intention. Although things may seem abstract (or whatever the adjective is), there's still a methodology. There's still planning and assembly. There's work that goes into it that requires forethought and intention and skill. You don't just wake up and say, oh I'm just gonna improvise and it'll sort itself out. You may not follow a traditional pattern, but it's still a process.

CM: It's an intuitive process, even for the shapes and the colors, right? You have a sense of what colors work well and what placements go together. That's intuitive thinking. So you're right. It's not without process.

AR: Yes, you have to make a definitive decision. Like Sharbreon said, when you're putting something together, you may say, "Oh, I just threw this together." But you made a decision as to what, where, and how.

SP: In keeping with our earlier points about quilts and perception, I'd be curious to hear from both of you about two things that I'd like to ground in the terms "urgency" and "importance." The first question is, what do you feel is most urgent or important about what is conveyed in this show, in particular? Second, what do you feel is most urgent or important as it relates to the current state of African American quiltmaking?

CM: I looked at most of the quilts in the show, and it was the standard improvisational fare. I always think there has to be some balance with other shows. I hate to say that, but there has to be some balance where the viewer can see other [styles] of works and not just think, "Oh, this is it." In the field, I think they're seeing it, because right now we're in a time in our lives, not unlike the Harlem Renaissance, where Black art is being shown and appreciated. This isn't only Black quilts, but Black art overall. In the past five years or so, it's been like working on cloud nine, because everybody's interested in how to showcase Black art. So quilts are very popular. Now, for those quilters that are interested in selling and hanging their quilts—they're having a field day! I see balance, which is wonderful to have in the show and the quilts. The other side of the coin is that it has to be seen as well as written about. These Black guilds are very active, and they have their yearly quilt shows, and many of them are publishing catalogs, which I love. So that documentation is key. It feels like a new day. We're coming along.

SP: Is that optimism I hear?

CM: There's always hope as long as there's a dollar to be made. Collectors want the next best thing out there. They're competitive. I know that because I've been subject to all sides of these conversations. They're out there and they're collecting quilts across the spectrum.

SP: A'donna, how would you respond to the prompt?

AR: Well, first I applaud the Berkeley Art Museum and Pacific Film Archive for recognizing and addressing the significance of African American quilts, specifically for their efforts in trying to be inclusive (the museum as a whole). For their attempts to portray these African American quilts and the quiltmakers accurately and [for] telling the truth. There are so many falsehoods out there that are attached to our quilts, and I know that Carolyn's received the brunt of this. Eli's collection is full of it. When Eli didn't know something, he made it up—from quilt patterns to how he obtained the item. Sure, he made an attempt to try, but when it's not true, it's just not true. I appreciate that this show is one route towards getting to the truth.

SP: Yes to truth telling! Thank you both for such thoughtful reflections and your time spent in conversation. Before we depart, is there anything else you'd like to share as a call to action?

CM: That's a long answer! I'll say this—documentation of quilts is very important. It's critical—critical to history and from a collector's point of view. It's important for me to be a good steward of the work, because I buy that work. It doesn't mean I am at liberty to do whatever I want with it. I'm still obligated to the quiltmaker and quiltmaker's family as to what I do with their creation. I'm not going to live forever, so I have to make sure that my collected works go to a good home where the general public can enjoy and study that work. Within my own community, I would like to see that we keep educating our people about the historic significance of what we do. That's one of the reasons I started the Women of Color Quilters Network, to let African American quiltmakers know not only the historical significance, but the monetary value of the work as well, so that they won't get cheated when they're selling their work. The quilter should educate themselves on the significance and the value of their quilts. Finally, we as Black artists must leave something behind for our families. We can't sell off everything. We can't give away everything to people outside of Black culture. We have to leave something to our families; we have to

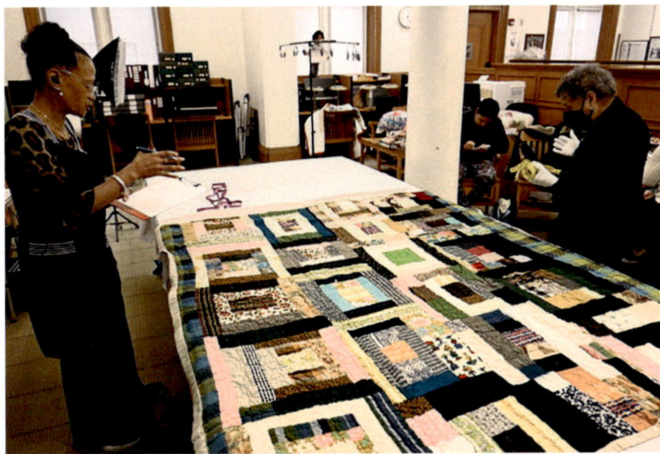

Fig. 49. Documentation day organized by the African American Quilt Documentation Study Group at the African American Museum and Library, Oakland, 2024

leave something to our community. Survival of the work for generations to come within our own communities. That's my call.

AR: I agree. What I have found is that when most people leave the southern region, time, work, the environment, and societal influences cause some to hold on to their family quilts and not continue the custom of quilting. These migrated quilts become either hidden away with their stories in boxes up under beds and in closets, or the family is unaware of the quilts' historic value, and tragically some quilt(s) end up moth-eaten in the basement or on the floor of the garage up under an old car. We need to continue to share the rich legacy that is tied to our quilts. They need to be studied and appreciated. That's why I founded the African American Quilt Documentation Study Group in 2015 (fig. 49). I started it because of what I didn't see in the State Projects of the 80s. I'd taken up quilting and started learning about groups like Gee's Bend, etc. Shortly after, I joined the American Quilt Study Group through Karen Alexander, who was the Pacific Northwest representative. Seeing the research at AQSG sparked my interest in history, which led me to the [state] documentation projects. After gathering whatever publications each state did online, I saw the lack of diversity across several states, including my own (Washington). At first, I was angry. Then I got mad with a purpose. After reading what the other states had done, I thought, "I could do this." I made a plan, created a guide, printed business cards and flyers, and took every chance I could to be a vendor at every African American event I could find. That's what started the Washington State Project focusing in on African American quilts. It was about educating the public and talking to them about family history.

Now, with relocating to California and the pandemic, things slowed down, but my mind couldn't rest. I said to myself, "A'donna, you did it in Washington and you've got a wider base of people here. Just see how it goes." In my heart, I knew this would be large-scale and far more comprehensive than anything I was doing on my own. So, that's when the African American Quilt Documentation Study Group evolved into a nonprofit. The Study Group encompasses the entire United States, if it's an African American quilt. I just felt we needed a platform that was committed to documenting and preserving our African American quilt history and making it available for research. We didn't have that, but we do now.

Carolyn has said dozens of times (and it's written in all her books) that quilts are not just warm blankets. In our culture, they symbolize such a powerful tool of expression, resistance, and hope. You don't get that story if someone just says, "Here's a picture of the quilt, here's the name, and these are the dimensions." Our history embedded in our quilts is rich, and it needs to be uncovered, recorded, and taught for our families and future generations. Now, who's going to do it if not we ourselves?

Notes

1. Roland L. Freeman, *A Communion of the Spirits: African-American Quilters, Preservers, and Their Stories* (Nashville: Rutledge Hill Press, 1996).
2. Cuesta Benberry, *Always There: The African-American Presence in American Quilts* (Louisville, KY: Kentucky Quilt Project, 1992).
3. Christine Humphrey, "Quilt Documentation Projects, 1980–1989: Exploring the Roots of a National Phenomenon" (master's diss., University of Nebraska-Lincoln, 2010). See also *Uncoverings* 35 (2014): 115–50, from the Research Papers of the American Quilt Study Group. From roughly 1980 to 1989, organizers across over thirty states completed state-wide quilt documentation projects. Humphrey notes that the success of the Kentucky Quilt Project inspired a nationwide interest in the archiving of quilts, their makers, and lesser-known histories.
4. Maude Wahlman, *Signs and Symbols: African Images in African-American Quilts* (New York: Penguin, 1993).
5. John Michael Vlach, *The Afro-American Tradition in Decorative Arts: Basketry, Musical Instruments, Wood Carving, Quilting, Pottery, Boatbuilding, Blacksmithing, Architecture, Graveyard Decoration* (Cleveland: Cleveland Museum of Art, 1978).
6. Eli Leon, *Who'd a Thought It: Improvisation in African-American Quiltmaking* (San Francisco: San Francisco Craft & Folk Art Museum, 1987).
7. Gladys-Marie Fry, *Stitched from the Soul: Slave Quilts from the Ante-Bellum South* (New York: Dutton Studio Books; in association with the Museum of American Folk Art, 1990).

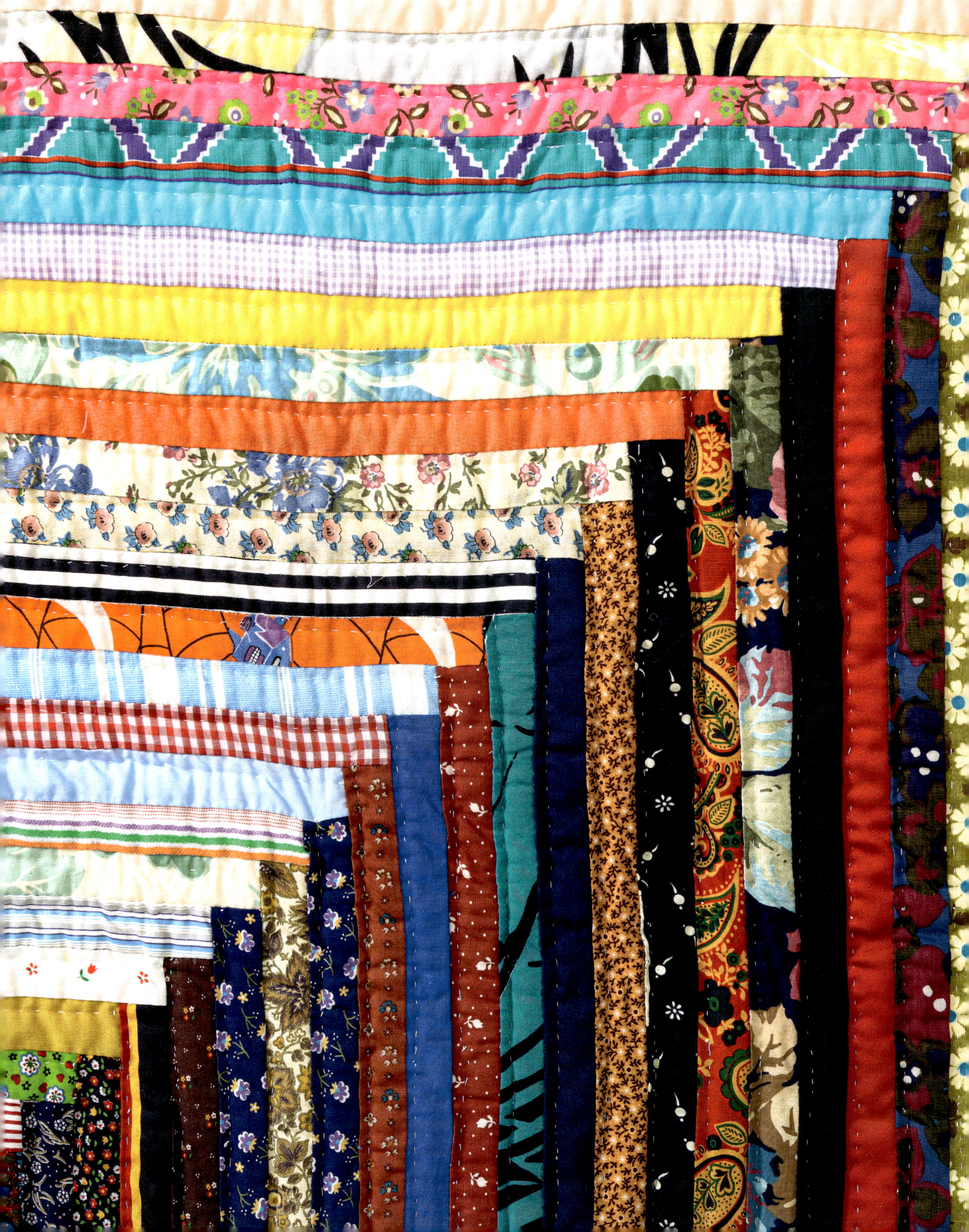

Collecting and Exhibiting Quilts

Bridget R. Cooks

I have been interested in, spoken about, and written on the topic of quilts and their relationships to makers, collectors, and museums for the past several years. The extraordinary gift of more than three thousand quilts from collector Eli Leon to the Berkeley Art Museum and Pacific Film Archive presents another opportunity to reconsider the meaning of possessing Black women's creativity. My work on quilts has led me to reflect on how museums and white collectors have differentiated between craft and art, and what collectors seek by acquiring the work of Black women quiltmakers. Addressing these topics can contribute to a critical understanding of how quilt collections are built, acquired, and exhibited, and how we may imagine practices that will better enable us to see quilts as part of a story of Black survival and liberation.

I begin with the artist Faith Ringgold, whose work has recently been seriously presented through the retrospective *Faith Ringgold: American People,* organized by the New Museum. This focused attention on Ringgold's oeuvre was long overdue. As the most visible quilt-based artist, Ringgold has influenced my thoughts about the discourse of quilts in the art world. In the 1980s, Ringgold began creating quilts that allowed her to tell a wide range of stories about memories, heroes, fantasies, and speculative futures. In these works, Ringgold combines text, image, and design, while challenging the denigration of quilts as "women's work." In the story quilt format, she developed a mature style.

Of all the story quilts, her arsenal of skills works together most critically in *The French Collection* (1991–97), a twelve-piece series in which Ringgold takes on as its subject the field of art history, along with its colonial partner, the museum (fig. 50). Art historian Richard J. Powell explains the artist's institutional critique: "The truths Faith Ringgold visually plies us with are (1) that women and men of African descent significantly figure in matters of art and art history, and (2) that audiences are capable of embracing not only an elitist, museum-sanctioned 'high art' but also a 'people's art' that knows no class boundaries or social distinctions."[1] Ringgold accomplished this in part by showing off her ability to copy artworks of canonical modern European painters, and, in the process, she subordinated the canon in the service of the critical development of a more inclusive contemporary art. Through this painted-quilt format, Ringgold engages in the creative destruction of the barrier between fine art and craft. As art historian Cheryl Finley notes, "Deeply embedded in the American craft tradition, the African and African Diaspora textile tradition, and the mythology of the Underground Railroad, the quilt became a palette on which Ringgold not only shares her talent as an artist, but also her experiences as a black woman."[2]

I think about what Ringgold had to go through to be recognized by the art museum. She had to quilt and paint, and explain art history, African American culture, African American women's history, and a speculative future and past. She had to do more artistic and intellectual work and provide more context than is required of most artists who are included in the permanent collections of art museums. She created the hybrid painting and quilt form that is a kind of cultural concession to "high-art" expectations. She met the art museum at least halfway, to show that she could fulfill the highest form of visual art. However, she insisted on bringing traditions of Black womanhood along with her.

Traditional quiltmakers signified through Ringgold's story quilts have not been interested in calling themselves artists. For example, we can think of the Gee's Bend quilters for whom the title "artist" was insignificant when they first received attention from the art world in the early 2000s.

Opposite: Detail of cat. 90

They were not concerned with the distinction between the categories of art and craft that had been a critical point of classification for American museums since their establishment in the nineteenth century. These categories are dependent upon distinctions of class, gender, and race. They make divisions between who belongs in the art museum and who doesn't; who is deemed civilized and uncivilized; and those who sit and those who squat.[3] For Black women, the shift in the status of quilts from craft to art has come at a price and has revealed the long-standing investments that museums have in social hierarchies. To fit through the narrow eye of the art-world needle, the quilters' stories, Christian faith, and testimonies to anti-Blackness in America would have to be left behind. Instead, their quilt tops were recognized as valuable because of their comparison to European paintings, something to which Ringgold gestures in her work.

In the last chapter of *Exhibiting Blackness: African Americans and the American Art Museum*, I discuss the 2002 blockbuster exhibition, *The Quilts of Gee's Bend*.[4] There I describe how the classification of quilts as art versus craft was a point of contention for some critics who berated art museums for presenting the quilts. One critic decried the exhibition for endangering the museum with an infestation of bedbugs.[5] The curators were also accused of trying to dupe audiences into thinking craft was art. In other critiques, the race, gender, and class identities of the quilters made the premise of the exhibition unbelievable.

Most critics missed what meaning the exhibition had for the women who made the quilts. Having the quilts in the museum was a way for them to share their Christian faith because of the spiritual practices that are a part of the process of making the quilts. Moreover, when a group of the quilters traveled to the openings and related programs of the exhibition, they would sing gospel songs for the audience as part of the celebration. The quilters wanted to share their Christian fellowship, the joy of singing and praying, that went into making the quilts.

I am struck by the disconnect between the Black women's lives, stories, and struggles and the desire for their work by white collectors. I also see a pattern, within and beyond the visual arts, concerning Black creativity and the white desire for possession of and intimacy with Black people and their things. The most prominent examples relevant to us today are William Arnett of the Souls Grown Deep Foundation and Eli Leon. Arnett amassed an incredible collection of art by Black artists who were not academically trained, including many, many quilts. What is so striking about Arnett, Leon, and other white collectors is their strong desire to possess and preserve stories of family and survival that were not theirs. Given the blatant history of anti-Blackness and its resurgence so dramatically in the last few years alone, we must ask some important questions regarding Black quilters and white collectors, a relationship that is obviously rife with racial tension–tension that continues a persistent and direct antagonism in the aftermath of slavery. So, I ask us to consider: Why this white preoccupation with Black possession? Were Arnett's and Leon's desires to be an ally to poor, Black women quilters? Why did they have such strong desires to possess the work of Black women who were outsiders to the art world? Why did these men desire a kind of intimacy with Black culture, and specifically Black women, through their collection of quilts?

Leon's bequest to BAMPFA included a box of archival documents. Among these papers are until-now-unpublished short essays that reveal his philosophy, process, and goal for collecting quilts by African American makers. For example, in the essay "Reclaiming a Missing Link" (pp. 186–188, this volume), Leon recalls being on the lookout for what he identified as Africanisms in contemporary quilts. His feeling of the thrill of the hunt is clear when he describes buying a quilt that was wrapped around the shoulders of another collector. Realizing that the seller did not have any information about the quilt's origins, Leon became both "crestfallen" and focused on solving a new mystery.[6] He found a woman named Lodesta, who was a relative of the man who had originally owned the quilt. He said that Lodesta was delighted to hear from him, because she "worried about the family's quilts and was relieved to learn that this one had found a good home."[7] She was also "amused" when she saw the quilt, because "it was the quilt they used the most."[8] Lodesta told Leon a powerful and sorrowful story about the quilter and the lives involved in the quilt's history.

> [The quilt] was made by Mother (Mary Lue) Brown, a woman who'd had a special relationship with Helen, the deceased wife of the man whose possessions had been auctioned. In the 1930's, Helen had gone to college with Mother Brown's daughter [Elfreda]. When Helen, an orphan, had had her first child, she'd had no one to help her. Mother Brown had stayed with her until she'd been able to handle the situation herself. The two formed an attachment that was to last a lifetime.[9]

In his telling of the story, Leon did not comment on the moving narrative around Black women's bonds, survival, and generosity all signified by the quilt. Leon did not state that he thanked Lodesta for sharing the provenance and for expressing the significance of the quilt's daily use. Nor did he return the quilt–likely the intuitive next step for sensitive people who were moved by Lodesta's revelation. He extracted information about the quilt and left Lodesta's

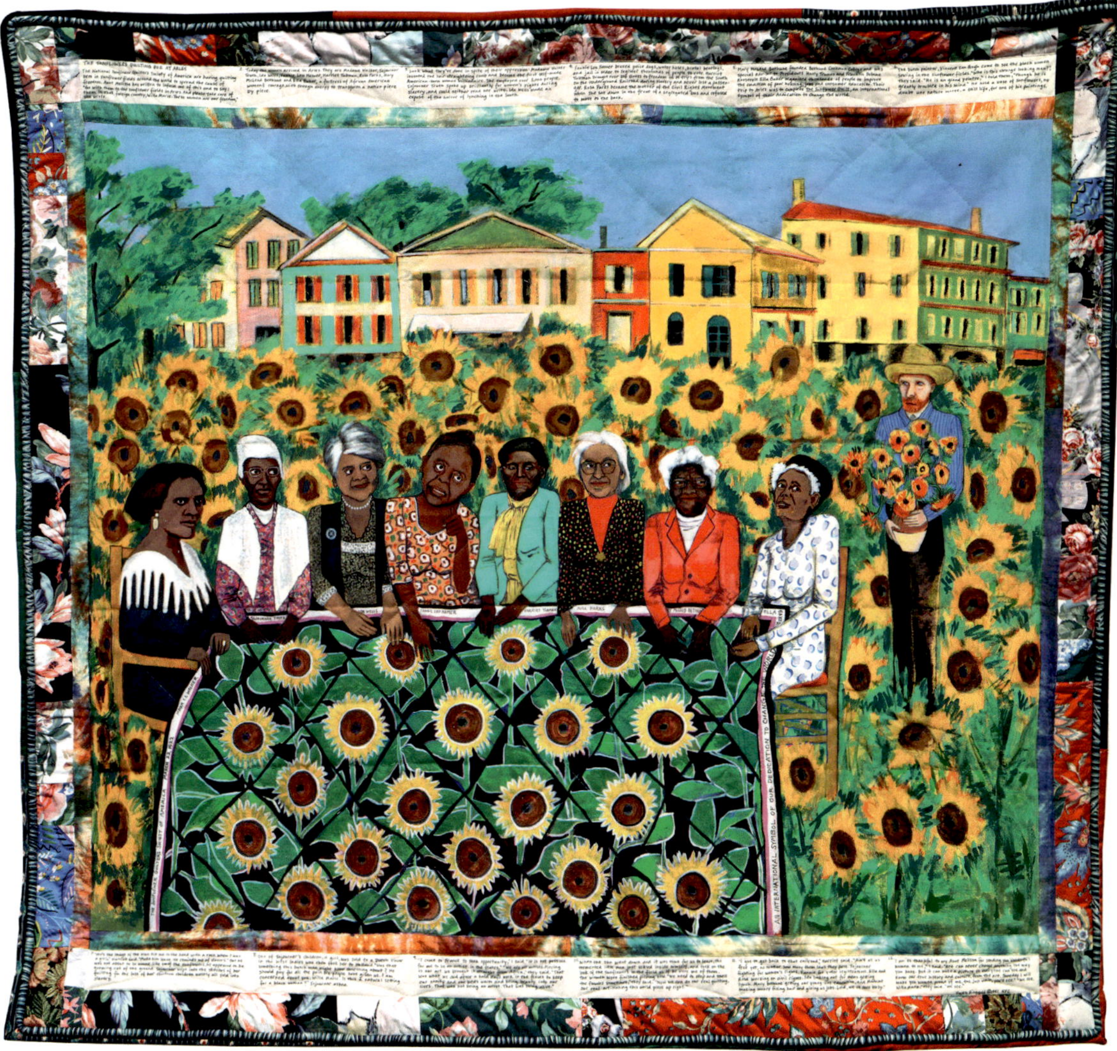

Fig. 50. Faith Ringgold, *The French Collection Part I, #4: The Sunflowers Quilting Bee at Arles*, 1991. Acrylic on canvas with pieced fabric border, 74 × 80 in. (188 × 203.2 cm). Private collection

home with a new lead to follow. Lodesta connected him with Elfreda, and he learned more about the quilt from her.

Instead of recognizing the opportunity to give the quilt to Lodesta or Elfreda, Leon expressed how exciting it was that *he* was the owner of the quilt. The purchase of the quilt was important to Leon, because it supported his theory of the influence of African cultures in the quilts by African American makers. He informs the reader that he later included the quilt in two exhibitions and lists the art institutions where the shows were presented. He states that with the provenance, the quilt, which he later called *Missing Link Strip Quilt*, "was destined [to] be of particular importance to my work."[10]

This desire for Blackness expands beyond the visual arts. I think of musician David Bowie's last album, *Blackstar,* in which, on the title track, he repeats, "I'm a Blackstar. I'm a Blackstar. I'm not a white star. I'm a Blackstar." As if stating it would make it true. The album was released on the day he died in 2016, emphasizing how he wished to be remembered as Black, although he was a white British international superstar. The desire to be connected to Blackness in some symbolic way manifests itself in white collectors of Black art, in the work of white museum curators, and in the hit songs of white rock musicians in ways that are remarkable.

What explains the desire for Black identity and white possession by white men in the arts? Certainly, it is not a desire for the whole of Blackness, as the late, great, cultural theorist and musician, Greg Tate, explains thoroughly in his classic work *Everything But the Burden: What White People Are Taking from Black Culture*. Tate clarifies that long-enacted desire that whites have had for Black style, Black cool, and a Black soul.[11] This desire has been enacted with violence in many forms, perhaps most theatrically in the practice of blackface, a practice that Eric Lott has explored in his book, *Love and Theft*, about the history of minstrelsy.[12] These examples demonstrate the expansive issue of white desire for Black possession. How do quilts figure into this

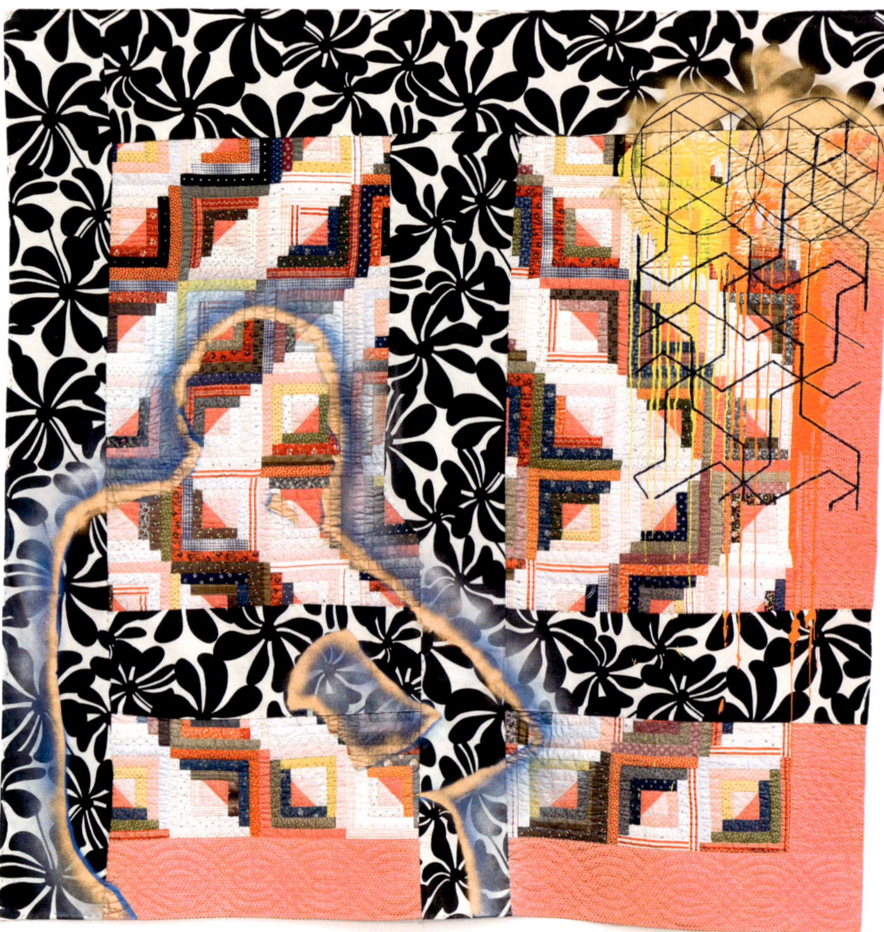

Fig. 51. Sanford Biggers, *Quilt 24*, 2013. Antique quilt, assorted textiles, acrylic, and spray paint, 77 × 79 in. (195.6 × 200.7 cm). Museum of Contemporary Art Chicago, Gift of Mary and Earle Ludgin by exchange, 2013.24

desire? What is this perceived "elevation" of quilts into art, and who is this elevation for?

Perhaps these white desires for Black women's creativity are about reparations and redemption. But who is being redeemed? The women's stories of spirituality and evangelism were not prioritized in collecting practices. The quilters and collectors did not have shared goals. The central desire in the relationship between the quilters and collectors belonged to the collectors. Leon left no room for other stories—the stories about Black women who would hide their quilts when they knew Leon was coming over, the Black women who would meet him on the porch so that he would not enter their house, stories that have circulated around the Bay Area quilting community. Leon is the hero of his stories.

Could it be that for these white collectors, Black women's quilts were *symbolic*, not personal? They considered the quilts as objects to be bought and possessed in ways other whites had once possessed Black people. The ownership of the objects gave the men status, it gave them collateral. It allowed them to make a name for themselves, and their insistence that the quilts were art and not craft gave them an entry point into the art world. The Black women and their quilts helped the men get over. What the men wanted and what the women wanted were unrelated. Black women who lived long enough to have their work recognized by an art world public have had the opportunity to secure economic support that demonstrated respect for their work. Selling a quilt to a collector, however, did not always come at a fair price, nor with any assurance that a collector would preserve the stories embodied in the quilt.

Now that thousands of quilts are in museum collections, we need to ask what museums can offer, what role they can play in this discourse of Blackness, creativity, and white possession. To the public, museums can offer education about

Black women's creativity, and move toward racial equity in their permanent collections. Museums can broaden the criteria that define who is validated as an artist and demonstrate a broader offering of aesthetics and cultural value. To the quiltmakers and their families, museums can potentially offer money and opportunities to share their stories. We think about the women from Gee's Bend singing a cappella songs at their openings and recording and releasing CDs. We can also imagine the influential workshops that can acknowledge and validate living Black quilters in communities served by the museums. The women whose quilts are part of permanent collections can be honored and paid for their role in connecting with the public in practical ways, such as speaking and teaching. In this way, their voices—from their mouths, not a spokesperson—can be acknowledged, heard, and seen.

I end with some thoughts about how this complicated, fraught relationship between Black artists and white collectors and museum curators might be addressed, and how contemporary artists have learned from Black women quiltmakers. I suggest that everyone consider the work of artist Sanford Biggers, whose incredible quilt exhibition, *Sanford Biggers: Codeswitch*, toured the country in 2021-22. For Biggers, quilts are valuable for their connection to the past and the future. He was particularly influenced to bring quilts into his art practice by *The Quilts of Gee's Bend*. By working through various media, including textiles, sculpture, performance, film, drawing, and painting, Biggers addresses diverse narratives of African American life. In his exhibition, Biggers presents his *Codex* series of antique American quilts modified through various techniques (fig. 51). It was inspired by the theory that quilts were used during the nineteenth century to mark safe houses along the Underground Railroad. The story proposes that quilts left hanging outside of a home were used as signposts for enslaved fugitives looking for a protected place to rest. Although there is no evidence for this theory, many historians agree that quilt-top patterns were used as mnemonic devices to help fugitives remember directions to free states and to encourage potential escapees to run away.

Intrigued by the stories of quilts and emancipation, Biggers's *Codex* series presents new visions of old designs in preparation for future moves toward Black freedom. The quilts are transformed by multidimensional surfaces, paint, and cuts. History, music, and movement are combined in his remixing of old and new. The results offer inventive strategies for imagining worlds of innovative change, migration, and design. Like Biggers, I'm interested in the *future* of quilts. It's a future inspired by the innovation within the past, and the ability of quilts to sustain Black life through everyday use and stunning creativity. If quilts were used as portals, safe-house markers, or mnemonic devices for Black liberation in the past, they can serve the same function in the future. Museums, as caretakers, or I hope, as caregivers for these objects, will play a role in assisting with Black liberation from possession.

Notes

1. Richard J. Powell, "Introduction: Faith Ringgold's French Connection," in Dan Cameron et al., *Dancing at the Louvre: Faith Ringgold's French Collection and Other Story Quilts* (New York: New Museum of Contemporary Arts; Berkeley, CA: University of California Press, 1998), 1-2.
2. Cheryl Finley, "Visual Legacies of Slavery and Emancipation," *Callaloo* 37, no. 4 (2014): 1031.
3. This phrase, taken from the essay by Fatimah Tobing Rony, "Those Who Squat and Those Who Sit: The Iconography of Race in the 1895 Films of Félix-Louis Renault," in *Camera Obscura* 28 (1992), is expanded upon in her book *The Third Eye: Race, Cinema, and Ethnographic Spectacle* (Durham: Duke University Press, 1996).
4. The exhibition was organized by the Museum of Fine Arts, Houston, and the Tinwood Alliance, Atlanta. It travelled to the Museum of Fine Arts, Houston (September 8-November 10, 2002); the Whitney Museum of American Art (November 21, 2002-March 9, 2003); the Mobile Museum of Art (June 14-August 31, 2003); the Milwaukee Art Museum (September 27, 2003-January 4, 2004); the Corcoran Gallery of Art (February 14-May 17, 2004); the Cleveland Museum of Art (June 27-September 12, 2004); the Chrysler Museum of Art, Norfolk, Virginia (October 15, 2004-January 2, 2005); the Memphis Brooks Museum of Art (February 13-May 8, 2005); the Museum of Fine Arts, Boston (June 1-August 21, 2005); the Julie Collins Smith Museum of Fine Art, Auburn, Alabama (September 11-November 4, 2005); the High Museum of Art, Atlanta (March 25-June 18, 2006); the de Young, Fine Arts Museums of San Francisco (July 15-December 31, 2006); and the Museum of Art, Fort Lauderdale (September 7, 2007-January 7, 2008).
5. Brook Barnes, "Art and Collecting: Museums Cozy Up to Quilts," *Wall Street Journal* (August 23, 2002): W12.
6. Eli Leon, "Reclaiming a Missing Link" (unpublished essay, March 20, 2005), Bequest of The Eli Leon Living Trust, BAMPFA, 1.
7. Leon, "Reclaiming a Missing Link," 3.
8. Leon, "Reclaiming a Missing Link," 3.
9. Leon, "Reclaiming a Missing Link," 4.
10. Leon, "Reclaiming a Missing Link," 2.
11. Greg Tate, "Introduction: Nigs R Us, or How Blackfolk Became Fetish Objects," in *Everything But the Burden: What White People Are Taking from Black Culture* (New York: Broadway, 2003), 9-10.
12. Eric Lott, *Love and Theft: Blackface Minstrelsy and the American Working Class* (Oxford: Oxford University Press, 2013).

Conversations

Adia Millett

> YES, quiltmakers are among the female warriors of yesterday, today, and tomorrow. To quote Laverne Brackens, "When sitting down to piece or quilt, one becomes focused and can meditate, visualize, think out, and solve all those problems the world keeps throwing at you, to keep you off balance. The quiltmaker is fighting a war to maintain her sanity. She is a warrioress. The process of quilt making helps her to win that war. . . . Nothing and Nobody can take away the peace and serenity."
>
> –Sherry Ann Byrd, 2023[1]

This beautiful quote came as an email response to an exhibition at the Institute of Contemporary Art in San José, in which quilts made by Sherry Ann Byrd and her mother, Laverne Brackens, were two of the four loaned to us from the University of California, Berkeley Art Museum and Pacific Film Archive. Then there was Phoebe (last name unknown), who created a quilt of denim pockets that inspired instant kinship (fig. 53). The collection of my partner's old jeans became the tool to respond with. And Flora Ates's quilt, with its bright colors and improv shapes, indicated a sense of liberation and play. Through their art, they spoke to me. I spoke back, and they responded. A conversation began that would expand way beyond the five of us, to so many people who made our works come together, but more importantly to the many viewers who began their own inquiries into an important dialogue.

I believe we are in conversation with everyone and everything. This collection of African American quilts contains thousands of voices, singing, laughing, crying, and speaking their stories. Our job is to listen and find ways to speak back.

I found my way to quilts through my grandmother. They were always around, but I didn't understand their value. What brought me to take a deeper look was my obsession with "craft." Back in the 90s and early 2000s, craft seemed like the underprivileged art form that would never truly be respected. In some weird way, I identified with it. I wanted to put anything crafty, that you could find in some middle-American home, on a pedestal. As a result, my early work consisted of miniature dollhouses, embroidery, ceramics, crochet, etc. But it wasn't until my grandfather died that I started to quilt. I asked my grandmother if we could make some small, quilted wall pieces out of his old clothes to give to his children. After that, I started spending time with a dear friend of mine, Roberta Andresen, who really taught me to quilt. I was hooked! I started seeing fabric as a tool to create a language. That language would open my eyes to seeing and hearing the languages of so many quiltmakers who made quilts to hold our spirits.

These intricate fabrics pieced together and then bound by endless hours of mending were not only relics for the future, but the function they provided left stories of warmth, protection, and strength. The stains, tears, and sun-drenched fades added more worth than preservation could ever provide. Lived experiences and endless wisdom are fused into these handmade gifts that often live longer than their makers.

What became true for me as I sat with the collection at BAMPFA was that preservation is so much more than putting these treasures on a wall or platform. The preservation of these works requires the recognition of the voices of the women who made them. If we forget the lives, the hands, the suffering, and the accomplishment of our grandmothers, mothers, aunties, and sisters, then the conversation ends. Who do we speak to, ourselves?

Opposite: Fig. 52. Adia Millett, *Quilted Water Warrior*, 2023. Cotton, rooster feathers, wool, cowrie shells, 74 × 52 in. (188 × 132.1 cm). Private collection

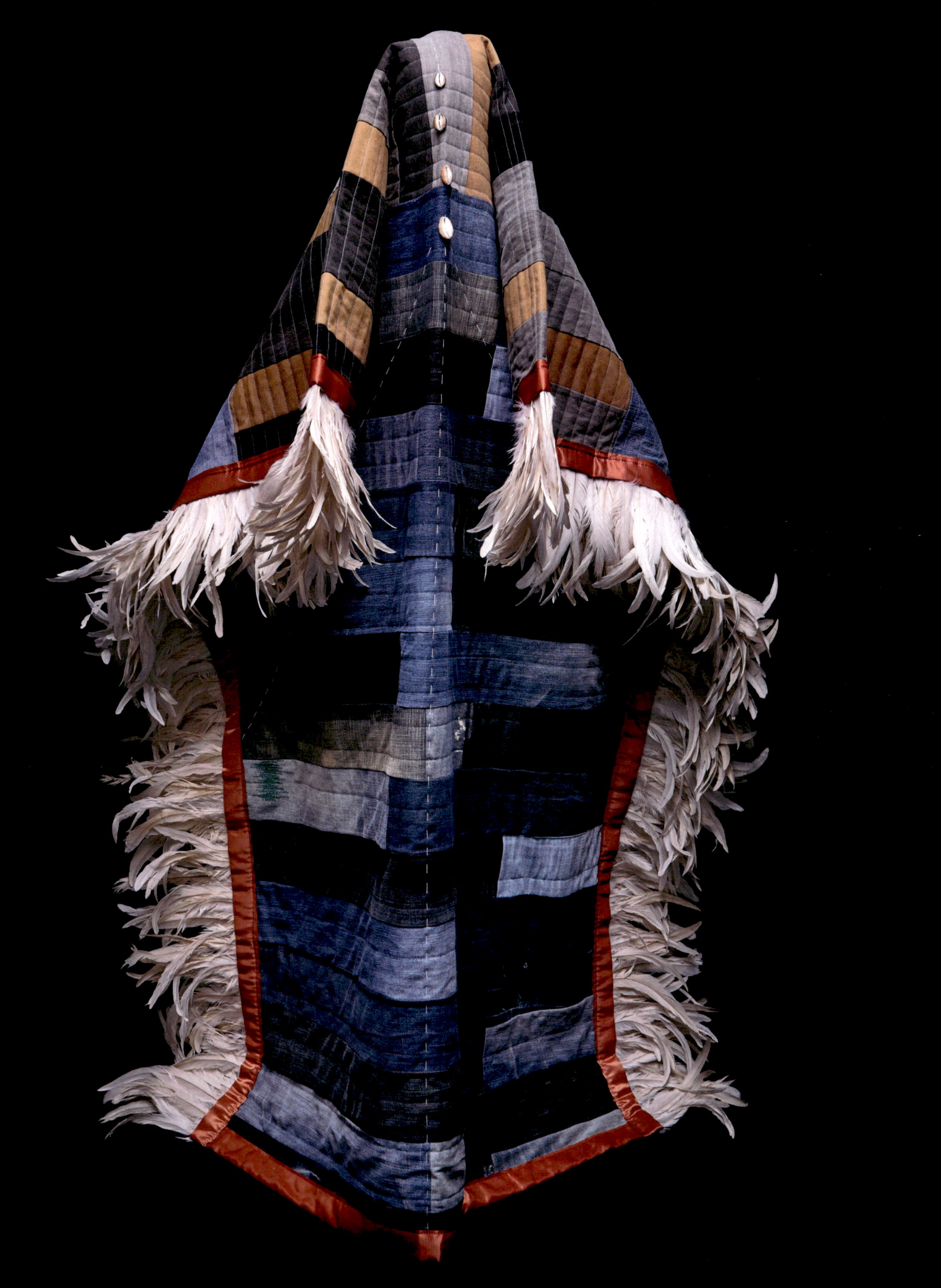

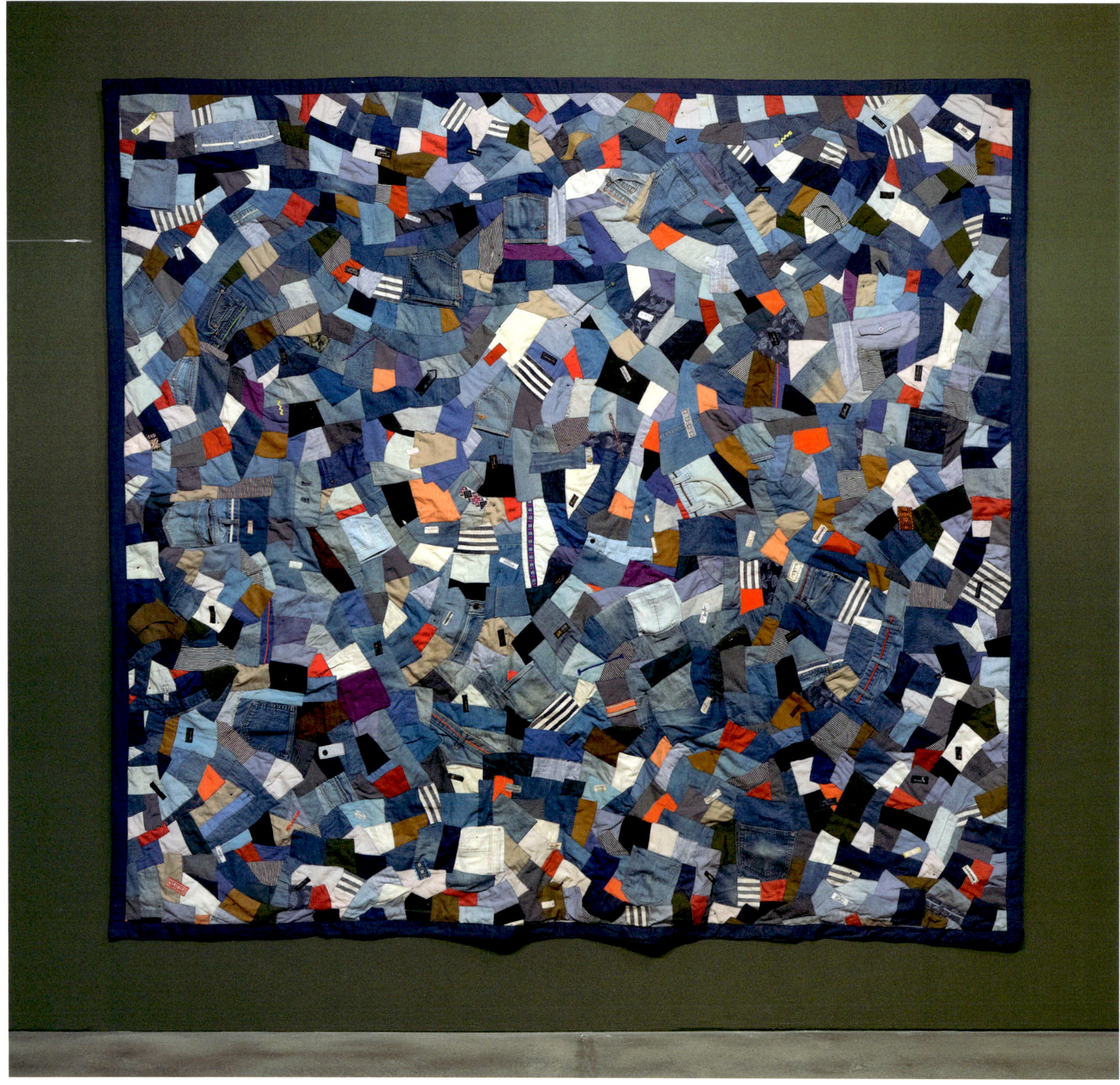

Fig. 53. Phoebe, Untitled (Denim Patchwork), 1960s–1980s. Cotton, 106 × 116 in. (269.2 × 294.6 cm). BAMPFA

Perhaps as artists, curators, collectors, and teachers we must passionately try to unpack the language these objects provide, the language that expands beyond words into the vast realm of creative choices. Quilters so gracefully share something deeply personal in their work. You can see their style, their morals, their mental health, their compromise, their playfulness, and their conviction. Furthermore, they do something our world needs desperately—they see outside of themselves, into their community.

Seeing Rosie Lee Tompkins's quilts and then being introduced to the other quilters' works that are part of the quilt collection forced me to wake up. They gave me the courage to trust myself and stop underestimating my value, and theirs. This is what powerful art can accomplish, but we must do a better job at engaging with respect and curiosity, not just with the art but with the makers, artists, and frankly, every human being we have the privilege to cross paths with.

Thank you, Elaine, for doing exactly that.

Notes

1. Sherry Ann Byrd, email message to Elaine Yau, September 14, 2023.

Grandma's Hand

Basil Kincaid

I feel myself walking, I notice the depth of my breath. The sky is gray but smells orange like fall. With each step I feel waves of energy cascading over me. Walking in the direction of the swelling force, the air thickens. As my left foot lands on cobbled stone, stepping off of moist grass and wildflowers delicately bound into supple living soil, I see how each wave of energy also carries what is now a faint gold luminescence. As my right foot meets the new terrain, I see that I'm holding the hand of a little brown-skinned child with long glistening hair in thick two-strand twists. They are brown but glow with a similar gold as the billows of luminous energy passing over us. Now I feel the rushes of light beating through my heart. Welling in my chest and behind my eyes is the sensation of a rising tide. As we get nearer to the source, I see an old Black woman standing on the stoop of a two-story row house. We continue our approach. It is clear now that this woman is the source of this immense energy that pulled us inward like warmth beckoning us from a frigid chill. As we draw closer, the waves of syrupy golden light become so powerful that it's taking all of my strength and focus to complete each step. A wave of energy hits me like a wall of water and now I see that the woman is my grandmother, my dad's mom. She's beautiful, standing strong like a volcano. With each of her breaths a ripple of flaxen aura pours up and out of the top of her head, a calm geyser, blanketing the landscape in her divinity. Even though her vitality is so powerful that I can barely breathe, I step forth. The child whose face I never saw and whose presence I often omit from the retelling for brevity is unfazed by the sheer auric force. At this point I'm in the street, at the mouth of the front yard. My eyes are transfixed on my grandmother. She can tell the energy is overwhelming me. She comforts me by saying, "It's ok . . . come on . . . I have something for you." I take this next step and see that the whole house that she is standing in front of is wrapped in a glorious quilt. My grandmother is also draped in and adorned with a quilt, sparkling like phosphorescence in the midnight sea. Within that final step my path was sealed in crystalline clarity. I was overpowered and overawed by the weight and intensity of her presence, flung abruptly into waking life.

I called my mom. As she picked up the phone, I exclaimed, "I got it!"

Prior to that dream, I had never done any sewing. But after, I felt compelled to learn sewing and quiltmaking. I felt and continue to feel compelled to create the vision of this house wrapped in quilt.

It was 2016 and I'd just returned from Ghana, where I completed a nine-month residency with Arts Connect International. During this time, I observed firsthand how connected people were to familial traditions. It inspired me to revisit my familial practices, and in this reconnection with family I was flooded with memories of my grandmother quilting.

Before I embarked on my quiltmaking journey, my art making was a technical and intellectual pursuit, influenced primarily by the Western canon of European art history, which perpetuates a notion of solitary genius. Traditionally, Black quiltmaking was done in the community; an artist might make the patchwork for the quilt top, but the actual quilting was very often done collectively. This collective practice is healing and allows for notions of collective care to enter the work. When I immersed myself in the practice of quilting, I immediately noticed how I don't feel alone. I feel my grandmother's spirit and I feel tapped into this deep, infinite well of source energy.

My grandmother's name was Eugenia ("Beanie") Townsend Kincaid. All through my life I'd been surrounded by and comforted by her quilts. I had memories of her hand- and machine-quilting, materializing patterned and

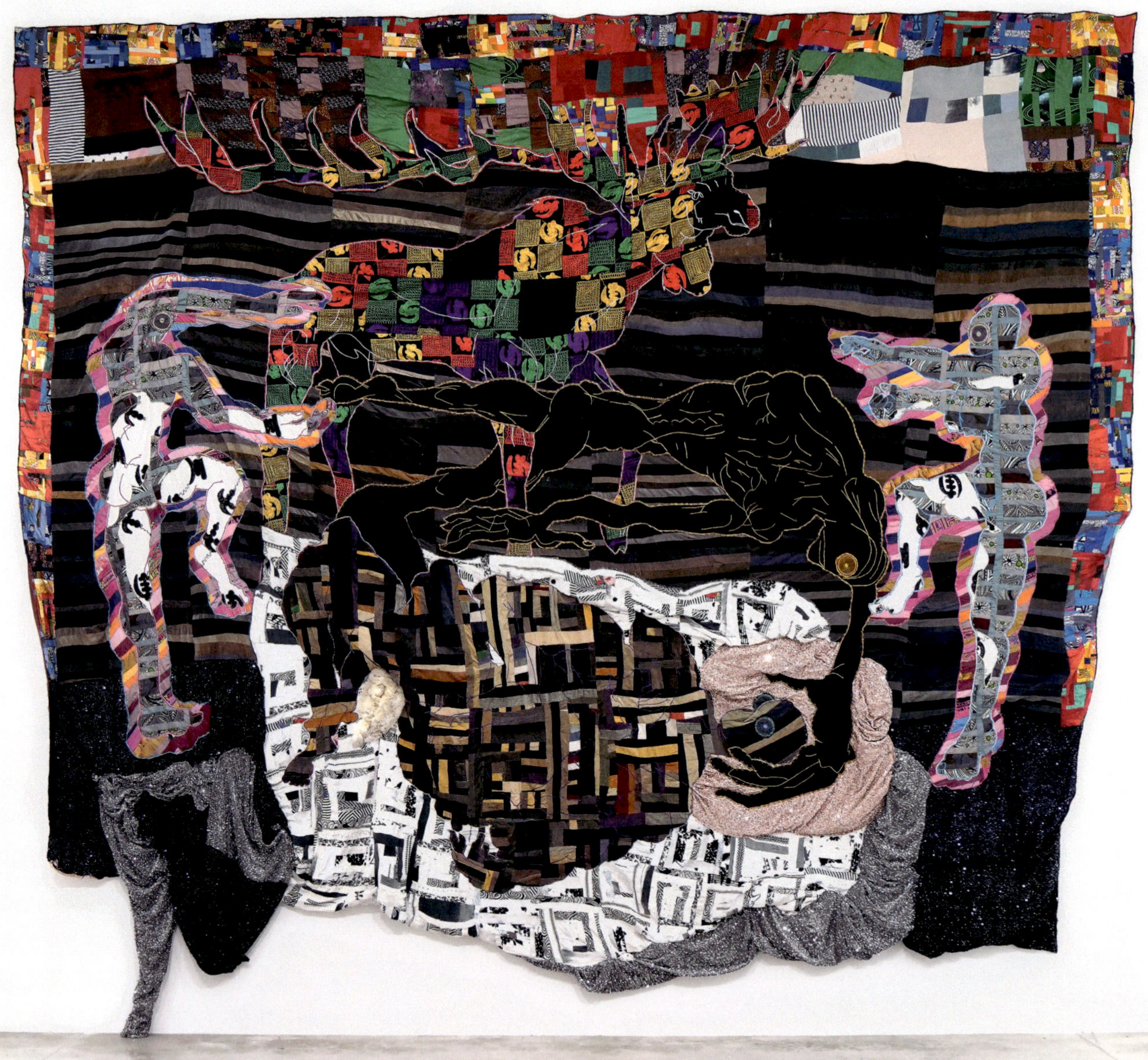

Fig. 54. Basil Kincaid, *The Fields We Lay and Turn with Horns*, 2023. Corduroy, kente, Ghanaian wax block fabric, cotton, wool, fur, polyester, sequins, embroidery floss, selected materials from previous performance works, curtains, on wall, 180 × 240 × 6 in. (457.2 × 609.6 × 15.2 cm). Rubell Museum, Miami

improvisationally pieced quilts. She even made figurative quilts, depicting dolls and other small and large figures—which I started to do in 2020.

Growing up, I spent summers with her in Arkansas, where my parents are from. I witnessed her love and generosity in the baskets of fresh fruits and vegetables she picked for us and the community. I remember her feeding the homeless, the mentally ill, anyone in need who ventured to knock on the farmhouse door, or call for her from the fence row. I witnessed her creativity and I witnessed her passion.

Her emphasis on nurturing empowers me in using my own style to expand my familial tradition, and evokes a great sense of purpose within me and a profound meaning within the work. My quilts sing and signal the depth of the medium, bringing glory and honor to the women in my family who carried the torch of the art but were not regarded as the magnificent multidimensional artists that they are and were. I love the description of the proliferation of Black American quiltmaking as rhizomatic because it is accurate in the sense that our practice is linked to the wealth of our spiritual life and alignment with source. At the beginning of my quilting practice eight years ago, I was studying the work of Dr. Joy Degruy and Paulo Freire and engaged in deep critical conversations with my brother, Matthew Kincaid, about a praxis of culturally relevant pedagogy. Within the study of these three scholars, I began to understand with greater intellectual clarity the layered nature of liberation within carrying forward the tradition of quiltmaking and

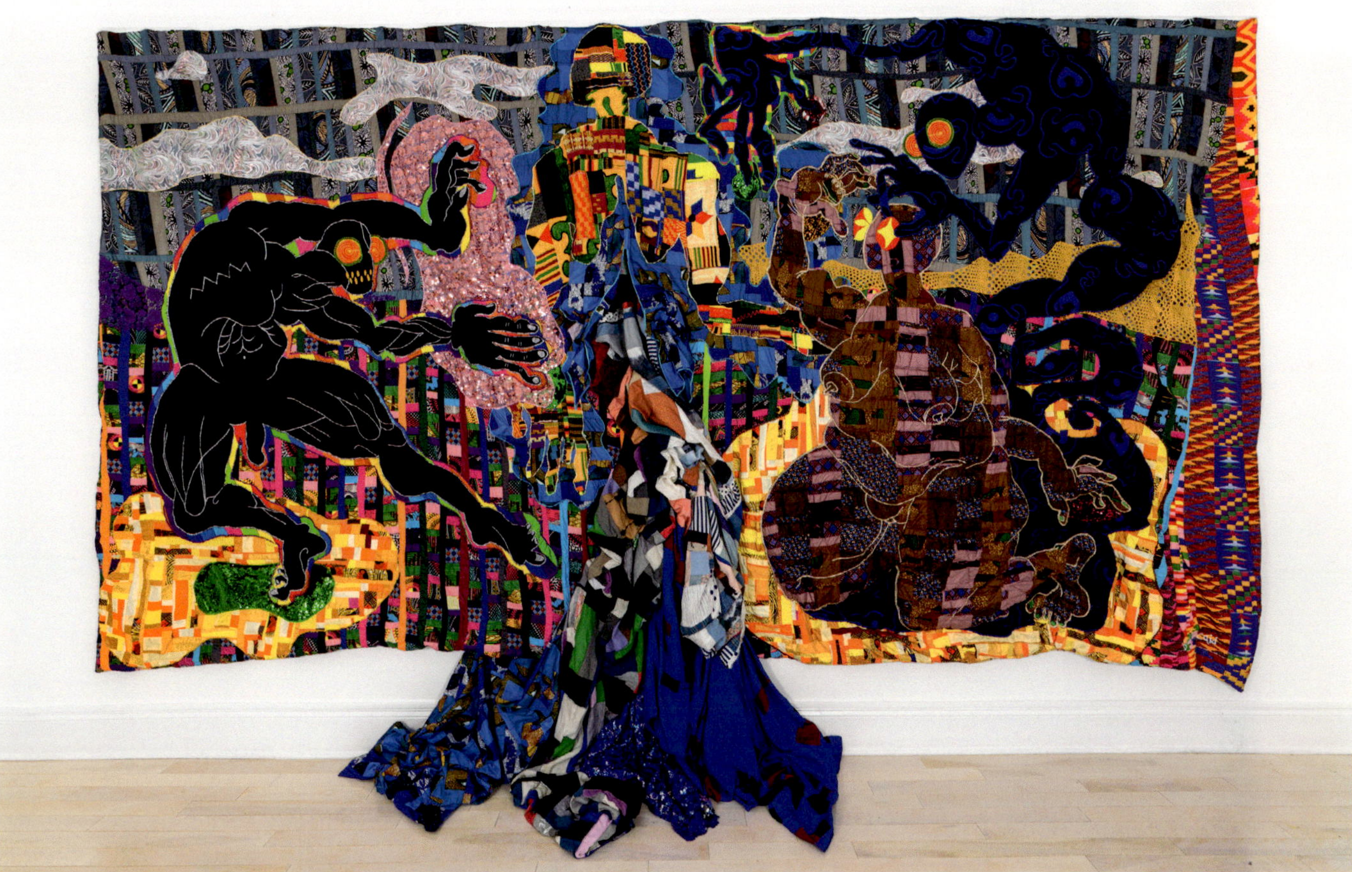

Fig. 55. Basil Kincaid, *The River*, 2017-2022. Quilt, 104 × 204 × 12 in. (264.2 × 518.2 × 30.5 cm). The Albertina, Vienna, Austria, OBJ40

quilt stewardship. Referring again to the Western canon—when I had the call to quilt, that pull shifted my focus away from this singular, unidimensional cultural image of the artist. Centering my practice within my family tradition, I felt empowered to honor my drive, purpose, roots, and instincts. The quilt became a necessary bridge between my purpose and liberation, and a mirror reflecting my innermost truth.

Quilting opened my eyes inward, and it got me to revisit and reevaluate my understanding of and relationship with painting and sculpture—beyond what academia has been able to capture and categorize—all the while providing an acute vehicle and stimulus for my performance work. Painting, while its definitions and concerns have expanded over the years, is still largely concerned with the principles of light, color, balance, rhythm, texture, composition, and opacity. Sculpture is centrally concerned with volume, space and negative space, shape, and at times shares overlapping concerns with painting. I feel strongly that quiltmaking within the Black tradition has always satisfied all of these formal concerns. However, quilting makes room for great(er) materiality in the sense that each material has had a lived experience and embedded memory: memorial content. The medium defies the constraints of categorization.

I believe this memorial content fuels intuition and improvisational quiltmaking. The practice of quilting and recognizing intuition as an elevated intelligence has catalyzed robust personal development in my life. I developed interest in using my contemporary artwork to highlight these areas of impact. In much the same way that quilts had been used historically to embody and transmit coded messages, I use the quilt through symbolism and allegory to retell familial and personal experiences, leaving breadcrumbs along my path of personal liberation for anyone who engages with my work.

I'm proud to say Quilting is my Inheritance—and within my Black experience, it's a spiritual gift. Quilts' contribution to contemporary art is vast and offers a deluge of previously missed opportunities within our art historical and cultural landscape. *Routed West: 20th Century African American Quilts in California* speaks to that, highlighting works from undersung artists who likely weren't known as such during their lifetimes. The impact of quilting on contemporary consciousness and on the contemporary art world must not be underestimated and will surely continue to expand beyond my most vivid dreams . . .

Quilts in Life

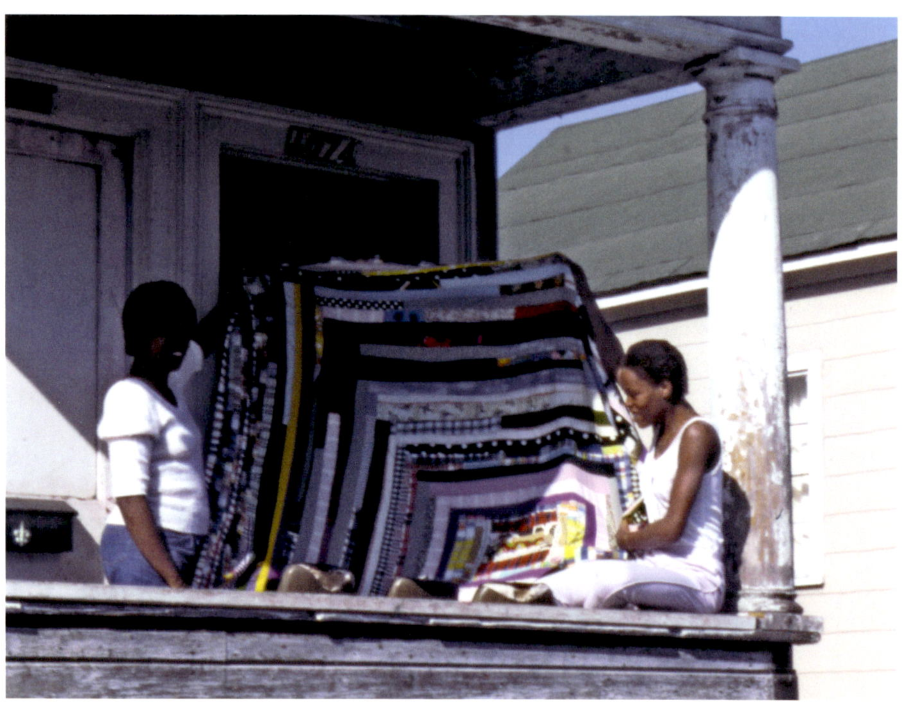

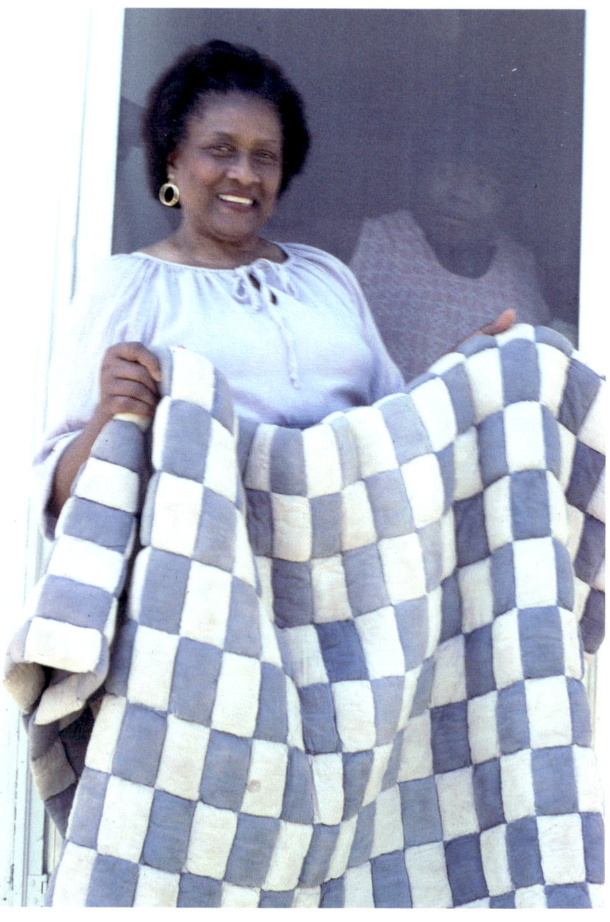

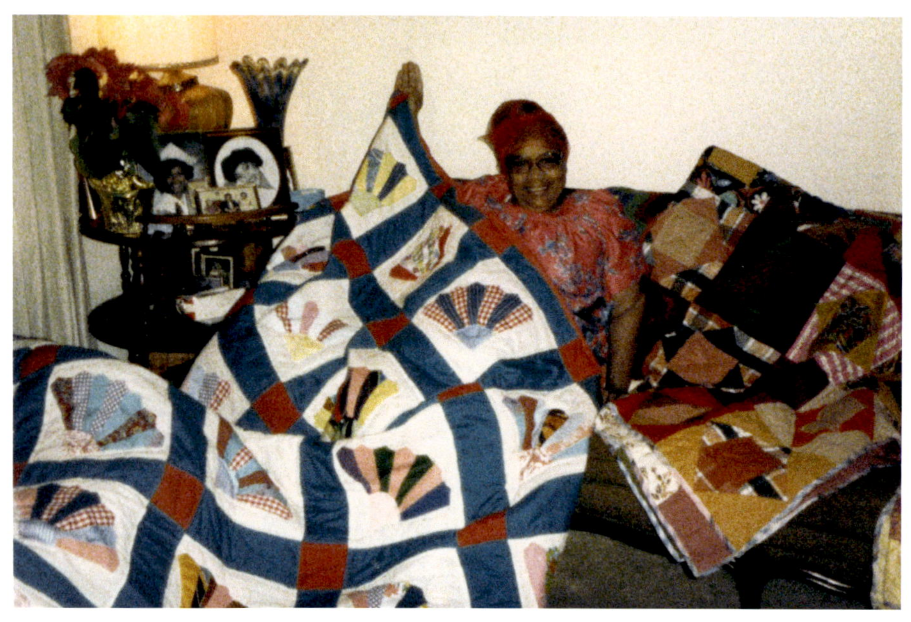

↖ Angelia Tobias and sister on their porch, Oakland, California, 1985

↑ Estella Brown with her Aunt Anne Crawford's quilt (cat. 13), 1981

← Mable Battle, 1985

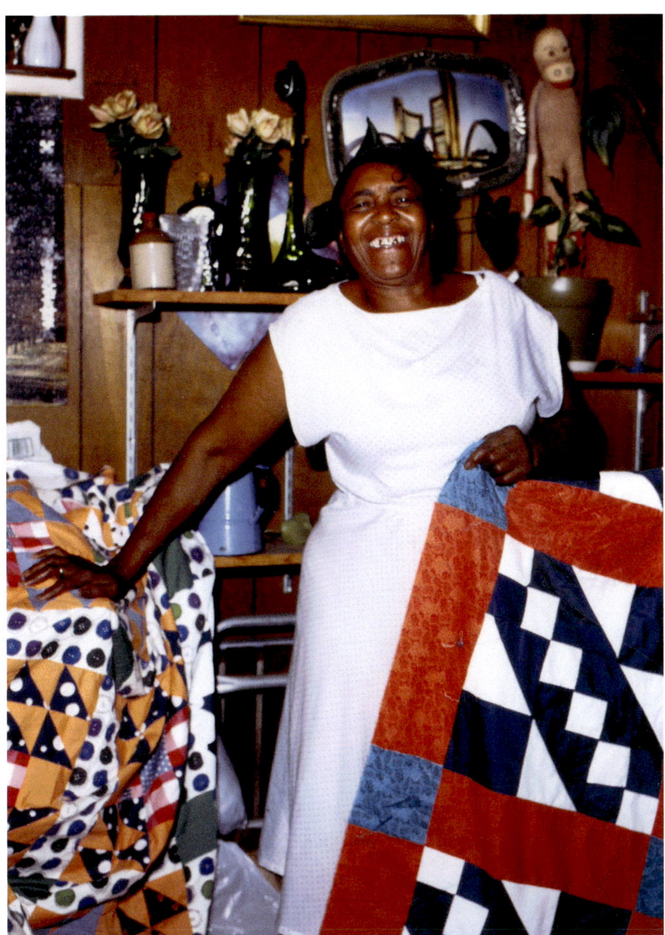

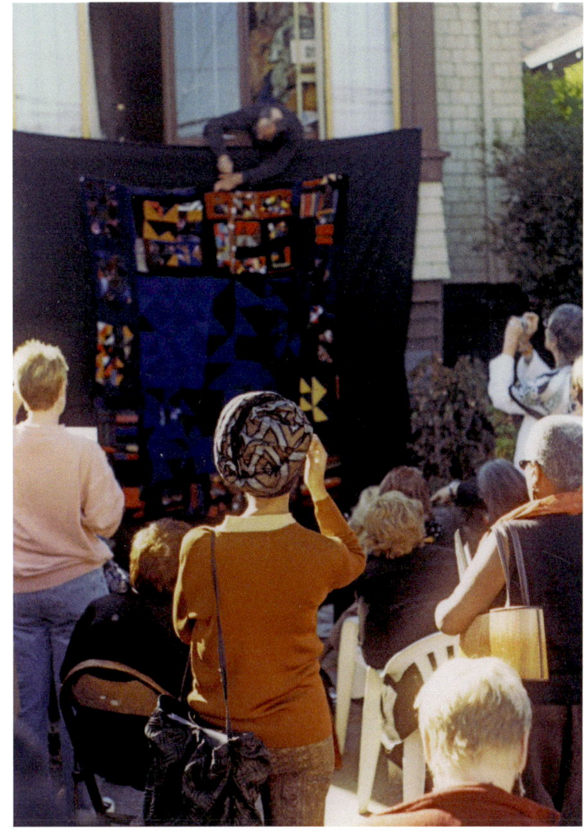

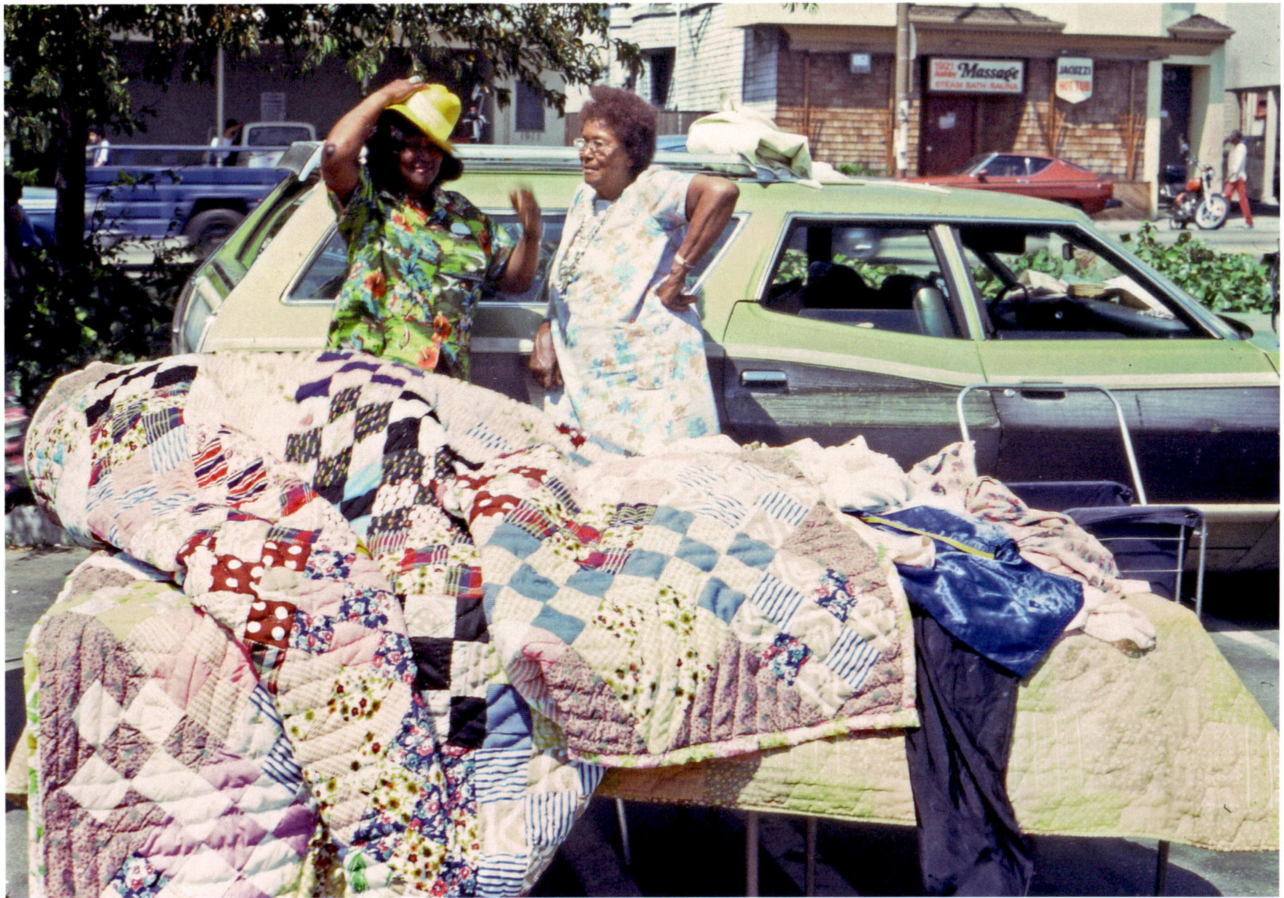

↑ Arbie Major, n.d.

↗ Yard show at Eli Leon's home, Oakland, early 1990s

→ Georgia Watkins and daughter at Berkeley Flea Market, 1981

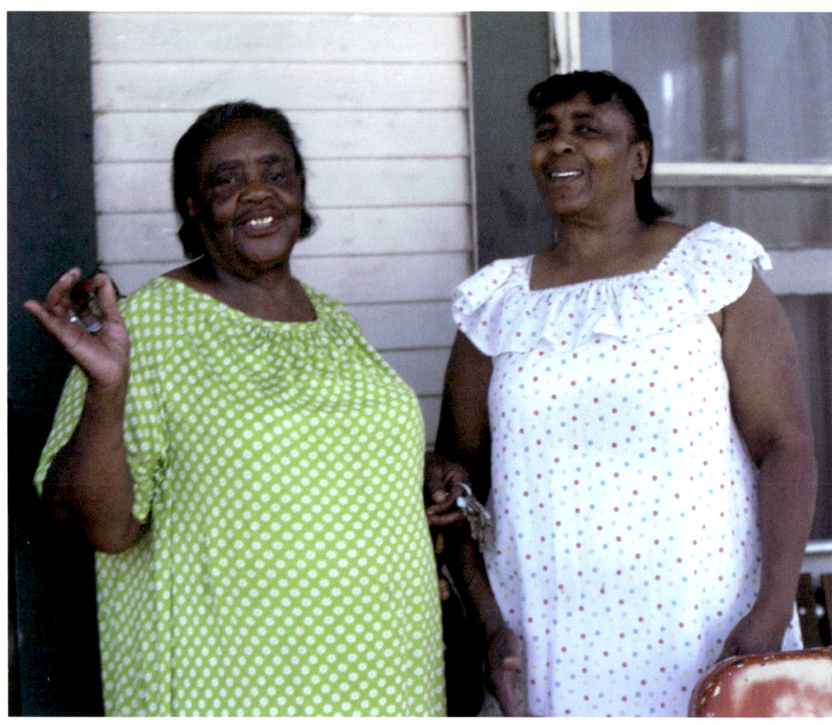

← Beauty Vaughns and Arbie Major, Fresno, California, 1984

↓ Beauty Vaughns's house, Fresno, California, 1984

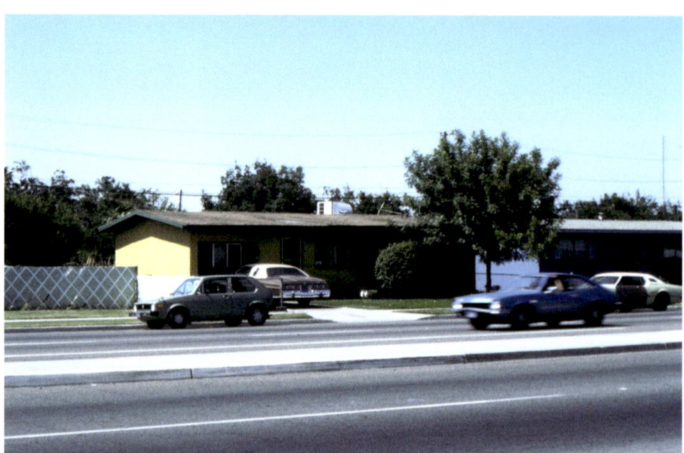

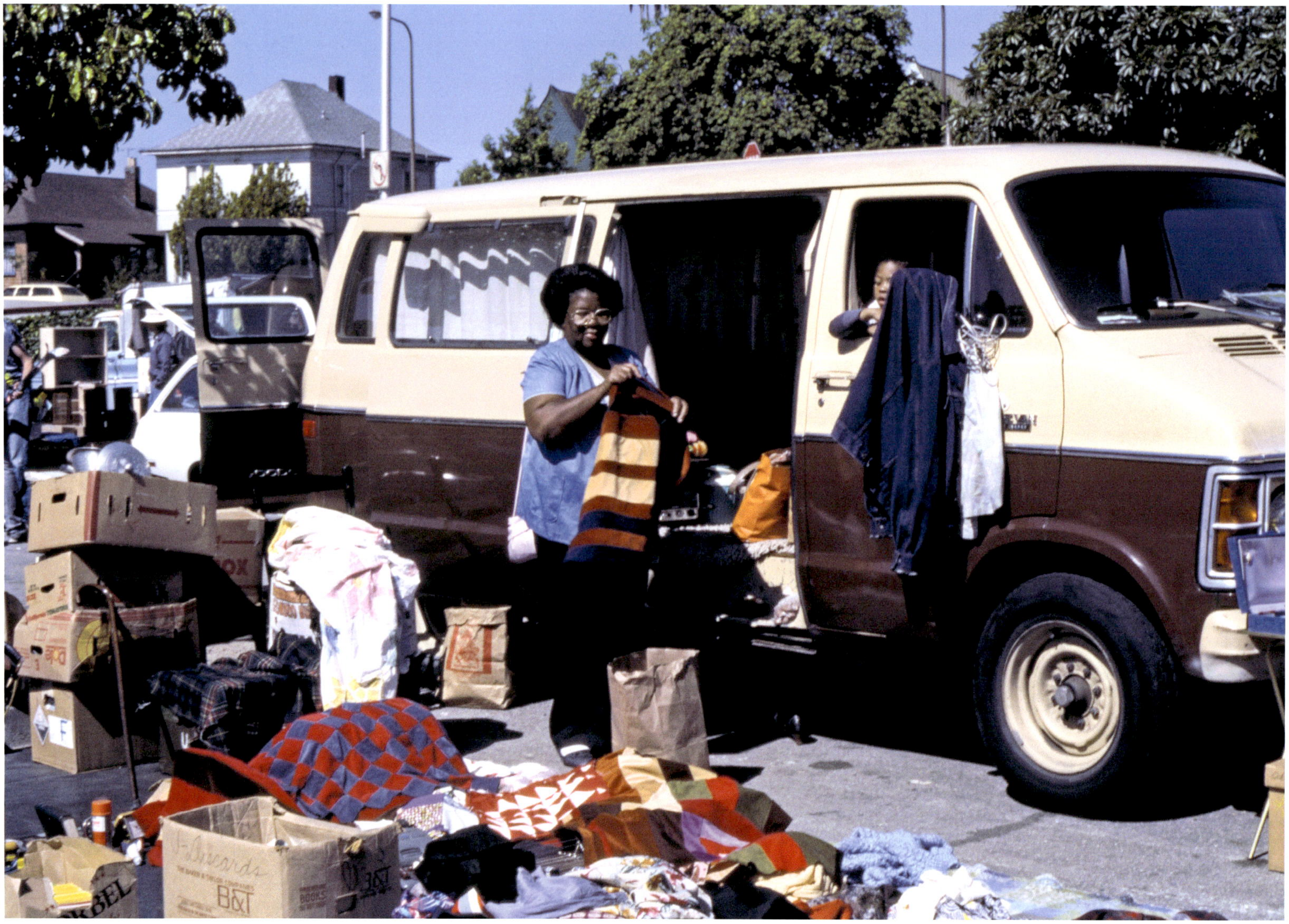

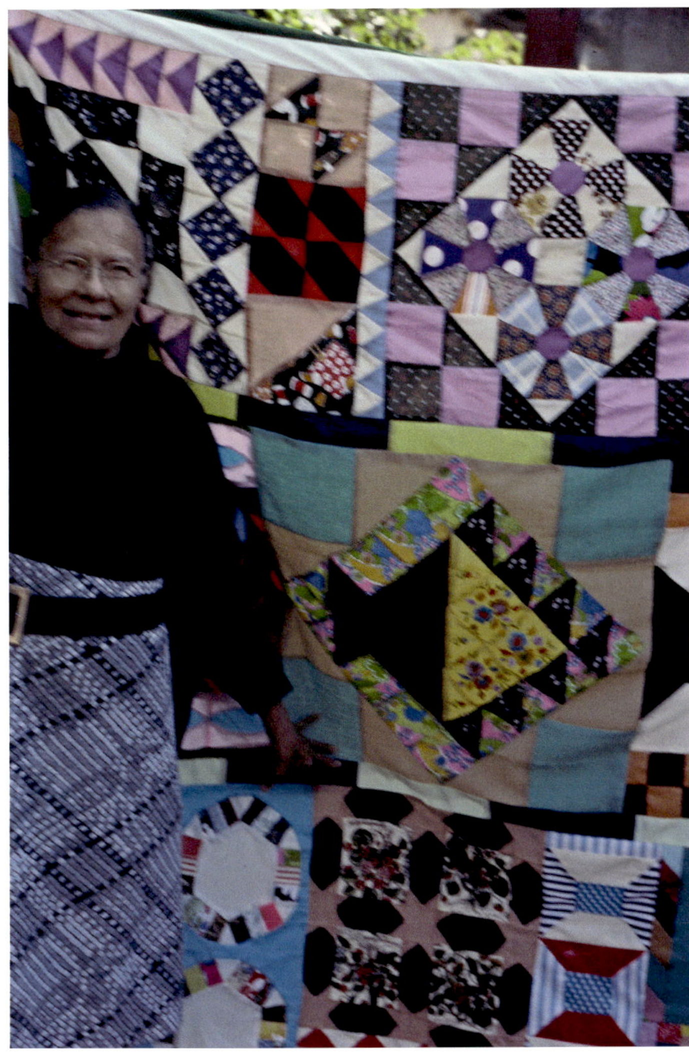

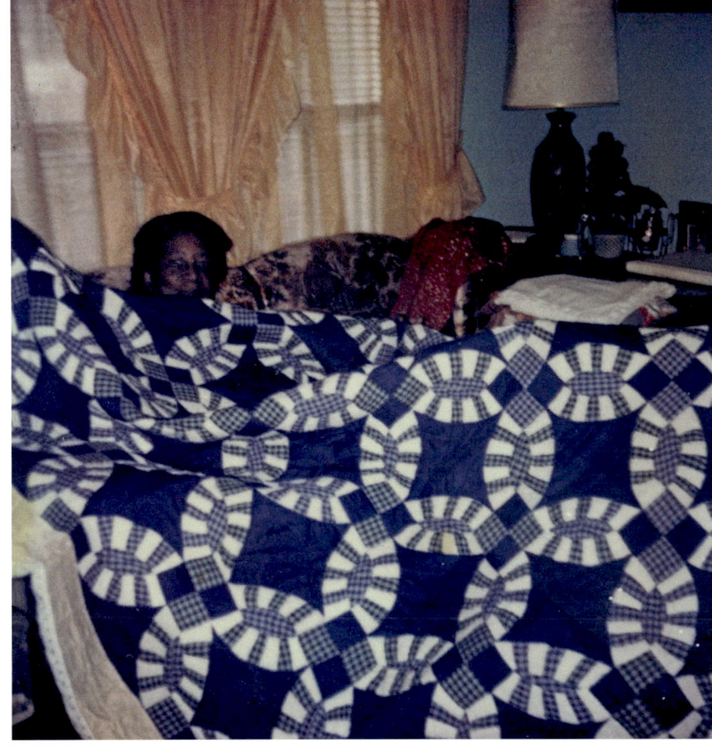

↑ Johnnie Wade standing with one of her quilts, 1987

↗ Laura Thompson, n.d.

→ Bessie Moore, Oakland, 1981

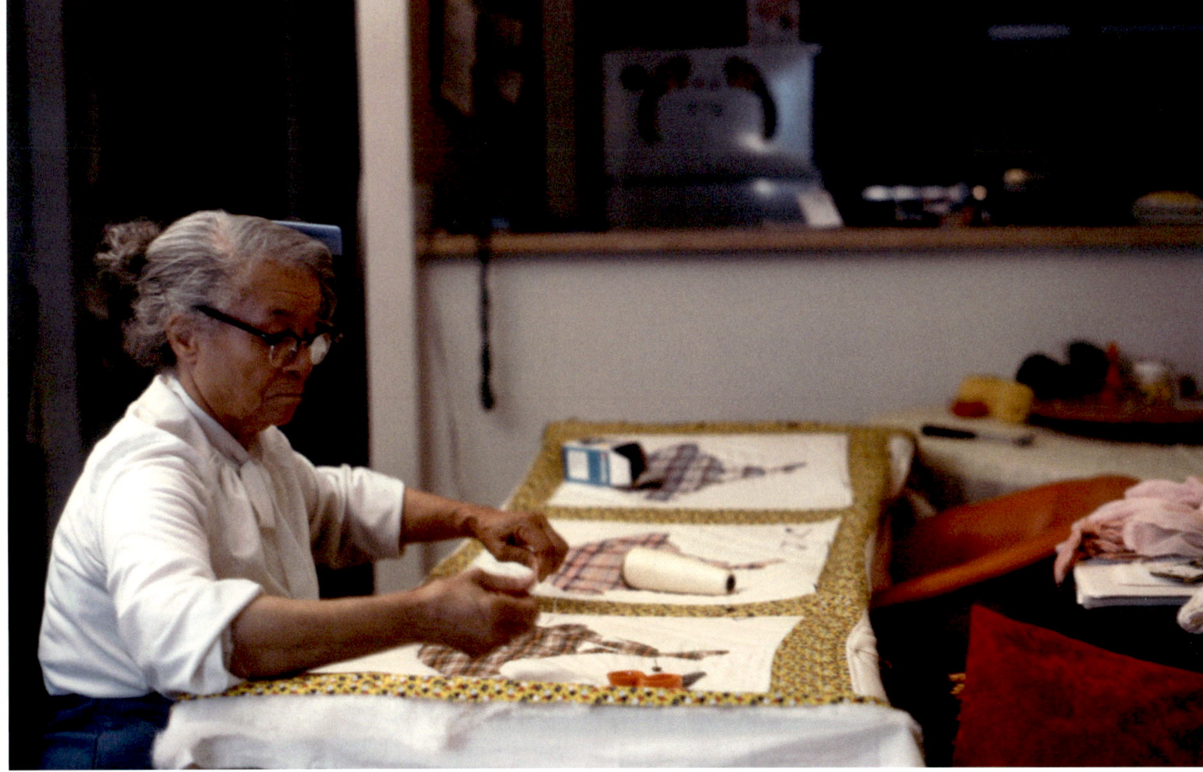

← Lee Wanda Jones at Berkeley Flea Market, 1988

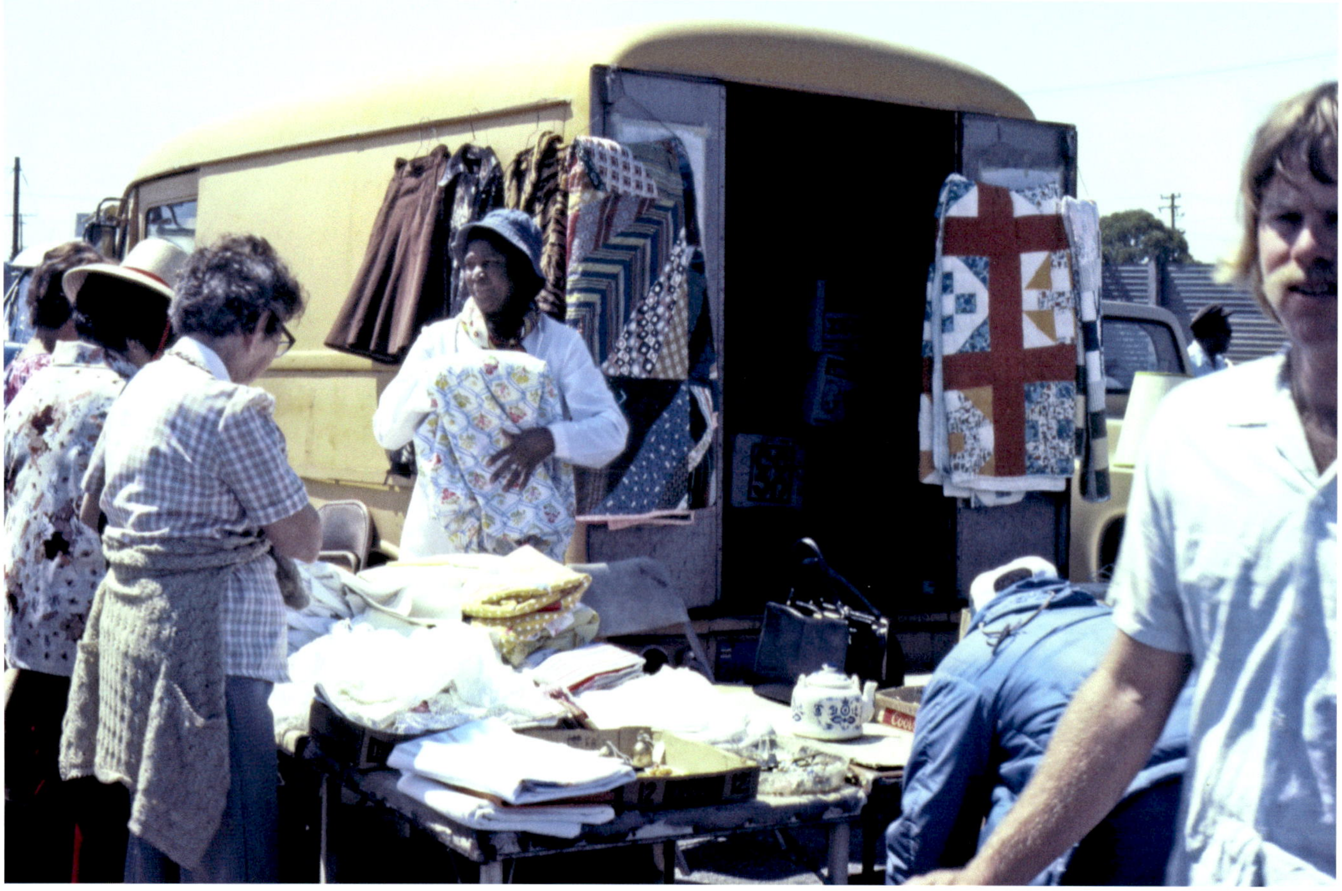

← Clara Decker at the Alameda Flea Market, early 1980s

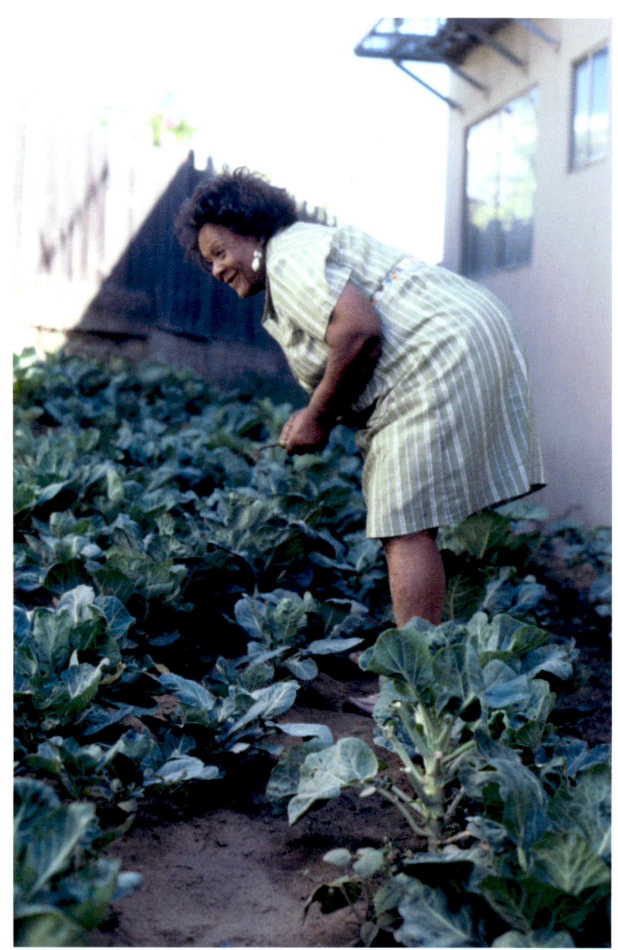

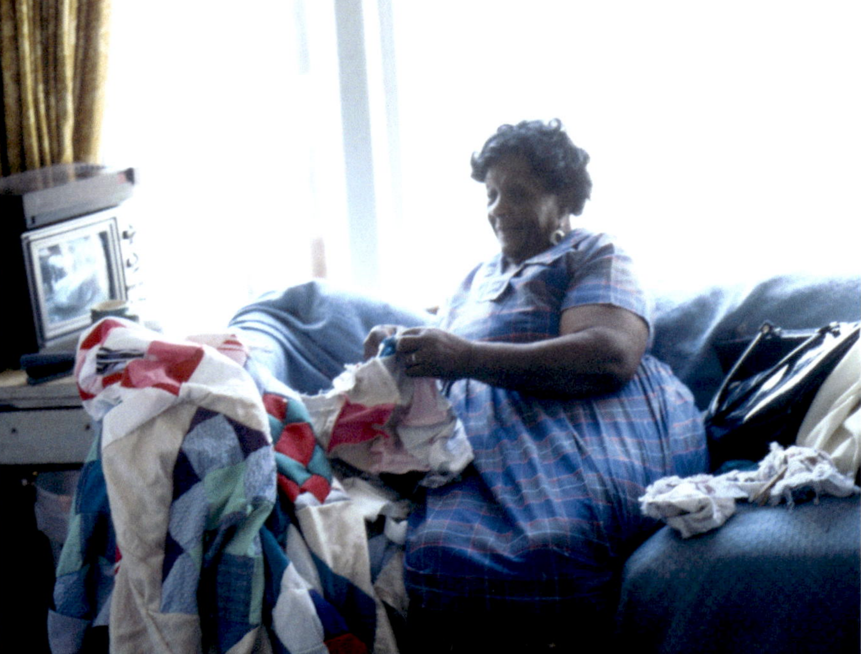

← Mattie Pickett in her garden, San Francisco, California, 1986

↑ Mattie Pickett quilting at her apartment, San Francisco, California, 1988

→ Isiadore Whitehead with a quilt she made for humanitarian relief, Oakland, California, 1984

↓ Willia Ette Graham with her quilt (cat. 26), San Francisco Craft and Folk Art Museum, 1987

↘ Quilt used as door hanging in Elzorah Abram's home, Oakwood, Texas, 1992

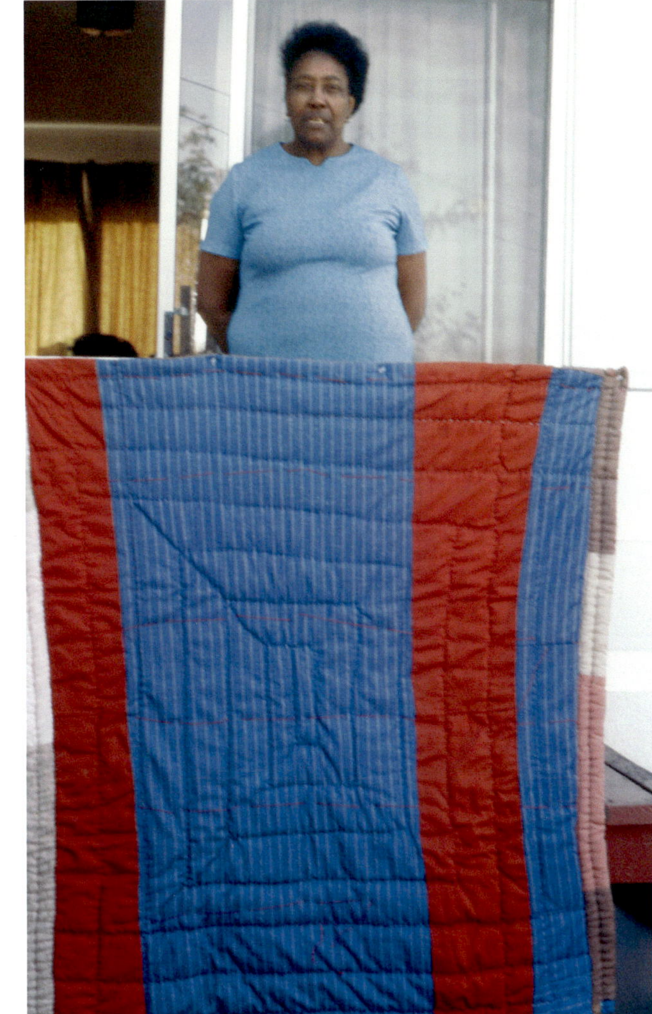

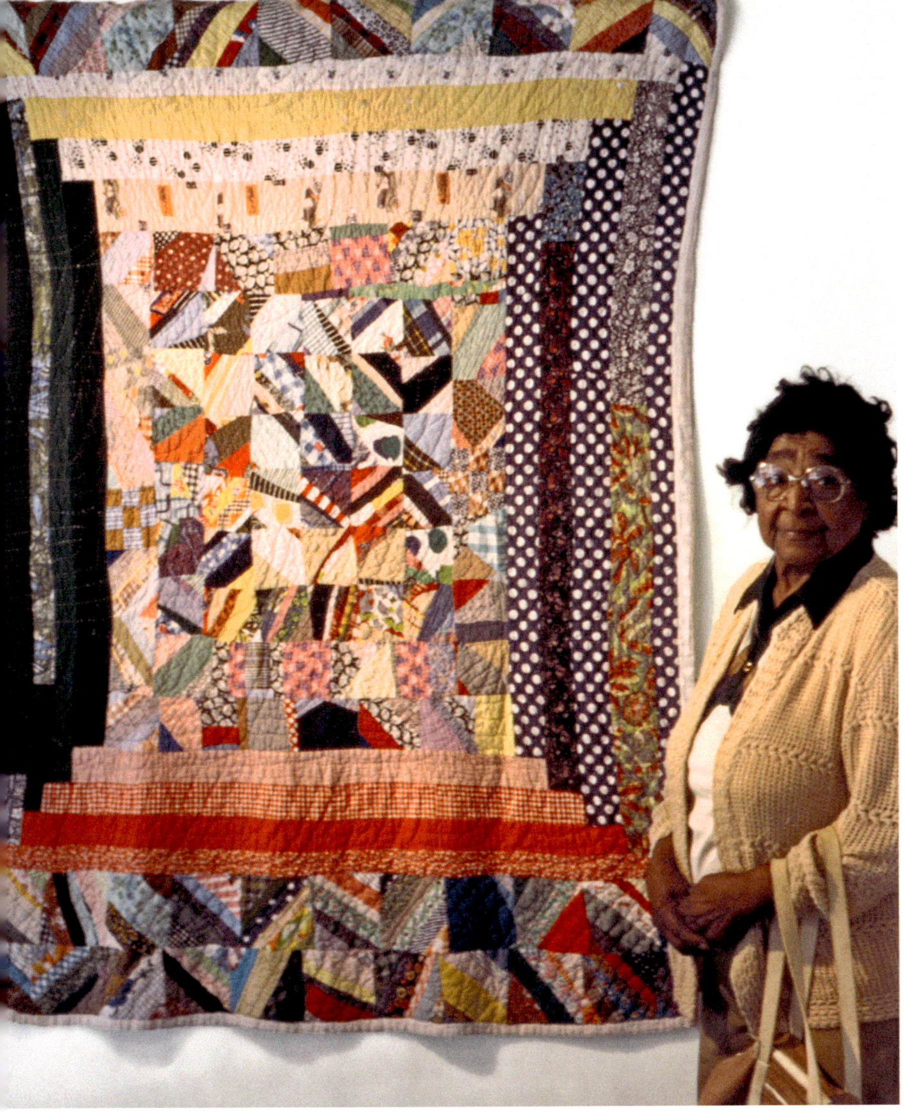

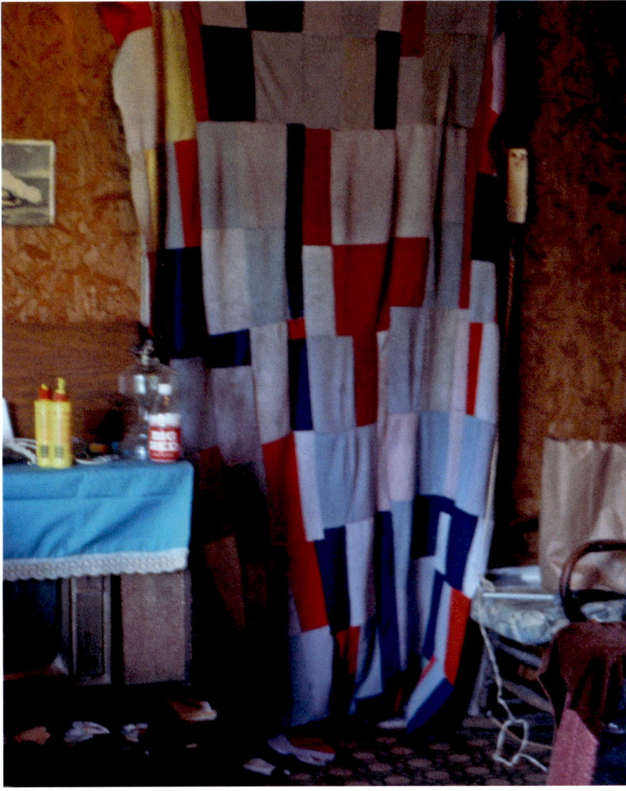

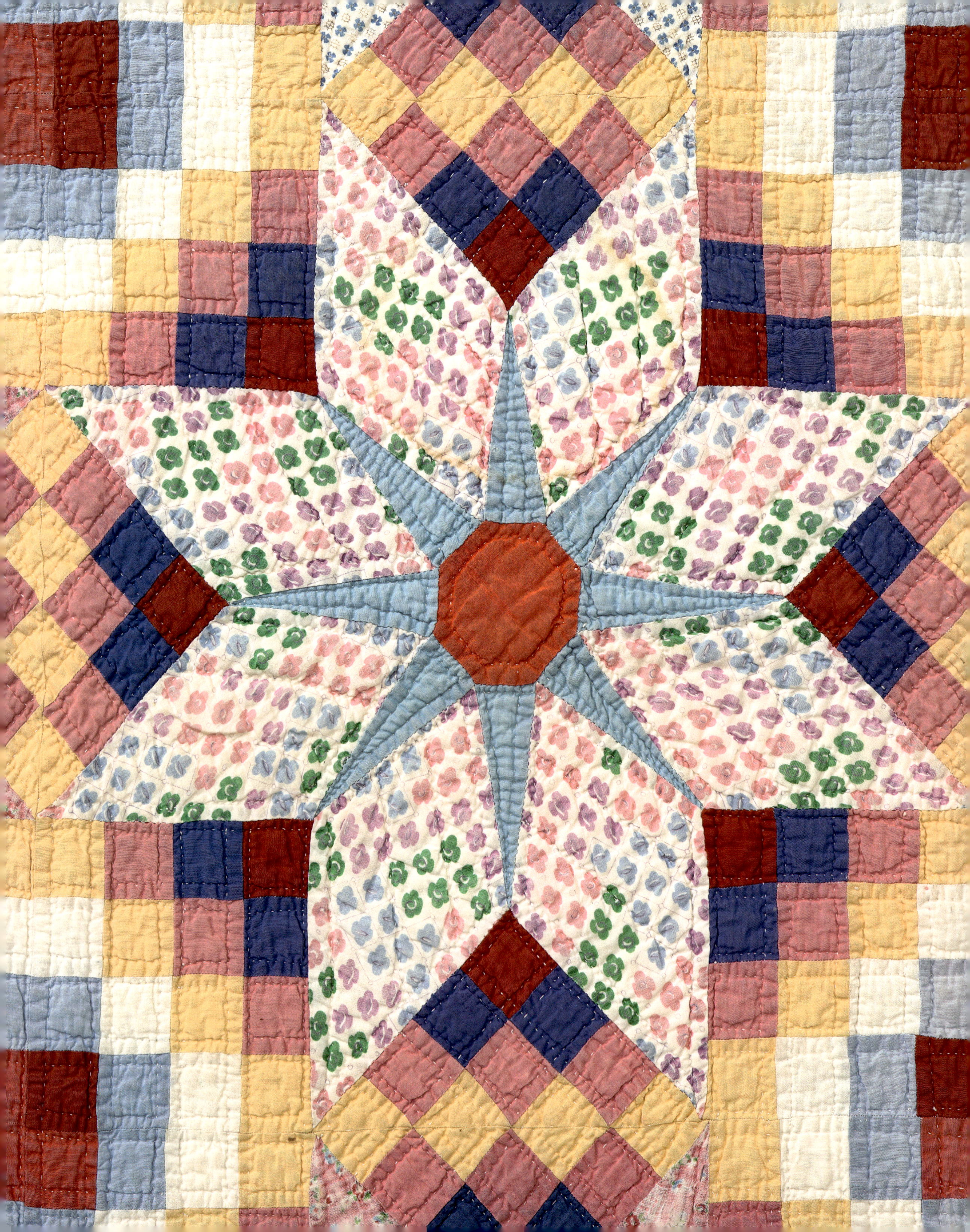

Quiltmaker Biographies

The following biographies are presented alphabetically, with kin grouped together in order of age from the eldest to the youngest, when applicable. Information has been gathered from public records, Eli Leon's archives, and, whenever possible, descendant families. As part of the ongoing work of recognizing individuals who are often unaccounted for in the historical record, these quiltmaker biographies, along with the quilts that have survived their makers, are offered here in the spirit of bell hooks's call to "state their particulars, to gather and remember." They seek to honor the interrelatedness of Black women's labor with the creative work of quiltmaking.

Elaine Y. Yau (EY)
Matthew Villar Miranda (MVM)

RACHEL HENRIETTA ADKINS

b. 1896, Marshall, Texas
d. 1976, Houston, Texas

A lifetime resident of Texas, Rachel Adkins was raised on the family farm in the Red Oak community outside of Marshall, Harrison County. She was an elementary school teacher and mother of ten children, of whom eight survived, including two sets of twins. As a quiltmaker, she preferred to reuse fabrics and waste as little as possible when creating quilts for her family. Adkins worked on a quilt frame that was suspended from the ceiling and could be hoisted up when needed. Zephyr Pruitt (1926–1993), her daughter, moved to California in 1958 and preserved several of her mother's quilts. EY

MARGARET GILLAM

b. 1922, Texas
d. 2002, Berkeley, California

Margaret Gillam's father and Rachel Adkins's mother were first cousins. As early as 1950, Gillam and her husband, Taft, lived at 832 Delaware Street, Berkeley, in a predominantly working-class neighborhood west of San Pablo Avenue. She was a domestic servant in a private home and Taft was a carpenter. Gillam first met Adkins's daughter Zephyr Pruitt in California, although their extended families both hailed from East Texas. EY

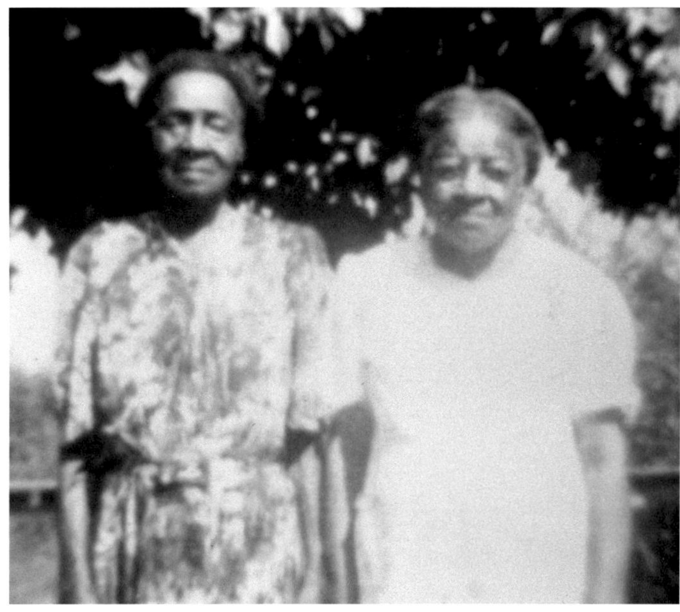

Lucinda Ballenger (left), with her daughter Mattie Ballenger Trimble, n.d.

LUCINDA BALLENGER

b. 1850s, Tennessee
d. 1919, Rusk County, Texas

Lucinda Ballenger (sometimes also appearing as "Ballinger") was born in Tennessee under slavery and sold from her mother. Her granddaughter Willia Ette Graham recalled that she lived in Henderson, Texas, with her three sisters, Charlotte, Adeline, and Ann. By 1880 she and her husband, William Ballenger, lived in Rusk County with twelve children, three of whom preceded her in death. Her daughter Louise Hicks was also a quiltmaker. MVM

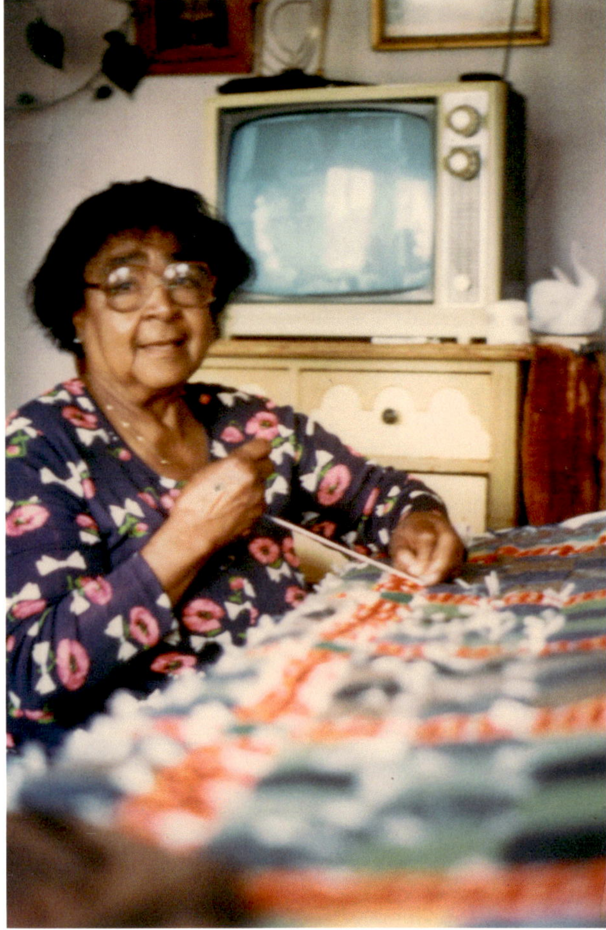

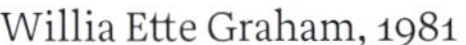

Willia Ette Graham, 1981

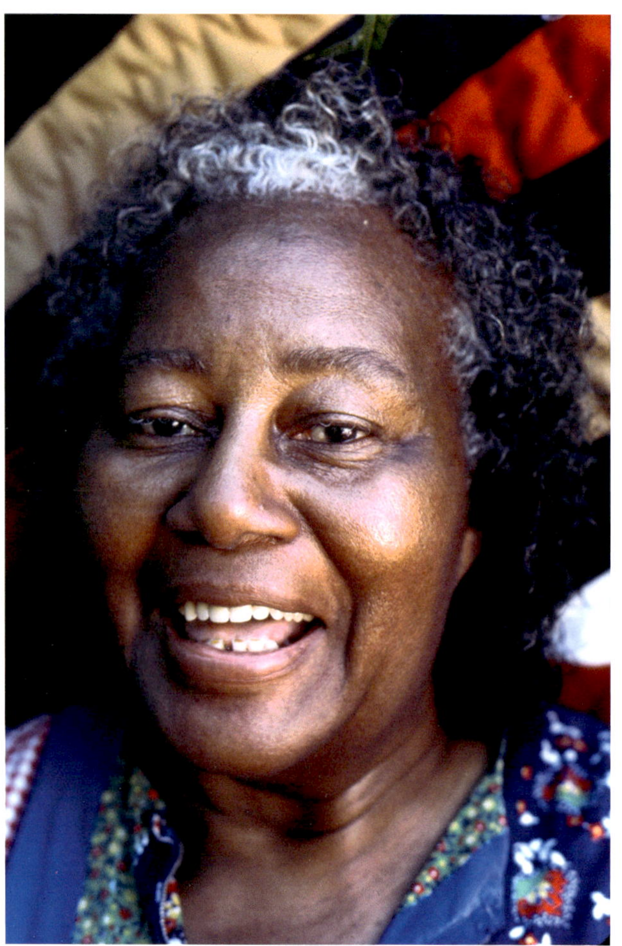

Irene Bankhead, 1987

LOUISE HICKS

b. 1872, Texas
d. 1957, Henderson, Texas

The daughter of William and Lucinda Ballenger, Louise Hicks was the eldest of twelve siblings and lived in the city of Henderson. She was married to Robert T. Hicks, with whom she raised several children, stepchildren, nieces, and nephews. She is laid to rest in New Prospect Cemetery in Rusk County, Texas. MVM, EY

WILLIA ETTE GRAHAM

b. 1903, Minden, Texas
d. 1997, Oakland, California

Continuing a rich lineage of quiltmakers in her family, Willia Ette Graham helped her mother, Louise Hicks, piece quilts from the age of around seven or eight until thirteen. Taking to sewing, she aspired to be a seamstress. Upon completing school in 1922, she taught school and worked as a domestic and beautician. She married in 1927 and raised three children from this union; after her husband's passing, she remarried in 1942. In search of better economic opportunities, she left Henderson, Texas, for Oakland in 1944 and joined the housekeeping department at the University of California, Berkeley, until her retirement in 1971. Through her association with Eli Leon, she was one of six women in the textile arts honored by the Women's Foundation in San Francisco. She was also featured in several network television programs, including one on ABC in 1988 and KGO TV's "A Stitch in Time" in 1991. Graham was affectionately known as "Dee Dee" by her family. MVM, EY

IRENE BANKHEAD

b. 1925, Prentiss, Mississippi
d. 2023, Oakland, California

Irene Bankhead recalled watching her mother, Evangeline Ball, make Nine Patch and star quilts while she was growing up, using remnants ordered from stores like Sears and Montgomery Ward, as well as scraps from the clothes she made for Irene and her four sisters. Bankhead began sewing and piecing when she was thirteen years old and participated in quiltmaking activities with her family and neighbors in Lake Providence, Louisiana. She completed her first quilt in 1942 and made covers for her children while working in a laundry in St. Louis. However, she did not quilt more frequently until arriving in Oakland in 1968, where she worked in a cannery.

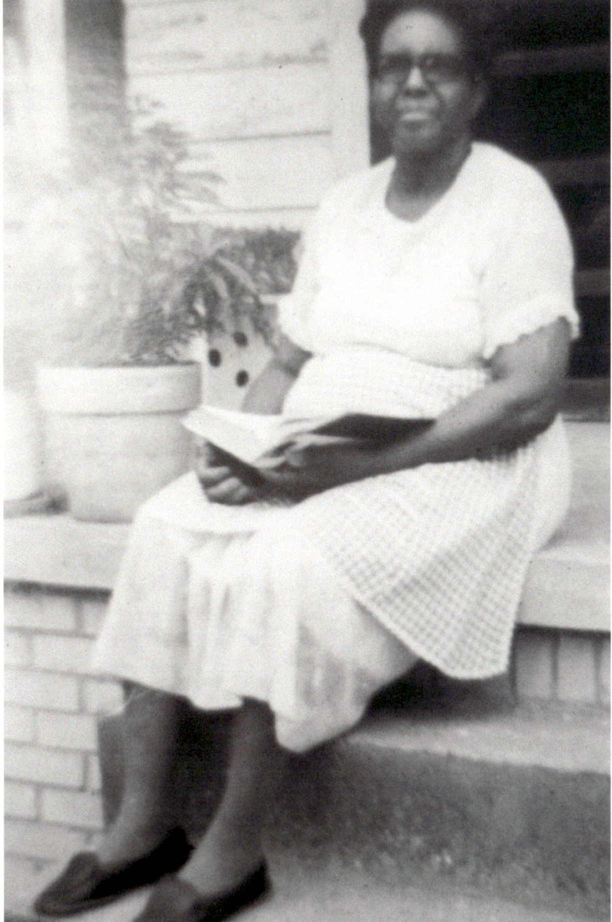

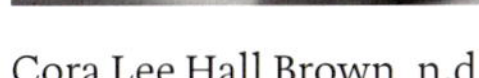

Cora Lee Hall Brown, n.d.

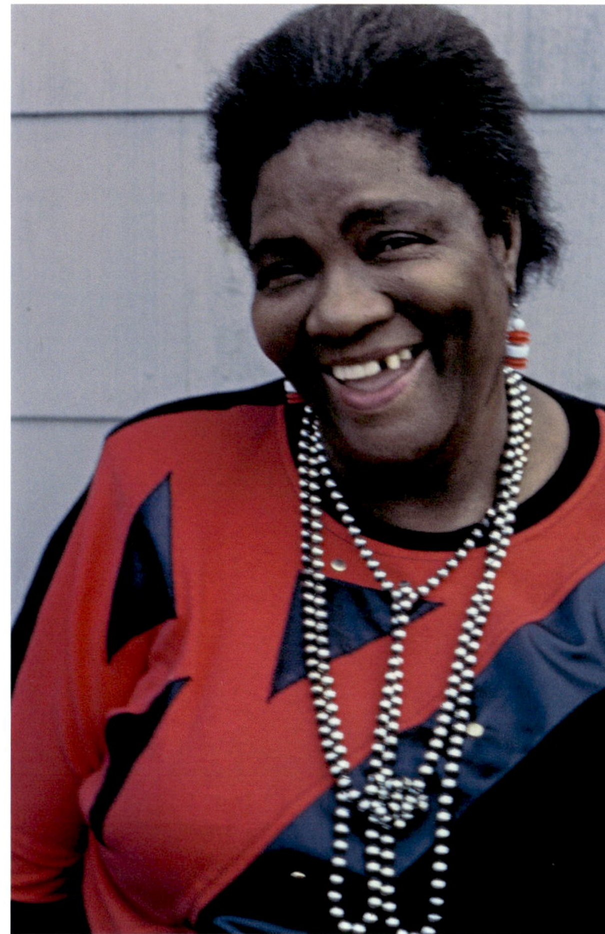

Gerstine Scott, 1988

She developed a personal approach to piecing, stating, "I just follow a pattern in my mind; then I work from that. . . . It's not that I try to make it to please somebody else. I just think, if this is something that I would use, then I know somebody else would use it."[2] In addition to making quilts for herself and to order–something she could pursue only after her children were grown–Bankhead quilted and finished hundreds of quilt tops for Eli Leon over the course of two decades. **EY**

CORA LEE HALL BROWN

b. 1900, Mount Enterprise, Texas
d. 1981, Mount Enterprise, Texas

The first child of Laura and David Hall, Cora Lee Hall Brown was affectionately known as "Sister" by her family. She was educated in Rusk County public schools. By the 1940s, she and her family lived in Shelby County, where she worked as a home economics instructor in Stockman and imparted life skills to women in her community. Mrs. Brown was also an expert seamstress and prolific quilter who learned to make quilts from her mother around the age of twelve. In the year leading up to her 1924 wedding, she intensified her quiltmaking, following the social expectations for a "homemaker." Several of these quilts were patterned and drafted after quilts Mrs. Brown had been gifted by her grandmother, Delia McLemore.

Relatives fondly remember Mrs. Brown's warmth and generosity, especially during their church's annual homecoming event in August: "We [would stay] up half the night talking, laughing, cooking, assisting her with her Sunday attire, and garnering her wisdom. Before journeying to church on Sunday morning, we would have had cooking lessons and the art of packing dinner in an extra-large cardboard box for a whole church family."[1] **EY with Alpheus Moss**

GERSTINE SCOTT

b. 1934, Henderson, Texas
d. 2001, Oakland, California

Gerstine Scott was born the youngest of twelve children and made her first quilt at the age of twelve. Her mother, Gertrude Lewis Ross, and grandmother Emma Shiner were her first teachers. By 1958, when she married Thomas J. Scott, she was living in West Oakland and working as a cook at the UC Berkeley Faculty Club. She spent her leisure time crocheting and making quilts, frequently enlisting her son to thread five

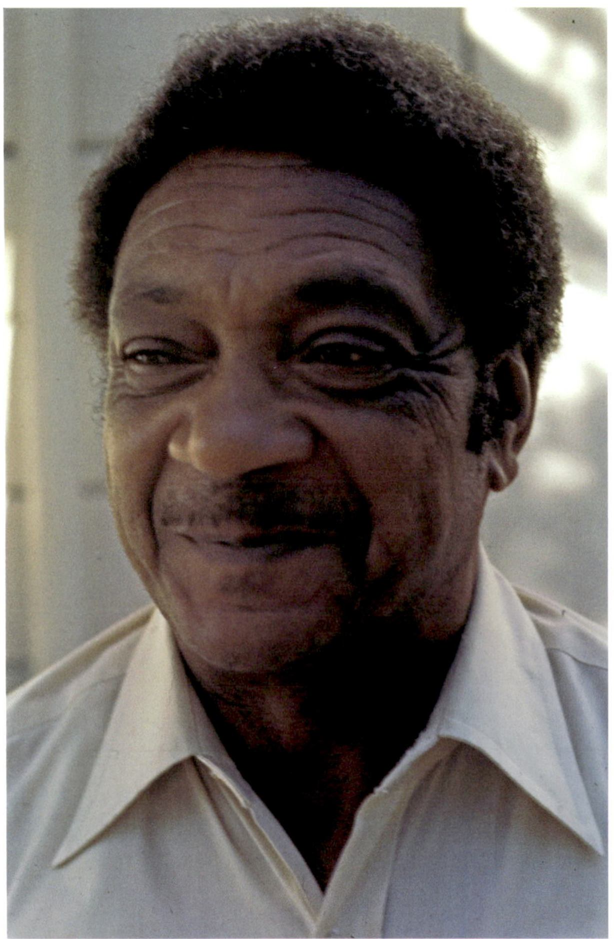

Charles Cater, 1985

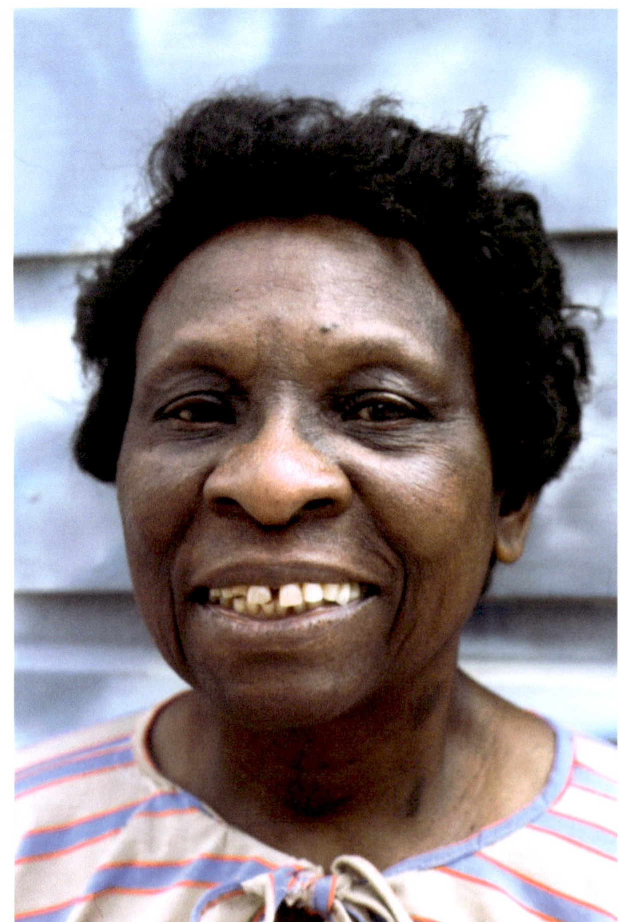

Willie Mae Chatman, 1991

needles at a time on Friday nights. When interviewed by Eli Leon, Scott expressed interest in teaching others to quilt and passing along the cherished values of handwork that she inherited from her foremothers, including her aunt Cora Lee Hall Brown. **EY with Douglas M. Hall**

MONIN BROWN

b. 1850, Virginia or Georgia
d. 1930, Macon, Georgia

HATTIE "STRAWBERRY" MITCHELL

b. 1854, Georgia
d. 1942, Macon, Georgia

Monin Brown and Hattie "Strawberry" Mitchell were sisters who were born into slavery and begin to appear consistently together in federal census records starting in 1900. By this time, they were living together at 6 Orchard Avenue in a segregated section of Macon, Georgia, known as Pleasant Hill, in a home purchased for them by William M. Johnston, their white employer. Before residing at Orchard Avenue, Brown was a live-in caregiver ("mammy") for Johnston's daughter Viola, and Mitchell cleaned their laundry at the Johnstons' antebellum home. Brown never married. Following Brown's death in 1930, Mitchell, who was widowed and whose son preceded her in death, lived with her niece Isabella Jones. While little is known about how they acquired their skills as quiltmakers and needlewomen, they were likely taught by older women relatives. **EY**

CHARLES H. CATER

b. 1928, Bibb County, Georgia
d. 1996, Oakland, California

Charles Home Cater was one of six children born to Patsy Moore and Willie Johnson. Taught by his grandmother, Annie Moore, he learned to sew by age five and made his first quilt at eight years of age. Cater moved to California in the early 1940s. He and his wife Barbara Ann created quilts together and sold them at their shop, "Cater's Nook," located at 3644 Grove Street, Oakland. His quilts were featured in KGO's network program, "A Stitch in Time" (1991), and were included in *Man Made: African-American Men and Quilting Traditions,* an exhibition curated by Gladys-Marie Fry at the Smithsonian

Institution's Anacostia Community Museum in 1998. He passed away in 1996 and is buried in San Joaquin Valley National Cemetery. MVM

WILLIE MAE CHATMAN

b. 1912, Homer, Louisiana
d. 2010, Virginia Beach, Virginia

Raised in Homer, Louisiana, Willie Mae Chatman learned to quilt from her mother, Mary Lewis, before she reached ten years of age. In 1945 Chatman moved to Richmond, California, with her husband, Latimore Chatman, and together they raised five children. In 1955 the couple moved to Berkeley. Chatman worked a variety of jobs at rest homes, school cafeterias, and Cal-Packard Canning, to which she dedicated thirty years of service. Among her many roles, she was a beloved, active member of McGee Avenue Baptist Church in Berkeley. MVM

LILY M. CHILES

b. 1918, Smetana, Texas
d. 2000, Oakland, California

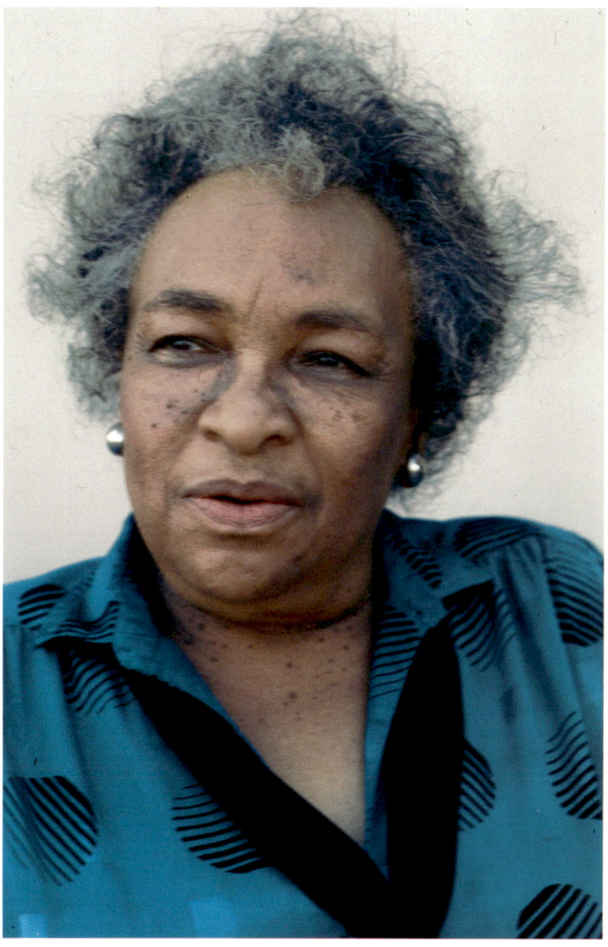

Lily Chiles, 1988

Lily Mae Chiles was born in the small rural town of Smetana in Brazos County, Texas, and spent her youth in Houston. She later moved to Galveston, where she married. During her time in Galveston, she owned a corner store and also worked as a beautician. In 1964 she moved to Oakland, where she served meals at local schools and convalescent homes. Following a car accident in 1972 that forced her into early retirement, she turned to quilting for peace of mind, building friendships, and the artistic challenge.

Chiles learned how to quilt from her paternal grandmother, Patsy Chiles—who, she fondly recalled, "taught me how to make a string quilt and cornmeal dumplings"[3]—and her mother, Ardella Jackson. Her first quilt was a Log Cabin pattern that she completed around ten years of age. In Oakland, Chiles frequently quilted with friends in the senior citizen club at New Hope Baptist Church, located at 36th and Market Streets, as well as with her daughter Geneva Rodgers and grandchildren Tina and Clarence Jackson. She also sold quilts at the Berkeley Flea Market, where friends would stop by to give her material. EY

RUTH CHARLOTTE CLAY

b. 1888, Arkansas
d. 1956, Oakland, California

TREVA M. CLAY

b. 1919, Fort Smith, Arkansas
d. 1989, California

Ruth Charlotte Clay spent part of her youth in Union County, Arkansas working on farms. In 1913 she married Robert Clay in Tulsa, Oklahoma, and they raised a family in Fort Smith, Arkansas, where Treva was born. According to census records, by 1940 the family (Treva and her siblings) was living in Oklahoma City, where Robert worked as a water carrier for a WPA project and as a trucker. By 1950, the three of them were living in West Oakland with another daughter, Lavoyce Clay. Treva was a store clerk at the Naval Supply Depot, and Robert was a hauler.

Despite having no occupation listed in any official records, Ruth was a dressmaker who also knew how to quilt and sometimes ordered quilt patterns from books. It is likely that Ruth taught Treva how to piece and that the two made quilts together. EY

CLARA BELLE COLEMAN

b. 1911, near Summit, Mississippi
d. 1985, San Francisco, California

Born Clara Belle Wallace, Coleman was raised in the household of her grandparents, Alex and Mary Cockerham, in Summit, Mississippi. In the federal census of 1940, Coleman was listed as a housekeeper in a private home and her husband, Jake, as a

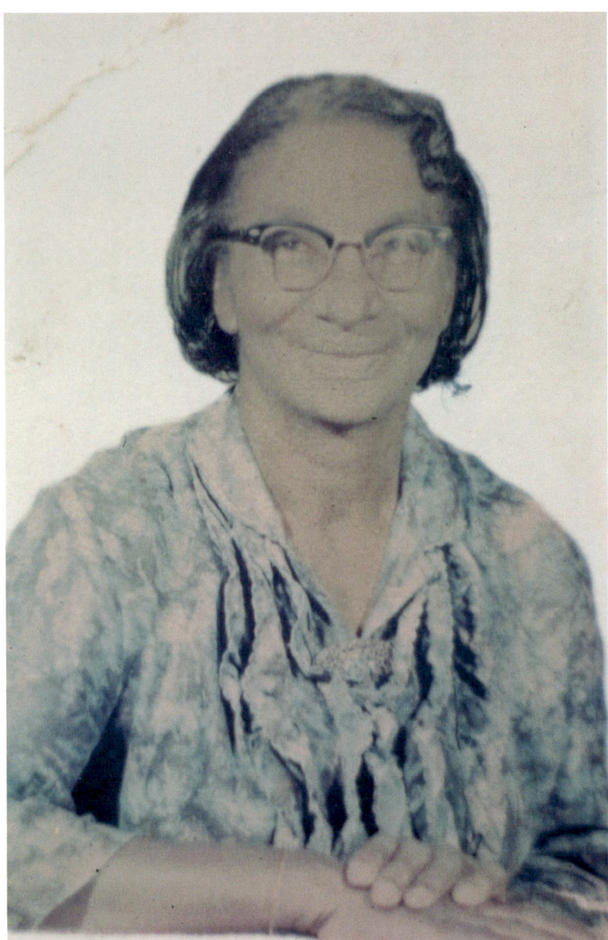

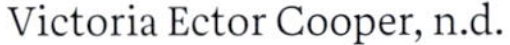

Victoria Ector Cooper, n.d.

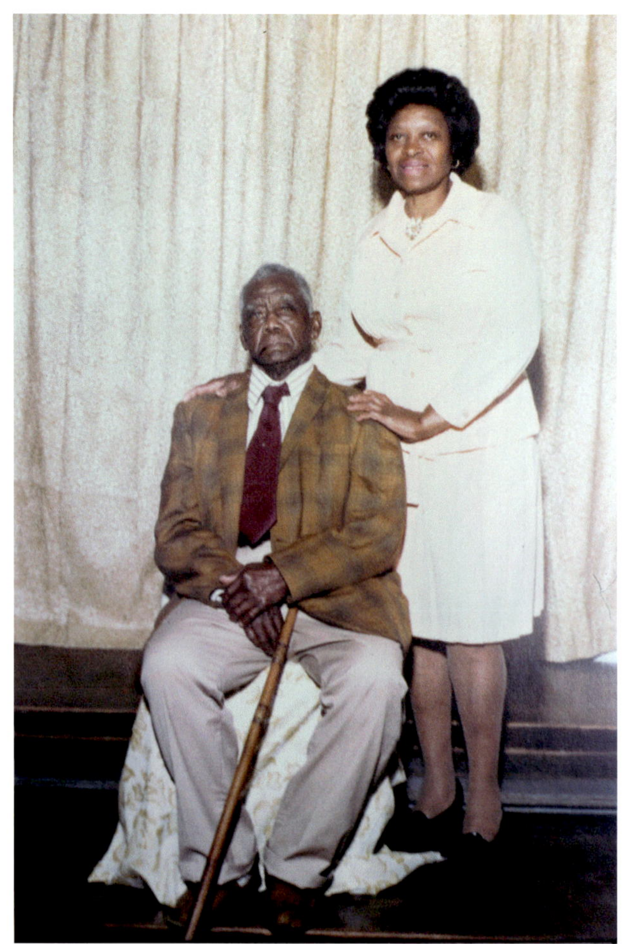

Thomas Covington with his daughter Mary Covington, n.d.

"common laborer" in McComb City. In 1945, they moved to California, where, by 1950, they lived with their niece, Annie Berry, in an apartment at 642 Hayes Street (between Buchanan and Laguna Streets). Their home was located in San Francisco's Western Addition, a district anchored by the Black businesses and clubs of Fillmore Street, where their neighbors were Black migrants from Arkansas, Texas, Louisiana, and Oklahoma. While it is not known if she was a quiltmaker, she owned at least two quilts that may have been either given to her or brought with her from Mississippi. EY

VICTORIA ECTOR COOPER

b. 1908, Henderson, Texas
d. 1996, Henderson, Texas

Victoria Ector Cooper was born to Ulcie Cooper and Tessie Jackson in the rural area of Henderson, Rusk County, Texas. By 1920, she and her family moved to Carlisle, where her father worked on a farm just outside of Henderson. She lived all her life in Texas, eventually passing away in her hometown in 1996. MVM

THOMAS COVINGTON

b. 1877, Lincoln County, Mississippi
d. 1979, Grand Bay, Alabama

Thomas Covington was born in Lincoln County, Mississippi, in 1877 to Martha and Arthur Covington, both of whom had lived under slavery and made quilts. Thomas and his wife, Laura Covington, raised six children in Wesson, Copiah County, Mississippi. He worked up to owning his own large farm. One of his daughters, Carlena White, recalled her father would "just sew what we had."[4] His Medallion quilt (cat. 41) was featured on the cover of the catalog for Gladys-Marie Fry's 1998 *Man Made* exhibition at the Anacostia Community Museum of the Smithsonian Institution. He pieced his last quilts in Grand Bay, Alabama, his final resting place. MVM

ANNIE CRAWFORD

b. 1884, Sugartown, Louisiana
d. 1950, Call, Texas

Born the second eldest daughter of Robert and Martha Smith, Annie Crawford raised her family in the farming area of Call,

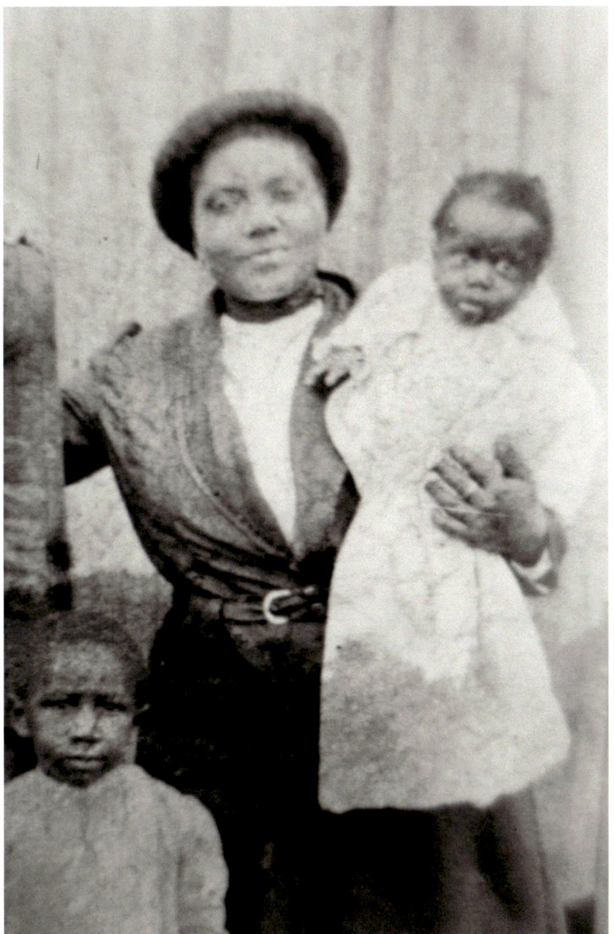

Annie Crawford with young child and baby, n.d.

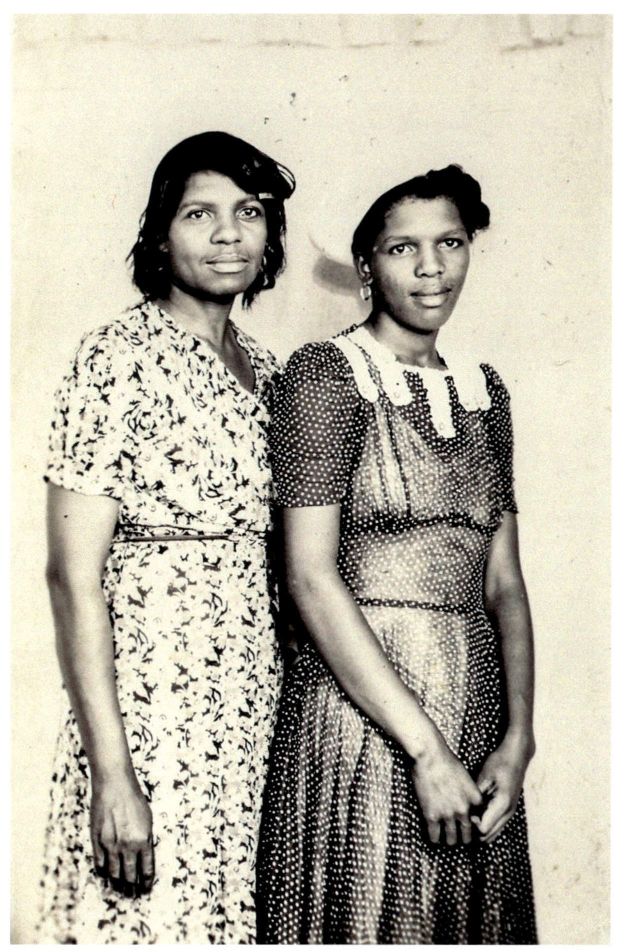

Zetta Dempsey's great-aunt Beulah Sanders (left) and mother, Mittie Nimmer Lawson (right), n.d.

Texas. According to Estella Brown, Crawford's niece who grew up in Oakdale, Louisiana, it was typical for their extended families to gather old clothes and salvage the strong fabric in the summer and make quilts in preparation for winter. They would place one quilt top in the frame in the morning and complete it by the evening.

The tobacco sack quilt (cat. 13) is Crawford's only known surviving quilt. Brown inherited it from Spurgeon and Clara Crawford, Annie's son and daughter-in-law, who moved to Berkeley sometime in the 1940s. EY

ANNA RUTH CROFIT

birth date and location unknown
death date and location unknown

Anna Ruth Crofit (possibly "Croft") lived in Pine Bluff, Arkansas, in the late 1980s. She had a sister, "Mama" Hayes, of Bakersfield, California. EY

ZETTA M. DEMPSEY

b. 1943, Bastrop, Louisiana
d. 2007, Bastrop, Louisiana

Zetta Dempsey and her younger sister, Beulah Lawson, were born in Bastrop, Morehouse Parish, Louisiana, to Milton E. Lawson and Mittie Nimmer Lawson. Both made their way to the East Bay by the early 1980s, at which time they had Oakland addresses.

Among Dempsey's possessions that Eli Leon acquired were two quilts, pieced blocks, and a pieced pillow constructed in a reverse Pine Burr pattern of 1940s fabrics (cat. 10), which were almost certainly made by her maternal grandmother, Lillie Lowe, and her great-grandmother Matilda Lowe. Ephemera also found with these patchwork materials offer additional clues to Dempsey's story, including information about family members who may have influenced her migration to California (cat. 11). Two official documents found in the cache of papers speak to the economic realities that shaped the lives of Dempsey's great-aunt Beulah Sanders and her husband, Albert. One is a notarized mortgage receipt from the Hopkins Company in Bastrop, and the other is a "Claimants Earnings Record and Benefit Determination" for Beulah from the Kaiser Corporation's shipyard in Vancouver. These papers suggest the

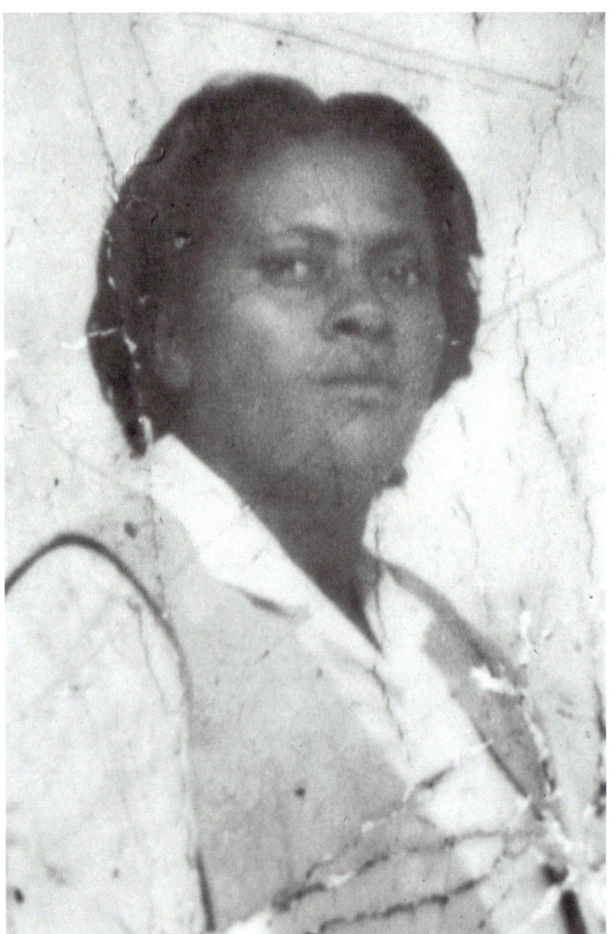

Odessa Doby, c. 1942–44

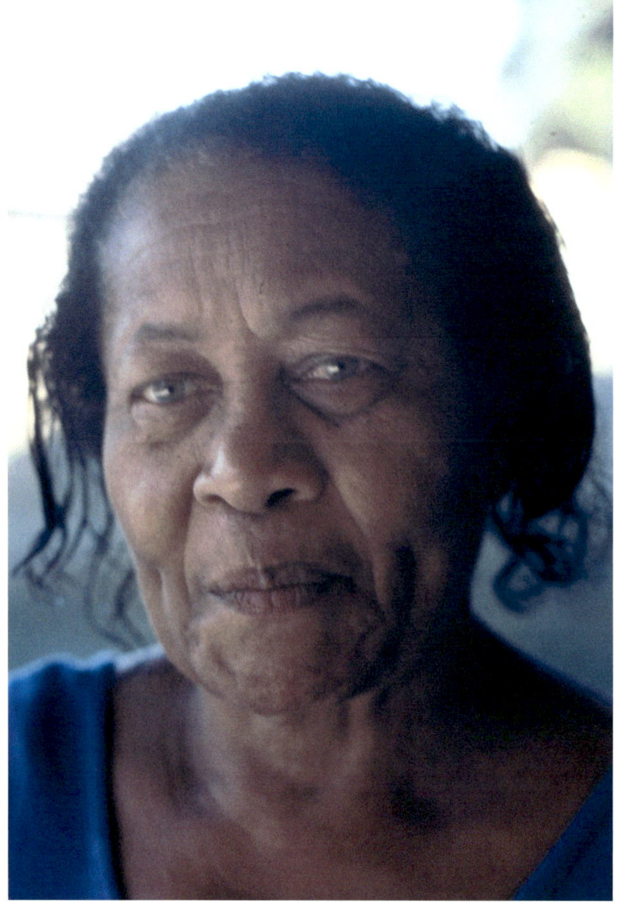

Florine Taylor, 1990

lengths to which her relatives traveled for work and wages, and the debts that they incurred at home in the South (by 1950 the couple moved back to Bastrop). Photographs—depicting a rural home and garden, other relatives and friends, and a section of Louisiana railroad tracks that was closest to their family home—along with a pamphlet from Mrs. Lena L. Haynes, Spiritual Advisor, add texture to an earlier period of Dempsey's larger family story. Likely retained as family keepsakes, these objects are evocative, poignant remains of everyday Black lives. **EY with Beulah Lawson**

ODESSA DOBY

b. 1912, Ozan, Arkansas
d. 1988, Ozan, Arkansas

Born to George and Rebecca Walker, Odessa Doby lived her entire life in Ozan, Arkansas. She first learned to quilt around ten years of age, starting with a Nine Patch. She was part of a quilting club during the 1920s and 1930s that met once or twice a week. Preferring to piece rather than quilt, she would piece tops for neighbors and elders who "needed cover."[5] She married Ira Doby in April of 1932 and supported her family working in local schools both as a bus driver and in cafeterias. **MVM**

FLORINE TAYLOR

b. 1922, Ozan, Arkansas
d. 2017, Nashville, Arkansas

The youngest of ten siblings (her sister Odessa Doby was the eldest), Florine Taylor was a lifetime resident of Ozan, Arkansas, and learned to piece from her mother by ten years of age, even reusing her mother's scraps for her dolls. She was a member of St. Mark CME Church and St. Peter CME Church in her hometown and attended Walnut Grove School and Clow Training Center, crucial hubs of Black community life during the segregation era. She married R.C. Taylor, a farmer in her home county, in September of 1943. She raised ten children: Maple Jean Swift, Leonard Taylor, R.C. Taylor Jr., Lancie Taylor, Audrey Taylor, Sharon Craven, Vanessa Swift, Gwendolyn Stewart, Stanley Taylor, and Carolyn Taylor. To support her family, she worked in the cafeteria at Lincoln High School, and as a teacher's aide at Washington Elementary School. **MVM**

LEE WANDA JONES

b. 1934, McCaskill, Arkansas
d. 2020, Fresno, California

Lee Wanda Jones (née Doby) learned to quilt at the age of eight by helping her mother, Odessa Doby, piece quilts. She sewed

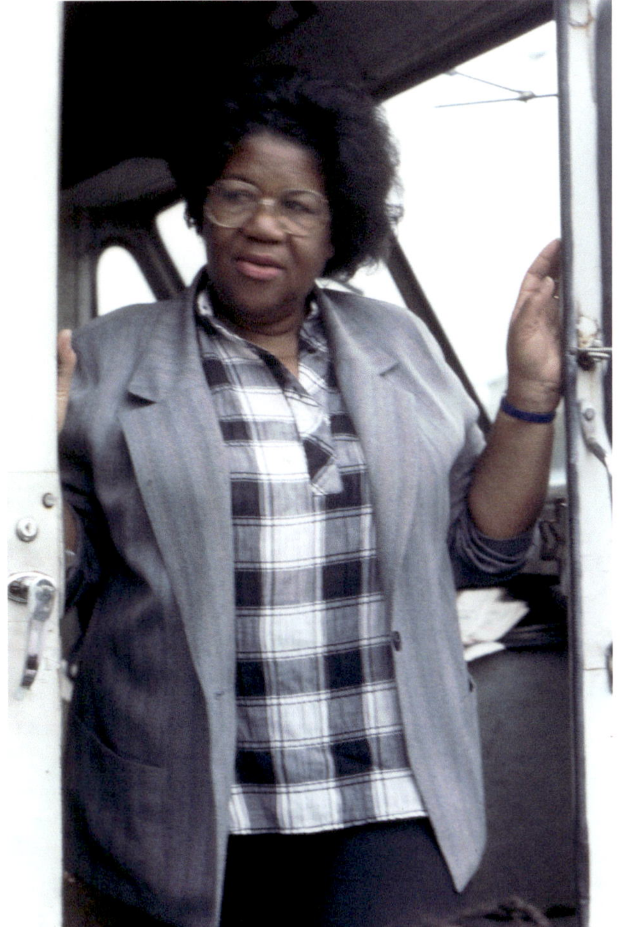

Lee Wanda Jones, 1989

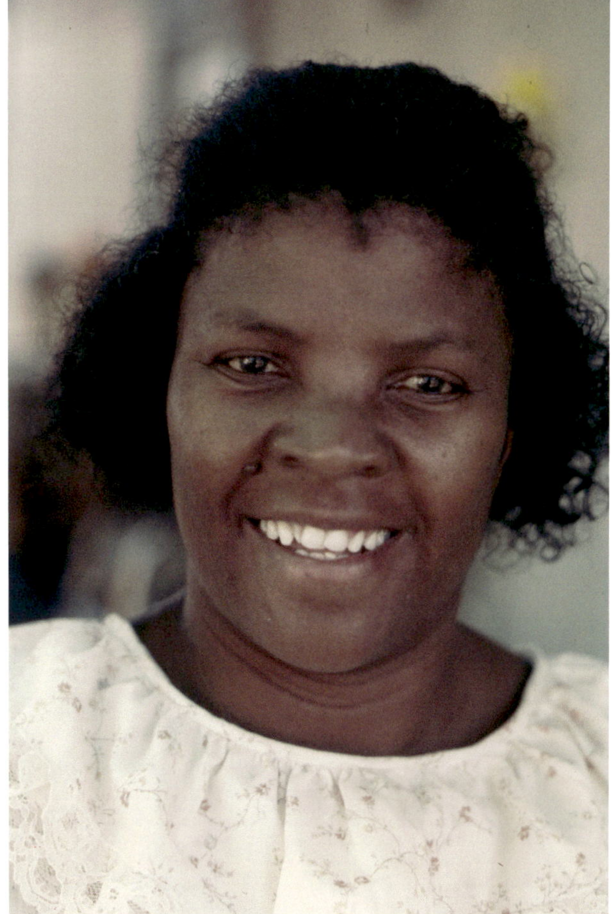

Maple Jean Swift, 1990

alongside her grandmother, Franny Doby, and her younger sister Burnell Doby Curry. She created her own patterns, making doll quilts or turning blocks into pillows. She used a variety of techniques, from "cornerstoning," or using the same pattern on all four corners of the quilt, to "stripping," or making blocks from long pieces of fabric. According to the federal census of 1950, she lived in Hempstead County, Arkansas, with her mother and father and three younger sisters. Two years later, she moved to Berkeley, where she worked as a nurse caring for the elderly, while also raising four children. She would later live between Fresno and Emeryville. MVM

MAPLE JEAN SWIFT

b. 1944, Ozan, Arkansas
d. 2019, Texarkana, Texas

Born in a large family, Maple Jean Swift came from a generation of quiltmakers and quiltkeepers in and around Ozan, Arkansas. Her grandmother taught her how to make her first quilt when she was eleven or twelve years old, and she often quilted patterns that her mother, Florine Taylor, or her community would pass on to her. While selling her quilts, she worked in factories and school cafeterias to provide for her family. Eli Leon noted her generosity and industrious spirit, writing, "She can machine-piece an eight-pointed star block in a half hour without measuring or using a pattern. Able to tack two comforters a day and 'still see about my babies and cook in between times.' She sells her productions or gives them to relatives and to people who have lost their home in a fire. In 1989 she made and sold about 50 bedcovers."[6] MVM

GLADYS CELIA DURHAM-HENRY

b. 1906, Butler, Texas
d. 1996, Butler, Texas

Gladys Celia Durham-Henry belonged to the fifth generation of the Durham family born in Texas. Her earliest known ancestor, known only as Gobi, fathered six sons in South Carolina. Five of them, along with their pregnant mother, were brought to Freestone County, Texas, by Robert Windfield Durham as slaves in 1862. Her grandfather, Rance Durham (1859–1950), who was born into slavery, was the first Black elected official in Freestone County after the Civil War. Her father, Willie Anderson Durham (1882–1965), farmed land inherited from Rance and ran a cotton gin and a syrup mill. Her grandmothers, Patsy Reddick Titus Manning (life dates unknown)

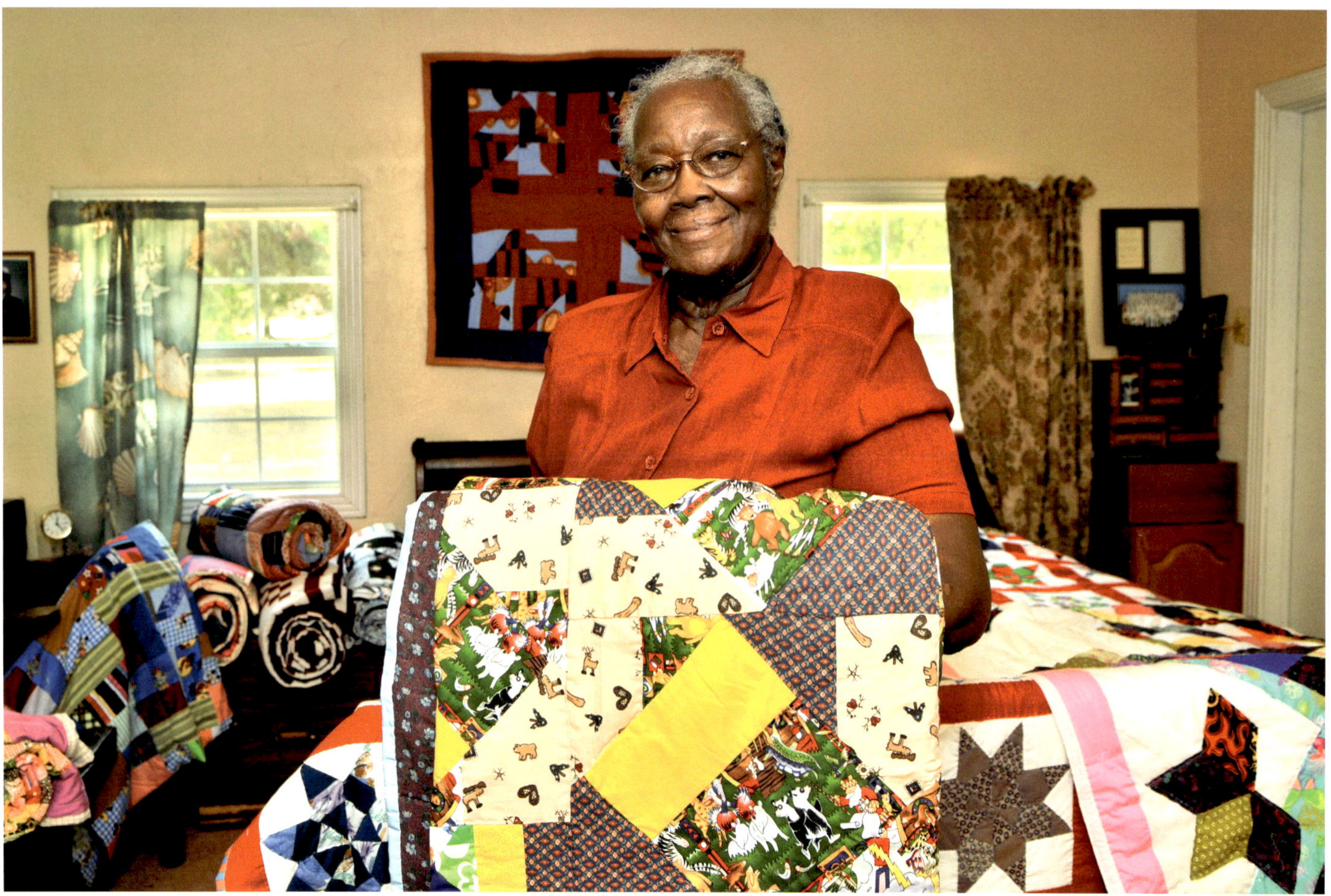

Laverne Brackens, 1992

and Chlora Dunbar-Titus (1826–1890), and mother, Ellen Anna Titus (1884–1929), were quiltmakers. They taught Gladys and her sisters Katie Mae Durham-Tatum (1917–2011) and Clara Venetta Durham-Peters (1902–1999) piecing and quilting.

She married Reverend Willie Elbert Henry Sr. in 1924, and together they had nine children. As a mother and farmer, Henry possessed an array of creative skills, from canning, sewing, and dressmaking to crocheting, knitting, and millinery. She also quilted alongside her mother-in-law, Elena Wade-Henry, and Willie's paternal grandmother, Delphia Joshua-Henry (1845–1934). She was introduced to Eli Leon through her granddaughter, Sherry Ann Byrd. Affectionately known as "Big Mama" by her family, she is one of six generations of quiltmakers in the Owen's Chapel community. Her quilts have been featured in several of Eli Leon's exhibitions, such as *No Two Alike: African American Improvisations on a Traditional Patchwork Pattern*. A selection of quilts made by four generations of her family is displayed permanently at the Chicago Police Department as part of the City's collection. **EY with Sherry Ann Byrd**

LAVERNE ARELLA HENRY-BRACKENS

b. 1927, Fairfield, Texas
lives in Fairfield, Texas

The second oldest of eight siblings, Laverne Arella Henry-Brackens grew up in eastern Texas. Her mother, Gladys Henry, her maternal aunts, and her grandmothers were all quiltmakers. From the age of six, Laverne was encouraged to learn to piece and make quilts. Nevertheless, as an energetic child, she preferred climbing trees to sewing. After getting married in 1945, she and her husband, Connie Brackens, had eight children. Connie Brackens died unexpectedly in 1964. To support her family, she worked in restaurants, managed a work crew that drove trucks for a local chicken farm from 1972 to 1987, and later worked as a cook for fourteen years in Mexia State School. In 1987, injuries sustained from an accident on the job prompted her early retirement. Rendered unable to stand for long periods of time and eager to keep her hands busy, Brackens began piecing quilts in the improvisational manner practiced by her foremothers.

That same year, her daughter Sherry Ann Byrd introduced Brackens to Eli Leon, who eventually purchased over three hundred quilts and tops from the artist and facilitated the exhibition of her work throughout the US. In 2011, Brackens was awarded the National Heritage Fellowship, the highest honor in folk and traditional arts. The city of Fairfield declared October 13, 2022, Laverne Brackens Day on the opening of her show, *The Art of the Quilt*. She continues to quilt today. **EY with Sherry Ann Byrd**

SHERRY ANN BYRD

b. 1951, Fairfield, Texas
lives in Fairfield, Texas

Sherry Ann Byrd is a sixth-generation quiltmaker in her family. Her earliest exposure to quilting came from observing her maternal grandmother, Gladys Henry, and occasionally helping her tack (or tie) tops to backings to complete a quilt. Between completing her undergraduate education at Sam Houston State University, moving to Richmond, California, in 1977, and supporting her growing family of nine with her husband, Curtis, she had little time to quilt. Yet she returned to quiltmaking in 1984 to cope with the grief of her son's stillbirth.

She began by making crib quilts and giving them away to friends, before making larger bed-sized quilts. After responding to Eli Leon's classified ad in 1986 and feeling encouraged by his interest in her quilts, Byrd kept building upon her love of art, history, and traditional handmaking that she had learned from Henry, and continued to develop her practice. While she can piece "precision" quilts, she prefers "M-provisational" quilts that encourage freedom and experimentation. Her quilts have been exhibited widely and can be found in the collections of the Fine Arts Museums of San Francisco, the Los Angeles County Museum of Art, the Bob Bullock Texas State History Museum, and the City of Chicago's Public Art Collection. In 1997, one of her quilts was included in British Airways' *Project Utopia*, a series of art commissions intended for the tailfins of its air fleet (it was never realized). In her capacity as the family griot, Byrd is currently at work on a series of story quilts that honor her ancestors in Texas and Africa. **EY with Sherry Ann Byrd**

BARALALESSA (BARA) BYRD-STEWART

b. 1975, Houston, Texas
lives in Teague, Texas

Bara Byrd-Stewart is the eldest daughter of Curtis and Sherry Ann Byrd, the granddaughter of Laverne A. Henry-Brackens, the great-granddaughter of Gladys C. Durham-Henry, and the five times great-granddaughter of Edward Ned and Chlorie Titus. She moved with her family to Richmond, California, at the age of two. Like her sisters, Bara is a seventh-generation quilter from the Titus family who first learned from her mother, their homeschool teacher, how to create tied doll quilts from scraps and two-piece outfits. She began hand-piecing and quiltmaking at the age of ten, while growing up in Richmond. Through a sewing class held at a close friend's home, she learned to use a sewing machine, which enabled her to make larger quilts. Her best quilt memories included waking up in the morning to find a brand-new quilt on her bed.

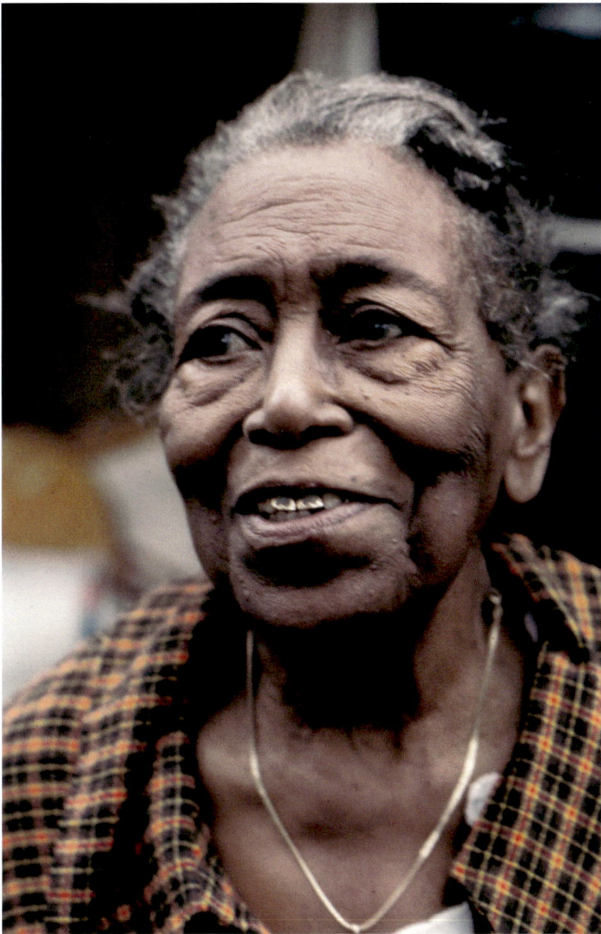

Joan Thompson, 1990

Although her first quilt was lost on the family's return to Texas in 1997, Bara's second quilt is featured in her mother's reversible story quilt, *Jazz with a Needle and Thread*. She frequently exhibits with other members of the Titus family of quilters. She resides in Teague, Texas, with her husband, Roy Stewart, and daughter, Kyla. **EY with Sherry Ann Byrd**

LOUISA FITE

b. 1891, Panola County, Texas
d. 1976, Panola County, Texas

Louisa Fite lived in Panola County, a region whose economy was driven by the cotton and timber industries in the early twentieth century. In 1911, she married Marvin Fite, who belonged to a family of farmworkers. Together, Louisa and Marvin raised six children. **MVM**

JOAN THOMPSON

b. 1915, Beckville, Texas
d. 2000, Carthage, Texas

Born to Louisa Fite and Marvin Fite in Beckville, Texas, Joan Thompson learned to quilt from her mother. According to the

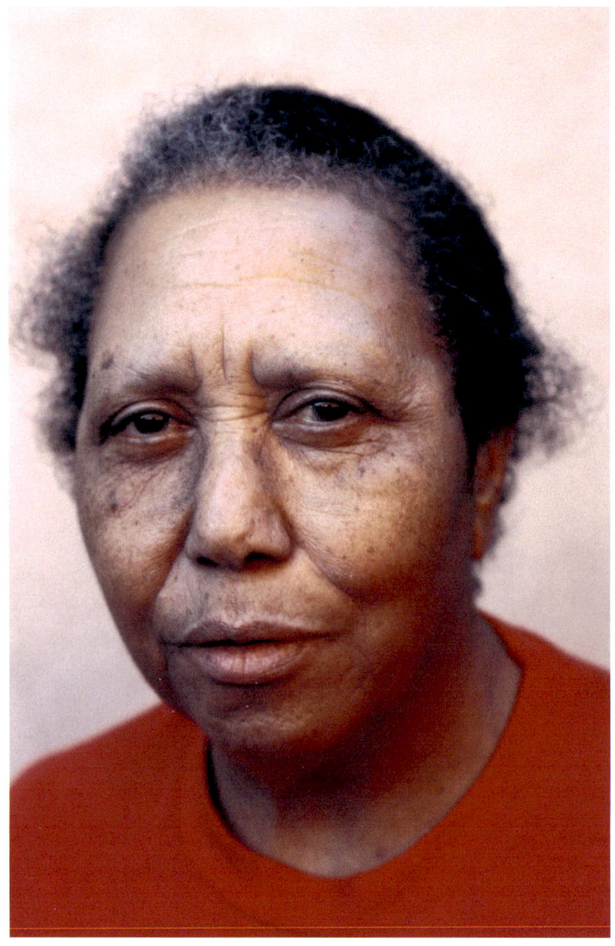

Selena Foster, 1985

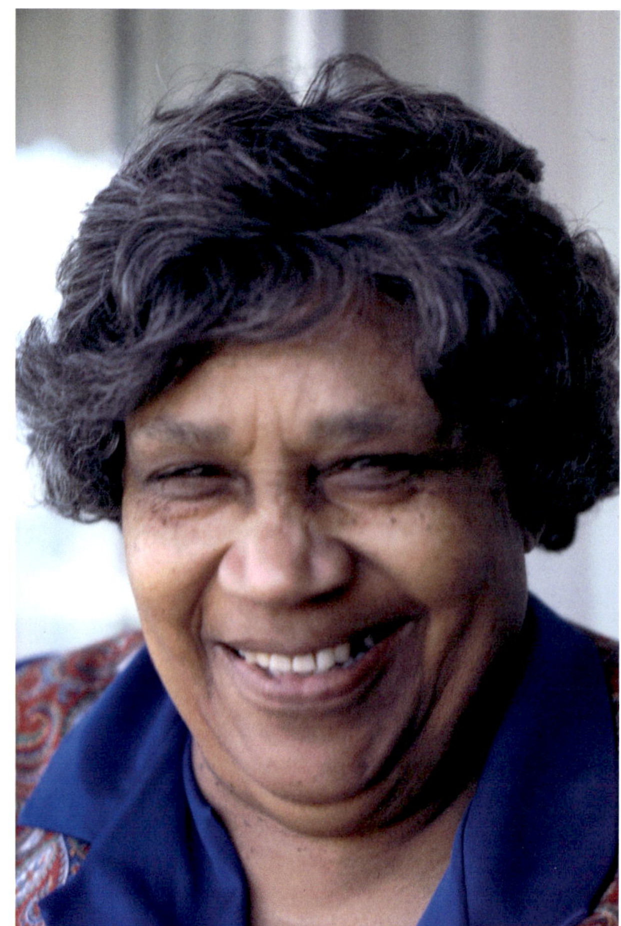

Mable Battle, 1985

federal census of 1940, she married Wallace Thompson and lived with their son and two daughters. By the age of 34, she supported her family through housekeeping, and gave birth to another son. Her final resting place is Holland Quarters Cemetery, an African American burial ground in Carthage, Panola County, on lands deeded to formerly enslaved people after the Civil War. MVM

SELENA M. FOSTER

b. 1916, Larissa community near Jacksonville, Texas
if deceased, death date and location unknown

Selena Foster was the second-eldest daughter out of nine children born to McKinley Anderson, a farmer, and Hazel Izora Anderson on her grandparent's farm in Cherokee County. Starting around age nine, she would piece quilts with her grandmother, recalling, "I threaded all of her needles every day before I would leave for school. Every little scrap of material that she had left over, that was mine to sew with."[7] At seventeen, she married Marvin Foster, and together they lived in Oklahoma and in Tyler and Forth Worth, Texas, before making the decision to move to California in 1944. Upon arriving in Richmond, Marvin worked at the Kaiser Shipyards, while Selena worked at Leo's Defense Diner. For the balance of their lives, they divided their time between Richmond and El Cerrito. Once the wartime economy had subsided, Marvin worked at a Cadillac dealership in San Francisco while Selena opened her short-lived restaurant called "Selena's Kitchen" with her mother-in-law, Mollie Bowen. Later, she worked at Eastman Factory in Oakland, making stationery and managing the company cafeteria.

In 1966, she underwent surgery that affected her ability to walk and use her hand, at which point she began to quilt more often as part of her recovery. In addition to making quilts, she eagerly sewed for her community, making pageant gowns for graduating high school seniors, and sang with the gospel choir at Easter Hill United Methodist Church. In 1986, she and her mother-in-law showed their quilts in the exhibition *To Keep Somebody Warm* at the Richmond Museum. In an interview with *The Tribune,* Foster said, "I've two daughters, a 98-year-old mother-in-law, and a grand baby that I help. I'm their everything, so I have to find time for quilting. I can sit down in the morning over a cup of coffee and quilt, and I can do it in the evening. I can get up and miss breakfast any morning and quilt."[8] She summed up her philosophy of life

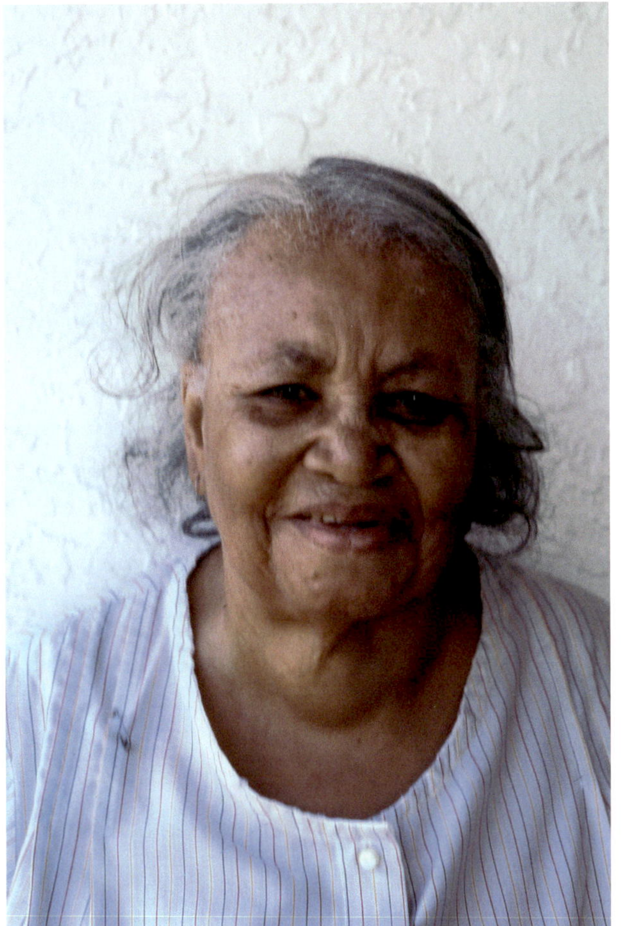

Missie Freeman, n.d.

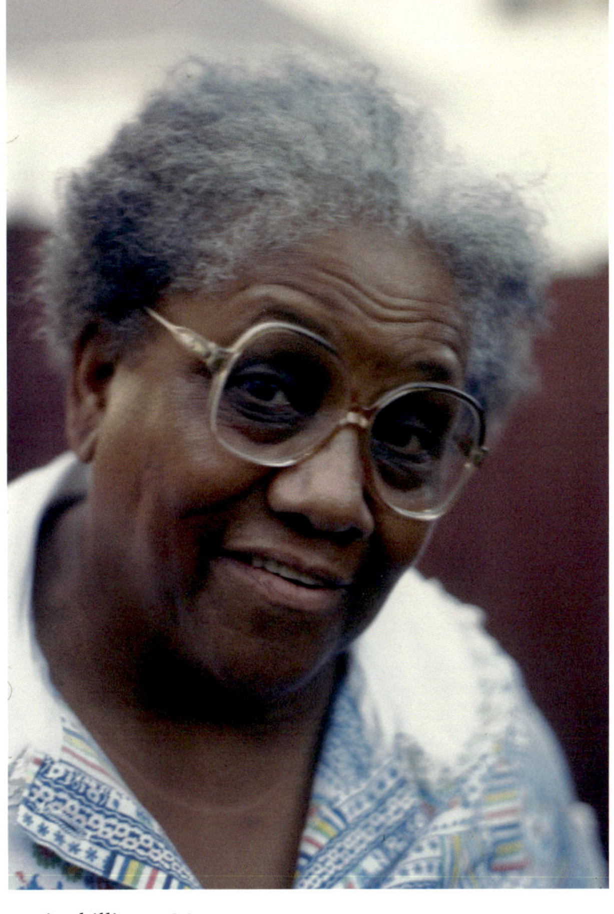

Bettie Phillips, 1986

and quilting this way: "I take your nothing and make something out of it."[9] MVM

MABLE O. BATTLE

b. 1918, Larissa community near Jacksonville, Texas
d. 2003, Richmond, California

Born Mable Anderson, Battle grew up in Cherokee County, Texas, as the fifth of ten siblings. She graduated from Frederick Douglass High School in Jacksonville. She married her childhood friend Cornelius Battle in Bakersfield, California, and in 1946 they moved to Fresno with their fourteen-year-old daughter, Lena. Cornelius was stationed at Hammer Field, while Mable was a housekeeper and vocational nurse before retiring. In 1951, the family moved to Richmond, where her older sister, Selena Foster, lived.

She recalls her mother quilting with and without patterns, sometimes using newspaper, but she eventually would discard the pattern and cut pieces without measuring. Battle sourced patterns in various ways, sometimes ordering pattern books and sometimes receiving them from other women. Among the over sixty quilts that Eli Leon collected from her, several are quilted by Foster, while others are pictorial quilts drawn from her Christian faith (she considered herself an evangelist). Of her quilt *A Vision*, for example, she credited God for the idea. She told Leon, "I would sort of blink my eyes like I'm looking at it, and pretty soon I see it. . . . It's sort of a vision; you know the Bible say without a vision, some people perish, so I don't want to perish, having no vision at all!"[10] MVM, EY

ALBERTA "MISSIE" FREEMAN

b. 1914, Castle, Oklahoma
d. 2005, Stockton, California

Missie Freeman was the eldest daughter of George and Sammie Freeman and grew up in Boley, Oklahoma. From an early age, she experienced profound hearing loss and did not speak more than a few words. Nevertheless, she performed all kinds of farming jobs, from chopping and picking cotton to milking cows and cooking for her family. She remained in Boley until 1967, the year her mother died, after which she relocated to Oakland so that her family could care for her. According to her sister, Bettie Phillips, Freeman was a skilled seamstress who could see a dress or pocketbook in a catalog and make it for herself or other family members. EY

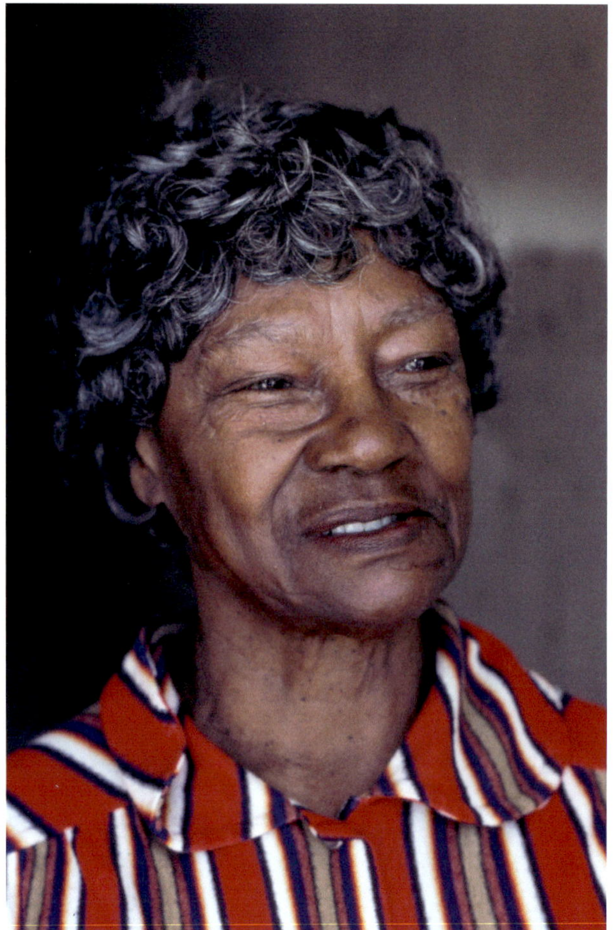

Annie Hawkins, 1981

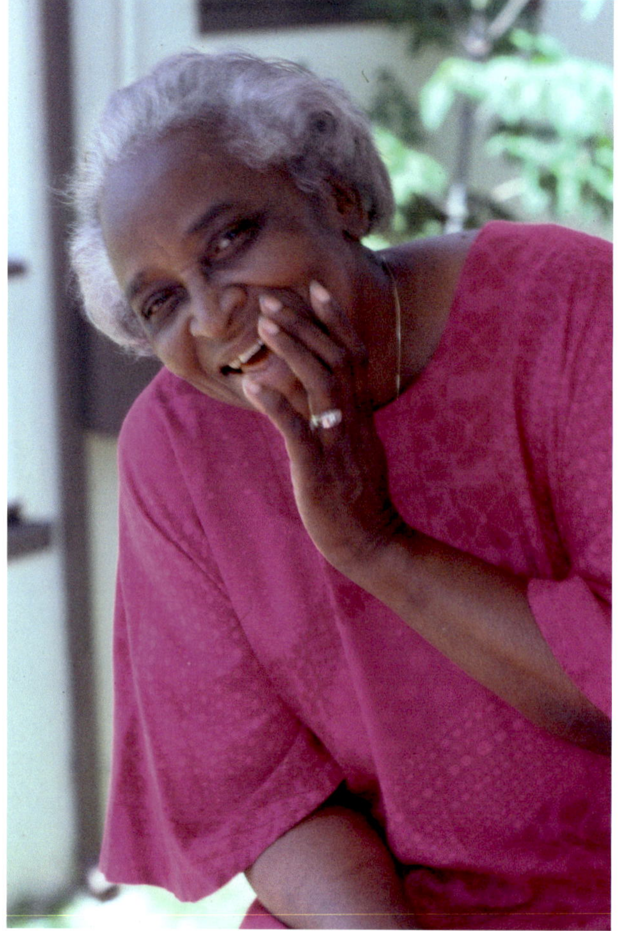

Mattie Lou Henderson, 1981

BETTIE LEVEDA PHILLIPS

b. 1916, Castle, Oklahoma
d. 2005, Oakland, California

Bettie Leveda Phillips was born the second daughter of eleven children in Castle, Oklahoma. She attended grammar school and high school in nearby Boley, which was one of fifty all-Black towns founded in Oklahoma. She left during the Great Depression, arriving in Pasadena, California, in 1937. After periods of living in Los Angeles (working in hotels), Dos Palos, Vallejo (working in the shipyards and later doing "daywork" cleaning houses), and Stockton (working as a cook in a children's home), she moved to Oakland in 1967, when her husband, Romeo, passed away. She lived there for the remainder of her life.

By her own account, Phillips was descended from several generations of women quilters, including her mother, Sammie Freeman, and her grandmother, Cherry Goree, from Louisiana. She learned to sew as a young girl, first by making doll clothes and appliquéing fabric onto dish towels. She made quilts throughout her adult life and, like her mother, was adept at both paper piecing and improvisational quilting, sometimes deriving patterns from everyday objects or ones that appeared in her dreams. EY

EMMA HALL

b. 1878, Louisiana
d. 1949, Sweet Home, Arkansas

Emma Hall was born to Pollie and Edward Bromdon in Louisiana. She worked as a farmer to support her family, which included four daughters (Rosie Huggins, Addie January, Zuline, and one whose name is unknown) and a son, James R. Hall. She lived in Pulaski County, Arkansas, for twenty years. Her son, James, inherited her personal effects, including several quilts, upon her passing in Sweet Home, Arkansas, in 1949.[11] Her final resting place is Zion Hill Cemetery, Pulaski County, Arkansas. MVM

LOUELLA HARRIS

b. 1903, likely Gregg County, Texas
d. 1991, Richmond, California

Louella Harris (née Jackson) spent her childhood in Gregg County in eastern Texas. It is unknown when she came to Richmond, California, but her daughter-in-law, Alice Hilliard of Oakland, owned and kept several of her quilts. EY

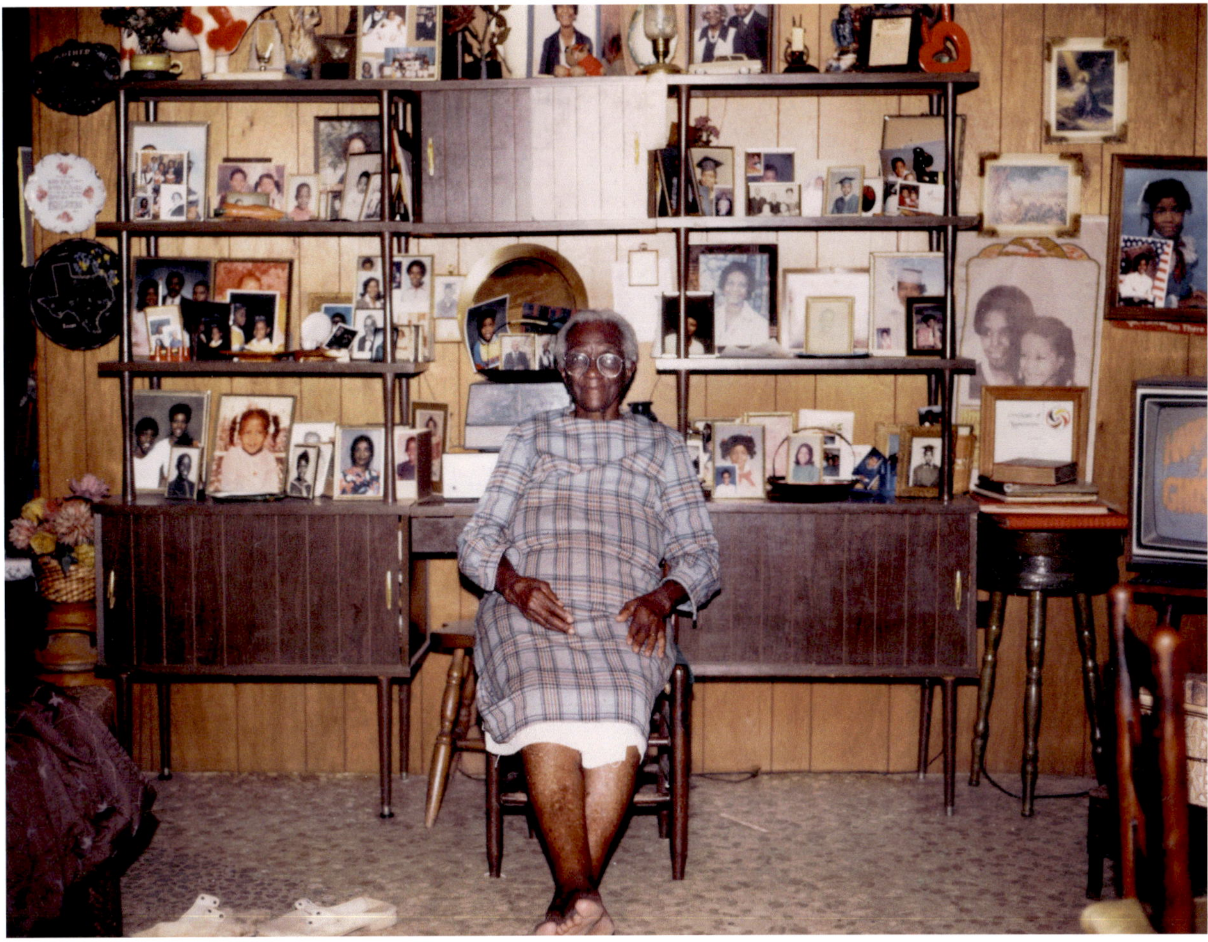

Roberta Lee Johnson, c. 1989

ANNIE HAWKINS

b. 1905, Alligator, Mississippi
d. 1990, location unknown

Born in Bolivar County in the heart of the Mississippi Delta, Annie Hawkins and her husband, Charlie, were farmers who came to Oakland in 1949. EY

MATTIE LOU HENDERSON

b. 1910, Clarksville, Texas
d. 1995, Alameda County, California

Mattie Lou Henderson (née Young) was born into a large farming family in Red River County, Texas, on the Oklahoma border near southwest Arkansas. She moved to the East Bay in 1947, the same year she remarried, and lived at different locations in West Oakland and Berkeley. Henderson had a variety of caregiving jobs, from cleaning private homes and serving food in schools to in-home practical nursing for the elderly and shopping for them.

She learned to quilt by watching her mother, Florence Young, who taught her basic sewing skills around the age of eight. However, it was not until 1975 that Henderson began quilting more regularly as a hobby. During this time, she preferred to purchase new fabrics from JC Penney and tended to measure and cut her pieces. As part of her practice, she occasionally modified patterns made by her friend Tennie Edwards. EY

ROBERTA LEE JOHNSON

b. 1903, Mount Enterprise, Texas
d. 2004, Mount Enterprise, Texas

Roberta Lee Johnson was born in Mount Enterprise, Texas, her lifetime home. Her parents, Lemontine Burgess and Aron Burgess, raised her and her siblings, Addie Faye Thompson (1928–1976), Hayward Johnson (1926–1996), and Millard L. Johnson (1931–2010). Growing up, she watched her mother quilt and eventually learned to quilt at the age of twenty-five from her mother-in-law, Georgia Ann. With her husband, Marion Johnson, she raised seven children, often quilting bedcoverings for her family to help them weather the Great Depression. Between 1928 and 1941, Johnson would earn a bachelor's degree to pursue a career in teaching, working in elementary school, high school, and adult schools for

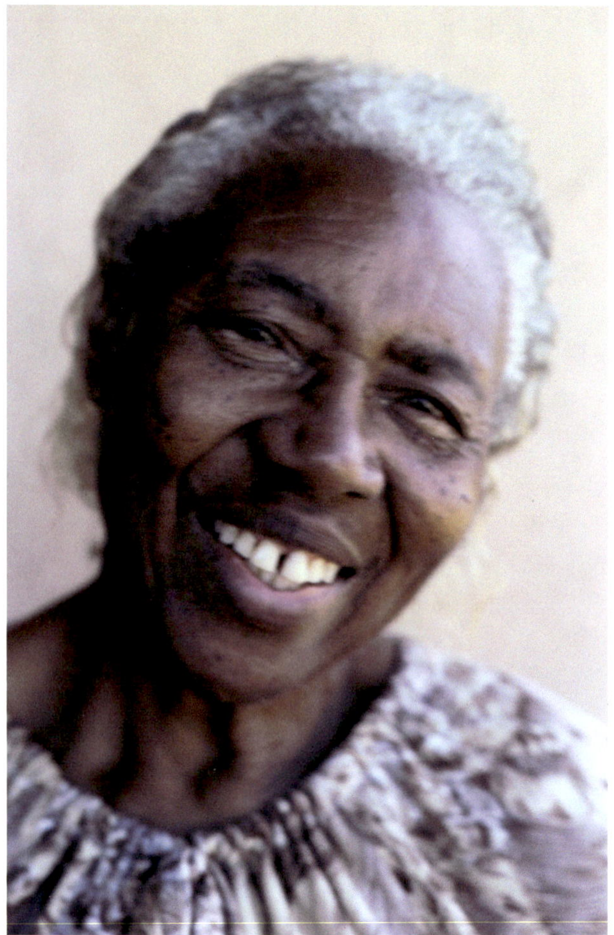

Atleaver Jones, 1991

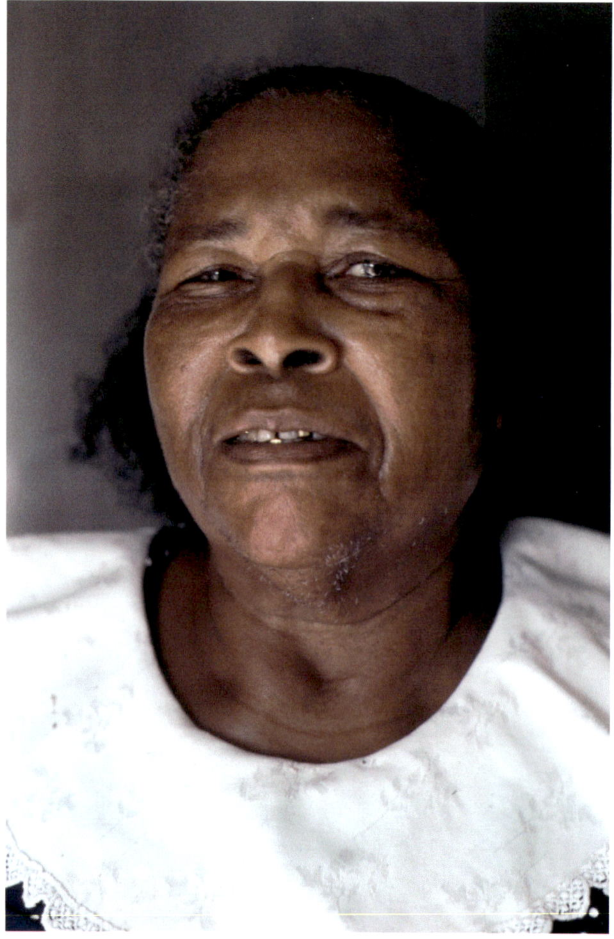

Georgia Lee Kidd, n.d.

forty-four years, prior to "the unceremonious dismissal of all the African-American teachers in her district upon court-ordered integration."[12] In her lifetime, she was a pillar of her community, honored by the Zion Grove CME Church of Cushing, Texas, in neighboring Nacogdoches County. MVM

KITTY GLADYS JONES

b. around 1900, location unknown
d. 1974, Forest, Mississippi

Kitty Gladys Jones is the aunt of Atleaver Jones's husband, Winey Jones. EY

ATLEAVER JONES

b. 1912, Le Flore County, Oklahoma
d. 2006, Fresno, California

According to the federal census of 1920, Atleaver Jones was the sixth child and only daughter of Lumpkin and Mattie Anderson. Descending from Texas and South Carolina, they were a farming family, and listed as working "on [their] own account." She married James Mickel in 1929, and they had three sons. In 1940, the entire family was living in Kennady, Oklahoma, and by 1950 they had relocated to Fresno, California, where Atleaver was working for a private employer, a local family. She and her second husband, Winey Jones, are buried in Fresno's Mountain View Cemetery. EY

GEORGIA LEE KIDD

b. 1921, Warren, Arkansas
d. 2004, Los Angeles County, California

Georgia Lee Kidd (née Neal, later Edwards) was a third-generation Arkansan: her parents and maternal grandparents were from Bradley County. She grew up in the country about twelve miles from Warren, Arkansas. According to the federal census of 1920 (the year just before she was born), her father, Ed Neal, was a log cutter for the public works and a WWI veteran, while her mother, Angie Slater Neal, had no occupation listed and likely worked in the home. She was living in Pennington, Bradley County, in 1940, before moving to Portland, Oregon, with her husband, Herman Edwards, and three children. By 1950, they were living in McNary, Arizona,

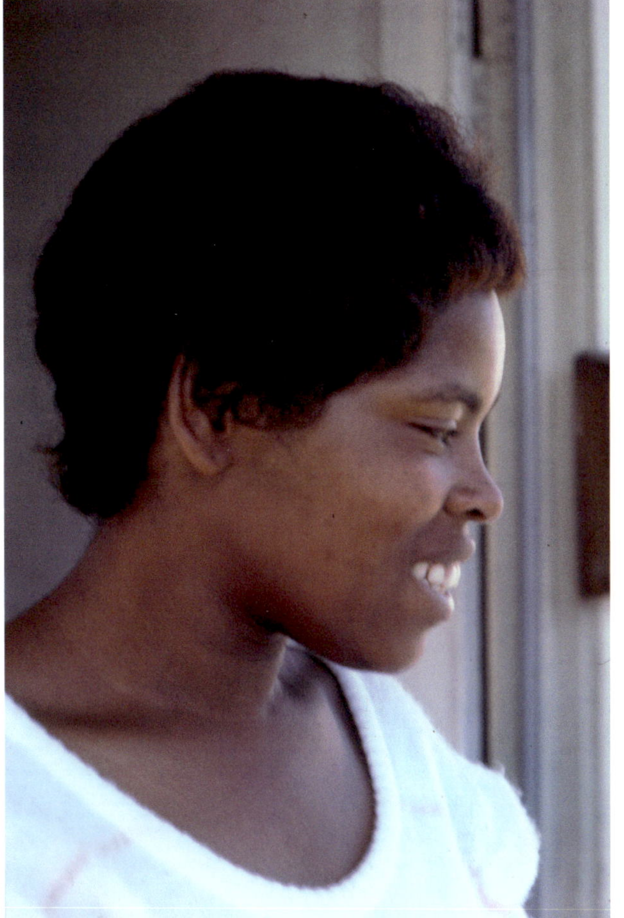

Angelia Tobias, 1985

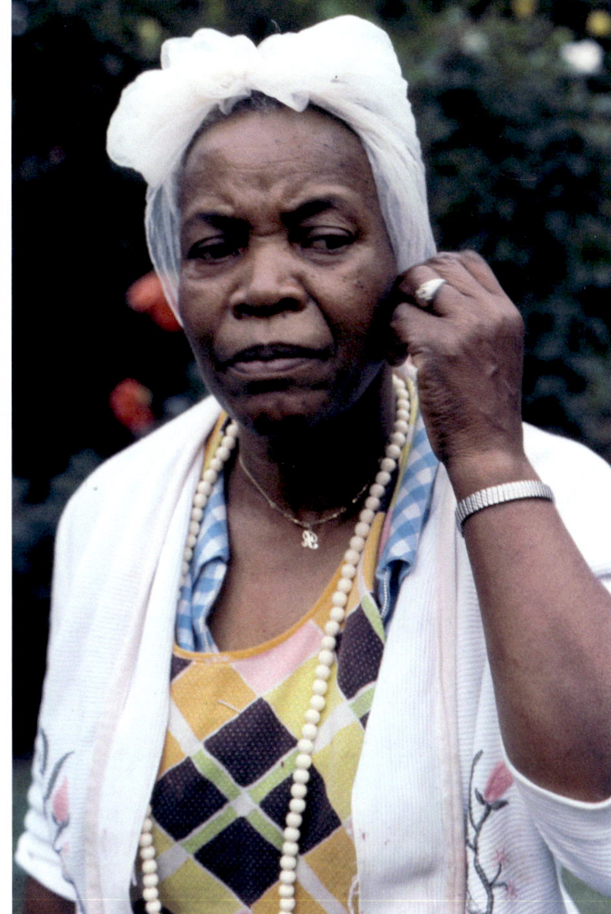

Ruby Lewis, 1981

where Herman worked at a lumber mill and she worked as a dishwasher. In 1951, she moved to Los Angeles but returned to Arkansas in 1980 and lived in the town of Camden. By 1984, she was living in Riverside, California. She died at the age of 83 and is buried in Rose Hills Memorial Park in Whittier, California.

Kidd learned to quilt around the age of nine from her mother, who imparted a sense of precision and neatness to her daughter's sewing practice. As a ten-year-old, she made doll quilts and had pieced her first large quilt using String blocks. A lifelong quilter, Kidd sometimes dreamed of quilt patterns, which she would then transfer into drawings. EY

DOROTHY EDWARDS

b. 1938, Bradley County, Arkansas
d. 1984, location unknown

When Dorothy Edwards was two years old, she was living in Pennington, Arkansas, with her father, Herman Edwards, who worked at a lumber mill, and her mother, Georgia Edwards (later Kidd), who worked in the home. By 1950, her family, including her grandfather Ed Neal, were living in McNary, Arizona, likely drawn to the town's thriving sawmill industry, which employed a predominantly Black labor force from Louisiana. While her whereabouts in later decades is unknown, she lived in Los Angeles for a time and collaborated with her mother on the quilt pictured as cat. 64 towards the end of her life, in Fordyce, Arkansas. EY

ANGELIA LAJUANA TOBIAS

b. 1955, Los Angeles, California
lives in Merced, California

Angelia Tobias has been sewing since she was twelve years old. She learned to quilt from her mother, Dorothy Edwards, and her grandmother, Georgia Lee Kidd. As an adult, she made and sold quilts to supplement her income from cleaning houses. She would typically have upwards of thirty tops available for people to select from and have her finish, usually by tacking.

Though Tobias pieces her quilts improvisationally, she selects fabrics that cohere aesthetically in any given quilt, such as corduroys, miscellaneous cotton prints, or fabrics with local sports team logos. She also applies her skills to an array of functional objects like potholders and dolls. EY

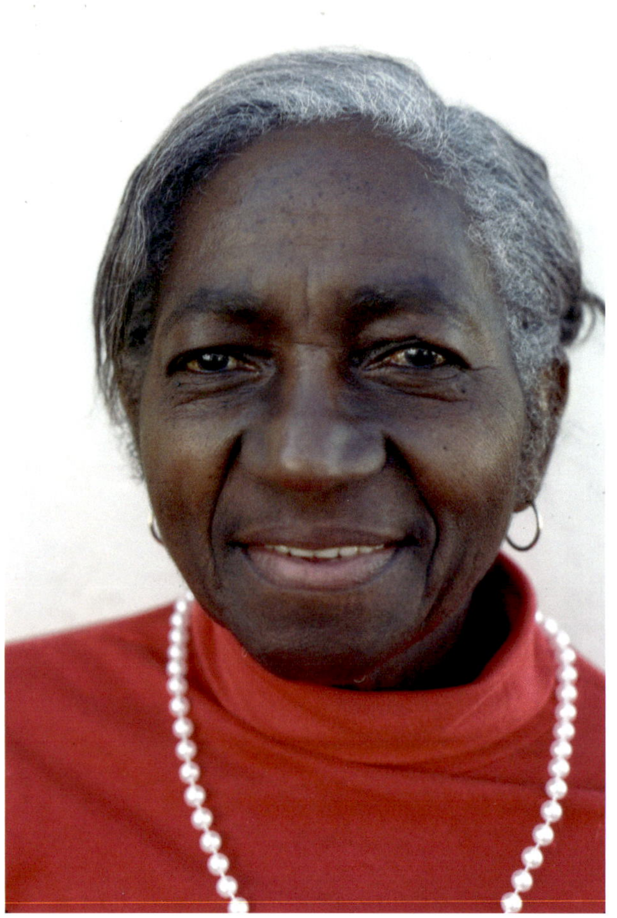
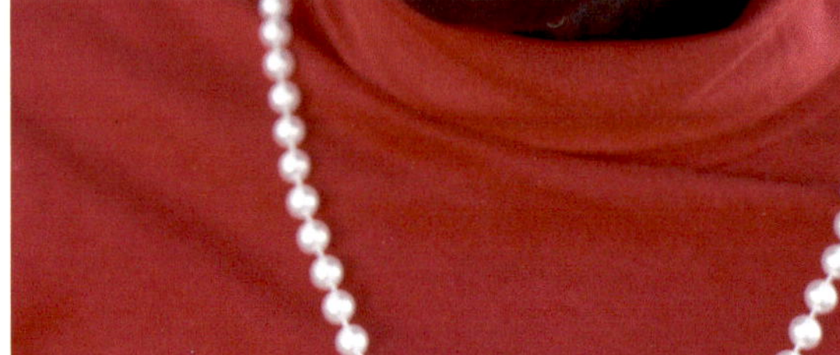
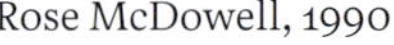

Rose McDowell, 1990

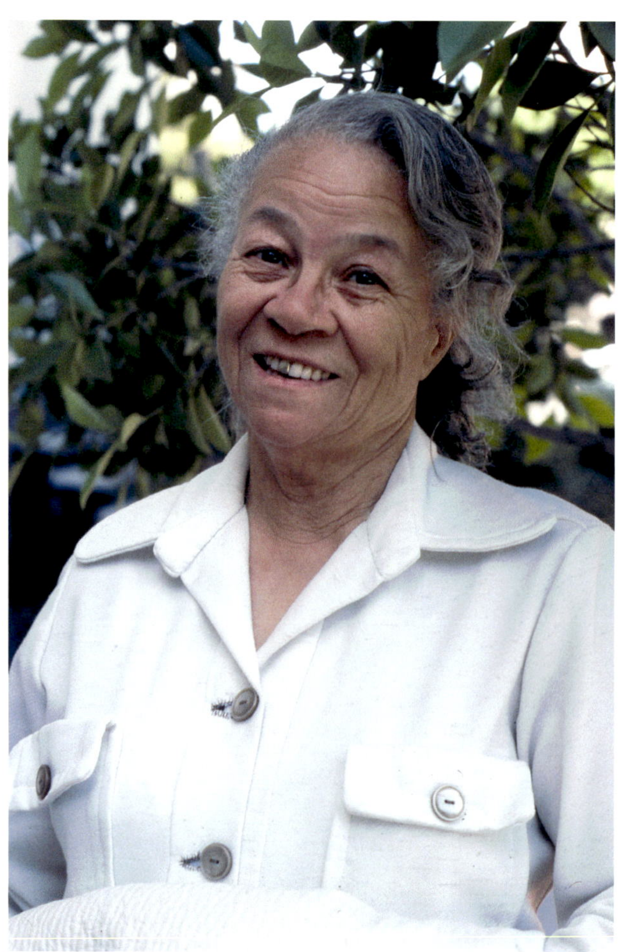

Bessie Moore, 1981

RUBY B. LEWIS

b. 1915, Wall Lake, Louisiana
d. 2006, El Sobrante, California

Ruby Lewis was born in the small town of Wall Lake, Ouachita Parish, Louisiana, to Willis Tucker and Josie Tucker. She learned to quilt at the young age of eight from her mother, grandmother, and other relatives. By 1950, she was living at 2411 Channing Way in West Berkeley with her husband, Wayland (who worked as a packer at the Naval Supply Depot), three children, sister, brother-in-law, nephew, and a lodger. She passed away in 2006. MVM, EY

ROSE McDOWELL

b. 1914, near Wilmington, North Carolina
d. 1998, Oakland, California

Rose McDowell belonged to a family of avid quilters that included her niece, Mable Everett, and her aunt, mother, and grandmother. Having lost her mother when she was two years old, she remembers being told that her mother and grandmother were both quilting by the age of seven; she cherished the quilts her mother had made. However, she did not start making quilts herself until she was an adult. Moving to Seaside, California, in 1950 and later settling in Oakland in 1960, MacDowell was mainly self-taught. She never belonged to a quilting group but occasionally took classes in East Oakland or at her church. She salvaged scraps of rayon or velvet from the faded window dressings of her husband's jewelry store, where he worked as a watchmaker. She would find a therapeutic calm in quilting and embraced unconventionality, arranging pieces on the floor and placing them backwards or upside down to make them fit. MVM

BESSIE MOORE

b. 1910, Cave Springs, Georgia
d. 1999, Corona, California

Bessie Ware (later Moore) was born to Luke Ware and Ada Braziel in Cave Springs, Georgia. After her father passed away, she moved around the northeastern part of the state, spending her childhood years in Rockmart. She learned quilting from her mother at around seven or eight years old and quilted alongside her sisters. Despite their poverty, she fondly recalls growing up in a loving family. She moved to California, where she would spend most of her life, first to Corcoran by 1947, then to Oakland in 1977, and later to Corona. She married twice and raised seven children. To help put them through school, she cleaned houses and worked in police stations while her husband worked hauling hay, ginning cotton, and also repairing TVs and radios.

While Bessie could piece without patterns (i.e., make "put togethers"), she more often quilted them and regularly made her own. Inspired by the natural life around her, she invented her own patterns from the leaves she found at her church, from an image of an olive vine on a box, or from a picture of a sunflower on the package of quilting cotton. She gave most of her quilts to friends, family, and especially her grandchildren: "I just think anybody that receives a quilt as a gift has really received something that they can cherish. Because a quilt is handmade . . . and it's so much time that has gone into 'em, and love, 'cause if you sit down and piece a quilt and then quilt it and give it to somebody, it's got to be because you think a lot of them."[13] **MVM**

SARAH MOORE

b. 1875, Caddo Parish, Louisiana
d. 1926, location unknown

Sarah Moore lived in Caddo and Jackson Parishes in northwestern Louisiana. By 1910, she and her husband, Lee Moore, lived in Boley, Oklahoma, with their four children. Boley was the largest and most renowned of Oklahoma's all-Black towns and was founded in 1903 by formerly enslaved people who decided to settle in the Indian Territory of the Creek Nation (land that would become part of the state of Oklahoma in 1907 and is within the present-day borders of the Muscogee [Creek] Nation). In this moment, when newly freed people could exercise self-determination, and in the context of their farming family, Sarah Moore passed quilting traditions across two generations including her daughter, Effie Edwards, and her granddaughter, Zula Mae Johnson. Moore's sister, Beulah Dye, was also a quilter. **EY**

EFFIE EDWARDS

b. 1895, Caddo Parish, Louisiana
d. 1969, Fresno County, California

The points along Effie Edwards's migration journey trace a life in pursuit of greater freedom. She was born Effie Moore in Caddo Parish, an area that ignominiously holds the record for the second highest number of reported lynchings in Louisiana.[14] By 1910, she had moved with her family to the all-Black town of Boley, Okfuskee County, Oklahoma, where she married Joseph "Levi" Edwards in 1914. For the next twenty years, they lived and worked on farms around Okfuskee and Blaine Counties, Oklahoma. Around 1942, Joseph headed towards Madera, California, to establish a livelihood before sending back for Effie and their children. By 1950, Effie worked as a housekeeper in Madera, where she is buried. **MVM, EY**

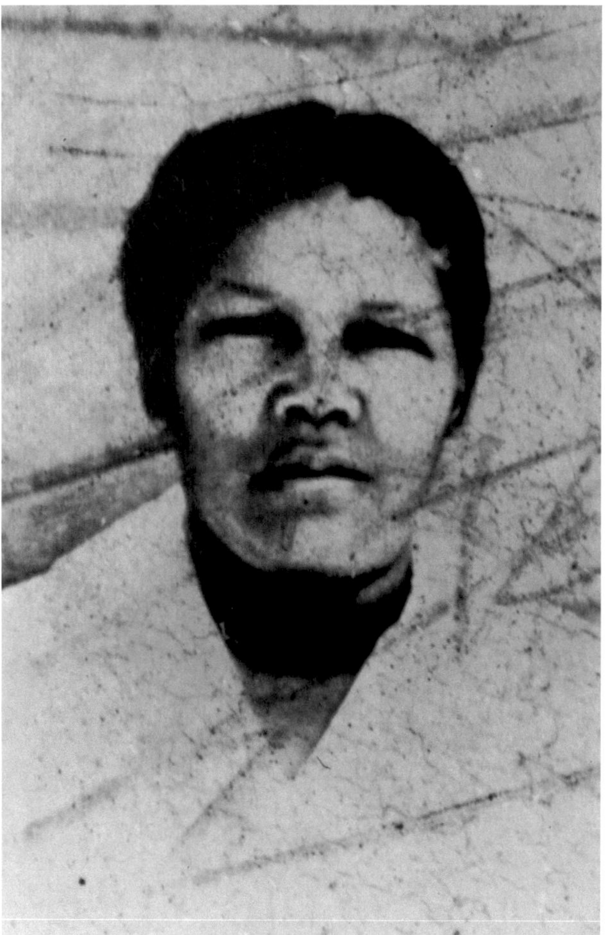

Effie Edwards, n.d.

ZULA MAE JOHNSON

b. 1925, Castle, Oklahoma
d. 2016, Richmond, California

Zula Mae Johnson was born Zula Edwards in Castle, Oklahoma, to Levi and Effie Edwards. At the age of three, her family moved to a farm in Watonga, Oklahoma, located roughly 140 miles west of Castle, near Oklahoma City. When she was seventeen, her father left for Madera, California, to work on a farm, with the rest of the family following him three months later. Johnson married Elijah Woodard in 1944 and later moved to Oakland and Los Angeles before returning to Madera. She married her second husband, Solomon Johnson, in 1954 and moved back to Oakland.

She learned to piece quilts as a young girl from her mother. She pieced her first quilt on paper at eight years old, progressing to a Nine Patch (what she called a "granny square") quilt

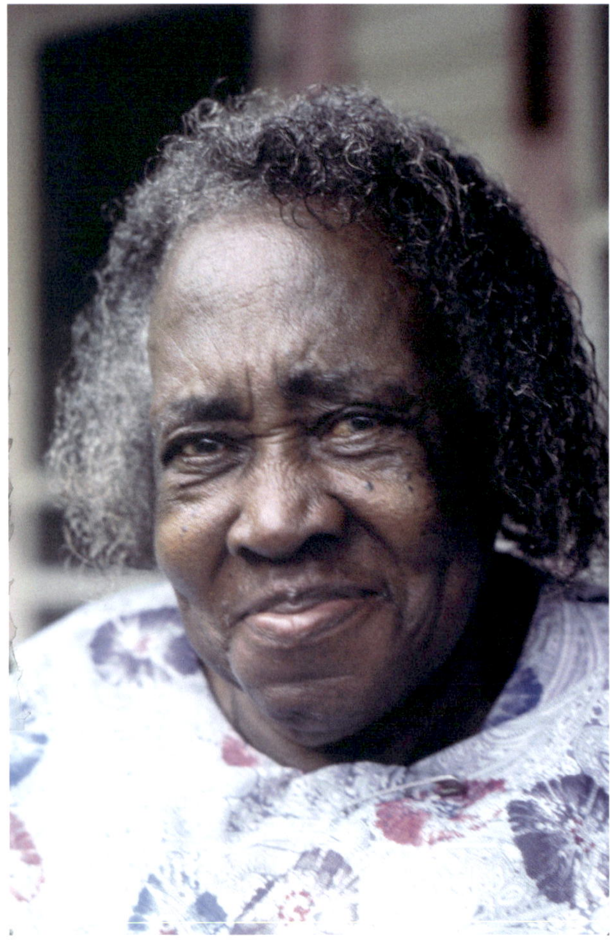

Elizabeth Munn, 1990

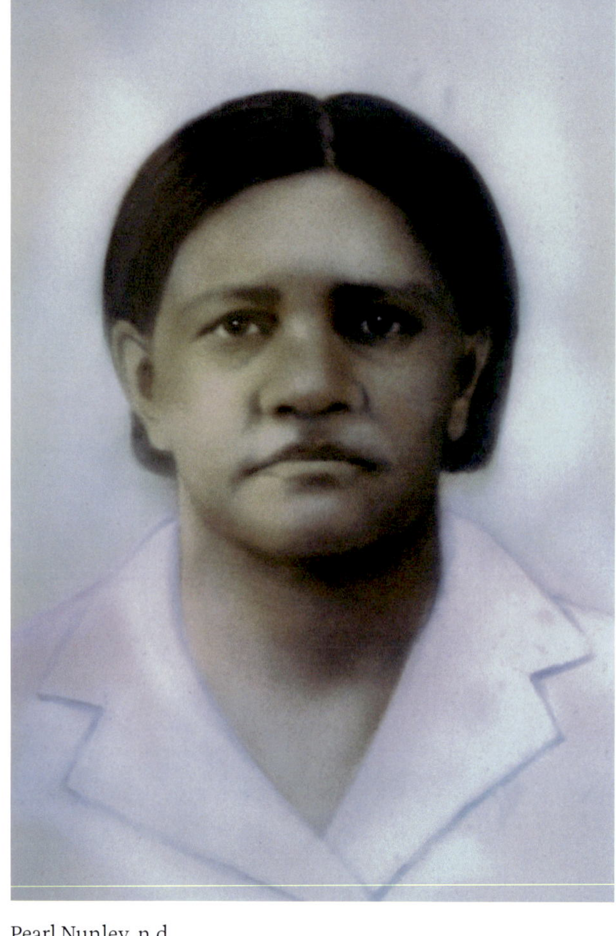

Pearl Nunley, n.d.

at the age of about ten or twelve. She quilted intermittently as a teenager but then returned to it more regularly after she had married and her kids had grown. She passed away in Richmond, California, where she rests in Rolling Hills Memorial Park. **MVM**

ELIZABETH MUNN

b. 1906, Hempstead County, Arkansas
d. 2000, Hempstead County, Arkansas

Born Elizabeth Stuart in 1906 in Hempstead County, Arkansas, Munn married William 'Willie' Munn in 1928 and raised seven children. She provided for her family by "contracting," where she and other workers would collectively harvest produce in agreement with a farm. She learned to quilt from her mother, first practicing by piecing string quilts on newspaper. She completed a whole quilt before the age of ten. As she developed her technique, she reused fabric so as not to waste any scraps. When Eli Leon interviewed her in 1990, she had sold nearly twenty-five quilts in a two-year period. She passed away in her hometown in 2000. **MVM**

ANNA NICHOLSON

b. 1902, Hinds County, Mississippi
d. 1969, Vallejo, California

Before moving to California sometime in the 1940s, Anna Nicholson (née Caldwell) had lived her entire life in Mississippi. Born in Hinds County, she had moved to Vicksburg in neighboring Warren County by the time her eldest son, Fudge, was born in 1918. By 1947, she and Fudge were living in Pittsburgh, California, with her husband, Lonnie; both her son and husband were employed at the Port Chicago Naval Magazine. Her youngest daughter, Rosalie, and Rosalie's husband, Thaddeus Brown (who rose to be San Francisco's Head Tax Auditor), lived across the Bay in what is known today as San Francisco's Visitación Valley neighborhood. A third child, Arthur, also moved to Oakland. Little is known about her background as a quiltmaker. **EY**

PEARL NUNLEY

b. 1888, Paraloma, Arkansas
d. 1952, Paraloma, Arkansas

According to the federal census of 1900, Pearl Nunley was the second eldest of six children born to Henry and Emma Graves.

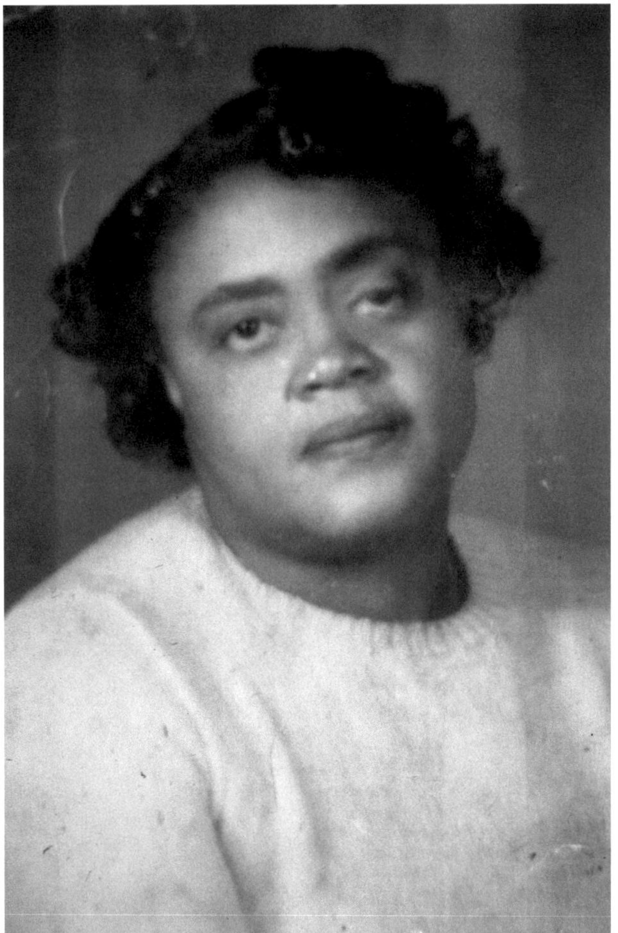

Beauty Vaughns, 1954

Arbie Major, 1950s

Her parents were born in 1862 and 1864, respectively, during the tumultuous years of the Civil War. During Reconstruction, the family remained in Sevier County, where they farmed land within a sharecropping system. Nunley and her husband, Alexander, were also farmers and raised four children: Henry, Anna, Earnestine (Beauty), and Arbie.

As a seamstress, Nunley could look at a pattern and cut it, recalled her daughters, Beauty Vaughns and Arbie Major. She insisted that any "mistakes" in piecing quilts should be undone and attempted again, in order for the pattern to look "right." EY

BEAUTY EARNESTINE VAUGHNS

b. 1911, Paraloma, Arkansas
d. 2005, Fresno, California

Beauty Earnestine Vaughns grew up working on the family ranch in Paraloma, Arkansas, picking and chopping cotton, among other crops. In 1950, she moved to Fresno, California, where she worked as a house cleaner and caregiver to the elderly while raising five children. She retired from wage labor in 1963, the same year she married her second husband, John H. Vaughns.

Vaughns learned how to sew and quilt from her mother, Pearl Nunley, at the age of seven, and she continued to quilt into adulthood. Preferring to piece according to patterns and from scraps–as her mother had taught her–Vaughns would turn to paper-piecing to use even the smallest of scraps. She sometimes sold her quilts to other working women who did not have the time or skill to make their own. EY

ARBIE MAJOR

b. 1915, Paraloma, Arkansas
d. 2013, Fresno, California

Arbie Major grew up in Paraloma, a community in the southwest part of Arkansas near Millwood Lake. After her mother, Pearl Nunley, passed away in 1952, she moved to Fresno, California. She lived for a period in Minnesota in the 1990s with her husband, Earsel Neal, before returning to Fresno, where her sister, Beauty Vaughns, also lived. Throughout her life, she performed domestic work.

She learned to quilt at the age of nine from her mother, who encouraged her to do "neat work." Like many quiltmakers, she first learned to piece using a Nine Patch pattern; by the age of sixteen, she was cutting and piecing quilts of her own. She continued to quilt throughout her life, preferring to work with patterns such as the Lily Pond and Lone Star. EY

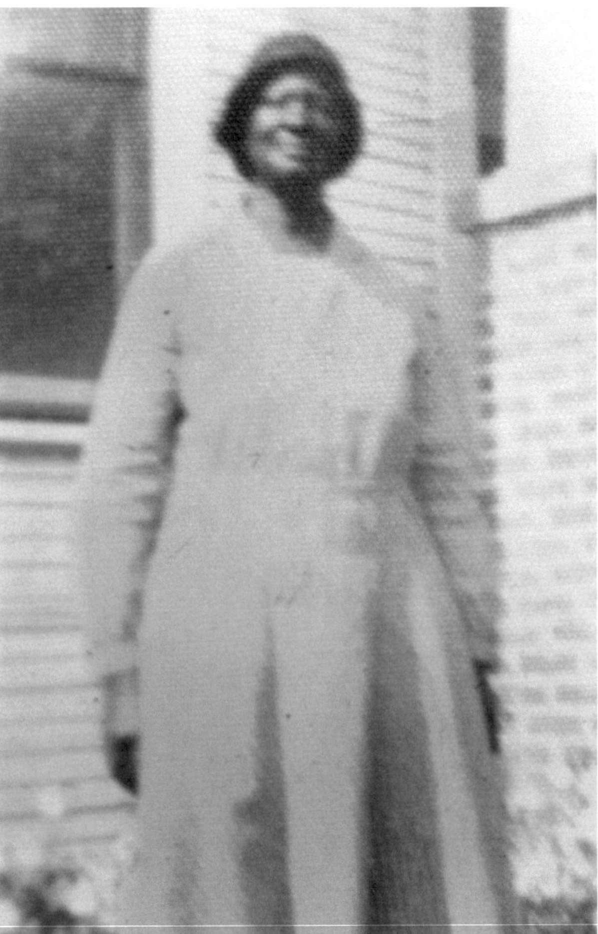

Chaney Ella Peace, 1930s

CHANEY ELLA PEACE
b. 1867, Louisiana
d. around 1965, Louisiana

Chaney Ella Peace lived most of her life near the community of Frierson in DeSoto Parish, Louisiana. She was a seamstress. Her parents, Ephraim and Susan Peace, were farmers who were born in South Carolina. She gave her niece, Lula Belle Zanders of Oakland, some of her tops before her death. EY

DOROTHY PERKINS
b. 1922, Nashville, Tennessee
d. 1995, Oakland, California

Dorothy Perkins learned to quilt from her grandmother, Tennessee Perkins, who used crossword puzzles as the basis for her patterns. While living in Oakland, she was a member of the Lighthouse Missionary Church of God in Christ located at 24th and Market Streets. EY

GRACIE PIGRUM
b. 1891, Leflore County, Mississippi
d. 1987, Darling, Mississippi

Gracie Pigrum (née Coleman) and her husband, Robert, were farmers in Quitman County, Mississippi. Their daughter, Mattie Lou Pigrum Taylor, moved to San Francisco and is buried in Cypress Lawn Memorial Park in Colma, California. EY

SUSAN PLESS
b. 1860s, location unknown
d. 1944, location unknown

Appearing in federal census records as "Pleiss", "Pliss," and "Pleos"–and described as both "mulatto" and "black"–Susan Pless (née Blackwell) lived most of her adult life on farms with her husband, Aaron Pless. In 1900, they were recorded as living in Tipton, Tennessee, with their six children. From 1910 onward, they were recorded as residing in east-central Oklahoma, first in Okfuskee County and then later in Red Fork, Tulsa County, by 1930. It is highly likely that they lived in or near Boley, one of Oklahoma's fifty historic all-Black towns, the place of residence listed on the marriage license of their daughter, Mary Jane Johnson (1890–1989). Johnson's daughter, Gracell Tate of Fresno, was the keeper of the quilt illustrated as cat. 23. EY

PEARLIE RAYFORD
b. around 1890, Arkansas
death date and location unknown

Pearlie Rayford lived in Cominto, Drew County, Arkansas, throughout the 1920s and 1930s, where federal census records for those decades indicate that she worked in farming and housekeeping as a "servant." She was 88 years old in 1979 and lived in Little Rock, Arkansas. EY

FRANCIS SHEPPARD
b. 1890, Coleman County, Texas
d. 1992, Las Vegas, Nevada

Francis Sheppard (née Burton) spent most of her life in Panola County, Texas, where she attended school and raised four children with her husband, Joe Sheppard. When she was about five or six years old, she first learned how to piece quilts from her mother, Ludy Parker, whom she recalled as being a great quilter. She pieced her first complete quilt at about age ten and would continue piecing during the summers when she did not have to complete household chores or pick and chop cotton. She found more time to piece after raising her family, including daughter Arbie Williams, and after the death of her husband. Initially, she made tops and quilts for her family; only later in life did she sell her quilts. EY

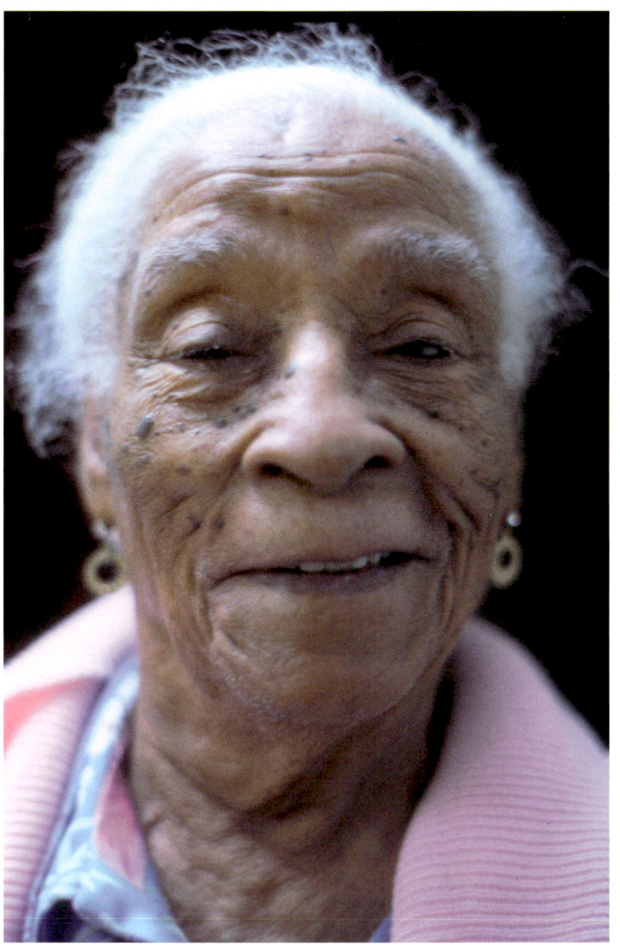

Francis Sheppard, 1987

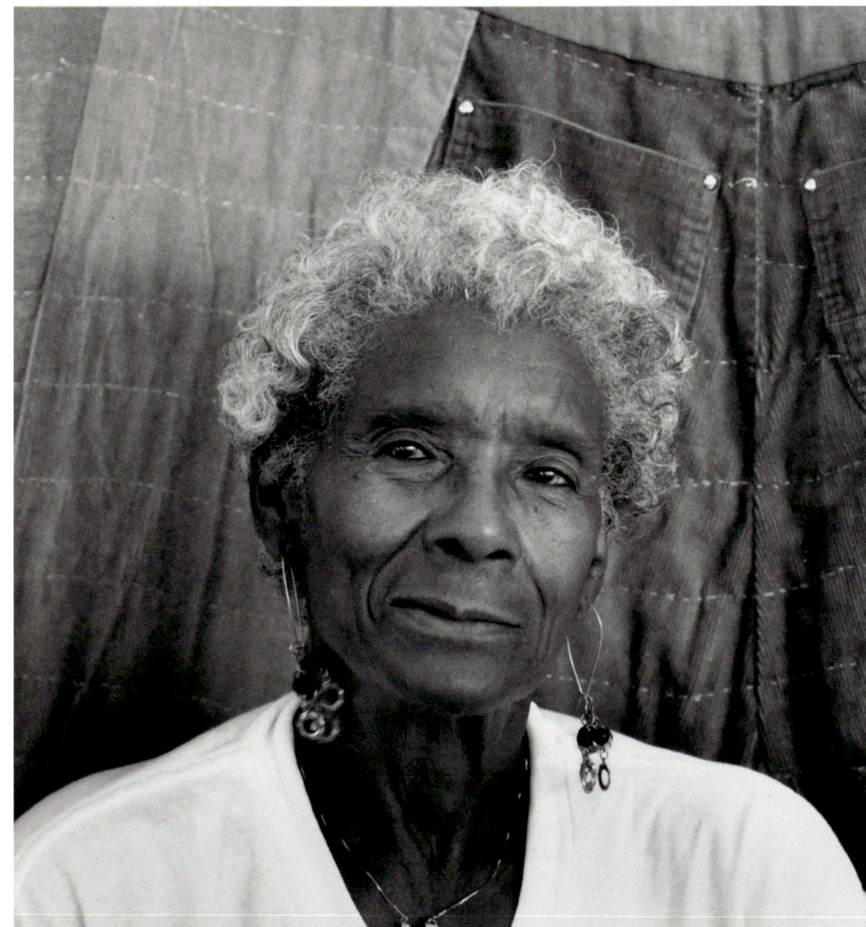

Arbie Williams, 1990s

ARBIE WILLIAMS

b. 1916, Perduca, Texas
d. 2003, Oakland, California

Arbie Williams learned to sew from her mother, Francis Sheppard, when she was eight years old and growing up on farms and ranches in Texas and Oklahoma. Between ten and twelve, she was piecing her own quilts, while continuing to perform her other chores and tasks for the family. As she recalled, "I could wash, I could cook, I could plow. I did anything the men's done and they never did say I was tired."[15] As a young woman living in a railroad worker's camp in Beckville, Texas, in the 1940s, she organized a small quilting group that made functional covers. Soon after, in 1945, she and her second husband, Johnnie Ramsey Williams, came to Oakland, California, for a second honeymoon. What began as a temporary visit became a permanent move. By 1950, Johnnie worked at the US Naval Supply Center while Arbie was raising their children, "keeping house," and working nights–a period that left little time for quilting.

Williams's return to quilting was prompted in the early 1980s, when she was a caregiver for Gussie Wells's ailing mother. To pass the time, Williams and Wells began making quilts side by side and often collaborating. Through Wells, she met Eli Leon. In addition to selling him her quilts, she was often commissioned by Leon to complete tops he collected that were made by others. While experienced in piecing traditional patterns, Williams is most celebrated for her britches quilts that retain the shape of the pants: "Bigger is better, it is, because you got a whole quilt together there without cutting it down."[16] In addition to being shown nationally in several of Leon's exhibitions, her work is in the collections of the Oakland Museum of California and the Fine Arts Museums of San Francisco. In 1991, she was named an NEA National Heritage Fellow along with Wells. Williams was a devout Christian and mother figure throughout her life. Her quilting legacy is carried on by her granddaughter Ophenia. EY

ANNIE MAE COOPER

b. 1919, Texas
d. 1996, Las Vegas, Nevada

Annie Mae Cooper was the second eldest daughter of Francis and Joe Sheppard. According to the federal census for 1950, she and her husband, Syble Collins, both worked at a basket factory in Panola, Texas. Towards the end of her life, she lived in Las Vegas, Nevada, with her mother. EY

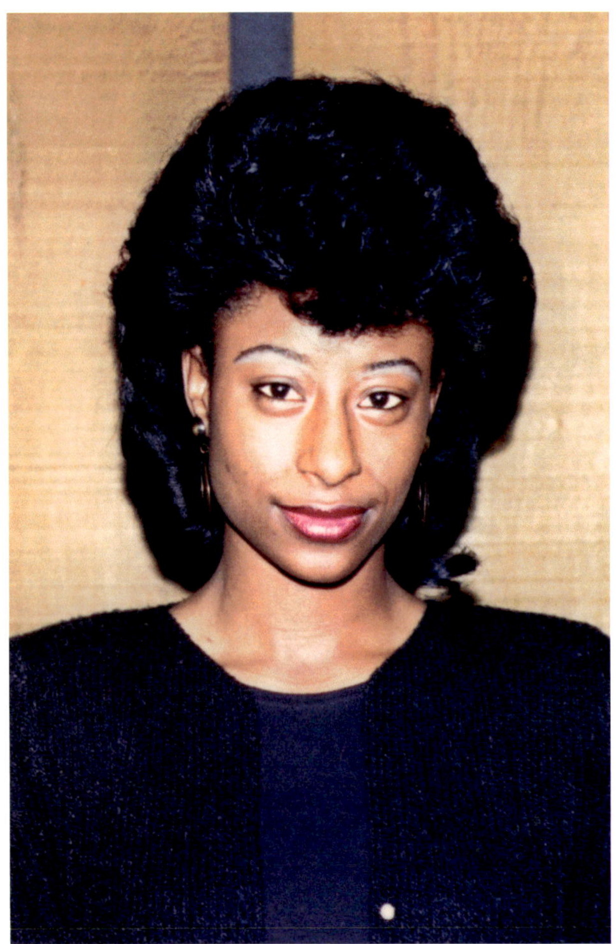

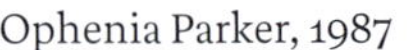

Ophenia Parker, 1987

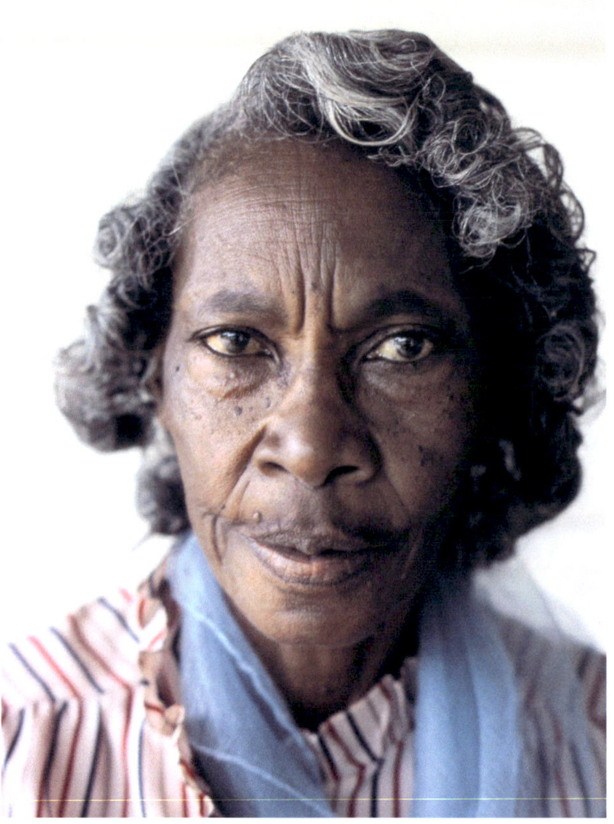

Minnie Skinner, 1992

OPHENIA R. PARKER

b. 1966, Oakland, California
lives in San Leandro, California

Ophenia Parker learned to quilt at the feet of her grandmother, Arbie Williams, great-grandmother, Francis Sheppard, and great-aunt, Annie Mae Cooper, as a little girl at 2546 14th Avenue in Oakland. Her first quilt was a one patch that she completed at the age of fifteen. While finishing school and working as a young adult, she did not have time to quilt. However, she returned to the art form in 1995, a time that coincided with an affirmation of her faith. What began as simply "something to do" has since become a practice that is deeply intertwined with the prayer and spiritual truth that has shaped her life. In addition to making quilts for sale, Parker is a writer whose first book, *The Courtship–Introduction*, published in 2023, carries a photo of one of her quilts. Her current and upcoming writing projects will also feature quilts as part of their stories and illustrations. **EY with Ophenia Parker**

MINNIE SKINNER

b. 1920, Houston County, Texas
d. 2003, Alto, Texas

A longtime resident of "The Flats" in Alto, Cherokee County, Texas, Minnie Skinner was born in 1920 to Lizzie and Felix Ross. She married William Skinner, who worked at a sawmill. She passed away in 2003 and is buried in St. Thomas Chapel AME Church Cemetery. **MVM**

BEATRICE SMITH

b. 1914, West Otis, Arkansas
d. 1996, Horatio, Arkansas

Beatrice Smith lived her entire life in Sevier County, Arkansas, near the Oklahoma state line. She grew up in a family of quiltmakers and she made her first quilt at the age of twelve. She worked as a housekeeper in private homes, while her husband, Curtis, whom she married in 1935, was a general laborer. **EY**

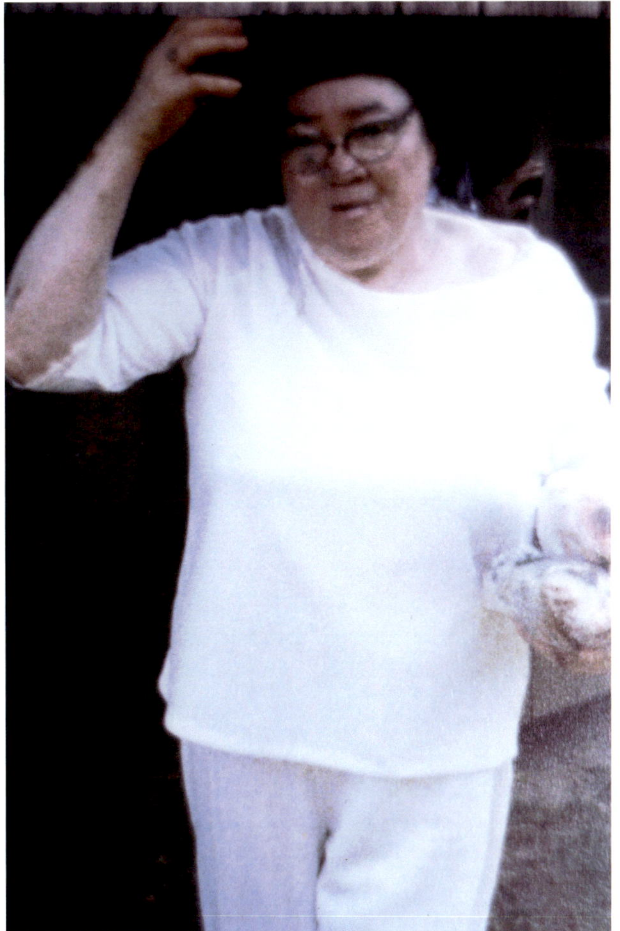

Beatrice Smith, 1985

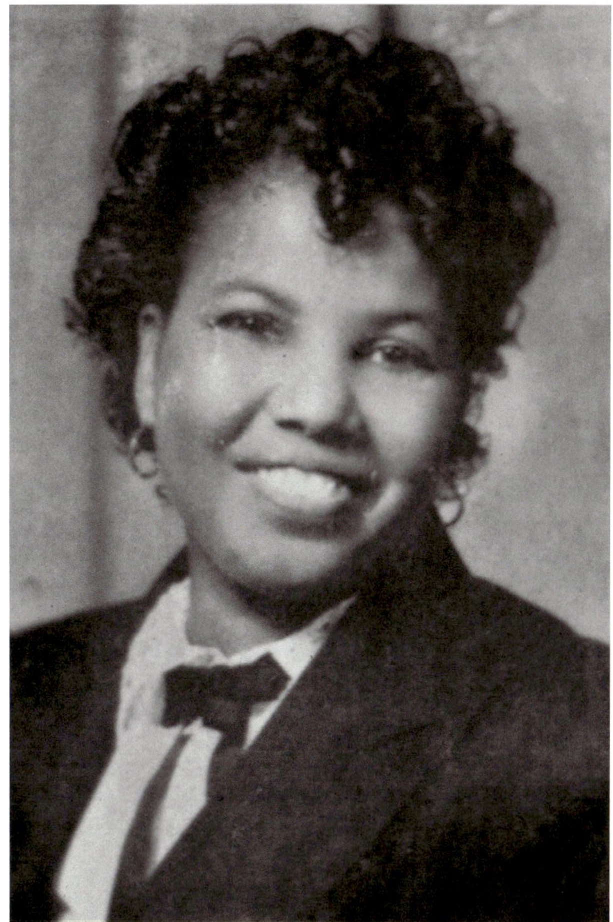

Jimmie Johnson, c. 1950s

EMMA SMITH

birth date and location unknown
death date and location unknown

Little information is available about Emma Smith, whose quilts were found in the unclaimed storage lot of her daughter, Dorothy Mae Jiles (b. 1919, Louisiana; d. 1987, San Francisco). It contained four completed quilts and thirteen quilt tops. EY

REBECCA SMITH

b. around 1864, Louisiana
d. 1956, Bastrop, Louisiana

One of four daughters of May and Lavina Williams, Rebecca Smith lived all her life in rural Louisiana, likely in the environs of Bastrop in Morehouse Parish in the northeastern part of the state. She and her husband, Raphael (sometimes listed as "Raife" or "Ralf" on census records), raised eight children, including Betty (later Betty Chafford). She passed away in her nineties. MVM

BETTY CHAFFORD

b. 1892, Bastrop, Louisiana
d. 1979, Contra Costa County, California

The eldest daughter and fourth of Rebecca and Ralf Smith's eight children, Betty Chafford lived in Morehouse Parish for nearly four decades. In the federal census of 1920, she and her husband, John Johnson, a farmer, had three sons named Almon ("Elmore" in subsequent census documents), Robert, and Roy. By 1940, she was living with Robert, Roy, and daughters Laura and Inez in Bastrop. She came to Oakland in 1941. By 1950, she was living at 663 32nd Street around the corner from Grove Street (now Martin Luther King Jr. Way) with her son Robert, who was a machine operator at the Moore Dry Dock, her daughter-in-law, Lula, and Robert's niece, Linda Barton. Chafford was known to have quilted with other family members. MVM

JIMMIE LUCILLE JOHNSON

b. 1914, Ouachita Parish, Louisiana
d. 1978, Oakland, California

Born in Ouachita, Louisiana, Jimmie Lucille Johnson was the fourth of seven children of Reverend James A. Chambers and

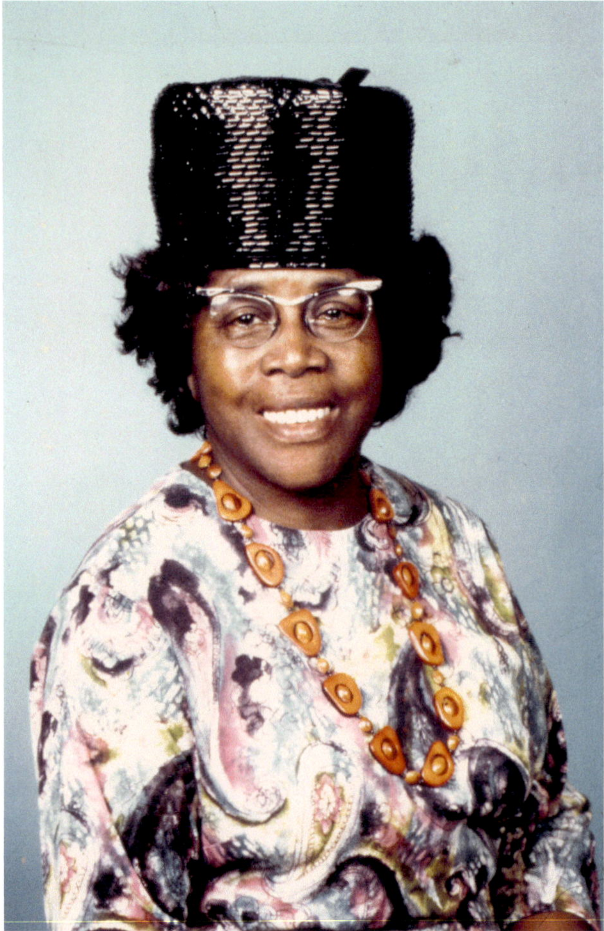

Eula Thomas, n.d.

Lenora Smith Chambers. In 1933, she married Elmore Johnson in Perryville, Louisiana; they had two children, Onzell Orell and Elmore Reginald. They relocated to Oakland, California, in 1942. Once there, Elmore worked at Moore Dry Dock and later for Lerner Steel Company until his 1973 retirement, while Jimmie cared for the home and family. She helped raise Laura Johnson (later Battise), Elmore's sister, along with their niece and goddaughter, Linda Barton White. Upon Elmore's death in 1988, his obituary offers warm insight into his and Jimmie's sense of hospitality that was anchored by their Christian faith: "The household headed by Brother Johnson was the gateway for many to a new life in California. Over the years, Brother Johnson extended his concern and home to many family members and friends as they sought shelter, a job and a new spiritual base in the area."[17] MVM, EY

LAURA JOHNSON BATTISE

b. 1924, Bastrop, Louisiana
d. 2016, Oakland or Richmond, California

Laura was born to John Johnson and Betty Smith in Bastrop, Louisiana, along with three older brothers. According to the federal census of 1930, she had moved with her mother and was living in an intergenerational household with a younger sister, Inez. As a teenager, she also lived with the family of her brother Elmore and his wife, Jimmie, also in Bastrop and including a young niece and nephew. They all moved to Oakland in 1942. By 1950, their household was at 597 30th Street and included Inez, Beverly S. Battise, aged four, and three boarders. Laura now appeared in the record as "Laura Battise," and her husband, Mitchell Battise, was recorded as being a welder (they would divorce in 1965). In the years immediately following the war, Laura was a machine operator in the upholstery industry. In her later years, she moved between Oakland and Vallejo. She passed away in 2016 at the age of ninety-two, leaving behind a large extended family in the East Bay. MVM, EY

QUINCIANA TATMON

b. 1893, Verdunville, Louisiana
d. 1995, Oakland, California

Born in Verdunville, Louisiana, to Winnie and William Rush, Quinciana Tatmon learned to quilt from her mother. In 1934, she traveled to California, where she would spend the rest of her life. According to a 1940 census, Quinciana lived in Oakland at 343 Center Street. She was married to Henry Tatmon, a railway worker, and raised her daughter, Annabelle Pace. MVM

EULA THOMAS

b. 1904, Oakland, Louisiana
d. 1982, San Leandro, California

Born to Ada Mae Harris and Charlie Wilson, a section hand for the local railroad, Eula and her four siblings (including a twin sister, Beulah) grew up in Bastrop, Louisiana. She married Commodore Thomas in 1934 in Ashley County, Arkansas. She moved to California around 1941 or 1942 and found work as a tailor at a men's clothing store near 9th and Broadway in Oakland. By 1943, she and her husband ran a clothing cleaning and pressing shop at 8th and Chester Streets, where she did alterations and tailoring. In addition to being an accomplished seamstress, she was an active member of the Rosette Civic and Social Club and was a teacher's assistant at an adult school in retirement. EY

MARY THOMPSON

b. 1908, North Little Rock, Arkansas
d. 2004, location unknown

Mary Thompson was born in North Little Rock, Arkansas, in 1908. She started to quilt at ten years old. Thompson supported her nine children as a domestic worker and moved to California in 1962. She and one of her daughters, Aurelia Foster, would often create quilts together. MVM

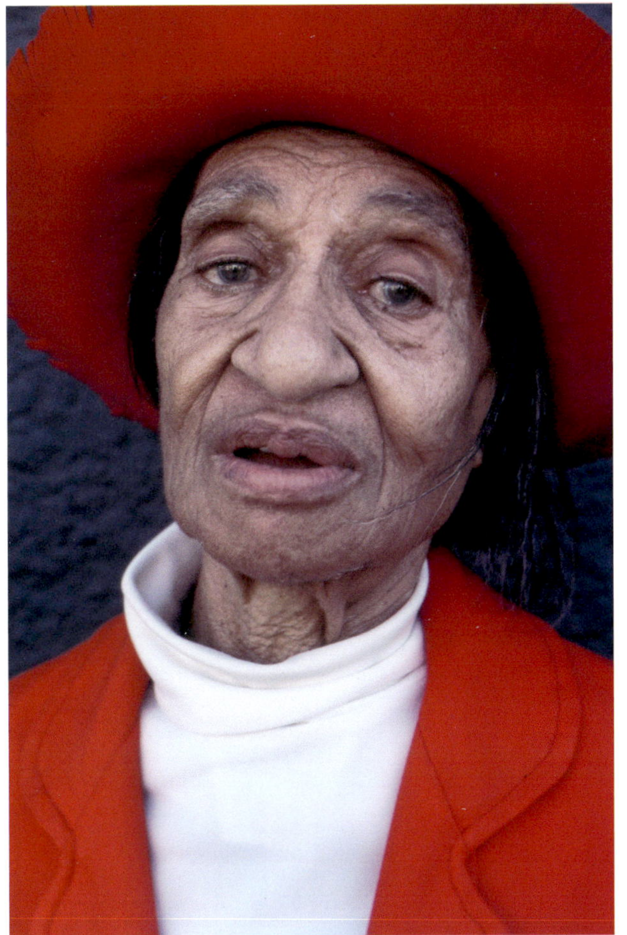

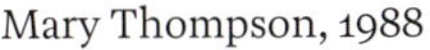

Mary Thompson, 1988

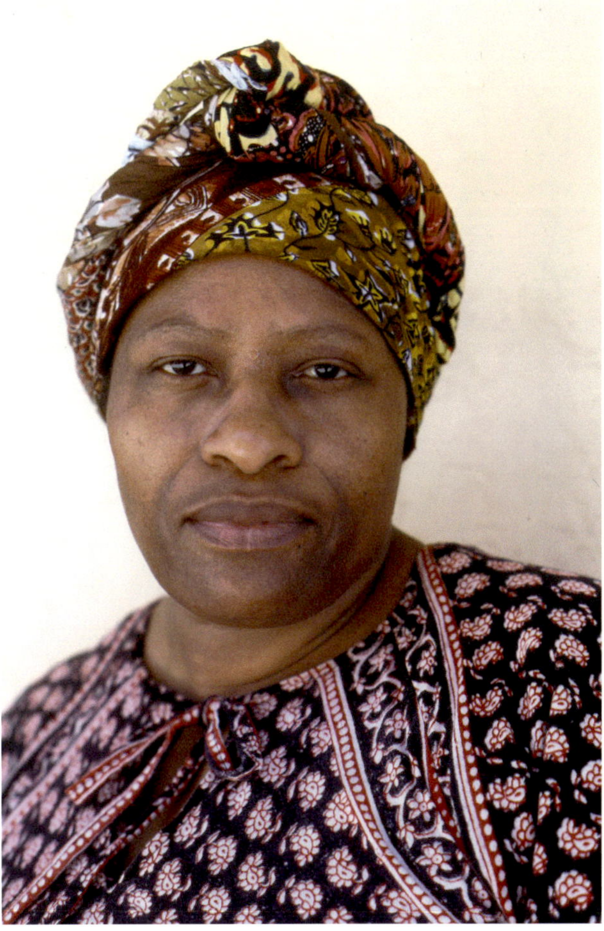

Rosie Lee Tompkins, 1997

AURELIA FOSTER

b. around 1927, location unknown
if deceased, death date and location unknown

Aurelia Foster was born in 1927 to Mary Thompson. She lived in the bustling Lower Haight neighorhood on Hayes Street in San Francisco between 1999 and 2002. MVM

ROSIE LEE TOMPKINS

b. 1936, Gould, Arkansas
d. 2006, Richmond, California

Rosie Lee Tompkins (a pseudonym adopted by Effie Mae Howard) was born in Lincoln County, Arkansas, to Sadie Bell and MacCurey Martin. The oldest of fifteen half-siblings, she grew up working within the sharecropping system, farming cotton. In 1958, she arrived in the Bay Area, where she took adult classes and worked as a practical nurse in convalescent homes. She married twice and raised five children and stepchildren in Richmond, California, and was an active member of the Beacon Light Seventh-Day Adventist Church.

Tompkins learned to quilt from her mother and other relatives, although she did not take it on as a serious pursuit until her adulthood in the 1970s. She made crazy quilts and pillows, selling them at local flea markets in Oakland, Marin City, Danville, and other locations. Preferring to work improvisationally and with repurposed materials, she also sought out lush fabrics such as velvet and beaded embellishments. Her deep spirituality is especially central to her later works, in which embroidered Christian scriptures and personal references serve as markers of her meditative process. Bolstered by Eli Leon's patronage and exhibitions—the two met around 1985—Tompkins has become an acclaimed artist, celebrated for her category-defying practice. The Berkeley Art Museum and Pacific Film Archive organized her retrospective in 2020. EY

JANE TRAYLOR

b. 1847, Louisiana
d. 1923, near Dean, Louisiana

Jane Traylor lived most of her life in Litroe and its surroundings, an area of Union Parish, Louisiana, bordered by the state line with Arkansas to the north and the Ouachita River to the east. According to her granddaughter, Alice Neal, Traylor was part Cherokee and part French by descent, despite being

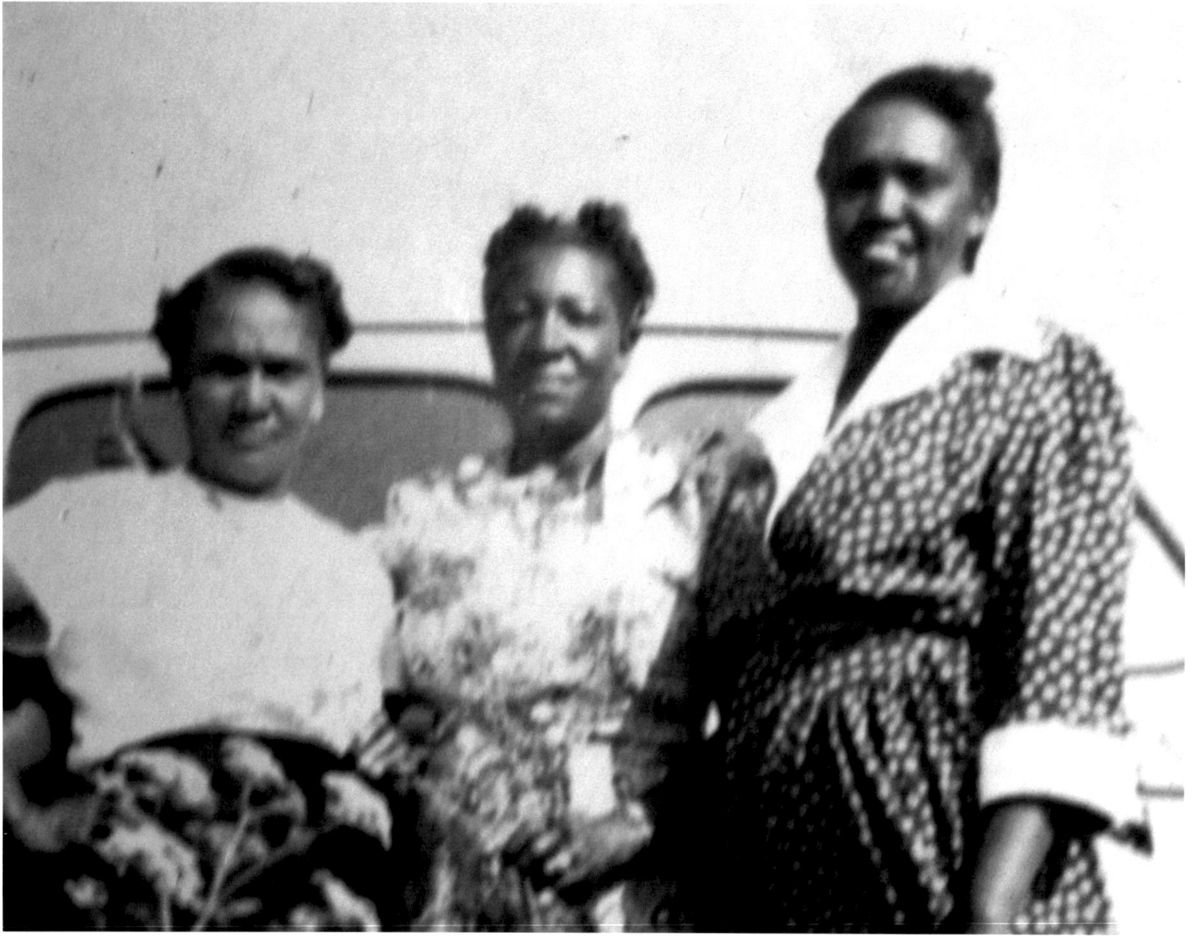

Alice Neal (right) with cousins, n.d.

recorded as "Black" on the federal census of 1880, along with her husband, Tyler Traylor (c. 1830–1920), who was a farmer. She learned to quilt, embroider, and make lace while enslaved. Due to her excellent sewing skills, she was put in charge of other women on the plantation. She eventually taught her daughter Mary (and likely her other four daughters) these same techniques. EY

ALICE NEAL

b. 1916, Marion, Louisiana
d. 1985, Oakland, California

Alice Neal was born in Marion, Union Parish, in northern Louisiana as one of eleven children of Don and Mary Bright. Her father was a farmer. Prior to getting married, her mother was a teacher, who, as Neal recalled, was not paid in wages but in "potatoes and peanuts." Neal was also a teacher, working with fifth and sixth graders in nearby Farmersville before arriving in California sometime in 1943 or 1944. She married Richard Neal, who worked as a "track man" at the Naval Supply Center while she worked at their grocery store at Athens Avenue in West Oakland.

Neal learned to quilt from her mother as early as she could "hold a needle," learning from patterns belonging to Bright and, later, from patterns she would order. She began quilting more regularly after getting married, when she realized that she had more time on her hands while working at the store. Her fine needlework can be attributed to her training from Bright, who Neal recalled was a "perfectionist" and who sometimes shortened her daughter's stitches that she deemed too long. Although several quilts survive in her extended family, Neal was the only one among her siblings to continue the tradition of quiltmaking. EY

SARAH T. TURNAGE

b. 1900, Mississippi
d. 1976, San Francisco, California

Born November 25, 1900, Sarah T. Turnage was married to Alonzo Turnage. Together they lived in Fair River, Lincoln County, Mississippi, as farmers. By 1940, Turnage was widowed and living with her son, Earl Archie, his wife, Helen, and their son, Lonnie, in Rankin County. By 1950, the family had divided, likely to seek better opportunities: Earl and Helen were living in Toledo, Ohio, where he was working as a janitor, while Turnage and Lonnie remained in Mississippi. The two

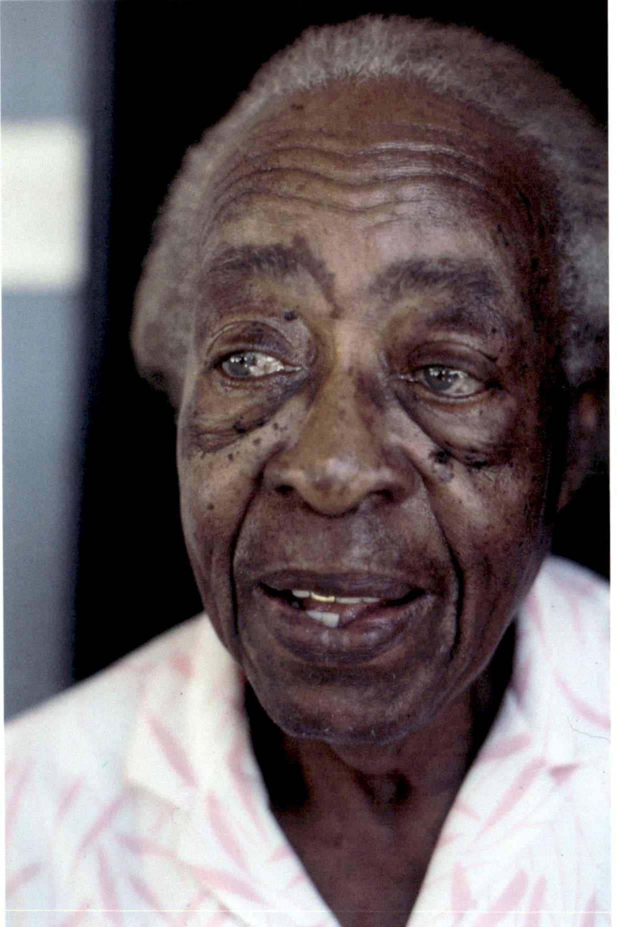

Venella Tyler, 1991

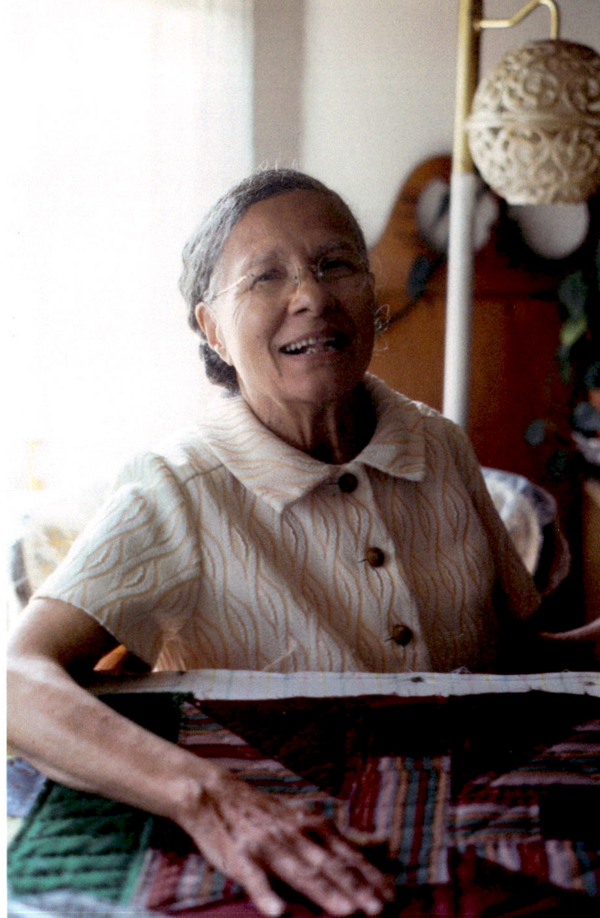

Johnnie Wade, 1988

eventually moved to San Francisco, probably after Lonnie's service in the Korean War. Known affectionately as "Mother T," Turnage was remembered fondly by her friend Julia Commer, a neighbor in San Francisco. EY

VENELLA TYLER

b. 1907, Calhoun City, Mississippi
d. 1996, Fresno, California

Born Venella Russell in Calhoun City, Mississippi, Tyler grew up in the countryside with her family, where quilting was a common activity. The quilters in her family often used fabric scraps from homemade clothing for their intricate quilts. She learned quilting from her mother at around eight years old, completing her first diamond-patterned quilt at age twelve. "She really learned that I was a designer too, because sometimes if I didn't see a pattern, I could, you know, make it up, figure it out in my mind, and I make the pattern."[18]

Married at eighteen to Arthur Tyler, she moved to Greenwood, Mississippi. There she sewed for others, bought fabrics, and raised three children while working as a midwife and nurse. She shared her experiences in interviews with Eli Leon, recounting walking long distances to aid patients and generously giving quilts to those in need or suffering tragic events like house fires.[19] During the 1920s she taught quilting to young girls in Mississippi and cherished the memory of her mother's influence in naming quilts after desired qualities. Tyler preferred using whole pieces of fabric to create quilts with precisely matching shapes and fondly recalled her mother's contrasting use of light and dark fabrics.[20] MVM

JOHNNIE ALBERTA WADE

b. 1908, Esperanza, Texas
d. 2015, Oakland, California

Born in the Mount Zion community near Esperanza, Montgomery County, Texas, Johnnie Wade (née Nelson) moved to Conroe, about forty miles north of Houston, at the age of seventeen. In 1944, she moved from Galveston to Oakland, where she lived the remainder of her life.

Wade learned to piece quilts from her mother, Sarah Nelson, as a young girl around seven or eight years old. However, she never learned to quilt until 1987, when she met Willia Ette Graham, who taught her around Graham's quilting frame.

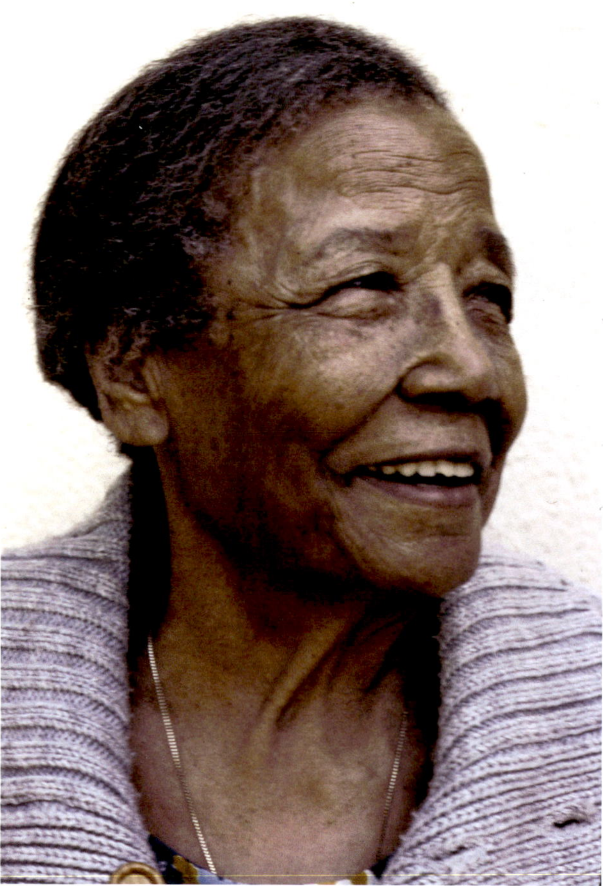

Gussie Wells, 1988

Encouraged by Eli Leon's interest in collecting quilts by African American artists, Wade quilted over one hundred quilts with Graham, her friend and mentor. EY

MAUDRA WALKER

b. 1898, Texas
d. 1979, San Mateo, California

Born at the turn of the twentieth century in Texas, Maudra Walker was living in San Mateo, California, by 1951. She spent the remainder of her life there. MVM

NAOMI WALKER

b. around 1911, Texas
death date and location unknown

Naomi Walker lived in Berwyn, Carter County, Oklahoma, a small farming community that was renamed Gene Autry in 1941, after the cowboy film actor purchased a nearby ranch. She cared for the home with her husband, Joe Walker–who appears in the federal census as a farmer, sawmill worker, and cotton ginner–and their four children. MVM

JOE WASHINGTON

b. around 1879, location unknown
d. around 1963, Wood County, Texas

Joe Washington's daughter-in-law, Ruby Richard, inherited some of his quilts when he came to live with her in the Fouke community near Hawkins, Texas. Corn and cotton were the main crops grown in this agricultural region located in Wood County, Texas. EY

GUSSIE WELLS

b. 1901, Princeton, Louisiana
d. 1994, Oakland, California

Gussie Wells was born to Robert Ely and Georgia Dixon in Princeton, Louisiana, a community near Shreveport. She lived in Galveston, Texas, in 1927, and later in New York City, where she worked various jobs in sawmills, hotels, and private homes. She stayed in New York until 1945 before moving to San Francisco, where she married Preston Wells around 1946 or 1947. While living in San Francisco, she worked in a bag factory, eventually saving enough to buy a house. In 1948, she traveled to Santa Rosa with her husband and daughter, Mattie Lee Davis (1916–1990), and bought a forty-acre ranch. According to the 1950 federal census, Wells was aged forty-eight and lived in Healdsburg in Sonoma County, California. The family sold the ranch a few years later and returned to San Francisco, where they ran a restaurant and housed tenants. In 1967 Gussie moved to Merced. In 1977 she moved to Oakland, where she retired and spent the remainder of her days.

Wells learned to quilt from her mother and grandmother by the age of ten. She took up quilting again with greater interest after befriending Arbie Williams, who was caring for Wells's mother. Wells was named a National Heritage Fellow in 1991, along with Williams, who was her frequent collaborator. MVM

ISIADORE WHITEHEAD

b. 1914, Magnolia, Arkansas
d. 2005, Oakland, California

Born in Columbia County in southwestern Arkansas, Isiadore Whitehead spent her young adult years in Monroe, Louisiana, where she married before moving to the Bay Area in 1942 with her two children (her mother arrived two years later). Whitehead was a certified welder in the Richmond shipyards. She studied at Laney and Merritt Colleges, receiving a nursing credential in 1967; she was also a school bus driver until her retirement in 1972. A devout Christian, Whitehead was baptized in the Jordan River and served as a deaconess at Oakland's Allen Temple Baptist Church.

Whitehead learned to quilt around the age of nine from her mother, grandmother, and other neighbors, all of whom were accomplished needlewomen. White continued to make

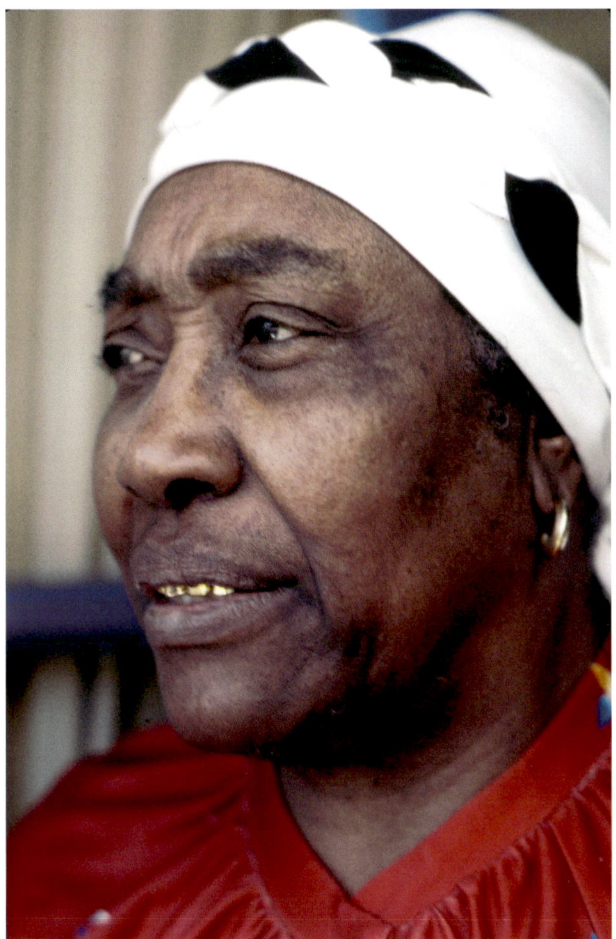

Isiadore Whitehead, 1984

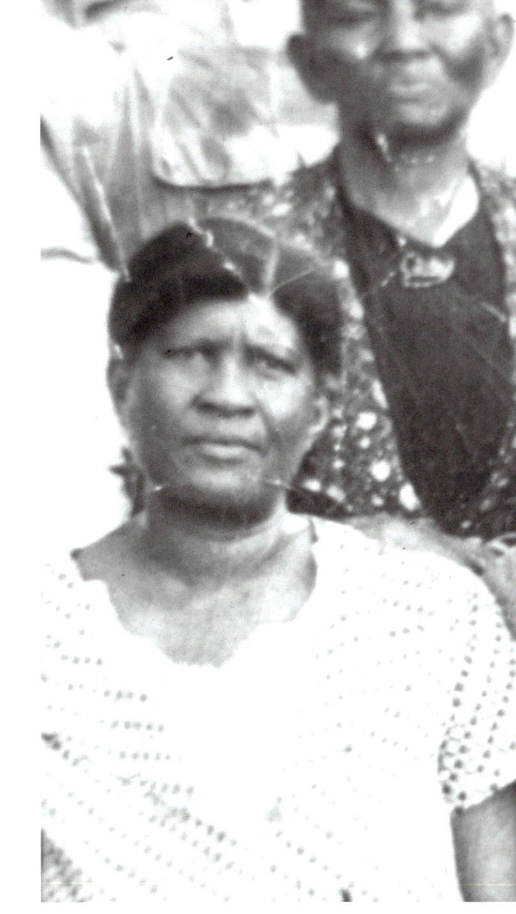

Warren Wise with his wife Bobbie, early 1930s

quilts as an adult, primarily for herself rather than for sale, favoring the use of patterns and repurposing of fabrics. In the mid-1980s, she channeled her creative and humanitarian energies into making one hundred quilts for an impoverished community in Ethiopia. "I don't want any money and I'm poor," she once explained, "but I have always given help to people who are suffering."[21] EY

BIDDIE M. WILSON

b. 1918, Waldo, Arkansas
d. 2000, Oakland, California

Biddie Wilson (née Porter) was born in Waldo, Arkansas, where her family members were farmers. Both her grandmother, Betty Smith, and her mother, Willie Smith, were quilters. Wilson started quilting at the age of ten by watching her mother. Though she preferred to make dresses, she made a number of quilts, enjoying the mixing of a variety of vibrant colors and engineering her own methodical patterns. She worked various jobs to support her family. She traveled to Oakland in the 1940s during World War II and lived in California for the rest of her life. MVM

WARREN WISE

b. 1889, Homer, Louisiana
d. 1960, Nevada County, Arkansas

Born in Homer, Louisiana, Warren Wise lived nearly all his life in the environs of southwestern Arkansas between Prescott in Nevada County and Wallaceburg in Hempstead County. He moved to Prescott when he was about nine years old. As an adult, he worked as a farmer and a carpenter and quilted in his spare time. He learned quilting from his mother and grandmother. His daughter, Lee Ester Townsend, remembers him cutting and piecing quilt tops. His work has been featured in the 1998 exhibition *Man Made: African-American Men and Quilting Traditions* held at the Smithsonian Institution's Anacostia Community Museum in Washington, DC, and curated by Gladys-Marie Fry, one of the first exhibitions to acknowledge the participation of men in quilting. MVM

MAKER ONCE KNOWN/UNIDENTIFIED ARTIST

More commonly referred to as "anonymous" or "unidentified artist," the unknown identity of a given quiltmaker remains so for any number of reasons. Part of the answer lies in the genre itself. For the most functional of patchwork quilts, makers would have had little reason to inscribe their names when everyday use, mending, and disrepair were accepted and expected aspects of their life cycles. Attributions could be verbally communicated among kin and community, as quilts circulated mainly within private homes, regardless of whether a quiltmaker's name was recorded.[22] Other reasons can account for the dearth of records for quilts. Oral histories may fail to be passed down, for example. Quilts' historical devaluation as "women's work" within Western fine art hierarchies has also resulted in a broad disregard for the medium until recent decades, engendering a situation where details about a quilt's creation are less likely to survive.

"Anonymous" in the context of African American quilt history is more often a name suppressed or unattested rather than withheld by the quiltmaker's choice. For much of the nineteenth century in the United States, anti-literacy laws directed toward the enslaved were a primary mechanism of suppression; when names do appear in the historical archive, they often represent Christianized or classical names assigned by white enslavers. Moreover, even with incremental civil rights progress made during the twentieth century, economic precarity and inequities are legacies of enslavement that have made Black people's connections with their belongings especially vulnerable to loss and separation. In other situations, quilts appearing at auction, flea markets, thrift stores, or curbsides are commonly the result of an owner dying or being pressed to discard it. With a quilt's value diminished (for that person or their family), thus begins the gradual uncoupling of the quilt from its story.

However, even without a name, signature, diary entry, or oral history attached to a quilt, we are not at a complete loss. Digitized genealogical records make familial and cultural information more accessible than ever before. The quilt and its provenance can yield clues and prompts for asking about a quilter's skill, aesthetic sensibilities, or intentions (cats. 8, 21, and 36). And in the end, one can still honor an absent name as someone known to themselves. A quilt left behind is, among other things, a material connection and testament to a quiltmaker's life. EY

Opposite: Detail of cat. 21

Notes

1. "Mrs. Cora Lee Hall Brown, 'Sister,' September 25, 1900–July 18, 1981" (unpublished personal remembrance, September 25, 2020), PDF file in the author's possession.
2. Irene Bankhead, interview by Eli Leon, 1984, African-American Quilt Maker Interviews, BAMPFA, CD004, 4/84 to 5/84, side B, track 3.
3. Lily Chiles, interview by Eli Leon, 1990, African-American Quilt Maker Interviews, BAMPFA, CD083, 12/87 to 2/88, side B, track 8.
4. Eli Leon, *Accidentally on Purpose: The Aesthetic Management of Irregularities in African Textiles and African-American Quilts* (Davenport, IA: Figge Art Museum, 2006), 89.
5. Leon, *Accidentally on Purpose*, 89.
6. Leon, *Accidentally on Purpose*, 88.
7. Selena Foster, interview by Judith K. Dunning, "A Longtime Richmond Resident from Cherokee County, Texas," On the Waterfront: An Oral History of Richmond, California (Berkeley: Regional Oral History Office, the Bancroft Library, University of California, 1992), 61.
8. Richard Spencer, "Quilt Display Weaves Colorful History of Richmond," *The Tribune,* May 7, 1986.
9. *The Tribune*, May 7, 1986.
10. Mable Battle, interview by Eli Leon, 1994–95, African-American Quilt Maker Interviews, BAMPFA, CD175, 10/94 to 10/95, side A, track 4.
11. Eli Leon, "But Now I See: African-American Quilt Revelations" (unpublished essay, January 5, 2006), Bequest of The Eli Leon Living Trust, BAMPFA, 11.
12. Leon, *Accidentally on Purpose*, 152.
13. Bessie Moore, interview by Eli Leon, 1987–1988, African-American Quilt Maker Interviews, BAMPFA, CD82, 12/87 to 2/88, side A, track 10.
14. "Explore the Map," *Lynching In America–Equal Justice Initiative*, https://lynchinginamerica.eji.org/explore/louisiana.
15. Arbie Williams, StoryCommons, https://storycommons.org/archives/arbie-williams/.
16. Arbie Williams, StoryCommons, https://storycommons.org/archives/arbie-williams/.
17. "A Celebration of Life for Brother Elmore Johnson," memorial program, January 8, 1988, Eli Leon Archives, BAMPFA.
18. Venella Tyler, interview by Eli Leon, 1991, African-American Quilt Maker Interviews, BAMPFA, CD152, 2/91 to 6/91, side B, track 5.
19. Tyler, interview by Eli Leon, 1991, CD152, 2/91 to 6/91, side B, track 8.
20. Tyler, interview by Eli Leon, 1991, CD152, 2/91 to 6/91, side B, track 10.
21. Loretta Green, "A Woman Blankets Ethiopia," [*Peninsula*?] *Times Tribune*, undated newspaper clipping, Eli Leon Archives, BAMPFA.
22. Prior to the mid-nineteenth century, names or initials could appear on quilts along with inventory numbers and dates for the practical purposes of managing household property and dower rights. Quilts made for more formal occasions or presentations, such as a wedding, fundraiser, or exhibition in a public arena (like a county fair), might also call for inscriptions or special dedications. In these contexts, signatures can refer not only to the quiltmaker, but also to supporters of a cause, members of a community, and other contributors to the making of a quilt. These varied social contexts invoked through names on a quilt contrast with the model of singular artistic genius that has long been prized within Western art. I am grateful to Julie Silber for her insights on this section and other thoughtful comments on this entry.

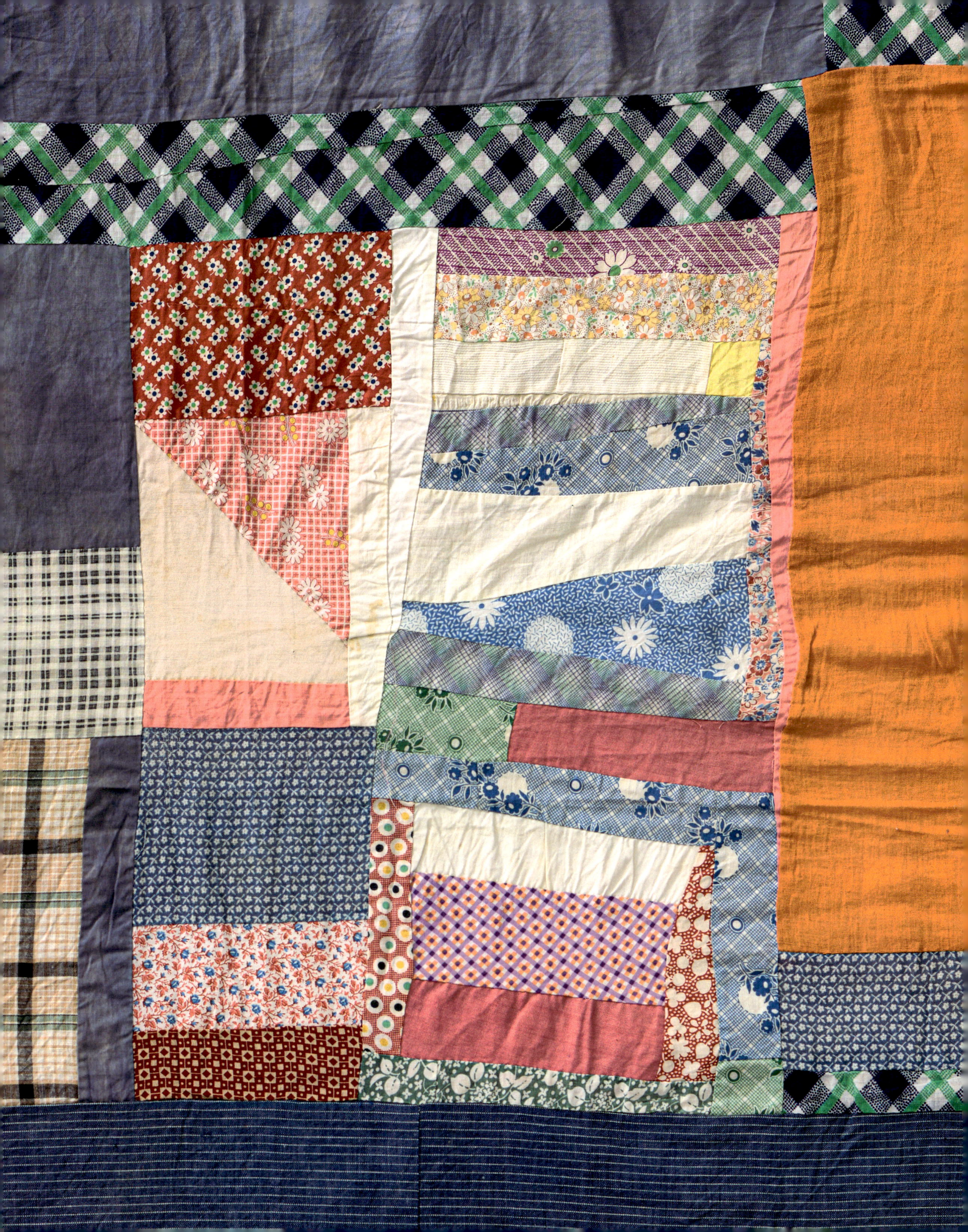

Exhibition Checklist

The objects listed below appear alphabetically by artist name. For quilts made by more than one person, the individual with the earliest contribution is listed first. Circa ("c.") is used when a probable date of construction is known; date ranges are given as estimates based on a combination of fabric dating and available information about the quiltmaker(s). Dimensions are given as length followed by width. All artworks are from the bequest of the Eli Leon Living Trust, University of California, Berkeley Art Museum and Pacific Film Archive, unless otherwise noted.

Rachel Adkins
Pieced c. 1970; Houston, Texas

Margaret Gillam
Quilted c. 1970; Berkeley, California

Esther Foss
Repaired 1990; Oakland, California

Untitled (Log Cabin, Courthouse Steps variation)
Cotton flannel, cotton feedsack, linen; hand pieced, hand quilted
81 × 75 in. (205.7 × 190.5 cm)
OBJ0491
Cat. 44

Lucinda Ballenger
c. 1900; Henderson, Texas

Untitled (Six Point Star variation)
Cotton; hand pieced, appliqué
76 × 71 in. (193.0 × 180.3 cm)
OBJ0363
Cat. 1

Irene Bankhead

Untitled (Half-Square Triangles)
1984; Oakland, California
Cotton/polyester blend, polyester; hand pieced, hand quilted
87 × 85 in. (221.0 × 215.9 cm)
OBJ0251
Cat. 66

Untitled (One Patch)
1996; Oakland, California
Cotton/polyester blend, rayon, polyester; hand and machine pieced, hand quilted
95 × 87 in. (241.3 × 221.0 cm)
OBJ2175
Cat. 107

Untitled (Bars)
2001; Oakland, California
Cotton, cotton/polyester blend; machine pieced, hand quilted
96 × 85 in. (243.8 × 215.9 cm)
OBJ2384
Cat. 111

Mable Battle
Pieced 1978–1979; Richmond, California

Selena Foster
Quilted 2004; Richmond, California

Untitled (Medallion)
Cotton, denim, polyester; machine pieced, hand quilted
78 × 84 in. (198.1 × 213.4 cm)
OBJ2488
Cat. 56

Mable Battle
Pieced 1995; Richmond, California

Willia Ette Graham
Johnnie Wade
Quilted 1995; Oakland, California

Post Oak Grapevine (Square in a Square, Nine Patch)
Cotton, cotton/polyester blend; machine pieced, appliqué, hand quilted
116 × 75 in. (294.6 × 190.5 cm)
OBJ2078
Cat. 105

Mable Battle
1997; Richmond, California

Untitled (T-shirt quilt)
Cotton, cotton/polyester blend; hand and machine pieced, hand quilted
96 × 65 in. (243.8 × 165.1 cm)
OBJ2266
Cat. 109

Laverne Brackens
Pieced 1990–1991; Fairfield, Texas

Willia Ette Graham
Johnnie Wade
Quilted 1992; Oakland, California

Untitled (Bars)
Cotton, cotton/polyester blend, polyester, velvet, other synthetic fabrics; hand and machine pieced, hand quilted
85 × 80 in. (216.0 × 203.2 cm)
OBJ3484
Cat. 91

Laverne Brackens
Pieced 1994; Fairfield, Texas

Willia Ette Graham
Johnnie Wade
Quilted 1994; Oakland, California

Untitled (Star put-together)
Cotton, cotton/polyester blend, polyester, rayon; hand pieced, hand quilted
76½ × 70 in. (194.3 × 177.8 cm)
OBJ2050
Cat. 104

Cora Lee Hall Brown
c. 1970; Mount Enterprise, Texas

Untitled (String Medallion with newspaper backing)
Cotton, cotton/polyester blends, newspaper; machine pieced
83 × 73 in. (210.8 × 185.4 cm)
OBJ1000
Cat. 45

Cora Lee Hall Brown
Pieced 1981; Mount Enterprise, Texas

Willia Ette Graham
Quilted 1985; Oakland, California

Untitled (One Patch)
Cotton, cotton/polyester blend;
hand pieced, hand quilted
77½ × 89½ in. (196.9 × 227.3 cm)
OBJ0263
Cat. 62

Monin Brown
Pieced possibly before 1930; Macon, Georgia

Hattie Mitchell
Pieced possibly before 1930; Macon, Georgia
Bordered and finished 1932; Macon, Georgia

Untitled (Patchwork)
Silk, rayon, cotton, sateen/satin, other synthetic fabrics; hand pieced, not quilted
66 × 58 in. (167.6 × 147.3 cm)
OBJ0316
Cat. 3

Bara Byrd-Stewart
Pieced 1988; Richmond, California

Irene Bankhead
Quilted 1989; Oakland, California

Untitled (Medallion, Broken Dishes Variation, Half-Square Triangles)
Cotton, polyester, flannel; hand pieced, hand quilted
62½ × 88½ in. (158.6 × 224.8 cm)
OBJ0853
Cat. 82

Sherry Ann Byrd
Pieced 1984, finished 1987; Richmond, California

Irene Bankhead
Quilted 1987; Oakland, California

Untitled (Double Medallion, Half-Square Triangles)
Cotton, polyester, cotton/polyester blend; hand and machine pieced, hand quilted
87 × 75 in. (221.0 × 190.5 cm)
OBJ0426
Cat. 67

Sherry Ann Byrd
Pieced 1990; Richmond, California

Irene Bankhead
Quilted 1990; Oakland, California

Untitled (Medallion)
Cotton, cotton/polyester blend, rayon;
hand pieced and quilted
95 × 75½ in. (241.3 × 191.8 cm)
OBJ1143
Cat. 87

Charles Cater
Pieced 1985; Oakland, California

Willia Ette Graham
Quilted 1986; Oakland, California

Sandy Diep
Repaired 1994; Oakland, California

Untitled (Medallion)
Cotton, polyester, cotton/polyester blend;
hand and machine pieced, hand quilted
88 × 93 in. (223.5 × 236.2 cm)
OBJ0353
Cat. 71

Betty Chafford
Rebecca Smith
1920s–1930s; Bastrop, Louisiana

Untitled (Shadow Star)
Cotton; machine pieced, hand quilted
88 × 69 in. (223.5 × 175.3 cm)
OBJ0180
Cat. 5

Willie Mae Chatman
1986; Berkeley, California

Untitled (Crossed Canoes or Evening Star)
Cotton, cotton/polyester blend, polyester, wool; hand and machine pieced, hand quilted
87 × 72 in. (221.0 × 182.9 cm)
OBJ0615
Cat. 75

Lily Chiles
Pieced and quilted 1991; Oakland, California

Clarence Jackson
Embroidered 1991; Oakland, California

Tina Jackson
Embroidered and quilted 1991; Oakland, California

Ruthie Love
Quilted 1991; Oakland, California

Untitled (Africa blocks)
Cotton, cotton/polyester blend;
appliqué, machine pieced, hand quilted
95 × 77 in. (241.3 × 195.6 cm)
OBJ1417
Cat. 92

Ruth Charlotte Clay
Treva Clay (?)
1930s–1940s; location unknown

Untitled top (Dresden Plate)
Cotton, flannel; hand and machine pieced, appliqué
79 × 65½ in. (200.7 × 166.4 cm)
OBJ1728
Cat. 6

Ruth Charlotte Clay
Treva Clay (?)
Pieced 1930s–1940s; location unknown

Irene Bankhead
Quilted 1998; Oakland, California

Untitled (Roman Stripe)
Cotton, cotton/polyester blend; hand and machine pieced, hand quilted
92 × 78 in. (233.7 × 198.1 cm)
OBJ1721
Cat. 7

Victoria Ector Cooper
1940s; Rusk County, Texas

Untitled (String Hexagons)
Cotton; hand pieced, hand quilted
80 × 71 in. (203.2 × 180.3 cm)
OBJ1174
Cat. 19

Thomas Covington
Pieced c. 1965; Grand Bay, Alabama

Irene Bankhead
Quilted 1997; Oakland, California

Untitled (Medallion)
Cotton, polyester, cotton/polyester blend; hand and machine pieced, hand quilted
79 × 62 in. (200.7 × 157.5 cm)
OBJ2284
Cat. 41

Annie Crawford
1933–1940; Call, Texas

Untitled (Puff quilt with tobacco sacks)
Cotton; hand pieced
69 × 58 in. (175.3 × 147.3 cm)
OBJ0038
Cat. 13

Anna Ruth Crofit
before 1983; Pine Bluff, Arkansas

Untitled (Snail's Trail or Indiana Puzzle)
Cotton, cotton/polyester blend, polyester; hand and machine pieced, hand quilted
94 × 71 in. (238.8 × 180.3 cm)
OBJ0916
Cat. 65

Odessa Doby
Pieced and quilted 1940s, Ozan, Arkansas

Willia Ette Graham
Restored 1987; Oakland, California

Untitled (Broken Dishes)
Cotton; hand pieced, hand quilted
71 × 64 in. (180.3 × 162.6 cm)
OBJ0532
Cat. 18

Dorothy Edwards
Georgia Lee Edwards
1983; Fordyce, Arkansas

Untitled (unidentified pattern)
Cotton, cotton/polyester blend, repurposed blanket batting (?); machine pieced, tied
78 × 71 in. (198.1 × 180.3 cm)
OBJ1311
Cat. 64

Louisa Fite
Pieced 1950s–1960s; Beckville, Texas

Joan Thompson
Quilted c. 1970; Holland Quarters community, Carthage, Texas

Untitled (Log Cabin)
Cotton, flannel; hand pieced, hand quilted
71 × 64 in. (180.3 × 162.6 cm)
OBJ1233
Cat. 34

Missie Freeman
1995; Oakland, California

Untitled top (Little Boy's Britches)
Cotton/polyester blend, polyester, rayon, linen; machine pieced
93 × 75 in. (236.2 × 190.5 cm)
OBJ2196
Cat. 106

Willia Ette Graham

Untitled (String Medallion)
Some blocks pieced before 1944; Texas
Completed 1950s; repaired 1985; Oakland, California
Cotton, cotton flannel, linen; hand pieced, hand quilted
71½ × 55½ in. (181.6 × 141 cm)
OBJ0064
Cat. 26

Untitled (original design)
1981; Oakland, California
Cotton; hand pieced
93 × 78 in. (236.2 x198.1 cm)
OBJ0060
Cat. 63

Willia Ette Graham
Pieced and quilted 1988; Oakland and San Francisco, California

Johnnie Wade
Quilted 1988; San Francisco, California

Untitled (Boots)
Cotton; hand pieced, hand quilted
92 × 82 in. (233.7 × 208.3 cm)
OBJ0643
Cat. 83

Emma Hall
c. 1940; Sweet Home, Arkansas

Untitled (Double Wedding Ring)
Cotton; hand pieced
71 × 71½ in. (180.3 × 181.6 cm)
OBJ0051
Cat. 16

Louella Harris
Pieced 1980s; Richmond, California

Willia Ette Graham
Johnnie Wade
Quilted 1994; Oakland, California

Untitled (Wheel of Fortune)
Cotton, cotton/polyester blend, other blends; hand pieced, hand quilted
81 × 77 in. (205.7 × 195.6 cm)
OBJ2045
Cat. 61

Annie Hawkins
Pieced c. 1969; Oakland, California

Willia Ette Graham
Quilted 1984; Oakland, California

Untitled (original design)
Cotton, cotton/polyester blend, rayon, other blends; hand pieced, hand quilted
78½ × 63 in. (199.4 × 160.0 cm)
OBJ0236
Cat. 42

Mattie Lou Henderson
c. 1984; Berkeley, California

Untitled (Sailboats)
Cotton, cotton/polyester blend, polyester; hand and machine pieced, hand quilted
87 × 86 in. (221.0 × 218.4 cm)
OBJ0471
Cat. 69

Gladys Henry
c. 1990; Butler, Texas

Crocheted rug
Cotton, cotton/polyester blend
35 × 38 in. (89.0 × 96.5 cm)
OBJ1505
Cat. 89

Gladys Henry
Pieced 1993; Butler, Texas

Rose McDowell
Quilted 1993; Oakland, California

Untitled (Double Medallion)
Polyester, rayon, other synthetic fabrics; hand and machine pieced, hand quilted
89 × 66 in. (226.1 × 167.6 cm)
OBJ1842
Cat. 93

Louise Hicks
c. 1939; Henderson, Texas

Untitled (Plain quilt)
Cotton; hand pieced, hand quilted
78 × 65 in. (198.1 × 165.1 cm)
OBJ0362
Cat. 15

Jimmie Johnson
Laura Johnson Battise
Pieced 1940–1978; Oakland, California

Arbie Williams
Bordered 1988; Oakland, California

Willia Ette Graham
Quilted 1988; Oakland, California

Untitled (Fifty-Four Forty or Fight)
Cotton/polyester blend; hand pieced, hand quilted
75 × 77 in. (190.5 × 195.6 cm)
OBJ0620
Cat. 27

Roberta Lee Johnson
c. 1928; Cushing, Texas

Untitled (One Patch, Strip)
Cotton, denim; machine pieced, hand quilted
90 × 70 in. (228.6 × 177.8 cm)
OBJ0941
Cat. 4

Zula Mae Johnson
1951; Oakland, California

Untitled (Crossed Canoes variation)
Silk, sateen/satin, cotton; hand and machine pieced
78 × 62 in. (198.1 × 157.5 cm)
OBJ0096
Cat. 31

Kitty Gladys Jones
Pieced before 1970; Forest, Mississippi

Atleaver Jones
Quilted c. 1978; Fresno, California

Untitled (Square in a Square)
Cotton; hand and machine pieced, hand quilted
84 × 69 in. (213.4 × 175.3 cm)
OBJ0899
Cat. 43

Lee Wanda Jones
c. 1985; Berkeley, California

Half Apron (One Patch)
Cotton, cotton/polyester blend; machine pieced
19 × 76 in. (48.3 × 193.0 cm)
OBJ0355
Cat. 73

Lee Wanda Jones
Pieced 1988; Oakland, California

Willia Ette Graham
Johnnie Wade
Quilted 1988; Oakland, California

Road to Nowhere
Cotton/polyester blend, rayon, sateen/satin, silk, other synthetic fabrics; hand pieced, hand quilted
81 × 55 in. (205.7 × 139.7 cm)
OBJ0733
Cat. 84

Ruby Lewis
c. 1985; Berkeley, California

Untitled top (One Patch)
Cotton, cotton/polyester blend, rayon, wool, polyester, linen, denim, cotton flannel; hand pieced
83 × 78 in. (210.8 × 198.1 cm)
OBJ0703
Cat. 74

Arbie Major
c. 1950–1952; Paraloma, Arkansas

Untitled (Snowball String)
Cotton, rayon, silk, cotton/polyester blend, sateen/satin; hand and machine pieced, hand quilted
76 × 71 in. (193.0 × 180.3 cm)
OBJ0197
Cat. 30

Maker Once Known/Unidentified Artist
c. 1930; Dunn, North Carolina

Unbleached feedsack
Cotton
36¼ × 18½ in. (92.1 × 47.0 cm)
OBJ3356
Fig. 17

Maker Once Known/Unidentified Artist
1930s; location unknown

Untitled (Four Patch Log Cabin variation)
Wool, other blends, polyester; machine pieced, not quilted
86 × 77 in. (218.4 × 195.6 cm)
OBJ0421
Cat. 8

Maker Once Known/Unidentified Artist
1930s; near McComb, Mississippi, or San Francisco, California

Untitled (Medallion)
Cotton, rayon, silk, wool, cotton/polyester blend, velvet, other synthetic fabrics; hand pieced, hand quilted
82 × 70 in. (208.3 × 177.8 cm)
OBJ0557
Cat. 9

Maker Once Known/Unidentified Artist
Pillow (Pine Burr)
1930s–1940s; location unknown
Cotton, polyester, other blends, other synthetic fabrics; hand pieced
16 × 16 × 3 in. (40.6 × 40.6 × 7.6 cm)
OBJ0534
Cat. 10

> *Found with:*
> Assorted ephemera and photographs from the estate of Zetta Dempsey
> 1920s–1980s; various locations
> OBJ0535
> Cat. 11

Maker Once Known/Unidentified Artist
1940s; location unknown

Untitled top (Medallion)
Cotton; hand pieced
67 × 70 in. (170.2 × 177.8 cm)
OBJ0153
Cat. 21

Maker Once Known/Unidentified Artist
c. 1990; Tutwiler, Mississippi

Handbag (Patchwork)
Cotton, cotton/polyester blend; hand and machine pieced, hand quilted
26½ × 12 in. (67.3 × 30.5 cm)
OBJ1127
Cat. 88

Hattie Mitchell
Appliquéd and embroidered 1906–1908, 1914; Macon, Georgia
Quilted and finished c. 1930; Macon, Georgia

Untitled (appliqué with embroidery)
Cotton; hand appliqué, hand piecing, hand quilted
96 × 62 in. (243.8 × 157.4 cm)
OBJ0319
Cat. 2

Sarah Moore
Some blocks pieced 1890s–1910s; Louisiana and/or Oklahoma

Effie Edwards
Pieced 1960s; California

Untitled top (Jacob's Ladder, T, Farmer's Daughter)
Cotton; hand and machine pieced
81 × 62 in. (205.7 × 157.5 cm)
OBJ0097
Cat. 37

Elizabeth Munn
c. 1951–1952; Ozan, Arkansas

Untitled (Roman Stripe Medallion)
Cotton; machine pieced, tied
80½ × 70 in. (204.5 × 177.8 cm)
OBJ1078
Cat. 32

Alice Neal
1955–1956; Oakland, California

Mary Bright Commemorative Quilt (with Dresden Plate, Monkey Wrench, Wild Goose Chase, Fan, Basket of Flowers, Star of Lemoyne, Nine Patch blocks)
Cotton, buttons, woven hat; appliqué, hand pieced, hand quilted
78½ × 62¾ in. (199.4 × 159.4 cm)
OBJ2973
Cat. 33

Anna Nicholson
1940s; Vicksburg, Mississippi, or California Bay Area

Untitled (Log Cabin, Barn Raising variation)
Cotton, wool, other blends, silk; hand pieced, tied
69 × 62 in. (175.3 × 157.5 cm)
OBJ3230
Cat. 20

Pearl Nunley
Beauty Vaughns
1940; Paraloma, Arkansas

Flower Garden (Sunflower variation)
Cotton, cotton/polyester blend, polyester; hand and machine pieced
71 × 78 in. (180.3 × 198.1 cm)
OBJ0190
Cat. 17

Ophenia Parker
God's Promise
Top completed 2005, finished 2023
Cotton
90 × 90 in. (228.6 × 228.6 cm)
Courtesy of the artist, Ophenia Parker
Not illustrated

Chaney Ella Peace
Pieced c. 1950; Shreveport, Louisiana

Bessie Moore
Quilted c. 1989; Oakland, California

Untitled (Royal Star, Dog Tooth Violet, and Britches variations)
Cotton, cotton/polyester blend; hand pieced, hand quilted
81½ × 62 in. (207.0 × 157.5 cm)
OBJ0006
Cat. 28

Dorothy Perkins
Pieced c. 1974; Oakland, California

Irene Bankhead
Quilted 1987; Oakland, California

Untitled (Crossword Puzzle)
Cotton/polyester blend, linen, polyester, wool, other synthetic fabrics; hand and machine pieced, hand quilted
93 × 69 in. (236.2 × 175.3 cm)
OBJ0493
Cat. 55

Bettie Phillips
1985; Oakland, California

The Fence
Cotton/polyester blend, cotton, polyester, wool, velvet, other synthetic fabrics, sateen/satin; machine pieced, tied
93 × 69 in. (236.2 × 175.3 cm)
OBJ0404
Cat. 70

Gracie Pigrum
1970s or early 1980s; San Francisco, California

Floor mat (Pine Burr variation?)
Polyester, wool, flannel, velour, other synthetic fabrics; machine pieced
33 × 22¼ in. (83.8 × 56.5 cm)
OBJ0255
Cat. 57

Susan Pless
Before 1944; Okfuskee County, Oklahoma

Untitled (Strip)
Corduroy, cotton, cotton/polyester blend, velveteen; machine pieced, hand quilted
82 × 75 in. (208.3 × 190.5 cm)
OBJ1815
Cat. 23

Pearlie Rayford
1930s–1940s; Little Rock, Arkansas

Untitled (Friendship Dahlia)
Cotton; appliqué, hand quilted
88 × 80 in. (223.5 × 203.2 cm)
OBJ0026
Cat. 12

Gerstine Scott
1989; Oakland, California

Untitled (Necktie quilt)
Polyester, rayon, silk, wool, other synthetic fabrics; hand pieced, hand quilted
94 × 85 in. (238.8 × 215.9 cm)
OBJ0795
Cat. 85

Francis Sheppard
Pieced 1980–1985; Las Vegas, Nevada

Irene Bankhead
Quilted 1991; Oakland, California

Untitled (Boston Puzzle or Marble)
Cotton/polyester blend, polyester, rayon, cotton, other synthetic fabrics; hand pieced, hand quilted
75 × 74 in. (190.5 × 188.0 cm)
OBJ0283
Cat. 60

Francis Sheppard
Pieced and quilted c. 1984; Las Vegas, Nevada

Arbie Williams
Pieced c. 1984; Las Vegas, Nevada

Annie Mae Cooper
Quilted c. 1984; Las Vegas, Nevada

Untitled (Jacob's Ladder variation)
Cotton, cotton/polyester blend, polyester, velveteen, other synthetic fabrics; hand and machine pieced, hand quilted
101½ × 92½ in. (257.8 × 235.0 cm)
OBJ1329
Not illustrated

Minnie Skinner
Late 1940s; Alto, Texas

Untitled (Patchwork with work clothes)
Cotton, denim, repurposed blanket batting; hand pieced, tied
79 × 66 in. (200.7 × 167.64 cm)
OBJ1543
Cat. 25

Attributed to Emma Smith
Possibly 1950s–1970s; Monroe, Louisiana or San Francisco, California

Untitled top (Medallion)
Cotton, cotton/polyester blend, rayon, polyester, linen; machine pieced
84 × 78 in. (213.4 × 198.1 cm)
OBJ1389
Cat. 36

Maple Jean Swift
Pieced 1960s; Ozan, Arkansas

Florine Taylor
Quilted 1960s; Ozan, Arkansas

Untitled (Medallion)
Cotton, cotton/polyester blend, other synthetic fabrics; hand and machine pieced, hand quilted
87 × 65 in. (221.0 × 165.1 cm)
OBJ1060
Cat. 39

Quinciana Tatmon
1950s–1960s; Oakland, California

Untitled (Fans)
Cotton; appliqué, hand pieced, hand quilted, tied
71 × 69½ in. (180.3 × 176.5 cm)
OBJ1674
Cat. 35

Florine Taylor
1987; Ozan, Arkansas

Untitled (One Patch with borders)
Cotton, cotton/polyester blend; hand and machine pieced, hand quilted
83 × 65 in. (210.8 × 165.1 cm)
OBJ1067
Cat. 81

Eula Thomas
Pieced 1971; Oakland, California

Willia Ette Graham
Quilted 1984; Oakland, California

Untitled (String)
Cotton, cotton/polyester blend, polyester; machine pieced, hand quilted
77 × 64 in. (195.6 × 162.6 cm)
OBJ0204
Cat. 54

Angelia Tobias
Pieced 1984; Oakland, California

Irene Bankhead
Quilted 1987; Oakland, California

Untitled (Medallion)
Cotton, corduroy, denim; hand pieced, hand quilted
77 × 67½ in. (195.6 × 171.5 cm)
OBJ0561
Cat. 68

Angelia Tobias
Pieced 1985; Oakland, California

Irene Bankhead
Quilted 1986; Oakland, California

Untitled (Patchwork)
Cotton, cotton/polyester blend, polyester, rayon, other blends; hand and machined pieced, hand quilted
80 × 69 in. (203.2 × 175.3 cm)
OBJ0389
Cat. 72

Angelia Tobias

Double-sided doll with patchwork clothes
1992; Oakland, California
Cotton, cotton or polyester blend, polyester, yarn; hand pieced
10 × 8½ in. (25.4 × 21.6 cm)
OBJ3427
Cat. 97

Doll with patchwork clothes and striped hat
1992; Oakland, California
Cotton, polyester; hand pieced
12 × 8 in. (30.5 × 20.3 cm)
OBJ3429
Cat. 98

Doll quilt (Patchwork)
1993; Oakland, California
Cotton; hand pieced
10½ × 9 in. (26.7 × 22.9 cm)
OBJ1902
Cat. 95, top

Doll quilt (Patchwork)
1993; Oakland, California
Cotton, cotton/polyester blend; hand pieced
12 × 10¼ in. (30.5 × 26.0 cm)
OBJ1906
Cat. 95, middle

Doll quilt (Patchwork)
1993; Oakland, California
Cotton; hand pieced
12 × 12 in. (30.5 × 30.5 cm)
OBJ1908
Cat. 95, bottom

Doll with yellow dress
1993; Merced, California
Cotton, polyester, cotton/polyester blend, yarn; hand pieced
14 × 9 in. (35.6 × 22.9 cm)
OBJ3433
Cat. 102

Sleeping Doll with braids
1996; Merced, California
Cotton, polyester, yarn; hand pieced
8 × 6½ in. (20.3 × 16.5 cm)
OBJ3438
Cat. 96

Doll with romper and lace trim
1996; Merced, California
Cotton, polyester, yarn, rubber bands, unknown filling; hand pieced, embroidered
22 × 19½ in. (arm span) (55.9 × 49.5 cm)
OBJ2195
Cat. 99

Doll with braided pigtails, cap, and red dress
1996; Merced, California
Cotton, polyester, rayon, yarn; hand pieced
8 × 6½ in. (20.3 × 16.5 cm)
OBJ3443
Cat. 100

Doll with braided hair and dress
1996; Merced, California
Cotton, cotton/polyester blend, polyester, yarn; hand and machine pieced
21 × 16 in. (53.3 × 40.6 cm)
OBJ3444
Cat. 101

Doll with jumpsuit and cap
1996; Merced, California
Cotton, polyester, yarn; hand pieced
8 × 6 in. (20.3 × 15.2 cm)
OBJ3442
Cat. 103

Rosie Lee Tompkins
Pieced 1986; Richmond, California

Irene Bankhead
Quilted 1987; Oakland, California

Untitled (Half-Square Triangles, Nine Patch)
Silk, polyester, cotton/polyester blend, sateen/satin, other synthetic fabrics; machine pieced, hand quilted
104 × 96 in. (264.2 × 243.8 cm)
OBJ0481
Cat. 76

Rosie Lee Tompkins
Pieced 1986; Richmond, California

Irene Bankhead
Quilted 1996; Oakland, California

Untitled (Half-Square Triangles)
Cotton, denim, cotton/polyester blend; machine pieced, hand quilted
103 × 67 in. (261.6 × 170.2 cm)
OBJ2130
Cat. 77

Rosie Lee Tompkins

Pillow (Half-Square Triangles)
1988; Richmond, California
Cotton, denim, cotton/polyester blend; machine pieced
12 × 10 in. (30.5 × 25.4 cm)
OBJ0842
Cat. 79

Pillow (Half-Square Triangles)
1997; Richmond, California
Cotton, denim, chintz, polyester, animal fur; machine pieced
16½ × 12 in. (41.9 × 30.5 cm)
OBJ2199
Cat. 78

Pillow (Half-Square Triangles)
1997; Richmond, California
Cotton, denim, chintz, other synthetic fabrics, animal fur; machine pieced
16 × 19½ in. (40.6 × 49.5 cm)
OBJ2234
Cat. 80

Untitled (Half-Square Triangles)
c. 2000; Richmond, California
Cotton, polyester, other blends, flannel, sateen/satin; machine pieced, tied
28 × 23 in. (71.1 × 58.4 cm)
OBJ3035
Cat. 110

Jane Traylor
Pieced c. 1918; Litroe, Louisiana

Alice Neal
Quilted early 1980s; Sacramento or Oakland, California

Untitled (Lotus Blossom or Whig's Defeat variations)
Cotton; hand pieced, hand quilted
70 × 78 in. (177.8 × 198.1 cm)
OBJ0181
Fig. 14

Sarah Turnage
Pieced 1970s; San Francisco, California

Aurelia Foster
Mary Thompson
Quilted 1990; San Francisco, California

Untitled (Fractured Log Cabin)
Cotton, polyester; machine pieced, hand quilted
64 × 72 in. (162.6 × 182.9 cm)
OBJ1253
Cat. 59

Venella Tyler
c. 1936; Greenwood, Mississippi

Untitled top (Pinwheel variation)
Cotton; hand pieced
73 × 64 in. (185.4 × 162.6 cm)
OBJ1320
Cat. 14

Beauty Vaughns
1963; Fresno, California

Untitled (Ocean Wave)
Cotton, linen, repurposed blanket batting (?); hand pieced
79 × 71 in. (200.7 × 180.3 cm)
OBJ0189
Cat. 38

Johnnie Wade
Pieced and quilted 1990; Oakland, California

Willia Ette Graham
Quilted 1990; Oakland, California

Untitled (Log Cabin)
Cotton, cotton/polyester blend; machine pieced
92 × 70 in. (233.7 × 177.8 cm)
OBJ1015
Cat. 90

Johnnie Wade
1996; Oakland, California

Untitled (Texas Star)
Cotton, cotton/polyester blend, polyester; hand and machine piecing, appliqué, hand quilted
86 × 90 in. (218.4 × 228.6 cm)
OBJ2135
Cat. 108

Maudra Walker
1960s–1970s; Oklahoma or San Mateo, California

Untitled (Strip)
Polyester, cotton/polyester blend, rayon, wool, other synthetic fabrics; hand pieced, tied
69 × 57 in. (175.3 × 144.8 cm)
OBJ1283
Cat. 40

Naomi Walker
After 1943; near Gene Autry, Oklahoma

Untitled (String crosses with newspaper backing)
Cotton/polyester blend, muslin, newspaper; hand pieced
13 × 13 in. (33.0 × 33.0 cm)
OBJ0598
Cat. 22

Joe Washington
1940s–1950s; near Hawkins, Texas

Untitled (Fifteen Patch variation)
Cotton, cotton/polyester blend, repurposed blanket batting; hand pieced, hand quilted
83 × 70 in. (210.8 × 177.8 cm)
OBJ1053
Cat. 24

Gussie Wells
Arbie Williams
Pieced 1989; Oakland, California

Irene Bankhead
Quilted 1989; Oakland, California

Untitled (Strip)
Rayon, cotton/polyester blend, other synthetic fabrics; machine pieced, hand quilted
90 × 65 in. (228.6 × 165.1 cm)
OBJ0790
Cat. 86

Isiadore Whitehead
c. 1970; Oakland, California

Chair with Double Wedding Ring seat cushion
Cotton/polyester blend, polyester; hand pieced
29 × 16½ × 27 in. (74.3 × 41.9 × 68.6 cm)
OBJ3485
Cat. 53

Drape (Double Wedding Ring)
Cotton, polyester, linen; hand pieced, hand quilted
82 × 41 in. (208.3 × 104.1 cm)
OBJ2530
Cat. 47

Drape (Double Wedding Ring)
Cotton, linen; hand pieced, hand quilted
82 × 42 in. (208.3 × 106.7 cm)
OBJ2531
Cat. 48

Drape with embroidered names (Double Wedding Ring)
Cotton, polyester, linen; hand pieced, hand quilted
79 × 54 in. (200.7 × 137.2 cm)
OBJ2532
Cat. 49

Drape with embroidered names (Double Wedding Ring)
Cotton, polyester, linen; hand pieced, hand quilted
82 × 57 in. (208.3 × 144.8 cm)
OBJ2533
Cat. 50

Floor mat (Double Wedding Ring)
Cotton, polyester, linen; hand pieced, hand quilted
28 × 40 in. (71.1 × 101.6 cm)
OBJ2528
Cat. 51

Floor mat (Double Wedding Ring)
Cotton, polyester, linen; hand pieced, hand quilted
40 × 52 in. (101.6 × 132.1 cm)
OBJ2529
Cat. 52

Untitled (Double Wedding Ring)
Cotton, linen, other blends and woven fabrics; hand pieced, hand quilted
106 × 90 in. (269.2 × 228.6 cm)
OBJ0252
Cat. 46

Arbie Williams
Pieced 1993; Oakland, California

Irene Bankhead
Quilted 1993; Oakland, California

Untitled (Overalls quilt)
Cotton, cotton/polyester blend, polyester, denim, velvet, other woven and synthetic fabrics; hand and machine pieced, hand quilted
72 × 65 in. (182.9 × 165.1 cm)
OBJ3227
Cat. 94

Biddie Wilson
1970s–1990s; likely Oakland, California

Untitled (Robbing Peter to Pay Paul, Jacob's Ladder)
Cotton, cotton/polyester blend, polyester; hand pieced, hand quilted
86 × 67 in. (218.4 × 170.1 cm)
OBJ2330
Cat. 58

Warren Wise
Pieced c. 1950; Prescott, Arkansas

Willia Ette Graham
Quilted 1985; Oakland, California

Untitled (Cross and Circles)
Cotton; hand pieced, hand quilted
81½ × 80 in. (207.0 × 203.2 cm)
OBJ3325
Cat. 29

Index

Notes: Pages with images are given in *italics*. Unattributed works are listed under Maker Once Known. *Quilt/s* and *quiltmaker/s* refer to African American quilts and makers, unless otherwise identified.

ILLUSTRATION CREDITS

BAMPFA respects the protected status of all copyrighted material and has made every effort to identify copyright holders and obtain permission for works appearing in this volume. Any omissions are unintentional. We welcome notification of any errors or omissions by rights holders who are located or who come forward after the time of publication, and we will work to make necessary arrangements at the earliest opportunity.

Cover: Bequest of the Eli Leon Living Trust, BAMPFA. Courtesy of Juanita McFall, granddaughter of the quiltmaker. Photo: Kevin Candland
Endpapers and frontispiece: Bequest of the Eli Leon Living Trust, BAMPFA. Courtesy the Descendants of Pearl Nunley. Photo: Kevin Candland

Figs. 1 and 30: Courtesy the Bancroft Library, University of California, Berkeley
Fig. 2: Courtesy the Richmond Museum of History & Culture, Richmond, California
Figs. 3–5: © The Dorothea Lange Collection. Photo: Dorothea Lange
Fig. 6: Eli Leon Archive, BAMPFA
Fig. 7: Eli Leon Archive, BAMPFA. Photo: Helen Wallis
Fig. 8: © The Colonial Williamsburg Foundation. Photo: Hans Lorenz
Figs. 9–10: Bequest of the Eli Leon Living Trust, BAMPFA. Courtesy the Family of Beatrice Smith. Photo: Kevin Candland
Figs. 11–12, 14, 21–22, 25–26, 37–38, and 40–42: Eli Leon Archive, BAMPFA. Photo: Eli Leon
Fig. 13: Bequest of the Eli Leon Living Trust, BAMPFA. Courtesy the Thomas Covington Family. Photo: Kevin Candland
Fig. 15: Eli Leon Archive, BAMPFA. Photo: Commercial Studios Photographers
Fig. 16: Eli Leon Archive, BAMPFA. Photo: Kevin Candland
Figs. 17, 23–24, and 35: Bequest of the Eli Leon Living Trust, BAMPFA. Photo: Kevin Candland
Fig. 18: Courtesy the International Quilt Museum, University of Nebraska-Lincoln
Figs. 19 and 44: © The University of North Carolina at Chapel Hill, 2024. Photo: Roland L. Freeman
Fig. 20: Photo: Deann Tyler
Fig. 27: © Condé Nast. Photo: Horst P. Horst, *Vogue*
Fig. 28: Courtesy the California Heritage Quilt Project
Fig. 29: © Edith Gross. Courtesy the artist, Carolyn Mazloomi, and Textile Center, Minneapolis. Photo: Carolyn Mazloomi, WCQN
Fig. 31: Courtesy the Environmental Design Archives, College of Environmental Design, University of California, Berkeley
Fig. 32: Courtesy the African American Museum and Library at Oakland, Oakland Public Library, Oakland, California. Photo: Harold Jenkins
Fig. 33: © The Regents of the University of California, The Bancroft Library, University of California, Berkeley. Photo: David Johnson
Fig. 34: Eli Leon Archive, BAMPFA. Courtesy the Willia Ette Graham Family
Fig. 36: © Estate of Mary Lue Brown. Los Angeles County Museum of Art. Digital Image © 2024 Museum Associates / LACMA. Licensed by Art Resource, NY
Fig. 39: Eli Leon Archive, BAMPFA. Photo: Mable Murphy
Fig. 43: Courtesy the Division of Anthropology, American Museum of Natural History, New York
Fig. 45: Courtesy Carolyn L. Mazloomi, WCQN. Photo: Rezvan Mazloomi
Fig. 46: Courtesy the artist
Fig. 47: © A'donna Richardson. Courtesy the artist
Fig. 48: BAMPFA Library. Courtesy Peggie Hartwell and Sharon Kerry-Harlan
Fig. 49: Courtesy A'donna Richardson
Fig. 50: © Faith Ringgold / ARS, NY and DACS, London. Courtesy ACA Galleries, New York 2022 and New Museum, New York
Fig. 51: © Sanford Biggers. Courtesy David Castillo Gallery, Miami, and Museum of Contemporary Art, Chicago. Photo: Nathan Keay, © MCA Chicago / Art Resource, New York
Fig. 52: © Adia Millett. Courtesy the artist and Institute of Contemporary Art San José. Photo: Shaun Roberts
Fig. 53: Courtesy the Institute of Contemporary Art San José
Fig. 54: © Basil Kincaid. Rubell Museum, Miami. Courtesy the artist, Venus Over Manhattan, New York, and Rubell Museum, Miami. Photo: Venus Over Manhattan, New York
Fig. 55: © Basil Kincaid. Courtesy the artist, Venus Over Manhattan, New York, and The Albertina Museum Vienna, Austria. Photo: Venus Over Manhattan, New York

Cats. 1, 15, 26, 63 and 83: Bequest of the Eli Leon Living Trust, BAMPFA. Courtesy the Willia Ette Graham Family. Photo: Kevin Candland
Cats. 2–9, 12–14, 16, 18, 21–25, 27–28, 31, 33–37, 39–40, 42–44, 46–59, 61, 64–66, 68–74, 81, 84, 88, 90, 92, 95–103, and 105–111: Bequest of the Eli Leon Living Trust, BAMPFA. Photo: Kevin Candland
Cat. 10: Bequest of the Eli Leon Living Trust, BAMPFA. Courtesy the Zetta Mae Dempsey Family. Photo: Kevin Candland
Cat. 11: Eli Leon Archive, BAMPFA. Courtesy the Zetta Mae Dempsey Family. Photo: Kevin Candland
Cat. 17: Bequest of the Eli Leon Living Trust, BAMPFA. Courtesy the Descendants of Pearl Nunley. Photo: Kevin Candland
Cat. 19: Bequest of the Eli Leon Living Trust, BAMPFA. Courtesy the Victoria Ector Cooper Family. Photo: Kevin Candland
Cat. 20: Bequest of the Eli Leon Living Trust, BAMPFA. Courtesy the Anna Nicholson Family. Photo: Kevin Candland
Cat. 29: Bequest of the Eli Leon Living Trust, BAMPFA. Courtesy Jimmy Stuart and the Wise Family. Photo: Kevin Candland
Cat. 30: Bequest of the Eli Leon Living Trust, BAMPFA. Courtesy of Juanita McFall, granddaughter of the quiltmaker. Photo: Kevin Candland
Cat. 32: Bequest of the Eli Leon Living Trust, BAMPFA. Courtesy the Elizabeth Munn Family. Photo: Kevin Candland
Cat. 38: Bequest of the Eli Leon Living Trust, BAMPFA. Courtesy of Douglas Washington, grandson of the quiltmaker: Photo: Kevin Candland
Cat. 41: Bequest of the Eli Leon Living Trust, BAMPFA. Courtesy the Thomas Covington Family. Photo: Kevin Candland
Cats. 45 and 62: Bequest of the Eli Leon Living Trust, BAMPFA. Courtesy the Cora Lee Hall Brown Family. Photo: Kevin Candland
Cats. 60, 86, and 94: Bequest of the Eli Leon Living Trust, BAMPFA. Courtesy Ophenia R. Parker. Photo: Kevin Candland
Cats. 67 and 87: Bequest of the Eli Leon Living Trust, BAMPFA. Courtesy Sherry Ann Byrd. Photo: Kevin Candland
Cat. 75: Bequest of the Eli Leon Living Trust, BAMPFA. Courtesy the Willie Mae Chatman Family. Photo: Kevin Candland
Cats. 76–80: © Rosie Lee Tompkins. Bequest of the Eli Leon Living Trust, BAMPFA. Courtesy the Effie Mae Howard Estate. Photo: Kevin Candland
Cat. 82: Bequest of the Eli Leon Living Trust, BAMPFA. Courtesy Bara Byrd-Stewart. Photo: Kevin Candland
Cat. 85: Bequest of the Eli Leon Living Trust, BAMPFA. Courtesy the Gerstine Scott Family. Photo: Kevin Candland
Cats. 89 and 93: Bequest of the Eli Leon Living Trust, BAMPFA. Courtesy the Descendants of Gladys Henry. Photo: Kevin Candland
Cats. 91 and 104: Bequest of the Eli Leon Living Trust, BAMPFA. Courtesy Laverne Brackens. Photo: Kevin Candland

4: Bequest of the Eli Leon Living Trust, BAMPFA. Courtesy the Effie Mae Howard Estate. Photo: Kevin Candland
10, 204, 222, and 255: Bequest of the Eli Leon Living Trust, BAMPFA. Photo: Kevin Candland
51: Bequest of the Eli Leon Living Trust, BAMPFA. Courtesy Laverne Brackens. Photo: Kevin Candland
54: Bequest of the Eli Leon Living Trust, BAMPFA. Courtesy of Douglas Washington, grandson of the quiltmaker. Photo: Kevin Candland
216 (top, left and right), 217 (bottom), 218 (bottom), 219 (top left and bottom), 220, 221 (right, top and bottom), 224 (right), 226 (left), 227, 230 (right), 231, 233–236, 238–240, 246 (right), 249 (left), and 251–253 (left): Eli Leon Archive, BAMPFA. Photo: Eli Leon
216 (bottom, left), 217 (top, right), 219 (top, right), 229 (left), 230 (left), 241, 244, 247 (right), and 248: Eli Leon Archive, BAMPFA
217 (top, left): Eli Leon Archive, BAMPFA. Courtesy of Douglas Washington and Juanita McFall, grandchildren of the quiltmakers. Photo: Helen Wallis
218 (top, left and right): Eli Leon Archive, BAMPFA. Courtesy of Douglas Washington and Juanita McFall, grandchildren of the quiltmakers. Photo: Eli Leon
221 (left) and 224 (left): Eli Leon Archive, BAMPFA. Courtesy the Willia Ette Graham Family. Photo: Eli Leon
223: Eli Leon Archive, BAMPFA. Courtesy the Willia Ette Graham Family
225 (left): Eli Leon Archive, BAMPFA. Courtesy the Cora Lee Hall Brown Family
225 (right): Eli Leon Archive, BAMPFA. Courtesy the Gerstine Scott Family. Photo: Eli Leon
226 (right): Eli Leon Archive, BAMPFA. Courtesy the Willie Mae Chatman Family. Photo: Eli Leon
228 (left): Eli Leon Archive, BAMPFA. Courtesy the Victoria Ector Cooper Family
228 (right): Eli Leon Archive, BAMPFA. Courtesy the Thomas Covington Family
229 (right): Eli Leon Archive, BAMPFA. Courtesy the Zetta Mae Dempsey Family
232: © Tom Pich. Courtesy Laverne Brackens. Photo: Tom Pich/NEA/LOC
237: Eli Leon Archive, BAMPFA. Photo: Helen Wallis
242 (left): Eli Leon Archive, BAMPFA. Courtesy the Elizabeth Munn Family. Photo: Eli Leon
242 (right): Eli Leon Archive, BAMPFA. Courtesy of Douglas Washington and Juanita McFall, great-grandchildren of the quiltmaker
243 (left): Eli Leon Archive, BAMPFA. Courtesy of Douglas Washington, grandson of the quiltmaker
243 (right): Eli Leon Archive, BAMPFA. Courtesy of Juanita McFall, granddaughter of the quiltmaker
245 (left): Eli Leon Archive, BAMPFA. Courtesy Ophenia R. Parker. Photo: Eli Leon
245 (right): Detail © The University of North Carolina at Chapel Hill, 2024. Roland L. Freeman Photographic Collection (70147), Southern Folklife Collection at Wilson Special Collections Library, University of North Carolina–Chapel Hill. Photo: Roland L. Freeman
246 (left): © Ophenia R. Parker. Courtesy Ophenia R. Parker
247 (left): Eli Leon Archive, BAMPFA. Courtesy the Family of Beatrice Smith. Photo: Eli Leon
249 (right): Eli Leon Archive, BAMPFA. Courtesy the Effie Mae Howard Estate. Photo: Eli Leon
250: Eli Leon Archive, BAMPFA. Photo: Commercial Studios Photographers
253 (right): Eli Leon Archive, BAMPFA. Courtesy Jimmy Stuart and the Wise Family

BAMPFA Staff, National Leadership Board, and Director's Cabinet

FULL-TIME STAFF
John D. Alexander
Alex Arzt
Karen Bennett
Beverly Bradley
Miriam Campos-Quinn
Elsa Cardona
Sean Carson
Gibbs Chapman
María Cisneros
Rick Dufrene
A.J. Fox
Steve Fujimura
Justin Glasson
Sherry Goodman
Alexis Gordon
Anthony Graham
Laura Graziano
Jeff Griffith-Perham
Alexis Gruzman
Zuri Guzman
Laura Hansen
Yuna Jeong
Eva Kalea
Douglas Katelus
Taylor Kobryn
Jess Kreglow
Lili Kromdyk
Daria Lugina
Kate MacKay
Basil Meier
Henrriette Mena
Mike Meyers
Matthew Villar Miranda
Nathalia Morán
Katelyn Nomura-Weingrow
Tausif Noor
Margot Norton
Scott Orloff
Susan Oxtoby
J Rivera Pansa
Ivet Ramirez
Nat Rees
Stephanie Reeves
Orlando Antonio Sánchez
Jason Sanders
Linda Scobie
Jessica Seville
Jon Shibata
Laurel Silverstein
Jesse Slee
Jim Sugarman
Victoria Sung
Dave Taylor
Alayna Tinney
Julie Rodrigues Widholm
David Wilson
Hong Wong
Caro Yagjian
Elaine Y. Yau

NATIONAL LEADERSHIP BOARD
Leslie Berriman
Penny Cooper
Marta Hall
Sara Guyer
Shannon Jackson
Rich Lyons
Julie Simpson
Cissie Swig
Paul Wattis

DIRECTOR'S CABINET
Lily Belcher*
Sharon Corwin
Brenda Drake
Ben Hermalin
Julie Huntsinger
Cathy Koshland
Isaac Julien
Sophia Limoncell-Herwick*
Annie Perrin
Favianna Rodriguez
Charmin Roundtree
Tabitha Soren
Cynthia Tongson
Catherine Wagner

* Student Committee Co-chairs

Contributors

Daphne A. Brooks
William R. Kenan, Jr., Professor of African American Studies, American Studies, Women's, Gender, and Sexuality Studies, and Music at Yale University

Bridget R. Cooks
Professor of African American Studies and Art History at the University of California, Irvine

Basil Kincaid
Artist based in Saint Louis, Missouri

Eli Leon
Collector, curator, and writer

Carolyn L. Mazloomi
Historian, curator, author, lecturer, artist, mentor, facilitator, founder of the African-American Quilt Guild of Los Angeles and the Women of Color Quilters Network (WCQN), Bess Lomax Hawes NEA National Heritage Fellow, United States Artists Fellow, Ohio Heritage Fellow, and American Craft Council Honorary Fellow

Adia Millett
Artist based in Oakland, California

Matthew Villar Miranda
Curatorial Associate at the Berkeley Art Museum and Pacific Film Archive

Sharbreon S. Plummer
Independent curator, public scholar, and Artistic Director at Threewalls

A'donna Richardson
Founder and Managing Director at the African American Quilt Documentation Study Group

Wendy M. Thompson
Associate Professor of African American Studies at San José State University

Elaine Y. Yau
Associate Curator and Academic Liaison at the Berkeley Art Museum and Pacific Film Archive

Published in conjunction with the exhibition *Routed West: Twentieth-Century African American Quilts in California*, organized by the University of California, Berkeley Art Museum and Pacific Film Archive, from June 7, 2025, to November 30, 2025.

Routed West: Twentieth-Century African American Quilts in California is curated by Elaine Y. Yau, Associate Curator and Academic Liaison, with Matthew Villar Miranda, Curatorial Associate.

The Henry Luce Foundation has provided generous lead support for the exhibition and accompanying catalog, including significant funding for research, conservation, and care of the African American Quilt Collection at BAMPFA. Major exhibition support is provided by the Shah Garg Women Artists Research Fund and the Terra Foundation for American Art. Additional support for the *Routed West* catalog is provided by Brenda and Michael Drake and by a grant from the Black Studies Collaboratory at UC Berkeley, an awardee of the Mellon Foundation's Just Futures Initiative. Conservation of the quilt collection was made possible by major grants from the Bank of America Art Conservation Project, the Save America's Treasures program of the Institute of Museum and Library Services, and the Office of the Chancellor at the University of California, Berkeley.

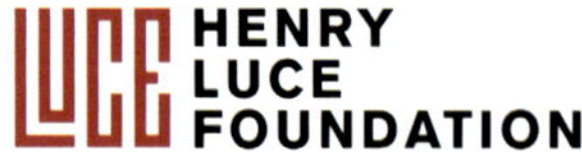

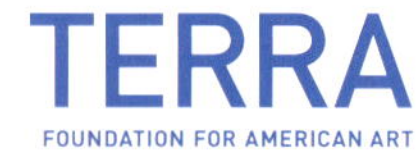

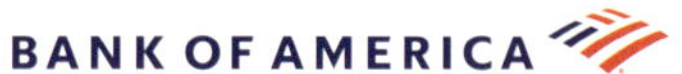

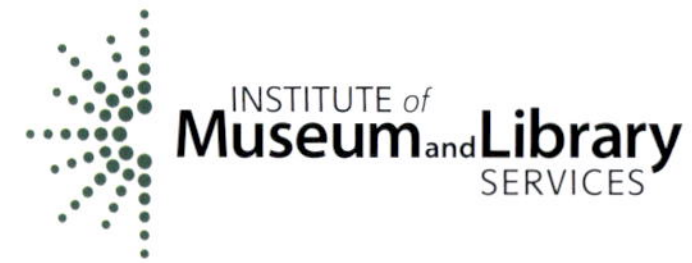

Published in 2025 by University of California, Berkeley Art Museum and Pacific Film Archive and DelMonico Books • D.A.P.

University of California,
Berkeley Art Museum
and Pacific Film Archive
2155 Center Street
Berkeley, CA 94720
www.BAMPFA.org

DelMonico Books
available through ARTBOOK | D.A.P.
75 Broad Street, Suite 630
New York, NY 10004
artbook.com
delmonicobooks.com

Library of Congress Control Number: 2024946273

ISBN 978-1-63681-159-8

UC Berkeley Art Museum and Pacific Film Archive
Julie Rodrigues Widholm, Executive Director
John Alexander, Director of Collections and Exhibitions
Elaine Y. Yau, Associate Curator and Academic Liaison
Matthew Villar Miranda, Curatorial Associate

Miko McGinty Inc.
Produced by Miko McGinty
Designed by Rita Jules
Typeset by Tina Henderson in Aneto and Yport

Edited by Eric Zeidler
Indexed by Kathleen Friello
Maps by Jonathan Corum

DelMonico Books
Mary DelMonico, Publisher
Karen Farquhar, Production Director

Printed and bound in China

Front and back cover: Detail of cat. 30
Endpapers: Detail from back of cat. 17
Frontispiece: Detail of cat. 17
Page 4: Detail of cat. 77

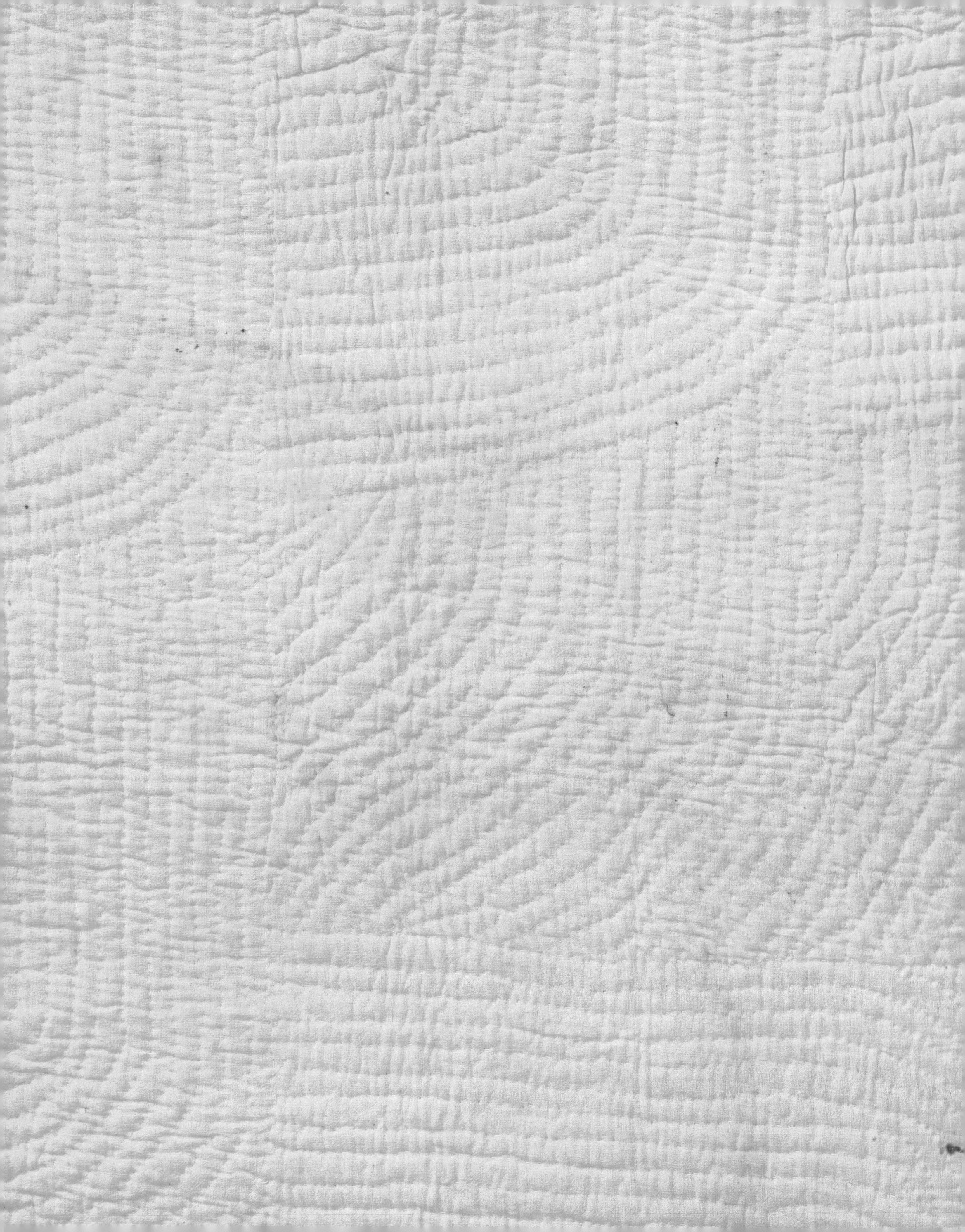